BRAIN SCANS OF AN ARTIST AND NONARTIST
WHILE SKETCHING A PORTRAIT

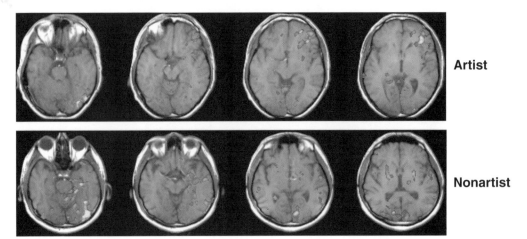

Artist

Nonartist

fMRI brain activity for a noted artist and a nonartist as each drew a sketch of a portrait. Both show activation of the right parietal lobe where facial processing is expected but the artist seems to show less activity suggesting efficient processing (From Solso, 2001).

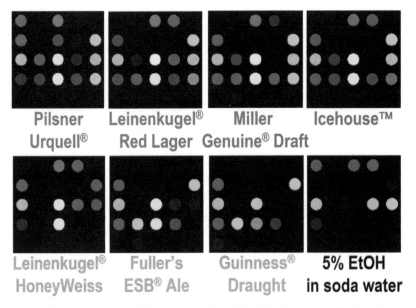

Pilsner Urquell®   Leinenkugel® Red Lager   Miller Genuine® Draft   Icehouse™

Leinenkugel® HoneyWeiss   Fuller's ESB® Ale   Guinness® Draught   5% EtOH in soda water

An artificial taste tester. The tastes and smells of the beers are displayed visually in colorimetric arrays

Can you solve it? What do an ancient corkscrew, a watch, and Bugs Bunny have in common? Can't figure it out? See Chapter 15. (Reprinted by permission of Dan Wagner.)

EIGHTH EDITION

Cognitive Psychology

Robert L. Solso

Late, University of Nevada, Reno

Otto H. MacLin

University of Northern Iowa

M. Kimberly MacLin

University of Northern Iowa

PEARSON
and

Boston ● New York ● San Francisco
Mexico City ● Montreal ● Toronto ● London ● Madrid ● Munich ● Paris
Hong Kong ● Singapore ● Tokyo ● Cape Town ● Sydney

Series Editor: Stephen Frail
Series Editorial Assistant: Mary K. Tucker
Marketing Manager: Karen Natale
Production Supervisor: Beth Houston
Editorial Production Service: Pine Tree Composition, Inc.
Composition Buyer: Linda Cox
Manufacturing Buyer: JoAnne Sweeney
Electronic Composition: Pine Tree Composition, Inc.
Cover Administrator: Linda Knowles

For related titles and support materials, visit our online catalog at www.ablongman.com.

Between the time website information is gathered and then published, it is not unusual for some sites to have closed. Also, the transcription of URLs can result in typographical errors. The publisher would appreciate notification where these errors occur so that they may be corrected in subsequent editions.

Library of Congress Cataloging-in-Publication Data

Solso, Robert L.
  Cognitive psychology / Robert L. Solso, Otto H. MacLin,
M. Kimberly MacLin.—8th ed.
      p. cm.
    Includes bibliographical references and index.
    ISBN 0-205-52108-8 (alk. paper)
    1. Cognition—Textbooks. 2. Cognitive psychology—
Textbooks. I. MacLin, Otto H., 1958– II. MacLin, M.
Kimberly. III. Title.
  BF311.S653 2008
  153—dc22
2007028725

ISBN-13: 978-0-205-52108-1
ISBN-10: 0-205-52108-8

Printed in the United States of America

10   9   8   7   6   5   4   3   2   1   11   10   09   08   07

In memory of Kathy Donovan
Professor of Psychology at the University of Central Oklahoma for 17 years

We dedicate this book to teachers everywhere who work tirelessly
to share their science with others, as Kathy did.

Thanks for the Memories. . .
Robert L. Solso
1933–2005

Contents in Brief

Contents

CHAPTER 12 | **Cognition across the Lifespan   333**

CHAPTER 13 | **Concept Formation, Logic, and Decision Making   373**

Preface

To Our Readers

Welcome to *Cognitive Psychology!* Whether you are a student, instructor, or a casual reader, we hope that you enjoy this book and learn much about the workings of the mind and brain.

When Bob Solso wrote the first edition of *Cognitive Psychology* more than thirty years ago it was particularly challenging because he had no example to follow except the now classic books by More (1939) and Ulric Neisser (1967) and the hundreds of articles and symposium papers that were available at the time. Bob was greatly influenced when he sat in on Ed Smith's class on cognition at Stanford University in 1974. Ed's organization of material is still in the background (although modified over the years) in the present book, and we have seen this style in the now several dozen texts in cognitive psychology that are available today and have influenced students and instructors alike in the United States and across the world. In fact, this book has been translated in Russian and Turkish, is printed in China, and there is an international edition, as well as this current edition.

As you may know, Bob passed away in January 2005. His memorial service was on Valentine's Day, so fitting for a man who loved life, people, science, and writing so much. We are proud to say that we were both PhD students of his and spent countless hours in seminars and informal discussions about cognitive psychology as well as the real importance of communicating our science to others. Thus, we feel it is our good fortune to carry on this book in the tradition he started over a quarter century ago. Through all the changes in this edition, we've done our best to retain Bob's vision of a text that honors the past and embraces the future of cognitive psychology. Let us know how we did.

As a side note: we had a lot of fun designing the cover. In Japanese symbolism the koi fish represents perseverance in adversity and strength of purpose. We honor Bob

Solso with this symbolism for his perseverance and strength in fighting his cancer with grace and humility which was an inspiration to all of us. Additionally the shape and pattern of the fish represent yin and yang which embodies harmony derived from conflicts. Bob hated conflict, and strove to find harmony with people cared about. We see other symbolism in the image as well regarding the universe, patterns, and even astrology (asks us about it sometime!) But all that symbolism aside, we think it looks cool!

To the Instructor

In this eighth edition we have retained the best features and content of the previous seven editions while adding important new material, and reorganizing the structure of the book to better reflect the order of cognitive processing. This has resulted in changing some chapter titles to better reflect their content, and moving some content that was distributed across multiple chapters into more centralized locations. Furthermore, some topics such as experts, that were previously given their own chapter have been moved to chapters relevant to that expertise. The remarkable advancements in cognitive neuroscience, not only in technology but also in data and their implications, are fully appreciated in the present edition, but we are clearly mindful that cognitive psychology is the study of the human mind: its biology, its thoughts, its reasoning process, its language, its memory. These subjects (and others) are the topics of cognition of which cognitive neuroscience is but one way to illustrate and explain cognitive functioning. We have retained many of the historical studies that have endured the test of time and the empirical test of science and, when appropriate, have added interesting new studies. There is a great temptation to substitute a new study for an old one (for the sake of "newness"), and in some instances, where the more recent paper illustrates a new facet of a problem, substitution is justified. However, in many cases an older study is perfectly clear and has been retained. We have also updated the explanations and examples of many of these older studies to better capture the interest of today's students.

Overview and Revisions to This Edition

Each chapter begins with preview questions we call "Hmmm . . . ?" These are the questions designed to capture students' interest and encourage them to wonder about these concepts prior to delving into the chapter material. We know that learning of essential knowledge is facilitated if the student has a clue about what he or she is expected to learn.

Most chapters begin with a brief review of the historical perspective on the topic presented. Since the field of cognitive psychology changes so rapidly, we believe it is important for readers to know something of the history of a topic so that they may understand new information within the context of past events. Most chapters correspondingly end with a recent study in cognitive neuroscience ("Spotlight on Cognitive Neuroscience"), and a review of a theoretically or methodologically interesting finding ("A la carte") that highlights an aspect of that chapter.

The "Cognition in Everyday Life" and "Try This!" boxes encourage the student to analyze or contemplate the immediate subject matter in terms of an everyday experience or an easy-to-do demonstration or thought experiment.

Discussions of the evolutionary basis of cognitive processes have been added throughout the text. The consciousness chapter has been completely revised to include important philosophical and cognitive viewpoints on consciousness while retaining the content on states of consciousness (e.g., sleeping, etc.). The content on language has been condensed to one chapter, and a new chapter, "Forgetting and Remembering," has been added. New coverage of cognition in older adults has been added to the development chapter. All chapters have been revised for clarity, new art additions, and updated references. Many new quotes have been added that are designed to cause the student to stop and think about the material and integrate what they know and what they are learning with the content of the quote. We also envision the quotes being used as effective lecture starters in the classroom.

In addition, we have revamped the resources at the end of each chapter. This section is now called the Student Resource Center and includes a study guide, key terms, and a starting points section. This section is designed to provide resources to the student to pique their interest in topics related to the chapter and as a concrete resource for starting a research project or paper. Thus, the section includes book and article listings, as well as movie titles and Internet search terms.

A test bank, instructor's manual, and companion website (www.ablongman.com/solso8e) are all available for your use. Because we wrote these supplements ourselves, we can assure you that the content matches the textbook content perfectly in terms of level, organization and quality.

While many chapter titles have changed, we have taken efforts to ensure that the returning instructor to this text will find that their course plans still map on well to the eighth edition.

1. Introduction and Research Methods
2. Cognitive Neuroscience
3. Attention, Sensation, and Perception
4. Object Recognition
5. Memory Models and Short-Term Memory
6. Memory Theories and Long-Term Memory
7. Forgetting and Remembering
8. Consciousness
9. The Verbal Representation of Knowledge
10. The Visual Representation of Knowledge
11. Language
12. Cognition across the Lifespan
13. Concept Formation, Logic, and Decision Making
14. Problem Solving, Creativity, and Intelligence
15. Artificial Intelligence

Many people have contributed to this book, and it is a pleasure for us to recognize them here. Feedback from instructors and students about what works and what doesn't is extremely valuable; this book is for you and we appreciate your feedback and continued use of this text. It's no small task reviewing a book (and doing it well). We'd especially like to acknowledge the reviewers of the Eighth Edition who spent a great deal of time to provide us with useful, constructive criticism. Their contribution has been priceless and many changes are a direct result of their input. Gary Klatsky, SUNY at Oswego; David Ludden, Lindsey Wilson College; Chris Niebauer, Slippery Rock University; Angelina MacKewn, University of Tennessee at Martin; Thomas Shaffer, South Dakota State University.

Thanks to our editor Stephen Frail for his support to the art department at Allyn & Bacon for collaborating with us on the cover design, and to Patty Donovan of Pine Tree Composition, Inc. for her tireless efforts in getting this book in (and through) production. Thanks go to Lucas Heuer, an undergraduate student at UNI, for his assistance in gathering materials for the instructor's manual and test bank, and to Dwight Peterson, our graduate student, who helps (and challenges) us at every turn. We owe a debt of gratitude to the Psychology Department's administrative assistants, Jeanne Marshall and Betty Bagenstos. They make our lives easier every day in big and small ways and we appreciate them so much. Thanks also to our friend Steve Knapp for his feedback, insight, news clippings, and quotes. We'd also like to thank our colleagues—you know who you are—and we thank you for your friendship and insight. And last, but not least, we thank our families for tolerating our absences and busy schedules, and especially to our sons Gage, Davis, and Ricardo for being so patient and so thrilled when the answer to the oft-asked question "Are you done with the book?" was "Yes!"

otto.maclin@uni.edu

Photo Credit: Karen Orders Photography

kim.maclin@uni.edu

Courtesy of Tim Crone

CHAPTER 1

Introduction and Research Methods

hmmm. . .?

1. What is cognitive psychology?
2. What disciplines contribute to cognitive science?
3. How did cognitive psychology emerge as a major force in psychology?
4. What is a cognitive model, and how have cognitive models been used to understand the mind?
5. How has cognitive neuroscience influenced the study of mind sciences, and what new directions in cognition might emerge because of this influence?
6. How has evolutionary cognitive psychology influenced thinking in cognitive psychology?

What Is Cognitive Psychology?

When you read and think about the question *what is cognitive psychology?*, you are engaging in cognition. Cognitive psychology deals with the perception of information (you read the question), it deals with understanding (you comprehend the question), it deals with thought (you determine whether you know the answer), and it deals with the formulation and production of an answer (you may say, "Cognitive psychology is the study of thinking"—you may also say, "I don't know!"). Cognitive psychology can also be viewed as the study of processes underlying mental events. In fact, cognitive psychology encompasses everything we do.

It will be useful to gain some perspective on what cognitive psychology actually is by exploring a cognitively demanding occupation—the job of an air traffic controller.

Air traffic controllers are responsible for the lives of airplane passengers and pilots and they coordinate the movement of air traffic to make certain that planes stay a safe

Air Traffic Controllers at work.

distance apart. This may sound easy to some people. Well, actually, it is a difficult job that some say is hours of boredom punctuated with moments of sheer terror. Read one controller's account of his job:

> "It's like a three-dimensional chess game. You must be able to concentrate on several things at the same time and be able to visualize moving aircraft that you're controlling. You'll have one aircraft 15 miles away at such and such an altitude then another will call in from 20 miles away in another direction and give an altitude. You're expecting another scheduled flight in the area shortly. You sit and think, what should I do? Rapid decision making, that's what it's all about. You're constantly updating your information and you must know what's going on in your section every minute, every second. The keys are quick thinking and clear communications. There's a lot of pressure . . . the consequences could be catastrophic."

How would the cognitive psychologist view the air traffic controller's job? A cognitive psychologist would view the air traffic controller's job by breaking it down into separate tasks and their related cognitive processes. For example, a basic breakdown might consist of several parts: (1) *external inputs* of weather reports, information displayed on the radar monitor, and radio contact with the pilot; (2) *selective attention* and *perception*

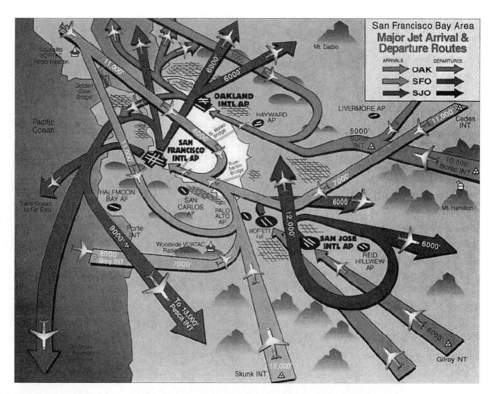

Approach/departure corridors for San Francisco Bay Area.

Courtesy of the FAA.

Cognition in Everyday Life

Throughout this book you will see these boxes where you will be presented with an everyday experience that is relevant to the current chapter's content.

Right now, and at any moment, just like the air traffic controller, you are involved in a myriad of cognitive activity. You have external inputs of this information on the page, and your surrounding environment (the quiet of the library, or the chaos of the student union or your residence hall); these inputs affect your selective attention of the text you are reading and ultimately your ability to accurately perceive this information; assuming you are able to pay attention and perceive, you are forming internal representations of this information, and those representations are stored in memory; you may also be engaging decision making (like how much longer you are going to read before you stop and whether or not you are going to take notes while you are reading) and finally, you may take some action (move locations because it is too loud, take notes, finish reading the chapter or stopping reading at the end of this box). You, right now, have a lot going on cognitively.

of the external inputs; (3) the formation of *internal representations* to be stored in *memory;* (4) *decision making* and planning, and finally, (5) taking *action* by typing into a keyboard or *communicating* to a pilot. While air traffic controllers are selected for their cognitive abilities, any job, any activity, has a lot going on cognitively.

By the time you finish reading this book you'll have a clear idea of these processes. For now, we're going to give you a brief history of cognitive psychology to lay the groundwork for the study of cognitive processes (such as the ones used by the air traffic controller).

The History of Cognitive Psychology in Brief

Of all the areas of psychology, cognitive psychology is likely to have the longest history, stemming back to early philosophers asking themselves where knowledge comes from and how it is represented in the mind. Eternal questions such as these are fundamental to modern cognitive psychology as it has been through the ages of humankind. The fascination with knowledge can be traced to the earliest writings. Early theories were concerned with the seat of thought and memory. Ancient Egyptian hieroglyphics suggest their authors believed that knowledge was localized in the heart—a view later shared by the ancient Greek philosopher Aristotle, but not by his mentor Plato, who held that the brain was the locus of knowledge.

Two perspectives have been proposed about how knowledge is represented in the mind. These are the empiricists' and nativists' viewpoints. The **empiricists** maintained that knowledge comes from experiences gained through the lifetime. For example, everything we know is learned. The **nativists** argued that knowledge is based on innate characteristics of the brain. In other words, we're born "hardwired" with some existing knowledge.

For example, the empiricists' perspective would be that you may have learned the Pythagorean Theorem, illustrated below, in high school: The sum of squares of the length of the sides of a right triangle is equal to the square of the length of the hypotenuse. No doubt your experience in high school geometry class led to that knowledge. However, the nativists might respond that the knowledge of triangles something that preexisted inside your brain before you were born, and was the basis for your understanding of the Pythagorean Theorem.

$$a^2 + b^2 = c^2$$

How can we find the height of this pyramid?

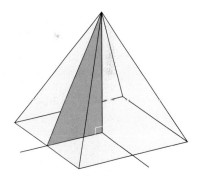

Solution: *by solving a right triangle.*

From a scientific perspective, neither case can be definitively proved, so the argument continues without one side winning over the other. Nowadays people take a more moderate perspective, as it is obvious that information gained from experiences is processed by an innately receptive brain that allows us to process and make sense out of these experiences, thus forming knowledge.

Some of the difficulty in this ongoing debate stems from our defining knowledge as the "storage and organization of information in memory," thus fitting the definition to two sides of the argument: The "storage" side suggests that experiences are important,

Plato   **Aristotle**

and the "organization" side suggests that some preexisting structural capacity exists in the brain. Renaissance philosophers and theologians seemed generally satisfied that knowledge was located in the brain.

The eighteenth century was also known as the **Period of Enlightenment** (The Renaissance), during which many technological, social, and political changes were taking place. Science started working without fear of repercussions from the Church. It was during this time when philosophical treatment of what would later be termed psychology was brought to the point where scientific psychology could assume a role. The British empiricists—George Berkeley, David Hume, and later, James Mill and his son John Stuart Mill—suggested that **internal representation** is of three types: (1) direct sensory events; (2) events that are stored in memory; and (3) transformation of these events in the thinking process. Hume's writing illustrates how philosophers talked about internal representations. "To form monsters, and join incongruous shapes and appearances, costs the imagination no more trouble than to conceive the most natural and familiar objects." In this quote, Hume speaks of internal representation and transformation and postulates that internal representations are formed according to definable rules, and that such formation and transformation takes time and effort. Although this was written in the 1860s, these assumptions underlie much of modern cognitive psychology.

During the nineteenth century, psychologists emerged from **philosophy** to form a discipline based on testable hypotheses and empirical data rather than on philosophical speculation. Conspicuous as a factor in this emergence was the activity of early psychologists. By the last half of the nineteenth century, theories of the **representation of knowledge** became dichotomized once again into structure and process. Wundt in Germany and his American student Titchener in the United States emphasized the structure of mental representation through their research on **introspection,** while Brentano in Austria emphasized the processes or acts of **mental representations.** Brentano considered internal representations to be static entities of little value in psychology. He took the study of cognitive acts of comparing, judging, and feeling to be the proper topics of psychology. These rival theories dealt with many of the same issues discussed 2,000 years before by Plato and Aristotle. However, unlike the philosopher who could only speculate, the psychologist could test ideas via experimentation.

About the same time, William James critically analyzed the new psychology that was developing in Germany and was being brought to America by students of Wundt, like Titchener. James established the first psychological laboratory in America at Harvard University, wrote the definitive work in psychology in 1890 (*Principles of Psychology*), and developed a well-reasoned model of the mind. James considered the subject matter of psychology to be our experience of external objects. Perhaps James's most direct link with modern cognitive psychology is his view of memory, which comprises structure and process. F. C. Donders and James Cattell, contemporaries of James, were performing experiments using the perception of brief visual displays as a means of determining the time required for mental operations. They published reports of experiments that dealt with topics we would today call cognitive psychology. The technique, subject matter, procedures, and the interpretation of results of these early scientists seem to have anticipated the emergence of the formal discipline a half-century later.

The Rise and Fall of Behaviorism

The representation of knowledge, as we have used the term, took a radical turn with the advent of twentieth-century **behaviorism.** The behaviorist views of human and animal psychology were cast in a framework of reducing experience to a **stimulus–response** psychology.

As a result, psychological studies of mental processes as conceptualized in the late nineteenth century suddenly became unfashionable, displaced by behaviorism. Studies of internal mental operations and structures—such as attention, consciousness, memory, and thinking—were laid to rest and remained so for about fifty years. Those who chose to study these topics were compelled to reframe their work in behaviorist terms. To the behaviorists, internal states were subsumed under the label of **intervening variables.** Intervening variables were defined as hypothetical constructs presumed to represent processes that mediated the effects of stimuli on behavior. And were consequently neglected in favor of making observations purely on behavior (the things that humans and animals did that could be objectively observed) rather than on the mental processes that were the underpinnings of behavior.

In 1932, some years before the **cognitive revolution** swept across psychology, behaviorist Edward Tolman from the University of California at Berkeley published his

I was educated to study behavior and I learned to translate my ideas into the new jargon of behaviorism. As I was most interested in speech and hearing, the translation sometimes became tricky. But one's reputation as a scientist could depend on how well the trick was played.

—George Miller writing about the cognitive revolution

Edward C. Tolman **(1886–1959).**
Developed the concept of a cognitive map.

Photograph courtesy of Archives of the History of
American Psychology, University of Akron, Akron,
Ohio 44303.

book *Purposive Behavior in Animals and Men.* In this seminal work, Tolman observed
that rats seemed to know the "lay of the land" when running a maze, rather than a series of stimulus–response connections. Tolman, conducted a series of ingenious experiments in which a rat was trained to find food by following a single winding pathway,
and found that it went in the general direction of where the food was instead of following the exact pathway. In other words, instead of learning simply how to get to the food,
it learned the relative location of the food, allowing it to use alternate, novel (untrained)
pathways when accessible. This ability to learn without being directly trained was problematic for the behaviorists. The animal, according to Tolman's interpretation, gradually

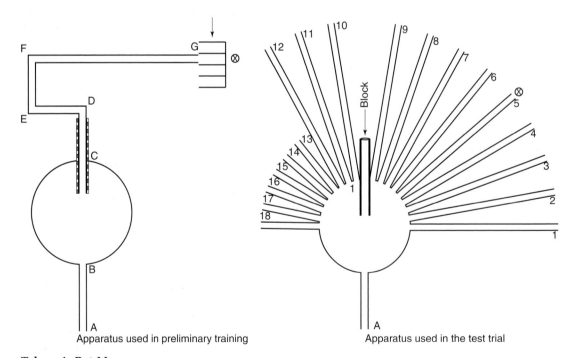

Apparatus used in preliminary training   Apparatus used in the test trial

Tolman's Rat Mazes.

Adapted from Tolman, Ritchie & Karlish (1946).

developed a "picture" of its environment that was later used to find the goal. This picture was called a **cognitive map.** The rats in Tolman's experiments exhibited their cognitive map by reaching a goal (the food) from a number of different starting points. This internal map was, in effect, the way information about their environment was represented. His postulate about cognitive maps in animals did anticipate the contemporary preoccupation with how knowledge is represented in a cognitive structure.

Another important event in 1932 occurred when Sir Frederick Bartlett from Cambridge University wrote *Remembering* in which he rejected the popular view at the time that memory and forgetting can be studied by means of nonsense syllables, as had been advocated by Ebbinghaus during the previous century. In the study of human memory, Bartlett argued, the use of rich and meaningful material under naturalistic conditions would yield far more significant conclusions than using arbitrary stimuli, such as nonsense syllables. Bartlett had participants read a story and then try to recall as much of the story as they could. He found that an important aspect of remembering a story was the participant's attitude toward the story. In Bartlett's words, "The recall is then a construction made largely on the basis of this attitude, and its general effect is that of a justification of the attitude." In effect, what you remember about a story is based on the overall impression created by the story. Subsequent recall of specific facts then tends to corroborate the participant's impression, thus distorting facts or filling in missing pieces.

From the earliest concepts of representational knowledge to recent research, knowledge has been thought to rely heavily on sensory inputs. That theme runs from the Greek philosophers, through Renaissance scholars, to contemporary cognitive psychologists. But are internal representations of the world identical to the physical properties of the world? There is mounting evidence that many internal representations of reality are not the same as external reality. Tolman's work with laboratory animals and Bartlett's work with humans suggest that information from the senses is stored as an abstract representation. Their ideas ran contrary to the *zeitgeist* of the 1930s, which was centered on the overt behaviors of animals and humans. Because behaviorism failed to fully account for their findings, these studies and others over the next twenty years would become influential in the downfall of behaviorism by influencing the thinking of future cognitive psychologists.

In the 1950s, interest again began to focus on cognitive processes. New journals and professional groups were founded as psychologists began more and more to turn to studying cognitive processes. As the study of cognitive processes became established with even greater clarity, it was plain that a brand of psychology different from that in vogue during the behaviorist-dominated 1930s and 1940s was emerging. In 1956, George Miller published his landmark article, "The Magical Number Seven, Plus or Minus Two: Some Limits on Our Capacity for Processing Information," which brought to the forefront the empirical evaluation of cognition.

The spark that set off what has become known as the cognitive revolution took place the same year that Miller published his paper. During the late summer of 1956, a symposium on information theory was held on the campus of MIT. Many of the leading figures in communication theory were in attendance and listened to talks by Noam Chomsky (linguistics), Jerome Bruner (thinking), Allen Newell and Herbert Simon (computer science), and George Miller (information processing), among others. The meeting had an indelible effect on many of its participants, and the general feeling was that something new was being created that would significantly change the way psychological processes could be conceptualized. Reflecting on the meeting several years later, George Miller (1979) wrote:

I went away from the Symposium with a strong conviction, more intuitive than rational, that human experimental psychology, theoretical linguistics, and computer simulation of cognitive processes were all pieces of a larger whole, and that the future would see progressive elaboration and coordination of their shared concerns. . . . I have been working toward a cognitive science for about twenty years, beginning before I knew what to call it. (p. 9)

As we have learned, a great portion of cognitive psychology deals with how knowledge is represented in the mind. The lively issue of representational knowledge has evoked the same fundamental questions over centuries: How is knowledge acquired, stored, transformed, and used? What is consciousness, and where do conscious ideas originate? What is the nature of perception and memory? What is thought? How do these abilities develop?

These questions reflect the essential issue of representational knowledge—how ideas, events, and things are stored in the mind. But it was not until the 1960s that Ulrich Neisser wrote the first cognitive psychology textbook that brought together these diverse topics representing the new discipline of cognitive psychology. Well, then, one might conclude that the rest is history (so to speak). However, cognitive psychology continued (and continues) to define itself by scientifically exploring the processes of the mind by incorporating new methodologies, disciplines, and thought in these areas.

Cognitive Psychology Is about Processing Information

When we say that cognitive psychology is about processing information, we mean that it is concerned with how we attend to and gain information about the world, how that information is stored and processed by the brain, how we solve problems, think and formulate language, and how these processes may be manifested as overt behaviors.

Neisser (1967) put it more precisely: " . . . the term cognition refers to all processes by which the sensory input is transformed, reduced, elaborated, stored, recovered, and used . . . it is apparent that cognition is involved in everything a human being might possibly do; that every psychological phenomena is a cognitive phenomena" (p. 4).

Cognitive psychology involves the total range of psychological processes—from sensation to perception, pattern recognition, attention, consciousness, learning, memory, concept formation, thinking, imagining, language, intelligence, emotions, and how all these things change through the life span (developmental considerations)—and cuts across all the diverse fields of behavior. The list is long because the scope of cognitive psychology is broad (See Figure 1.1).

Cognitive Metaphors, Models, Theories, and Perspectives

Metaphors

People often use **metaphors** to describe cognitive processes. For example, memory can be thought of in terms of a file cabinet, a computer, a puzzle, or a video camera. Each of these metaphors of memory provides a convenient way to think about the structure

FIGURE 1.1

Principal research areas of cognitive psychology.

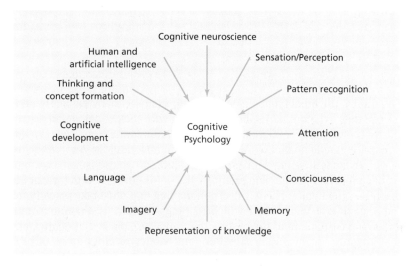

and function of memory. As useful as metaphors are, they can also be misleading. For example, we are often asked to provide consultation to jurors to explain memory processes. We have to make clear that in fact memory is not like a video camera. Ultimately what we are asked to do is to discuss memory based on cognitive models. Models are essentially a testable, more detailed form of a metaphor. As such, they help us understand the actual memory process. Models though are still only a representation of the actual biological process of memory. Some benefits of models are that they help us communicate processes to others, and they help scientists make predictions based on the model.

Models

A **model** is an organizational framework used to describe processes. Models are based on inferences drawn from observations. Their purpose is to provide an understandable representation of the character of the observation and to aid in making predictions. Models are useful in conceptualizing cognitive processes for analytic purposes. **Formalism** is the rules underlying the model. Formalism is a means to represent the rules used in the establishment of a model. When models lose their vitality as analytical or descriptive tools, they are revised or abandoned. Although, we use models to help understand cognitive processes, we could just as easily use a model to describe and understand the process of ordering a take-and-bake pizza. See Figure 1.2.

While ordering a pizza is a well-understood process for most of us, we can examine it further (we can model it). We see that there is a series of stages or activities linked together in a linear fashion such that you proceed through the stages one after the other.

FIGURE 1.2

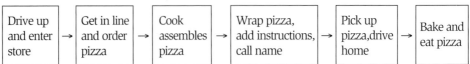

So initially, the model helps us understand the process by explicitly describing it. Models can do even more for us, however. Even with this model, it can be used to make predictions. One could predict that if someone entered the store, they would come out with a pizza. A simple prediction, but a prediction nevertheless. Another benefit of the model is we can study it as the entire series of stages, or we can isolate our inquiry to one particular processing stage. For example, the get-in-line-and-order-pizza stage has several discreet components. There is decision making that must take place (where is the end of the line? thin or thick crust? which toppings?). There is a communication process between the customer and the cashier that must take place that is integral to the outcome that includes exchanging information, and money or other forms of payment. This is a useful model because it describes the process, allows for inquiry about various aspects of the process, and aids in predictions about the process.

So going back to our video camera metaphor for memory, we can see how it may be useful for an individual to think about memory as a video camera on a day-to-day basis. It is like a video camera because it allows us to consider issues such as focusing on an object, recording an object or scene, and playing it back. However, in the context of a juror in court (or in any setting where it is important to be accurate and precise), this metaphor is simplistic and misleading because that is not how our memory works. Instead, a cognitive model of memory is more accurate and more useful. Like the pizza model, it is descriptive, allows us to focus on particular aspects of the process, and aids in predictions. In describing memory to jurors, a cognitive model of memory, such as the straightforward one below (See Figure 1.3), not only helps illustrate the memory process, but allows for jurors to evaluate eyewitness memory.

Now you might be thinking, "That model is still pretty similar to a video camera." You're right, in part. However, the model, being without the trappings of what we know about video cameras, helps us be more specific and accurate about the memory process. One common misperception when thinking about memory as a video camera is that we can rewind to a particular scene or select a particular incident from the past to view, and view it exactly as it occurred, and this is simply not the case. In fact, this three-stage model allows us to go in and talk about any one of the stages in detail (just as in the

FIGURE 1.3

pizza example). And thus, we are able to explain to jurors about how memories are encoded, and how that encoding is different in the brain than it is on a VHS tape or DVD.

So let's turn to a more complex model than pizza ordering or a three-stage model of memory. Models can be complex, multistaged, and not solely linear. In other words, a model can indicate processes that occur at the same time. Recall what our air traffic controller discussed at the beginning of the chapter. This job involves specific tasks and specific cognitive processing for these tasks. There are applied cognitive psychologists who study air traffic controllers so that they may make predictions about their performance (and to presumably reduce costly errors). These researchers rely on cognitive models to conceptualize these tasks and processes. As can be seen in Figure 1-4, this model takes into consideration external events, perceived events, and resulting behaviors. It's more than that. But it serves as an illustration that not all processes are linear, some interact with each other, sending information back and forth, as is the case with perceived events and external events (noted by the double-headed arrows). And, there is also a feedback loop from behaviors (e.g., communications) back to external events.

FIGURE 1.4

A model for the cognitive tasks of an Air Traffic Controller.

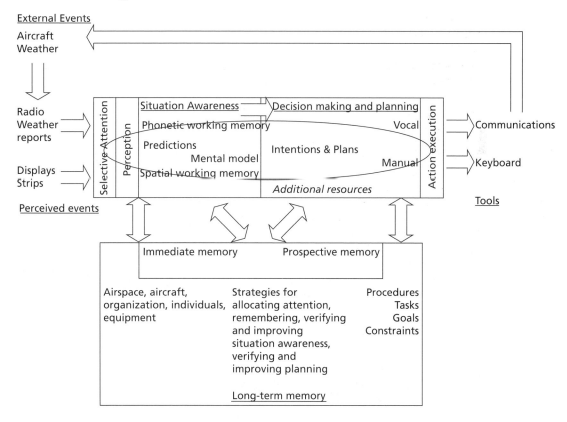

Theories

A theory, on the other hand, is an attempt to explain some aspect of the process, with some theories being more substantiated than others. **Theories** attempt to explain particular aspects of phenomena and are often used to test hypotheses. For example, Darwin's theory of evolution is an attempt to explain how the natural world has changed over time. While it is "just a theory" it is well substantiated by a tome of data. You can test theories by collecting data that will ultimately support or disprove the theory.

Perspectives

There are several perspectives in cognitive psychology that have been influential in the thinking and development of the discipline. Perspectives guide scientists' research questions and the evaluation of their findings. We cover four such perspectives: information processing, neuroscience, computer science, and evolutionary psychology.

Information Processing   The **information processing** perspective is generally related to a time-ordered sequence of events, and many cognitive models use this approach. This perspective begins with a set of three assumptions. Cognition can be understood by analyzing it into a series of (mostly) sequential stages. At each stage unique processes take place on incoming information. The eventual response is assumed to be the outcome of this series of stages and operations. Each stage receives information from preceding stages and then performs its unique function. Because all components of the information processing model are in some way related to each other, for convenience we can think of the sequence as starting with incoming information.

One of the first and most frequently cited models based on this perspective dealt with memory. In 1890, William James expanded the concept of memory to include primary memory and secondary memory. Primary memory was hypothesized to deal with immediate events, and secondary memory with permanent, "indestructible" vestiges of experience. This was as follows (See Figure 1.5):

Although James's model was rather simplistic, a later revision of the model by Waugh and Norman (1965) satisfied many of the demands for a representative model. As such, the new model allows for the generation of hypotheses and predictions. (See Figure 1.6.) However, it is still overly simplistic, compared to today's memory models. Not all human memory processes and storage systems can be accurately described using this model, thus it was inevitable that more complex models have evolved.

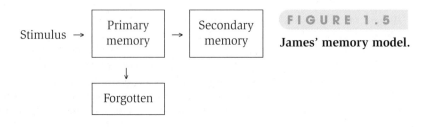

FIGURE 1.5

James' memory model.

FIGURE 1.6

Modified Waugh and Norman memory model.

Adapted from Waugh and Norman (1965).

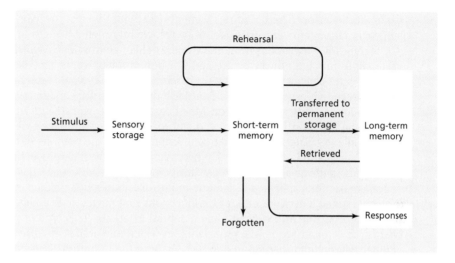

The James model and the Waugh and Norman model both are based on a sequence of events. A stimulus is presented, we detect it through the sensory system, we store and transform it in memory, and we react to it. You may have noticed that models of human cognition bear some resemblance to the sequential steps involved in computer processing, indeed, cognitive psychologists have borrowed heavily from the computer metaphor.

Neuroscience   The **neuroscience** perspective focuses on the underlying brain functions that produce cognitive experience. During the early years of cognitive psychology, little attention was given to physiological psychology or neuroanatomy, possibly due to the reliance on the computer metaphor. Moreover, neuroanatomy and related areas seemed to be so far removed from, and bore little resemblance to, cognitive topics such as perception, memory, and thinking.

Much of the early information on the brain and its functions resulted from head traumas incurred during wars and accidents. For example, during World War I, neurosurgeons treating victims of shrapnel wounds to the brain learned a great deal about the specialized functions of the brain (e.g., which areas were associated with vision, speech, hearing, etc.) as well as the general functioning. It was presumed that behavioral deficits were related to specific areas of the brain that were damaged, which led researchers to deduce that those areas were responsible for particular psychological functions. This is similar to reverse engineering where engineers take something apart to see how something works.

The central issue neurologists struggled with was whether the brain was a holistic organ, with cognitive functions distributed throughout its infrastructure, or whether functions were localized and tied to specific regions. For example, did learning a specific fact take place in a localized area of the brain, or was learning distributed throughout many parts of the brain? Among the most prominent scientists who grappled with these issues was Karl Lashley. In his experiments, Lashley lesioned (surgically removed) specific parts of the brains of rats after they had learned to run a maze (Lashley, 1929). He demonstrated that maze-running performance declined according to the total amount of the brain destroyed. There was no correlation between performance and the specific location of the lesion. These findings were at odds with those of the World War I neurosurgeons. This controversy was later to be resolved through advances in neuroscience.

Significant progress has been made in the field of neuroscience, which comprises investigations into both the structure and function of the brain. In the 1960s, researchers found structural elements involving the cerebral cortex that would later have a direct impact on cognitive psychology. Some of these discoveries were made at the Johns Hopkins School of Medicine by Vernon Mountcastle, whose work dealt with the cerebral cortex—the top layer of the brain, thought to be involved in higher mental processes. Mountcastle (1979) discovered that connections among the neurons of the cortex were more numerous than had previously been thought. As well as processing information using serial pathways, perhaps most intriguing was the discovery that the system of neural connections appeared to fan out and be distributed in a parallel array. The parallel array formed a network of neural connections that ranged over a large territory, with functions occurring at the same time in several locations. This type of processing is in contrast to serial or sequential processing, in which one neural impulse is passed on to another neuron, and then on to another. The way the brain functions, according to the parallel view, is that processing networks are distributed throughout the cortex rather than localized. Mountcastle's research helps reconcile the World War I neurosurgeons' and Lashley's findings, essentially indicating that they were both correct. The neurosurgeons were correct because localized parts of the brain associated with vision, speech, motor actions, and so on, are specialized only in the sense that they receive inputs and make outputs associated with those functions. Lashley's work is confirmed in that some studies have found that many functions are actually distributed throughout the brain. This makes sense if you use the Internet as a metaphor for how the brain is wired. The Internet essentially consists of individual computer servers located around the world (like your university server where you have your email account). These provide specific services to localized groups of people (like the students and faculty at your university). The majority of the servers are interconnected with each other. So if one goes down, the network itself remains largely unaffected. For example, if your university server goes down, you will be unable to check your email and surf the Internet through that account. However, other people in the world using the Internet will be largely unaware of this situation unless they are trying to send you an email, or trying to access your university's webpages.

Computer Science   Although Pascal, Descartes, and other philosophers dreamed of computing machines centuries ago, it was not until only about sixty years ago that computers were invented, and the discipline of **Computer Science** was born. Computers gained enormous acceptance and are presently used in virtually every aspect of modern life. They also have had a philosophical impact on the way scholars view the mind, in addition to being an important tool for scientists interested in studying the mind. Originally, computers were thought to be wonderful number crunchers capable of performing a multitude of complex mathematical operations in a fraction of the time required by

Electrical Numerical Integrators and Computer (ENIAC), US Army, 1946.

U. S. Army Photo.

humans. In fact, some of the earliest computers were developed by the military to help solve mathematical equations used in targeting military sites. However, it was quickly discovered that computers could be more than super calculators and that they could perform functions that resembled human problem solving and intelligent behavior.

What computers do well (i.e., perform high-speed mathematical functions and abide by rule-governed logic) humans do poorly, relatively speaking. And what humans do well (i.e., form generalizations, make inferences, understand complex patterns, and have emotions) computers do not do so well, if at all. For example, if we ask you to find the square root of 2.19 by hand, it will probably take you several minutes; a computer can solve this problem in milliseconds. On the other hand, one area where computers are still not as good as humans is in face recognition. Computers can "recognize" a face if it is programmed into its database. However, they can't make inferences about age, gender, or affect when it sees a new face. This humans can do in milliseconds.

The next generation of cognitive computer scientists is working toward building computers that are structured and process something like a brain. Computer scientists took what they knew about neural networks in the brain and created computers with artificial neural networks. These are complete with layers of interconnected electronic surrogate neurons, whose organizational "hardware" mimics the "wetware" of the brain, and they contain programs that mimic the functions of organic neural networks.

For example, David Rumelhart, James McClelland, and the PDP Research Group (1986) have developed a neurally inspired model based on the kind of neural processing mechanism that is the human mind. Not only is the brain interconnected, the brain

David Rumelhart (left) and James McClelland. Formalized the neurally inspired PDP model.

sends along excitatory and inhibitory signals within the network. Excitatory signals tell neurons to pass on the information. Inhibitory signals tell neurons to not pass on the information. For example, the brain does not store memory in any single neuron or probably even in any local set, but it does store memory in an entire ensemble of neurons distributed throughout several parts of the brain. If two neurons are simultaneously activated, the bond (the excitatory or the inhibitory nature of the connection) between them is strengthened. On the other hand, if one is activated and another inhibited, the bond is weakened. Computer scientists that use these types of models referred to them as **parallel distributed processing** (PDP). "These [PDP] models assume that information processing takes place through the interactions of a large number of simple processing elements called units, each sending excitatory and inhibitory signals to other units" (McClelland, Rumelhart, & Hinton, 1986, p. 10). Because they are modeled after the brain, PDP models not only help us understand the processes of the brain, but also understand the structure. See below for a diagram of a neural network.

A Typical Neural Network

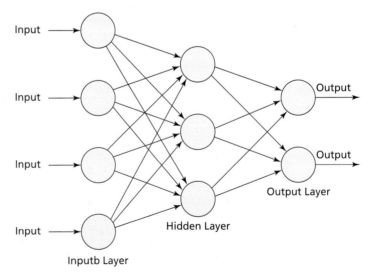

The similarities between the human brain and the computer have not always been clear, however, we know now that there are fundamental differences between the internal workings of computers and the internal workings of the brain. Nevertheless, the computer perspective continues to have a profound and generally positive impact on the continued development of the discipline of cognitive psychology.

Evolutionary Psychology   This perspective is based on the idea that cognition is best understood from a functionalist approach. In other words, what function does a particular cognitive process serve in the context of physical and social evolution? Recall that evolutionary theory as laid out by Charles Darwin evaluates physical and behavioral traits in terms of how adaptive they are to the organism, and further, to what extent those traits lead to reproductive success, and thus the passing on of one's genes to the next generation. One of the confusions about evolutionary theory lies in people's mistake in recognizing exactly what environmental pressures are being referred to as having shaped a particular trait. Cosmides and Tooby (1997) explain it very well:

> The environment that humans—and, therefore, human *minds*—evolved in was very different from our modern environment. Our ancestors spent well over 99% of our species' evolutionary history living in hunter-gatherer societies. That means that our forebearers lived in small, nomadic bands of a few dozen individuals who got all of their food each day by gathering plants or by hunting animals. Each of our ancestors was, in effect, on a camping trip that lasted an entire lifetime, and this way of life endured for most of the last 10 million years.
>
> Generation after generation, for 10 million years, natural selection slowly sculpted the human brain, favoring circuitry that was good at solving the day-to-day problems of our hunter-gatherer ancestors—problems like finding mates, hunting animals, gathering plant foods, negotiating with friends, defending ourselves against aggression, raising children, choosing a good habitat, and so on. Those whose circuits were better designed for solving these problems left more children, and we are descended from them.
>
> Our species lived as hunter-gatherers 1000 times longer than as anything else. The world that seems so familiar to you and me, a world with roads, schools, grocery stores, factories, farms, and nation-states, has lasted for only an eyeblink of time when compared to our entire evolutionary history. The computer age is only a little older than the typical college student, and the industrial revolution is a mere 200 years old. Agriculture first appeared on earth only 10,000 years ago, and it wasn't until about 5,000 years ago that as many as half of the human population engaged in farming rather than hunting and gathering. Natural selection is a slow process, and there just haven't been enough generations for it to design circuits that are well-adapted to our post-industrial life. (p. 9)

Thus, cognitive processes can be interpreted in terms of the long-term biological and evolutionary history of the species. William James, John Dewey, and other **functionalists** examined psychological processes in terms of their function of how they allow us to adapt to changes in the environment. For example, James would ask "Why do we have memory?" "How does it help us survive and adapt?" According to Darwin's theory, and modern conceptualizations of it (Tooby & Cosmides, 2001), features or traits that are adaptive are present because they were selected for (because they serve a

*M*ind and world . . . have evolved together, and in consequence are something of a mutual fit.

—*William James*

survival function) and passed on to subsequent generations; byproducts of evolution perform no function of their own, but are present because they are related to traits that do have a function (like fearing harmless vs. poisonous snakes); and finally, noise, which is random variation that may introduce strange, nonfunctional traits into a species (e.g., sneezing when exposed to the sun) (Cosmides & Tooby, 1997).

Following this logic, James would say if memory exists (thus has not been selected out), it must have a function. A major premise of the **evolutionary perspective** is the supposition that there are universal human cognitive attributes and that these common and widely shared attributes of the mind are a result of evolved psychological mechanisms. Roger Shepherd (1987) formulates the perspective of evolutionary psychology this way:

> I seek general psychological laws that underlie all specific mental processes and behaviors, despite their apparent variation between individuals, cultures or species. Moreover, I seek an evolutionary origin of such general psychological laws in the properties of the world that have been so pervasive and enduring as to be relevant for a broad spectrum of species. (p. 254)

One of the benefits of the evolutionary perspective is that it puts a constraint on theories and models that people would develop by forcing them to consider the utility and overall benefit of a particular process or trait. Thus, if there was no benefit, why would such a process or trait exist? Researchers interested in face recognition, for example, had to argue that the ability to recognize other faces was so important that a specific area of the brain was designated for that function or process. In other words, it was adaptive to have such an ability. In fact, neuroscience has subsequently demonstrated such a specialized area in the temporal lobe of the brain.

The Relationship between Cognitive Psychology and Cognitive Science

A byproduct of the cognitive revolution is that scholars from categorically discreet areas—including linguistics, computer science, developmental psychology, and cognitive psychology—got together and focused on their common interests such as the structure and process of cognitive abilities. Collectively, these individuals created a united front to defeat behaviorism. For example, Noam Chomsky held that the brain had a language acquisition device that functioned beyond what could be explained with the stimulus–response behaviorism psychology. Similarly, Piaget, at the time, laid out important stages of cognitive development that children go through, which again could not be explained solely in behaviorists' terms. Computer scientists contributed a perspective that computer processing could be a way to conceptualize brain processing. These scientists maintained their own distinct methodologies, literatures, and lines of scientific inquiry, but they held together and remained united in their interest in cognition and in their goal to bring the scientific study of these processes to the forefront. This scientific collective became known as cognitive science.

Today, **cognitive science** relies heavily on the following areas as an interdisciplinary field: computer science, philosophy, psychology, neuroscience, linguistics, and anthropology (see below). Scientists in these areas, interested in cognitive processes, might refer to themselves as a cognitive scientist if they have expertise in two or more of these areas. Due to the interdisciplinary nature of the field, one can find cognitive science courses taught in departments besides psychology, such as philosophy and computer science. Cognitive science is strongly influenced by computer science, with courses in cognitive science focusing on computer modeling, artificial intelligence (AI), and neuroscience. While cognitive psychology deals with these topics, it focuses unapologetically on all aspects of human cognition. This fundamental knowledge then becomes the infrastructure for the specialized interests of scientists in other disciplines.

One of the reasons why computer science is dominant in cognitive science is its ability to construct and test cognitive models. The benefit of a computer model is that it can simulate a process and provide output. The parameters of the model can then be adjusted until the results of the simulation maps onto data from behavioral studies. Once this occurs, then cognitive scientists can run further simulations to predict how humans would respond under hypothetical circumstances. The benefit of computer modeling is that it is not

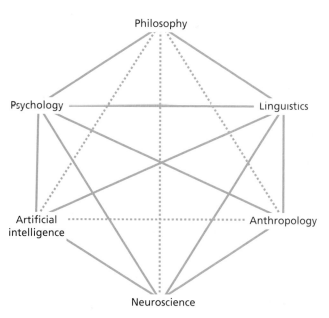

Gardner's Hexagon. Connections among the cognitive sciences. Key: Unbroken lines = strong interdisciplinary ties. Broke lines = weak interdisciplinary ties.

...the AI community may well turn out to be for the cognitive sciences what mathematics broadly has been for all sciences. If mathematics is the queen of sciences, AI could earn the mantel of the Prince of Wales of Cognitive Science.

—*Unknown*

as resource intensive (in terms of time and money) as compared to having humans participate in numerous experiments. The computer program is capable of running thousands of simulations in the time it would take to collect data from one human research participant, making them a powerful research tool. An additional benefit of the computer simulations is that modern high-speed computers, as we said before, are capable of running PDP (neural network) models that are designed to process more similarly to the human brain.

An example of a cognitive model versus a PDP model from face recognition is given below. The benefit of the computer model is that the elements of the model are interconnected, and the parameters are capable of being adjusted to accurately produce re-

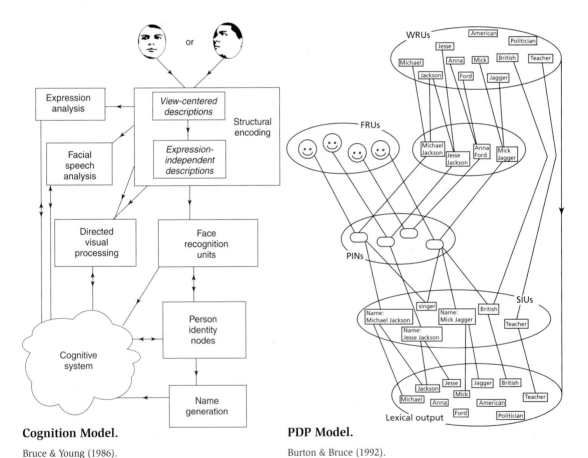

Cognition Model.

Bruce & Young (1986).

PDP Model.

Burton & Bruce (1992).

sults similar to human face recognition. The cognitive model *describes* the process; the computer model *simulates* the process.

While computer science might dominate cognitive science, effectively the root of cognitive science is cognitive psychology, because by and large all of these areas are interested in fundamental cognitive processes and resulting behaviors.

Research Methods

The methods of cognitive psychology stem from those used by early German researchers studying memory, association, and processes. These tools became the mainstay of experimental psychology. As cognitive psychology began to form and become interdisciplinary, methods from other fields were borrowed and modified for use in the study of cognitive processes. Research methods are the tools by which we come to know and understand, as well as test ideas and develop new ones. We provide a brief overview here.

There are many research methods available to the psychological scientist. Some allow researchers to *describe* phenomena (**observational studies**) and another allows researchers to *explain* phenomena (an **experiment**). Through an experiment, cause and effect can be determined, making this a useful tool of cognitive psychologists.

Throughout the book you will encounter examples and details of experiments and studies conducted by cognitive psychologists. We provide here a brief description of these different methods as a primer of sorts to assist you in understanding the cognitive processing itself and the studies we are going to present.

Before we start talking about the methodologies themselves, we need to introduce you to definitional issues (conceptual vs. operationalized), as they are central to the study of cognitive processes. An example of a conceptual definition is the situation where a motorist is "drunk." There is a general understanding of what "drunk" means (this is the conceptual definition), but it does not tell us precisely how much or what the motorist drank. An **operational definition** requires that you specify the concept precisely and explicitly, thereby turning the abstract into something concrete. The interesting (and creative) aspect of this part of the research process is that you the researcher determine what the operational definition is dependent on your research question and interests. Thus, "drunk" could be operationalized in any number of ways, including physiological definitions ("drunk" = a blood alcohol level of .08), observational definitions (rating or scoring behavior as in a roadside sobriety test), or self-report definitions (asking the individual directly via interview or questionnaire).

Another common feature of methodology, regardless of the specific method, is the unit of analysis. The **unit of analysis** is the primary entity or focus of your study, and is ultimately what is measured. The best way to understand the unit of analysis is to determine what is actually being measured. For example, if you are collecting data on the neural firing of a specific cell, your unit of analysis is the cell. If you are collecting IQ data on children, your unit of analysis is the individual child. If you are measuring the number of words exchanged between two individuals within a 5-minute period, your unit of analysis is the conversation. If you are measuring the number of times a team commits fouls, your unit of measurement is at the group level of the team. Units of analysis can even be geographical (at the city, state, or country level) or artifacts (books, photos, drawings), among others. Cognitive psychology primarily uses as its unit of

If we are to achieve results never before achieved, we must expect to use methods never before tried.

—*Francis Bacon*

analysis the individual. Other areas of psychology, and disciplines such as sociology and anthropology, rely more heavily on other units of analysis. But either way, it is important to ask yourself what is the unit of analysis that the researcher is using.

Each type of research method also rests on some particular assumptions. We will alert you to these assumptions in each section.

The two main types of methods we are going to cover can loosely be categorized into the following: (1) measuring psychological correlates to the physical world, and (2) documenting unique cases. However, due to the interdisciplinary nature of the fields there is often overlap. We will try to keep within these categories as best as possible.

Measuring Psychological Correlates to the Physical World

Methods that fall into this category are those that specifically measure a reaction or response to an external event in the physical world. As were the early philosophers, early researchers were interested in how the physical world was translated into the mental world and what were the limits of these perceptions of the external world. This interest continues today.

Psychophysics   **Psychophysics** is the scientific study of the relationship between stimuli (specified in physical terms) and the sensations and perceptions evoked by these stimuli. This assumes that there is a functional relationship between a psychological (psycho) state and a physical (physics) stimulus. For example, Weber was interested in a person's ability to detect weight. If a person was holding a weighted object, how much weight can be added before they can detect a difference. This came be known as just noticeable differences. One of the great contributions of Weber's study was that these weight detections followed mathematic principles such that one could predict a just noticeable difference by calculating a formula, and thus had lawful properties.

Psychophysicists were interested in perceptual thresholds. Fechner established a variety of psychophysics methods that include, but are not limited to, absolute threshold, difference of threshold, and method of adjustment. A study in absolute threshold of the perception of light, for example, might have the experimenter systematically increasing the intensity of light from absolutely dark, up to the point where the sensation was noticed by the observer. The unit of analysis for psychophysics was typically an individual, in actuality the researcher him- or herself. They operated as the observer and conducted these experiments on themselves. Even today it is not uncommon to read a research ar-

Child engaged in a just-noticeable-difference task.

ticle on visual perception and see a graph of data containing the initials of a singular observer, oftentimes the author. One of the assumptions made in psychophysics is that we all perceive in a similar manner, therefore, it is not problematic for the researcher to measure his or her own perceptual experiences. Psychophysics include some of the oldest methods in psychology.

Single-Cell Studies **Single-cell studies** have been used by researchers such as Hubel and Wiesel (1959) who mapped out the visual cortex of cats (see figure, page 26, for experiment setup). They shared a Nobel Prize for this work, and Hubel was later honored by having the Hubel space telescope named after him. Single-cell studies are invasive in that the researcher must open the skull of the subject. Therefore, these studies are seldom conducted with humans and are thus typically conducted with animals under humane guidelines of research. The scientists reasoned that since cells communicated via electrical impulses, a meter on the end of a very small probe (finer than a human hair) could enter a cell without damaging it. The probe would then measure electrical activity of the cell, and thus we could evaluate the perceptual experience at the cellular level. What Hubel and Wiesel essentially did was to restrain the cat and present visual stimuli (dots or bars moving across a screen) and systematically insert the probe into the visual cortex of the cat until they measured an electrical response. The assumption is that if the cell responds to the visual stimulus there is a relationship between that stimulus and that particular cell. Single-cell recordings have also been used in other areas of the brain such as the lateral geniculate nucleus (LGN) and the cerebral cortex.

Single cell study on a cat.

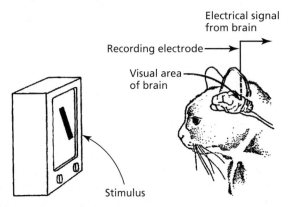

Reaction-Time Studies   **Reaction-time studies** are the hallmark of cognitive psychology. They are used to study cognitive processes. Early studies conducted in Wundt's lab referred to the use of mental chronometry and are illustrated by Donder's complication studies. These studies basically examined the amount of time it took to complete a simple task such as responding to a white light being turned on and comparing that to the amount of time it took to respond to a yellow light being turned on. Early researchers believed that the difference between these two times could be used to infer the additional processing that was used to discriminate between the yellow and white lights. Reaction-time studies funadamentally rely on the assumption that cognitive activity takes time and that one stage is completed before the other starts. Thus, many studies in cognitive psychology evaluate how long it takes to respond to stimuli or engage in a particular task. Another example was conducted by Roger Shephard of Stanford University who found that it

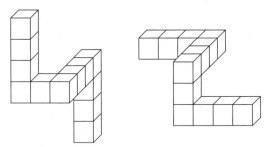

Based on Shepard & Metzlar's "Mental Rotation Task"

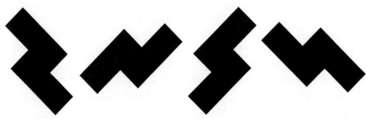

Mental Rotation task based on Canonical Orientations

took longer for research participants to mentally rotate an object 45 degrees compared to 15 degrees (see previous page for sample objects). Remember, this is mentally, not actually rotating the object, and thus Shephard concluded that mental events correspond to physical properties of the real world.

Priming Studies   In priming studies a stimulus is briefly presented (a prime) and then, after a delay, a second stimulus is presented and a participant is asked to make some judgment regarding the second stimulus, such as, "Is the second stimulus the 'same' as the first?" **Priming studies** have been used by cognitive psychologists for several generations, and a type of simple priming (cueing participants to make a response) can be found in the early history of experimental psychology, dating back to the nineteenth century. With the advent of the tachistoscope (a device that allows the brief presentation of stimuli and measures response time), computers, and, more recently, brain imaging technology, priming experiments have become increasingly popular. The rationale behind priming experiments, especially those designed to test semantic effects, is that by activating one item that may be related to another item, the acceptability of the second item is enhanced. This effect is called the semantic priming effect.

A second type of effect called the object priming effect is similar to semantic priming. Typically, there are two stages. The first stage consists of the presentation of an object, say, a line drawing of an airplane, followed by an interval that may be as brief as 100 milliseconds or as long as several months. In the second stage, a second object, similar to the original but commonly changed, rotated, elaborated, or degraded in some way (for example, some of the contours may be left out), is presented and the participant's accuracy and (sometimes) reaction time are measured. In some instances, the reverse procedure is used; that is, the participant sees a degraded form and then is asked to identify a completed object. Control participants get the same treatment but without the presentation of the first item. (See Tulving & Schacter, 1990, for further details.)

Eye-Tracking Studies   A lot of the brain is used for processing visual information. And because we can only get in what we are looking at, researchers have developed techniques to determine exactly where a person's eye fixation is at any given moment. Because eye movements are often involuntary, thus you can't just ask the person what he or she was looking at, objective measures of eye movements were necessary. One area where eye tracking has been particularly useful has been in the study of reading. Using eye tracking, researchers can evaluate exactly where in a word or sentence a person is looking and where they look next. Through **eye tracking studies,** researchers have found that people with dyslexia have different eye movements than people without dyslexia. The assumption is that the brain directs the eyes to locations in the visual world important to carry out cognitive functioning.

Lateralization Studies   In efforts to localize brain function, researchers discovered that the two halves of the brain may be responsible for different types of cognitive functions. This was the case with the Broca's and Wernicke's areas that were responsible for speech and language, as they were located (lateralized) on one side of the brain (the left side). Researchers then began to look for functions that were unique to the left or right side of the brain. There have been two lines of studies, one being less invasive than the other. The noninvasive technique to study lateralization of function is to briefly present a stimulus in either the right visual field or the left visual field. Due to the unique architecture of the visual system, images presented to the left visual field are processed in the right hemisphere and images presented in the right visual field are processed in the left hemisphere. The participant is required to make a timed response depending on the stimulus presented. This is not to say that information presented to the left hemisphere is not ultimately processed by the right hemisphere. Information is in fact communicated to the other hemisphere primarily through the corpus collosum, a structure that consists of a thin ribbon of axons. The assumption underlying these types of **lateralization studies** is that if an object is presented to the left hemisphere, but ultimately needs to be processed by the right hemisphere, it will take longer to respond than if that object had originally been presented directly to the right hemisphere. In the 1960s research was performed by Michael Gazzaniga at University of California, Santa Barbara, using humans undergoing preventative surgery for their extreme epilepsy. In order to reduce the spread of an epileptic seizure, surgeons severed the corpus collosum, thus severing communication between the hemispheres. This invasive surgery was warranted by the potential benefit of the reduced seizures. Using a lateralized presentation of stimuli, Gazzaniga was able to study hemispheric lateralization without the "cross-talk" between the hemispheres. Over time, other pathways that were responsible for communicating between the hemispheres to a lesser degree became more adept at this function and lateralized differences reduced to some extent.

Documenting Unique Cases

Case Studies   We stated earlier that sometimes psychologists can study brain processing through a process of reverse engineering. As in the case of World War I soldiers injured by shrapnel, or other people with stroke or degenerative diseases that may render a portion of the brain functionless, the researcher can examine the cognitive deficit and attribute that to the damaged area. These are referred to as clinical **case studies** and are observational in nature. They are not experiments. These deficits occur to a relatively small percentage of the population, so what we find are a few well-documented cases of individuals. Oftentimes their initials are used to protect their privacy. Early research on naturally occurring deficits was difficult because it was nearly impossible to determine where the neurological damage occurred. Obviously if there was external damage from shrapnel, there was some indication of where the damage occurred. In two well-known cases, Broca and Wernicke, researchers found deficits in speech perception and production with their patients. While they were able to document the cognitive deficits, they were not able to localize the damage until the patients had died and autopsies were able to be performed. Today, we have imaging techniques that allow us to study people such as they are while they are still living. The assumptions are that there are localized areas for specific functions and that they are not solely dependent on a network of neurons.

Imaging Studies   Localization of function has been greatly advanced by technology that allows us to create images of the brain. **Imaging studies** can be categorized as imaging that shows structure, imaging that shows process, and imaging that shows both structure and process. Imaging for structure is useful for providing details on neurological damage, as well as developmental change, whereas imaging for process allows us to determine where and when something happens. These will be covered in greater detail in the next chapter. However, we want to point out some of the assumptions underlying these studies. The assumption is that some of the imaging techniques rely on monitoring blood flow to specific regions to the brain. Blood is used to carry oxygen to regions and carry away metabolic waste. It is presumed that the areas involved in cognitive activity will require a greater amount of oxygen and generate a greater amount of waste and thus more blood will be directed to that area.

Ethics

Researchers study cognitive processes of humans and animals. What is tolerated with animals is not always acceptable with humans. For example, using invasive probing of the brain may be tolerated in very rare presurgical procedures in humans is fairly well accepted in research on cats and primates. Similarly, what may be tolerated in adults may not be tolerated in children. For example, some imaging techniques require the use of radioactive isotopes, which may be harmful to children and not so much for adults. Regardless, all research has to comply with federally mandated ethical guidelines. Research on animals has recently come under scrutiny by organizations like PETA (People for the Ethical Treatment of Animals) even though it may fall under legally accepted guidelines. This debate is ongoing and has been volatile at times with people breaking into laboratories to free animals used in experimentation. When properly conducted, studies using animals have provided us with valuable data that could not have been obtained otherwise. As with our fellow scientists in medicine and biology, you have to weigh the benefits with the costs to both the quality of life of the animal and the quality of life gained by humans.

To the Student

This book will lay out for you the main topic areas in cognitive psychology. We have tried to do this in a way that is useful and interesting. In this chapter we have provided you with a preliminary understanding of what cognitive psychology is and a summary of its history. We've also introduced to you to some of the features you will see throughout this book. The quotes were chosen not necessarily because somebody famous said them, or that they necessarily agree with what is being said in the book, but rather because they are thought-provoking and should spur discussion (so take a second and read them!). The Cognition in Everyday Life boxes are meant to guide you in recognizing cognitive processes all around you. These are important in helping you understand the cognitive processes others experience as well as you (so read them!). The Try This! feature encourages you to experience a cognitive process yourself. These are important to do because experiencing these draws your attention to cognitive processes that may otherwise go unnoticed (so do them!). The Spotlight on Cognitive Neuroscience reviews a neuroscience article relevant to the chapter. And finally, the A La Carte section covers an interesting research area and current findings relevant to the chapter.

At the end of every chapter you will find the Student Resource Center (SRC). This section provides you with a study guide that summarizes the main points of the chapter, a key terms section, and Starting Points, which is a section that provides you with books and journal article titles if you want or need more information (say for a book report annotated bibliography or research paper), movie titles that reflect the chapter's

A La Carte

Face Recognition

Recent advances in DNA testing have led to the exoneration of hundreds of citizens who were falsely convicted for crimes they did not commit. Psychological researchers have poured through the evidence used to convict the exonorees and the leading cause of misidentification was faulty eyewitness evidence. The traditional methodology, developed by social psychologists, for examining eyewitness identification in the laboratory involves showing the participant a staged crime typically using a brief video clip of a theft. The participant is then shown a photo lineup either on paper or using a computer, with the participant making only one identification response (MacLin, Zimmerman, & Malpass, 2005). Because so few data points are obtained, hundreds of participants are required for a study. Cognitive psychologists, on the other hand, traditionally have conducted face recognition studies to examine how people are able to recognize faces on a day-to-day basis. A typical face recognition study involves showing participants many photo images of faces during an "encoding" phase. After a delay period, the recognition phase begins. Participants are presented with the original faces from the encoding phase mixed with the equivalent number of new faces they had not previously seen. Their task is to indicate which faces were seen previously ("old") and which were the "new," recently added faces. With this methodology, many data points ("old/new" responses) are obtained, thus fewer participants are required. Additionally, more advanced statistical analyses can be conducted including the use of signal detection measures. Meissner et al. (2005) put a new twist on the old eyewitness identification methodology by combining the typical eyewitness study with a typical face recognition study. In their new paradigm, participants were shown eight faces during the encoding phase. They were later shown sixteen lineups with varying numbers of lineup members during the recognition phase, allowing the researchers to study the effects of lineup size. The results indicated that as the number of lineup members increased, discrimination accuracy decreased. While this may not be surprising, results from such studies can help researchers to make recommendations to law enforcement agencies about the optimal size and presentation manner a lineup should have. However, the main contribution of this study was to demonstrate that a more efficient method of data collection based on sound cognitive psychology methodology could replace the old methodology developed long ago by social psychologists.

relevant principles, and search terms for you to further pursue the topic online (many search engines are available; the terms we present are designed for Google). The intent for the SRC is to help you do well on your quizzes, tests, and research projects, and to help you develop a lifelong understanding of your cognitive processes.

Student Resource Center

STUDY GUIDE

1 Cognitive psychology is concerned with how we acquire, transform, represent, store, and retrieve knowledge, and how that knowledge directs what we attend to and how we respond.

2   One commonly adopted model is the information processing model, which assumes that information is processed through a series of stages, each of which performs a unique function.

3   Two questions raised by the information processing model are:
(a) What are the stages through which information is processed?
(b) In what form is knowledge represented?

4   Cognitive psychology uses research and theoretical approaches from major areas of psychology, including neuroscience, perception, pattern perception, attention and consciousness, memory, representation of knowledge, imagery, language, developmental psychology, thinking and concept formation, human intelligence, and artificial intelligence.

5   Historical antecedents of modern cognitive psychology include Greek philosophy; eighteenth-century empiricism; nineteenth-century structuralism; and the neocognitive revolution influenced by modern developments in communication theory, linguistics, memory research, and computer technology.

6   The main theme of the cognitive revolution is that internal processes are the subject matter of psychology. This is in contrast with behaviorism, which proposes that response or behavior is the true subject matter of psychology.

7   Conceptual science is a useful metaphor devised by humans to help comprehend "reality." Psychologists devise conceptual models in cognitive psychology with the aim of developing a system that reflects the nature of human perception, thought, and understanding of the world.

8   Cognitive models are based on observations that describe the structure and processes of cognition. Model building can make observations more comprehensible.

9   The information processing model has dominated cognitive psychology, but other models, occurring in computer science and in neuroscience, have been combined with cognitive psychology to form cognitive science.

10 Parallel distributed processing (PDP) is a model of cognition in which information is thought to be processed in a way similar to neurological networks. Those networks suggest that neural processing occurs simultaneously, in different regions, with simple connections being either strengthened or weakened.

11 Evolutionary cognitive psychology is an approach to cognition that draws on evolutional psychology and biological psychology in a unitary system of knowledge.

KEY TERMS

behaviorism	ethics
case studies	evolutionary perspective
cognitive map	experiment
cognitive revolution	eye-tracking studies
cognitive science	facts
computer science	formalism
empiricists	functionalists

imaging studies

information processing

internal representation

intervening variables

introspection

lateralization studies

mental representation

metaphors

model

nativists

neuroscience

observation studies

operational definition

parallel distributed processing (PDP)

period of enlightenment

perspectives

philosophy

priming studies

psychophysics

reaction time studies

representation of knowledge

single-cell studies

speculation

stimulus response

theories

unit of analysis

Starting Points

Books and Articles

● Howard Gardner has written a lively history of cognitive science in *The Mind's New Science*, which is highly recommended. Karl Pribram, a neurophysiologist, has a thoughtful article in *American Psychologist* entitled "The Cognitive Revolution and Mind/Brain Issues." Posner (ed.), *Foundations of Cognitive Science*, and Neisser, *Cognition and Reality: Principles and Implications of Cognitive Psychology*, will serve to introduce several issues in cognitive psychology. The best source to gain a perspective on American psychology, including the emergence of cognitive psychology, is Ernest Hilgard's *Psychology in America: A Historical Survey*. A good account of the schism between behaviorism and cognitive psychology can be found in the lively book by Bernard Baars, *The Cognitive Revolution in Psychology*. Interesting new views on adaptive cognition may be found in Barkow, Cosmides, and Tooby, eds., *The Adapted Mind: Evolutionary Psychology and the Generation of Culture*, and Gazzaniga, ed., *The Cognitive Neurosciences* (especially Section X) and *The New Cognitive Neurosciences*. Some useful entries may be found in *The MIT Encyclopedia of the Cognitive Sciences*, edited by Wilson and Keil.

Search Terms

● Science a gogo

● Exploratorium

● Center for Evolutionary Psychology

● History of Psychology

Cognitive Neuroscience

hmmm. . .?

1. What is the mind–body issue?
2. What is the basic foundational principle of cognitive neuroscience?
3. What is the relationship between neuroscience and cognitive psychology
4. Identify the major parts of the central nervous system.
5. Describe the basic anatomy and functions of the brain.
6. How did early studies of the brain lead to an understanding of localization of function?
7. How useful have imaging techniques been in understanding psychology?
8. How has split-brain research aided in our understanding of the function of the brain?

Is the brain really a device? Can it be thought of as a machine, as the quote above tells us? In this chapter, we explore these issues by learning about the structure and function of the brain and nervous system as a whole.

Exploring the Brain: The Frontier Within

Cognitive neuroscience is the brain-based approach to cognitive psychology. Humans have always wondered what was over the next hill, what was in the valley, and where the river began. And, in the past, the great explorers of the world—Columbus, Lewis and Clark, and Cook—saw and discovered wondrous new things. Today, scientists have turned their explorations inward to an even more fundamental territory than the geography of the earth, one that is far more intimate, far more enigmatic, and far more stubborn in giving up its secrets. The territory that the cognitive neuroscientists have set their sights on discovering and exploring is the complex world of the brain.

While the dimensions of the globe are vast and its terrain complex, the brain is small in size (its tofu-like mass weighs only about three pounds) and its information processing capacity is seemingly infinite. The intricate network of neurons in the human brain and their interconnections make up the most complicated system known to humankind. The capacity of the human brain for the computational analysis of sensory signals and the understanding of itself and the universe are staggeringly complex. Everything we experience, from love to hate, and everything we do, from swinging a baseball bat to playing classical guitar, arises out of the activity of neurons. Let us look into this wonderful computational system by first understanding its physical and functional properties.

And, while the gross geography of the human brain has been known for some time, the specific geography and functions of the brain are still being reported in the scientific literature.

This exploration of the world of the brain has been aided tremendously by imaging technology that allows us to see through the solid wall of the skull. Like the ancient mariner who charted dangerous seas, safe lagoons, and "widow-maker" reefs, cartographers of the mind are mapping areas in which visual processing, semantic analysis, auditory interpretation, and myriad other cognitive functions take place. This chapter is the tale of discovery that has led us up to modern research in cognitive neuroscience— but by all means, there is much to still learn about our closest frontier—the brain.

Cognition in Everyday Life

Smoking Addiction

*E*very day we are learning more about the geography of the brain and its function. Recent research (Naqvi, Rudrauf, Damasio, & Bechara, 2007) indicates that a particular part of the brain (the insula) may be directly responsible for the strong urge to smoke among those who are addicted. These researchers stumbled upon a case study whereby an individual who had smoked forty cigarettes a day for fourteen years had a stroke. And when he woke up from the stroke, he had no urge to smoke. He did not "decide" to quit or make any conscious effort to quit. His brain did the quitting for him, because the stroke did damage to the insula, a part of the brain known to control conscious urges. However, no one knew that it might be such a critical neural substrate responsible for smoking addiction, such that damage to it would result in immediate termination of the addictive behavior. To confirm their hunches, they studied other smokers who had experienced strokes and found similar findings. The study is small ($N = 20$), but a promising start to understanding the brain's localization of addiction as well as providing a starting point for pharmacological intervention for ceasing addictive behaviors. Finally, findings such as this underscore how truly difficult it is to quit smoking. The brain has been altered by the smoking behavior, and short damage to this brain region, quitting is a difficult task indeed. Changing your mind may be one thing, but changing your brain is pretty tough (though not impossible).

Logbook: The Twenty-First Century—Brain Sciences

Much of the excitement in cognitive psychology is due to developments in a discipline that combines cognitive psychology and neuroscience, a specialty called **cognitive neuroscience.** The scientific field of cognitive neuroscience received its name in the late 1970s in the backseat of a New York taxicab. Michael Gazzaniga, a leader in split-brain research, was riding with the great cognitive psychologist George Miller on the way to a dinner meeting for scientists from Rockefeller University and Cornell University, who were to study how the brain produces what we experience as the mind. A topic in need of a name. Out of that taxi ride came the term "cognitive neuroscience." Before discussing the details of cognitive neuroscience, let's briefly consider the larger question of how cognitive neuroscience fits into the mind–body dichotomy contemplated by scientists and philosophers for centuries and reexamined by cognitive neuroscientists equipped with imaging technology.

Mind–Body Issues

To fully appreciate the story we are going to begin to tell you, you need to suspend for a moment your reality of instant access to information and imagine yourself in the world of the early thinkers and scientists. Imagine that the smartest people around did not know how the mind and body interacted, and whether they were two different entities or one in the same. Enter Descartes.

One of the early questions that philosophers had was how the body moved. Descartes gave an example of a person putting his hand in the fire and sensing the heat energy and

A modern day reflex arc.

without even thinking pulling their arm back. How did that all work? Was this some kind of mechanical feature or was this part of a deliberate thought process?

Descartes believed that the "filaments" connecting the hand to the brain moved and activated the brain, which released fluids that enabled the arm to remove the hand from the fire. He called this the **reflex arc.** As absurd as this may seem, Descartes based this idea on modern machines at the time. During this period, giant cuckoo clocks were being made where on the hour human figures would emerge and move using the gears and springs from the clock. Also popular at the time were water gardens, which included human-like automatons that moved their arms and legs using hydrolic water power. By combining these two types of technology, it made sense for Descartes that that's how our nervous system worked.

Since Descartes, philosophers have been preoccupied with questions about the relationship between the mind and the body. We know now that everything psychological (mind) is simultaneously neurological (body). Remarkably, we humans occupy these two worlds at the same time.

The world consists of physical things that exist in time and space, like rocks, trees, clocks, and machines. These things have physical properties that follow physical laws, such as the laws of gravity, which govern falling objects and the laws of centrifugal force, which control the action of rotating objects. In the case of living things, they also include neurological laws, which regulate the transmission of an impulse from one neuron to another. While we are not saying that the body is akin to a rock (or a tree, for that matter), but it is in the physical world (like a rock and a tree) and some would argue that the body is fundamentally separate from the mind.

The world of the mind is populated by memories, ideas, thoughts, images, and so on. These too are governed by laws, though finding them is sometimes more difficult than finding those that govern the physical world.

Because, traditionally, we have set out to find rules in the two worlds using different techniques, many philosophers and scientists have thought that these worlds are fundamentally different and fundamentally separate. This dichotomous conclusion is based on the assumption that one world is focused on the physical universe (body) while the other is centered on the mental universe (the mind). The separation of mind from body is intuitively logical, or self-evident, but the interaction between the worlds is equally self-evident. Your mental inability to concentrate on a test may be related to the physical harm you inflicted on your body at last night's poker party.

The **mind-body issue** is not settled. Some philosophers argue that the only real world is the world of the mind and that the physical world is an illusion. Conversely, some argue that the only real world is the physical world and that the mind is ultimately a function (and byproduct) of the activities of the brain. A frequent criticism of the latter position is that it robs humanity of its lofty, idealistic spirit, to, for example, reduce "love," to neural firing.

While the dualist believes that the mind and body can coexist, one basic problem is trying to figure out how the mind is connected to the body and vice versa. There are various ideas about the mind–body relationship. What do we mean when we talk of the mind? We are talking about the things that are done by the brain, for example, thinking, holding things in memory, perceiving, and judging, as well as the more complex experiences our cognitive system allows us, like love, grief, composing music, and making jokes. The mind, in this sense, comprises the processes carried out by the brain.

The brain has physical properties. It is made of up neurons. The brain is in a constant state of flux, never rests totally, and is always teeming with electrochemical activity. However, the physical architecture of the brain is relatively stable. For example, the network of neurons, the location of major landmarks on the cortex, the areas of the brain that are related to functions such as sensory experiences, motor control, and vision, change very little. What takes place in the brain—the brain processes—changes more readily. Minds tend to be more dynamic than brains. We can change our thoughts rapidly and without much obvious structural change in the brain, even the the pattern of electrochemical transmissions may be extremely dynamic. Our conscious thoughts may shift swiftly from the ridiculous to the sublime, from inner space to outer space, and from sacred to profane in less time than it takes to read this sentence. The physical changes in neural activity cause changes in the mind, while the basic anatomical structure of the brain, of course, remains stable.

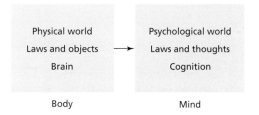

Physical world		Psychological world
Laws and objects	$\longrightarrow$	Laws and thoughts
Brain		Cognition
Body		Mind

This constantly changing dynamic nature of the mind could be what inspired James to equate thought as a stream of consciousness. However, even though minds tend to be dynamic, they also have their consistencies; our general mode of thinking, our attitudes toward religion, our aspirations, our view of the family, and so on, are reasonably stable. As we progress through the chapter, how cognitive psychology and neuroscience have, after centuries of debate, for the first time in the intellectual history of our species, shed some light on the topic that is both reliable and scientifically valid.

The Central Nervous System

We know now that our **central nervous system** (CNS) is much more complex than a system of filaments and fluids. While the CNS consists of the spinal cord and brain, our discussion focuses on the brain, with particular attention to its structure and processes.

The basic building block of the CNS is the **neuron,** a specialized cell that transmits information throughout the nervous system (see Figure 2.1). The human brain is made of densely packed neurons. Some estimates place the number at more than 100 billion (about the number of stars in the Milky Way), each of which is capable of receiving and passing neural impulses to sometimes thousands of other neurons and is more complex than any other system known to be in existence. Each cubic inch of the human **cerebral cortex** contains about 10,000 miles of neurons, which connect the cells together (Blakemore, 1977). Figure 2.2 presents a view of the interconnectivity of neurons in the human brain. Compare this drawing with the diagram of a neuron (see Figure 2.1), and try to locate the dendrites and axons in Figure 2.2. At any given time, many of the cortical neurons are active, and it is thought that cognitive functions such as perceiving, thinking, awareness, and memory are carried out by the simultaneous firing of neurons located throughout this complex neural network. It is difficult to imagine the vast number of neurons that are simultaneously activated within the intricate infrastructure supporting the system. If we have difficulty imagining that (or conceptualizing 10,000 miles of neurons between Washington DC, and Toyko)—imagine the difficulty in understanding other complexities of the brain. There is the paradox: Because the brain is so complex, it may never fully understand itself no matter how hard we try. So is it overly optimistic to think we will ever discover the workings of the mind? Possibly, however, we do know a lot about the building block of the brain, the neuron.

The Neuron

There are perhaps as many as a thousand different types of neurons (see Kandel, Schwartz, & Jessell, 1991), each of which carries out specialized functions in a variety of locations.

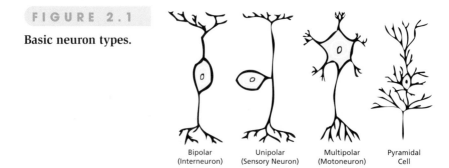

FIGURE 2.1

Basic neuron types.

Bipolar
(Interneuron)

Unipolar
(Sensory Neuron)

Multipolar
(Motoneuron)

Pyramidal
Cell

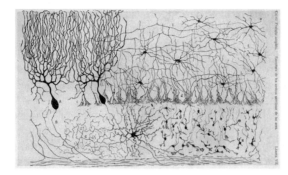

FIGURE 2.2

Drawing from Ramon y Cajal's first publication on the central nervous system, showing the five classes of neurons in the cerebellum. A, Purkinje cell; D, stellate cell; F, Golgi cell; H, granule cell; S, basket cell axons.

From the Instituto de Neurobiologica see "Ramon y Cajal," Madrid, Spain.

The four main parts of the neuron include the following: (See Figure 2.3)

1. The **dendrites** receive neural impulses from other neurons. Dendrites are highly arborized, suggesting the branches and twigs of a tree.

2. The **cell body** is responsible for housekeeping. It receives nutrients and eliminates waste products by filtering them in and out of the permeable cell wall.

3. The **axon,** a long, tubular pathway in which signals are transmitted from the cell body to other cells by means of junctures known as synapses. Axons in the brain may be tiny or may reach up to one meter or more in length. Large axons are surrounded by a fatty substance called the myelin sheath, which acts as a type of insulation that speeds up the transmission of the neural impulse.

FIGURE 2.3

The structure of a neuron.

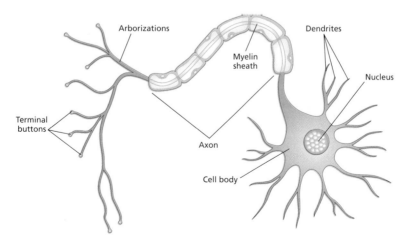

4. The axon terminates at **presynaptic terminals.** They are near the receptive surface of dendrites of other neurons. While not connected, the presynaptic terminal and the dendrites of other neurons combine to form the **synapse.**

Although the synapse is not part of the actual structure, it may have one of the most important jobs because this is where chemical information is exchanged from one neuron to another in the form of chemicals called neurotransmitters. Electrical charges travel through the axon. When they reach the dendrite, neurotransmitters are released. Traveling through the synaptic cleft to the receptor sites is the next neuron's dendrite. This chemical neurotransmitter changes the polarity, or electrical potential, of the receiving dendrite. A **neurotransmitter** is a chemical message that acts on the membrane of the dendrite of the receiving neuron (see Figure 2.4). One class of neurotransmitter has an inhibitory effect, which tends to make the next neuron less likely to fire. Another class has an excitatory effect, which makes the next neuron more likely to fire. Currently, over 100 different chemical substances are known or suspected of functioning as neurotransmitters (Borodinsky et al., 2004). Some seem to perform ordinary functions, such as maintaining the physical integrity of the cells. Others, such as acetylcholine, seem to be related to learning and memory.

At birth, not all synaptic connections are complete, nor are all neurons completely myelinated (see Figure 2.5); however, no new neurons will be generated. In other words, the neurons you are born with are the ones you have available to you for a lifetime (and you will lose some too through natural aging or injury). One might assume then that we would have the ability to generate new dendrites to create more connections between neurons. However, this likely is not the case after about the age of 2. Thus, in adults, synapses do not propagate (Kornack & Rakic, 2001). But fortunately, in adults, the average cell body and dendrite have the capacity to receive about 1,000 synapses from other neurons, and the average axon has the capacity to form synapses to about 1,000 other neurons.

This has not been without controversy. Research into **neurogenesis** during the late 1990s using nonhuman primates suggested that new neurons were able to form in the primate cortex. However, more recent research indicates that in fact the generation of new neurons is not common and probably only occurs in the hippocampus.

The speed with which impulses move along the axon is related to its length. In the smallest axon, **neurotransmission** creeps along at about 0.5 meters per second (about 1 mile per hour), while in the largest axons the rate is 120 meters per second (about 270 miles per hour). These speeds are slow compared to modern computer processors, which can transfer information many thousand times faster. The brain is always alive with electrochemical activity, and an excited neuron may fire as often as 1,000 times per second. The more times a neuron fires, the more effect it will have on the cells to which it synapses.

Human knowledge is encoded; it is not localized in any single neuron. It is believed that human cognition takes place in the large patterns of neural activity that are distributed throughout the brain, function in parallel, and operate by means of excitatory or inhibitory connections, or "switches." A number of different theories, including the influential theory of Donald Hebb (1949), have been proposed that address the issue of the connection strengths between units. In a simplified version of a connectionist model, in any neural connection where A synapses with B, if A exciting B leads to a satisfactory

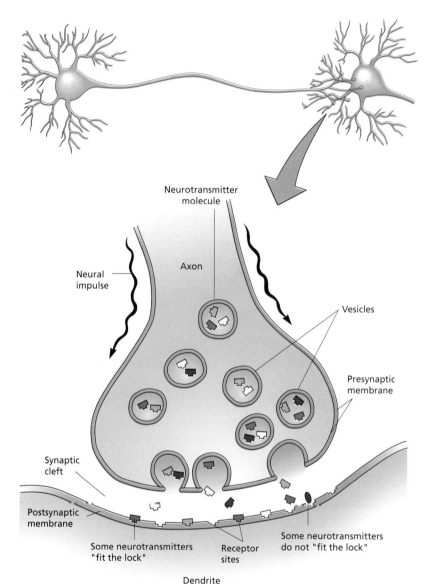

FIGURE 2.4

Synaptic transmission. Neurotransmitters in the axon of one neuron are released into the synaptic gap by means of a neural impulse. These neurotransmitters stimulate receptor molecules embedded in the membrane of the postsynaptic neuron.

Neurotransmitter molecule

Neural impulse

Axon

Vesicles

Presynaptic membrane

Synaptic cleft

Postsynaptic membrane

Some neurotransmitters "fit the lock"

Receptor sites

Some neurotransmitters do not "fit the lock"

Dendrite

outcome (either cognitively or behaviorally), the weight of that connection will be increased so that in the future A will have the ability to excite B even more. This makes sense because whatever cognitive function is being carried out by A → B, if it is adaptive we want it to be carried out again. However, if the outcome is unsatisfying, the weight of the connection will be reduced to the point that the outcome will be inhibiting. It is no coincidence that the basic assumptions underlying these parallel distributed processing (PDP) models are similar to these neural models.

FIGURE 2.5

Neural networks from birth to 2 years of age. A human baby has almost all of its neurons at birth. However, the connections among neurons continue to grow, reaching astronomical numbers. A small sample is shown here.

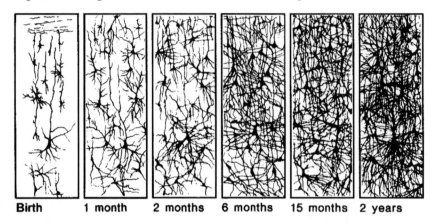

| Birth | 1 month | 2 months | 6 months | 15 months | 2 years |

The Anatomy of the Brain

The early anatomists discovered the structure and function of animals and humans by dissecting them after death. Upon opening the body, they could quickly view easily discriminable structures, and from those structures, infer function. A tubal structure (like the intestine or a blood vessel) could be inferred to carry substances. A sack structure (like the stomach or bladder) could be inferred to store substances. This early exploration into the body gave us a wealth of information about the structure and function of the body. The early brain scientist, however, had a bit more of a challenge in front of him (back then it was almost always a him). Open the skull and the most noticeable thing is that the brain appears to be composed of two halves and overall is a soft mass of ridges. Deeper in the brain, there are no hard structures and few easily identifiable features. Those structures that are discriminable from one another don't offer immediate inferences to their function. However, extensive study did demonstrate discrete structures.

Donald O. Hebb **(1904–1985).** Early researcher in neurocognition whose seminal ideas are frequently used in connectionistic models.

*E*volution has encased the brain in a rock-hard vault of bone, wrapped it in layers of tough membrane, and cushioned it in a viscous bath of cerebral spinal fluid. These protective shields post particularly difficult challenges for scientists who would like to observe human brain activity directly.

—*Gordon Bower*

The brain is divided into two similar structures, the right and left **cerebral hemispheres.** These hemispheres have as their first layer the cerebral cortex, a thin, gray, moist material densely packed with the cell bodies of neurons and short, unmyelinated axons. The cerebral cortex is only about 1.5–5 millimeters (¼ inch) thick. Because it is deeply convoluted, the surface area of the cortex is greater than it appears. The ridges between the folds are called **gyri** (singular, gyrus), and the grooves are called **sulci** (singular, sulcus). Deep and prominent sulci are called fissures. If the cortex were spread out, it would measure about 324 square inches, or about three times the amount seen on the surface. The convoluted cortex, with its characteristic walnut appearance, increases the surface area of the brain without increasing the size of the skull, a clever biological adaptation that enables the human animal to retain its mobility, without being encumbered by a very large head, which increases survival probability. It is within the cerebral cortex that human thought, sensation, language processes, and other cognitive functions take place.

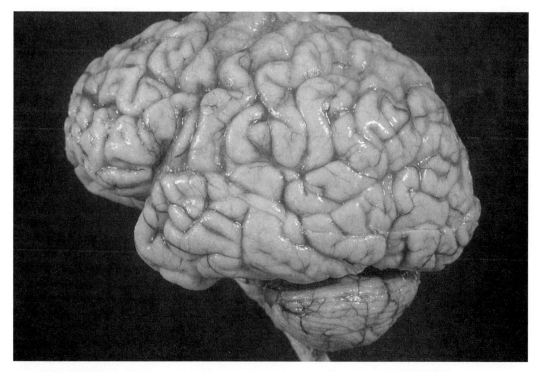

The human brain.

The Cerebral Cortex   The cerebral cortex has been the focus of attention for over 100 years because it seems to be the site of thinking and cognition. While cognition (perception, memory, problem solving, language processing, and memory) engages many sections of the brain, the cerebral cortex, that thin veneer of densely packed cells, is what we commonly think of as "the brain," although one should note that many intricate and necessary body and cognitive structures rely on other parts of the brain.

The cortex is the most recent of the brain structures to evolve. Some creatures, such as fish, have no cortex; others, such as reptiles and birds, have a less complex cerebral cortex. On the other hand, mammals such as dogs, horses, cats, and especially primates have well-developed, complex cerebral cortexes. In humans, the cortex is involved in perception, speech, complex actions, thinking, language processing and production, and other processes that make us different from other mammals.

Lobes of the Cerebral Cortex   The cerebral cortex is divided into four major sections, some of which are delineated by major fissures. These four areas are the frontal, temporal, parietal, and occipital lobes (see Figure 2.6). Although each lobe is associated with specific functions, it is likely that many functions are distributed throughout the brain.

Frontal Lobes. Responsible for impulse control, judgment, problem solving, controlling and executing behavior, and complex organization.

Temporal Lobes. Processes auditory signals, hearing, high-level auditory processing (speech), face recognition.

Parietal Lobes. Integrates sensory information from various senses, manipulation of objects, visual-spatial processing.

Occipital Lobes. Visual processing, receives information originating from the retina, processes information and passes it on to relevant areas, also known as the striate cortex.

Sensory-Motor Areas   Scientific work on the motor areas of the brain may be traced to the nineteenth century when studies of electrical stimulation to various parts of the cortex of lightly anesthetized dogs resulted in twitching reactions, as a mild current to the frontal lobe led to a reflexive reaction in the forelimb. These early researchers discovered that these mild currents were processed contralaterally. That is, sensory information from the spinal cord (signals from your hand touching a rabbit) enters the left side of the body, crosses over, and is initially processed in the right hemisphere. Also, the

Cerebral Cortex-controls thinking and sensing functions, voluntary movement

Corpus Callosum-relays information between the two cerebral hemispheres

Hypothalamus-regulates temperature, eating, sleeping, and the endocrine system

Pituitary Gland-master gland of the endocrine system

Thalamus-relays sensory information to the cerebral cortex

Midbrain-reticular activating system carries messages about sleep and arousal

Pons-relays information between cerebral cortex and cerebellum

Cerebellum-coordinates fine muscle movement and balance

Medulla-regulates heartbeat and breathing

Spinal cord-relays nerve impulses between brain and body and controls simple reflexes

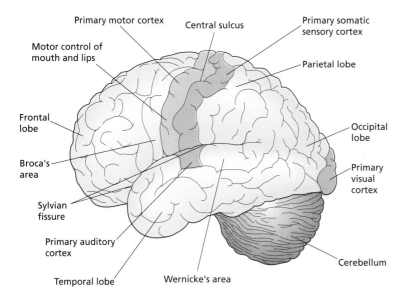

Primary motor cortex

Central sulcus

Primary somatic
sensory cortex

Motor control of
mouth and lips

Parietal lobe

Frontal
lobe

Occipital
lobe

Broca's
area

Primary
visual
cortex

Sylvian
fissure

Primary auditory
cortex

Cerebellum

Temporal lobe

Wernicke's area

FIGURE 2.6

The major areas of the human cerebral cortex. Here the frontal, parietal, occipital, and temporal lobes are shown. The primary motor cortex is shown (shaded) and also the primary somatic sensory cortex (dark shading). Two important functional areas used for generating words and understanding speech are shown: Broca's area (anterior to the primary motor cortex) involved in speech production, and Wernicke's area (posterior to the sensory cortex) involved in comprehension of spoken words.

motor areas of each hemisphere controls movements of the opposite side of the body. Later contributions of electrical stimulations of the human brain were conducted by Canadian researcher Roger Penfield who applied mild electric shocks to human patients just prior to surgery, which elicited verbal reports of long forgotten memories. Mapping the sensory and motor areas of the brain in other mammals, including humans, soon followed, and a general picture of topographic size and function emerged. The more important a function, such as the forepaw manipulation in raccoons (raccoons depend on forepaw activity for eating and building), the greater the size of the motor cortex allocated to this part of the anatomy. The raccoon has a relatively large motor cortex devoted to the forepaws, say, in comparison to a dog (see Welker, Johnson, & Pubols, 1964). Mapping of the sensory area has shown that delicate electrical stimulation of various parts of the regions is associated with corresponding sensations in the opposite side of the body associated with the sensory cortex being aroused. Stimulation in the somatosensory area associated with the hand, for example, might create a tingling sensation in the hand on the opposite side of the body. As with motor allocation, parts of the body rich in sensory functions, such as the human tongue, occupy a larger part of the sensory cortex. See the table on the previous page for a summary of structures.

Discovering Cortical Functioning

Early Studies in Localization

People have known about some of the relationships between cognition and the brain for centuries through patients who have suffered lesions, tumors, hemorrhages, strokes, and other pathologies. Alas, the link between brain and thought was usually made postmortem after opening the skull of a recently deceased person and then reconstructing his or her behavior with brain anomolies. Now, live, fully functioning people are used to show what parts of the brain are functioning when specific cognitive activities are practiced. More on that later, but now, a brief history of some early discoveries.

Early scholars believed that the brain had little to do with thought and perception. Aristotle, for one, ascribed such functions to the heart. Much later, the practice of phrenology held that character, personality, perception, intelligence, and so on, were exactly localized in the brain (see Figure 2.7).

Phrenologists received early scientific support from neurologists, who discovered that some brain functions were related to specific areas. Phrenologists believed that the brain was like a muscle and could be exercised. They believed that personal characteristics, aptitudes, and emotions could be measured by examining protrusions and indentations on the outer surfaces of the skull. Using their metaphor as a muscle, areas that were well developed pushed out of the skull. Areas that were less developed created valleys. These specific areas had designated characteristics associated with them. For example, Silas Hubbard discovered bumps corresponding to consciousness and conjugal love. Many of the phrenologists were proscribed to logical positivism, which emphasized the nurture aspect of the nature–nurture continuum. And they believed that if you could identify the deficits in someone's personality through phrenology, that you could develop characteristics such as forthrightness. Part of the movement also emphasized changing environments to make children into better adults.

However, though they gained some support, and helped fuel the **localization** of brain function, little support was found for phrenology as a science. **Phrenology** is portrayed as being scientific, but ultimately cannot be supported by the standards of scientific research.

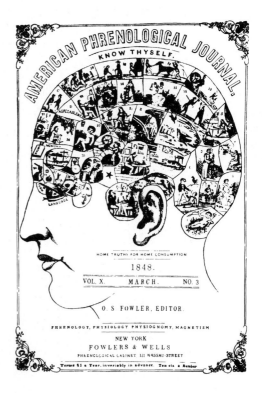

F I G U R E 2 . 7

Cover of the American Phrenological Journal (1848).

Such research is typically called **pseudoscience,** which literally means false science. Other areas of pseudoscience are aromatherapy (using essential oils in healing practices), craniometry (proscribed that the larger your head the smarter you were), and physiognomy (features of the face tell us something about the character of the person). Recently, intense debate has centered on intelligent design as being a pseudoscientific counterpart to evolution.

One of the earliest examples of localization of function came from a case example involving Phineas Gage. Gage was a foreman working on railroads who was working with dynamite to prepare for the laying of railroad tracks. Railroad workers used a large iron tool called a tamping spike. One of its many uses was to compact dynamite inside of holes drilled into rock. One day the dynamite exploded, sending the tamping iron up through Gage's jaw, through his frontal cortex, exiting his head and landing some distance away. While it was a miracle that Gage survived the initial accident, it was further surprising that he survived infection and late-1800s medicine. Prior to the accident, Gage was well regarded as a kind and upright man, and he was now irreverent and disdainful to his friends and colleagues. This led early scientists to believe that the frontal lobe was responsible for the controlling of people's temperament.

This notion that the frontal lobes were responsible for temperament led to the development in the 1930s to a practice called psychosurgery, influenced by the research of Antonio Moice who found that destroying portions of the frontal lobe of monkeys produced a calming effect. Influenced by this research, Walter Freeman and his colleagues developed a technique to perform psychosurgery on the frontal lobes of humans, relieving them of bad behavior such as aggressive impulses. This technique became known as frontal lobe **lobotomy** and Freeman refined his surgical technique to literally insert an ice pick device into the brain through the eye sockets and rotating it to destroy sections of the frontal lobe.

Psychosurgery is still used today in very rare cases to control disorders such as obsessive–compulsive disorder, depression, and severe seizures.

Clearly the phrenologists and lobotomists were off to the wrong start; however, they were on the right track in terms of being curious about the localization of function in the brain. This inspired French neurologist Pierre Flourens, who considered phrenology nonsense, to

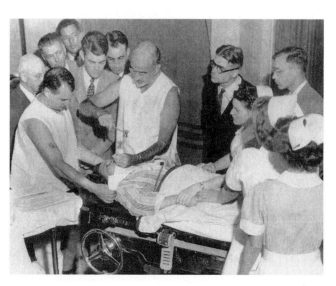

A transorbital lobotomy. Freeman operating at Western State Hospital, Washington State, in July 1949.

THE FAR SIDE® By GARY LARSON

"Whoa! *That* was a good one! Try it, Hobbs—just poke his brain right where my finger is."

set out and disprove phrenology. In his investigations, he excised portions of the human brain and examined the effect of the surgery on behavior. He concluded that motor and sensory functions are not a matter of simple localization in specific regions, as suggested by other researchers, but that these functions are also distributed in other parts of the brain. Traumas or injuries to the brain seemed to affect all higher functions equally.

This position was later called the **aggregate field theory,** which argued against localization and supported the view that the brain operates as a holistic organ, with cognitive processes distributed throughout. There is a compromise view, which seems consistent with the best knowledge in the field. It holds that some mental attributes are localizable to specific regions, or constellations of regions, within the brain. These include control of motor responses, sensory terminals, vision, and some language processing. However, many functions—especially higher-order cognitive processes such as memory, perception, thinking, and problem solving—are divided into subfunctions, which are distributed throughout the brain.

Early support for localization of function can be traced to the nineteenth century. Especially important is the work of French neurologist Pierre Paul Broca, who studied aphasia, a language disorder in which the patient has difficulty speaking. This disorder is

Areas of the brain involved in aphasia and language.

Language Symptomology in Aphasia			
	TYPE OF APHASIA	SPONTANEOUS SPEECH	COMPREHENSION
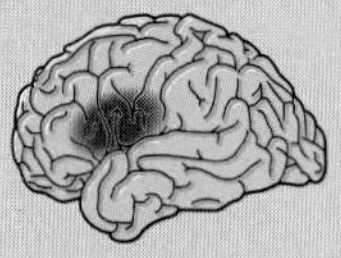	Broca's aphasia	Nonfluent	Good
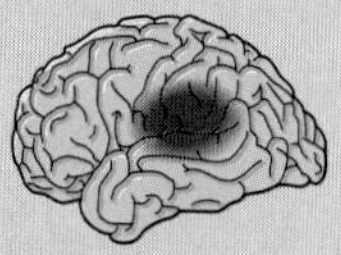	Wernicke's aphasia	Fluent but makes no sense	Poor
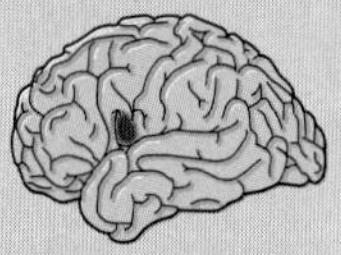	Conduction aphasia	Fluent	Good
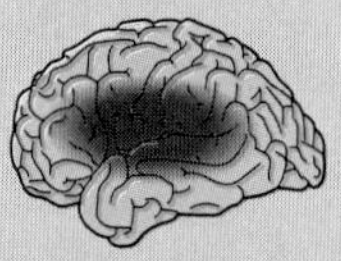	Global aphasia	Nonfluent	Poor
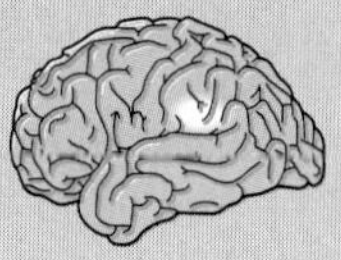	Subcorticle aphasia	Fluent or nonfluent	Variable

commonly found in stroke victims. Postmortem examination of aphasics' brains revealed lesions in the area now called Broca's area (see Figure 2.8). In 1876, the young German neurologist Karl Wernicke described a new type of aphasia, which was characterized by the inability to comprehend rather than the inability to speak. In fact, the speech was fluent, but made no sense.

Wernicke agreed with earlier scholars that certain mental functions are localized but that these are, for the most part, concerned with simple perceptual and motor activities. Complex intellectual processes such as thinking, memory, and understanding result from the interactions among the perceptual and motor areas. Support for this position came around the turn of the century, when the Spanish physiologist Santiago Ramon y Cajal showed that the nervous system is made up of discrete elements, or neurons.

What had been a mosaic concept of the mind (conceptually not far removed from the phrenological view, without the bump readings) was now a connectionist concept:

complex cognitive functions take place and can be understood in terms of the network of links among neurons. Furthermore, Wernicke suggested that some functions are processed in parallel in different parts of the brain. Wernicke's hypothesis about the brain and its functions proved to be important to modern cognitive psychologists.

Redundant processing of information, as suggested by the parallel processing theory, might appear wasteful and contrary to the view that animal systems are efficient to the point of parsimony. However, it is arguable that involved biological systems are usually redundant. Certainly this is true in the case of reproduction, where many times more eggs are produced than are fertilized and, among many species, many times more offspring are spawned than grow to maturity. Redundancy in nature is likely to play a central role in survival and adaptability. Perhaps redundant and parallel processing of neural information by humans increases our chances for survival and procreation. Thinking, and the science of cognition we now enjoy, are the serendipitious byproducts of these primary functions.

The theories of Flourens, Broca, and Wernicke on the relationship between the brain and behavior were expanded by the American psychologist Karl Lashley of Harvard University. Lashley, however, was not concerned with aphasia in humans but with the locus of learning in rats. In his influential book *Brain Mechanisms and Intelligence* (1929), Lashley expressed his interest in brain injuries and behavior, with the aim of shedding light on the issue of localization versus generalization of functions. To study such phenomena, he examined lesions in the brains of rats to determine their effects on the animals' ability to master a complex maze. Small areas of damage to a rat's brain did not have much effect on maze performance. Because no specific area seemed tied directly to learning, Lashley concluded that learning was not confined to specific neurons. Lashley developed a theory called mass action, in which the importance of individual neurons is minimized and memories seem to be distributed throughout the brain. Lashley (1950) concluded that "there are no special cells reserved for special memories." The importance of these ideas lies in their suggestion that the brain operates in a holistic rather than compartmentalized manner. (About the same time, Alexander Luria was developing similar ideas in Russia.) These findings may appear to contradict those of Penfield's electrical stimulation of the brain, thus shrouding the results of Penfield in a controversy.

Recent studies of memory and blood flow (which is thought to reflect neural activity) suggest that some memory functions may be associated with certain areas of the brain but perhaps not to the precise degree suggested by earlier data (see Penfield, 1959). This is not to suggest that Penfield's observations are necessarily erroneous, but rather that

Karl Lashley **(1890–1958).** Developed the principle of mass action. APA president, 1929.

Photo courtesy of Harvard University Archives.

they are difficult to replicate. We now believe that the brain contains areas associated with specific functions (such as motor reactions) but that the complete processing of this class of information also engages other parts of the brain. Other functions (like thinking) seem to be widely distributed throughout the brain. It should probably be clear to the reader by now that the brain operates in both a localized and **mass action** manner.

Next let's examine a sample of the existing experimental and clinical studies of brain structure and processes.

- Many mental functions seem to be localized to specific regions or constellations in the brain, such as motor regions and sensory terminals. However, in addition to the regional concentration of these functions, further processing appears to take place in different sites.

- Many higher-order mental functions (thinking, learning, and memory, among others) seem to involve several different areas of the cerebral cortex. Neural processing of this class of information is redundant in the sense that it is distributed throughout the brain and processes in parallel at many locations.

- Damage to the brain does not always lead to a diminuation of cognitive performance. This may be due to several factors. In the first place, the damage may be due to parts of the brain that are related to performance in subtle ways or in areas of the brain that perform redundant functions. Also, cognition may be unaffected because the intact connections can take over the original function or the intact connections can be arranged in a way that allows them to accomplish the primary task.

A Tale of Two Hemispheres

As we've alluded to before, if you removed the cranium from any person, you would see a brain with two plainly visible parts. Each part is about the size of a fist, known as the right and left hemispheres of the cerebral cortex. Even though they appear identical, the two parts of the cortex differ widely in function. This difference in humans has been known for centuries, and it has also been observed in most mammals and in many vertebrates.

The earliest written reference to the brain is found in Egyptian hieroglyphs written during the seventeenth century B.C. The hieroglyphic character for the brain is shown here. According to the eminent Egyptologist James Breasted, it has been found eight times in ancient writings. In one source, known as "The Edwin Smith Surgical Papyrus," found in the rare book room of the New York Academy of Medicine, the author describes the symptoms, diagnoses, and prognoses of two patients with head wounds. The early Egyptians knew that injuries to one side of the brain caused an affliction in the opposite side of the body.

The purpose of contralaterality is still not completely understood but has contributed to the theory that the two hemispheres carry out distinctively different functions. There has been a profusion of scientific (see Kandel et al., 1991; Kupferman, 1981; Sperry, 1982) and popular (see Ornstein, 1972) ideas about the functions of the hemispheres. (One even proposes that people can be classified as "right-brained" or "left-brained" thinkers.)

Clinical evidence for contralaterality was first recorded by the ancient Egyptians, but the scientific confirmation of opposing functions emerged during the last century, when brain surgeons noted that tumors and excisions in the left hemisphere produced different effects from similar pathology in the right hemisphere. Left-hemisphere damage

Roger Sperry **(1924–1994).** Nobel
Laureate, introduced split-brain
research, which opened a new area
of research with far-reaching
implications regarding the brain.

resulted in language impairment, while patients with damage to the right hemisphere were
observed to have difficulties dressing themselves. Further indications of hemispheric
specialization appeared in the 1950s, when physicians treating patients with severe
epilepsy cut the **corpus callosum**—the massive bundle of nerves that connects the two
hemispheres, allowing them to pass information back and forth (see Bogen & Vogel,
1962). By severing this connective tissue, communication between the two main structures of the brain was greatly reduced. Surgeons hoped to confine the effects of an epileptic seizure originating in one hemisphere from traveling to the other hemisphere.
Apparently, this worked, however, such radical surgery is not commonly done today.

Split-Brain Research   Also in the 1950s, Roger Sperry at the California Institute of
Technology conducted research on animals concerning the effect of severing the corpus
callosum. This is also referred to as a split-brain procedure. The main goal of this research was to determine different functions associated with each hemisphere. Of particular interest was the finding by Myers and Sperry (1953) that cats that had undergone
this procedure behaved as if they had two brains, each of which was capable of attending to, learning, and remembering information independent of the other.

Using this procedure, **cerebral commissurotomies,** Sperry and his colleagues, notably
Michael Gazzaniga, had an opportunity to study human patients who had undergone this
surgery. In one study (Gazzaniga, Bogen, & Sperry, 1965), they observed that a patient who
was given a common object, such as a coin or comb, in his right hand could identify it verbally, since information from the right side crosses over to the left hemisphere, where language processing is centralized. However, if given a coin or comb in the left hand, the patient
could not describe it verbally; he could point to it, but only with his left hand. The reason
why he could only point at it with his left hand is that the right side of the brain controls
the left hand and the right side of the brain could identify the object but couldn't name it.

The studies conducted by this group and others indicated that, indeed, the left hemisphere is associated with special functions such as language, conceptualization, analysis, and classification. The right hemisphere is associated with integration of information
over time, as in art and music, spatial processing, recognition of faces and shapes, and
such tasks as knowing the way around a city or getting dressed. These findings tend to
support the argument for localization of functions. However, subsequent work indicated
that the right hemisphere was capable of more linguistic processing, especially written
language, than was initially believed. In addition, younger patients exhibited well-
developed capacities in both hemispheres (Gazzaniga, 1983). Overall, these observations

Try This

Eye Movements and Hemispheric Processing

Try this little experiment. Ask a friend to answer this question: "What does it mean when we say, 'Facts are the abridgment of knowledge?'" Did your friend's eyes move to the right? Now ask, "Imagine your home and count the number of windows." Did the eyes look to the left? In general, especially among right-handed people, ac-

tivation of left-hemisphere functions—those associated with language processing—are accompanied with right-body activities or right-sided orientations, while right-hemisphere functions— those associated with visual and/or spacial tasks—are accompanied with left-body activities.

suggest that there is considerable plasticity in the developing human brain and that functions are not as clearly separated as they once were believed to be, but rather are shared by various regions and hemispheres.

Given the radical nature of invasive surgery on the brain, scientists have looked to other ways to explore the functions of the brain, including hemisphere specialization.

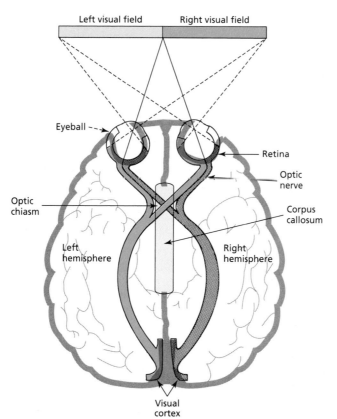

FIGURE 2.9

Visual Pathway. Note that half of the nerve fibers from each eye cross over to the opposite hemisphere at the optic chiasm and half do not.

Much of the current work in the field of hemisphere specialization has dealt with visual perception, which has a unique system of processing contralateral information. Consider the visual system's anatomy in relation to the hemisphere (see Figure 2.9).

The unique structure of the visual system allows us to study hemispheric specialization. Each eye is constructed such that visual information from the left side of the page you are reading now strikes the right side of the retina. Visual information from the right side of the page strikes the retina on the left side. Again we see this principle of contralaterality. This principle applies to both eyes (see Figure 2.9). The retinas of the eyes have long axons that travel from the retina to the lateral geniculate nuclei, which act as an intermediate processing center for the visual system. For each eye, these axons are bundled up in two separate pathways. The axons from the left part of each eye travel to the left hemisphere of the brain. Equally, the axons from the right part of each eye travel to the right hemisphere. As a result, some optic information has to cross over through the optic chiasm to get to its designated hemisphere, as shown in Figure 2.9. Since the left side of the eye receives information from the right side of the visual world, the left hemisphere processes the information from the right side of the page.

If we briefly present a stimulus (an object) on a computer screen to one side of the visual field and if that presentation is faster than the eye can move, the visual information is going to only one side of the retina, and thus only to one hemisphere. If the object were on the screen longer, the eye would have a chance to move, thus capturing the image on both sides of the retina, and thus sending information to both hemispheres. We can control which hemisphere gets that visual information by removing the stimulus from the screen before the eye could move, thus ensuring that only one hemisphere is receiving the visual information.

If the corpus callosum is cut, as in the split-brain procedure, then information detected by, say, the right retina of the right eye would be "trapped" in the right hemisphere. Likewise, information detected by the left retina would be limited to the left hemisphere.

Is the ability to share information lost after split-brain surgery (see Figure 2.10)? To find out, Gazzaniga, using the method described above, one hemisphere of a patient was presented with the word "bow"; the other hemisphere saw the word "arrow." If the information is shared between hemispheres the patient should be able to say "bow and arrow" or draw a bow and arrow. The patient in fact did draw a bow and arrow, and it was assumed that the two hemispheres were able to somehow communicate with each other, despite the severed corpus callosum. How could this be? The researchers thought that it was possible that the patient could draw each picture independently without realizing the integrative concept of bow and arrow. A better test would be to take two that when combined create a new object altogether. For example, if the patient is presented with the words "sky" and "scraper," if they are not integrating them, the patient would draw a sky and a tool-like scraper (Figure 2.10). If the information is integrated, the patient would draw a tall building.

When presented with the words "sky" and "scraper" to opposite hemispheres, the patient drew the two separate objects (sky and a scraper tool). The next question they had was whether the ability to synthesize was dependent on both hemispheres communicating, or was it possible for each hemisphere on its own to synthesize information? They presented words such as "ice" and "cream" into the right hemisphere only, and the patient drew with his left hand an ice cream cone, as opposed to ice cubes and a cup of milk.

The impressive bilateral nature of the hemispheres is found in a demonstration by Levy, Trevarthen, and Sperry (1972). In this experiment, a split-brain patient was asked to look at a fixation point at the center of a screen. Two faces were combined where half

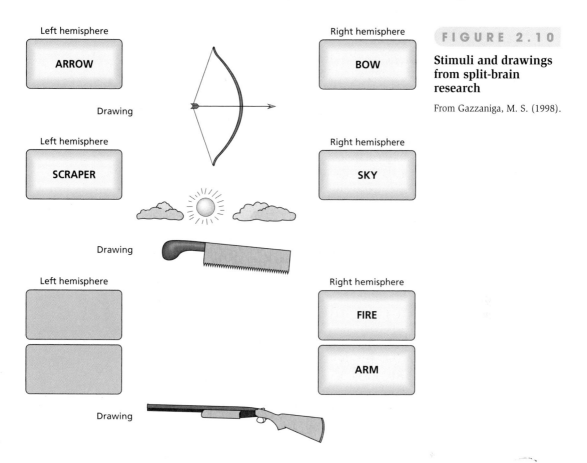

FIGURE 2.10

Stimuli and drawings from split-brain research

From Gazzaniga, M. S. (1998).

of the resulting face was a man and the other half was a woman. The face was briefly flashed on the screen (Figure 2.11).

The participant did not report anything unusual about the composite, even though each hemisphere perceived a different face. When asked to describe the face, the participant verbally described a man's features, supporting the verbal nature of the left hemisphere. However, when asked to recognize the face from an array of photographs, the participant picked the woman's photo, supporting the pictorial nature of the right hemisphere (see Bradshaw & Nettleton, 1981; Springer & Deutsch, 1984). Clearly there is specialization in the hemispheres and that specialization cannot be used by the other hemisphere without benefit of the corpus callosum.

Cognitive Studies with Participants with Intact Corpus Callosums   Because of the curious neural pathways involved in visual processing, it is possible to do lateralization experiments with participants whose corpus callosum is intact. Obviously, it is far easier to find unimpaired participants than commissurotomized ones, and, as a consequence, a great number of cognitive experiments have been done with this population. Also, the procedure is relatively straightforward, and the apparatus is conventional. Typically, a person is screened for handedness because left-handed people sometimes have language in the right hemisphere, thus they are often excluded from these sorts of studies.

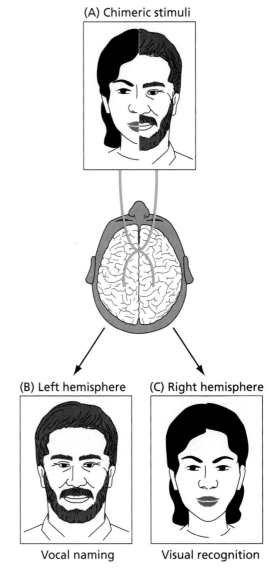

(A) Chimeric stimuli

FIGURE 2.11

Display of chimeric face (A) used with commissurotomized patients. Each hemisphere appears to register separate images: the left (B) records a man's face, the right (C) a woman's. When asked to describe the face, the participant verbally labels it as a man's, but when asked to point out the face among a display of faces, the participant selects the woman's face.

(B) Left hemisphere

(C) Right hemisphere

Vocal naming

Visual recognition

They are also screened for gender because women have been known to have thicker corpus callosums, thus facilitating the exchange of information between the two hemispheres. They too are often excluded from this type of research. These research restrictions leave us with right-handed males. The participant is asked to look at a fixation point presented in the center of a computer screen. A word, a color, or some other type of visual information is then momentarily presented either to the right or left of the fixation point. Information presented to the right of the fixation point crosses over to the left hemisphere, and information to the left crosses over to the right hemisphere. The participant is then typically asked to make some type of decision about the visual information (e.g., "Was it a word?"), and his reaction time is recorded. The rationale behind the design is that if information is normally processed in one or the other hemisphere, then access to that information should be fast; if information is initially processed in the "wrong" hemisphere, it must pass over to the "correct" hemisphere to be processed, and that operation takes time. It should be noted that the amount of time involved in these experiments is very brief indeed, and a difference of 50 milliseconds is considered large.

Researchers have successfully used the technique of presenting a brief stimulus to the right or left **visual field** to evaluate information processing. In general, these findings have confirmed that the left hemisphere is superior at words and letters, and the right hemisphere is superior at spatial processing. Other studies have indicated differences in gender (Boles, 1984), in auditory processing (Ivry & Lebby, 1993), during sustained visual attention (Whitehead, 1991a, 1991b), and in handedness (Annett, 1982). These studies have also suggested that the type of visual stimuli has differential effects, depending on the hemisphere in which the material is processed (Boles, 1987).

The adaptive function of laterality is less clearly understood than the fact that it does appear consistently, especially in humans. One intriguing hypothesis by Corballis (1989) gives the phenomenon an evolutionary basis: human evolutionary history reveals that right handedness, tool use, and the development of left-hemispheric mechanisms for language use developed in hominids as long as 2 or 3 million years ago and set the stage for the development of more complex functions. Corballis writes, "Beginning some 1.5 million years ago with the emergence of the larger brained *H. erectus,* tool culture became more complex. However, a truly flexible tool culture and the rapid, flexible speech of modern humans may not have developed until later still, perhaps 150,000 years ago, when *H. sapiens* emerged in Africa, to subsequently populate the globe" (p. 499). According to Corballis, the evolution of hemisphere specialization may be associated with flexibility of thought and generativity or the ability to combine elements using rules to create new associations—be they words, sentences, or more complex tools. Genrativity may be uniquely human and is associated with the left cerebral hemisphere. Corballis's theory is fascinating, but it should be considered in light of studies done on language processing and tool use by chimpanzees and apes, providing evidence that these skills may not be uniquely human (see Gardner & Gardner, 1969).

Impressive as they are, these experiments regarding the dissimilar nature of the hemispheres need to be considered in a larger context. Although a sizable number of careful experiments and demonstrations have indicated that some functions are located in specific areas of the cortex, it is likely that cerebral processing is also distributed throughout other areas in the brain. Even in the case of hemisphere specialization, the brain seems to operate as a holistic organ. It should be noted that many of the research paradigms reported here involved patients whose corpus callosums had been severed and were designed to demonstrate the bilateral nature of the human brain. In normal humans the connective tissues are intact, and the two hemispheres operate cooperatively with massive "communication" between them.

Cognitive Neuroscience

These early studies on lobotomies, phrenology, and localization of function were precursors to modern cognitive neuroscience. Neuroscientists are scientists who study neuroscience, or the branch of science that encompasses the study of neuroanatomy,

*T*he task of cognitive neuroscience is to reverse-engineer the brain: to dissect its computational architecture into functionally isolable information-processing units, and to determine how these units operate, both computationally and physically.

—*Cosmides & Tooby*

neurophysiology, brain functions, and related psychological and computer models of brain functioning. Because of the efforts of neuroscientists, hypothetical constructs such as memory types and language processing are no longer so intangible but seem to have specific neurophysiological correlates. Furthermore, microscopic structures of the brain, when viewed as neural networks, seem to be related to larger components of human cognition, such as memory, perception, problem solving, and the like. In some ways, cognitive neuroscience is a meeting ground to further explore the long-standing issues surrounding mind and body. Cognitive neuroscience, as Richard Thompson of the University of Southern California states, ". . .is the natural marriage of neuroscience and cognitive science—loosely speaking, the study of brain and mind" (2000, p. 411).

Perhaps another generation will view such gross demonstrations of cortical neural activity, which correspond to equally gross categories of thinking, as a primitive attempt to use knowledge from two previously disparate sciences to understand the central mechanisms of human cognition. This early work will be remembered as a turning point in both cognitive psychology and neuroscience, and the exciting part for contemporary students of cognition is that they will witness and, in some cases, create a new science of the mind.

Cognitive Psychology and Cognitive Neuroscience

What are the two fields getting out of the marriage called cognitive neuroscience? How do they mutually benefit? There are several reasons contemporary psychologists are using information and techniques from neuroscience and neuroscientists are using cognitive psychology. These include:

- The demand to find physical evidence for theoretical structures of the mind. The search for the properties of the human mind stretches back to the beginning of history, if not before, but has been constantly frustrated because of the tenuous nature of the supporting evidence. The development of sophisticated equipment has made it possible to materially identify the presence of important psychological processes such as language, perception, form identification, thinking, memory, and other cognitive functions.

- The need on the part of neuroscientists to relate their findings to more comprehensive models of brain functioning and cognition. Even if it were possible to

*T*he function of the brain. . .is to generate behavior that is appropriate to your environment.

—*Cosmides & Tooby*

identify every minute detail of neurological functions, this would tell us little about the network and systems properties that are essential to the understanding of cognitive effects and the way we humans perform everyday activities, from the profound to the profane.

- The clinical goal to find correlates between brain pathology and behavior (symptoms). For generations neurologists have been concerned with the way in which brain traumas, lesions, infarctions, thrombosis, and tumors affect behavior and with the procedures and might alleviate related symptoms. These concerns require a precise understanding of brain functioning and psychology. Conversely, psychologists interested in the psychological treatment of organically impaired patients require better understanding of the physical causes of such behavior.

- The increased involvement of neurological functions in models of the mind. Specifically, cognitive psychologists interested in parallel distributed processing (PDP), also called connectionism or neural network systems, are interested in finding psychological models consistent with neurological structures and functions.

- The work of computer scientists who are attempting to simulate human cognition by developing computer software that behaves in a way that is similar to the way in which the human brain behaves. These approaches to brain and computer are sometimes called neural network archcitectures. They include the subspecialty perceptrons, which is the simulation of neural networks in computer architecture. The word "perceptron" was first used in 1957 by Frank Rosenblatt, a Cornell Aeronautical Laboratory scientist, who built one of the first neural networks. Such developments of computer architecture and function require detailed understanding of brain architecture and function.

- The development of techniques that allow scientists to peer into the human brain and that reveal structures and processes never seen before. These include positron emission tomography scans, computed axial tomography scans, magnetic resonance imaging, and electroencephalography. These largely noninvasive tools are possible because of advances in computer technology and brain-scanning techniques.

Understanding the adaptive problems our ancestors faced guides the search for models of cognition that solve them, and the neural basis of those cognitive strategies. There are four questions that we can use to consider the importance of tying together cognitive psychology and cognitive neuroscience (adapted from Cosmides & Tooby, 1997). (1) Where in the brain are the neural circuits that control specific types of cognition? (2) What kind of information is being processed by these circuits? (3) What types of cognitive strategies do these circuits embody? and (4) What were these neural circuits (and resulting cognitions) designed to accomplish in a hunter-gatherer context? These questions serve to force us to consider that the neurophysiological basis for cognition was formed via natural selection, and therefore must have served to solve problems that our ancestors faced.

The Neuroscientists' Toolbox

This section is designed to provide you with some basic information on some very complex technologies. We want you to come away with a clear understanding of the type of information each technology provides the researcher. You'll be able to apply this basic

T A B L E   2 . 2

The Neuroscientist's Toolbox

Acronym	Name	Device	Information Captured	Display	Information Gained
EEG	Electroencephalogram	Electrodes on scalp	Electrical signals (neural activity)	Graph	How long it takes to process stimuli
CT	Computed Axial Tomography	X-ray scanner	Density of tissue	3D image	Brain structure
PET	Positron Emission Tomography	Radioactive scanner	Regional cerebral blood flow (glucose use)	3D color coded image	Brain function
MRI	Magnetic Resonance Imaging	Electromagnetic scanner	Density of hydrogen atoms	3D image	Brain structure
fMRI	Functional Magnetic Resonance Imaging	Electromagnetic scanner	Density of hydrogen atoms	3D images	Brain structure and function
MEG	Magnetoencephalography	Electromagnetic scanner	Magnetic fields (from nerve cell activity)	3D image	Brain function
TMS	Transcranial Magnetic Stimulation	Wand that emits magnetic charge	Neural activity	Used with EEG or MEG	Brain function; subjects' reported experiences during testing
Micro CT	X-ray micro tomography	X-ray scanner	Density of material	3D image	Structure of very small objects

understanding throughout the book and build on this information when reviewing figures (like the one on the inside cover of this book) and study findings in later chapters. Table 2.2 summarizes the technology.

Fifty years ago, neuroscientists had only a few tools and techniques to use in the direct observation and exploration of the human brain. These included ablations (damaging tissue by excising or freezing), single-cell recordings, postmortem examinations, and animal studies. Psychologists, on the other hand, invented a whole arsenal of techniques in which the mind revealed itself, such as the momentary presentation of stimuli and measuring of reaction time. New instruments have been invented that have profoundly accelerated our understanding of the brain and, for our purposes, spun off a new breed of scientist who is part neuroscientist and part cognitive psychologist. The new technology was originally developed for the diagnosis of brain disorders, but it has now become a valuable research tool for scientists interested in studying the mind. These methods have led to important new discoveries in the study of human cognition and have already proved to be an integral part of the future of cognitive neuroscience.

EEG

Electroencephalography (EEG) records electrical signals from neural activity in the brain, using a series of noninvasive electrodes placed on the scalp. The electrical signals recorded by the electrodes are sent to instruments that display the signals. Early EEGs were hooked up to pens that traced the signals onto constantly moving graph paper, however, these have been replaced by computer displays. EEGs can show us how long it takes to process stimuli, but they cannot show us structures, anatomy, or the functional regions of the brain.

Alan Gevins and his colleagues of the EEG Systems Laboratory in San Francisco developed a "super" EEG system, called Mental Activity Network Scanner (MANSCAN), which can record as many as 250 images of cerebral activity per second. EEG recordings are also lightning fast—as fast as one-thousandth of a second, which is a real advantage over other imaging techniques that, in some instances, require many seconds to capture an image.

Many of the new techniques allow us to see the brain and its function in one way or another, with apparatuses similar to that shown in Figure 2.12. In such procedures a patient is placed in the center of the scanning instrument, which records impressions from within the cranium or other parts of the body. The scan produces a cross-sectional image of the brain or other body part. The impression is first enhanced by a computer, then color coded, and finally displayed on a computer monitor. Photographs and/or hard copies of the display are often made. There are several types of brain scans in general use: the computed axial tomography (CT) scan, the positron emission tomography (PET) scan, magnetic resonance imaging (MRI), and magnetoencephalography (MEG).

CT Scans

Computed axial tomography (CT) is the process of using computers to generate a three-dimensional image showing the structure of the brain from flat (in other words, two-dimensional) X-ray pictures. The machine rotates around the skull, bombarding it with thin, fan-shaped X-ray beams. The beams pass through the brain and are recorded on sensitive detectors on the opposite side of their source. This procedure is different from a conventional X-ray examination, which gives only one view of the body part. Also, with conventional X-rays, large molecules (such as calcium in the skull) absorb the rays and partially occlude the organs behind them. The CT scan rotates the X-ray beam 180 degrees, resulting in numerous "pictures" of the same organ and producing an internal cross section, or "slice," of the body part. This graphic cross section, called a tomogram, has become critical in medical diagnosis. An even more sophisticated version of the CT technique, the dynamic spatial reconstructor (DSR), shows internal structures in three dimensions. One advantage of CT is the ubiquity of the machines. As of the mid-1990s, more than 10,000 scanners were in use in American hospitals. Also, recent technology has helped solve one of the problems with this technique. The temporal resolution, or shutter speed, had been about 1 second, with the result that dynamic processes (even the heartbeat) appeared blurred. Now, an ultrafast CT has been developed that speeds up processing so that previously blurred images are now clear. Additionally, a new CT imaging technique is called x-ray microtomography. This technology uses CT to scan via a microscope which allow for 3D images of very small structures (a 5mm fossilized fish eyeball, the tine structures of the inner ear, and the root structure of a human molar tooth (Uzon, Curthoys, & Jones, 2006). The full utility of this technology is yet to be determined.

FIGURE 2.12

Brain scanning techniques.

A. Overall procedure for obtaining brain scans with a video display.

B. CT scan procedure in which low-intensity X-ray beams scan the brain.

C. PET scan procedure, in which radioactive tracers are detected by peripheral sensors.

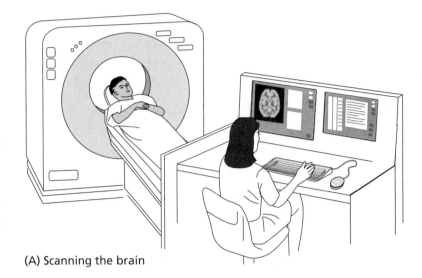

(A) Scanning the brain

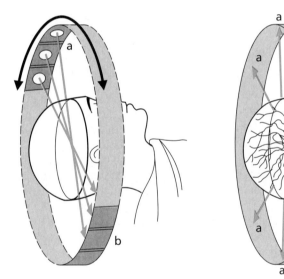

(B) CT scan procedure   (C) PET scan procedure

PET Scans

Positron emission tomography (PET) is used to scan for glucose use in the brain. PET scans differ from CT scans in that they use detectors to measure radioactive particles in the bloodstream to measure regional cerebral blood flow (rCBF) Figure 2.13. Active parts of the brain require blood flow, and hence, more radioactive tracers amass in operative areas. These tracers emit rays, which can be converted to visual maps. The computer codes the glucose absorption data to show varying levels of activity in a color-coded

Functional MRI

PET

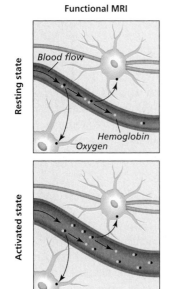

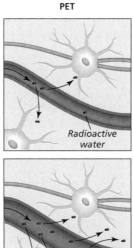

Resting state

Blood flow

Hemoglobin
Oxygen

Radioactive
water

Activated state

FIGURE 2.13

Blood flow to the brain provides the signals detected by functional MRI and PET. When resting neurons (top) become active (bottom), blood flow to them increases. MRI (left) detects changes in oxygen levels, which rise in the nearby blood vessels when they are activated. PET (right) relies on the increased delivery of injected radioactive water, which diffuses out of the vessels to reach all parts of the brain.

Raichle, *Scientific American,* April 1994. Reprinted with permission from Jared Schneidman Design.

map. Red usually indicates more active areas and blue usually indicates less activate areas. The application of PET scans to cognitive neuroscience has been particularly useful for measuring brain functioning. At Lund University in Sweden, research scientists Jarl Risberg and David Ingva (see Lassen, Ingvar, & Skinhoj, 1979), working in collaboration with Steve Petersen, Michael Posner, Marcus Raichle, and Endel Tulving, have pioneered the use of PET scans in cognitive psychology (see Posner, Petersen, Fox, & Raichle, 1988). PET technology is more expensive compared to CT scanners. Some advances in PET studies have been in the type of tracers injected into the blood. Early studies were based on inhaling a radioactive isotope. Nowadays, a different isotope is used that can be injected intravenously, which allows for high-resolution maps to be made in a few seconds (Risberg, 1987, 1989; Tulving, 1989a, 1989b), thus giving the researcher considerable latitude in collecting cognitive data.

MRI and fMRI

Magnetic resonance imaging (MRI) scans provide still images of structures of the brain. In the MRI technique the body is surrounded with very powerful electromagnets that align the nuclei of hydrogen atoms found in water. From these measures, it is possible to infer varying densities of hydrogen atoms and their interaction with surrounding tissues. Since hydrogen reflects water content, it is possible to use the MRI for diagnostic and research purposes. One of the main drawbacks of the technique, until recently, was the time it took to form images using MRI technology. Because it required long exposure time, the technique was acceptable for viewing static biological structures. However, it was nearly useless for rapidly changing cognitive functions. It is now possible using fMRI to apply high-performance image acquisition techniques to capture an image in as little as

30 milliseconds, which is brief enough to record fast-paced cognitive functions. fMRI (functional magnetic resonance imaging) detects increased blood flow to activated areas of the brain, thus displaying function and structure.

MEG

Magnetoencephalography (MEG) uses a machine that measures brain activity from the outside of the head by detecting the faint magnetic fields that brain activity produces. MEG produces an activity map or functional image of the brain. Of all the brain scanning methods, MEG provides the most accurate resolution of nerve cell activity (to the millisecond).

TMS

Transcranial magnetic stimulation (TMS) is used in conjunction with EEG or MEG to evaluate the effects of changes in brain electrical activity on perceiving and thinking. A magnetic charge is directed via a wand placed on the head and pointed to a specific location in the brain for a very short period of time. This charge alters the neural functioning; these effects on brain functioning can be seen in the output of the EEG or MEG, as well as in terms of the person's responses to the cognitive and perceptual tasks he or she is engaged in at the time.

Micro CT

A new CT imaging technique is called x-ray microtomography. This technology uses CT to scan via a microscope which allow for 3D images of very small structures (a 5mm fossilized fish eyeball, the tine structures of the inner ear, and the root structure of a human molar tooth (Uzon, Curthoys, & Jones, 2006). The full utility of this technology is yet to be determined.

Research Using Imaging Techniques: Examples of PET

Of particular interest to cognitive psychologists is the use of cortical blood flow patterns in memory research. As you'll recall, PET and fMRI measure blood flow. Endel Tulving has developed a theory of memory that posits two unique types: episodic (memory for personal events) and semantic (memory for general knowledge). In one experiment studying two types of memory by Tulving (1989b), participants were asked to think silently about an event in their lives (an episodic memory) and then to think about something general. The research was conducted with a PET scanner. Recall that PET scans work by injecting a tracer into the participant's bloodstream. The results of one participant's rCBF are shown in color on the inside front cover of this book. While expertise is required to fully interpret these scans, one can still see general differences in the patterns of blood flow, suggesting increased neural activity associated with different regions of the brain. Basically, it appears that episodic memory is identified by greater activation of the anterior portion of the cerebral cortex, and semantic memory is associated with greater activation of the posterior regions. It seems safe to conclude that episodic and semantic memory systems involved different brain processes and that each has its own location. This in turn suggests that we may have multiple memory systems, an idea long held in cognitive psychology. Data from this PET study supports other observations from clinical studies of patients with brain damage who have episodic memory loss.

In another attempt to find a direct correlation between cognitive processes and brain activity, Michael Posner, Steven Petersen, and their colleagues at the McDonnell Center for Higher Brain Functions at Washington University conducted a series of PET experiments dealing with the processing of words by the normal, healthy brain (Petersen, Fox, Posner, Mintun, & Raichle, 1988). There were four stages of the experiment: (1) a resting stage; (2) the appearance of a single word on a screen; (3) the reading of the word aloud; and (4) the production of a use for each word (see Figure 2.14). Each of these

FIGURE 2.14

Are words processed in the same place in the brain? Not at all, according to PET studies of word processing. When participants are presented with a word to view, parts of the occipital region are activated (A). When they are listening to words, the superior temporal cortex is activated (B); when they are speaking, parts of the primary motor cortex (C) are activated; and when they are generating verbs, the frontal lobe and middle temporal cortex are implicated (D) (after Petersen et al., 1988).

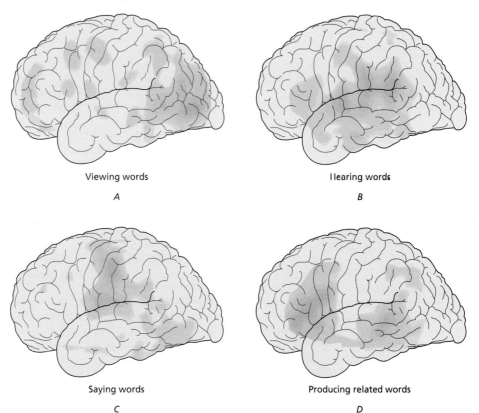

Viewing words
A

Hearing words
B

Saying words
C

Producing related words
D

Steven Petersen. Along with colleagues at Washington University (St. Louis), Petersen has done pioneering work with PET and cognitive processes.

stages produced its own pattern of activation, allowing the researchers to localize the different cognitive functions associated with seeing, speaking, and producing words. This is also evidence for more holistic processing, with words in general being processed using vast areas of the brain (i.e., there isn't a little "word spot" in the brain). When a participant looked at a word on a screen, the occipital region of the cortex was activated; when the participant was hearing a word, the central part of the cortex was activated; when speaking a word, motor regions were activated; and when asked to produce related words (e.g., if the word "cake" appeared, the participant was to produce a verb related to that word, such as "eat"), the associative region produced the greatest amount of activity, but other general activity throughout the cortex was also observed.

A la carte

Adaptation to Faces

Although cognitive neuroscience technology has been around for a while, much of what we currently know about the brain and cognition was discovered before the widespread use of modern imaging techniques. In the early 1900s researchers used the method of adaptation to help discover how the physiology of the brain worked. Gibson and Radner (1937) used a tilted line to demonstrate the "tilt aftereffect" where an observer would fixate on a line that was not quite vertical (e.g., "\"). After a short period of fixation, the observer would be said to be in a state of adaptation. They were then shown a straight line (e.g., "|"), which as a result of their adaptation would appear tilted in a direction opposite the adapting stimulus (e.g., "/"). Gibson used his findings to argue the existence of neural substrates that were "tuned" to orientations of lines. Hubel and Weisel (1968) would later use single-

cell recordings to locate these orientation-specific cells in the visual cortex of cats. One theory of how adaptation works is that neurons selectively tuned to the adapting stimulus become fatigued. When the vertical line is presented, nonfatigued neurons "overreact," causing the perception of a tilted line in the opposite direction. Similar results have been found for neurons selective for motion and others for color, for example. Using the method of adaptation, researchers have learned a considerable amount about perception and cognition. It was previously thought that adaptation to complex objects such as faces was not possible. Recently researchers demonstrated that not only was adaptation using faces possible, but that it could be used to examine specialized areas of our brain responsible for recognizing faces (MacLin & Webster, 2001). Researchers have since used adaptation to examine neural selectivity of gender and ethnicity of faces (Ng, Ciaramitaro, Anstis, Boynton, & Fine, 2006). For a demonstration of how adaptation to faces works, check out the three faces below. Two of the faces belong to American politicians and the third face is a morph of the two. If you stare at the image of President George W. Bush for just a few minutes, the morph in the middle is perceived to look more like John Kerry. This may be due to the cells responsible for recognizing President Bush becoming fatigued, thus when you look at the morph, only the cells that are involved with recognizing Kerry are fully functioning.

  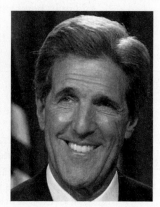

Photos courtesy of Michael Webster.

Student Resource Center

STUDY GUIDE

1   The mind–body issue has been debated for centuries. The term *mind* refers to the functions of the body, specifically the brain.

2   Using studies of regional cerebral blood flow (rCBF), Tulving found specific regions of the brain that are active during episodic memory processing and other regions that are active during semantic memory processing.

3   Cognitive neuroscience is the scientific study of the relationships between cognitive psychology and neuroscience. Several reasons exist for the alliance between psychology and neuroscience. These include the need to find physical evidence for theoretical properties of the mind, the need among neuroscientists to find more comprehensive models of brain and behavior, the need to find relationships between brain pathology and behavior, the increased use of neurally inspired models of cognitive science, the increased use of computers to model neurological functions, and the invention of techniques that enhance the ability to depict brain structures more clearly.

4   The basic building block of the nervous system is the neuron, whose principal parts are the dendrites, cell body, axon, and synaptic juncture where neurotransmission takes place.

5   Neurologists have long debated whether the functions of the brain could be localized. The conclusion is that some gross functions are localized (for example, speech) but that functions are generally distributed throughout the brain.

6   Brain scientists have developed techniques that allow high-resolution graphic depictions of brain activity. These techniques include MRI, PET, and CT scans as well as other imaging procedures.

7   Split-brain and cognitive research has indicated that processing of information in the right hemisphere differs from that in the left hemisphere.

KEY TERMS

aggregate field theory
axon
cell body
central nervous system
cerebral commissurotomy
cerebral cortex
cerebral hemispheres
cognitive neuroscience
Computed Axial Tomography (CT)
contralaterality
corpus callosum
dendrites
electroencephalography (EEG)
fissures
frontal lobe
gyri/gyrus
lobotomy
localization
magnetic resonance imagery (MRI)
magnetoencephalography (MEG)

mass action
mind–body issue
neurogenesis
neuron
neurotransmission
neurotransmitters
occipital lobe
parietal lobe
phrenology
positron emission tomography (PET)
presynaptic terminals
pseudoscience
psychosurgery
reflec arc
sulci/sulcus
synapse
temporal lobe
transcranial magnetic stimulation
    (TMS)
visual field

STARTING POINTS

Books and Articles

● The field of cognitive neuroscience is relatively recent, and some of the best references are to be found in current issues of journals. Germane periodicals include *Science, Brain and Behavioral Sciences, Cortex, Journal of Neurophysiology, Psychobiology, Nature, Brain,* and *Brain and Cognition,* among others. Corballis's article "Laterality and Human Evolution" appears in *Psychological Review* (1989), and Land and Fernald is in the *Annual Review of Neuroscience,* Volume 15.

● Some books of interest are Restak, *The Mind;* Blakemore, *Mechanics of the Mind;* Ornstein, *The Psychology of Consciousness;* and Benson and Zaidel, eds., *The Dual Brain: Hemispheric Specialization in Humans.* More specialized, but highly recommended, are Kandel, Schwartz, and Jessell, *Principles of Neural Science* (3rd edition); Thompson, *The Brain: A Neuroscience Primer* (2nd edition); and Squire and Butters, eds., *Neuropsychology of Memory* and an edited behemoth by Gazzaniga called *The Cognitive Neurosciences.* Of particular interest in the Gazzaniga volume are introductory chapters on memory, by Tulving; on consciousness, by Schacter; on language, by Pinker; on thought and imagery, by Kosslyn; and on attention, by Posner.

Movies

- Awakenings (1990)—Effects of L-Dopa
- A Scanner Darkly (2007)—Futuristic brain damaging drug
- Mind over Matter (2006)—A man's struggle with brain cancer

Search Terms

- Neuroguide
- The Whole Brain Atlas
- Comparative Mammilian Brain Collection
- 10% Brain Myth
- Neuropsychology Central

Sensation, Perception, and Attention

hmmm . . . ?

1. Why are sensation and perception important topics to cognitive psychologists?

2. How do illusions help us understand perception?

3. What are iconic storage and echoic storage, and how do they help us understand the "real" world?

4. How do cognitive psychologists define *attention*? Name several examples of attention in everyday life.

5. What are the major theories of attention and the experimental support for them?

6. What do we mean when we talk about "processing capacity" and "selective attention?"

7. What is "automatic processing?" Give some examples of automatic processing from your everyday life experiences.

8. What have cerebral imaging techniques told us about attention?

A good advertisement is one which sells the product without drawing attention to it.

— *Doug Ogilvy*

*A*ny man who can drive safely while kissing a pretty girl is simply not giving the kiss the attention it deserves.

—*Albert Einstein*

As you woke today, you fired up your cognitive computer, which had been turned off for the night. When you were jolted out of an unconscious state by the ringing of an alarm clock, you sensed the auditory world; when you opened your eyes, you caught sight of the visual world; when you splashed water on your face, you sensed the tactile world; when you inhaled the rich aroma of freshly brewed coffee, you enjoyed the olfactory world; and when you nibbled on a fresh roll, you savored the gustatory world. Five senses—five windows to the world—only five ways to know the world. Yet, contained within those five conduits to the "real world" are the basic means by which we comprehend everything from Picasso to punk rock, not to mention the ocean's mist, Bach, perfume, Dostoevski, peppermint candy, sunsets, and physical intimacy.

In this chapter we find out how we humans use the **computational brain** to *perceive* information about the environment, *attend* to the world, and *process information* during the initial stages.

We begin by examining the perception of sensory signals because this is the initial step in the processing of information. At the heart of this process is the brain, whose task it is to understand and, in effect, make sense out of the things being fed into it from the **peripheral nervous system.** That system is made up of nerves that lie outside the spinal cord and the brain and are involved in sensation and perception.

The Computational Brain

The peripheral nervous system and brain are largely designed to perceive and cogitate—to see and understand, for example. Steve Pinker expressed it well in his book *How the Mind Works:* "The mind is a system of organs of computation, designed by natural selection to solve the kinds of problems our ancestors faced in their foraging way of life, in particular, understanding and outmaneuvering objects, animals, plants, and other people" (1997, p. 21). We see, hear, smell, taste, and feel the sensations of the world as the first link in a chain of events that subsequently involves coding stimuli; storing information; transforming material; thinking; and, finally, reacting to knowledge (see Figure 3.1).

The concept of the computational brain is based on the idea that the mind is what the brain does—it processes information. When we engage in "higher-order cognition"

The stages of information processing showing external phenomena and internal processes and structures.

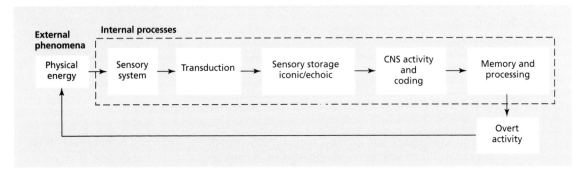

—thinking about how to find a better job or figuring out where to meet our friends on Thursday night to study for a Friday exam—we are doing a type of computation.

As shown in Figure 3.1, physical energy that falls within the limited range of human detection stimulates the sensory system, is transduced (converted to neural energy by sensory organs), is briefly held in a sensory storage, is subjected to further processing by the central nervous system (CNS) and coded, and may be passed on to memory systems for processing. The results can initiate responses that become part of the stimulus field for further processing. (A large portion of this book deals with the very complex and abstract processing of information that takes place in the memory systems and the computation of that information.)

It is useful to keep in mind that the flowchart shown in Figure 3.1 is just a model of the hypothetical stages through which information is processed. It is certainly not the case that the brain is arranged more or less as shown in the illustration, but this model has value as a visual conceptualization of the various stages of information processing postulated in cognitive psychology. Cognitive psychologists have the capability to see the activation of the brain as information is being processed. Techniques (such as those mentioned in the previous chapter) suggest that the stages shown in this figure are analogous to actual physiological processes. With imaging techniques, the dream of scientists throughout the twentieth century to observe the locus of brain activities associated with cognitive processes is rapidly becoming a reality. Some of these findings and trends are shown in this chapter and in later chapters on memory and higher-order cognition.

Sensation and Perception

In cognitive psychology we refer to the physical (external) world as well as the mental (internal) world. The interface between external reality and the inner world is centered in the sensory system.

Sensation refers to the initial detection of energy from the physical world. The study of sensation generally deals with the structure and processes of the sensory mechanism and the stimuli that affect those mechanisms (see Table 3.1). **Perception,** on the other

TABLE 3.1

The Five Senses

Sense	Structure	Stimulus	Receptor
Vision	Eye	Light waves	Rods and cones
Hearing	Ear	Sound waves	Hair cells
Taste	Tongue	Chemicals	Taste buds
Smell	Nose	Chemicals	Hair cells
Touch	Skin	Pressure	Nerve cells

hand, involves higher-order cognition in the interpretation of the sensory information. Basically, *sensation* refers to the initial detection of stimuli; *perception* to an interpretation of the things we sense. When we read a book, listen to our iPod, get a massage, smell cologne, or taste sushi, we experience far more than the immediate sensory stimulation. Sensory events are processed within the context of our knowledge of the world, on culture, expectations, and even who we are with at the time. These give meaning to simple sensory experiences—that is perception.

Vision

While all our senses provided us with valuable information about our environment, vision, by far provides the most critical information. **Vision,** the act of sensing a small section of electromagnetic waves referred to as light, is made possible because of the eye's unique structure. Light rays enter the eye through the **cornea** and **lens,** which focus an image on the **retina.** The recognition of a pattern, whether a simple two-dimensional black-and-white form or a complex three-dimensional colored form, is always represented on the retina as a two-dimensional[1] form. From these two-dimensional representations on the retina, higher-order perception—including the illusion of three-dimensionality—is made possible when the impulses are passed along the visual pathway to the **visual cortex** and, when combined with existing knowledge, lead to the recognition of, say, our grandmother when we see her.

The visual system is one of the most complex of all sensory systems. The human eye has about 7 million **cones,** which are sensitive to well-illuminated stimuli (photopic), and about 125 million **rods,** which are sensitive to poorly illuminated stimuli. This distribution of rods and cones in the retina is not even. Cones are concentrated in the **fovea,** and are responsible for color and fine vision and rods are spread away from the fovea. There are no rods in the fovea. Interestingly, the visual experience at the retina is two-dimensional (without depth) and color blind (it is not until the neural inputs are combined

---

[1]The image that falls on the retina occurs over a period of time, which some might consider another dimension.

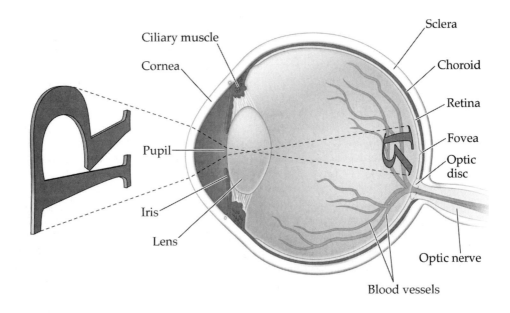

SENSATION AND PERCEPTION, Figure 2.2 © 2006 Sinauer Associates, Inc.

later on that the perception of color emerges). Electromagnetic waves are transduced into electrochemical signals, which are the "language" of the brain. These signals are passed through three layers of cells located *in front* of the retina, actually blocking some light from reaching the retina. These layers consist of several types of cells: horizontal, bipolar, amacrine, and ganglion cells. **Ganglion cells** have relatively long axons that are bundled and travel through a hole in the retina called the blind spot, back to a transfer station of sorts called the **lateral geniculate nucleus** (LGN). The LGN received the majority of information from the retina and passes a majority of its information to the **visual cortex** (also referred to as the striate cortex). By the time the signal reaches the visual cortex, signals have been reduced to small units such as lines and their orientations (Hubel & Wiesel 1959). These are then sent from the visual cortex to the cerebral cortex along pathways (also referred to as the "what" and "where" pathways) to different locations depending on how the signals are initially interpreted.

Several ongoing projects are attempting to emulate human vision using computers, which have been built on the information just presented. At this time it is impossible to build an artificial eye with millions of sensors. What has been built is a television "eye" with a 512 × 512 array (which has 262,144 pixels, or "picture elements") that crudely simulates the human eye. The pixels can be turned on or off, and light intensity can be further simulated by computer programs. Identifying visual boundaries of real objects has also been successfully simulated (see Marr, 1982, for details). We shall return to computer vision in Chapter 15. We turn our attention to models of human visual information processing.

Our experiences in the world guide our perception, but so do forces that guide the development of the biology and cognitive systems in the first place. Cosmides and Tooby (1997) provide us an interesting example:

> You have sensory receptors that are stimulated by the sight and smell of feces—to put it more bluntly, you can see and smell dung. So can a dung fly. But on detecting the presence of feces in the environment, what counts as appropriate behavior for you differs from what is appropriate for the dung fly. On smelling feces, appropriate behavior for a female dung fly is to move toward the feces, land on them, and lay her eggs. Feces are food for a dung fly larva—therefore, appropriate behavior for a dung fly larva is to eat dung. And, because female dung flies hang out near piles of dung, appropriate behavior for a male dung fly is to buzz around these piles, trying to mate; for a male dung fly, a pile of dung is a pickup joint.
>
> But for you, feces are a source of contagious diseases. For you, they are not food, they are not a good place to raise your children, and they are not a good place to look for a date. Because a pile of dung is a source of contagious diseases for a human being, appropriate behavior for you is to move away from the source of the smell. Perhaps your facial muscles will form the cross-culturally universal disgust expression as well, in which your nose wrinkles to protect eyes and nose from the volatiles and the tongue protrudes slightly, as it would were you ejecting something from your mouth.
>
> For you, that pile of dung is "disgusting." For a female dung fly, looking for a good neighborhood and a nice house for raising her children, that pile of dung is a beautiful vision—a mansion. (p. 4)

So why is there such a difference in perception between the fly and the human of the same sensory (chemical) experience? Cosmides and Tooby (1997) argue that our sensory system, subjected to the forces of natural selection, has adapted to solve problems, in this case the problem of staying healthy (for humans) and finding food (for the dung fly).

Illusions

The distinction between sensations and the perceived interpretation of those experiences—in effect between what our sensory system receives and what the mind interprets—has occupied a central position in perception and cognition. The study of the relationship between the physical changes of the world and the psychological experiences associated with these changes is called **psychophysics.**

Psychophysicists use measurements of the physical and psychological quality of the same sensory stimuli. Sometimes reality and perception do not match, as in the case of perceptual **illusions.** A well-known example is the Müller-Lyer illusion (see Figure 3.2), in which two equal segments of a line seem unequal. The explanation of this illusion is probably partly influenced by our past experiences, which have taught us to expect that certain shapes are far away and others close. On the other hand, some argue that this illusion (and many more like it) reflects deep-seated invariant structures of the brain. Illusions are important to psychophysicists, not because they point out fault in our ability to perceive, but rather because they provide insight into how our perceptual system

A

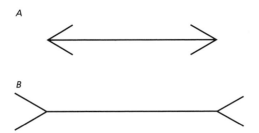

B

FIGURE 3.2

The Müller-Lyer illusion. Which line (A or B) looks longer? They are the same length. Even knowing this cannot upset the illusion.

works. For example, the circles in the rotating snake illusion (Figure 3.3) appear to move because **luminance** changes in the pattern, moving from darker to lighter luminance. The illusion plays out only in the periphery of our vision as a direct glance to the moving circle halts the perception. This suggests that the peripheral vision interprets (processes) changes in luminance as motion (Kitaoka & Ashida, 2003). Artist M. C. Escher knew about illusions and invented several of his own when creating his art as seen in Fig-

FIGURE 3.3

Rotating snakes by Akiyoshi Kitaoka.

ure 3-4. Here the visual cues of proximity and distance and of the behavior of running water do not appear consistent with each other.

Prior Knowledge

The relationship between perception and prior knowledge of the world is manifested not only in simple geometric illusions but also in the interpretation of scientific data. For example, consider holes found in an archaeological dig. If your knowledge of the tribe in question led you to the hypothesis that their huts had been rectangular, you would tend to "see," rectangle patterns representing the floor plans of huts. Conversely, other hypotheses might

FIGURE 3.5a

Duck or rabbit?

FIGURE 3.5b

Young woman or old lady?

lead you to interpret the pattern of various holes differently. Suppose you had reason to believe that the huts were triangular. You could just as easily outline along those lines, selecting "relevant" and "irrelevant" holes. Perceptions are influenced by past knowledge, previous hypotheses, and prejudices, as well as sensory signals. For example, the illusions shown on this page can each be interpreted in two very different ways. Figure 3-5a can be seen as a duck or a rabbit. Figure 3-5b can be seen as a young woman or old lady. Which image you see is dependent upon your perspective and cues in the environment (like your professor saying, "Find the animal in Figure 3-5a"). Most people are usually able to be prompted to see the other image that they first had not initially noticed; however, it is not possible for people to see both images at once. Alternatively, images that are ambiguous to their figure and ground can have multiple interpretations. You probably are familiar with the vase/profile image where you can see either a vase or two profiles by "pushing" the figure back to the ground and vice versa (Figure 3.6a). Another example is camouflage, where natural images are difficult to perceive against their backgrounds (see Figure 3.6a and 3.6b).

So, the way we perceive the primary information of the world is greatly influenced by the way the sensory system and brain are initially structured—we are "hard-wired" to perceive the world in a certain way—*and* by our past experiences, which give abundant meaning to the initial sensation of stimuli. If past learning did not influence our perception, the curious lines on this page you are now reading, which we call letters, would not be perceived as parts of words and the words would be devoid of meaning. We learn what visual (and auditory, tactical, gustatory, and olfactory) signals mean.

During World War II researchers were working with a new technology at the time called radar. As you probably know, radar emits a signal, which is reflected off of an object. The returned signal is then displayed on a monitor as a blip (computer monitors back then were only green with a black background—imagine how difficult it might be to interpret a green blip on a black background). Trained Navy operators were able to interpret the signals enabling them to differentiate hostile from friendly vessels. Researchers discovered that performance depended on expectations based on previous knowledge and expectations. If many reports of enemy vessels were reported, operators would misidentify blips identi-

FIGURE 3.6b

Where's the dog?

Courtesy of Karen Orders Photography.

FIGURE 3.6a

Faces in profile or vase?

fying friendly vessels as enemies. This began a line of research that examined how perceptual performance is based on expectations, now known as **signal detection theory.**

Sensory-Brain Predisposition

There is another side to the sensory and perceptual process that is supported by studies of the physical makeup of the sensory system and the brain. The sensory system is composed of the receptors and connecting neurons of the five senses (hearing, sight, touch, taste, and smell). Each of these senses has, to a greater or lesser degree, yielded its secrets through the effort of physiologists, physicians, and physiological psychologists throughout the past 150 years. Knowledge about the brain and its role in perception, on the other hand, has been slow to develop, partly because of the brain's inaccessibility. Direct observation of the workings of the brain typically involved the removal of a portion of its skull, the hard calcified case, which had evolved over millennia for the very purpose of keeping the brain from harm's way, or the postmortem scrutiny of brains by physicians interested in finding the neurological basis for symptoms. These studies indicated some general features, such as the well-known contralaterality of the brain, which dictates that cerebral damage to one hemisphere will result in a deficiency in the opposite side of the body. Other traumatic episodes, such as getting rapped on the back of the head in the region called the occipital lobe, result in "seeing stars." We "see" bright flashes, and yet the eye does not detect such things. This is due to what is called **labeled lines** (also the law of specific energy), which means that nerves are connected to a specific sensory function. If the nerves are stimulated they will be perceived as originating from the particular nerve they are associated with. This is why a bump to the occipital lobe creates the sensation of "seeing stars."

Seeing stars of liberty.—Philadelphia Inquirer.
© 2001 HARPWEEK®

Cognitive scientists have been able to observe the sensory, perceptual, and cognitive processes of the brain without removing the skull or clobbering people on the cranium. These techniques involve both behavioral data, such as reaction time experiments, and imaging technology, as discussed in the previous chapter (PET, CT, fMRI, and the like). It is now possible to "see" the workings of the brain as it perceives information about the world and how those perceptions are routed through the neural labyrinth of the brain.

Evolutionary psychologists may ask, what is the rationale for our sensory, perceptual, and cognitive system as a reflection of the world? How might these functions be adaptive? The windows of the mind, the human sensory system, emerged with the physical changes that occurred in our evolving planet. Very simple organisms developed specialized cells that reacted to light, and over millions of years, those cells became more and more specific in operation until, in time, something resembling an eye emerged (see Figure 3.7). With the evolution of the eye, the brain also emerged. A large portion of our brain is dedicated to our visual experiences. It's nice to see the world, but it's even nicer to understand what the world means! The eye and other sensory organs are as stupid as the brain is wise. For example, the retina of the eye is essentially color blind; the brain interprets color based on the retinal experience. Conversely, a wise brain without sensory input is devoid of essential knowledge of the world. Sensations of the world and what they mean are as much a function of the biologically fixed mechanisms as they are of the past history of the observer.

Everything We Know Is Wrong

It is useful to use a metaphor for the various elements of the sensory system. We can think of the sensory system as windows that are open to external reality. Only the sensations that are detected and passed on by our receptors are available for higher-level processing, and because the system is limited in its receptivity, our knowledge is necessarily restricted. Imagine yourself in a busy city. There are too many sights, sounds, and smells to take them in all at once. It is likely that we overemphasize the importance

FIGURE 3.7

FIGURE 3.7

Stages in the evolution of the eye

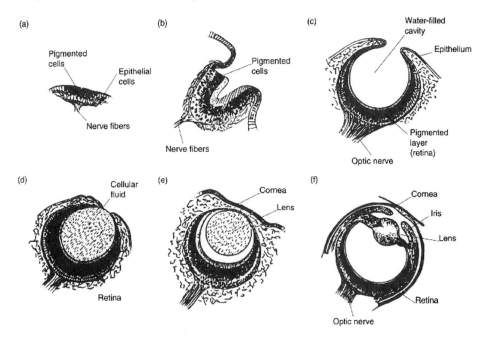

of the features of our physical universe that we can detect, while underemphasizing the importance of those we do not perceive. Consider how our view of "reality" would change if our eyes could "see" infrared radiation but could not "see" the normally visible part of the electromagnetic spectrum we refer to as light. Would our day and night schedules be the same? What would be the effect on history, on marketing, on fashions, on philosophy—indeed, on the whole of society? Most importantly, consider the effect on how we conceptualize reality. Because we apprehend reality through such limited (hence, distorting) channels, we are forced to conclude that everything we know is wrong. However, within the limits of our sensory apparatus, we are able to rough out a descriptive system of how we process the immense amount of information that we can detect, being mindful that the reality of our immediate world is many times more bustling than that sensed.

Our view of the perceptual process, then, is that the detection and interpretation of sensory signals is determined by stimulus energy sensed by the sensory systems and brain, and knowledge stored in memory prior to an experience.

A portion of cognitive research is concerned with the question of how the sensory systems and brain distort sensory information. It now seems that the things stored in our memory are abstract representations of reality. The apple you see, of course, is not stored in your head. Light reflecting off of the apple is abstracted such that all the information you need to know (i.e., what it looks like, smells like, feels like, tastes like, etc.) is stored in your memory. The key to the processing of sensory information and its cognitive interpretation seems to be the abstraction of information. At the sensory level, information is very specific, whereas on the interpretation level, information is commonly abstract. Our view of the world is determined by the integration of what we know (in an abstract sense) with what we sense (in a specific sense). Now, we turn to another aspect of perception—the question of how much information can be detected in a moment's glance.

Perceptual Span

How much we can experience at a brief exposure is called **perceptual span,** an early component in the processing of information. We know that the world is teeming with stimuli, a huge number of which are within the range of sensory detection. How many of these sensations are available for further processing? To better understand this we must discriminate between two hypothetical structures—preperceptual sensory storage and short-term memory.

We apparently have a **sensory store** that is capable of quick decisions based on brief exposure to events. Common knowledge confirms this notion. If we close our eyes, we continue to "see" the world; if a piece of music ceases, we still "hear" it; if we remove our hand from a textured surface, we still "feel" it. Each of these sensory memories fades rapidly, however, and most are soon forgotten. What are the boundaries of these transitory impressions? How long do they last? How much information about the world can be perceived in how short a time?

The first experiment investigating perceptual span dealt with vision, not only because vision is an important sense but also because it is somewhat easier to exercise experimental control over visual than over other stimuli (touch or taste, for example). Visual studies also had a practical side in that they were related to the rapidly developing research in reading. (Many early studies of the perceptual span were concerned with the amount of information that could be grasped in a brief period.) University of Paris Professor Emile Javal (1878) had observed that reading was not done by smoothly scanning a line of text but was a matter of jumping from one fixation point to another. These jumps are known as **saccades.** Reading, or the gathering in of textual material, took place at the fixation points, not during the saccades (Cattell, 1886a, 1886b; Erdmann & Dodge, 1898).

These early studies indicated that the most information that could be gathered during a single exposure was about four or five letters of unconnected matter. It is important to recognize that the conclusions of these early reading studies were based on what participants reported seeing. This failed to take into consideration the possibility that the perceptual span was greater than four or five letters, but that the participant was conscious of—that is, recalled having perceived—only four or five. One explanation of this phenomenon of capacity being greater than recall is that at least two cognitive stages are called into play when reporting the number of letters (1) the perceptual span and (2) the recall of immediate impressions. Until a series of critical experiments later proved it wrong, the immutable "fact" remained for sixty years that on average 4.5 letters constituted the perceptual span in reading.

In all, these critical experiments had two major effects on cognitive psychology. First, our understanding of the capacity of the perceptual span was significantly changed; second, the processing of information came to be viewed as taking place in successive stages, each of which operated by different principles. This latter result was to strengthen the "boxes in the head" metaphor as a way of representing hypothetical cognitive structures.

Iconic Storage

Neisser (1967) called the persistence of visual impressions and their brief availability for further processing **iconic memory.** There is some question as to whether the term *memory* is properly applied to these sensory phenomena. *Memory* to many (if not most) cognitive psychologists suggests coding and storage of information in which higher-order cognitive processes are used. Although iconic memory does involve some storage, recent findings suggest that it seems to be independent of higher-order processes such as attention. Iconic storage is essentially a stack of snapshots of the visual field. Each one lasts about a second. The purpose of these snapshots is to give the brain time to catch up with the visual information it is receiving from the eye.

Many researchers have found that incoming information is accurately represented in iconic memory but disappears quickly (between 250 ms to 4s) if not passed on to further processing states. The question arose whether, while making a verbal report—that is, "reading" visual information out of a rapidly fading sensory register—the participant loses some information. If this were the case, then the amount of information reported to be contained in the perceptual span would be only the amount of information reported before it faded away. In other words, the number of letters reported was a joint function of iconic fading and the time required to report the visual information.

George Sperling (1960) reasoned if the icon (or visual impression) was fading as participants were attempting to report the whole list of letters in the iconic store, it might be possible to report just a portion of the list. If he could devise a way to test partial memory or portions of the list, he could measure the actual amount of iconic storage. Sperling developed a partial-report technique in which for 50 milliseconds a participant was presented with a list of letters such as the following:

R	G	C
L	X	N
S	B	J

If participants try to recall nine letters, the chances are they will recall only four or five. Immediately following the display of each row of letters, however, Sperling presented one of three tones—a high-, medium-, or low-pitched one. (Thus, in the foregoing example, *RGC* might have been cued by a high tone, *LXN* by a medium-pitched tone, and so on.) The tones served to cue the participant to recall the first, second, and third rows of letters, respectively. In other words, they were able to provide a "partial report" of the information. The result was that each line was recalled correctly nearly 100 percent of the time. Since the participant did not know in advance which of the three rows would be cued for recall, we can infer that all nine letters were equally available for recall; therefore, the sensory store must hold at least nine items. Another feature of Sperling's work was that it varied the time between the display of the letters and the presentation of the tone, making it possible to gauge the length of time before the iconic store faded completely. If the tone was delayed more than 1 second, recall dropped to the level expected in whole-report examinations (see Figure 3.8).

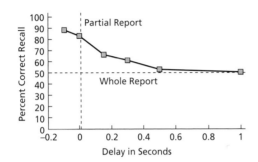

FIGURE 3.8

Sperling's partial report. The percentage of letters correctly recalled decreased as the delay in the auditory cue increased. After about 0.5 seconds performance falls to whole-report performance.

Adapted from Sperling, 1960.

To estimate the decay properties of this very brief store of information, studies have been done in which one interval between the letter display and the onset of the cue (a tone or a bar marker) was varied. The effect on recall indicated that the duration of the icon is about 250 milliseconds (¼ seconds).[2]

Echoic Storage

If we have an iconic memory store for vision, do we have a memory store for other senses? If we can "see" after the visual stimuli have passed, can we "hear" after auditory stimuli have passed? Apparently so. Neisser (1967) has dubbed the sensory memory for audition **echoic memory.** Echoic storage is similar to iconic storage in the sense that the raw sensory information is held in storage (in order that the pertinent features can be extracted and further analyzed) for a very short time (again, for about 250ms to 4s). As with iconic storage, which allows us additional time to view fleeting stimuli, echoic storage allows us additional time to hear an auditory message. If we consider the complex process of understanding common speech, the utility of echoic storage becomes clear. Auditory impulses that make up speech are spread over time. Information contained in any small fraction of speech, music, or other sound is meaningless unless placed within the context of other sounds. Echoic storage, by briefly preserving auditory information functions as a "glue" to hold our auditory world together.

To test for echoic memory, Moray, Bates and Barnett (1965) used stereo equipment with multiple speakers to generate an auditory experience that would parallel that of Sperling's experimental method. Moray and colleagues placed the participants in the center of four loudspeakers (in other experiments they fitted them with quadraphonic earphones) that permitted four messages to be presented simultaneously—much as the

---

[2]This is about the same time as that of the above-mentioned fixation period in reading, and some have speculated that during reading, readers briefly record visual information—words and letters—and move on to further images only after the image is recorded.

participant might experience sound at a party or at the center of a Beethoven string quartet. In each of these examples, a participant can attend to one voice (or signal) or another. In Moray's experiment, the message was a series of one to four letters of the alphabet presented through two, three, or all four channels simultaneously. As in the early visual experiments, the participant was asked to repeat as many letters as possible in the whole-report condition. In the partial-report portion of the experiment, four lights, corresponding in position to the sources of the sound, could be illuminated to cue the participant as to the channels from which he or she should recall the letters. The lights were presented 1 second after the audio signal terminated. Results, indicating that recall for partial report of auditory cues was superior to that for whole reports, were interpreted as supporting the notion that auditory information was also briefly held in sensory storage.

An even closer analogy to the Sperling partial-report technique is found in an experiment by Darwin, Turvey, and Crowder (1972). Through stereo headphones, participants were presented a matrix of auditory information (comparable to the visual display described earlier) consisting of three triplets of mixed random digits and letters. What the participant heard was three short lists of three items each, such as the following:

Left Ear	Both Ears	Right Ear
B	8	F
2	6	R
L	U	10

The time for the presentation of all items was 1 second. Thus, a participant would hear, simultaneously, "B" and "8" in the left ear, and "F" and "8" in the right. The subjective experience is that right- and left-ear messages can be localized as emanating from their source, and the "middle message" (which usually emanates from a signal present in both ears simultaneously) appears to come from inside the head. This technique was similar to the technique involving three visual rows used by Sperling. Recall was measured either by means of the whole-report or partial-report techniques. A visual cue (a bar) was projected onto the left, middle, or right portion of a screen in front of the participants. As with the visual studies, delaying the cue made it possible to trace the decay of memory. Darwin and his colleagues delayed the visual recall cue by 0, 1, 2, and 4 seconds. Apparently, echoic storage lasts up to 4 seconds but is most vivid during the first second after auditory stimulation.

We have reviewed two of the sense modalities through which information is detected: vision and hearing. Unfortunately, not enough data have been collected on taste, olfaction, or touch to allow us to make a definitive case for or against an early perceptual memory store for these senses corresponding to the iconic and echoic storage of vision and audition. Some evidence has been presented that suggests our tactile sense involves a somewhat analogous early store (Bliss, Hewitt, Crane, Mansfield, & Townsend, 1966). Bliss developed a system using air jets that stimulated the twenty-four interjoint segments of the fingers and had participants memorize letters of the alphabet associated with the stimulus points. Results were similar to those found with other memory stores already mentioned with a higher degree of accuracy with partial report relative to whole report.

Function of Sensory Stores

The seminal work discussed previously on vision and audition has given the field of cognitive psychology important constructs that help explain the information-processing chain of events. What is the overall purpose of these brief and vivid sensory impressions of external reality? How do they fit into the larger reality of cognitive psychology? How are they adaptive?

Remarkably little attention has been directed toward integrating theories of sensory information into the larger scheme of human events. One speculation concerning iconic and echoic storage is that the extraction of information from the external, physical world follows a law of parsimony. Given the astronomical amount of sensory information that continuously excites our nervous system and the limited ability of higher-order cognitive systems to process information, only a small fraction of sensory cues can be selected for further processing.

This consideration seems to apply to vision and audition: It seems appropriate, even necessary, for the sensory system to hold information momentarily so further processing of pertinent items may take place. In reading, for example, an accurate impression of letters and words may be necessary for comprehension, and in listening it is likely that everything from understanding conversations to appreciating music is contingent on the exact recording of auditory signals.

It seems that a delicate balance exists between selecting the appropriate information for further processing and rejecting the inappropriate information. Temporary, vivid, and accurate storage of sensory information, as exists in echoic and iconic storage, seems to provide us with a mechanism by which we can select only the pertinent information for further processing. By preserving the complete sensory impression for a brief period, we can scan the immediate events, picking out those stimuli that are most salient and fitting them into the tangled matrix of human memory. When all works properly, no more and no less information is coded, transformed, or stored than is necessary for humans to carry on a normal existence. The speculation of Edwin Boring (1946) a long time ago seems compatible with this notion: "The purpose of perception is economy of thinking. It picks out and establishes what is permanent and therefore important to the organism for its survival and welfare."

Iconic storage, echoic storage, and storage of other sensory information allow us the opportunity to extract only the information to be subjected to further processing. The very limitations of the human nervous system prohibit the recording and processing of all, or even a sizable fraction, of the bits of information available from our brief sensory store.

Our capacity for complex processing of visual stimuli may be understood in terms of sensory storage; the ability to read may well be based on iconic storage that allows us to extract meaningful features from the visual field while discarding those extraneous stimuli that are unimportant. Similarly, our capacity to understand speech may well be based on echoic storage that allows us to hold auditory cues briefly in the presence of new ones so that abstractions can be made on the basis of phonetic context.

The development of brief sensory stores may have been an essential component in evolution. Their function as survival mechanisms is purely speculative, but it is plausible that they allow us to perceive "everything" and yet attend to only the essential components of our percepts, making for the most economical system evolved. Sensory storage gives us the time to extract critical features for further processing and action.

Attention

When we think of attention we think of things like "pay attention," "give me your attention," "stand at attention," and "center of attention." Without ever examining the cognitive process of attention, one gets the idea that attention is a valued resource. In this next section we discuss attention as an important, and valuable, cognitive mechanism.

More than a hundred years ago, William James wrote that "everyone knows what attention is." He explained that

> It is the taking possession by the mind, in clear and vivid form, of one out of what seem several simultaneously possible objects or trains of thought. Focalization, concentration of consciousness are of its essence. It implies withdrawal from some things in order to deal effectively with others. (1890, pp. 403–404)

When we talk about attention today from the standpoint of a cognitive psychologist we refer to attention as a cognitive process that selects out important information from the world around us (through all of our five senses) so that our brain does not get overloaded with an overwhelming amount of information. Is this what happens to children with attention-deficit disorder (ADD)?

It is improbable, of course, that James meant that we know all there is to know about attention. We did not in 1890, and we do not now. However, through a number of carefully designed experiments on attention, it has been possible to define the issues involved, and several models have emerged that present an overall perspective on the issue. This section is primarily about the emergence of attention as a component of cognitive psychology and includes exciting developments in cognitive neuroscience.

This child is clearly the center of attention.

Soldiers at attention.

We shall use this general definition of **attention:** "the concentration of mental effort on sensory or mental events." Research on attention covers five major aspects of the topic: processing capacity and selective attention, level of arousal, control of attention, consciousness, and cognitive neuroscience.

Many of the contemporary ideas of attention are based on the premise that there are available to the human observer a myriad of cues that surround us at any given moment. Our neurological capacity is too limited to sense all of the millions of external stimuli, but even were these stimuli detected, the brain would be unable to process all of them; our information processing capacity is too limited. Our sensory system, like other kinds of communication conduits, functions quite well if the amount of information being processed is within its capability; it fails when it is overloaded.

The modern era of attention was introduced in 1958 by Donald Broadbent, a British psychologist, who wrote in an influential book, *Perception and Communication*, that attention was the result of a limited-capacity information-processing system.[3] The essential notion of Broadbent's theory was that the world is made up of many more sensations than can be handled by the perceptual and cognitive capabilities of the human observer. Therefore, in order to cope with the flood of available information, humans selectively attend to only some of the cues and tune out much of the rest.

It was long thought that we can attend to one cue only at the expense of another. If we attempt to understand simultaneous messages, especially of the same sensory modality, some sacrifice must be made in accuracy. For example, we may be able to attend to the highway while we drive a car (a highly practiced habit that has turned highly automatic) and even listen to the radio at the same time, but it is difficult to attend simultaneously to more than one cue of the same modality—such as two auditory cues or two visual cues. It is even difficult to operate at peak performance when we are confronted with two conceptual tasks, as in the case of mentally dividing a dinner check for seven people and being asked for the time. Likely, you'll be able to provide the time, but you'll have to start the more complex task of your tab-dividing calculation over again.

---

[3]The impact of this work was not limited to the topic of attention but had a profound effect on the emergence of cognitive psychology as a whole.

Donald Broadbent **(1926–1992)**.
Opened up the field of attention and information processing.

Our everyday experience tells us that we attend to some environmental cues more than others and that the attended cues are normally passed along for further processing, while unattended cues may not be. Which are attended to and which are not seems to stem from some control we exercise over the situation (such as looking at the instant replay to see whether the football player stepped out of bounds) and from something relating to our long-term experience (such as reading a technical report to find a certain fact). In either situation, the attention mechanism focuses on certain stimuli in preference to others, although at times it may appear so, not all of the "extraneous" stimuli are necessarily excluded entirely from attention; they may be monitored or toned down.

This is particularly evident with auditory cues, such as at a party, where we may attend to one voice while being mindful of other surrounding ones. Most of us have had the experience of having our attention drift from the voice of our conversation partner to that of someone imparting a choice bit of gossip in another conversation. It is easy to tune in to the voice recounting the gossip while we attempt to conceal our inattention to our current conversation partner when we find we have lost track of whatever he or she was saying in the first place.

Another case might be that of watching an opera at the point at which two characters begin "talking" (singing) at the same time. Opera abounds with such multiple signals. You may try to hear all, find it only confusing, and so tune in to one, continuing to hear, but not understanding, the other. Or while you are watching a football game with all of its multiple action, it is difficult to watch all players at the same time. In the sense that we are regularly bombarded with a profusion of sensory signals and are called upon to make choices as to which are to be attended to, all of one's waking existence is comparable to these examples whether we are aware of it or not.

Five issues of attention have been illustrated in these examples:

1. *Processing capacity and selectiveness.* We can attend to some, but not all, cues in our external world.

2. *Control.* We have some control over the stimuli we attend to.

3. *Automatic processing.* Many routine processes (such as driving a car) are so familiar they require little conscious attention and are done automatically.

4. *Cognitive neuroscience.* Our brain and CNS are the anatomical support for attention, as well as all cognition.

5. *Consciousness.* Attention brings events into consciousness.

Cognition in Everyday Life

The Absentminded Professor (Student?)

Within a period of a few weeks, a professor we know applied skin cream, which was packaged in a tube almost identical to toothpaste, to his toothbrush and started brushing his teeth before realizing his error; he measured water in a coffee pot, placed the pot on the coffee maker, turned it on, and, after seeing that nothing was happening, realized he had failed to pour the water into the coffee maker's tank; and while lecturing on kinetic art (and thinking about an experiment with dancers) used the term *kines-* *thetic art.* Most people do silly things like this every day.

As an exercise in critical thinking about attention, keep track of your own absentminded behaviors for several days and then organize them into types. It is likely that you will find most of the errors are due to automatic processing (your brain is on "automatic pilot") and/or you are attending to something else ("head in the clouds").

To use the opera or football game as an example, you attend to only a minor portion of the activity. You are likely to attend selectively, focusing on some cues (such as the person who is speaking or carrying the football) more than others. One reason you attend selectively is that your ability to process information is restricted by **channel capacity.** Think of bandwidth on the Internet. Second, you have some control over which features you choose to attend to. For example, while two characters may be talking simultaneously, you can exercise some control over the one to which you will listen, or in the case of a football game, you attend to one of the players, such as the center. Third, your perception of events is related to your automatic processing of material. Fourth, recent investigations into the cognitive neuroscience of attention have suggested that the attention system of the human brain is separate from other systems of the brain, such as the data processing systems. These recent discoveries have implications for cognitive theories of attention as well as serving as a bridge between neuroscience and cognitive psychology. Finally, those things that you attend to are part of your conscious experience. These five issues occupy center stage in the research on attention.

Next, some important areas related to attention will be covered.

Consciousness   Largely stimulated by the work of Sigmund Freud, psychologists for more than a century have been interested in the dichotomy between the conscious and the unconscious aspects of the mind. Freud believed the conscious level was responsible for thoughts and perceptions, while the unconscious level was responsible for fears and immoral urges, for example. One problem in accepting Freud's dichotomy of consciousness (especially by the behaviorists) is that his theories lacked objective substance and empirical support. Nevertheless, experiments by cognitive psychologists as well as case studies from psychoanalysts have supported Freud's view of the dichotomous mind.

Subliminal Perception   In psychophysical (and physiological) terms a *limen* is considered the sensory threshold at which a stimulus is barely perceptible. Literally, subliminal is below the sensory threshold, thus imperceptible. However, **subliminal perception** often refers to stimuli that are clearly strong enough to be above the psychological limen but do not enter consciousness, and is technically referred to as sub-raliminal (above limen). Public interest in subliminal messages began in the late 1950s when advertisers briefly flashed messages between frames at a movie theater in attempts to increase sales of popcorn and soda. Since then subliminal messages have been reported in a variety of sources such as naked women in ice cubes, demonic messages in rock 'n roll music, and recent presidential campaign advertisements.

The efficacy of subliminal messages is centered in debate. The question of being able to perceive signals that are below perceptual threshold is problematic for many research psychologists, who regard this as pseudoscientific. How can we "hear" without hearing? Yet studies of attention clearly show that it is possible to retain information that has been neglected. The topic of subliminal perception is closely related to perceptual **priming,** in which the display of a word is so brief that the participant cannot report seeing it, however, the word actually facilitates the recognition of an associate to that word without any conscious awareness of the process. Furthermore, several studies (Philpott & Wilding, 1979; Underwood, 1976, 1977) have shown that subliminal stimuli have an effect on the recognition of subsequent stimuli. Therefore, some effect of the subliminal stimuli is observed.

Filter location. Contemporary models of attention focus on where the selection (or filtering out) of information takes place in the cognitive process. Inherent in many of these filter theories is the notion that people are not aware of signals in the early part of processing of information but, after some type of decision or selection, pass some of the signals on for further processing. The models typically differ based on early or late selection depending on where the filter location is hypothesized.

Processing Capacity and Selective Attention

The fact that we selectively attend to only a portion of all cues available is evident from various common experiences, such as those described earlier. This selectivity is often attributed to inadequate **channel capacity,** our inability to process all sensory cues simultaneously. This notion suggests that somewhere in the processing of information a bottleneck exists, part of which is due to neurological limitations (see Figure 3.9). This bottleneck may not be a limitation but may actually be adaptive. Consider the circuit breaker in your home or apartment when it shuts down because you are running the microwave, the toaster, and the dishwasher simultaneously from the same circuit. Rather than shutting down our cognitive processes, the cognitive system restricts the amount of stimuli entering to avoid overloading. **Selective attention** is analogous to shining a flashlight in a darkened room to illuminate the things in which we are interested while keeping the other items in the dark. With respect to the amount of information we respond to and remember, however, there appears to be a constraint in cognitive power in addition to these sensory limitations. Thus, we carefully aim the attentional flashlight, process that which we attend to, and disregard (or moderate) the other information.

*T*he simple act of paying attention can take you a long way.

— *Keanu Reeves*

FIGURE 3.9

The bottleneck in information processing.

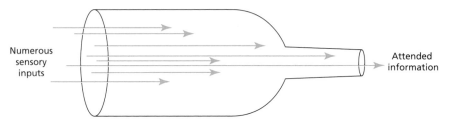

Numerous
sensory
inputs

Attended
information

From a communication perspective, our capacity to react to a signal is related in part to how "clean" it is, that is, how free of competing information or "noise" it is. This is known as the signal-to-noise ratio. You might have experienced this if you have ever watched a foreign movie with subtitles, and you tried to read the subtitles and translate words the actors are saying at the same time; or when you are deciding to purchase something with packaging that has bilingual instructions. If you attend to only one cue—say the English—you can decide if you want the product; however, if you puzzle over the compound stimuli, switching attention from one to the other may create cognitive interference, complicating the decision to buy. Researchers have designed an experimental paradigm to measure cognitive interference called the Stroop task (named after John Stroop who discovered it in 1935). The basic task presents the participant with a display of color names such as red, yellow, blue, and green, which the participant is asked to read. Simple enough, however, the font color of the words are incongruous to the color names, making it a particularly difficult task as the colors and the color names compete, creating cognitive interference. This task is useful in investigating attention-deficit hyperactivity disorder (ADHD).

Auditory Signals

The information processing approach to attention largely grew out of auditory research, but since that time visual as well as semantic research has emerged. Early research by Cherry (1953) led to the development of an experimental procedure called **shadowing,** now a standard method of studying auditory attention. In shadowing, a participant is asked to repeat a spoken message while it is presented. The task is not difficult if the rate of speech is slow, but if the speaker talks rapidly, the participant cannot repeat all the information that comes in. Unlike the eyes that pass information to both cerebral hemispheres, each ear passes information only to the contralateral hemisphere. And although the ears are accustomed to receiving information out of phase (a noise on one side of the

*T*here is no such thing as an attention span. People have infinite attention if you are entertaining them.

— *Jerry Seinfeld*

room will reach the near ear sooner than the ear on the far side), the brain automatically adjusts for the temporal offset by perceptually combining the two audio inputs into one signal. Cherry's experiments, however, had an added feature: using headphones two auditory messages were simultaneously presented—one to be shadowed and the other ignored. Cherry (1966) observed:

> The remarkable thing is that over very wide ranges of texts [the subject] is successful, though finds great difficulty. Because the same speaker reads both messages, no clues are provided by different qualities of voice, which may help in real-life cocktail party conversation. (p. 280)

Despite the ability of participants to shadow,[4] Cherry found that they remembered little of the message they repeated. Perhaps most of the processing of information was done in a temporary memory, so there could be no permanent storage and understanding of the message. The unattended messages received by the "deaf" ear were even (understandably) more poorly remembered. When the unattended message was speech, the participants did report that they recognized it as speech, but a change from English to German in the unattended speech was not noticed. The ability to focus on one message and reduce processing from other information seems to be an important human attribute; it allows us to regulate information without overloading the capacity for information processing.

What can we conclude from Cherry's observation? Since many of the major cues were eliminated in his experiments, the participant must have tuned in to more subtle cues, thought to be related to the regularities of our language. In the course of our lifetime, we gather an immense amount of knowledge about phonetics, letter combinations, syntax, phrase structure, sound patterns, clichés, and grammar. Language can be understood when presented in one ear even when another auditory signal is presented in the other ear because we are capable of attending to contextual cues and immediately checking them with our knowledge of the language. Anomalous messages (those that don't conform to the normal grammatical and lexical structure) must have powerful signal characteristics before being admitted. Highly familiar messages are processed more easily.

But what happened to the "forgotten" unshadowed message? How much, if any, information sinks in from unattended channels? In one experiment (Moray, 1959), information to the "deaf" ear was not retained by participants listening to the opposite channel, even though some words were repeated as many as thirty-five times. Even when Moray told them that they would be asked for some information from the unattended channel, they were able to report very little. Moray then took a significant step: he prefaced the message in the unattended channel with the participant's name. Under those conditions, the message was reported more frequently. (Isn't this also true at a party? Someone on the other side of the room says, "And I heard that Jack is . . ." At that moment all the Jacks in the room and those who know Jacks, who until then were completely engrossed in other conversations, turn a live ear to the person speaking). The intrusion of an interesting event that gains one's attention has been appropriately dubbed the **cocktail party phenomenon.** (Has it happened to you?)

However, the need to attend to one message is apparently strong, and with the exception of special information (like your name), little other than the attended message

---

[4]Some professors often suspect students are shadowing when they are taking lecture notes. One of our own professors used to say, "It goes in the ear and out the pencil."

Modern day cocktail party phenomenon.

Courtesy of Brian Westbrook.

is admitted. There is no evidence to suggest that the ears are not being equally stimulated on the sensory level. Nor is there any evidence that one of the messages does not reach the auditory cortex. There is, however, some evidence that different parts of the cortex are involved in attention, while other parts are involved in information processing (Posner, 1988), a topic addressed later in this chapter.

Models of Selective Attention

Remember from Chapter 1 that models are often used in cognitive psychology. Models are hypothetical cognitive structures often represented by boxes and arrows. Models are important because they help researchers organize the data they have collected and they direct research by allowing researchers to make predictions/hypotheses and then test them. We next review models of selective attention, attention used to focus on incoming stimuli. These are the filter model, the attenuation model, and the late attention model.

The Filter Model: Broadbent

The first complete theory of attention was developed by Broadbent (1958). Called a **filter model,** the theory, related to what has been called the *single-channel theory,* is based on the idea that information processing is restricted by channel capacity.

Broadbent argued that messages traveling along a specific nerve can differ either (a) according to which of the nerve fibers they stimulate or (b) according to the number

Try This

Selective Attention

Read the message in **bold type** *starting with the word* **among.** *Somewhere* **Among** *hidden on a* **the** *desert island* **most** *near the* **spectacular** *X islands, an* **cognitive** *old* **Survivor** *abilities contestant* **is** *has* **the** *concealed* **ability** *a box* **to** *of gold* **select** *won* **one** *in a* **message** *reward* **from** *challenge* **another. We** *Although* **do** *several hundred* **this** *people* **by** *(fans,* **focusing** *contestants,* **our** *and producers) have* **attention** *looked* **on** *for it* **certain** *they* **cues** *have* **such** *not as* **found** *type it* **style.** *Rumor* **When** *has* **we** *it* **focus** *that 300* **our** *paces* **attention** *due* **on** *west* **certain** *from* **stimuli** *tribal* **the** *council* **message** *and* **in** *then* **other** *200* **stimuli** *paces* **is** *due* **not** *north* **X marks clearly** *the* **spot identified.** *Apparently* **However** *enough* **some** *gold* **information** *can* **from** *be* **the** *had* **unattended** *to* **source** *purchase* **may** *the* **be** *very* **detected** *island!*

What did you read? Can you tell anything about the message that appeared in *this type?* If so, what words caught your attention and why did they? Several cues helped keep you on the right course; these include the physical nature of the stimuli, the meaning of the sentences, and the syntax. Cues from the unattended message may have distracted you. You may have been distracted by interesting or meaningful words (i.e., *gold, Survivor, tribal*) or distinctive visual cues (i.e., *300, 200, X*). In everyday life we focus our attention on some stimuli at the exclusion of others. Note the next time you do this, and let your instructor (and us!) know about your example.

---

of nerve impulses they produce. (Neuropsychological studies have disclosed that high-frequency signals and low-frequency signals are carried by different fibers.) Thus, when several nerve fibers fire at the same time, several sensory messages may arrive at the brain simultaneously.

In Broadbent's model (see Figure 3.10), these would be processed through a number of parallel sensory channels. (These channels were assumed to have distinct neural codes and could be selected on the basis of that code. For example, a high-pitched signal and a low-pitched signal presented simultaneously could be distinguished on the basis of their physical characteristics even though both would reach the brain simultaneously.) Further processing of information would then occur only after the signal was attended to and passed on through a selective filter into a limited-capacity channel. In Figure 3.8 we saw that more information can enter the system than can be processed by the limited-capacity channel. Broadbent postulated that, in order to avoid an overload in this system, the selective filter could be switched to any of the sensory channels.

Intuitively, the filter theory seems valid. It is obvious that we have a limited information-processing capacity. To make some meaning out of what we hear, the brain may attend to one class of impulses (based on physical characteristics), much as a crossover filter in audio equipment is capable of detecting messages (electrical impulses) of one frequency level or another and sending each such message on to its respective speaker for more processing. When the situation calls for it, we can switch our attention to another channel. However, if selection is on the basis of the physical qualities of signals, as Broadbent originally thought, then switching attention should be unrelated to the content of the message.

FIGURE 3.10

Information-flow diagram accommodating views of recent theories.

Adapted from Broadbent (1958).

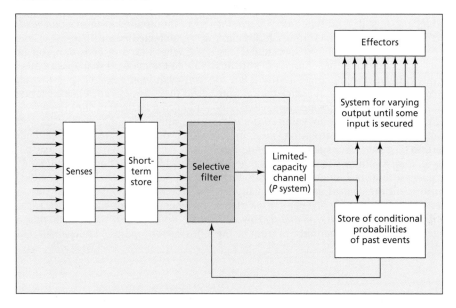

In an early experiment, Broadbent (1954) used the **dichotic listening task** to test his theory. Research participants were presented with three digits in one ear and, at the same time, three different digits in the other ear. Thus, he or she might hear:

Left ear	Right Ear
6	4
2	9
7	3

In the first condition, participants were asked to recall the digits by ear of presentation (i.e., 493 and 627). In the second condition, participants were asked to recall the digits in the sequence in which they appeared. Since two digits at a time were presented, the participants could recall either member of the pair first but had to report both before continuing through the sequence. Thus, in this condition, the participant could report the digits in this manner: 4, 6, 9, 2, 3, 7.

In both experimental conditions, recall was less than expected. In the first condition, participants were correct about 65 percent of the time; in the second, 20 percent of the time.

Broadbent interpreted the difference to be a result of having to switch attention between the sources more often in the second condition. In the first condition, where participants were asked to recall all the items from one ear and then all those from the other, they could attend to all the stimuli from one "channel" and then all those from the second (the latter, presumably, having been held briefly in some memory system). In the sequence condition, however, participants would have to switch their attention at least three times—for example, from left to right ear, then back from right to left, and once more from left to right.

Broadbent (1981) and others have extended the concept to memory. We all carry within us a large number of memories of past events—for example, knowledge of dozens of friends, schedules of forthcoming events, memories of past experiences, thoughts about family members, and so on. Yet, at any moment in our personal history, we can recall only a small subset of these memories while the others remain in the background waiting to be used. Broadbent's connection between selective perception and memory raises important theoretical as well as practical issues but, more important for our current discussion, reminds us that selective perception is not confined to a narrow range of phenomena—it touches almost every other cognitive system.

Broadbent's theory has not gone unchallenged. Gray and Wedderburn (1960) presented to alternate ears the syllables composing a word (in sequence) and random digits, so that when a syllable was "heard" by one ear, a digit was "heard" by the other. For example:

Left Ear	Right Ear
OB	6
2	JEC
TIVE	9

If Broadbent's filter theory (based on the physical nature of auditory signals) was correct, the participants, when asked to repeat what they had "heard" in one channel, should have spewed out gibberish—for example, "ob-two-tive" or "six-jec-nine"—just as participants reported 4, 6, 9, 2, 3, 7 when they heard 4 and 6 simultaneously (4 in the right ear and 6 in the left ear), and then 9 and 2, and so on. They didn't; they said (in the case of our example), "objective," thereby showing their capacity to switch rapidly from channel to channel to extract meaning.

In a second experiment, Gray and Wedderburn presented phrases (such as "Mice eat cheese" or "Dear Aunt Jane") instead of syllables. For example:

Left Ear	Right Ear
Dear	3
5	Aunt
Jane	4

As in the experiment with syllables and digits, the participants tended to "hear," in this example, "Dear Aunt Jane"; thus, they again grouped the message segments by meaning. In Gray and Wedderburn's words, "subjects were acting intelligently in the situation."

The Attenuation Model: Treisman

One problem with the filter model is the detection of meaningful information through an unattended channel. Moray (1959) found that participants noticed their own names from the unattended channel about one-third of the time. We also know from common experience that we can monitor a second message while attending to another. A parent in church may be engrossed in a sermon, ignoring a crying child in the background. The preaching is clearly understood, and the cries of children bother not our serene parishioner. However, let the faintest whisper be emitted by the listener's own child, and that signal is heard as clearly as Gabriel's trumpet. Broadbent was not entirely wrong. His original theory postulated that the selection filter does occasionally admit one or two highly "probable" (likely to occur, given the context) words through the unattended channel.

To explain the fact that participants could sometimes hear their own names through the unattended channel, Treisman suggested that in the participant's "dictionary" (or store of words) some words have lower thresholds for activation. Thus, important words or sounds, such as one's own name or the distinctive cry of one's child, are activated more easily than less important signals. Her elegant model retains much of the architecture of Broadbent's model while accounting for the empirical results obtained by Moray (see Figure 3.11).

Treisman demonstrated that we tend to follow the meaning rather than attend to the message from only one ear, even when told to report the message received in that one ear. In one experiment Treisman (1964a) had French–English bilingual participants shadow a passage from Orwell's *England, Your England.* In one ear the voice spoke in English; in the other, French. Unknown to the participants, the passages were the same but slightly offset in time. As the offset interval was gradually reduced, many participants noticed that the two messages were the same in meaning. It would appear that the "unattended" voice was not cut off from the participants' knowledge of the second language.

Treisman's data and those of other researchers once seemed at odds with the filter model. As though some cerebral "executive," before it analyzed signal characteristics, had to make a decision to do so. Obviously, some initial screening of information must take place. According to Treisman, the first of these filters evaluates the signal on the basis of gross physical characteristics and more sophisticated filters then evaluate the signal in terms of meaning. The initial screening takes place by means of an attenuator, or perceptual filter—a device that regulates the volume of the message and that intercedes between the signal and its verbal processing. Treisman's model suggests that "irrelevant messages" are heard with a "dull," not "deaf," ear.

One way to better understand what Treisman had in mind when she suggested an attenuator is to examine how attenuators are used in radar detection. Attenuators are

Anne Treisman. Developed an attenuation model of attention.

FIGURE 3.11

Comparison of Broadbent and Treisman models. The Broadbent switch filter does not allow unattended information to pass. While Treisman's model reduces the unattended information to a weak signal that is passed to a perceptual dictionary, if the dictionary signal is amplified to a level of importance.

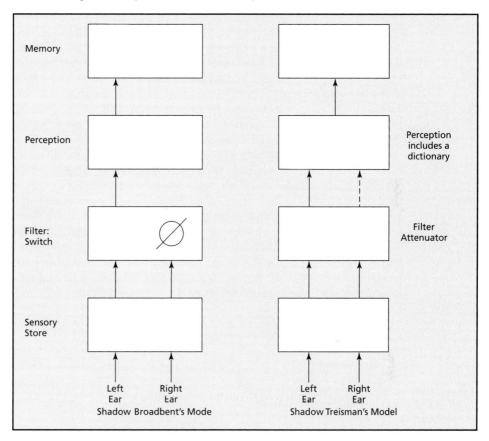

used in radar to reduce the amplification of the sonar signal to reduce noise from faraway objects, thus maintaining a proper signal-to-noise ratio.

These questions have sparked debate as to exactly what attributes Treisman ascribed to the attenuator. She clarified her position with regard to the attenuator, when she wrote to Bob Solso:

> My suggestion was that the attenuator treats *all* [emphasis added] unattended messages alike, regardless of their content. The effects of probability, relevance, importance, etc., are all determined within the speech recognition system, exactly as they are for the attended message if it arrives with a low signal-to-noise ratio. . . . The only difference between unattended and attended messages is that the unattended message has its overall signal-to-noise ratio reduced by the selective filter, and therefore

fails to excite lexical entries for any of its content except a few words or phrases with unusually low detection thresholds. The attenuator selects only on the basis of general physical properties such as location or voice quality. (1986, p. 123)

Visual Attention

Thus far, we have concentrated on the auditory aspects of attention, but all sensory experiences (visual, auditory, olfactory, gustatory, and tactile)[5] are governed by rules of attention. Vision, color, and form perception have received the greatest amount of analysis outside of audition. Consider the stimuli in Figure 3.12. Here, you can "see" the cluster of +s in a field of large Ls. In experiments of this type, Treisman and her colleagues and Julesz (1971) along with his colleagues have found that when visual elements are distinctive, as the +s are in Figure 3.12, the boundaries jump out to the viewer within 50 milliseconds—this is called the **pop-out effect.** This "pop-out" allows for a parallel search of the stimuli. You can take in all the information from the +s simultaneously or all at once. The Ts require more effort and, they certainly do not jump out of the context as the +s do. Yet, the compositional elements are identical (that is, a + is made up of two lines at right angles to each other, as is a T). Because the visual system "sees" the Ts to be similar to the background Ls, it requires a serial search of the items—you have to scan each item until you find the Ts (they are in the lower right quadrant).

Both Treisman and Julesz hypothesize that two different processes in visual attention are operating. In the first stage (see Figure 3.13), there is an initial, *preattentive process* (a kind of master map of an image) that scans the field and rapidly detects the main features of objects, such things as size, color, orientation, and movement, if any.

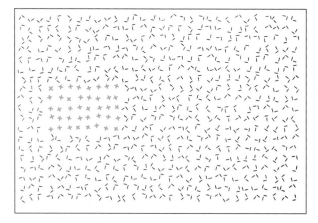

FIGURE 3.12

It is possible to "see" the rectangular cluster of +s in the figure but more difficult to "see" the Ts. The first stage of attention seems to be a preattentive scanning, which surveys the general field and yields basic information, such as seeing the +s. Seeing the Ts (in the lower right quadrant) requires focal attention.

From J. R. Bergen and B. Julesz, *Nature, 303,* 696–698, Figure 1. Reprinted by permission.

[5]Shift your attention from the visual reading of this text to another modality, say, touch, and focus on the pressure you feel on your left foot by your shoe. Think about it. Now try to center your attention on each of the other senses, and spotlight the experiences associated with each sensation.

FIGURE 3.13

A model of the stages of visual perception and attention. Initially, some basic properties of a visual scene (color, orientation, size, and distance) are encoded in separate, parallel pathways that generate feature maps. These maps are integrated into a master map. Focused attention then draws on the information from the master map to analyze in detail the features associated in a selected region of the image.

From Treisman (1988).

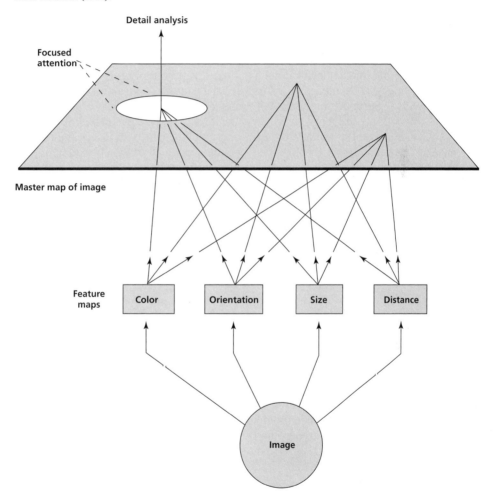

Then, according to Treisman, different properties of the object are encoded in specific **feature maps,** which are located in different parts of the cortex.

Just where and when filtering occurs has been a long-standing issue in attention research. Both Broadbent and Treisman place their filter just before perceptual processes. Others have placed the bottleneck later on past the analysis stage (Deutsch & Deutsch, 1963; Norman, 1968). For this to be correct both channels must pass equally through the analysis stage, with responses from each channel being passed though a response filter. If in fact we have a late filter, then why is information then lost to the "deaf" channel? Supporters of the late filter model argue that information that is not personally important is forgotten quite rapidly. Support for the late filter is derived in part from the research findings of Donald MacKay (1973) who had participants in a dichotic listening task where an ambiguous sentence similar to the Groucho Marx quote was presented to the attended ear (e.g., "He rode/rowed to the city"). In the unattended ear the participant would hear either the word "bicycle" or "boat." If the word literally fell to a "deaf" ear then it should not affect the interpretation of the ambiguous sentence. However, when participants were asked to choose between "he went to the city by land" versus "he went to the city by sea," their choice was indeed influenced by information in the deaf ear. This appears to be very much like the subliminal priming studies discussed earlier. If the prime presented in the unattended channel had been filtered out prior to processing the semantic meaning of the sentence, it would not have had the opportunity influence it.

Since the appearance of Broadbent's original notion of attention in the 1950s, which not only influenced a whole generation of researchers including Treisman but also was important in the development of a limited-capacity model of information processing, a dozen or more theories have been put forth, all of which modify or attack some of his basic notions. Unfortunately, some have portrayed Broadbent's theory as an either/or theory, in which information is processed either in one channel or in another. That characterization is wrong. What Broadbent (1958) wrote was "Once again we cannot say simply 'a man cannot listen to two things at once.' On the contrary, he receives *some* [emphasis added] information even from the rejected ear: but there is a limit to the amount, and details of the stimulus on the rejected ear are not recorded" (p. 23). No single theory of attention has replaced the original one, although much of the research has helped clarify specific issues involved in human attention.[6]

Automatic Processing

People are confronted by myriad stimuli while at the same time participating in several activities. For example, as we drive a car, we may look at a map, scratch, talk on a cell phone, eat a hamburger, put on sunglasses, listen to music, and so on. In terms of allocation of effort, however, we are (hopefully) directing more attention to driving than to other activities, even though some attention is allocated to these other activities. Highly practiced activities become automatic and thereby require less attention to perform than do new or slightly practiced activities. This relationship between **automatic processing** and attention has been described by LaBerge (1975):

> For example, imagine learning the name of a completely unfamiliar letter. This is much like learning the name that goes with the face of a person recently met. When presented again with the visual stimulus, one recalls a time-and-place episode which subsequently produces the appropriate response. With further practice, the name

---

[6]We also want to point out that in many areas of cognitive psychology, several competing theories often exist. Some are outdated and reported for historical significance. Others directly compete with no clear victor...yet.

emerges almost at the same time as the episode. This "short-circuiting" is represented by the formation of a direct line between the visual and name codes. The process still requires attention. . . . and the episodic code is used now more as a check on accuracy than as the mediator of the association. As more and more practice accumulates, the direct link becomes automatic (Mandler, 1954). . . . At this point the presentation of the stimulus evokes the name without any contribution by the Attention Centre. Indeed, in such cases, we often observe that we cannot prevent the name from "popping into our head." (p. 52)

LaBerge's concept may help account for quite a lot of human activity under stressful conditions. Norman (1976) has provided us with an apt example. Suppose that a diver is entangled in his or her scuba apparatus while beneath the surface. To survive, the diver needs to release the equipment and gradually float to the surface. Norman points out:

Practicing the release of one's weight belt over and over again while diving in a swimming pool seems a pointless exercise to the student. But if that task can be made so automatic that it requires little or no conscious effort, then on the day that the diver needs to act under stress, the task may get performed successfully in spite of the buildup of panic. (p. 66)

In the 1986 movie *Alien*, Gorman is asked how many times he has been dropped into combat:

Ripley: How many drops is this for you, Lieutenant?
Gorman: Thirty eight . . . simulated.
Vasquez: How many *combat* drops?
Gorman: Uh, two. Including this one.
Drake: Sh—.
Hudson: Oh, man . . .

While simulations may not equate to actual experience, the benefit is that some of the associated processes will become automatic.

Can You Rub Your Belly and Tap Your Head Simultaneously?

With one finger, tap out the rhythm to a well-known song, such as "Happy Birthday to You." Wasn't that easy? Now, with a finger on the other hand, tap out "Row, Row, Row Your Boat" (or some other well-known song.) That too is easy. Now, tap out both songs simultaneously. Can you do it? Why not? With a great deal of practice, you may be able to do this successfully. If you can, it is likely that you learned to do it by tapping out one tune so well that you could do it on "automatic pilot" while attending consciously to the other. Accomplished piano players do similar tasks with practice. It is likely that the simultaneous processing of such acts is regulated by a motor timer in the cerebellum—that large structure in the very hind part of the brain resembling a cauliflower—but other parts of the brain are also involved.

I once shot an elephant in my pajamas. How he got in my pajamas—I'll never know.

—*Groucho Marx*

For automaticity of processing to occur, there must be a free flow of information from memory to the person's control of actions. Practice Helps!

The automatic processing of information was given much needed structure by Posner and Snyder (1974, 1975), who describe three characteristics of an automatic process:

- An automatic process occurs without intention. In priming experiments, the effect operates independently of intention or conscious purpose on the part of the research participant. For example, it is easier to recognize the word *NURSE* after seeing the word *DOCTOR*.
- Automatic processes are concealed from consciousness. As pointed out in the previous example, priming effects are mostly unconscious. We do not "think" about automatic processes, which suggests the third characteristic.
- Automatic processes consume few (or no) conscious resources. We can read words or tie a knot in our shoelaces without giving these activities a thought. They take place automatically and without effort.

The importance of studies of automaticity may be that they tell us something of the complex cognitive activity that seems to occur outside of conscious experience. Furthermore, skills such as typing, scuba diving, playing the violin, driving a car, playing tennis, and even using the language correctly and making social judgments about other people are likely to be well-practiced ones that, for the most part, run automatically. Skillful performance in these matters may free consciousness to attend to the more demanding and changing onslaught of activities that require attention. The topic of automaticity engages the most enigmatic of topics in psychology: consciousness, a topic which is discussed in Chapter 5.

The Cognitive Neuroscience of Attention

Studying attention from a cognitive neuroscience perspective provides the opportunity for finding neurological support for earlier findings, as well as determining the location of various attentional processes in the brain.

Attention and the Human Brain

The connection between attention and the human brain was originally investigated by correlating attentional deficits associated with brain trauma. This early work was largely

Cognition in Everyday Life

Visual Search, Automaticity, and Quarterbacks

It's third and long, and your home team is down by 6 points late in the fourth quarter. The football is near the center of the field, and a rookie quarterback is called on to perform a task that involves a complex visual search, selection of a target, and an execution of a reasonably practiced motor act, performed under great pressure before thousands of frenzied football fans. This task, which is repeatedly performed throughout America, provides us with an interesting example of visual search, automaticity, and cognition. First, the quarterback must hold in memory a play that involves knowledge about the routes his receivers are to run. Then he must factor into his cerebral formula the defensive formation. And, finally, he must calculate the probabilities of successful candidates to receive the ball and fling the ball to that target.

Two stages of this process can be identified: A memory-retrieval task (remembering the play and routes) and a perceptual-judgment task (defensive evaluation and probabilistic judgments of success). By repeated training, each of these tasks may be vastly improved to the point that they become "automatic"—something like practiced tennis players, ballet dancers, or even chess players (see Chapter 4) perform. The trouble is that quarterbacks do not get an opportunity to practice to the degree that they can perform automatically (and about the time a professional player hones his skill to that level, his bell has been rung so many times he is ready to retire to sports announcing).

Several researchers have become interested in the automaticity problem in sports—including Arthur Fisk and Neff Walker at Georgia Institute of Technology, who have used a computer-based training system which contains film excerpts from actual games from the vantage point of the quarterback. The quarterback watches these scenes, which last about 6 to 8 seconds, and using buttons, he selects the receiver he would throw the ball to. The program then buzzes or beeps if he selects the wrong or right receiver. Another aspect of the process is actually throwing the ball and hitting a moving target. That process may be performed over and over again without a full complement of players, while the "thinking" part of the game might be turned over to computer simulation which trains people to become automatons. Perhaps in this new century all sorts of training programs will be made available for home use.

confined to neuropathology. For example, a lesion or stroke in one part of the brain might be associated with a type of attentional deficit. Unfortunately, pathological observations were commonly based on strokes and gunshot wounds, which know no boundaries, and, thus, the specific locus of the brain damage involved in specific kinds of attention problems remained veiled. There was an additional problem in that specific pathological observations were frequently based on postmortem examinations, which allow for, to say

Michael I. Posner. Did seminal work in attention, memory, and cognitive neuroscience, which has opened up new areas of cognitive psychology.

the least, minimal interaction between the subject and observer. Pathological studies did, however, suggest that attention was partly tied to a specific cortical region. Recently, researchers interested in attention and the brain have engaged techniques, developed in both cognitive psychology and brain science, which significantly expand our understanding of this relationship. Furthermore, there is an impressive catalog of techniques to draw upon in both disciplines that do not require the subject to die, to suffer a massive stroke, to take a bullet in the head, or to surrender to a surgical procedure in order for observations to be made. The focus of these recent efforts has generally been in two areas: research and diagnosis/testing.

1. There is the search for correlates between the geography of the brain and attentional processes (Corbetta, Miezin, Dobmeyer, Shulman, & Petersen 1991; Hillyard, Mangun, Woldorff, & Luck, 1995; Mountcastle, 1978; Pardo, Fox, & Raichle, 1991; Posner, 1988, 1992; [especially] Posner & Petersen, 1990; Whitehead, 1991a 1991b; Woldorff et al., 1993). These studies have made use of the full range of cognitive techniques discussed in this chapter (for example, dichotic listening, shadowing, divided attention, lexical decision tasks, shape and color discrimination, and priming) and remote sensing devices used in neurological studies (e.g., MRI and PET scans) as well as traditional reaction-time experiments.

2. Techniques developed in the cognitive laboratory are used as diagnostic tests or in the investigation of pharmacological agents that supposedly act selectively on the attentional process (Tinklenberg & Taylor, 1984).

   Consider the matter of finding correlates between brain anatomy and attention. There appear to be anatomically separate systems of the brain that deal with attention and other systems, such as the data processing systems, that perform operations on specific inputs even when attention is directed elsewhere (Posner, 1992). In one sense, the attention system is similar to other systems (the motor and sensory systems, for example) in that it interacts with many other parts of the brain but maintains its own identity.

Attention and PET

Current research on attention has used brain imaging technology (mainly PET), and although it is impossible to report all of the recent studies, it is possible to showcase some work being done in this important area of cognitive neuroscience research by some of its foremost scientists. The basic methodological technique for PET investigations is discussed in Chapter 2. It is important to remember that this is a procedure in which blood flow rates in the brain are evaluated by means of radioactive tracers. As the brain metabolizes nourishment through use, more blood is called for. These actions are monitored by means of radioactive sensors and transposed by a computer into a geographic map of the cortex in which "hot spots," regions of concentrated blood flow, are identified.

Typical of these experiments is the work of Petersen and his colleagues (Petersen, Fox, Snyder, & Raichle, 1990) in which research participants were shown words, nonwords that resembled words, and consonant strings. As shown in Figure 3.14, the areas activated for words and regular nonwords (but not consonant strings) were the ones shown with an oval (left figures). Curiously, patients who suffer lesions to these

FIGURE 3.14

The areas of the cerebral cortex of the human brain involved in attention. Attentional networks are shown by solid-colored shapes on the lateral (outside) and medial (cross-sectional) surfaces of the right and left hemispheres. It appears that the parietal lobes are involved in the attentional network (see x's); the right frontal lobes are related to vigilance; and the diamonds are part of the anterior attention network. The word processing systems, are related to visual word form (o's) and semantic associations (o's).

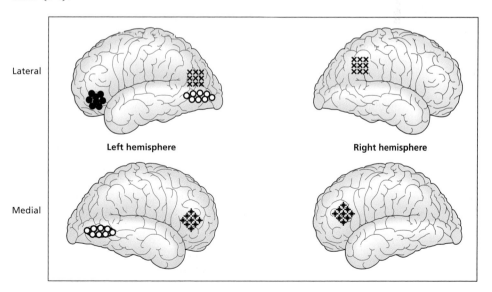

areas frequently are unable to read words but may read letter by letter. For example, shown the word *sand,* these patients cannot read it but can say the letters one by one (*s-a-n-d*). Through this action, the string is (probably) represented into an auditory code. Other areas of the brain take over the functioning, and these patients can say what the word is. Additional studies of the brain by means of PET show other areas involved in specific types of attention, as shown in Figure 3.14. Each of these designated areas of the brain is involved in selective attention in different ways, and to thoroughly understand the nature of the brain in attention, it is necessary to consider the topic of awareness and consciousness. The current state of knowledge of the role of the cerebral cortex in awareness and attention is that the attentional system produces the contents of awareness in the same way as other parts of the brain, such as the visual system, and organizes the way other sensations are processed, such as how the visual world is perceived.

Spotlight on Cognitive Neuroscience

Visual Attention

Paul Downing, Jia Liu, and Nancy Kanwisher (2001) used fMRI and MEG to study visual attention. Not only do they focus on finding the neural correlates of this type of cognitive function, but they also then use that information to test theories of attention. The spatial and temporal resolution of fMRI and MEG afford the opportunity to pinpoint the neural locations of activity resulting from particular stimuli and task activities. Downing and his colleagues capitalize on previous research that has shown that the fusiform face area (FFA) of the brain responds selectively to faces and the parahippocampal place area (PPA) responds to places and houses. Using this information, they conducted a study to evaluate object-based attention. Using activity in FFA and PPA as dependent variables, they had participants focus their attention to either the direction of a moving stimulus or to the position of a still item. The stimuli were a transparent house and a transparent face superimposed one over the other. The moving stimulus was sometimes the face and sometimes the house (with the corresponding still stimulus being the opposite). So half of the time the participants were told to pay attention to the house and the other half of the time to the face. They found that when participants attended to a moving house, activity was higher in the PPA, compared to a moving face. Alternatively, when participants attended to a moving face, activity was higher in the FFA, compared to a moving house. When they were instructed to attend to the still item, the reverse occurred: When attending to the static face while the house was moving, activity was higher in the FFA, and when attending to the static house while the face was moving, activity was higher in the PPA. They conclude that "task-irrelevant features in each display received more attention when they were associated with the attended object, compared to an ignored object at the same location, implicating object-based selection uniquely" (p. 1334).

Downing, P., Liu, J., and Kanwisher, N. (2001). Testing cognitive models of visual attention with fMRI and MEG. *Neuropsychologia, 39*(12), 1329–1342.

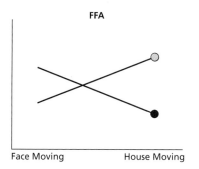

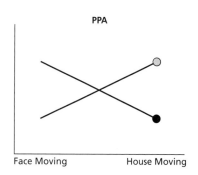

A la carte

High-Speed Police Chases

We have all probably seen news clips of chase scenes where police are in hot pursuit of an offender, with vehicles speeding through the city streets putting bystanders and oncoming traffic in jeopardy. A high-speed chase places considerable demands on the police. If cognitive psychologists can uncover what information the police are attending to and how they process that information, better training methods can be developed to keep the police and the innocent bystanders safer. Crundall, Chapman, Phelps, and Underwood (2003) conducted such a study using clips of pursuits (occurring both day and night) and eye-tracking equipment to measure eye fixations while police watched the chase scenes. Eye fixations are assumed to equate to visual processing. In other words, the visual information looked at is the visual information being processed. The researchers wanted to know if the police looked primarily at the vehicle ahead, or if they were also looking for peripheral information that may be related to innocent bystanders. Compared to novice drivers, police had a greater sampling rate and a greater spread of search for the daytime clips, indicating that they spent more time looking at the periphery than did the novice control group, indicating that they were more aware of their surroundings and more prepared to respond should a hazard arise. However, Crundall and his colleagues found little difference between the two groups for the night-related clips. It is likely that the fleeing vehicle is more salient at night. This is problematic as hazards my go unnoticed at night. This information can be of great value in developing educational and training procedures for night pursuit that could save innocent lives.

Student Resource Center

STUDY GUIDE

1   Cognitive psychologists are interested in perception because cognition is presumed to be a consequence of external events, sensory detection is influenced by previous experiences, and knowledge about sensory experience may tell us how information is abstracted at the cognitive level.

2   *Sensation* refers to the relationship between the physical world and its detection through the sensory system whereas *perception* involves higher-order cognition in the interpretation of sensory signals.

3   Illusions occur when one's perception of reality is different from "reality." Illusions are often caused by expectations based on past experiences.

4   The perceptual process consists of the detection and interpretation of reality as determined by the stimulus sensed, the structure of the sensory system and brain, and previous knowledge.

5   Studies of perceptual span concern the basic question of how much we can experience from a brief exposure.

6   Reporting stimuli perceived from a brief presentation is a dual-stage process: (1) the perception, or actual sensory registration, and (2) the recall, or ability to report what was registered before it fades.

7   Partial-report techniques address the problem of confounding sensory capacity with recall ability.

8   Iconic storage holds visual input and appears to be independent of subject control factors (e.g., attention). Capacity is estimated to be at least nine items with a duration of approximately 250 milliseconds. Echoic storage holds auditory input with a duration of about 4 seconds.

9   Iconic and echoic storage may allow us to select relevant information for further processing, thus providing one type of solution to the problem of capacity limitations inherent in the information-processing system.

10 Attention is the concentration of mental effort on sensory or mental events. Many contemporary ideas about attention are based on the premise that an information-processing system's capacity to handle the flow of input is determined by the limitations of that system.

11 Research on attention covers five major aspects: processing capacity and selectiveness, control of attention, automatic processing, the cognitive neuroscience of attention, and consciousness.

12 Capacity limits and selective attention imply a structural bottleneck in information processing. One model locates it at or just prior to perceptual analysis (Broadbent).

13 The attenuation model of selective attention proposes a perceptual filter, located between signal and verbal analyses, which screens input by selectively regulating the "volume" of the message. Stimuli are assumed to have different activation thresholds, a provision that explains how we can hear without attending.

14 Recent work in cognitive neuroscience has studied attention and has sought correlates between parts of the brain and attentional mechanisms.

KEY TERMS

attention
attention model
automatic processing
channel capacity

cocktail party phenomenon
computational brain
cones
cornea

dichotic listening task	pop-out effect
echoic memory	priming
feature maps	psychophysics
filter model	retina
fovea	rods
ganglion cells	signal detection theory
iconic memory	selective attention
illusion	sensory store
labeled lines	saccades
lateral genicultate nuclear	sensation
lens	shadowing
luminance	subliminal perception
perception	vision
perceptual span	visual cortex
peripheral nervous system	

Starting Points

Books and Articles

Historically, Broadbent's *Perception and Communication* is an important work and still makes interesting reading. Gregory's *The Oxford Companion to the Mind* is an intellectual tour de force to be enjoyed by anyone interested in ideas, cognition, and attention. Highly recommended papers include Kihlstrom's article "The Cognitive Unconscious" in *Science;* Cowan's article in *Psychological Bulletin;* Posner and Petersen's chapter, "The Attention System of the Human Brain," in the *Annual Review of Neuroscience;* Pashler's "Doing Two Things at the Same Time" in *American Scientist;* and, for a touch of automaticity and PDP, Cohen, Servan-Schreiber, and McClelland's article (1992). Gazzinaga's edited volume, *The Cognitive Neurosciences,* contains some detailed chapters by leading authorities in the field. Recent issues of *Perception and Psychophysics, Cognitive Psychology, American Journal of Psychology, Journal of Experimental Psychology: Human Perception and Performance,* and *Memory and Cognition* frequently carry reports on the subjects discussed in this chapter.

Movies

- The World is not Enough (1999)—Man who can't feel pain
- How Does It Feel? (1976)—The brain's use of information from the senses
- Altered States (1980)—The effects of sensory deprivation
- K-PAX (2001)—A man learning about the world
- At First Sight (1999)—A blind man regains his vision
- Little Miss Sunshine (2006)—One character figures out he is color blind
- Oversight (2001)—Perception versus reality

Search Terms

- BioMotion Lab Demos
- Channel capacity
- The Soundry
- Mythbusters—Pirates eye patch
- Mythbusters—Breaking glass with voice
- Subliminal perception
- Synesthesia
- Exploratorium

Object Recognition

hmmm. . .?

1. What are the main issues regarding object recognition?

2. What is constructive perception? Direct perception?

3. What is Gestalt psychology, and how does the theory account for perception?

4. What are the main features of the following ideas regarding pattern recognition: template matching, geon theory, feature analysis, and prototype formation?

5. What is priming, and why is it considered important in cognitive psychology?

6. How do experts (such as chess masters) organize visual patterns?

*T*he lowest form of thinking is the bare recognition of the object. The highest, the comprehensive intuition of the man who sees all things as part of a system.

—*Plato*

What familiar objects have you seen so far today? If you are like most people, the number of things you saw and identified was huge. Now, for the harder question: How were you able to recognize so many objects rapidly and accurately (or not so accurately, in some cases)?

Our ability to recognize familiar types of things is a spectacular human characteristic. This attribute allows us to recognize an old friend in a crowd of faces, to identify a song from a few notes, to read words, to enjoy the taste of a vintage wine, or to appreciate the smell of a rose. Pattern recognition and the ability to recognize objects is a cognitive ability that we mostly perform seamlessly, rapidly, and without much effort. We use object and pattern recognition all the time, yet the cognitive structures that support recognition are only recently understood. How is it that we recognize someone we know? For example, how does one recognize their grandmother? Is there a template in our mind so unique that your grandmother fits? Is there a generalized grandmother prototype allowing one to recognize her under a variety of circumstances (with or without glasses, with or without her hair up)? When we see someone who looks familiar to us, do we look at each feature (eyes, nose, mouth, etc.) and analyze them against a "master" list of features for that person? Some researchers have hypothesized the existence of a **grandmother cell**—a single neuron that fires when it receives visual signals constituting someone familiar to them. These important questions are addressed within this chapter on pattern and object recognition. Keep in mind that although our discussion deals primarily with visual patterns that quite often lead to object recognition, other forms of patterns—auditory, tactile, and so on—can also be involved in pattern recognition. As we proceed through the chapter we will often use the words "pattern" and "object" interchangeably. This is not to say that they are the same thing, but unless specified, what we state about patterns applies to objects (smells, touch, etc.).

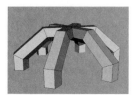

What is the above object? Although you have never seen this before, your brain has already attempted to make sense of it. It has already confirmed that you have never seen this before, but you have seen something like it previously. A structure? A lunar lander? Perceptual cues, such as shadowing, allow us to see that it is three-dimensional. This is a good example of how our automatic processes attempt to make sense of our visual world. As we shall see, even everyday **pattern recognition** involves a complex interaction between sensation, perception, memory, and a cognitive search for identification of

113

TABLE 4.1

Principle	Example
• Recognize familiar patterns promptly and with a high degree of accuracy.	• We easily recognize the faces of our friends, the interior of our house, and street signs.
• Evaluate and understand unfamiliar objects	• Even though we may have never seen an unusual shape, our visual-perceptual system can analyze it and create a three-dimensional representation.
• Accurately perceive objects that are placed or rotated at different angles.	• We recognize a coffee cup, even though it may be upside down.
• Identify objects partly hidden from view, occluded, or in some other way "noisy."	• We infer that hidden parts of objects exist, as in the case of the lower torso and legs of TV reporters.
• Perform pattern recognition quickly, with subjective ease, and automatically.	• We move through a world in which shapes and objects are constantly changing, and yet we process this information swiftly and without undue effort.

the experience. As complex as the process of object recognition is, it is also performed more or less accurately within a fraction of a second. From both laboratory studies (and common knowledge), we know that we can recognize and evaluate familiar and even unfamiliar objects quickly, and accurately (see Table 4.1).

Perceptual Theories

As we discussed in the previous chapter, we are bombarded with information about the physical properties of the world through the windows of our five senses. There is so much information that temporary sensory stores and elaborate sensory filters are required to help determine what and how much information can be passed along to our brain. The big question is what happens to that information. How does it become the perception of an object such as a car, or the smell of sour milk, or the texture of silk? In this next section we introduce some theories of perception that researchers have developed over time to help explain and understand how a sensation becomes the perception of a pattern or object.

Perceptual psychologists have developed two major theories of how the world is perceived by humans. One theory, **constructive perception,** holds that people "construct" perceptions by actively selecting stimuli and merging sensations with memory. Another theory, **direct perception,** holds that perception consists of the direct acquisition of information from the environment.

Recall in earlier chapters mention of top-down and bottom-up processing. Radar technicians may interpret a blip on the radar screen solely based on the size and shape of the image (bottom-up) or they may use information about the presence of enemy vessels in their interpretation (top-down). Constructive perception uses a top-down strategy while direct perception uses a bottom-up strategy.

Cognition in Everyday Life

Perception of Depth

*L*aunched in 1977, two American spacecraft called *Voyager* were sent hurtling through space on their way to the stars. These space vehicles are extraordinary in that attached to each is a gold-coated phonograph record, which, when decoded by creatures from some distant civilization, will tell about our planet and culture. Each record has about 90 minutes of music, sounds from the earth, greetings in 60 languages, and 118 "photographs" of people and planet. What, if anything, might intelligent inhabitants from an alien civilization make of this information? More important for human cognitive psychologists, what assumptions about human perception and information processing are embodied in this task?

Photographs 61 and 62 have been reproduced to illustrate the assumptions we make about human and alien perception of complex forms. In photograph 62 (below left) a Bushman hunter

and (presumably) his son are hunting a small, horned, four-legged animal. Most humans easily discern that the animal is larger than the absolute size in the photograph. The ability to adjust for size is called size constancy. In the right photograph scientists created a silhouette of the three principal forms in the photograph along with measurements of the animal and the boy. It was anticipated that an alien would be able to use these measures to understand the concept of depth perception, which we humans take for granted. However, when we consider the probably unique evolutionary history of homo sapiens and other creatures, it is unlikely that even these cues would be sufficient for complete and immediate understanding. We humans bring to form perception a myriad of cognitive and physiological attributes that produce a singular impression that, as far as we know, is special among intelligent beings.

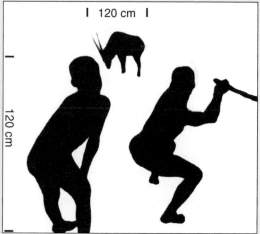

Diagram by Jon Lomberg. From *Murmurs of Earth: The Voyager Interstellar Record,* by Carl Sagan, F. D. Drake, Ann Drugen, I. Ferris, Jon Lomberg, and L. S. Sagan. Random House, Inc. Photography by N. R. Farbman, *Life Magazine,* Time, Inc., in Sagan et al. (1978).

Constructive Perception

The theory of constructive perception is based on the notion that during perception we form and test hypotheses regarding percepts based on both what we sense and what we know. Thus, perception is the combined effect of what comes in through our sensory system and what we have learned about the world through experience. When you see a friend approaching from a distance, you recognize him because his features, his nose, his eyes, his hair and so on, are sensed by your eye *and* because you have knowledge that he usually can be seen at this time at this place. You may even be able to recognize him in spite of the fact that he may have grown a goatee recently or changed his hair style or is wearing sunglasses. According to the constructivists, these changes in the pattern of the original stimuli still allow you to recognize him accurately because of **unconscious infer-ence,** a process by which we spontaneously integrate information from several sources to construct an interpretation. We see, according to the constructivists, as much with the brain and its rich supply of knowledge about the world as with the eyes (and other sensory organs) that provide us with the raw sensory input. The theory is closely aligned with "top-down" processing and is consistent with the view of many cognitive psychologists working on problems in visual pattern recognition, such as Jerome Bruner, Richard Gregory, and Irvin Rock. The theory may be traced back to the classic work of Hermann von Helmholtz writing at the turn of the twentieth century about visual perception.

Direct Perception

Direct perception holds that information in the stimuli is the important element in perception and that learning and cognition are unnecessary in perception because there is enough information in the environment to make an interpretation. The leading proponent of the theory was the late James Gibson (1966, 1979) and his followers at Cornell University including James Cutting (1986, 1993) who stated that "Direct perception assumes that the richness of the optic array just matches the richness of the world" (p. 247). The idea, which has gained support among ecologically minded psychologists, is that the stimulus contains sufficient information for correct perception and does not require internal representations for perception. The perceiver does minimal work in perception because the world offers so much information, leaving slight demand to construct perception and draw inferences.

During Gibson's time most research on perception was conducted in the laboratory using very simple stimuli such as colored lights, however, Gibson reasoned that visual cues, such as linear perspective, relative size, explored in the lab, are not relevant for depth perception in real-world scenes. He found support for his notion when he was involved in pilot selection during World War II and found that those pilots who performed well on depth-perception tests were no better at flying a plane, which requires a high level of performance as well as depth perception, than those who scored poorly on such tests. He concluded that the traditional set of cues for depth was not adequate for real-world perception. The direct perception view shares many features of the "bottom-up" theory of form perception, which will be discussed shortly.

Each of these two theories of perception has a legion of ardent supporters and, at least on the surface, seems to represent directly opposing and irreconcilable propositions. Yet, at another level of analysis the theories can be seen as complementary rather than contradictory. The constructive view of perception is intuitively appealing as, after all, when you perceive the words on this page as you are reading, you "understand" their meaning *because* you have semantic knowledge of what they mean; when you look at a piece of art you perceive its significance because of your information about the artist, the materials used, and its context. These examples of "perception" seem to rely on knowledge, experience, and learning—all of which direct our attention to and meld with internal representations of the mind. On the other hand, what could be more natural than perception that emphasizes the completeness of the information in the receptors and suggests that perception occurs simply, naturally, and directly without complicated internal representations and circuitous information processing routines?

Our view is that both theories work well to explain perception but they focus on different phases of the process. The direct-perception view is important for our understanding of perception for two reasons: It calls to attention the significance of sensory stimuli, suggesting that the processing of these is simple and direct and that cognition and perception are natural, ecologically based phenomena—a position harmonious with the cognitive evolutionary perspective discussed in Chapter 1. While direct perception may help us understand some of the early perception of sensory impressions, the constructive-perception theory is useful in understanding how sensory impressions are comprehended by the thinking brain. The deductive attribute of humans (and other animals) in perceiving "reality" is not only useful in the comprehension of stimuli that are *not* complete (e.g., seeing your friend without his goatee) but are necessary for the survival of the species.

Visual Pattern Recognition

Beyond the two general theories described above, there are several specific theories that have gained support over time, although not all have equal support. These theories are computational theory, Gestalt theory, bottom-up and top-down processing, template matching, feature analysis, prototype theory, and an integrated form of perception theory. It should be noted that each of these viewpoints may share some theoretical features with other viewpoints; the distinction provides an organizational framework for our discussion of these viewpoints.

Subjective Organization

From a constructivist perspective the brain is interpretive. It uses heuristics and algorithms to process information signals. A heuristic can be considered a good guess based on "rule of thumb" that most often results in the correct outcome, whereas an algorithm is like a specific set of rules that lead to a predictable outcome. Because the brain relies on heuristics, it will make errors. These errors are often the basis of perceptual illusions causing us to see things in the physical world that do not exist.

An intriguing feature of human vision is the tendency to "see" things in the physical world that do not exist. These illusions are the result of not only the sensations from the outer world but also the predisposition of the visual/cognitive system in distorting what really exists in the real world. By studying illusions, cognitive psychologists are able to understand the relationships between external physical phenomena and the way the mind organizes such stimuli in "internal representations."

FIGURE 4.1

Kanizsa Triangle. Can you see a floating white triangle? Does it physically exist or does it exist only in your mind's eye?

One class of illusions that illustrates the way the mind naturally organizes visual stimuli and is important to object recognition is called **illusory contours.** In Figure 4.1 an example of an illusory contour is shown. Illusory contours are percepts of forms where the forms exist in the perceptual-cognitive system, not in the stimulus. They appear to be in front of the other shapes, rather than the ground (or background), and have a real perceptual presence, although the observer seems to have the feeling that they are not really "real."

Look at Figure 4.1. What do you see? It is likely that your "mind's eye" sees a hovering equilateral triangle in the center *even though there is not a physical triangle.* Yet, you see it! Furthermore, the illusionary triangle has well-defined features; for example, it is whiter than the surrounding area and it tends to float above the background. In addition, the lines of the illusory triangle appear even though only a fraction is defined by the slits in the three defining circles. The illusion of the triangle is so compelling that after one views it for several seconds and then covers the outer black circles the *triangle persists.* Perhaps the persistence of the triangle is caused by **lateral inhibition,** or the tendency of adjacent neural elements of the retina to inhibit surrounding cells, thus accentuating contours. (For more information, see Coren, 1991; Kanizsa, 1976; Lesher, 1995; Lesher & Mingolla, 1993.) Even though one can create the phantom triangle, there is still a feeling that this figure is an illusion and not a physical triangle.

There are a number of explanations for these illusions. From an evolutionary perspective, the need to see forms, edges, and motions (as well as faces, some might add) was an imperative necessary for survival. Thus, even in the absence of real lines or forms, our sensory-cognitive system used partial information to fabricate these forms in an effort to make comprehensible a seemingly chaotic world. This explanation is rooted in the evolution of survival mechanisms, and creatures who evolved the ability to perceive these types of figures were able to disambiguate figure from ground when an important figure was nearly the same color or luminance as the background. Some theorists (e.g., Ramachandran, 1987) propose that the perception of illusory contours is a means for canceling the effects of camouflage.

Gestalt psychologists argue that we create subjective illusions because of the tendency to see simple, familiar figures of good form in our environment. This is known as

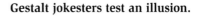

Gestalt jokesters test an illusion.

Pragnanz and it is considered to be a primary law of Gestalt perception. Having good form explains the answer to the question, "What is the most likely visual organization of environmental stimuli?"

Gestalt Theory

The way we organize and classify visual stimuli was studied by adherents of **Gestalt psychology** during the early part of the twentieth century, although perception was only one part of their overall theory. **Pattern organization** to these early Gestalt psychologists involved all stimuli working together to produce an impression that went beyond the sum total of all sensations.

Some patterns of stimuli, according to the founder of the Gestalt movement Max Wertheimer (1923), tend to be naturally (or "spontaneously") organized.

Other Gestalt laws include, for example, the law of proximity, similarity, closure, symmetry, continuity, and common fate. Because of pragnanz, we see the arrangements of the eight dots below to be either a square or a circle, however, when they fail the good form test, we simply see an abstract form. Arranged differently we see a straight line of dots. If we arrange the dots so every other one is shifted, we no long see a line, we now see four sets of two-dot patterns because of the **proximity** of the dots relative to each other. If we change the fill pattern of the dots below we now perceive two rows of dots due to the law of similarity.

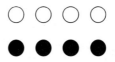

Some patterns of stimuli seem to be classified the same way by many people. For example, if shown this pattern of visual stimuli,

most people would recognize it and label it a square. This is called closure. **Closure** extends to other complex objects such as these:

According to the Gestalt psychologists, we seek **symmetry** when perceiving patterns such as the jagged lines below which form a tree.

When objects are not symmetrical they stand out. Faces are perceived to have a high level of symmetry, however, this is often not the case when an image of a face is split center wise and the same-side halves are combined, they reveal asymmetries that have been "touched up" by our perceptual system, as seen in the photos below.

Consider also the way the eye "naturally" organizes the direction in which the triangles are pointed[1] in Figure 4.2. Look at this figure for several seconds, and you will see the orientation shift from one direction to another and yet another. One explanation of

[1]For a much more detailed analysis, see Palmer (1989, 1999).

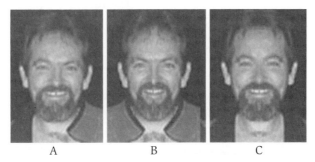

A   B   C

Faces are perceived as symmetrical when often they are not. Photos B and C look like separate images of one of the authors; however, they are composite or cherimic faces based on the original photo, A.

this change is that the mind's eye is constantly searching for alternate perceptual organization. In this instance, the stimuli that impinge on the retina are identical, but the interpretation is different. Although the reorganization may occur spontaneously, it can also be voluntarily controlled. Such demonstrations show the influence of higher-order mental processes on visual perception.

When faced with the task of disentangling a perceptual scene, we are said to be using the law of **continuity.** Continuity allows our mind to continue a pattern even after it physically stops. **Common fate** suggests things going in the same direction belong together and therefore should be grouped together. Examples are flocks of birds, schools of fish, and even sailboats.

The influence of past memories on form perception can also be seen in Figure 4.3. Examine the two figures briefly. What do you see? In Figure 4.3A, people generally see a stable two-dimensional object, and in Figure 4.3B an unstable three-dimensional one. However, if you look closely, you will see that both figures are identical except that they are misaligned by 45 degrees. Why do we have this radically different perception of two nearly identical patterns? One constructivist reason is that through past experience we see boxes positioned in the orientation shown in Figure 4.3B. This reminds us of a box that has three dimensions. The form in Figure 4.3A is unboxlike. At best, it would be an odd orientation for a box. We do not easily see the dimensionality associated with a box, but we do see a symmetrical two-dimensional object that appears to be two squares held up by a frame. Although this powerful illusion may be particularly compelling for people

FIGURE 4.2

Look at this display of triangles. In which direction do they point? Look again. Does the direction change? Can you control the direction?

FIGURE 4.3

Effect of orientation on perception.
Which of these forms appears to be three-dimensional?

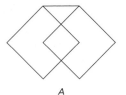

A

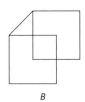

B

growing up in Western civilization, would the illusion hold for people who might not come into contact with boxes or angular forms in their everyday lives? Probably not. (See Deregowski, 1980, for further discussion.)

A conspicuous assumption of the early Gestalt psychologists—especially Köhler (1947)— was that spontaneous organization of a pattern was a natural function of the stimulus itself and only minimally related to past experience with the object. Although the controversy about the source of "natural organization" continues, a considerable number of experimental reports (some based on cross-cultural observation) support the notion that "natural organization" of patterns is directly tied to the perceptual history of the human subject.

Study of pattern recognition by cognitive psychologists has extended the work of the early Gestalt psychologists. Some recent cognitive psychologists have concentrated on the "internal" structures and processes that are associated with complex pattern recognition rather than emphasizing the characteristics of simple stimuli. Following are some of these models and the patterns on which they are based.

Canonic Perspectives

One extension of the ideas expressed by the Gestaltists can be seen in the work with canonic perspectives. **Canonic perspectives** are views that best represent an object or are the images that first come to mind when you recall a form. If we ask you to think of a common object, say, a blender, the image that comes to mind is likely to be the canonic perspective and not, say, looking down from the top. Research in this area is important, since it combines findings from Gestalt psychology with prototype formation, a topic that is covered in some detail later in this chapter.

If your canonic perspective of a blender is the same as ours, you conjured up a view of a blender that is generally from the front, rotated to the left a few degrees, and viewed from a slightly elevated position. You did not "see" it from directly above, from the back, with a large cookie jar occluding part of it, or from the perspective of a tiny ant crawling over the buttons. However, each of these perspectives is possible. (Much more is reported on visual imagery in Chapter 8.)

Canonic representations may be formed through experience with similar members of a category (called **exemplars**). As interesting (if not entertaining) as these views might be, they fall outside the confines of empirical science. For several years we have been asking people all around the world to "draw a cup and saucer," and some of the renditions are shown in Figure 4.4. There is some variation in the drawings, as a result of varied artistic ability and personal idiosyncrasies, but the remarkable feature of this little experiment is that most people—from Palo Alto, CA, to Waterloo, IA, to Chicago, to London, to Istanbul—drew basically the same "cup and saucer." The first author's drawing of a

When we think of a blender, chances are we construct an image with a canonical perspective rather than other, less informative perspectives such as looking straight down onto it.

"cup and saucer," a bird's-eye view of those objects shown in Figure 4.5, meets the criterion of the task and, when identified, is easily recognized. It is also conspicuously different from the other sketches because it is not canonic; yet, when you are told what it is, you "see it" easily.

One theoretical explanation of the generality of canonic perspectives is that, through common experience with objects, we develop permanent memories of the most representational view of an object and of a view that discloses the greatest amount of

FIGURE 4.4

Canonic cup caper connected cognitively.

Reprinted with permission of Sylvan Kornblum.

FIGURE 4.5

Improbable view. Cup and saucer —bird's-eye view.

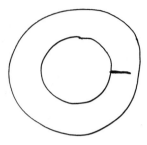

information about it. Thus, studies of canonic perspectives tell us something about form perception, but they tell us much more about human information processing, prototype formation (or the typicality of objects as represented in memory), and economy of thinking and, in the above-mentioned case of the cup caper, efficiency in communication.

Experimental data have supported these conclusions. Palmer, Rosch, and Chase (1981) photographed a series of horses from different perspectives (see Figure 4.6). Par-

FIGURE 4.6

Twelve perspective views of a horse. Used in Palmer, Rosch, and Chase experiment (1981) with mean "goodness" ratings.

Reprinted by permission of Sylan Kornblum.

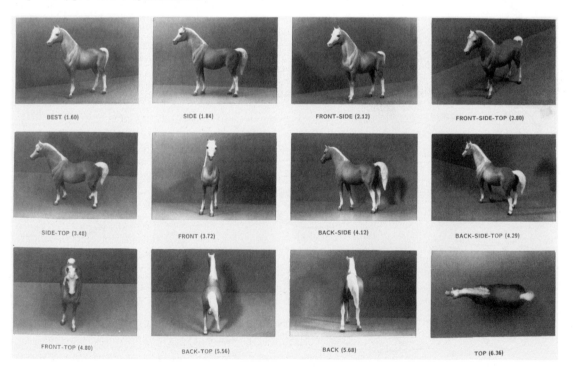

ticipants rated the perspectives for typicality and familiarity. In a second part of the experiment, subjects were shown the photographs of the horse and other objects (e.g., a camera, a car, a piano, etc.) that had been similarly evaluated and were asked to name the objects as rapidly as they could. Not surprisingly, the canonic views were identified most quickly, with reaction times increasing as a function of the rated distance away from canonicality. It should also be noted that the visual system still operates with a reasonable degree of efficiency, even when evaluating less than "perfect" figures.

Vicki Bruce and her colleagues (1987) found that the faces are better recognized when seen from a three-quarter view. Support for the three-quarter canonical view of faces comes from single-cell studies examining cells specialized in recognizing faces. When shown a variety of faces in varying perspectives, some cells responded more actively when the three-quarter view faces were presented.

There are several probable reasons that reaction times are generally longer for less canonic pictures: (1) Fewer parts of the object may be discernible. Look at the back view in Figure 4.6. How much of the horse can you see by looking at its rear? Not much. (2) The best (canonic) view (figure in the upper left) is one that is most commonly experienced. We "see" blenders, chairs, cars, telephones, and horses from one orientation more than others and, therefore, that view is more familiar to us. (3) The canonic view is an idealized, or best, view of the object. Through endless impressions of the world, we form a mental picture of a class of objects in which the epitome of the class is represented in memory. When we ask you to imagine a blender, it is likely that your impression is one of a garden-variety blender, not one of an unconventional model with a weird shape. The same principle works for recalling dogs, horses, sports cars, and birds. This view is consistent with theories of prototype formation, which are discussed shortly.

Bottom-Up versus Top-Down Processing

How do we recognize a pattern? Do we identify a dog because we have first recognized its furry coat, its four legs, its eyes, ears, and so on, or do we recognize these parts because we have first identified a dog? The question of whether the recognition process is initiated by the parts of the pattern, which serve as the basis for the recognition of the whole (**bottom-up processing**), or whether it is primarily initiated by a hypothesis about the whole, which leads to its identification and subsequent recognition of the parts (**top-down processing**).

Some theorists (e.g., Palmer, 1975b) have suggested that, under most circumstances, the interpretation of parts and wholes takes place in top-down and bottom-up directions simultaneously. As an example of the interactions of part-to-whole and whole-to-part strategies, Palmer cites the recognition of parts of a face with context and without context. As shown in Figure 4.7, the parts of a face that can easily be recognized in context are somewhat ambiguous when seen alone, although recognizable when more detail or information is supplied. Expectations play a role in processing. As Palmer puts it,

> How can someone recognize a face until he has first recognized the eyes, nose, mouth, and ears? Then again, how can someone recognize the eyes, nose, mouth, and ears until he knows that they are part of a face? This is often called the parsing

FIGURE 4.7

Facial features. Recognizable in the context of a whole face in profile (A) are less recognizable out of context (B). Differentiated more fully and realistically (C), the features are more recognizable.

From Palmer (1975b).

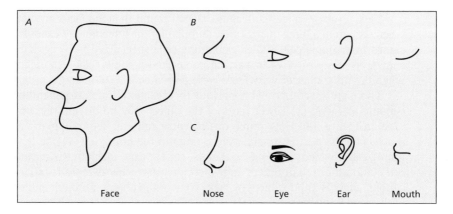

paradox. It concerns the difficulties encountered with either a pure "bottom-up" (part-to-whole) or a pure "top-down" (whole-to-part) strategy in interpretive processing. (1975b, pp. 295–296)

It is likely that top-down processes may take time to acquire. Researchers examining face recognition have found that faces can be interpreted by features (featural) and by the configuration of the features (configurational), which is superior over just features when recognizing faces. Susan Carey at Harvard University and her colleague R. Diamond (1977) found that young children have difficulties using the configurational information and often make mistakes when a face is new (previously unseen) but is wearing a hat or a scarf belonging to another previously seen face. The scarf looks familiar so they think the person is familiar.

We expect to see certain objects in various contexts, for example, a stethoscope in a physician's office, silverware in a kitchen, a computer in an office, and a hydrant in a street scene. It is likely that this world knowledge is what facilitates identification of objects in familiar contexts and hinders identification of objects in inappropriate ones. Several investigations of this "context effect" by Biederman and his colleagues (Biederman, 1972; Biederman, Glass, & Stacy, 1973; also see the section, "Geon Theory" later in this chapter) have shown that, when a person searches for objects in real-world scenes (e.g., objects in a campus scene or street scene), recognition, accuracy, and time required to identify objects are related to the appropriateness of the objects' location in the scene.

From these and similar studies on word and letter identification in context, it is clear that the perception of objects is greatly influenced by the person's expectation as determined by the context.

Cognition in Everyday Life

Object Recognition

Oping for a matched set of chairs, which two would you buy? How did you come to that conclusion? What factors entered into your decision?

See discussions of template matching, priming, and feature analysis for additional thoughts.

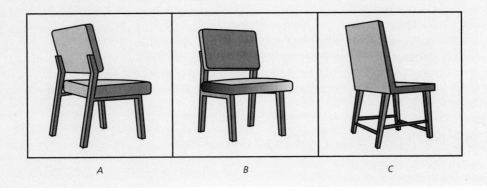

A   B   C

Template Matching

One early theory how the brain recognizes patterns and objects is called **template matching.** A template in our context of human pattern recognition refers to an internal construct that, when matched by sensory stimuli, leads to the recognition of an object. This lock-and-key idea of pattern recognition holds that a great number of templates have been created by our life experience, each template being associated with a meaning. Thus, the visual identification of a shape—say, a geometric form—would occur as follows: The light energy reflecting from the form falls on the retina and is transduced to neural energy, which is transmitted to the brain. A search is made among existing templates which corresponds to the neural pattern. If a template is found that matches the neural pattern, then the person recognizes it. After a match between the form and its template is made, further processing and interpretation of the form may occur.

Template matching, as a theory of pattern recognition, has some strength as well as some weakness. On the positive side, it seems apparent that to recognize a shape, a letter, or some visual forms, some contact with a comparable internal form is necessary. The objects in the external reality need to be recognized as matching a memory in the long-term memory. On the negative side, a literal interpretation of the template matching theory meets with some difficulty. For example, if recognition is possible only when a 1:1 match is found between the external object and its internal representation, then an object with even slight misalignment between itself and the template would not be recognized. Such a rigorous interpretation of the theory would imply that countless millions of templates need to be formed to correspond to each of the varied geometric forms we see and recognize.

The ease with which we identify visual patterns in our daily life may lead us to think that the process is simple, but if we try to duplicate pattern recognition by some artificial means, we find success elusive. Take, for example, the recognition of a letter and the development of word recognition. Although it may take several years to become a skilled reader, once we have learned to identify the orthographic configuration that makes up a word, we can immediately recognize that word in various contexts, pronounce it, and recall its meaning. How would you simulate the initial process of letter recognition in a machine or computer? One way would be to have each of the twenty-six letters stored in a computer memory. Then, each time a letter was scanned by an optical device, the perceived visual configuration would key the memory (template) associated with that letter. Thus, the word *CARD* would be analyzed as C-A-R-D, with *C* fitted into the slot in memory corresponding to the configuration *C. A* would find a match in the *A* slot, and so on. "Voilà!" our computer may exclaim, "I'm reading letters." However, what if we ask it to recognize the letters in *card?* There are no lowercase configurations in its memory. The solution is simple, you might assert: increase the memory to include lowercase letters. However, how would our computer read (as

Cognition in Everyday Life

Face Recognition: Neurons vs Pixels

*T*he ability to recognize faces is quite a feat for humans, yet we are remarkably good at remembering hundreds if not thousands of faces. Specialized cells have been located in the inferotemporal cortex of primates that are selectively tuned for recognizing faces (Desimone et al., 1984). Recognizing faces for a computer is an altogether different task. Recently casinos and other places of public gathering have installed computers for the purpose of recognizing wanted suspects. Computers have been designed to recognize faces by effectively reducing the facial image into pixel values and then computing these values using factor analysis. Once the faces are factor analyzed into what are called Eigenfaces, they can be stored in the computer's memory along with other information about the suspect (name, why they are wanted, etc.). In a split second the computer cameras located in public can decompose a face in the crowd into its Eigenface components and compare it to faces stored in the computer. A template for each face must be stored on the computer. If there is no template, the face cannot be recognized. One interesting aspect of the Eigenfaces is that once you know the formula for faces (see below), you can create new composite faces. Such systems have been developed for law enforcement (Tredoux, 2002).

Courtesy of Colin Tredoux.

we can) the letters in ꓭᐯꓵꓳ or *Card* or C ꓮꓣ D or ꓳꓮꓣꓷ? Of course, the process of reading involves a much more complex process than simple letter identification. The technique used by computers (of matching specific letter configurations against specific configurations in its memory) is called template matching, and it works something as a key in a lock does. A key's configuration of ridges and slots needs to correspond exactly to a lock's configuration if it is to release the lock. In template matching, if the visual configuration corresponds to a compatible memory representation, information, in terms of pattern recognition, is released. In the preceding example of the computer, the method of template matching to recognize various anomalies in the word *CARD* encountered difficulties, much as a bent key might in releasing a lock.

Geon Theory

An alternative to an unyielding template model is a theory that posits that the human information processing system has a limited number of simple geometric shapes that may be applied to complex shapes. One theory, which also bears some resemblance to feature analysis (discussed later in the chapter), was developed by Irving Biederman of the University of Southern California and adopts such an idea. Biederman's concept of form perception is based on the concept of the **geon,** which stands for "geometrical ions." It proposes that all complex forms are composed of geons. For example, a cup is composed of two geons: a cylinder (for the container portion) and an ellipse (for the handle). (See Figure 4.8 for examples of geons and objects.) Geon theory, as espoused by Biederman (see Biederman, 1985, 1987, 1990; Cooper & Biederman, 1993) proposes that the recognition of an object, such as a telephone, a suitcase, or even more complex forms, consists of *recognition by components* (RBC) in which complex forms are broken down into simple forms. Geons are 24 distinct forms and, like the letters of the alphabet,

Cognition in Everyday Life

The Remarkable Versatility of Human Form Perception

ꞋSꞋSSꞋsSSꞋ
SSSꞋSꞋꞋSSS
sSꞋSSSꞋSS s
SꞋSꞋSSꞋSSS
SSꞋSꞋSSS

*M*ost of us are familiar with the many font options available in the drop down menu of your word processor. Even the most ornate (or silly) font is legible. Shown here is a diverse collection of letters, which we easily recognize as variations of the letter *S*. However, it is unlikely that we have seen and formed a precise memory for all of these versions. We can do this task, and many other similar pattern recognition tasks, because we have formed an impression of various classes of objects, such as an *S*, and are able to apply that information to a wide class of similar forms.

FIGURE 4.8

Geons and objects. Objects are represented as configurations of geons, which are simple visual volumes.

From Biederman (1990). Reprinted by permission of MIT Press.

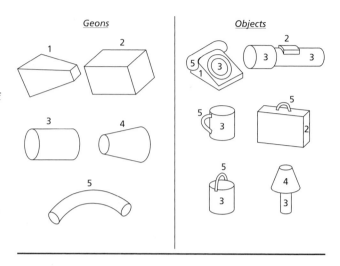

Geons   *Objects*

make up a type of system. When combined, they fabricate more complex forms, much as the words on this page are composed of letters. The number of different forms that can be generated by combining primitive shapes is astronomical. For example, three geons arranged in all possible combinations yield a total of 1.4 billion three-geon objects! However, we use only a fraction of the total possible number of complex forms. Biederman estimates that we use only about 30,000, of which we have names for only 3,000.

One test of geon theory is in the use of degraded forms, as shown in Figure 4.9. Which of these figures (A or B) is easier to identify?

In the illustration, 65 percent of the contour has been removed from a common object. In the cup on the left (A), the lines from the middles of the segments were removed, which still allows the viewer to see how the basic segments are related. In the cup on the right (B), the deleted lines are from the vertices, which include critical corners that relate segments one to another. Biederman presented objects of this type to participants for 100 milliseconds. He found that when the connecting lines were removed (A), a correct identification was made about 70 percent of the time; when the vertices were deleted (B), the number of correct identifications was about 50 percent. Thus, consistent with a theory that holds that object identification is grounded on seeing basic forms, the removal of critical relational information made the object harder to see than when such information was provided.

Irving Biederman has advanced our understanding of object recognition through innovative experiments and theories, especially geon theory.

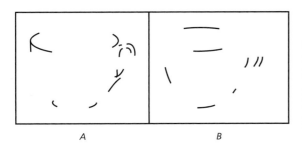

FIGURE 4.9

Sixty-five percent of the contour has been removed from a cup. Centered at either midsegments (A) or vertices (B).

From I. Biederman, "Human Image Understanding: Recent Research and a Theory" in *Computer Vision, Graphics and Image Processing*, 1985, *32*, 29–73. Copyright 1985 Elsevier. Reprinted by permission.

Understanding object recognition has been sought via two approaches. One approach focuses on looking for domain-general explanations, whereby the brain and cognitive system have general processes to recognize a wide range of objects (e.g., general geometry of objects; Biederman, 1990). The other approach is domain-specific such that the brain and cognitive system has "functionally distinct category-specific recognition systems" (Tooby & Cosmides, 2000). Evidence for a domain-specific approach to object recognition lies in research on the recognition of specialized objects in the world (e.g., faces, animals, plants, landmarks, among others; Caramazza & Shelton, 1998; Duchaine, 2000). Duchaine (2000) in particular points out that by virtue of the fact that people with prosopagnosia (those who cannot recognize faces) can recognize other classes of objects provides evidence for a domain-specific structure for object recognition.

The use of priming techniques raises an important issue for cognitive psychology; that is, the presentation of the prime, or initial, stimulus seems to activate a whole range of response tendencies of which the observer is not conscious. This nonconscious activation is called *implicit memory* as contrasted with *explicit memory,* which involves the conscious recall of previous experiences. In the example shown in Figure 4.10, it is unlikely that participants consciously thought about the second type of chair when they saw the first. For this reason, the type of memory being tested is called implicit memory.

An application of the priming technique discussed in Chapter 1 in which a component theory of object recognition was tested can be found in Biederman and Cooper (1991). To

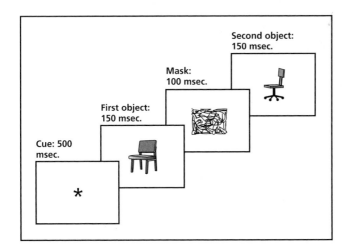

Second object:
150 msec.

Mask:
100 msec.

First object:
150 msec.

Cue: 500
msec.

FIGURE 4.10

Sequence of events on a 0° orientation difference. "Different" trial with familiar objects in the same-different task. Only if the two exemplars of the chair were the same, whatever the orientation in depth, were the participants to respond "same." (The designation of orientation on different trials was arbitrary.)

Cognition in Everyday Life

Geons and Art?

Pablo Picasso, the great abstract painter, was influenced by Paul Cézanne, the great impressionist painter. Cézanne encouraged Picasso to examine the nature of "cones, cylinders, and spheres" as he believed that complex paintings should be organized around these "basic" forms. Picasso took the advice seriously and experimented with assembling a painting with these basic forms, which eventually led to cubistic renditions.

Pablo Picasso, "Girl Before a Mirror," ©2007 Estate of Pablo Picasso/
Artists Rights Society (ARS), New York.

test the recognition of common forms (e.g., a piano, a flashlight, or a padlock), participants were first primed with outline drawings of figures in which parts of the lines were missing. For each of these a corresponding drawing was shown in which the name of the object was the same as the prime, but the type of object differed (e.g., the prime was a grand piano, but the object was an upright piano—see Figure 4.11). The results indicated that the **priming effect** was visual rather than conceptual. This is consistent with other findings in studies of short-term memory.

Complementary Image 2

Same Name,
Different Exemplar

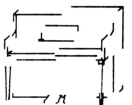

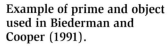

Example of prime and object used in Biederman and Cooper (1991).

© 1991 by Elsevier. Reprinted with permission.

Feature Analysis

Another approach to the problem of how we extract information from complex stimuli is **feature analysis.** This theory holds that object recognition is a high-order processing of information that is preceded by a step in which complex incoming stimuli are identified according to their simpler **features.** Thus, according to this approach, before the full-blown pattern of visual information is appreciated, its components are minimally analyzed. On a simple visual level, a word (e.g., *ARROW*) is not immediately translated into its definitional or visual representation in our memory (e.g., "a pointed shaft shot from a bow" or "→"). Neither is it read as "arrow," nor are the individual letters perceived as (A-R-R-O-W), but rather the features, or components, of each character are detected and analyzed. Thus, the *a* of *arrow* may be fractured into two diagonal lines (/ \), one horizontal line (—), a pointed head (^), an open bottom (/—\), and so on. If the recognition process is based on feature analysis (and there is good evidence to support this), the earliest stages of information processing are more complex than we might first guess. To appreciate the complex sensory and perceptual (and motor) apparatus necessary for "simple" perception and reaction, think of what is involved in hitting a tennis ball in flight. In a fraction of a second, we are able to judge its shape, size, speed, color, trajectory, spin, and anticipated location. Our brain must translate all of this information (which is recorded in only two dimensions on the retina) into a motor reaction, which, if successful, allows us to return the ball. In addition to the fact that this takes place in only a flash of time, much of the information is constantly changing (e.g., the ball's relative size, speed, and trajectory).

Two lines of research—neurological and behavioral—have supported the featural-analysis hypothesis. First, we review single-cell experiments by Hubel and Wiesel (1959, 1963; Hubel, 1963b) that give direct evidence of the type of information coded in the visual cortex. These researchers inserted small wires, or microelectrodes, in the visual cortex of a lightly anesthetized cat or monkey and then studied the neural activity that resulted as simple patterns of light were projected onto a screen directly in front of the animal's eyes. By recording excitation of single nerve cells and amplifying the resulting electrical impulse, they found that some cells respond only to horizontal lines, while others respond only to vertical lines. In other experiments they found that some cells are sensitive to edges of visual stimuli, some to lines, and still others to right angles. Figure 4.12

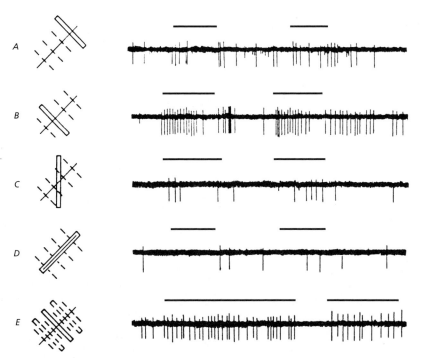

F I G U R E 4.12

Responses of a cell in the cortex of a very young kitten to stimulation of the eye with a light slit. A to E indicate the orientation of the light slit (heavy bar) relative to the receptive field axis (dashed lines). For example, in E, the slit was oriented as in A and B but moved rapidly from side to side. The corresponding horizontal lines with vertical slashes indicate cell response over time with E showing the greatest amount of neural activity and D showing the least.

From Hubel and Wiesel (1963). Reprinted with permission from the American Physiological Society.

shows the amplified brain activity in a cortical cell of a young (and visually inexperienced) kitten correlated with specific orientations of a light slit (A to E) that was presented on a screen within the vision of the animal. Horizontal bars above each activity recorded indicate periods when light was visible. Hubel (1963b) concluded that the development of these cortical codes of perceptual forms was innate and specific to each cell.

One can now begin to grasp the significance of the great number of cells in the visual cortex. Each cell seems to have its own specific duty; it takes care of one restricted part of the retina, and it responds best to one particular shape of stimulus and to one particular orientation. Let's look at the problem from the opposite direction. For each stimulus—each area of the retina stimulated, each type of line (edge, slit, or bar), and each orientation of stimulus—there is a particular set of simple cortical cells that will respond. Changing any of the stimulus arrangements will cause a whole new population of cells to respond. The number of populations responding successively as the eye watches a slowly rotating propeller is scarcely imaginable.

The complex and awkward mechanism of breaking patterns into simpler features, then, may be not only within the realm of neurological possibility but also neurologically necessary. That is, feature analysis may be a stage in information processing that must occur before higher-level object recognition can take place.

Eye Movements and Object Recognition

A direct approach to feature analysis is observation of eye movements and eye fixation. This line of research presumes that the eye makes saccades related to the visual information being extracted and if you gaze for a relatively long time at a certain feature in a pattern, you are extracting more information from it than from a feature only cursorily viewed. The results of the fixation experiments by Yarbus (1967), a Russian psychologist, are shown in Figure 4.13.

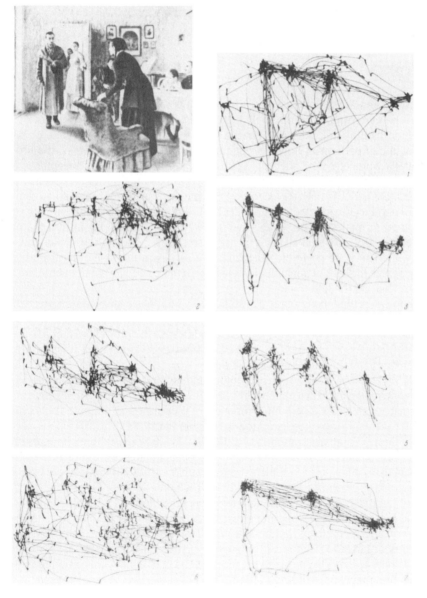

FIGURE 4.13

Records of eye movements of participant examining picture at upper left. Trace 1 was made when participant examined picture at will. Subsequent traces were made after participant was asked to estimate the economic level of the people shown (Trace 2); judge their ages (3); guess what they had been doing before arrival of the "visitor" (4); remember their clothing (5); remember their positions (and those of objects) in the room (6); and estimate how long the "visitor" had not seen the "family" (7).

From Yarbus (1967). Reprinted by permission from Kluwer Academic.

Yarbus suggests that the more information carried by a feature (e.g., the people or relationships in the illustrations shown), the longer the eyes stay fixed on it. He also concludes that the distribution of fixation points is a function of the participant's purpose. In one series, the participant was asked to make certain estimates regarding the complex pattern (e.g., the material circumstances of the family and the ages of the people). Under these circumstances the focus tends to be on those features most important to the participant's purpose. For example, when participants' goals were to discriminate ages their eyes rested longer on the faces in the painting. Thus, the perception of features within complex patterns seems not only to depend on the nature of the physical stimuli but also to engage higher-order cognitive processes, such as attention and goals.

Prototype Matching

An alternative to template matching and feature analysis as a means of recognizing objects is **prototype matching.** It seems likely that, rather than form specific templates or even features for the numerous different patterns we are called upon to recognize, some kind of abstraction of patterns is stored in memory and that abstraction serves as a prototype. A pattern would then be checked against the prototype and, if a resemblance were found, the pattern would be recognized. Prototype matching in humans seems to be more compatible with neurological economy and memory search processes than template matching, and it also allows for recognition of patterns that are "unusual" but in some way related to the prototype. In this system, we may, for example, form a prototype of the letter *S*, against which all other *S*s are evaluated in terms of how closely they fit the prototype. Where the degree of mismatch is great, as in the case of letters other than *S*, we recognize the lack of a match and reject the letter as an *S;* we may then search for a prototype that fits the letter better.

Evidence for prototype matching is all around us, and it has a strong intuitive credibility. For example, we recognize a Volkswagen, even though it may be of a different color or shape or have a lot of fancy doodads that are at odds with the prototype in our head. A prototype in this sense is not only an abstraction of a set of stimuli, but it is also the epitome or the "best" representation of the pattern.

Although the argument seems to favor prototype matching over template matching, you might ask whether an exact match between image and template is necessary or whether templates only serve as an approximation of the image that unlocks the memory. If the latter were the case, however, how could you make the fine distinctions necessary for common visual discrimination? Consider, for example, the close featural similarity of *O* and *Q,* and *B, P,* and *R*. Although these visual patterns are similar, we seldom confuse them. In effect, then, templates cannot be sloppy, for if they were, we would make many errors in pattern recognition—and we seemingly do not.

As a theory of pattern recognition, then, template matching has utility in computer programs (bar-code reading, etc.) but, in its rigid form, inadequately accounts for the diversity, accuracy, and economy of human pattern recognition. To sum up, pattern recognition presumes an operation conducted in memory. At the simplest level, it is safe to assert that a pattern is identified by some process that matches sensory information with some trace held in a repository of information.

Abstraction of Visual Information

As we have suggested, template matching may occur at one level of visual recognition, but at another level prototypes may be used. This view holds that a prototype is an abstraction of a set of stimuli that embodies many similar forms of the same pattern. A prototype allows us to recognize a pattern even though it may not be identical (only similar) to the prototype. For example, we recognize a diverse number of *S*s, not because they fit neatly into cerebral slots but because the members of the class *S* have some common properties.

The empirical studies seeking evidence concerning prototypes as a means of pattern recognition have largely addressed the questions of how prototypes develop and by what process new exemplars are quickly classified. The question is not new; Bishop Berkeley (cited in Calfee, 1975) worried about it a long time ago:

> In his mind's eye all images of triangles seemed to have rather specific properties. They were equilateral or isosceles or right triangles, and he searched in vain for a mental image of the "universal triangle." Although it is easy to define verbally what we mean by a triangle, it is not clear what the "perfect" triangle looks like. We see lots of different kinds of triangles; from this variety what do we create in our mind as the basis for recognizing a triangle? (p. 222)

Berkeley's speculative odyssey for the "perfect" triangle spanned several centuries and was finally empirically studied, in what has itself become a classic experiment, by Posner, Goldsmith, and Welton (1967). They searched for the prototype of a triangle (and other forms) and then measured participants' reaction to other forms that were something like the prototypical one. In the first part of their experiment, they developed a series of prototypes (see Figure 4.14) formed by placing nine dots in a 30 × 30 matrix (standard,

FIGURE 4.14

The four prototypical patterns and four distortions of the triangle pattern used by Posner, Goldsmith, and Welton in their study.

Adapted from Posner, Goldsmith, and Welton (1967).

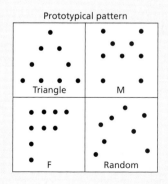

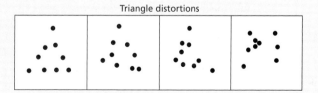

20-squares-per-inch graph paper). These formed either a triangle, a letter, or a random arrangement, which served as prototypes. Four distortions of each of these original forms were made by shifting dots from their original positions. (Figure 4.14 also shows the distortions of the triangle pattern.) Participants were shown each of the four distortions one at a time and asked to classify the pattern by prototype. After participants classified each pattern (by pressing a response button that indicated how they classified the pattern), they were provided feedback on which of their choices had been correct; the prototype was not presented during this part of the experiment.

From this first experiment it was evident that the participants had learned to classify distorted patterns of a specific prototype into a common category, while other patterns, derived from another prototype, were sorted into another common category. The original task was followed with a transfer task, in which participants were asked to classify a series of patterns into one of the three previous categories. The new sets of patterns were composed of (1) old distortions, (2) new distortions (based on the original prototypes), and (3) the prototypes themselves. The old distortions were easily correctly classified (with an accuracy level of about 87 percent). More importantly, the prototypes (which the participants had never seen or classified) were correctly classified about equally well. The new distortions were classified less well than the other two types. Because the prototypes were as accurately classified as the old distortions, it would seem the participants had actually learned something about the prototypes—even though they had never seen anything but distortions of them.

The remarkable feature of this experiment is that the prototype was classified correctly about as frequently as the original learned distortion and more frequently than the new (control) distortion. Posner and his colleagues argue that information about the prototype was abstracted from the stored information (based on the distortion) with a high degree of efficiency. Not only are prototypes abstracted from distorted exemplars, but also the process of pattern learning involves knowledge about variability. The possibility that the correct classification of the prototype was based on the familiarity of the prototype (triangle, *F,* and *M*) was dealt with in an experiment by Petersen, Meagher, Chait, and Gillie (1973). Their results indicated that prototypes and minimally distorted test patterns of highly meaningful configurations were more easily identified than meaningless prototypes and minimally distorted test patterns. However, where the degree of distortion was great, the opposite was true; that is, the highly meaningful prototype was less often identified than the one with low meaningfulness. Their results are not inconsistent with Posner and his team but tease out the interaction between what Berkeley may have called the "universal triangle" and its distortion. Apparently, we abstract prototypes on the basis of stored information. Well-learned forms do not seem to accommodate as wide a range of distortion as less well-learned forms. Bishop Berkeley's search for the perfect triangle has led to the conclusion that all triangles are equal, but some are more equilateral!

Pseudomemory

In an experiment of prototype formation that embodied the Franks and Bransford procedure, Solso and McCarthy (1981b) found that participants falsely recognized the prototype as a previously seen figure with greater confidence than they identified previously seen figures. This phenomenon is called **pseudomemory.** They hypothesized that a prototype is formed on the basis of frequently experienced features. These features, such as individual lines in a figure or parts of a human face, are stored in memory. A general index of the strength of the memory for features can be determined by the frequency of exposure to the feature. Frequently perceived features are, in general, more likely to be permanently stored in memory than are rarely perceived features. Furthermore, it may be that the rules that govern the relationships between features in a pattern are not as well incorporated in memory as the memory for features themselves. Thus, we can conceptualize the process of acquiring knowledge about a pattern as consisting of two stages: acquisition of information about the features of the pattern and acquisition about the relationships between the features. Perhaps the most intriguing part of the puzzle of prototype formation is the evidence that the two stages appear to develop at different rates as we acquire knowledge about a pattern. It is something like a race in which two runners run at different rates. The faster runner is analogous to feature learning, and the slower runner is analogous to learning relationships.

In the Solso and McCarthy (1981b) experiment, a prototype face was composed from an Identikit, a face-identification system used in police work that consists of a series of plastic templates, each representing a facial characteristic such as hair, eyes, nose, chin, and mouth. From each of the three prototype faces selected, a series of exemplar faces was derived ranging in similarity to the prototype face (see Figure 4.15). Participants were shown exemplar faces and then a second set of faces, which contained some of the original faces, some new faces that were scaled in their similarity to the prototype face, and the prototype face. The participants were asked to judge the faces as being members of the previously seen set or new faces and to rate the confidence of their impression. As can be seen in Figure 4.16, not only did participants rate the prototype faces as an old (previously seen) face, but they also gave those faces the highest confidence ratings (an example of pseudomemory).

From the foregoing we can draw some conclusions about visual prototype formation and use. The previously cited research indicates that we (1) form a prototype on the basis of averaging the characteristics of its exemplars; (2) acquire some specific information about prototypes when we deal only with exemplars; (3) acquire some general information about the common properties of prototypes, with well-known prototypes yielding less generous inclusiveness than less familiar (or recently learned) prototypes; (4) judge exemplars in terms of their transformational proximity to prototypes; and (5) form prototypes on the basis of abstractions from exemplars and then evaluate the relationship between forms of the prototypes on the basis of their distance from the prototype as well as from other individual examples.

Theories of Prototype Formation

From the above-mentioned experiments and many other studies, two theoretical models of prototype formation have emerged: the central tendency theory and the attribute frequency theory. In the **central-tendency theory,** a prototype is conceptualized as representing the average or mean of a set of exemplars. The research of Posner and his colleagues (1967) tends to support this theory. Posner and Keele (1968), for example, believe that a prototype is represented mathematically by a hypothetical point in multidimensional space at which the

Prototype face and exemplar faces used in Solso and McCarthy (1981b). The 75 percent face has all the same features as the prototype face except the mouth; the 50 percent face has different hair and eyes; the 25 percent face has only the eyes in common; and the 0 percent face has no features in common with the prototype face.

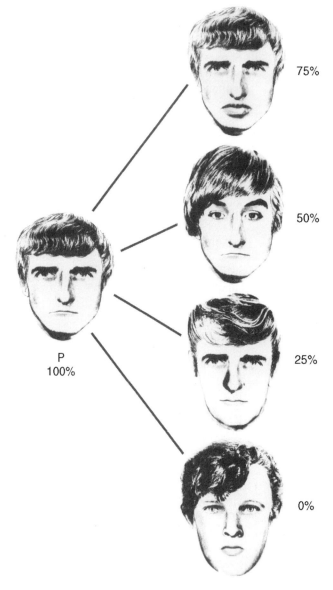

means of the distances along all attributes intersect. We can see in the Posner and Reed experiments how people form a prototype that is an abstraction of a figure. Thus, the prototype is an abstraction stored in memory that represents the central tendency of the category.

The second theory, called the **attribute-frequency theory,** suggests that a prototype represents the mode or most frequently experienced combination of attributes. The experiments of Franks and Bransford, Neumann (1977), and Solso and McCarthy support this theory. In this theory a prototype is synonymous with the "best example" of

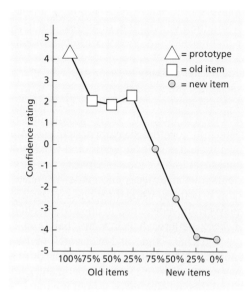

FIGURE 4.16

Confidence ratings for prototype face, old faces, and new faces.

From Solso and McCarthy (1981b).

a set of patterns. A prototype is a pattern that incorporates the most frequently experienced features expressed in a series of exemplars. While the prototype is often unique because it is made up of a unique combination of attributes (think of the unique geometric forms in Frank and Bransford's experiment or the unique faces in Solso and McCarthy's experiment), the features themselves have been previously experienced. The features (the geometric components, or face parts) are the building blocks of the prototype. Each time a person looks at a pattern, he or she records both the features in the pattern and the relationship between the features. However, according to the attribute-frequency theory, upon the introduction of a prototype (which incorporates many of the previously perceived attributes), an individual believes he or she has previously seen the figure because the attributes have been stored in memory. Since the relationships between the features have been seen fewer times than the features (in most experiments the exemplars are shown only once), knowledge about the relationships of features is less well stored in memory than is the knowledge about features.

Pattern Recognition among Experts

Chess Players

So far our perceptual displays have been simple. How are more complex patterns viewed? Chase and Simon (1973a, 1973b) studied this problem by analyzing the complex pattern made by pieces on a chessboard and the way chess masters differed from ordinary players. In this case a pattern is comprised of a constellation of objects (as opposed to features making up objects). Intuition may tell us that the cognitive differences between the two are a matter of how many moves ahead the master player can think. The intuition is wrong, at least according to the research of de Groot (1965,

1966), who found that master players and weaker players thought ahead about the same number of moves, considered about the same number of moves, and had a similar search for patterns of moves. It may be that master players even consider fewer alternative moves, while the weaker player wastes time looking at alternatives that are totally inappropriate. What is the difference? One is the master's ability to reconstruct a pattern of chess pieces after viewing if for only a few seconds; the weak player has great difficulty in doing so. The key to this observation is in the nature of the pattern: it must make sense. If the pieces are arranged in a random order, or illogically, then both masters and beginners do equally poorly. Perhaps the masters put together several chess pieces into chunks or patterns, much as we might put together letters to form words, and words to form sentences. Experienced masters, then, would seem to have greater capacity to reproduce the pattern because they are able to encode the bits and pieces into chess schemata.

Chase and Simon checked this hypothesis using three types of participants—a master, a Class A player (a very strong player), and a beginner. In one experiment their participants were asked to reconstruct twenty chess patterns in plain view—half from the middle games and half from end games selected from chess books and magazines. In this task, two chessboards were placed side by side and the participant was to reconstruct on one chessboard the arrangement of chess pieces shown on the other. In a second experiment, participants scanned a chess pattern for five seconds and then reconstructed it from memory. Chase and Simon found that scanning time was about the same for the master and the Class A player and the beginner, but that the time spent in reconstructing was much less for the master than for the others (Figure 4.17); Figure 4.18 shows the number of pieces correctly placed. Further analysis of these data indicated that the ability to see chunks, or meaningful clusters, of chess pieces made it possible for the better players to gather more information in the given time.

The Chase and Simon experiment has significant theoretical implications. Chunks of information held together by abstract relationships may constitute the basis for a theory of pattern syntax. Bits of information without any meaningful context or grouping are hard to encode, be they letters, geometric forms, notes, or chess pieces; however, when fitted into a meaningful structure (such as poetry, architecture, music, an elegant chess defense), they become significant because they are easily abstracted in terms of a common

F I G U R E 4 . 1 7

Scanning and reconstruction times for chess players of three levels of skill.

Adapted from Chase and Simon (1973a).

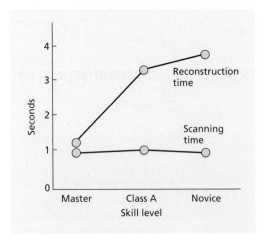

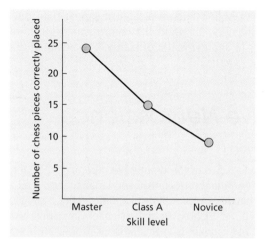

FIGURE 4.18

Distribution of correct placement of chess pieces by players of three levels of skill. Players were shown original pattern for 5 seconds.

Adapted from Chase and Simon (1973a).

grammar. Modern information theorists have developed pristine models of the mind based on structural levels. We have witnessed the growth of structural grammar in language, in music, in body responses, in graphic tasks, and in chess problems. A prevalent human attribute, applicable to all sensory forms, may be the tendency to code information into higher-order abstractions of reality into which new information is fitted. The above-mentioned experiments on chess perception, and other experiments in which immediate stimuli are abstracted, support this postulate.

Object Recognition—The Role of the Perceiver

We have covered quite a lot of territory in this chapter on object recognition: bottom-up and top-down processing; template matching; computer simulation of object recognition; feature analysis; physiological components in object recognition; prototype matching; cognitive structure; letter identification; and forms, faces, and chess problems. In most of these topics it has been hard to isolate specific functions of object recognition without calling on other cognitive systems. Throughout our discussion, we have occasionally considered the influence that context and redundancy have on object recognition and learned that both of these factors bear directly on the recognition of sensory stimuli. The one system that seems to crop up time and again is memory. Object recognition seems to involve several lower-order systems, such as visual storage, analysis of features, synthesis of features, and prototype matching. However, object recognition in humans also involves memory. In our natural environment the world is filled with sensory stimuli, which, when organized and classified, create a recognition of an object or pattern. The stimuli themselves are empty of meaning, existing in their primitive form whether or not we perceive them. They do become meaningful when analyzed into higher-order patterns. Look and listen to your immediate environment. What do you see and hear? What do you smell, taste, or feel? Certainly, you do not perceive raw, vacuous stimuli (even though we are confident that these stimuli excite our sensory system), but you do sense things that mean something to you. The bell in the distance, the tree outside a window, the series of letters on this page, and the smell of fresh bread are all examples of stimuli that, when recognized by the brain, take on a fuller meaning than the physical structures that they excite. That meaning is provided by our memory for these events, which casts immediate experiences in a larger realm of reality. The meaning of sensory stimuli is provided by the perceiver.

Spotlight on Cognitive Neuroscience

Pattern Recognition in the Brain

It is known that the two hemispheres of the brain have different "specialities" or, in other words, functional asymmetries. Fine motor control and language use tend to be focused in the left hemisphere (of right-handed people). Spatial abilities tend to be focused in the right hemisphere. Margaret Funnell, Paul Corballis, and Michael Gazzaniga were interested in demonstrating that the right hemisphere is specialized for processing spatial information. To do this, they solicited the help of J. W., a 45-year-old, right-handed man, who had received a callosotomy (severing of the corpus collosum) at age 25 to control severe epilepsy. By using a "split-brained" patient, they were uniquely able to determine the functioning properties of each side of the brain, because the hemispheres are unable to communicate with one another as can someone who has an intact corpus collosum. Using a variety of stimuli (colored images of objects, black-and-white line drawings of objects, and abstract geometric forms), they found that both hemispheres were able to encode the stimuli but that the left hemisphere was poor at recognizing spatial differences in the stimuli (e.g., if an object was presented next to its mirror image, the left hemisphere did not notice the difference). They concluded that the left hemisphere is directed more toward pattern recognition, and the right hemisphere is directed more toward the analysis of spatial information (like understanding that the object and its mirror image were different images due to orientation).

Funnell, M. G., Corballis, P. M., and Gazzaniga, M. S. (1999). A deficit in perceptual matching in the left hemisphere of a callosotomy patient. *Neuropsychologia*, 37(10), 1143–1154.

Student Resource Center

STUDY GUIDE

1 The ability to identify and process visual patterns and objects has been approached from several theoretical positions: Gestalt psychology, bottom-up versus top-down processing, template matching, feature analysis, and prototype recognition.

2 Gestalt psychologists proposed the perception of visual patterns to be organized according to the principles of proximity, similarity, and spontaneous organization.

3 Object recognition may be initiated by the parts of the pattern, which are then summed (bottom-up processing), or as a hypothesis held by the perceiver, which

(continues on p. 146)

A la carte

I Never Forget an Eigenface

In order for us to see, our visual system first breaks down an object into basic components such as lines and orientations, and then reconstructs the images in our visual cortex. Researchers have developed computerized systems that break faces down into basic components or building blocks called eigenfaces (see figures). Faces can be reconstructed by recombining the eigenface in their original order. Researchers, such as Colin Tredoux (2002) at the University of Capetown in South Africa, have discovered that the eigenfaces can be combined to create novel or fictitious faces. Tredoux and others have been working on computerized systems to help victims create digital composites of their assailants. With Tredoux's system, a series of ficti-tious faces are randomly generated. Using a pointing device, the witness can select several faces that may resemble the person they saw. Under the assumption that similar faces will contain similar building blocks, the program then analyzes the selected faces for the eigenfaces they may have in common. The ID program then generates a new population of faces based on the common eigenfaces. With each new population, the fictitious faces begin to converge on the mental image the witness has in his or her head until one can be selected as most similar. A system such as Tredoux's is more useful than traditional facial composite construction programs because it deals with real mathematical properties of faces.

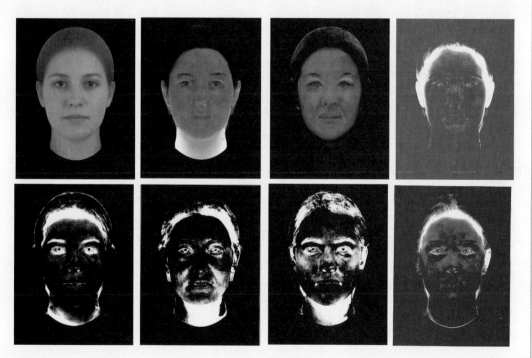

The first eight eigenfaces (computer-generated images) of a frontal image set of 278 faces.

Ten images and their reconstruction by increasing numbers of eigenfaces.

Courtesy of Colin Tredoux.

leads to recognition of the whole and subsequent recognition of the components (top-down processing).

4   Experimental work indicates that object perception is greatly influenced by contextually derived hypotheses.

5   Template matching holds that object recognition occurs when an exact match is made between sensory stimuli and a corresponding internal form. This position has conceptual and practical utility, but it is unlikely as an explanation for many complex cognitive processes, such as our ability to interpret unfamiliar shapes and forms correctly.

6   Feature analysis asserts that object recognition occurs only after stimuli have been analyzed according to their simple components. Data from neurological and behavioral experiments lend support to this hypothesis.

7   Prototype formation asserts that object perception occurs as a result of abstractions of stimuli, which are stored in memory and serve as idealized forms against which patterns are evaluated. Two models proposed by prototype theory are the central-tendency theory, which states that a prototype presents the mean or an average of a set of exemplars, and the attribute-frequency theory, which states that a prototype represents the mode or a summation of the most frequently experienced attributes.

8   Visual object recognition in humans involves visual analysis of input stimuli and long-term memory storage.

KEY TERMS

attribute-frequency theory
bottom-up processing
canonic perspective
central-tendency theory
closure
constructive perception
continuity
direct perception
exemplar
features
feature analysis
geon
Gestalt psychology

grandmother cell
illusory contours
lateral inhibition
pattern organization
pattern recognition
priming effect
prototype matching
proximity
pseudomemory
symmetry
template matching
top-down processing
unconscious inference

STARTING POINTS

Books and Articles

● Most of the readings recommended for Chapter 3 are relevant to this chapter. Other sources include Reed, *Psychological Processes in Pattern Recognition;* Humphreys (Ed.), *Understanding Vision;* Murch, *Visual and Auditory Perception;* and McBurney and Collings, *Introduction to Sensation/Perception.* Rock's book *The Logic of Perception* is an important addition to the field. Lesher's article on illusionary contours in *Psychonomic Bulletin & Review* (1995) is excellent.

Movies

● ET (1982)—Learning about new objects
● The Da Vinci Code (2006)—A symbolist sees and tracks down patterns in art

Search Terms

● Eyetricks
● Illusion Gallery
● Galaxy 200

Memory Models and Short-Term Memory

hmmm . . .?

1. **How much information can you hold in STM?**

2. **What is "chunking" of information, and how does it increase our capacity for storing knowledge?**

3. **How is information coded and retrieved from STM?**

> *G*od gave us memories that we might have roses in December.
>
> —*J.M. Barrie*

> *M*emory is the cabinet of the imagination, the treasury of reason, the registry of conscience, and the council chamber of thought.
>
> —*St. Basile*

Memory is central to most all cognitive processes. No wonder memory was prominent in the writings of early investigators—William James in America and Hermann Ebbinghaus in Germany. Memory as a research topic was neglected when American psychology became consumed with an interest in behaviorism. However, out of the behaviorist approach of the first half of the twentieth century evolved an interest in how what we learned was stored and transformed in memory. This interest in memory captivated the attention of experimental psychologists who formulated elaborate models of mental representations of how information was stored and retrieved. One of the enduring models of memory was that originally proposed by William James, although the model has undergone significant elaboration. That model maintained that memory was dichotomous in nature: some things are perceived and enter memory and then are lost, and other things stay in memory forever. The concept of short-term memory, which is the theme of this chapter, was born.

Dualist Models of Memory

James

Early interest in a dualistic model of memory began in the late 1800s when James distinguished between immediate memory, which he called **primary memory,** and indirect memory, which he called **secondary memory.** James based much of his depiction of the structure of memory on introspection, and he viewed secondary memory as the dark repository of information once experienced but no longer easily accessible.

William James **(1842–1910).** Philosopher, physician, psychologist whose dual-memory concept served as the basis of modern theories of memory. Author of *Principles of Psychology,* 1890.

According to James, primary memory, closely related but not identical to what is now called **short-term memory** (STM), never left consciousness and gave a faithful rendition of events just perceived. Secondary memory, or **long-term memory** (LTM), was conceptualized as paths, etched into the brain tissue of people but with wide individual differences. For James, memory was dualistic in character, both transitory and permanent. However, little scientific evidence was presented to distinguish operationally between the two systems. That happened about 75 years later, when the relationship between primary memory and secondary memory was described by Waugh and Norman (1965), as shown in Figure 5.1. In their early model, an item enters primary memory and then may be held there by rehearsal or may be forgotten. With rehearsal, the item enters secondary memory and becomes part of the permanent memory.

James's dualistic memory model made good sense from an introspective standpoint. It also seems valid from the standpoint of the structural and processing features of the brain. Later, evidence for two memory states would come from physiological studies.

Performance by animals in learning trials is poorer when the trials are followed immediately by electroconvulsive shock. That this is the case (while earlier learning is unaffected) suggests that transfer from primary memory to secondary memory may be interfered with (Weiskrantz, 1966). Furthermore, there is a large body of behavioral evidence—from the earliest experiments on memory to the most recent reports in the psychological literature—that supports a dualistic theory. A primacy and recency effect for paired associates was discovered by Mary Calkins, a student of William James. When a person learns a series of items and then recalls them without attempting to keep them in order, the primacy and recency effect is seen whereby items at the beginning (primacy) of the list and the end (recency) of the list are recalled best (see Figure 5.2). This effect is consistent with a dual memory concept.

While the **primacy-recency effect** is pretty robust, there is a notable exception to this called the **von Restorff effect** in which a letter in the middle of a list is novel, relative to the other list items. For example, imagine a list of 20 digits, with the letter *A* located in the middle of the list. Most if not all people will remember this middle item.

Because primacy and recency effects had been known for a long time, their incorporation into a two-process model of memory seemed a logical step. In such a model, information gathered by our sensory system is rapidly transferred to a primary memory store and is either replaced by other incoming information or held there by rehearsal. With a lot of other information coming in, as in list learning, information held in STM is bumped

F I G U R E   5 . 1

Model of primary and secondary memory systems.

Adapted from Waugh and Norman (1965).

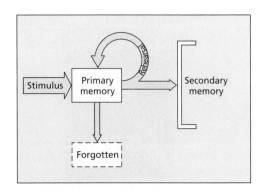

FIGURE 5.2

Free recall in a serial task.

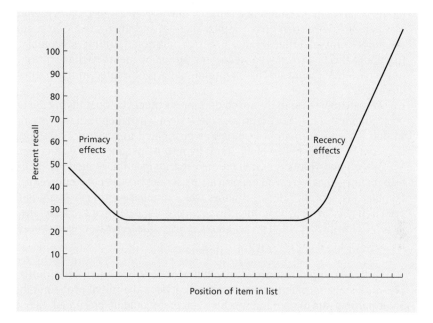

out by new information. Take, for example, how items from a list might be entered into STM. Since rehearsal is required to transfer information into LTM, the first items on the list will have more rehearsal time and a greater opportunity to be transferred. As the middle items from the list come in, they compete with each other and bump each other out. While items at the end of the list aren't rehearsed as long, they are still retained in STM at the time of recall given the recency in which they were learned.

We can trace the **storage capacity** of STM by identifying the point at which the recent curve begins to emerge. The number of items in that span is rarely larger than eight, thereby lending support to a dual memory model that includes a STM system that has limited capacity.

Mary Whiton Calkins **(1863–1930).**
Discovered the primacy-recency effect.

Waugh and Norman

The first modern behavioral model was developed by Waugh and Norman (1965). The model is **dualistic,** containing a primary memory and a secondary memory. Waugh and Norman borrowed freely from James's model and illustrated their model by means of the model shown earlier (Figure 5.2). An additional, unintended contribution was introducing the "boxes in the head" metaphor of memory that showed memory as a flow chart–like diagram. This metaphor soon proliferated in the cognitive psychology literature.

Waugh and Norman improved on James's model by quantifying the properties of primary memory. This short-term storage system was taken to have very limited capacity, so that loss of information from it was postulated to occur not as a simple function of time, but by displacement of old items by new items, once the storage limit was reached.

Waugh and Norman examined the capacity of primary memory by using lists of sixteen numbers that were read to participants at rates of either one number per second or four numbers per second. The last number was a number previously heard in the list and was used as a cue (along with a tone) that signaled the participant to recall the number immediately following the initial presentation of the probe. A typical series of numbers might be:

7 9 5 1 2 9 3 8 4 6 3 7 0 6 0 2 (tone)

In this example, the correct recall would be 9 because it follows the probe number (2). In this instance, ten items intervene between the initial probe number and the cue. Since participants did not know which number would be presented, they could not focus their attention on any one number and rehearse it. Waugh and Norman were interested in what happens to the items in STM that are not recalled. They propose that the items could fade or **decay** from memory, or that they are replaced (interfered with) by newer numbers. The purpose of presenting numbers every second or quarter second was to determine whether forgetting was a function of decay (due to time) or **interference** (by other list items). If forgetting was a function of decay, participants should remember more items in the four-second presentation, and fewer items in the one-second presentation. If it is due to interference, then there should be no difference in the number of items recalled for either presentation rate. As can be seen in Figure 5.3, the rate of forgetting for the two presentation times is similar, indicating that interference is a greater factor than decay.

Atkinson and Shiffrin

The proliferation of the boxes in the head explanation for human memory was well under way when Atkinson and Shiffrin (1968) reported their model, the framework of which was based on the notion that memory structures are fixed and control processes are variables. Atkinson and Shiffrin share the dualist concept of memory described by Waugh and Norman but postulate far more subsystems within STM and LTM. The early models of memory, according to Atkinson and Shiffrin, were too simplistic and not powerful enough to handle the complexities of attention, comparison, retrieval control, transfer from STM to LTM, imagery, coding sensory memory, and so on. In their model (Figure 5.4), mem-

FIGURE 5.3

Examining decay and interference in STM.

Adapted from Waugh and Norman (1965).

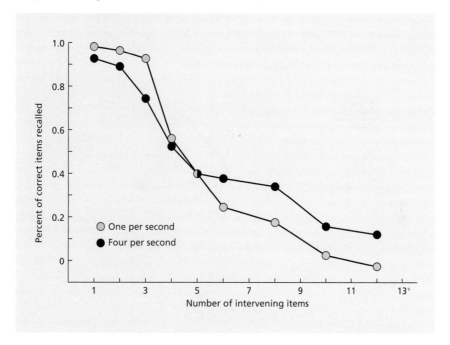

ory has three stores: (1) the sensory register, (2) the short-term store, and (3) the long-term store. A stimulus is immediately registered within the appropriate sensory dimension and is either lost or passed on for further processing.

Atkinson and Shiffrin make an important distinction between the concepts of memory and memory stores; they use the term "memory" to refer to the data being retained, while "**store**" refers to the structural component that contains the information. Simply indicating how long an item has been retained does not necessarily reveal where it is located in the structure of memory. In their model, this information in the short-term store can be transferred to the long-term store, while other information can be held for several minutes in the short-term store and never enter the long-term store. The short-term store was regarded as the working system, in which entering information decays and disappears rapidly. Information in the short-term store may be in a different form than it was originally (e.g., a word originally read by the visual system can be converted and represented auditorially). Information contained in the long-term store was envisioned as relatively permanent, even though it might be inaccessible because of interference of incoming information. The function of the long-term store was to monitor stimuli in the sensory register (and thus controlling information entering the short-term store) and to provide storage space for information in the short-term store.

FIGURE 5.4

Model of memory system with control process expanded. Solid arrows indicate paths of information transfer; dashed arrows are connections permitting comparison with information arrays as well as potential paths for signals that activate transfer, rehearsal mechanisms, and so forth. Long-term store is postulated to be permanent; short-term store, no more than 30 seconds (without rehearsal); and the sensory register, a few hundred milliseconds.

Adapted from Shiffrin and Atkinson (1969).

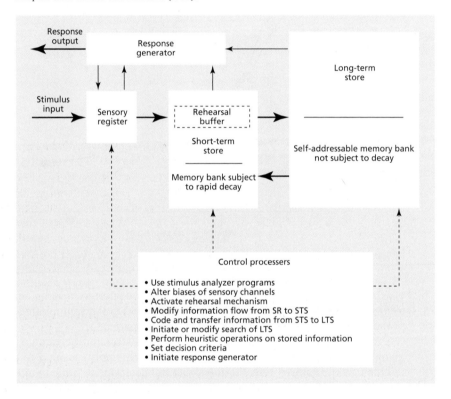

Short-Term Memory

When we think of memory, we often think of the expansive repository of information and knowledge. This aspect of our memory is commonly referred to as long-term memory (LTM). Although eclipsed in capacity, STM plays an integral role in the memory process. Additionally, its minimal storage capacity is matched by limited processing capacity, and not only that, there is a constant trade-off between storage capacity and processing capabilities. (see Table 5.1)

But just how limited is STM? How would you measure it? Lloyd Peterson and Margaret Intons-Peterson (1959; see also J. A. Brown 1958—given their near simultaneous work in this area, the resulting paradigm has been termed the **Brown-Peterson technique**) demonstrated that our capacity to store information in a temporary bank is severely limited and

TABLE 5.1

Characteristic Sensory and STM Storage Systems.

Storage Structure	Processes				Cause of Failure to Recall
	Code*	Capacity	Duration	Retrieval	
Sensory "store"	Sensory features	12–20 items[†] to huge	250 msec–4 sec	Complete, given proper cueing	Masking or decay
Short-term memory	Acoustic, visual, semantic, sensory features identified and named	7 ± 2 items	About 12 sec; longer with rehearsal	Complete, with each item being retrieved every 35 msec	Displacement, interference, decay

*How information is represented
[†]Estimated

susceptible to loss if we do not have the opportunity to rehearse the information. Their experiment represented a turning point in our experimental conceptualization of STM and, along with other seminal experiments, books, and studies, helped launch what was to become the cognitive revolution. Prior to this time the distinction between STM and LTM had been made on the bases of neurological structures (see Hebb, 1949) and psychological concepts (see James, 1890). Now, the distinction could be made using experimental data.

In the experiment done by the Petersons, participants were read a three-letter cluster such as JQD and given a three-number cluster to begin counting back from. Participants were asked to count backward to prevent them from rehearsing the letters. For example, the experimenter might say "C-H-J, 5-0-6" and then the participant would be required to count backward by 3s from 506, responding "506, 503, 500 . . ." until a certain amount of time had passed. Then the participant was asked to recall the three-letter cluster. By varying the amount of time passing, the Petersons could evaluate how long the three-letter cluster remained in STM without rehearsal. The dramatic effects of preventing rehearsal are shown in Figure 5.5, which shows that recall seriously eroded when participants were not allowed to rehearse the three-letter cluster.

As can be seen in Figure 5.5, the percent of clusters recalled declines linearly (and dramatically) as delay is increased, until it levels at about 15 seconds delay. These results suggested that if information is not rehearsed it drops out of STM. These findings implied

Lloyd Peterson and
Margaret Intons-Peterson.
Discovered the duration
of short-term memory.

FIGURE 5.5

The percent of clusters recalled when rehearsal was prevented by counting backwards.

Adapted from Peterson and Peterson (1959).

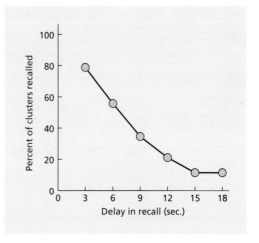

that STM existed and had characteristics quite unlike the permanent repository of information (LTM). Hundreds of subsequent experiments have given support for the Peterson study and a good picture of the characteristics of STM. In this chapter we review some of the distinguishing features of STM and how they fit into our understanding of memory processing and theories. Based on the work of the Petersons and others, supporting arguments for two memory stores can be summarized as follows:

- Casual introspection suggests that some things are remembered for a short time and others for a long time.
- Psychological experiments suggest that the retrieval of some information in memory is characteristic of a short-term function, whereas retrieval of other information is characteristic of long-term function, for example, primacy and recency data.
- Physiological studies indicate that short-term functions can be interrupted, whereas long-term function seems to remain intact, which is discussed in the next section.

Cognitive Neuroscience Support

Neurophysiological findings suggest that separate memory stores could be located structurally within the human brain. The original studies appeared about the same time as the Petersons' psychological experiment, but they dealt with clinical patients who experienced some form of physical trauma or brain lesion. The most famous case, that of H. M., was presented by Canadian researcher Brenda Milner (1966). H. M. had severe epilepsy, and following a medical workup, a bilateral surgical excision was done to relieve him of the symptoms. This procedure removed parts of the temporal lobe, including the hippocampus. Although the patient's epilepsy improved, he became profoundly amnesic and could not store new information in LTM, yet his STM was unimpaired. His memories formed before the operation were intact and he even performed well on standard IQ tests, yet he could not learn the names or recognize the faces of people he met since the operation. He could converse normally with Milner when she visited him but did not recall her previous visits. H. M.'s STM seemed intact, but his ability to form new

LTMs was lacking. But the problem was nothing could be updated in his LTM. He perpetually thought he was 27 years old and that the year was 1957 (the year of the surgery). Milner tested his recall using a series of numbers. He recalled them immediately or shortly thereafter, but could not retain the information for prolonged periods of time. Because the lesions took place in the temporal lobe and hippocampus, it is apparent that these sites contain important memory structures. Specfically, it seems that the hippocampus is an interim depository for LTM in which early experienced information is processed and then transferred to the cerebral cortex for more permanent storage. However, H. M. could learn a new skill and retain that information over time. For example, a standard skill task in a laboratory is a **mirror reversal task** (see Figure 5.6). Participants find this task difficult at first, but with practice become quite adept at drawing the figure while looking in a mirror (just like most of us become fairly proficient at shaving or applying makeup while looking in a mirror). Ironically, although H. M.'s skill improved, he had no memory

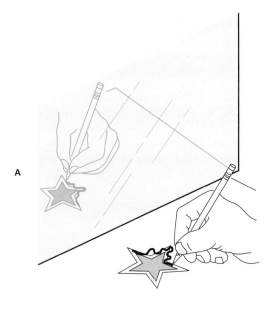

A

FIGURE 5.6

A. Mirror reversal task. The task is to trace between the star and its outline while viewing in a mirror.

B. H.M.'s skill acquisition. Data show improvement on mirror reversal task (a procedural memory) over a 3-day period.

From Blakemore (1977).

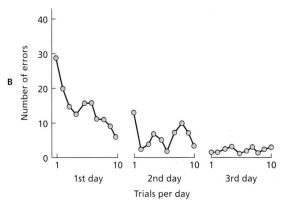

of doing the task before. This was a startling discovery that changed the way STM and LTM were conceptualized. Patients such as H. M. with temporal lobe lesions can learn implicit types of tasks that involve perceptual and motor skills, but cannot transfer other types of information to LTM.

There is also the case of K. F. studied by Warrington and Shallice (1969) whose LTM functioned properly but he had great difficulty learning a series of digits, indicating problems with his STM. This is an important finding because it demonstrates what is known as a double dissociation. Double dissociations are used to demonstrate the existence of two separate processes, in this case, STM and LTM. In H. M.'s case, we saw that the lesion affected LTM but not STM, but this is not sufficient evidence to say that STM and LTM are two separate processes. However, with the additional information from the case of K. F., who has difficulties with STM and not LTM, provides the necessary and sufficient evidence to support two separate processes. Other examples of double dissociation exist for people and unfamiliar faces (Malone et al., 1952) and rote verbal and arithmetic knowledge (Dhaene & Cohen, 1997).

Working Memory Model

The formulation of the Brown-Peterson technique of measuring the capacity of STM and the case of H. M. firmly entrenched the concept of STM as a distinct memory system. Not only was STM seen as separate from LTM based on behavioral data, but also it had a physiological basis as confirmed through neurological studies of patients with brain-damage. Still, the notion of a dualistic memory system that simply dichotomized memory into STM on one and LTM on the other, without any further refinements, was soon to be challenged by British researcher Alan Baddeley and his colleagues (Baddeley & Hitch, 1974; Baddeley, 1986, 1990a, 1990b, 1992). Baddeley proposed a working memory model that temporarily holds and manipulates information as we perform cognitive tasks.

Working memory can be conceptualized as a type of workbench in which new and old information are constantly being transformed, combined, and updated. Working memory challenges the view that STM is simply another "box" in the head—a simple processing station along the way to either being lost or sent on to LTM.

The concept of working memory also challenges the idea that the capacity of STM is limited to about seven items. Baddeley argues that the span of memory is determined by the speed with which we rehearse information. In the case of verbal material, he proposed that we have a phonological loop that contains the phonological store and articulatory process in which we can maintain as much information as we can rehearse in a fixed duration (see Figure 5.7).

Take the following example. Read the following five words and try to repeat them without looking back at them:

WIT, SUM, HARM, BAY, TOP

How did you do? Most people are very good with shorter words. Now try these:

UNIVERSITY, OPPORTUNITY, ALUMINUM, CONSTITUTIONAL, AUDITORIUM

Here, the task is much harder, and on average, only 2.6 items are recalled. The important factor, according to Baddeley, is that the longer words require more time to say. The

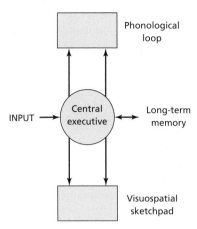

FIGURE 5.7

Diagram illustrating Baddeley & Hitch's (1974) working memory model.

gist of the idea is that we can rehearse in the **phonological loop** only a limited amount of information and one determinant is the time to vocalize the word.

The second component of working memory is the **visuospatial sketchpad** which is similar to the phonological loop but is responsible for visual and spatial tasks, which might include remembering sizes and shapes or the speed and direction of moving objects. The sketchpad is also involved in the planning of spatial movements such as exiting a burning building. The phonological loop and visuospatial sketchpad are regulated by a central executive, which coordinates attentional activities and governs responses. The **central executive** acts much like a supervisor who decides which issues deserve attention, which will be ignored, and what to do if systems go awry.

Shortly after the working memory model was introduced, researchers concentrated on finding out more about the phonological loop, the visuospatial sketchpad, and the nature of the central executive using conventional psychological measures. Lately, however, cognitive neuroscience measures have been applied to the model with considerable success. Cabeza and Nyberg (1997) have shown that the phonological loop is related to bilateral activation of the frontal and parietal lobes as measured by PET scans. And, in a study done by Haxby, Ungerleider, Horwitz, Rapoport, and Grady (1995), the visuospatial sketchpad activates different areas of the cortex. Here it was found that shorter intervals activate the occipital and right frontal lobes while longer intervals implicate areas of the parietal and left frontal lobes. Increasingly, observations made possible by brain-imaging technology are being applied to models of memory, and more and more parts of the puzzle of memory are being solved. Baddeley (2000) updated his model to include the episodic buffer. The episodic buffer is a limited capacity system that combines information from LTM and the visuospatial sketchpad and phonological loop with the central executive. The revised model acknowledges that information from the systems are integrated.

Capacity of STM

Where the Petersons explored the duration of STM, Miller in his seminal work (1956) studied the capacity of STM, concluding that STM holds about seven units. Miller cites that the earliest recorded evidence of the limited capacity of STM seems to have come from Sir

William Hamilton, a nineteenth-century philosopher, who is said to have observed: "If you throw a handful of marbles on the floor, you will find it difficult to view at once more than six, or seven at the most, without confusion." Similarly, Jacobs (1887) read aloud a sequence of numbers, in no particular order, and asked his listeners to write down immediately as many as they could recall, with seven being the average. Based on these and many other instances and observations, Miller hypothesized that our capacity to process information is limited to about seven, give or take two. Miller hypothesized that these limitations are due to some common underlying mechanisms that would later be known as STM.

STM and Chunking   That STM holds seven units regardless of the type of data involved seems paradoxical. Obviously, a string of words has greater information content than a string of letters. For example, chances are that presented the string *T, V, K, A, M, Q, B, R, J, L, E, W,* you could recall about seven letters, and presented the string *towel, music, boss, target, salad, church, money, helium, sugar, parrot, music, chicken,* you would again recall about seven items (depending on the rate of presentation). However, by inspecting the amount of information recall (at least in terms of letters), it is obvious that more information is recalled with words than with letters alone. Miller (1956) offered an explanation as to how items are coded in STM. He postulated a model of memory in which seven units or chunks of information could be held. Individual letters, counted as separate pieces of information, and, as such, each letter would fill one slot of seven available slots. When letters composed a word, however, they were chunked into one-word units, so that each of these word units also occupied only one slot in STM. Thus, the perceived increased capacity (in terms of the total number of letters) of STM was achieved through the **chunking** of letters into word units. Chunking is important because it offers an explanation of how so much information is processed through STM, without posing a bottleneck in the information processing sequence.

LTM and Chunking   The capability of STM to handle a vast amount of information, then, is facilitated by our ability to chunk information into meaningful units. However, chunking cannot occur until our LTM has provided the meaning of these units. The relationship between LTM and chunking was nicely illustrated in an experiment by Bower and Springston (1970), in which participants were read a letter sequence and asked to recall the letters. In one condition, the experimenters read the letters in three-letter chunks, that, with the help of LTM, have meaning (e.g., CSI, LOL, MTV, IBM). In another condition they read the letters in meaningless chunks (e.g., CS, ILO, LMT, VIB, M). There can be little doubt that the meaningful letter chunks were more readily recalled, illustrating the role of LTM in STM and chunking.

Coding of Information in STM

Information in STM can be auditory, visual, or semantic, depending on the type of information or the task demands placed on the person. For example, if asked, "How many siblings do you have?" one might respond, "Three" because that information is readily available in auditory form. However, if asked, "How many windows are in your apartment?" you will likely have to conjure up a mental image and do a virtual walk-through of your home before you could come up with "seven." Additionally, STM can be coded semantically, which relates to the meaning of objects.

Auditory Code STM seems to operate by means of an **auditory code,** even if the information is produced by a nonauditory code such as a visual one. For example, in our window example, while you are using a visual code to generate the information, you "count" and report the number in an auditory code. Although recent evidence suggests some overlap in codes, the predominant coding of information in STM seems to be auditory.

Support for auditory predominance comes from an often-cited early experiment by Conrad (1963). Conrad found that STM errors were made on the basis of auditory rather than visual characteristics. In Conrad's experiment he presented letters that sounded alike (e.g., B, V), and from these he created sets of six letters to be presented to the participant. Letters were presented in either an auditory or visual mode (i.e., they either hear or saw the letters). It was hypothesized that participants who heard the letters would make mistakes based on letters sounding alike. Participants who read the letters would make mistakes based on the visual structure of the letters. Overall, it was hypothesized that the associated memory is primarily acoustic and that more errors would occur with the participants who heard the letters. As can be seen in the table below, more errors in fact did occur in the auditory condition.

Auditor

Provided Letter

Response Letter	B	C	P	T	V	F	M	N	S	X
B	.	171	75	84	168	2	11	10	2	2
C	32	.	35	42	20	4	4	5	2	5
P	162	350	.	505	91	11	31	23	5	5
T	143	232	281	.	50	14	12	11	8	5
V	122	61	34	22	.	1	8	11	1	0
F	6	4	2	4	3	.	13	8	336	238
M	10	14	2	3	4	22	.	334	21	9
N	13	21	6	0	20	32	512	.	38	14
S	2	18	2	7	3	488	23	11	.	301
X	1	6	2	2	1	245	2	1	184	.

Visually

Provided Letter

Response Letter	B	C	P	T	V	F	M	N	S	X
B	.	18	62	5	83	12	9	3	2	0
C	13	.	27	18	35	15	3	12	35	7
P	102	18	.	24	40	15	8	8	7	7
T	30	46	70	.	38	18	14	14	8	10
V	56	32	30	14	.	21	15	11	11	5
F	6	8	14	5	31	.	12	13	131	16
M	12	6	8	5	20	16	.	146	15	5
N	11	7	5	1	19	28	167	.	24	5
S	7	21	11	2	9	37	4	12	.	16
X	8	7	2	2	11	30	10	11	69	.

Cognition in Everyday Life

Make That Call

*Y*ou call directory assistance to get a friend's phone number. The electronic voice gives you a telephone number, say, 969-1391. Presumably that number must be retained in STM until you can complete the call. How do you keep it alive? Chances are (if you don't write it down) that you repeat it to yourself either aloud, or subvocally (in your head) "969-1391, 969-1391," and so on. This practice is one of maintaining an auditory representation of the digits in STM. Thus, from the standpoint of common sense, we hold information in STM by auditory rehearsal. You may argue, however, that the source of the information (the electronic voice) was auditory, which biased the nature of STM storage. In fact, the same auditory rehearsal is likely to occur even if you find the number in the phone book, which is a visual stimulus. In whatever manner the information may be represented, storage in STM seems to be auditory.

Visual Code   Evidence suggests that STM may also code information by means of a **visual code.** Posner and his colleagues (Posner, 1969; Posner et al., 1969; Posner & Keele, 1967) found that, at least part of the time, information is coded visually in STM. In their experiment, letter pairs were presented that were identical in name and form (AA, aa) or same in name but different in form (Aa), or different on both counts (AB, aB). Participants were to indicate, by pressing a button, whether the two letters were the same. Letters were presented one at a time with varying time periods in between: 0 seconds (thus, letters were presented simultaneously), .5 seconds, 1 second, or 2 seconds. The researchers hypothesized that if the letter pairs were processed auditorally, it should take no longer to process AA than Aa. However, if the visual code was important, it would take longer to respond to Aa than AA. As can be seen in Figure 5.8, it takes longer to respond to letter pairs that are same in name but different in form (Aa) than it takes to respond to AA.

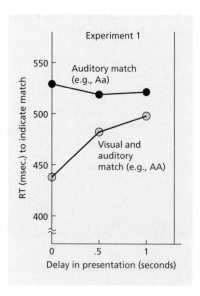

FIGURE 5.8

Posner's letter-matching experiment. A function of delay for visual and auditory matches.

Adapted from Posner et al. (1969).

However, as the delay increases, the advantage for same form pairs diminishes as the STM has the opportunity to convert the visual code into an auditory one.

In summary, information would appear to be represented in STM auditorially and visually. Consider next the possibility that semantic codes also function in STM.

Semantic Code   **Semantic codes** are those that are related to meaning. The question addressed in this section is whether semantic (hence, meaningful) information can be represented in STM. Several experiments indicate that it can. The first of these was conducted by Delos Wickens and his colleagues (Wickens, 1970, 1972; Wickens, Born, & Allen, 1963; Wickens, Clark, Hill, & Wittlinger, 1968; Wickens & Engle, 1970). Most of the experiments by Wickens and his colleagues are based on use of proactive inhibition (PI). PI is a phenomenon whereby recall of a list of words is impaired if previous memorized lists were semantically related. For example, if a participant is asked to memorize a list of related words (say, the names of fruit), they might recall about 90 percent of the list. Then, suppose they were asked to memorize a second list of fruit. Recall for the second list can be as low as 30 percent. Furthermore, if a participant is required to learn yet a third list of fruit, recall will continue to decline. This proactive inhibition indicates that semantic information is being processed in STM because it is interfering with the words on subsequent lists. So what happens when a fourth list that is semantically unrelated is memorized? Recall increases dramatically. This is referred to as release from PI.

Not only was Wickens (1973) interested in release from PI, but he was also interested in the effect of the degree of relatedness of the lists on release from PI. Wickens assigned participants to five different conditions. All five groups were required to complete three trials where they memorized lists of fruit (it could have been any semantic category: cars, dogs, etc). As can be seen in Figure 5.9, participants did worse in each subsequent trial. On the fourth trial, participants were given lists of either professions, meat products, flowers, vegetables, or another list of fruit (this was the control group). Wickens hypothesized that release from PI would be greatest with categories with the least semantic relationship to fruit; thus recall should be highest for professions and meats than for flowers and vegetables because professions and meats are the least related to fruit, and thus, the release from PI is greatest. Data from this study support his hypothesis.

George Miller. His book *Language and Communication* (1951) shaped the direction of psycholinguistics and cognitive psychology. APA president, 1969.

FIGURE 5.9

Results from typical release-from-PI experiments.

From Wickens (1973).

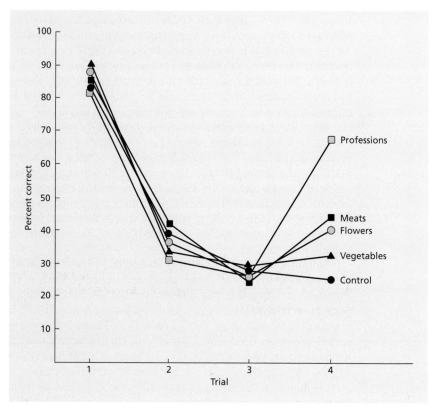

Retrieval of Information from STM

The modern era of information processing was significantly influenced by an experimental technique developed by Saul Sternberg (1966, 1967, 1969). This technique involves a serial scanning task in which the participant is shown a series of items such as numbers, each for 1.2 seconds. It is presumed that these items become stored in the participant's STM. After the participant has memorized the list, he or she pushes a button and is immediately presented with a comparison number that may or may not have been included in the initial list. The participant's task is to compare the number with the list in their memory and to indicate if it was indeed in the list. Each new trial contains a different list. The experimenter may vary the size of the list from one to six numbers, which is well within the capacity of STM. Basically this task (now called the **Sternberg task**) requires the participant to search through a list of numbers in order to make the comparison. A search such as this could be self-terminating where the participant reports (and stops searching) when he or she has encountered the number. Conversely, the participant could engage in an exhaustive search where he or she searches the entire list before reporting the presence or absence of the number. For example, with a seven-item search, if it took 10 ms to check each item, on average, it should take 400 ms to report if the item is present in the fourth position, using a self-terminating search strategy. However, if the search was exhaustive, and each number is examined before reporting, it should take on average 700 ms to provide a response. Thus, reaction time should reflect the time it takes to search through the list in memory and may serve as a basis for delineating STM structure and laws of retrieval of information from the structure. The longer the list, the greater the reaction time because more information in STM requires more time to access. Two other findings, however, are surprising. One is that the reaction times changed uniformly according to the number of items in the list (see Figure 5.10). Each additional item in the list increase the reaction time in the exact same increment. The second surprise has a far-reaching impact on views of how we retrieve information from STM. Reaction time to identify a number were nearly identical to reaction times to indicate that the item was not there. Keep in mind that an exhaustive search must be conducted if the number is not there. Therefore, that the reaction times were identical for present and absent numbers indicates that an exhaustive search was conducted even when the item was present (even when early in the list).

FIGURE 5.10

Sternberg Task. Reaction time as a function of number of items in the list. Reaction time increases linearly for each additional list item. Reaction time for item-present and item-absent lists are similar, suggesting an exhaustive search.

Adapted from Sternberg (1969).

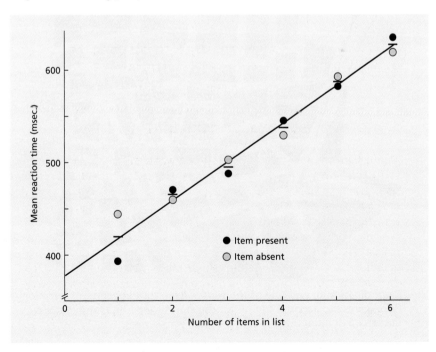

A la carte

Working Memory in Navigation

The ability to navigate through our world is an important skill with obvious adaptive benefits. Even in today's modern society navigation is so important that automobiles are armed with global position systems telling us to turn left at the next intersection. Yet how do we remember how to get from Point A to Point B without the GPS prosthetic? Researchers from Scotland and Italy (Garden, Cornoldi, & Logie, 2002) investigated the role of working memory in our ability to navigate. The working memory model includes a visual-spatial component as well as an auditory-verbal component. So they could determine which component, if any, was relied on for navigation, the researchers had participants engage in a word task, a spatial-tapping task, or mixed task combining both words and spatial tapping while learning a route through Venice based on a map (see figure). Participants were tested on their ability to learn the route by showing them segments of the map and then asked to identify which segment was correct. The suprising results of the study indicate that suppressing the verbal articulatory loop caused the participants to make more errors than the spatial demand task, indicating that verbal codes are used during encoding of maps. The researchers next had participants learn a map by actually walking through the streets rather than looking at the map with similar results, although the walk-though was found to demand a greater overall amount of cognitive resources.

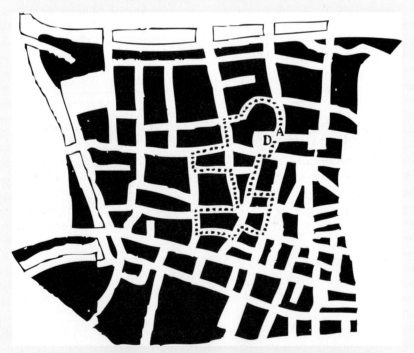

Example of map and one of the routes used for experiment. Location D indicates the departure point for the start of the route, and location A the arrival point at the end of the route.

Cognition in Everyday Life

Attention and Memory

"You'll never learn anything if you don't pay attention!" admonished many a third-grade teacher—more than once. While it is possible to learn things without conscious attention, a phenomenon called incidental learning, it is true that learning and memory are enhanced if we pay attention.

In everyday life, we are constantly being bombarded with stimuli, usually in the form of advertising and news headlines, that demand our attention and frequently create a need in us to buy. It is almost as if advertisers and newspaper editors equate attention with memory and, in order to attract our attention, present outlandish, paradoxical, or incongruous themes. Take a few minutes each day for a week to record these provocative events. Consider some of the issues raised in the previous chapter regarding attention and its influence on memory.

Similar results have been observed over a wide range of stimuli, including letters, words, colors, faces, and phonemes, with the slope of the reaction time function sometimes more steep or less steep, but the relationship between present and absent items remaining the same.

Student Resource Center

STUDY GUIDE

1 Memory can be categorized as STM and LTM and working memory. Each has distinctive features.

2 Short-term memory capacity is limited to about seven items, but the density or amount of information per item can be increased by chunking (e.g., regrouping letters into words).

3 Patients with lesions to the temporal lobe of the hippocampus show that these structures are involved in the storage of long-term memories.

4 Chunking procedures in short-term memory require accessing information from long-term memory.

5 Coding of information in short-term memory involves at least visual, acoustic, and semantic codes. Evidence suggests visual coding occurs before acoustic and semantic coding.

6 High-speed short-term memory retrieval appears to operate by means of an exhaustive rather than a self-terminating process.

7 Memories seem to be stored locally and generally.

KEY TERMS

auditory code
Brown-Peterson technique
central executive
chunking
decay
dualistic
interference
long term memory
mirror reversal task
phonological loop
primacy-recency effect

primary memory
secondary memory
semanitc code
short term memory
storage capacity
store
Sternberg task
visual code
visuospatial scratchpad
von Restorff effect
working memory

STARTING POINTS

Books and Articles

● Among the most readable books that contain lively discussions of STM are Klatzky, *Human Memory: Structures and Processes;* Baddeley, *The Psychology of Memory;* Lindsay and Norman, *Human Information Processing;* and Norman, *Memory and Attention* (1st or 2nd ed.).

● On a more advanced level are Tulving's chapter "Episodic and Semantic Memory" in his *Organization of Memory: Quo Vadis?* and Kennedy and Wilkes, eds., *Studies in Long Term Memory.*

● Neisser's *Memory Observed* and Tulving's *Elements of Episodic Memory* are also recommended highly. Klatzky's book *Memory and Awareness* is a highly readable account of memory research from an information processing perspective. *Practical Aspects of Memory,* by Gruneberg, Morris, and Sykes, has some interesting chapters. Cohen has written a fascinating memory book called *Memory in the Real World,* which is recommended.

● See also *Memory & Cognition,* Vol. 21, 1993, which is largely devoted to the topic of short-term memory.

Movies

● Memento (2000)—A man with short-term memory problems

● Finding Nemo (2003)—A fish with short-term memory problems

Search Terms

● The World Memory Championships

Memory Theories and Long-Term Memory

hmmm . . .?

1. What is procedural memory? declarative memory?

2. What is meant by *level of recall, levels of processing,* and *self reference effect?*

3. What is episodic and semantic memory?

Except for the innate reflexes we are born with, everything we know about us and our world is in our long-term memory. Our ability to deal with the tiny slice of sensory events that constitutes the present in the ongoing continuum of time seems to be the main function of our transitory STM, while our ability to experience the past and to use that information to process the present is the function of our LTM. In one sense, our LTM allows us to live in two worlds simultaneously (the past and the present) and, by doing so, allows us to understand the continuous flood of immediate experience. LTM must be pulled into STM where it's incorporated and used to understand the ongoing stream of information of the moment.

LTM's most distinguishing feature is its diversity—of codes, abstraction of information, structure, capacity and permanence. The capacity of LTM seems limitless, and its duration, virtually endless. To understand this, we consider first the neurological aspects of LTM, its capacity and duration, how information is stored, and types of memory.

Localization and Distribution of LTM

For centuries scientists have known that the brain is involved in memory; without a brain we would be senseless, mindless, and well . . . without memory. The tricky part is to determine where memories reside in the brain, and how information in LTM is stored in the brain. If you learn a second language, where is that stored? Are the lyrics to your favorite song stored with the tune?

The current studies into the cognitive neuroscience of memory are straightforward in content. They involve the plotting of functions on the topography of the brain, the routing of memory traces, and the identification of the neural changes in the brain associated with memory formation and change. Many of the techniques used in these studies have been discussed earlier and, in general, include the use of brain imaging technology (e.g., PET scans, MRI, and EEG recordings), electrical probes of the brain (e.g., use of minute electrical stimulation for the prompting of memories), the use of chemicals and drugs that affect neurotransmission at the synapse (e.g., the use of pharmaceutical agents in the treatment or study of memory enhancement or reduction), and the study of pathological types presenting unusual memory deficits.

The location of memories is throughout the brain, as well as in particular locations. For example, PET studies show that the frontal area of the brain is involved in deep processing of information, such as determining whether a word describes a living or nonliving thing (see the work of Kapur, Craik, et al., 1994; Kapur, Scholey, et al., 1994; Tulving, Kapur, Craik, Moscovitch, & Houle, 1994), which would suggest that that type of memory operation is highly specialized. However, other regions of the brain are also involved, only to a lesser degree. This principle of specialization and distribution applies to other types of memory operations and storage systems (see Zola-Morgan & Squire, 1990).

Some brain regions are essential in the formation of memories. These regions include the hippocampus and the adjacent cortex and thalamus, as indicated through the study of clinical patients who suffer damage in these areas. However, the hippocampus itself does not provide permanent long-term storage of memories; if it did, then H. M. would not have had access to his memories prior to the surgery. Many permanent long-term memories are stored and processed in the cerebral cortex. It is well established that sensory information is passed along to specific brain regions. Information from the eyes and ears, for example, is passed to the visual cortex and auditory cortex, respectively. It is likely that long-term memories for these types of sensory experiences are also stored in or near these areas. However, and this is one of the many complex issues in brain science, sensory experiences are multifarious. When you read the words in the previous sentence, the information from your eyes is processed in the visual cortex, but when you consider the meaning of the word "multifarious," you use other parts of your brain to subvocalize the word, and another part of your brain to Google it.

In summary, although models of memory represent memory as a box, in reality, it's really not like that at all. It's spread throughout the brain; it's an active process that involves many areas of the brain, with some areas being more specialized than others.

Capacity of LTM

It is hard to imagine the capacity and duration of information contained in LTM, but we can make some reasonable estimates of these characteristics. Even the most obscure information is readily available to us. For example, you can remember and "see" the place you first tried sushi, your phone number, the strategy for how to win your latest Xbox games, where you parked your car, and the name of your first pet, and yet many of these events were not in your conscious awareness until they were brought up. Even in an era when the information capacity of computers is vast, the capacity of the human brain for storing detailed information over long periods (and in so small a space) remains unequaled.

A remarkable demonstration of the ability to recognize pictures over a very long time was provided by Shepard (1967). From a large number of highly memorable pictures (e.g., advertisements in magazines), he selected 612. The pictures were projected one at a time onto a screen at a rate set by the participant. After the participant viewed the 612 pictures, a recognition test was given in which 68 of the 612 were shown paired with one new picture each. The participants were to indicate which of each pair was the picture they had previously viewed. The immediate recognition task yielded a very high percentage of "hits," 96.7 percent. Two hours later, in the part of the experiment particularly germane to our discussion of very long-term memory, the participants were again asked to judge another set of old/new picture pairs of photographs. This time, 99.7 percent of the pictures that had already been seen were recognized. Participants were able to recognize the already viewed pictures very well, even after a week. Participants were subsequently given recognition memory tasks of the sort after 3 days, 7 days, and 120 days. Further support for the capacity of LTM has been found by Standing, Conezio, and Haber (1970). They presented 2,560 color slides to participants and found that recognition ranged from 97 percent to about 63 percent over a year. Somewhat more interesting is the decline in recognition scores after 4 months. Did memory for the picture surface, or did other images intervene and confuse the participants? The data gathered after 3 days and

7 days would suggest that the memory for pictures was encoded in the participants' LTM and that the decline of recognition memory after 4 months would appear to be a function of intervening images. Others have demonstrated the capacity of LTM using 10,000 pictures (Nickerson, 1965, 1968; Standing, 1973).

Cognition in Everyday Life

Making Modular Memories

The brain's real estate keeps getting subdivided. Neuroscientists have been busy for the past three decades parceling up the visual cortex, where the brain starts to process signals coming in from the eyes, into ever-smaller, specialized plots. Some of these areas respond to color, some to shape, and some to movement. But when we think about objects, we recall all of these qualities, so it seemed logical for scientists to assume that, higher up in the brain, this disparate information gets spliced together in areas where memories are formed and cognition takes place. But now a team from Yale University has shown that similar subdivisions exist even in the prefrontal cortex, which is involved in forming temporary, working memories. Some areas chiefly respond to "what" an object was, while others respond to "where" it was located.

"Memory is modular; it's not all in one device," says neuroscientist Patricia Goldman-Rakic, one of the researchers. "This is the first physiological evidence separating out those modules." She and her colleagues Fraser A. Wilson and Séamas P.Ó. Scalaidhe report that neurons in two regions in monkeys' prefrontal cortex respond to different visual cues. Neurons in an area known as the inferior convexity (IC) retain information about an object's color and shape for a short period after the object has disappeared from view. Neurons in an adjacent area encode an object's location.

"This is really right on the forefront" of memory research, says Jon Kaas, a neuroscientist at Vanderbilt University in Nashville, Tennessee. Kaas notes that these results are the first good functional evidence showing that separate perceptual pathways continue into the prefrontal cortex. And if further studies reveal working memory centers tied to the other senses, Kaas believes it would suggest that memories are divided up by their qualities much like image qualities—motion and shape, for example—are divided up in other cortical regions. "But that is a big if," he says.

Finding that working memory is specialized in at least two ways, say other scientists, shows that such memories appear to form in a parallel fashion, and that there's no central memory manager putting everything together. "The assumption in the past has sort of been that there will be a next level [of processing] that will reintegrate everything," says John Allman, a neurophysiologist at the California Institute of Technology. "But there just isn't much evidence for that."

Memory maps. Areas in the prefrontal cortex seem to recall different aspects of an image.

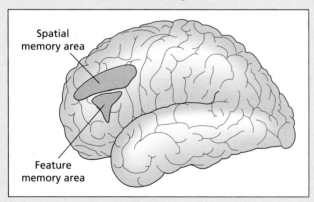

Spatial memory area

Feature memory area

Reprinted with permission from "Making Modular Memories," Science, 260:1876. *Copyright* © 1993 AAAS.

Theoretical Analysis of Expertise

Chase and Ericsson (1982) have explained extraordinary memory operations in terms of three principles that account for skilled memory and how experts exploit their LTM to perform unusual tasks.

1. The **mnemonic encoding principle** (organization) asserts that experts encode information in terms of a large existing knowledge base. Is his STM capacity larger? It is doubtful. More likely, he is using existing knowledge to chunk new information.

2. The **retrieval structure principle** (access) states that experts use their knowledge of a subject (e.g., typing, chess, baseball, selection of stocks) to develop abstract, highly specialized mechanisms for systematically encoding and retrieving meaningful patterns from LTM. This ability allows experts to anticipate the informational needs of a familiar task and to store new information in a format that will facilitate its retrieval.

3. The **speed-up principle** (speed) states that practice increases the speed with which experts recognize and encode patterns. In addition, experts are also able to retrieve information from LTM more quickly than novices. If LTM storage and retrieval are facilitated with extensive practice, then the extent to which new information can be processed is seemingly unlimited.

One ingredient almost overlooked in our discussion of experts is practice, the theme of a detailed analysis by Ericsson, Krampe, and Tesch-Römer (1993). It would seem that underlying the development of experts are hours and hours of dedicated practice. The adage "practice makes perfect," although too simplistic to qualify as a scientific principle is nevertheless of great significance in the nurturing of skill and expertise.[1] Although simple, mindless, brute practice seems counterproductive but distributed, "intelligent" practice is positively related to expertise.

Duration of LTM

Permastore—Very Long-Term Memory   Some interesting data have been gathered on the fate of **very long-term memories** (VLTM). An important study that talks about the duration of LTM was conducted by Bahrick, Bahrick, and Wittlinger (1975). In their ambitious effort to trace the longevity of memory, they tested 392 high school graduates for memory of names and photos of classmates selected from old yearbooks. In this cross-sectional study, nine retention intervals were tested, ranging in length from 3.3 months to almost 48 years. In this study, participants were first asked to recall the names of all the members of their graduating class. Next, a picture recognition task was given in which photographs from the participants' yearbooks were randomly presented for an

---

[1]Several years ago the late Bill Chase gave a talk on experts in which he promised to tell the audience what it would take to become a grand master chess player. His answer: "Practice." After the talk, the first author asked Chase how much practice. "Did I forget to say how much?" he asked quizzically. "Ten thousand hours."

identification task. A third task was to recognize names of their classmates from a list. The fourth and fifth tasks were to match pictures with the names, and names with pictures, respectively. Finally, a picture-cueing task was given in which the participant was to recall the name of one classmate from his or her picture. It is noteworthy that the recognition level for the faces of former classmates was astonishingly high (about 90 percent over 34 years), while name recognition and name matching declined after 15 years. The sharp decline in recognition and recall data after about 35 years of stability may reflect some degenerative process in memory due to the age of the participant. The ability to match names with faces and picture recognition remains the same over a very long period, about 90 percent from 3.3 months to 34 years (see Figure 6.1). The data gathered by Bahrick and his colleagues confirm the notion that VLTM does indeed exist, and last for a very long time and

FIGURE 6.1

VLTM for faces and names.

Adapted from Bahrick, Bahrick, and Wittlinger (1975).

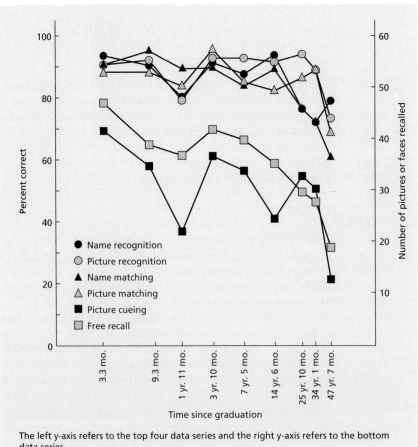

The left y-axis refers to the top four data series and the right y-axis refers to the bottom data series.

the stability of recognition memory over such a long time is surprising. The results suggest that recognition memory for distant events affect by the degree of initial encoding and the distribution of rehearsal. To address these issues of encoding and rehearsal, Bahrick et al. had participants fill out a questionnaire regarding how well they knew each person and their own level of participation in high school, as well as after high school to assess behaviors such as reviewing their yearbook and attending reunions.

VLTM for Spanish—Evidence for Permastore?   In another study done by Bahrick (1984; Bahrick & Phelps, 1987), memory for Spanish over a span of fifty years was examined. Students (N = 733) who had learned Spanish in high school participated in this study. Spanish tests of reading comprehension and recall and recognition tests for vocabulary, grammar, and idioms were given. In general, Bahrick found that the more thoroughly Spanish had been initially learned, the better the performance on the subsequent test (see Figure 6.2). However, the degree of VLTM is, if not surprising, gratifying to all who plan to live a long life. Knowledge of Spanish, in general, declined most sharply during the first three years and then reached a stable state, for about another thirty years. Some drop-off of knowledge, especially reading comprehension, was noted after about twenty-five years. However, much of the originally learned Spanish was still usable after fifty years. This "permanent" memory is referred to by Bahrick as permastore, and it would seem that memory for Spanish, and presumably other foreign languages, remains reasonably viable for a very long time.

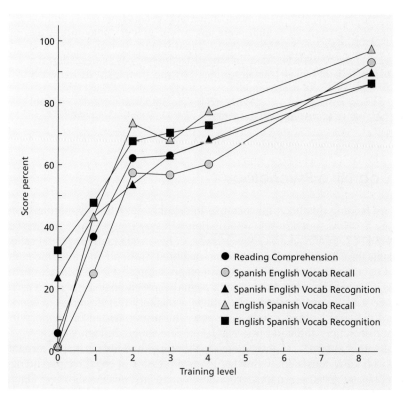

FIGURE 6.2

Recall of Spanish as a function of amount of training.

Adapted from Figure 2, "Semantic memory content in permastore: Fifty years of memory for Spanish leaned in school," by Bahrick, Harry P., *Journal of Experimental Psychology: General*, 113(1), March 18, 1984, 1–29. Reprinted by permission.

Try This

VLTM

Throughout our lifetime we gather countless impressions of our world and carefully store many as treasured memories. Elderly people seem to have an especially rich store of preserved impressions, and like discovering a flower pressed between the pages of a cherished book, once-vivid impressions can be recovered from the pages of memory. In talking with elderly people, it is almost as if they draw a book from memory, open it, and begin to recount its contents; then they turn to another section, tell of its contents, and, finally, carefully return the book to its original place so that it can be found again. Take a moment to call a grandparent and ask him or her to tell you about his or her childhood. Jot down the memories.

One of us once asked members of a cognitive psychology class to visit with elderly neighbors or relatives to record some very long-term memories. The following is a brief sample of one of the papers:

"I was born in 1885. . . . My mother died when I was 8 years old so I lived back and forth with relatives and went sometimes to school in the city of Kahoka, Mo., which consisted of about 5 rooms and sometimes to the country school named Star, which was only 1 room where more than one

grade was taught. Star School had windows all around looking out on the trees, a blackboard at the front and a little porch and cloakroom where you entered. . . . For entertainment we had the county fair, exhibiting all the local products. There were rides such as the Ferris wheel and merry-go-round, and pony rides. They sold ice cream cones and had lemonade stands. These items sold for 5 cents each. . . . I remember my Uncle John taking me to these events as well as one time when he took me to a show which featured hypnosis. . . . When we were sick they would give us a spoonful of Ayres sarsaparilla, a patent medicine bought at the drug store. . . . I hope this information will help you with your school project, and that you'll come and see me soon. Your Great-grandmother Menke." (Thanks to Scott Menke. May 24, 1987)

Notice that Great-grandmother Menke recounted "important" events from her childhood that were important to her: pony rides, ice cream cones, and lemonade stands. She also had a strong visual memory as evidenced by her accurate recall of the floor plan of her early school.

What were the important events in your grandparents' life? What will yours be?

VLTM and Cognitive Psychology

Assuming you are reading this book for a course in cognitive psychology, perhaps you have asked yourself, "How much of this information will stay in my LTM?" An answer to that question can be found in an article by Conway, Cohen, and Stanhope (1991) called "On the Very Long-Term Retention of Knowledge Acquired Through Formal Education: Twelve Years of Cognitive Psychology." The experimenters sampled a large number of students (N = 373) who had completed a course in cognitive psychology as long ago as 12 years. The former students were asked to complete a memory test designed to assess their retention of material learned a long time ago. The test consisted of memory for proper names of researchers and concepts. The results are shown in Figure 6.3.

Retention of names showed a slightly more rapid decline than the recall and recognition of concepts, a finding consistent with what many professors of cognitive psychology (and we suspect other subjects) see in much shorter retention intervals. As shown in Figure 6.3A, the recognition of both names and concepts follows the same trend. In Figure 6.3B

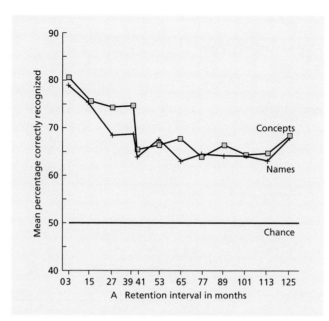

FIGURE 6.3

A. Mean percentages of correctly recognized names and concepts across retention intervals.

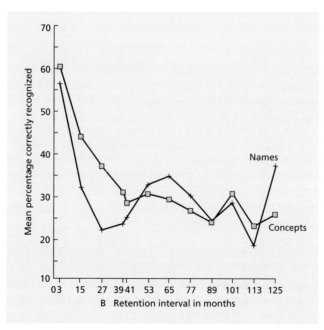

B. Mean percentages of correctly recalled names and concepts across retention intervals.

From the *Journal of Experimental Psychology: General, 120,* 395–409. Copyright © 1991 by the American Psychological Association. Reprinted with permission.

we see a much sharper initial decline in the recall of names and concepts. An interesting, if not altogether expected, finding was a high relationship between grades and VLTM scores. It pays to study or, an alternative hypothesis, it pays to have a good memory.

These data are consistent with the landmark experiments of Bahrick and his colleagues in the sense that VLTM for information, be it old class chums or STM/LTM

Results of Shepard's recognition test.

Adapted from Shepard (1967).

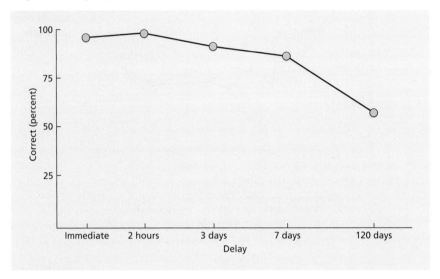

dichotomy, declines rapidly at first and then levels off and remains at a sustained level, above chance, for many years. The finding that concepts are retained longer than names needs some interpretation. It is likely that new names, which the student is (presumably) poorly motivated to commit to LTM (what value is it to know, in the long run, that Bahrick, Bahrick, and Wittlinger collected important data on VLTM?), would be variously associated with other memories of the principle of VLTM, namely, that people tend to forget rapidly at first and then not much. Ebbinghaus, a name (like his nonsense syllables) likely to be forgotten, continues to be right. Finally, one has to suspect that the emphasis placed on names versus concepts by individual professors, and perhaps even the emphasis placed on these things in the text used, might influence the results, although we hasten to add that the results are entirely consistent with previous studies of VLTM and support the main conclusions found by others.

Memory for Pictures A remarkable demonstration of the ability to recognize pictures over a very long time was given by Shepard (1967). From a large number of highly memorable pictures (for example, advertisements in magazines), he selected 612. The pictures were projected one at a time onto a screen at a rate set by the participant. After the participant viewed the 612 individual pictures, a recognition test was given in which 68 of the 612 were shown paired with one new picture each. The participants were to indicate which of each pair was the picture they had previously viewed. The immediate-recognition task yielded a very high percentage of "hits," 96.7 percent. Two hours later, in the part of the experiment particularly germane to our discussion of VLTM, the participants were again asked to judge another set of old/new pairs of photographs. This time 99.7 percent of the pictures that had already been seen were recognized. Participants were subsequently given recognition memory tasks of the same sort after 3 days, 7 days, and 120 days. As can be seen in Figure 6.4, participants were able to recognize the already viewed pictures very well, even after a week. Similar results have been reported by Nickerson (1965, 1968) and Standing (1973) using 10,000 pictures. Standing, Conezio, and Haber (1970) presented 2,560 color slides to participants and found that recognition ranged from 97 percent to about 63 percent over a year. Somewhat more interesting is the decline in recognition scores after about 4 months. Did memory for the picture fade, or did other images intervene and confuse the participants? The data gathered after 3 days and 7 days would suggest that the memory for pictures was encoded in the participants' LTM and that the decline of recognition memory after 4 months would appear to be a function of the intervention of confusing images. In the next section we consider the effects of loss of information or the inability to recall information from memory.

Autobiographical Memories

Autobiographical memories are memories of an individual's past history. Although personal memories have always been a topic of interest among nonspecialists, they also have been the subject of several interesting psychological studies. One reason these types of memories are interesting is that they are about the individual and his or her unique history. The person—you, your friend, or anyone—is the focus of autobiographical memories. The individual is the expert, since no one knows his or her life better. These memories also can tell us quite a lot about an individual's personality and concept of self.

The contents of personal memory do not comprise an even collection of sensory impressions. Our LTM does not record information unintelligently, but rather it is highly selective in choosing its contents. We remember close relatives, the look of our first car, the first time we had sex, school colors, the name of our hometown, heroes, bullies, and villains, a few cute things our children did, the floor plan of our home, and mother's good china. Contrary to our best intentions, we do not "remember this night forever," or "never forget you," or "think about you every day." We forget a lot of things, and sometimes those things that are very dear to us at the moment fade rapidly. Others remain forever. The contents of one's personal memory are not unlike the contents of one's attic—more a selective collection of important and odd memories than an indiscriminate stowing of all sensory impressions in our cerebral warehouse.

Autobiographical memories, if not perfect, are generally quite good. Objective data on this topic are hard to come by (after all, who can contest a personal memory?), but some researchers (e.g., Field, 1981) have interviewed various members of the same family, the "facts" of whose personal history could be validated by other members of the family. Such recollections as "I'm sure I had tonsillitis on July 3, as it was just before the Fourth of July and I had to miss the parade on Main Street" can be verified by checking with other family members and consulting medical records. Validating studies show a correlation of about +0.88 between family members when asked factual questions. A much lower correlation of about +0.43 is reported for emotions and attitudes (Field, 1981). Of course, we all know families in which the correlation between family members' attitudes is negative. Fortunately, some enterprising psychologists have undertaken the herculean task of keeping a record of their daily activities and then sampling their memories of these activities. One of these studies by Linton (1982; see also Wagenaar, 1986) concentrated on the recollection of episodic experiences over a 6-year period. Each day she wrote on cards a brief description of at least two events that happened on that day. Every month she selected two cards at random; she then tried to recall the events written on the cards and fix the date of the

FIGURE 6.5

Percent of items forgotten during six years.

From Linton (1982).

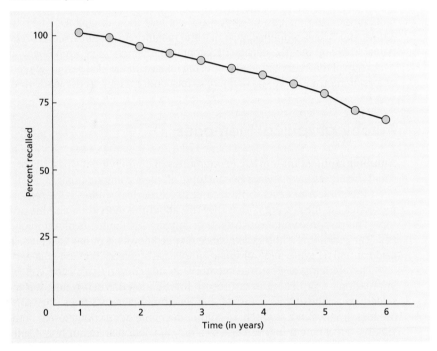

events. She also rated the memory for its saliency, or importance, and for emotionality, both at the time of recall and at the time of writing the card. Linton's results (see Figure 6.5) contained a few surprises. The rate of forgetting was linear, not curvilinear, as many forgetting curves from the time of Ebbinghaus onward have been. From this, we can infer the significant conclusion that memory for everyday, episodic events over a long period of time becomes gradually less available and that the ability to retrieve these items deteriorates at a steady rate. Linton noted two types of forgetting. One was associated with events repeated over time, such as attending committee meetings. In memory, meetings merged with other meetings. A second type of forgetting was associated with events that she simply forgot. One surprise was the failure to find a strong relationship between the rated importance and emotionality of memory and its recallability. This finding is contrary to "common knowledge" and some other studies, but it is consistent with the "I'll never forget this night" pledge and the subsequent inability to recall the night.

LTM Storage

One explanation of how long-term memories are formed and ultimately stored is based on the early pioneering work done by Donald Hebb. The simplified version of his notion of LTM is that information in STM is converted to LTM if it is rehearsed in STM long enough. This is because in STM a reverberating circuit of neural activity takes place in the brain, with a self-exciting loop of neurons. If the circuit remains active for a period, then some chemical and/or structural change occurs and the memory is permanently stored in LTM. If information is combined with other, existing meaningful memories, then memorability is enhanced.

Some experiences are remembered better than others. Exciting, ego-involving, or even traumatic experiences seem to stick in memory better than complicated lectures, for example. Research on animals suggests a role of increased glucose levels in the formation of memories. Furthermore, when an exciting event occurs, the adrenal medulla increases secretion of epinephrine (adrenaline) into the bloodstream, which is known to enhance the consolidation of memory (McGaugh, 1990). It is likely that epinephrine does not directly stimulate the brain's synapses, but rather converts stored glycogen to glucose, thereby raising the glucose level in the blood, which nourishes the brain. Some experimental research supports the notion that directly injecting glucose after learning enhances future memory of the event (Gold, 1987; Hall & Gold, 1990).

Codes

In LTM, information is coded acoustically, visually, and semantically. These three types of **codes** in LTM can be readily illustrated. Many of us have experienced a **tip of the tongue** (TOT) state (Brown, 1991, Schwartz, 1999), where you can remember some aspects of the item you are trying to recall but not all. In a TOT state, attributes of the item trying to be recalled are accessible, but the names of the items remains out of reach. For example, we were on a road trip in California, and as a tangent to the conversation we were having, we ended up trying to remember the name of a particular type of diet soda. It was not readily retrievable, and soon became the focal point of the conversation. The TOT state was very strong. Rather than recalling the name of the soda, we remembered that it was a short name, with a strong consonant sound at the end, in a pink can, that it wasn't readily available anymore, and that it was known for its saccharine taste. One of us remembered that we first tried it at the beach one summer in Oregon, and that it was for years her cousin's favorite drink. This TOT state completely supplanted the original conversation and was a source of distraction for several hours, until finally, seemingly out of the blue, the word Tab came to mind, rushed out of the mouth, and brought relief (and an end) to the search process.

Level of Processing

As we've already stated, meaningful things get stored, but in advance, how does the brain know that something is meaningful? It may use a heuristic of amount of effort and time. Perhaps the brain takes cues from other parts of the cognitive system. For example, the more energy we put into processing may be a cue to its importance and meaningfulness. Research on level of processing incorporates the ideas that the brain is using cues to discern the meaningfulness of information before it determines how it should be processed.

Craik and Lockhart's (1972) research on **level of processing** incorporates the general idea that incoming stimuli are subjected to a series of analyses starting with shallow sensory analysis and proceeding to deeper, more complex, abstract, and semantic analyses. Whether a stimulus is processed at a shallow or deep stage depends on the nature of the stimulus and the time available for processing. An item processed at a deep level is less likely to be forgotten than one processed at a shallow level. At the earliest level, incoming stimuli are subjected to sensory and featural analyses; at a deeper level, the item may be recognized by means of pattern recognition and extraction of meaning; at a still deeper level, it may engage the person's long-term associations. With deeper processing a greater degree of semantic or cognitive analysis is undertaken. Consider word recognition, for example. At the preliminary stages, the visual configuration may be analyzed according to such physical or sensory features as lines and angles. Later stages are concerned with matching the stimuli with stored information— for example, recognition that one of the letters corresponds to the pattern identified as *A*. At the highest level, the recognized pattern "may trigger associations, images or stories on the basis of the subject's past experience with the word" (Craik & Lockhart, 1972, p. 675).

The significant issue, in Craik and Lockhart's view, is that we are capable of perceiving at meaningful levels *before* we analyze information at a more primitive level. Thus, levels of processing are more a "spread" of processing, with highly familiar, meaningful stimuli more likely to be processed at a deeper level than less meaningful stimuli.

That we can perceive at a deeper level before analyzing at a shallow level casts grave doubts on the original levels-of-processing formulation. Perhaps we are dealing simply with different types of processing, with the types not following any constant sequence. If all types are equally accessible to the incoming stimulus, then the notion of levels could be replaced by a system that drops the notion of levels or depth but retains some of Craik and Lockhart's ideas about rehearsal and about the formation of memory traces. A model that is closer to their original idea but that avoids the box notion is shown in Figure 6.6. This figure depicts the memory activation involved in proofreading a passage as contrasted with that involved in reading the same passage for the gist of the material. Proofreading, that is, looking at the surface of the passage, involves elaborate shallow processing and minimal semantic processing. Reading for gist, that is, trying to get the essential points, involves minimal shallow processing, or "maintenance rehearsal" (held in memory without elaboration), but elaborate semantic processing. As a result of some studies (Craik & Watkins, 1973; Lockhart, Craik, & Jacoby, 1975), the idea that stimuli are always processed through an unvarying sequence of stages was abandoned, while the general principle that some sensory processing must precede semantic analysis was retained.

Level of Processing versus Information Processing   Information processing models of memory have generally stressed structural components (e.g., sensory store, STM, and LTM) dealing with processing (e.g., attention, coding, rehearsal, transformation of information, and forgetting) as operations that are tied (sometimes uniquely) to

Fergus Craik. Challenged traditional ideas of memory with the concept of levels of processing.

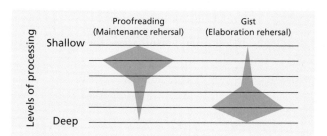

FIGURE 6.6

Memory activation in two kinds of reading.

Figure based on drawing kindly supplied by F. I. M. Craik.

the structural components. However, another approach is to postulate process and then to formulate a memory system in terms of these operations. Craik and Lockhart have taken just such a position, and their implicit criticism of the information-processing model (along with Neisser, 1976) suggests that it is falling on hard times.

Where information-processing models of memory stress the sequence of stages through which information is moved and processed, this alternate viewpoint argues that memory traces are formed as a by-product of perceptual processing. Thus, the durability of memory is conceptualized as a function of the depth of processing. Information that is not given full attention and is analyzed only to a shallow level is soon forgotten; information that is deeply processed—attended to, fully analyzed, and enriched by associations or images—is long lasting. The levels-of-processing model is not free of criticism (see Baddeley, 1978, Craik & Tulving, 1975). The criticism includes that (1) it seems to say little more than that meaningful events are well remembered, a mundane conclusion; (2) it is vague and generally untestable; and (3) it is circular in that any events that are well remembered are designated "deeply processed," with no objective and independent index of depth available.

One clear difference between the boxes-in-the-head theory (Waugh and Norman, and Atkinson and Shiffrin) and the levels-of-processing theory (Craik and Lockhart) is their respective notions concerning rehearsal. In the former, rehearsal, or repetition, of information in STM serves the function of transferring it to a longer-lasting memory store; in the latter, rehearsal is conceptualized as either maintaining information at one level of analysis or elaborating information by processing it to a deeper level. The first type, maintenance rehearsal, will not lead to better retention.

Craik and Tulving (1975) tested the idea that words that are deeply processed should be recalled better than those that are less so. They did this by having participants simply rate words as to their structural, phonemic, or semantic aspects. Typical of questions used are the following:

Structural: Is the word in capital letters?
Phonemic: Does the word rhyme with *WEIGHT*?
Semantic: Would the word fit the sentence
                  "He met a _____ in the street"?

Craik and Tulving measured both the time to make a decision and recognition of the rated words. (In another experiment, recall was also measured.) The data obtained (Figure 6.7) are interpreted as showing that (1) deeper processing takes longer to accomplish and (2) recognition of encoded words increases as a function of the level to which they are processed, with those words engaging semantic aspects better recognized than those engaging

FIGURE 6.7

Initial decision latency and recognition performance for words as a function of the initial task.

From Craik and Tulving (1975).

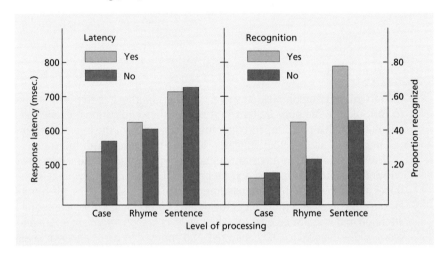

only the phonological or structural aspects. Using slightly different tasks, D'Agostino, O'Neill, and Paivio (1977); Klein and Saltz (1976); and Schulman (1974) obtained similar results.

The previous studies support the idea that memory is a function of how initial information is first encoded; semantically encoded information is better recalled than perceptually encoded information. Adopting a cognitive neuroscience perspective on this topic (some philosophers refer to this perspective as "biological reductionism"), one searches for the anatomic substrata of the strong memory effect associated with levels of processing. Fortunately, just such an investigation has been done by Kapur, Craik, et al. (1994) using PET imaging technology with exhilarating results. The task used in the experiment conducted by Kapur and his colleagues was similar to the studies mentioned previously. In one condition participants were asked simply to detect the presence or absence of a letter in a word (e.g., Does the word contain the letter *a*?), and in another condition different participants studied each word and were asked whether it represented something that was living or nonliving. In the first condition, the processing was considered to be shallow; in the second, deep. Behavioral responses (yes or no) to these questions were recorded by means of clicking a computer mouse, but the momentous data were the activation of specific brain areas as recorded by PET images using O_{15}-labeled water that were gathered during the performance of these two tasks. The behavioral data indicated that participants had substantially better recognition memory for the words processed at the deep level (living or nonliving thing) than for words processed at the shallow level (*a* or no *a*). The results of the PET images are shown in Figure 6.8.

Here the differences between the two groups showed a significant increase in cerebral activation in the left inferior prefrontal cortex during the semantic deep task as compared with the perceptual shallow task. In the present study it appears that the left prefrontal region, which was associated with enhanced memory performance, may be the

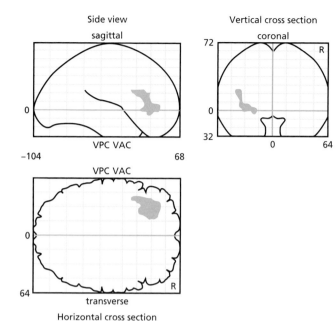

Side view
sagittal

Vertical cross section
coronal

VPC VAC

VPC VAC

transverse

Horizontal cross section

FIGURE 6.8

The regions of the brain that show increased cerebral blood flow in deep processing (living and nonliving) condition. The upper-left figure is a side view, with the frontal areas to the right and occipital lobe to the left. The upper-right figure is a vertical cross section. The grid and numbers represent standard coordinate spaces. VPC is a vertical line through the posterior commissure, and VAC is a vertical line through the anterior commissure.

Reprinted with permission from the National Academy of Sciences.

locus of this type of memory storage. The complete understanding of memory process, of course, must consider cognitive processes, neural activity, and memory performance integrated into an overall theory of memory.

Self-Reference Effect

New light was shed on the levels-of-processing concept when Rogers, Kuiper, and Kirker (1977) showed that self-reference is a powerful factor. Using a method similar to that of Craik and Tulving (1975), participants were asked to evaluate a list of 40 adjectives after they had been assigned to one of four conditions: structural, phonemic, semantic, and self-referent, with structural representing the most shallow encoding and self-referent representing the deepest encoding. In all four tasks, the participants were shown one of the four task questions, then the adjective appeared, and then they were required to answer yes or no for each question. In the structural task, participants were asked whether the adjective presented was in the same size type as the cue question ("Big letters?"). In the phonemic task, participants were presented with a word and asked whether or not it rhymed with the presented adjective ("Rhymes with?"). In the semantic task, participants were presented with a word and asked whether or not it was synonymous or not with the presented adjective ("Means same as?"). Lastly, in the self-referent task, participants were asked if the presented adjective described them ("Describes you?").

As in the Craik and Tulving study, it was hypothesized that words more deeply encoded (by virtue of the type of question posed), would be better recalled than more shallowly encoded ones. After the participants rated all of the words, they were asked to free-recall as many of the words they had rated as possible. As predicted, recall was poorest for words rated structurally and ascended through those phonemically rated and semantically rated.

FIGURE 6.9

The effect of self-reference on recall. Combined mean recall for both yes and no ratings as a function of the rating task.

Data from Rogers, Kuiper, and Kirker (1977).

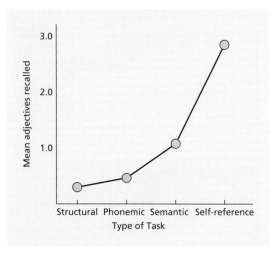

Self-reference words were recalled best. Figure 6.9 shows the recall data from the study. From these data, it is clear that words rated on a self-reference task lead to greater recall, which suggests that self-rating functions are a powerful encoding strategy.

Modifications of the original experiment have been conducted in several laboratories with the results being about the same. Some have argued that self-reference tasks are stored in some special memory system. Certainly, if you are asked to evaluate a personality trait as being self-descriptive, such as greedy, loving, or angry, you are engaging a very powerful **self-schema** (Markus, 1977), an organized system of internal attributes that is constellated around the topic of "I, me, mine." Since we all know a great deal about ourselves (and are emotionally, if not intellectually, deeply invested in ourselves), we have a rich and elaborate internal network available for storing self-information. Because of these complex internal self-structures, we can more easily organize new information as it might refer to ourselves than other, more mundane information (see Bellezza, 1992, for several important studies on this theme). Whether or not these self-rating memories are stored in different parts of the brain remains a question, but it is a good hunch that plenty of precious brain space is given over to information about the self.

Cognition in Everyday Life

Had Your Feelings Hurt Lately? You Probably Gained a Memory

All of us may have overheard an inconsiderate remark made about us, such as "she has bad breath" or "he is money-grubbing." Sometimes the remark is an ethnic or racial slur or refers to one's sexual preference. The affront may be related to our own deepest self-doubts: He or she is ugly; is too tall; has a long neck; has a homely nose; is poor; has AIDS; is bald; is alcoholic; is a slut; and one that is particularly prevalent in America, is fat! These self-referent caustic remarks have one thing in common: They are memorable, even if they are not true. Think about your own offensive remarks directed toward another person. How long will the memory of these remarks last? Why do we burn these sometimes careless statements so deeply into our memory? What are the cognitive reasons behind the memorability of personally abusive statements?

A Connectionist Model of Memory

The approach to memory earlier espoused by Tulving found direct correlates between neural activities and types of memory. The connectionist model, developed by Rumelhart and McClelland and others (1986), is also neurally inspired but attempts to describe memory from the even finer-grained analysis of processing units, which resemble neurons. Furthermore, since Tulving's model is derived from observations of brain activities, the connectionist model is based on the development of laws that govern the representation of knowledge in memory. One additional feature of the PDP model of memory is that it is not just a model of memory; it is also a model for action and the representation of knowledge.

Jets and Sharks   Memory systems of the sort just described have been studied by McClelland (1981) and McClelland and Rumelhart (1985), who illustrate how this system of content-addressable memory would work in a PDP model. In Table 6.1 are the names of several nefarious (and hypothetical) characters who live in a bad neighborhood (also make-believe). A subset of the units that represent this information is shown in Figure 6.10. In this figure, the groupings on the periphery enclose mutually exclusive information. (For example, Art cannot also be Rick.) All of the characters' attributes are connected in a mutually excitatory network. If the network is well practiced, that is, if the connections between units are established, then we can retrieve the properties of a given individual.

Suppose you want to retrieve the attributes of Ralph. By probing the system with Ralph (there is only one Ralph in the system), you can recall that he is a Jet, in his thirties, attended junior high school, is single, and is a drug pusher. In effect, we have recalled a representation of Ralph. In other words, Ralph is what he is. However, if we access the system from another angle and with less than complete information, we would end up with ambiguous results. For example, if we search for a person who is a Jet, is in his thirties, attended junior high school, and is single, we retrieve two names—Ralph and Mike. In this example, more information would be needed to be specific. (Police investigations are conducted with a similar network of inclusiveness and exclusiveness.)

One of the qualities of the **connectionist model** of memory is that it can account for complex learning, the type of memory operations we encounter in everyday life. These operations might involve the learning of a category or prototype formation. These processes are far more involved than the learning of nonsense syllables, as originally done by Ebbinghaus and reported in the beginning of this chapter.

The connectionist model of memory has won many disciples in the past few years. Its popularity is due in part to its elegant mathematical models, its relationship to neural networks, and its flexibility in accounting for diverse forms of memories.

Schemas and Gist

Many investigators have concentrated their efforts on psychological processes involving memory and how memory can be affected by the retrieval process. The best known of the investigations of the reconstruction of memory was done by Sir Frederic Bartlett of Cambridge University and reported in his remarkable book *Remembering: A Study in Experimental and Social Psychology* (1932). In this book Bartlett describes several experiments

Attributes of Members Belonging to Two Gangs, Jets and Sharks

Name	Gang	Age	Education	Marital Status	Occupation
Art	Jets	40s	Jr. High	Single	Pusher
Al	Jets	30s	Jr. High	Married	Burglar
Sam	Jets	20s	College	Single	Bookie
Clyde	Jets	40s	Jr. High	Single	Bookie
Mike	Jets	30s	Jr. High	Single	Bookie
Jim	Jets	20s	Jr. High	Divorced	Burglar
Greg	Jets	20s	High School	Married	Pusher
John	Jets	20s	Jr. High	Married	Burglar
Doug	Jets	30s	High School	Single	Bookie
Lance	Jets	20s	Jr. High	Married	Burglar
George	Jets	20s	Jr. High	Divorced	Burglar
Pete	Jets	20s	High School	Single	Bookie
Fred	Jets	20s	High School	Single	Pusher
Gene	Jets	20s	College	Single	Pusher
Ralph	Jets	30s	Jr. High	Single	Pusher
Phil	Sharks	30s	College	Married	Pusher
Ike	Sharks	30s	Jr. High	Single	Bookie
Nick	Sharks	30s	High School	Single	Pusher
Don	Sharks	30s	College	Married	Burglar
Ned	Sharks	30s	College	Married	Bookie
Karl	Sharks	40s	High School	Married	Bookie
Ken	Sharks	20s	High School	Single	Burglar
Earl	Sharks	40s	High School	Married	Burglar
Rick	Sharks	30s	High School	Divorced	Burglar
Ol	Sharks	30s	College	Married	Pusher
Neal	Sharks	30s	High School	Single	Bookie
Dave	Sharks	30s	High School	Divorced	Pusher

From McClelland (1981). Reprinted by permission.

in which brief stories, prose passages, pictures, and Native American picture writings were used to study the remembering (and forgetting) of meaningful material. The procedures were simple. Participants were given a short story or other material. They read it and then free-recalled what they could remember after a certain period. In other cases a story would be told to a person, who then retold it to another, who then retold it to another, with each retelling a reproduction of the previous story. By examining the contents

FIGURE 6.10

Sample of units and connections needed to represent the characters in Table 6.1. Bidirectional arrows indicate that units are mutually excitatory. Units within each cloud are mutually exclusive (that is, one cannot belong to both the Jets and the Sharks).

From McClelland (1981). Reprinted by permission.

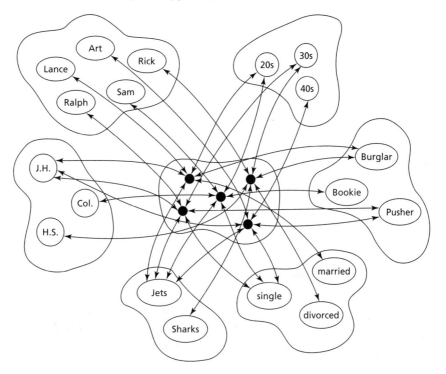

of the reproduced versions of the stories, it was possible to analyze both the nature of the material coded and the nature of the material forgotten.

Here is the original story:

The War of the Ghosts

One night two young men from Egulac went down to the river to hunt seals, and while they were there it became foggy and calm. Then they heard war-cries, and they thought: "Maybe this is a war-party." They escaped to the shore, and hid behind a log. Now canoes came up, and they heard the noise of paddles, and saw one canoe coming up to them. There were five men in the canoe, and they said: "What do you think? We wish to take you along. We are going up the river to make war on the people."

One of the young men said: "I have no arrows." "Arrows are in the canoe," they said. "I will not go along. I might be killed. My relatives do not know where I have gone. But you," he said, turning to the other, "may go with them."

Sir Frederic Bartlett **(1886–1969)**.
Studied language processing and memory in
a natural context.

So one of the young men went, but the other returned home. And the warriors went on up the river to a town on the other side of Kalama. The people came down to the water, and they began to fight, and many were killed. But presently the young man heard one of the warriors say: "Quick, let us go home: that Indian has been hit." Now he thought: "Oh, they are ghosts." He did not feel sick, but they said he had been shot.

So the canoes went back to Egulac, and the young man went ashore to his house, and made a fire. And he told everybody and said: "Behold I accompanied the ghosts, and we went to fight. Many of our fellows were killed, and many of those who attacked us were killed. They said I was hit, and I did not feel sick."

He told it all, and then he became quiet. When the sun rose he fell down. Something black came out of his mouth. His face became contorted. The people jumped up and cried.

He was dead.

After a delay of a day or more, participants reproduced the story more generally and as shorter, than the original story using a more informal style. Additionally, there were numerous omissions and some transformations. For example, familiar words replaced less familiar words (*boat* replaced *canoe,* and *fishing* replaced *hunting seals*).

Days later participants again would be asked to recall the story. Stories reproduced a second time were abbreviated. For example, the proper name (*Kalama* in the original) was missing and the excuse "I might get killed" reappeared after being missing from the first retelling.

Six months later another recall measure was made. In these reproductions, all unusual terms, all proper names, and references to supernatural powers were dropped.

Finally, one participant was asked to recall the story after 2 years and 6 months. He had not seen the original version during that time and, according to his own statement, had not thought of the story. His account is a good example of the reconstructive nature of memory. He maintains the gist of the story, but many details are lost or changed:

Some warriors went to wage war against the ghosts. They fought all day and one of their number was wounded.

They returned home in the evening, bearing their sick comrade. As the day drew to a close, he became rapidly worse and the villagers came round him. At sunset he sighed: something black came out of his mouth. He was dead.

Only the barest rudiments of the story remain. Little elaboration of details can be found, and several themes appear that seem to be related to what the participant thought should happen, rather than what actually did happen in the story. For example, in this passage the wounded man finally dies. When? at sunset . . . naturally! It would appear that this theme is part of the popular folk history of our subject; it certainly isn't in the original version.

Based on these assumptions, Bartlett (1932) was able to analyze how memory is reconstructed:

- *Omissions.* Specific information drops out. Also, information that is illogical or does not fit into the participants' expectations are not readily recalled.
- *Rationalization.* Some information is added that would help explain certain incongruous or illogical passages.
- *Dominant theme.* Some themes seem to become prominent, and other details are then related to the dominant theme.
- *Transformation of information.* Unfamiliar words are transformed to more familiar ones.
- *Transformation of sequence.* Some events are characterized as happening earlier in the story, others later.
- *Participant attitude.* The attitude of a participant toward the material determines the degree of recollection.

In making analyses on these bases, Bartlett used the concept of **schema** to account for his results. Schema, in his view, refers to an active organization of past reactions or past experiences. Incoming stimuli all contribute to the buildup of an organized schema.

Types of Memory

In general, we can think of LTM as the repository of all things in memory that are not currently being used but are potentially retrievable and important. Some of the general categories of the type of information contained in LTM (Bower, 1975) is arranged according to its possible adaptive function.

- Spatial Ability. Information about our location in the world and of potentially important objects in it. This knowledge allows for more effective maneuvering in the environment.
- Physical Properties of the World. Allows us to safely interact with objects in the world.
- Social Relationships. It is important to know who our friends and family are and who we can trust. Detecting enemies is critical.
- Social Values. Knowledge about what is important to the group.
- Motor Skills. Tool use, manipulating objects.
- Perceptual Skills. Enable us to understand stimuli in the environment from language to music.

Clearly the diversity of knowledge found in LTM has evolved to allow us to be successful in our environment. On a day-to-day basis, memory feels structured and orderly.

Therefore, the main research questions related to LTM are how it is organized. There is a large body of research that suggests specific information is stored within a well-structured and highly practical network. This concept implies that new information entering LTM does not require synthesis of a new network (which would defeat the utility of organization, as each event would require its own system), with an endless number of minor organization schemes the result. Instead, new information is typically stored within existing organizational structures.

As we discussed previously, our memory system not only stores information, it processes and directs information. Depending on the type of information, or importance, different organization schemes will be employed in LTM (see figure below). You can see that LTM can be divided into explicit (declarative) and implicit (nondeclarative) memory. Explicit memory is further organized into episodic and semantic memory. Implicit memory is divided into procedural and emotional memory. Within these categories of implicit and explicit memory are several subtypes as well.

Explicit memory relies largely on the retrieval of conscious experiences and is cued using recognition and recall tasks. **Implicit memory,** on the other hand, is expressed in the form of facilitating performance and does not require conscious recollection.

Types of Long Term Memory

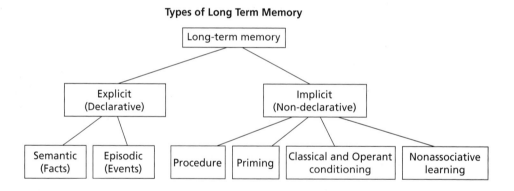

Autobiographical Memories

The contents of LTM are not a storage bin of everything experienced. LTM has a control function where personally relevant and meaningful information gets special attention. Autobiographical memories are memories of an individual's past history. Although personal memories are of interest to all of us, they also have been the subject of psychological research. We've already talked about autobiographical memories in terms of duration of LTM, now let's turn to autobiographical memories as a special type of long-term memory.

Autobiographical memories, if not perfect, are generally quite good. They typically contain information regarding emotion, self-description, specific and events, and life history. Objective data on this topic are hard to come by (after all, how do you prove or disprove an individual's personal recollection of something?). Some researchers, though, have overcome this issue. For example, Field (1981) interviewed various members of the same family, to ascertain which "facts" in a personal memory could be verified by other members of the family. Such recollections like "I'm sure I had tonsillitis on July 3, because it was just before the Fourth of July, and I had to miss the parade and fireworks display" can be verified by checking with other family members and consulting medical records. These types of studies show a high correlation (about .88) between family members' recollection of events. A much lower correlation (about .43) was found when recollections were about emotions or attitudes.

Knowing *What* and Knowing *That*

Our pursuit of the neurocognitive basis of representational knowledge continues with studies of **declarative** and **procedural** (or nondeclarative) **knowledge.** As previously mentioned, declarative knowledge is explicit and includes facts and episodes, while procedural knowledge is implicit and is accessible through performance. We may know that a bicycle has two wheels, a handlebar, and a frame (declarative knowledge), but we can only demonstrate that we know how to ride it (procedural knowledge) by actually doing so. One way to test for declarative and procedural knowledge is through priming and recognition experiments.

Priming, you may recall, is a test in which a research participant is given a cue, usually a word, that is in some way related to the target, usually an associated word. The prime facilitates the recognition of the target. For example, if we give you the word *TABLE* (the prime), your recognition of the word *CHAIR* (the target) is facilitated. Priming is thought to tap procedural knowledge, because the response is implicit and there is a more or less automatic activation of existing pathways. Therefore, if amnesic patients demonstrate positive performance on a priming task, we could conclude that their procedural knowledge would remain intact; if they performed poorly on a word recall task, we could conclude that their declarative knowledge was impaired. Several experiments have confirmed this hypothesis (e.g., Shimamura & Squire, 1984).

Episodic and Semantic Memory

Tulving (1972, 1983, 1986, 1989a, 1989b, 1993) classified memory into two types: episodic and semantic. Because it was assumed that a single memory state existed in LTM, Tulving's classification is important.

Episodic memory is a "neurocognitive memory system that enables people to remember past happenings" (Tulving, 1993, p. 67). Thus, memories of a particular experience (e.g., seeing the ocean, getting kissed for the first time, going to a good Chinese restaurant in San Francisco) constitute episodic memory events. These events are always stored in terms of "autobiographical reference." Episodic memory is quite susceptible to change and loss, but it is important in forming the basis of recognizing events (e.g., people and places) encountered in the past. These memories lack much of the formal structure that we impose on other information, notably that stored in semantic memory.

Semantic memory is the memory of words, concepts, rules, and abstract ideas and is necessary for the use of language. In Tulving's words:

> It is a mental thesaurus, organized knowledge a person possesses about words and other verbal symbols, their meaning and referents, about relations among them, and about rules, formulas, and algorithms for the manipulation of these symbols,

Endel Tulving. Hypothesized two types of memory, episodic and semantic, and demonstrated different cortical activity associated with each.

concepts, and relations. Semantic memory does not register perceptible properties of inputs, but rather cognitive referents of input signals. (p. 217)

When we use the word *blue*, we probably do not refer to a specific episode in our memory in which this word was used, but rather to the general meaning of the word. In our daily life we frequently retrieve information from semantic memory that is used in conversation, in solving problems, and in reading a book. Our capacity to process diverse information in rapid succession is attributable to a highly effective retrieval process and well-organized information in semantic memory.

Semantic memory and episodic memory differ not only in their contents but also in their susceptibility to forgetting. The information in episodic memory is lost rapidly as new information is constantly coming in. However, the knowledge that is required to multiply 5 × 3 is not susceptible to forgetting. Episodic memory gets a constant workout (and changes as a consequence of it), whereas semantic memory is activated less often and remains relatively stable over time.

According to Tulving, the system of memory that best accounts for the complexity and adaptability of the human creature is a three-part classification system: procedural, semantic, and episodic memory. (The latter two components have been described previously.)

These three systems are thought to be monohierarchical in that the lowest system, procedural memory, contains the next system, semantic memory, as its single entity, while semantic memory contains episodic memory as its single specialized subsystem. Although each of the higher systems depends on and is supported by the lower system(s), each system has unique capabilities.

Procedural memory, the lowest form of memory, retains connections between stimuli and responses and is comparable to what Oakley (1981) referred to as associative memory. Semantic memory has the additional capability of representing internal events that are not present, while episodic memory allows the additional capability of acquiring and retaining knowledge of personally experienced events.

Cognitive Neuroscience Support

Supporting evidence for semantic and episodic memory has been dramatically demonstrated by Tulving (Tulving 1989a, 1989b; Tulving et al., 1994), who has presented physical documentation for memory systems. Two types of studies have been reported. In one Tulving describes a case study of a man known as "K. C.," who suffered brain damage from a motorcycle accident, which severely damaged the right parietal-occipital and the frontal-parietal regions of his brain. The second is an imaging study.

In the fall of 1980, a thirty-year-old man, identified in the literature as "K. C.," suffered a serious motorcycle accident while returning from work to his home in Toronto. This unfortunate accident has provided psychology with a vivid example of the neurological nature of episodic and semantic memory. As a result of the accident, K. C. knows many things but cannot remember anything.

K. C. has semantic memory but not episodic memory. He knows, for example, that his family has a summer cottage and where it is located. He can even point out its location on a map. He knows that he spends some weekends there but cannot remember a single occasion when he was at the cottage or a single event that happened there. He knows how to play chess but cannot recall having played chess before with anyone. He knows he has a car and knows its make and year, but he cannot remember a single trip he took in it. Equally deficient is his ability to conjure up images about his future. Alas, K. C. seems to be frozen in a cognitive world that knows no past and anticipates no future.

The regions of the brain most severely injured included the left frontal-parietal and right parietal-occipital areas. K. C. remains densely amnesic, but the type of amnesia is remarkable. He has difficulty remembering normal, everyday, conscious experiences. He cannot bring back to conscious awareness "a single thing that he has ever done or experienced" (1989b). However, he is not mentally retarded, he is able to carry on what appears to be normal conversation, he can read and write, he can recognize familiar objects and photographs, and he is aware of what he has done for a minute or two after he has done it. Apparently, K. C.'s accident caused serious damage to the part of the brain necessary for the functioning of episodic memory and, to a much lesser extent, the semantic system.

The second type of study indicates the cortical locus of semantic and episodic memory by measuring regional cerebral blood flow (rCBF). Because the technique and findings were discussed in Chapter 2 and briefly at the beginning of this chapter, they are not repeated here, except in summary. By measuring the flow of blood in the cortex (which is interpreted as an indication of localized neural activity) with a modified PET scanning procedure, it was possible to create a cortical map of the brain during different memory operations. When a person engaged in semantic memory activities, specific regions of the brain "lit up," whereas episodic activities led to the activation of other areas of the cortex.

In the case of the mapping of the areas of the brain associated with specific memories and memory functions, three sites seem to be directly involved, although it should be emphasized that memory functions are distributed throughout the brain. These sites are the cortex, the outer surface of the brain thought to be involved in higher-order cognition such as thinking, problem solving, and remembering; the cerebellum, the cauliflower-looking structure at the base of the brain involved in the regulation of motor functions and motor memory; and the hippocampus, an S-shaped structure deep inside both cerebral hemispheres that is believed to process new information and route it to parts of the cortex for permanent storage. (It is likely that the hippocampus was damaged in C.W.'s case, discussed later, since past memories were intact but new memories were difficult to form.) Studies of the brain now suggest that two types of memories, **procedural memory** and **declarative memory,** are associated with these major structures. Procedural memory deals with motor skills, such as handwriting, typing skill, and (probably) our ability to ride a bicycle; it resides primarily in the cerebellum. Declarative memory consists of information and knowledge of the world, such as the name of a favorite aunt, the location of the nearest pizza parlor, and the meaning of words, plus a vast lot of other information; it is stored in the cerebral cortex.

Through the use of new techniques, the structural architecture of the human brain is becoming better known. Of even greater interest to cognitive psychologists are discoveries of the functional properties of the brain; their interrelationships; and their relationship to memory, perception, emotions, language, and other cognitive processes. As a result of these discoveries, psychologists have hypothesized that two types of memory exist: short-term and long-term memories. A wealth of psychological data supports such a notion, but now it appears that additional physiological evidence exists based on the structural and processing characteristics of the brain.

Also, it is becoming evident that sensory information is routed to the cortex soon after it is experienced. There, temporary links are formed among neurons and persist only briefly, but long enough for uncomplicated actions to take place, such as remembering a telephone number long enough to dial. In order for these impressions to become permanent a process called **long-term potentiation (LTP)** must occur. This is the tendency of nerve cells that have been exposed to a rapidly repeated stimulus to enhance their response tendencies for an extended period of time. LTP has been observed at hippocampal synapses in mammals. One theory suggests that the dendrites stimulated in this way sprout new growth, which facilitates long-term memories. Long-term declarative memories are thought to begin as the cerebral cortex sends information to the hippocampus, a process that strengthens the memory by rapidly and repeatedly exciting the neural circuit in the cortex. The strengthening of long-term memory may be achieved through voluntary actions, such as repeating a telephone number over and over again, or, in some instances, through involuntary actions, such as might occur in the case of a traumatic or emotional experience. For example, we may vividly recall the details of an automobile accident without conscious rehearsal of the event.

In summary, although much yet remains to be learned about the neurobiology of memory, some things are established. Physical events from the external world, such as light and sound energy, are detected by the sensory system, transduced to nerve impulses, and transmitted to the brain. From there they are initially analyzed and simultaneously routed to other centers, including the hippocampus area where, among other functions, their emotional content is assessed. This trace (sometimes called an **engram**) is further rerouted to the cortex and other locations where neurochemicals are activated, sometimes leading to the formation of permanent memory traces so that when the same or similar sensory impression is perceived, the memory trace may be activated. With this basic understanding of the neurocognitive structure of memory, we now turn to the traditional psychological studies and theories of memory.

Spotlight on Cognitive Neuroscience
Autobiographical Memory

Autobiographical memory can be thought of in terms of lifetime periods and general events within those lifetime periods. There are several brain sites that when injured produce disruption in autobiographical memory. This has led researchers to believe that autobiographical memory is a sequence process distributed across the brain and that is why a brain trauma in a variety of locations produces autobiographical memory deficits. Analysis of retrograde amnesiac patients (who have known areas of brain injury) resulted in a cognitive model of autobiographical memory that demonstrates this complex sequence process. Specific events appear to be represented in the posterior regions that are accessed by the autobiographical, "superordinate" memory system, via networks in the frontal and temporal lobes. This superordinate process can be disrupted at any point along that temporal sequence process. Therefore, loss of autobiographical memory is not a loss of the memory itself but is due to problems in the process of accessing that memory.

Conway, M. A. and Fthenaki, A. (2000). Disruption and loss of autobiographical memory. In F. Boller and J. Grafman (Eds.), *Handbook of Neuropsychology,* 2nd ed., Vol. 2.

A la carte

Nuns and Alzheimer's

Based on evidence from a study examining long-term memory permastore, we are able to retain a considerable amount of information in our long-term memories. Neurological disorders such as Alzheimer's disease initially appears as short-term memory deficit, but the long-term memory is affected in advanced stages. In extreme cases the patient cannot eat or move about without help. The causes are not clear, although some factors that may reduce the onset of Alzheimer's disease have identified with diet and exercise. An interesting source of information about Alzheimer's has come from David Snowden who began studying a group of elderly nuns living in Minnesota in 1986. The nuns belonged to the School of Sisters of Notre Dame, an organization that kept excellent health and biographical records, plus it provided a homogeneous lifestyle, making this an instant longitudinal study for Snowden once he was given permission to use the archived records. Another important aspect of this study is that the nuns agreed to have regular checkups and give blood and DNA samples. They also agreed to donate their brains post mortem. This is important because a definite diagnosis of Alzheimer's disease can only be made by examining the extent of the brain damage at death. Snowden and his colleagues found a strong correlation between the content of biographical writings (idea units) provided by the nuns and postmortem brain weight, indicating that the more articulate the nun was, the less her susceptibility to Alzheimer's disease (Riley, Snowdon, Desrosiers, & Markesbery, 2005). Findings such as these have led medical experts to recommend "exercising" the brain with activities such as reading and doing crossword puzzles.

Healthy brain

Alzheimer's brain

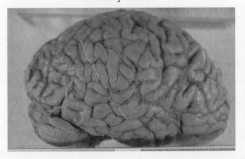

Courtesy of University of Kentucky Sanders-Brown Center on Aging.

Student Resource Center

Study Guide

1   Modern brain imaging technology (e.g., PET) has been useful in identifying specific brain structures associated with memories.

2   The cognitive neuroscience of memory shows that the cerebral cortex, the cerebellum, and the hippocampus are all involved in memory storage and processing.

3   The levels of processing hold that memory is a byproduct of analyses performed on incoming stimuli, with memory trace durability a function of the complexity or depth of those analyses.

4   Analysis of PET data indicates that the left prefrontal area of the brain is involved in deeper processing.

5   Information processing models and the levels-of-processing position differ with respect to the importance of structure and process and to the nature of rehearsal. Information processing theories generally emphasize structure and maintenance rehearsal, whereas the levels-of-processing position stresses processing and elaborative rehearsal.

6   Tulving emphasizes memory as a multiple system involving both systems and principles and proposes a three-part classification that includes procedural, semantic, and episodic memories. Recent observations have suggested that semantic and episodic memories are associated with localized cerebral activity.

7   The PDP model of memory postulates processing units that bear some resemblance to neurons. Mental processes, including memory, take place through a system of interconnecting units.

Key Terms

autobiographical memories
codes
connectivist model
declarative knowledge
declarative memory
engram
episodic memory
explicit memory
implicit memory
levels of processing
long-term potentiation

mnemonic encoding principle
procedural knowledge
procedural memory
retrieval structure principle
schema
self-scheme
semantic memory
speed-up principle
tip of the tongue
very long-term memory

Starting Points

Books and Articles

● A popular book by Baddeley called *Your Memory: A User's Guide* is a good place to begin your reading. Historically interesting is the first book on memory by Ebbinghaus (1885), which has been translated from German to English and is available as a paperback. A classic in psychology is William James's *Principles of Psychology,* also recently reprinted; it is recommended not only because of its historical significance but also because some of James's speculations have become an integral part of the contemporary literature in cognitive psychology.

● Several books that give an excellent overview of memory are Parking's *Memory* and Baddeley's, *The Psychology of Memory;* Adams's, *Learning and Memory;* and Daniel L. Schacter's popular book *Searching for Memory.* Rubin's edited book *Autobiographical Memory* also has many good chapters.

● Most authoritative for particular models of memory are the original sources. These are generally more technical than the summary presented in this chapter, but they are understandable with some effort. Suggested are Waugh and Norman's article in *Psychological Review;* Atkinson and Shiffrin in Spence and Spence, eds., *The Psychology of Learning and Motivation: Advances in Research and Theory;* Craik and Lockhart's article in *Journal of Verbal Learning and Verbal Behavior;* Tulving in Tulving and Donaldson, eds., *Organization of Memory;* and Tulving's article in *The Behavioral and Brain Sciences. Varieties of Memory and Consciousness: Essays in Honor of Endel Tulving,* edited by Roediger and Craik, and *Current Issues in Cognitive Processes: The Tulane Flowerree Symposium on Cognition,* edited by Izawa, are recommended.

● Some current studies on the cognitive neuroscience of memory are particularly suggested, including Petersen et al. in *Nature;* Petersen et al. in *Science;* and most of the *Proceedings of the National Academy of Sciences,* Volume 91, 1994, which is largely devoted to the work of Tulving and his colleagues.

Movies

● Bridges of Madison County (1995)—Through her mother's diary, a daughter comes to know her mother's autobiographical memories

● Memory Collector (2005)—A girl gives away a painful memory only to want it back as an adult

● Remembering Jim Thatcher (2006)—A man is told he can only take one memory to heaven

Search Terms

● Exploratorium

Forgetting and Remembering

hmmm . . . ?

1. What kinds of information do you forget? What things do you easily remember?

2. What mnemonic systems do you use? Why do you think they work?

3. Describe some people you know who have extraordinary memory abilities.

4. What makes an "expert"?

In the practical use of our intellect, forgetting is as important as remembering.

—*William James*

The existence of forgetting has never been proved: we only know that some things do not come to our mind when we want them to.

—*Nietszche*

Historical Perspective

It is unlikely that Hermann Ebbinghaus, who lived in Germany and wrote the first scientific account of memory experiments (*On Memory,* 1885), could have foreseen the impact his work would have throughout the history of the study of memory. Consider the circumstances that prevailed during this time. Even though everyone "knew" what memory was and philosophers had speculated about its purpose for years, no systematic formulation of memory structure had been tested, no sophisticated analytic apparatus was available, and no database of previous experimentation existed. Thus, his exploration of the unknown properties of memory was undertaken with little information and limited tested apparatus to guide him. He did have a hunch that sensations, feelings, and ideas that had at one time been conscious remained hidden somewhere in memory.

The *zeitgeist* in which Ebbinghaus worked deemed that memory could be understood by looking at formed ideas and then working backward to find their source. Ebbinghaus reversed this procedure; he studied how memory developed and, by so doing, was able to bring under scientific control the variables that were previously inseparable from memory. His search for the answer to the question of how memory is formed (and lost) required that he develop a task that was unknown to his experimental subject. Since Ebbinghaus was not only the theorist and experimenter but also his own research subject, he faced the problem of finding something to teach

Hermann Ebbinghaus **(1850–1909).** The first to present systematic studies of memory and forgetting. Wrote *On Memory* in 1885.

FIGURE 7.1

Ebbinghaus's forgetting curve for
nonsense syllables.

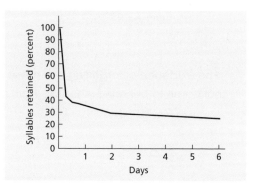

himself that he didn't already know. He ended up using nonsense syllables—non-word, three-letter consonant–vowel–consonant sequences. The resulting "words" ZAT, BOK, and QUJ were born to be forgotten and so they were. Ebbinghaus tenaciously rehearsed list after list of nonsense syllables and then tried to recall them after 20 minutes, 1 hour, 8–9 hours, 1 day, 2 days, 6 days, and 31 days. Figure 7.1 shows just how much he forgot.

Theories of Forgetting

But why does forgetting occur? We cover reasons why our memory fails us, putting us in the situation of "not remembering."

The first thing to consider is whether or not the information got into the brain in the first place. Was the sensory system not working (e.g., you're wearing ear plugs and can't hear)? Were your attentional energies not directed toward relevant stimuli in the environment (e.g., you're looking the other direction when a guy steals your friend's purse—and you don't see him)? If the information does not get into the brain via our sensory receptors as mediated by our attentional system, then there is no information to remember later (see diagram of memory processes, next page). This is called **failure to encode** and refers to the problem of failing to put material into LTM. However, sometimes we are not aware that the information did not enter memory. You may be surprised how poorly you did on an exam because you've never missed a class; but if you regularly space out, or do other work, the information never got into your LTM to retrieve later. You have probably also experienced failure to encode when you are introduced to someone and just a short time later cannot remember his or her name. You may not have "forgotten" the name at all; rather, it is likely it never entered your memory system in the first place. Another factor that can contribute to encoding failures is stress. The Yerkes-Dodson Law (Yerkes & Dodson, 1908) posits that very low and very high levels of arousal impair memory and other cognitive processes (see figure, next page). When arousal is so strong that it leads to forgetting, the memory may be nothing more than the emotional portion of the experience, lacking in details (Metcalf, 1998).

Basic Memory Process

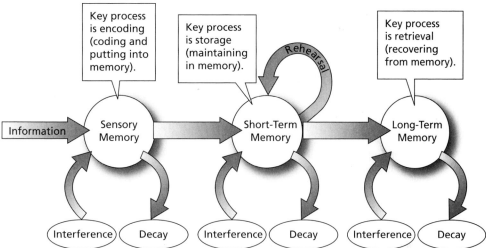

Consolidation failure is memory loss due to organic disruption while the memory trace is being formed, resulting in poorly formed memories that are experienced as forgetting. STM works properly, but the shifting of information into LTM is hampered.

Amnesia is forgetting caused by problems in the brain. It is not caused by a mere bonk on the head as you see in the movies, and very rarely results in loss of information about the self and your identity. It can be caused by disease processes (like Alzheimer's

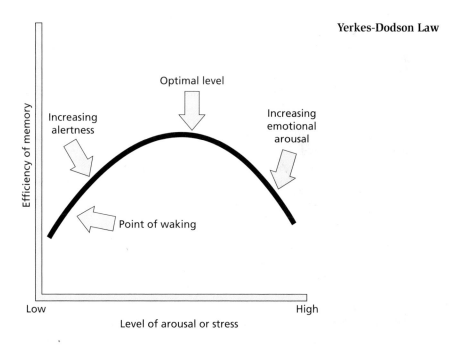

Can't remember to forget you.

—*From the movie* Memento

and Korsakoff's syndrome) as well as traumatic brain injury. Alzheimer's disease causes memory problems and recent research indicates that it may be due to protein molecules unnecessarily binding to glutamate, which then prohibits glutamate from doing its job in activating memory processes in the brain (Hoe et al., 2006). Korsakoff's syndrome causes memory problems due to a serious Vitamin B_1 deficiency. A person with long-term, extreme alcoholism often does not eat enough food to get this necessary vitamin. The result is damage to the brain because the brain cells cannot process glucose (necessary for survival) without Vitamin B_1. People with Korsakoff's have memory loss for recent events, and often do not realize they have a problem, and will make up, or **confabulate,** details to fill in what they cannot remember. **Retrograde amnesia** is memory loss for events prior to the brain injury ("retro" = "old"—old memories are lost). Most typically the memories lost are the five or ten minutes prior to the accident (often a concussion). The trauma to the brain (via a car accident or a particularly hard tackle) interrupts normal memory storage. Thus we see that retrograde amnesia has some roots in consolidation failure.

The results of a study by Lynch and Yarnell (1973) support this. These researchers interviewed football players who had received head traumas. The interviews, after a brief neurological examination, were conducted within 30 seconds after the injury. The players were also interviewed 3 to 5 minutes after and (as the situation permitted) every 5 to 20 minutes thereafter. (Uninjured players served as controls.) In the interviews immediately after the trauma, the players accurately recalled the circumstances. For example, "[I was hit] from the front while I was blocking on the punt." However, 5 minutes later they were unable to recall any of the details of the play. For example, "I don't remember what happened. I don't remember what play it was or what I was doing. It was something about a punt." It seems that the details of occurrences just prior to an amnesia-inducing event are stored temporarily in memory but are not passed on to (or consolidated in) permanent memory.

Some people, however, may lose months or years of past history following a **temporal gradient** whereby the memory loss is most severe for the events just prior to the injury and decrease incrementally the further back in time, thus leaving the oldest memories often intact. **Anterograde amnesia** is memory loss for events after the injury ("ante" = "after"—new memories are unable to be formed). In the event of a brain injury, patients will often experience both retrograde and anterograde amnesia, such that they cannot remember the few minutes prior to the accident, and when they wake up they often will not remember the first few visits by family members and doctors. See diagram depicting the memory problems with

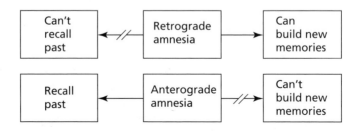

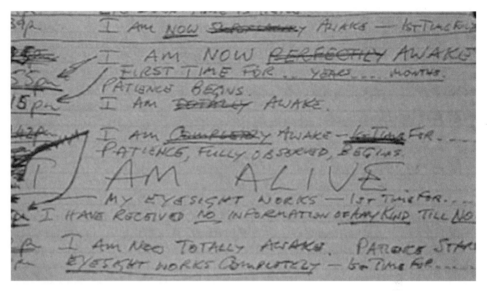

A sample from Clive Wearing's diary.

these two types of amnesia. Very rarely though, someone experiences total anterograde amnesia such as in the case of Clive Wearing. Wearing contracted a quite common virus (herpes) that normally causes only cold sores. For Wearing, though, the virus attacked his brain, destroying his hippocampus and parts of his temporal and frontal lobes. This resulted in a profound inability to lay down new memories. His whole world resides in a time span of anywhere from about 1–5 minutes. As soon as his attention is directed to anything else, he immediately forgets what just happened. Every moment, thought, and encounter is new. He resorts to keeping diaries to try to keep track of his day, but even those result in feelings of frustration and confusion. See a sample of Clive's diary, above.

Given that people with amnesia uniquely (and prominently) display the dual nature of memory, they have often been scientifically studied. In one study, Cohen and Squire (1980) found that patients with amnesia could acquire the skill involved in reading words from a mirror-reversed display, but when questioned later about the task, they could neither remember the words nor the skill they had demonstrated.

Similarly, patients with amnesia can learn the best solution to a puzzle, such as the "Tower of Hanoi." The "Tower of Hanoi" puzzle contains several rings of descending size stacked on top of each other on a peg. There are also two empty pegs. The task is to move the entire series of rings to one of the other pegs, moving only one ring at a time and always placing a smaller ring on the larger one. To solve this puzzle, considerable parts of the cognitive system must be intact and operable. Specifically, it requires procedural memory. Patients with amnesia are deficient in episodic and declarative memory, which is why they can perform this task as well as people without amnesia (though they don't remember doing it).

Decay is the fading of memory over time or through disuse. This may occur in STM (you remember the operator's recitation of a phone number just long enough to find a pen, or your cell phone). Decay can also occur in LTM where information that is not accessed simply slips away. Ebbinghaus's experiment described previously is an example of decay.

*I*t's harder now than it was in December—now I miss those small things, like his smile, his wink, his grabbing my hand, his laugh and he had such expressive eyes—but these are also the things I never want to forget so there you have it—the good and the bad.

—*Karen Martin*

Interference is the confusion or entanglement of similar memories. **Retroactive interference** is when new memories hurt the recovery of old memories ("retro" = "old"— old memories are hurt). For example, as a freshman in high school you may have been assigned a locker, and upon learning your new locker combination may not be able to remember your old locker combination from middle school—one that you used for two years! **Proactive interference** happens when old memories hurt the recovery of new memories ("pro" = "new"—new memories are hurt). For example, as a student on a university campus, you may occasionally drive to school, and repeatedly have to park far, far away. One day, you luck out and get a very close parking space. At the end of the day, where do you find yourself? Wandering around the far, far away parking lot looking for your car. The new memory (your close parking spot this morning) was hurt by the old memory (where you usually park).

Retrieval failure is the inability to find the necessary memory cue for retrieval. This state may be temporary, or at times can be long term. The encoding specificity principle (Tulving & Thompson, 1973) says that specific encoding operations determine the type of memory trace stored. The type of memory trace determines what retrieval cues will be successful at gaining access to the memory trace. The overlap of operations present at encoding with those present at time of retrieval determine the success of retrieval and the number of cues possible to lead to retrieval. For example, Godden and Baddeley (1975) sought to examine the role of context on memory retrieval. They had participants memorize a list either under water or on dry land, and then had them take a memory test under water or on dry land. What they found was that when learning and testing occurred in the same context (dry land–dry land or under water–under water) that memory was best. Memory was poor (in other words, they forgot) when the contexts were different (dry land–underwater, and vice versa). It should be noted that learning on dry land and being tested on dry land resulted in the highest retrieval rates, because that is a context that is readily familiar to us (more so than studying while snorkeling). Retrieval failure is problematic in that it is indistinguishable from decay and failure to encode. This can be particularly problematic for people who need to try to accurately assess memory (like detectives who need to question a witness about their memory). Continuing to prod for a memory that is not there (due to decay or failure to encode) can actually create a false memory.

Motivated forgetting is the knowing repression of memories, usually to avoid dealing with traumatic experiences. When people refuse to talk or think about a traumatic experience they may start to forget it.

Repression is the pushing (unknowingly) of threatening thoughts, memories, or feelings out of conscious awareness. Freud's original conception of repression was that it was done unconsciously to protect the ego. He posited that dreams, hypnosis, and free association were the means to tap into these memories. Repressed memories are those in

*M*emory can change the shape of a room; it can change the color of a car. And memories can be distorted. They're just interpretations, they're not a record, and they're irrelevant if you have the facts.

—*From the movie* Memento

which a person might exclude from consciousness a particularly painful memory, such as child sexual abuse. Under psychotherapy, these memories may be consciously recalled. The repression is not a conscious process (as in motivated forgetting). There is debate about the validity of repressed memories, and while some reports of repressed memories of child sexual abuse may indeed be real, we do know that some in fact are not. Recovered "memories" are often very detailed, which is contrary to how the event was encoded (under traumatic circumstances that were so stressful that for years it is "forgotten").

Memory Errors

Next, we turn to the situation where a memory is recalled, but it is incorrect. As we discussed in the previous chapter, much of memory is reconstructive. The brain does not provide instant access to exact replicas of information from the outside world stored in our memory systems. Rather, that information is pieced together to form memory. Memory can also be constructive. This means that prior experience, postevent information, perceptual factors, social factors, and even one's desire to remember certain events over others influence what we recall. This influence can be in the form of a constructed, new, but factually incorrect, memory. Unlike the factors discussed previously that inhibited the encoding or retrieval of a memory, the following factors produce a memory, but it is a false one.

False Memories

Roediger and McDermott (1995) experimentally demonstrated that they could quite easily instill false memories in participants. This study is easily replicable in the classroom environment with groups, or even here, as you read this book. Students read (or have read to them) the following list: Rest, Nap, Sheets, Night, Snooze, Bed, Doze, Pillow, Dream, Snore, Awake, Tired, Wake, Blanket, Slumber, Nap, Yawn, Drowsy. Now quick, close your book and write down as many words as you can remember (for real, do it!).

Okay, now that you're back. The researchers found (and we've demonstrated it over and over again in our classes), that participants recall many of the words accurately, but a large number of them recall the word "sleep"—check your list, did you recall sleep? Don't be surprised if you did. The semantically similar and strongly associated words in the list created the false memory of having read (or heard) the word "sleep." Roediger and McDermott's (1995) study on false memories of words is an experimentally important step to understanding the more complex problem of eyewitness memory errors.

Loftus and Palmer (1974) found that false memories could be constructed based on the types of questioning that were used to elicit the memory. Participants viewed clips

Elizabeth Loftus. Her work on malleability of memory has been frequently applied to eyewitness identification cases.

of car accidents and were asked to estimate the speed of the cars. The independent variable was the word used in the basic question: "About how fast were the cars going when they X each other?" where X equaled *hit, smashed, collided, bumped,* or *contacted.* They found that the word "smashed" produced the fastest estimated speeds (with an average of 40.8 mph) and "contacted" produced the slowest estimated speeds (with an average of 31.8 mph). Results clearly indicated that the estimated speeds were not due to the actual speed of the vehicle but rather to the word choice in the question. The false memory went beyond just the speed estimate and included "remembering" broken glass at the scene, when in fact there had been none! This study and others have led to important advances in understanding the role that leading questions can have in tainting memory.

While some repressed memories of traumatic childhood events are undoubtedly real (as discussed previously), it is argued by Loftus and others that some "recovered" memories are actually false, and are stories about events that did not occur, but are constructed (perhaps without awareness) by virtue of the therapeutic techniques used and possibly even to satisfy the demands of a therapist (Loftus, 1993a, 1993b; Loftus & Ketcham, 1991; Loftus & Polage, 1998). These false memories can be created by leading questions, hypnosis, guided imagery, and encouragement by the therapist to participate in group therapy with other survivors of child sexual abuse (some undoubtedly real) who share their stories and further contaminate memory.

Loftus and Pickrell (1995) sought to experimentally evaluate the possibility of creating complex false memories (beyond word lists and car crashes). They developed what is called the "lost in the mall" technique. The participants were given short narratives of childhood events provided by family members, except for one, false event created by the researchers. This event was about having been lost in the mall at around five or six years old and having been found by an elderly person after much distress and concern. Approximately 25% of the participants came to believe this nonevent, even reporting details that were not part of the original narrative. This technique has been shown to create false memories for even much more rare events than being lost, like being a victim of a vicious animal attack (Porter, Yuille, & Lehman, 1999), as well as in some cases create very "rich" false memories that include details and recalled emotions for a false event (Loftus & Bernstein, 2003). False memories have also been shown to be created for very recent events, and thus are not subject to other memory considerations (like forgetting). Kassin and Kiechel (1996) found that they could quite easily make people believe that they had ruined an experiment by pressing a forbidden button on a computer keyboard. When confronted (meant to be at least theoretically applicable to interrogation), 69 percent of the participants signed a "confession", 28 percent came to believe they had engaged in the act (when they had in fact not), and 9 percent actually created additional (false) details supporting their equally false memory.

Remembering

It should be apparent by now the ability to remember and to forget are functional and important in their own right. Being able to remember where you parked your car, that you are driving to the store or not to work, and friends and enemies are as important as being able to forget last week's grocery list, infomercial phone number, or harsh words exchanged with a friend. Much of remembering and forgetting is under the control of neural processes that regulate these processes without effort. However, sometimes we are in situations where we have to memorize things to ensure that we won't forget and in some ways override our natural tendency to let information decay over time, and take control over our memory processes. Nowadays we can call our home from our cell and leave a message to ourselves, we can text-message to not forget something, or we can even take a photo from our cell phone. This technology has of course not always been available and surprisingly enough, the technology to print books in mass production is relatively new. In fact, prior to that, only a small percentage of people knew how to read and write, and yet without those skills people can and do remember many things. In the following sections we review some mnemonic systems that not only have been helpful for people to memorize things of importance, but also cast light on how our memory systems work.

Factors that Enhance Memory

As we've discussed previously, directing attentional resources to stimuli in the environment increases the likelihood of memory entering the sensory system and entering STM. Maintenance rehearsal will keep information looping in STM, and elaborative rehearsal pushes information from STM into LTM. We also know by now that the encoding specificity principle can lead to increased retrieval of memories from LTM by providing cues that help gain access to the memory trace. Research in the area of memory consolidation has shown that people who learned tasks based on declarative memory (paired associates) or procedural memory (mirror tracing) showed increased memory of the tasks if they slept during the retention interval (as opposed to being awake during the retention interval). Specifically, non-REM sleep aids in declarative memory, and REM sleep aids in procedural memory (Plihal & Born, 1997). Another way to increase memory is through techniques designed to enhance encoding and aid in retrieval, called mnemonics. We cover these in the next section.

---

*Y*ou are going to have to learn to use your memory.

—*From the movie* Ray

Mnemonic Techniques

A **mnemonic** (the *m* is silent: ne-mahn'-ick) is a technique that enhances the storage and the recall of information in memory.

In Greek mythology, Mnemosyne (from which the word *mnemonic* is derived) was the mother of the nine muses of arts and sciences. Memory was considered the oldest and most revered of all mental skills, from which all others are derived. It was believed that if we had no memory, we would have no science, no art, no logic.

There are dozens of devices to aid (or in some cases replace) memory. Speeches are normally delivered from notes; television performers use teleprompters; salesclerks retrieve items from stock with the help of visual indexes; and physicians check symptoms in handbooks. Early Greek and Roman orators used the mnemonic technique called the method of loci to remember their speeches; religious people have used beads or prayer wheels to facilitate the recitation of formal prayers; and the oral folk history of numerous groups is filled with vivid imagery, which enhances memory. The late Alex Haley, author of *Roots,* indicated that much of the oral history preserved among his African American ancestors was rich in imagery.

Method of Loci   The **Method of Loci** is traced to Simonides who was able to remember the location of every guest at a banquet by their seat at the table. The way the method of loci works is to associate certain objects with certain places. While Simonides was able to associate each individual with his seat, others have used familiar places and environments to mentally place objects to later be remembered in deliberate locations. Therefore, by mentally visiting the place and going to those locations, the individual is able to recall those items. These locations (loci) can be a room, a familiar path, or even a mansion.

There is empirical support that the method of loci is effective at remembering certain types of information (Bower, 1970a, 1972). Suppose you were asked to go to the store to pick up five items. You might be worried that you would forget an item, or come back with the wrong stuff. You could use the method of loci with your house as a place to store the to-be-remembered grocery items:

hot dogs	driveway
cat food	garage interior
tomatoes	front door
bananas	coat closet shelf
whiskey	kitchen sink

Peg Word System   The **peg word system,** or peg list system, has several forms, but the basic idea is that one learns a set of words that serve as "pegs" on which items to be memorized are "hung," much as a hat rack has pegs on which hats, scarves, and coats may be hung. In one variation of this basic system, you learn a series of rhyming pairs, such as the following:

one is a bun	six is a stick
two is a shoe	seven is a heaven
three is a tree	eight is a gate
four is a door	nine is a line
five is a hive	ten is a hen

After the peg list has been learned, you "hook" a set of items to the pegs. One way this can be done is by imagining an interaction between the peg word and the TBR word. For example, if the first word in a series of TBR words is *milk,* it can be imagined to interact with *bun* (remember "one is a bun") in some way. The more bizarre and implausible the image, the better the likelihood of recalling the TBR item. In this example, you might think of milk being poured over a bun. If the next TBR item is *bread,* you might associate it with the peg word *shoe* by imagining a shoe kicking a loaf of bread in half. The use of peg word mnemonics in the memorization of a shopping list is illustrated in Figure 7.2.

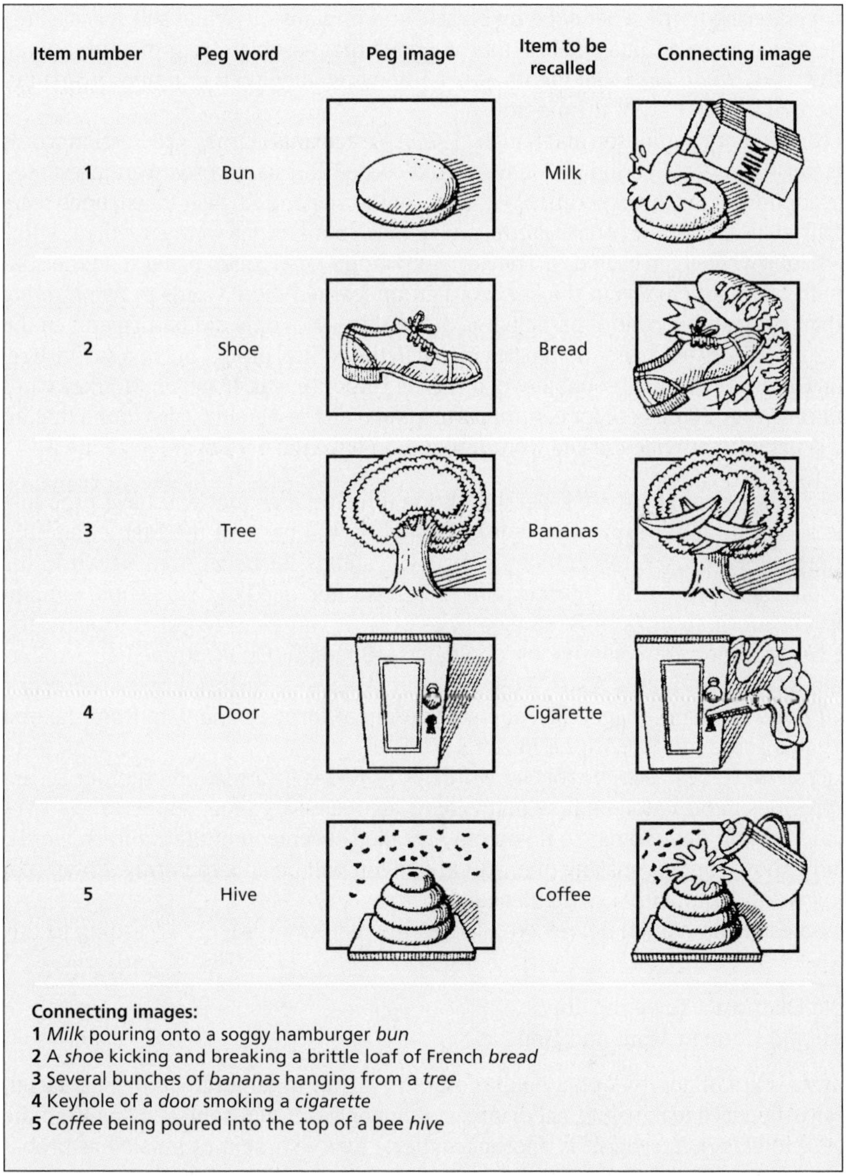

Item number	Peg word	Peg image	Item to be recalled	Connecting image
1	Bun		Milk	
2	Shoe		Bread	
3	Tree		Bananas	
4	Door		Cigarette	
5	Hive		Coffee	

Connecting images:
1 *Milk* pouring onto a soggy hamburger *bun*
2 A *shoe* kicking and breaking a brittle loaf of French *bread*
3 Several bunches of *bananas* hanging from a *tree*
4 Keyhole of a *door* smoking a *cigarette*
5 *Coffee* being poured into the top of a bee *hive*

FIGURE 7.2

Memorization using peg word mnemonics.

From G. Bower (1973).

Key Word Method   A slightly different form of the peg word technique is the **key word method,** which is useful in learning, foreign language vocabulary (Atkinson 1975; Atkinson & Raugh 1975, Raugh & Atkinson, 1975).

Suppose your native language is English, and the foreign language you are learning is Spanish. And suppose you want to learn the Spanish word *arbol* (which means *tree*). The first task is to associate an English word that sounds like arbol. The "bol" in arbol sounds like bowling alley. Bowling alley and tree. Now we have two words we have to associate together through imagery: bowling and tree. We could imagine a tree with bowling balls instead of fruit, or a bowling alley, and instead of pins there's a bunch of small trees—each adhering to the tenet of being bizarre and implausible while still successfully linking the concepts in an image. Now that we have that association in memory, when we hear the word *arbol,* we recall the image of a bowling alley with tiny trees instead of pins and remember that arbol means tree.

In an experiment by Atkinson and Raugh (1975), participants learned 120 Russian words (40 words per day over a period of 3 days). Prerecorded Russian words were presented through headphones; for the experimental group, key words and English translations were presented visually, and for the control group, only English translations were presented. Three training sessions were given each day. The key word group fared much better than the control group. In fact, participants in the key word group learned more words in two training sessions than comparable control participants did in three. Not only did participants in the key word group initially do better than participants in the control group, but in a surprise recall session 6 weeks later, the probability of a correct response was 43 percent for key word participants and only 28 percent for control participants. The researchers also found that, in general, it is better to provide the key word rather than have the participant generate it.

Verbal Techniques   There are several additional techniques that you have probably used. One is based on **acronyms,** or words formed on the basis of the first letters in a phrase or group of words. *LAN,* in today's parlance, stands for **L**ocal **A**rea **N**etwork. It's not just about making a verbal shortcut, but rather, is often used to help people remember important information as in PASS (see page 213). If you were required to learn the following list of important cognitive psychologists—Shepard, Craik, Rumelhart, Anderson, Bower, Broadbent, Loftus, Estes, Posner, Luria, Atkinson, Yarbus, Erickson, Rayner, Vygotsky, Intons-Peterson, Piaget, Sternberg—you might form an anagram from the first letters into this acronym: *SCRABBLE PLAYER VIPS.*

The acronym serves as a cue for the words, it provides information on order (if important), provides information on how many items are necessary to remember, and serves as a reminder for omitted words. So if you only recalled seventeen of the eighteen words, you not only know you are missing one, you know you will be able to narrow down that the missing word starts with a particular letter.

The names of the cranial nerves are learned by anatomy students according to this rhyme:

> On Old Olympia's Towering Top
> A Finn and German Vault and Hop

The nerves are olfactory, optic, oculomotor, trochlear, trigeminal, abducens, facial, auditory, glossopharyngeal, vagus, accessory, and hypoglossal. (Of course, going from the *G* in *German* to *glossopharyngeal* is another matter!) Every student of music has probably learned "*E*very *G*ood *B*oy *D*oes *F*ine" for the lines and "FACE" for the spaces of the

Cognition in Everyday Life

Easy-to-use on a fire:

Just remember the *"P-A-S-S" method*

PULL   ▼

Pull the pin
on the fire
extinguisher

AIM   ▼

Aim the fire extinguisher
at the base of the fire
(stand 6 feet from fire)

SQUEEZE   ▼

Squeeze the
handle of the
extinguisher.

SWEEP   ▼

Sweep the extinguisher
left to right while aiming
at base of fire.

An everyday example of an acronym used to teach people how to correctly use a fire extinguisher.

musical staff. The acronym *ROY G BIV* is composed of the initial letters of the names of the spectral colors: *r*ed, *o*range, *y*ellow, *g*reen, *b*lue, *i*ndigo, and *v*iolet.

In these examples the mnemonic uses the first letter of the to-be-remembered word. It appears that the initial letter carries the greatest amount of information of any letter in a word, which would suggest that words are coded in LTM according to initial letters— as, for example, in the indexing of a dictionary. The second most important letter tends to be the last one (but the rule is frequently violated in the case of words ending in *s*, *d*, and *e*—letters that give little information). Crossword puzzle addicts are likely to be familiar with this phenomenon. If the initial letter is cued by a mnemonic system, it is generally the most salient letter cue possible.

Support for the cueing potential of initial letters has been demonstrated by Solso and Biersdorff (1975). Participants were asked to recall a list of words. A word that was not recalled was then cued by either its first letter, something associated with the word in common experience, or a word that rhymed with the TBR word. If the participant still failed to recall the word, dual cues were presented, for example, the first letter *and* an associate. The rhyme, letter, and associate cue all aided the participants in recall, but, most important for our present discussion, if the results due to guessing were compensated for, the initial-letter cue was the best for recall.

Bédard and Chi (1993) state that "the studies (of expertise) have shown that a large, organized body of domain knowledge is a prerequisite to expertise." What is knowledge? Before you read further, formulate your own definition of knowledge and relate it to expertise.

Experts in the field of expertise and knowledge believe that knowledge can be classified in terms of its quantity or its structure. Experts have a greater quantity of domain-specific knowledge—a fact that is self-evident (an expert in carpentry knows far more about his or her craft than a novice). More important, however, is the way experts *organize* their knowledge. Experts organize knowledge in ways that make it more accessible, functional, and efficient.

The use of mnemonic techniques may increase one's specific knowledge base (a prerequisite for expertise), but the organization of knowledge is also vital.

Another related system is to form an **acrostic,** or a phrase or sentence in which the first letters are associated with the to-be-recalled words. Kings Play Chess on Fine Grained Sand is an acrostic many biology students use to remember: kingdom, phylum, class, order, family, genus, species. Sentences that are bizarre, personally meaningful, or visual are easiest to remember. In a moment we will look at how these methods might be used practically, as in the case of remembering the name of a new acquaintance or the recall of words and concepts—hopefully, this material will come in time to help with your next social encounter or examination.

You might ask, which mnemonic technique works "best"? Douglas Herrmann (1987) found that some techniques work well for some types of material, while other techniques work well for other types. Specifically, for paired associate learning, imagery mediation worked best; for free-recall learning, the story mnemonic seemed to be superior; while for serial learning, the method of loci worked well. In another assessment of mnemonic techniques, Garcia and Diener (1993) found that when tested over a week the methods of loci, peg word, and acrostics proved to be about equal in effectiveness.

Recall of Names   It is so important to remember the names of faces that sometimes politicians even hire people to help them remember who they know. It is embarrassing to recognize someone but for the life of you can't remember his or her name.

Lorayne and Lucas (1974) found that the learning of a name in association with a face involves three steps. The first, remembering the name, may be done by paying close attention to the way the name is pronounced and then by forming a substitute name or phrase for it. For example, the name *Antesiewicz,* pronounced something like "Ante-sevage," can be remembered as "Auntie-save-itch"; *Caruthers* as a "car with udders"; and *Eberhardt* as "ever hard"; and so on. These substitute names are rich in their imaginal properties. All of us can make up an image of these substitute names, some of them most bizarre (and may lack a degree of political correctness).

The second step involves searching for an outstanding feature in the person's face—a high forehead, a beard, unusual glasses, a crooked nose, full cheeks, warts, dimples.

The final stage involves associating a substitute word with an outstanding feature. Thus, if you are introduced to a man whose name is Wally Kelly, whose distinguishing features are a receding hairline and ample belly, the *W* made by his hairline may serve as a cue for Wally, and the belly, a cue for Kelly. Of course, if you forget the code, you may mistakenly call him Walter Stomach.

Extraordinary Memories

From our examples of mnemonics you get the impression that it takes a lot of effort to make good mnemonics. However, some people are so skilled with mnemonics that they occur almost spontaneously with very little effort.

People with unusual or extraordinary memory may be classified as either professional mnemonists, those who consciously apply a mnemonic technique, or spontaneous mnemonists, those whose capacities seem to have developed more or less naturally without conscious effort and without use of a technique or trick.

Although there are numerous anecdotal accounts of people with phenomenal memories, they are most difficult to authenticate. There are several accounts of such people, however, about whom much is known, and a few of these people have been studied intensively. Accounts of some of these are presented here.

S.: Luria

The most celebrated case of extraordinary memory (and also one of the best documented) is that of S. (S. V. Shereshevskii), whose capabilities were studied by the distinguished Russian psychologist A. R. Luria (1960, 1968). The semiclinical study began in the mid-1920s when S. was working as a newspaper reporter. He changed jobs several times and finally became a professional mnemonist.

S. was able to recall without error a list of words that was increased to 30, to 50, and to 70. Luria reports that "in order to imprint an impression of a table consisting of twenty numbers, S. needed only 35 to 40 seconds, . . . a table of fifty numbers required somewhat more time . . . 2½ to 3 minutes" (1968, p. 21).

Several months later when Luria asked S. to recall the list, he did so as accurately as he had on the first occasion. Luria performed numerous experiments of the same sort with similar results. S. did not seem to forget—even if it involved nonsense material—after days, months, or even years!

Alexander Luria **(1902–1977)**. Made basic discoveries in neuropsychology and wrote book on S.

Luria observed that S.'s phenomenal memory was accompanied by extreme **synesthesia,** a condition in which sensory information from one modality (e.g., auditory) evokes a sensation in another modality (e.g., visual).

These synesthetic components seemed important in S.'s recall process, since they provided a background for each item to be recalled.

S. also used the method of loci as a mnemonic. When presented with a series of items to be remembered, he would mentally distribute them along a familiar street in Moscow, starting at Pushkin Square and going down Gorky Street, and then recall the items by taking a mental walk along the same street using familiar landmarks as visual cues for retrieving the items. Errors arose on rare occasions from misperception rather than forgetting. For example, S. forgot a pencil because he "placed" it in front of a picket fence and didn't "see" it when he mentally passed that location.

S.'s vivid imagery also tended to interfere with his ability to understand prose, and abstract poetry seemed particularly difficult. He reported that, when listening to a voice, each word spoken elicited an image, which sometimes "collided" with others. When he read, he reported a similar type of imaginal interference. For example, the simple sentence "The work got under way normally" caused this reaction: "as for *work,* I see that work is going on . . . but there's that word *normally.* What I see is a big, ruddy-cheeked woman, a *normal* woman . . . then the expression *got under way.* Who? What is all this? You have industry . . . and this normal woman—but how does it all fit together? How much I have to get rid of to get the simple idea out of the thing!"

It appears that in S.'s case, his enormous capacity and the longevity of information are related to a combination of things, including imagery, synesthesia, and mnemonics.

V. P.: Hunt and Love

Hunt and Love (1972) discovered V. P., whose extraordinary memory rivals that of S. The case of V. P. is particularly interesting to cognitive psychologists for two reasons: V. P. demonstrated an unusually expansive memory, and, perhaps more important, he was clinically evaluated by a team of cognitive psychologists who used controlled experimental methods to text his abilities.

Hunt and Love had V. P. read a story. After 6 weeks, he was able to recite the story almost verbatim, indicating that V. P.'s LTM was extraordinary. His STM was tested using the Brown-Peterson technique.

E.: A Case of Photographic Memory

During most courses in cognitive psychology, a student will inevitably ask something like, "What about photographic memory? Aren't there some people who can look at a page and tell you verbatim everything they have seen?"

It is not well documented in the literature, but one case of photographic memory is reported by Stromeyer (1970). Elizabeth is a very intelligent, skilled artist who teaches at Harvard. She can mentally project an exact image of a picture onto a surface. Her image appears to be an exact copy of the original, and Elizabeth can look at the image and describe it in detail. Psychologists call this **eidetic imagery** (a talent sometimes found in children) rather than the more trendy *photographic memory.* Elizabeth's ability is not restricted

Recall by V. P. and twelve control subjects of three-consonant trigrams.

Adapted from Hunt and Love (1972).

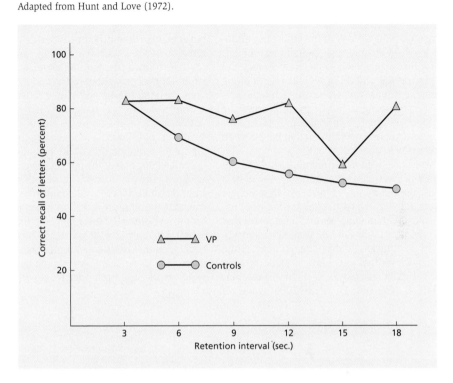

to visual images; she can also visualize, say, a poem in a foreign language she had read several years earlier. She can "copy" a line from the top of the poem or bottom equally well by writing as fast as she can, an ability that came in handy in high school examinations.

V. P.'s performance and those of twelve control participants are shown in Figure 7.3. It appears that V. P.'s recall is much better over time than that of the control participants, which would suggest that he is able to retain meaningless trigrams even in the presence of interfering tasks (which are believed to block rehearsal). V. P. did comment that, because of his knowledge of many languages, he was able to associate the meaningless trigrams in the experiment with a meaningful word. If this is the case, then the Brown-Peterson technique may be a test for his ability to store a meaningful chunk of information (a form of organization) over a brief period of time.

A la carte

China, Comets, and Hibernation: Using the Method of Loci

The method of loci is one of the oldest mnemonics. It involves imagining a distinct and familiar pathway, imagining items to be remembered, and then placing the objects in well-lit places along the imagined pathway. One simply remembers the objects by taking an imaginary stroll down the path. Since the method of loci is one of the oldest mnemonics, one might think that we know all there is to know about it. That is not the case. Researchers have been experimenting with the parameters or conditions that optimize recall of a text passage and minimize mistakes. Researchers in Padua, Italy (along with others), have been experimenting with mnemonics and have found that items presented orally are best remembered using the method of loci as an encoding strategy, while lists that are written out are best using rote rehearsal. This is referred to as the oral presentation effect. Moe and Di Beni (2005) gave all

participants three different types of passages to remember: (1) a narrative passage about China, (2) a descriptive passage about comets, and (3) an expository passage about hibernation. Participants were randomly assigned to three different groups where they either (1) imagined their own unique pathway, (2) used a pathway provided by the researchers, or (3) used a rehearsal method instead. So the presentation rate of the passages could be controlled for; half of the passages were presented on a computer monitor, the other half were played from an audio tape. Results confirm the hypothesis that the oral presentation effect is strongest for the self-generated loci group and that rehearsal is best when reading the passage. The researchers concluded that using mnemonics takes effort and if you plan to use them, you should be well aware which work best and under what conditions.

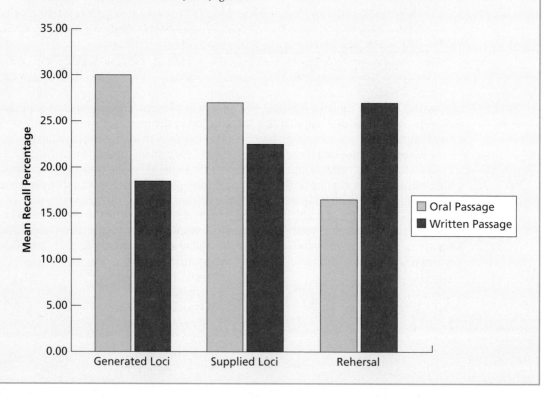

Student Resource Center

STUDY GUIDE

1   A mnemonic is a technique that facilitates storage, or encoding, and the recall of information in memory.

2   A variety of mnemonic techniques have been devised and involve such strategies as imagery and mediation (e.g., method of loci and peg word system), phonemic and orthographic characteristics (e.g., word and number recall), phonemic cues and imagery mediation (e.g., name recall and key word method), and semantic organization.

3   The success of mnemonics in facilitating memory is attributed to their assistance in organizing information.

4   Studies of individuals with exceptional memories indicate that their abilities involve a variety of mnemonic technique combinations: method of loci, imagery, and modified peg word system; method of loci, imagery, and synesthesia (e.g., S.); and semantic mediation (e.g., V. P.).

5   Studies of the expert portrait painter H. O. showed that the part of the brain involved in associative processing was more active than in a novice whereas the novice showed relatively greater activation of the facial-processing area. Also, studies of eye movements and fixations and hand actions of the artist show attributes unique to the expert.

6   Studies of experts show that they excel in their own domain, perceive meaningful patterns, are fast, utilize LTM and STM well, represent a problem at a deep level, analyze a problem qualitatively, and have self-monitoring skills.

7   Some ordinary people have been trained to perform exceptional mathematical computations and remember long strings of numbers. They do so by efficiently utilizing knowledge in LTM.

8   Skilled performance is achieved through organization of material, access to knowledge, speed of encoding patterns, and practice.

KEY TERMS

acronym
acrostic
amnesia
anterograde amnesia
confabulate
consolidation failure
decay
eidetic imagery
failure to encode
interference
key word method

mnemonic
Method of Loci
motivated forgetting
peg word system
proactive interference
repression
retroactive interference
retrograde amnesia
retrieval failure
synesthesia
temporal gradient

Starting Points

Books and Articles

● Popular books on mnemonics that are quite good include Cermak, *Improving Your Memory;* Lorayne and Lucas, *The Memory Book;* Yates, *The Art of Memory;* Young and Gibson, *How to Develop an Exceptional Memory;* Hunter, *Memory: Facts and Fallacies;* and Luria, *The Mind of a Mnemonist.* S. B. Smith has written a book about mnemonics called *The Great Mental Calculators: The Psychology, Methods, and Lives of Calculating Prodigies, Past and Present.* Also recommended is *Practical Aspects of Memory* by Gruneberg, Morris, and Sykes; J. R. Anderson's *Cognitive Psychology* and *Cognitive Skills and Their Acquisition;* and *Memory: Interdisciplinary Approaches,* edited by Solomon et al. An edited collection by Chi, Glaser, and Farr, *The Nature of Expertise,* is especially recommended. Jean Bédard and Michelene Chi have an article called "Expertise" in *Current Directions in Psychological Science* (1993), which is a good summary of knowledge and Ericsson, Krampe, and Tesch-Römer have an article in *Psychological Review* (1993) that is one of the best articles on the topic of expert performance and highly recommended as is Ericsson and Charness's article "Expert Performance" in *American Psychologist.*

Movies

● 50 First Dates (2004)—Anterograde amnesia

● Eternal Sunshine of the Spotless Mind (2004)—Forgetting

● Memento (2000)—Anterograde amnesia

● The Long Kiss Goodnight (1996)—Retrograde amnesia

● The Bourne Identity (2002)—Forgetting

● The Butterfly Effect (2004)—Repression

Search Terms

● The World Memory Championship

● The real life version of the movie Memento

● Clove Wearing

● The brainman

Consciousness

hmmm . . . ?

1. What are you consciously aware of at this instant? Now define *consciousness.* How does your definition compare with the text's definition?

2. What important historical events led to the contemporary studies of consciousness?

3. What is a "prime," and how has priming research told us about conscious and unconscious processes?

4. What is explicit and implicit memory?

5. How can consciousness be studied scientifically?

6. What are the stages of sleep?

7. What are some theories of consciousness?

8. What function does consciousness serve in everyday life as well as for our species?

*W*hen we understand consciousness . . . consciousness will be different.

—*Daniel Dennett*

Consciousness, once central to psychology then banished as unscientific, has now returned in full glory. It is a topic that simply will not disappear, and for good reasons. This last great mystery of science spans psychology, philosophy, and neuroscience. Topics such as subjective experience, awareness, dreams, drugs, and meditation all fall in the realm of the study of consciousness. We spend most of our waking lives engaged in conscious activity, and even during sleep some murmur of awareness is present. Otherwise, how do we wake to the alarm, the cry of our own baby, or a bucket of cold water in the face? When full consciousness returns from deep sleep, a massive change in electrical activity takes place all over the brain, as the fast, small, and irregular waves of waking EEG replace the large, slow, and regular hills and valleys of deep sleep. At the same time, we humans report a rich and varied array of conscious experiences: colors and sounds, feelings and smells, images and dreams, the rich pageant of everyday reality. Because these reports of conscious experience are so perfectly synchronized with brain activity, psychologists infer that they reflect a single underlying reality, the reality of waking consciousness. We begin this chapter with the following definition: **Consciousness** is the awareness of environmental and cognitive events such as the sights and sounds of the world as well as of one's memories, thoughts, feelings, and bodily sensations. By this definition consciousness has two sides. Consciousness includes a realization of environmental stimuli. For example, you might suddenly become mindful of a bird's song, a sharp toothache, or the visual recognition of an old friend. Consciousness also includes one's cognizance of mental events—those thoughts that result from memories and your own internal sense of awareness and self. For example, you might think of the name of the bird, the telephone number of your dentist, or how shy you get in large groups.

These internal, often private thoughts are every bit as important as external stimuli are in determining who we are and what we think. Throughout the day, we all have a myriad of conscious experiences caused by the sights and sounds of the world and an untold number of internal conscious experiences caused by our inner thoughts which privately unmask our personal reactions and feelings.

For scientists interested in consciousness, a fundamental question centers on how the mind emerges from brain activity. This is called the **hard problem** of consciousness (Chalmers, 1995). While brain activity is observable by others, the "mind is observable only to its owner" (Damasio, 1999, p. 4). This fascinating conundrum has led scientists to study consciousness from the smallest pulse of brain activity to the complexity of the subjective experience of smelling a rose. The fear that some have is, as Damasio (1999) has pointed out, that somehow by uncovering the neurological basis of conscious experience that we cheapen the wonder of the mind and all that makes us human. Not so. "By understanding the mind at a deeper level, we will see it as nature's most complex set of biological phenomena rather than as a mystery with an unknown nature. The mind will survive explanation, just as a rose's perfume, its molecular structure deduced, will still smell as sweet" (Damasio, 1999, p. 9).

*A*ll that we are is the result of what we have thought. The mind is everything. What we think, we become.

—*Buddha (563–483 BCE)*

History of Consciousness

Scientific psychology began in the nineteenth century as the study of conscious experience. In the famous words of William James, "psychology is the science of mental life," by which he meant conscious mental life (James, 1890/1983, p. 15). Long before this more formal inquiry, philosophers and lay people contemplated questions regarding the mind and the self. In the early part of the twentieth century the topic of consciousness was nearly banished from psychology by adherents of the dominant psychological ideology, namely behaviorism, led by John Watson and later B.F. Skinner. The "holy war for the mind of man" was fought during the last half of the twentieth century, with cognitive psychologists battling for the return of consciousness as an important topic (if not *the* important topic) in psychology on one side, and behaviorists struggling to maintain a purely objective science on the other. Consciousness would not disappear, and the anticonsciousness (dare we would say unconscious) forces were destined to lose the contest—not because objective psychology was untenable, but because the methods and doctrine were imperious to the point that authentic topics were considered taboo. Few scientific positions can survive narrow-mindedness, and the behaviorist zealots who closed their eyes to vital psychological phenomena, such as memory, imagery, and consciousness, lost the academic high ground to be replaced by cognitive psychology and neuroscience. While much of psychological behavior may be accounted for in behavioristic terms, many other topics, such as consciousness, are not adequately addressed. In recent years consciousness has become more "conscious" in the minds and writings of psychologists, philosophers, and cognitive neuroscientists than any other topic dealing with the mind.

Gradually, however, learning theories were being challenged by theories of memory, perception, and internal representations of mental processes. *Information processing* and *cognition* became buzz words, and consciousness—a topic that simply would not go away no matter how scorned by the behaviorists—began to creep into the psychological literature after a half century of neglect. And the scientists experimenting with the concept were not the psychedelic-loving beatniks of Haight-Asbury attempting to reach higher and higher levels of "consciousness." The 1990s proved to be a crowning decade for the study of consciousness with a "surge" of publications and scientific interest (Zeman, 2001). Interest in the topic continues to grow.

We need constructs to help us study things, especially things as seemingly abstract as consciousness, as they enable us to operationalize our variables to study phenomena. One of the problems is that the constructs help, but they also can hinder because they have such a profound role in guiding our studies and interpreting our data. If too narrow in scope, we may end up knowing a lot about some areas, and not enough of others. Zeman (2001) breaks down consciousness into four categories: (1) the waking state where we perceive and interact; (2) experience, which is our moment-to-moment awareness of what is going on around us; (3) our mental state, which includes our beliefs, hopes, intentions, and desires; and (4) our sense of self, which includes self-recognition, self-knowledge, feeling ownership over the thoughts, ideas, and feelings in your head. These are all very important areas, and we touch on aspects of them in this chapter. But how close does this get us to knowing about consciousness proper?

Oftentimes, while theories are typically what guide research, challenges can be an important driving force to make discoveries (consider Russia's challenge to race the U.S. to the moon, and Christopher Reeve's challenge to find a cure for spinal cord injury). Challenges direct resources (both intellectual and monetary) toward solving important problems or reaching important goals. As we stated earlier in the chapter, philosophers have long been interested in consciousness, while psychology has only recently reestablished its connection with consciousness. Cognitive neuroscientist Francis Crick, who won the Nobel Prize for his role as co-discoverer of the structures of DNA in the early 1950s, and Christof Koch, whose PhD is in nonlinear information processing, have been promoting consciousness as a problem to be solved by neuroscientists. They argue that most neuroscientists do not attempt to study consciousness because (1) it is considered a philosophical problem, best left to philosophers and (2) that it is premature to study it at the moment. Disagreeing with these two points, Crick and Koch challenge these assumptions by saying that consciousness is an emergent product of brain activity and as such there must be a neurological correlate of consciousness. At any given moment some neurological activity is involved in consciousness while other activity is not. If this is the case, and since much of the brain activity is localized in its functions, it might be possible to sort out those processes not involved in consciousness from those that are (Crick & Koch, 1998). Their challenge to find the neural correlate of consciousness has riled and inspired scientists and philosophers alike. These critics (Noe & Thompson, 2004; among others) argue that searching for a **neural correlate of consciousness** is unnecessarily reductionistic, and that pinpointing a brain region associated with a perceptual experience does not per se mean that the locus of consciousness has been discovered. However, as Chalmars (2000) has put it: "the search for a neural correlate of consciousness provides a project that is relatively tractable, clearly defined, and theoretically neutral, whose goal seems to be visible somewhere in the middle distance. Because of this, the search makes an appropriate centerpiece for a developing science of consciousness, and an important springboard in the quest for a general theory of the relationship between physical processes and conscious experience."

Framework for Consciousness: AWAREness

The study of consciousness has expanded beyond philosophical debates and scientific focus solely on various states of consciousness. It has become widely interdisciplinary and rising in prominence as a theoretically and methodologically active discipline. Here, we pre-

---

Consciousness is now largely a scientific problem.

—*Francis Crick*

Francis Crick
with a model
of DNA.

sent a general framework of consciousness called **AWAREness** (Solso, 2003; MacLin, MacLin, & Solso, 2007), which incorporates some central themes as well as some new ideas. The main features of the framework include **A**ttention, **W**akefulness, **A**rchitecture, **R**ecall of knowledge, and the **E**motive. In addition, there are several secondary attributes included with this framework. These are novelty, emergence, selectivity, and subjectivity.

The five elements of consciousness in the AWAREness framework are an attempt to reduce the variance in defining the subjective experience we call consciousness. Only one of the elements, architecture, deals with a physiological process; the rest deal with psychological processes. All contribute to consciousness and many interact.

Attention: the focusing of cognizance on external or internal things. We are able to direct our attention, and hence our consciousness, to external or internal events. This part of consciousness has been referred to as a "spotlight" and is similar to the spotlight metaphor of attention in which a concentrated beam of light is shone in the direction of interest. While visiting the beach, for example, you may attend to the beach birds at one moment and then swing your "spotlight" to a ship at sea, and then to a sunbather. We are constantly moving the focus of our attention and likewise shifting the contents of our consciousness. Our attention to objects is not arbitrary, but is driven by a "searching eye" looking for details that, combined and integrated into our larger world knowledge, form the basis of a more comprehensive consciousness. Because objects are seen very clearly only when they are in the very center of our visual field, our eyes are in fact literally moving from detail to detail in what lies before them.

In addition to external cues, we may turn our attention inside and reflect on personal thoughts, memories, and images. You may at this moment bring to consciousness the image of a famous person. You are equally adept at bringing to consciousness thoughts and memories from your past, which is a shared feature with the recall of knowledge.

Wakefulness: the continuum from sleep to alertness. Consciousness as a state of wakefulness implies that consciousness has an arousal component. In this part of the AWAREness framework, consciousness is a mental state, experienced throughout one's lifetime, in one's daily experience. For example, last night you slept and now (presumably) you are awake—two radically different states of consciousness. If you drink a cup of strong coffee, you might be even more awake. Thus, we first think of consciousness as having various levels of AWAREness and excitation. We may alter our state through meditation, drugs, or intensive attention. Wakefulness in the above context is very similar to arousal, which has been studied extensively by cognitive psychologists and which influences attention.

Architecture: the physical location of the physiological structures (and their related processes) that underpin consciousness. A defining aspect of consciousness is that it has some architecture or physiological structure. Consciousness is thought to have a home in the brain and may be identified through a type of investigation of the neural correlates of consciousness, discussed earlier. For over a century neuroanatomists have been dissecting the brain to discover its functions using refined techniques. In 1908, Korbinian Broadman analyzed the cellular organization of the cerebral cortex and, by use of staining techniques available at the time, was able to identify 52 distinct types of cells that were hypothesized to represent different types processes. The science of cellular structure and functionality was born. Some cells are specialized in hearing, some in speech, some in motor performance, some in vision, and the like. Following this lead, and using up-to-date imaging techniques, the logical extension of this work's to localize the part, or parts, of the cortex implicated in consciousness.

Cognitive neuroscientists are faced with a daunting task of unraveling the many strands of consciousness. Consider the neurons pictured on the next page. Consciousness is not a single process carried out by a single neuron, but is sustained by many neurological processes associated with the interpretation of sensory, semantic, cognitive, and emotional phenomena that are both physically present and imaged. For example, many psychological processes and the resulting behavior are carried out at an unconscious level—driving your car, returning a rocket tennis serve, recoiling at the sight and sound of a cranky rattlesnake. These actions seem to be automatized through experience. Other actions require conscious intervention, such as deciding which movie to go to, which museum to visit, or whether a given painting is beautiful or ugly. For these we need conscious AWAREness of a complex sort. Simple reflexive behavior of the sort that a frog might make when capturing a fly won't do. It appears that different parts of the brain handle conscious decisions that might involve deciding whether Will Smith was good in the movie *I, Robot* or if the movie would have been better if Willem Defoe played the part than deal with unconscious actions such as returning the fast tennis serve. Another example of consciousness being sustained in the brain is language, which occupies a sizeable portion of the left hemisphere of the brain. Language contributes to consciousness in hugely important ways such as giving semantic identification and organization to an object. Indeed, the whole brain seems to be involved in different aspects of conscious AWAREness.

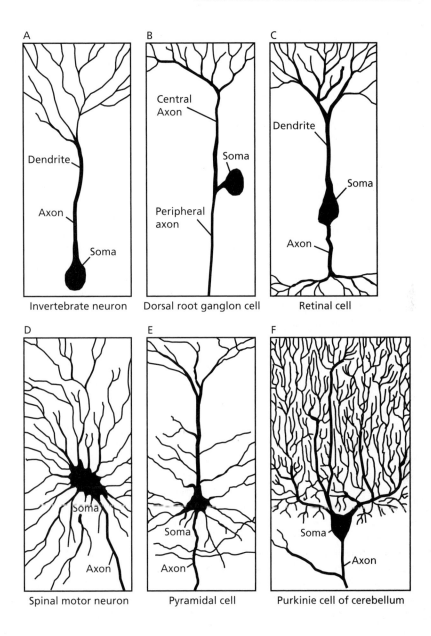

A — Invertebrate neuron
- Dendrite
- Axon
- Soma

B — Dorsal root ganglon cell
- Central Axon
- Soma
- Peripheral axon

C — Retinal cell
- Dendrite
- Soma
- Axon

D — Spinal motor neuron
- Soma
- Axon

E — Pyramidal cell
- Soma
- Axon

F — Purkinie cell of cerebellum
- Soma
- Axon

Recall of Knowledge: the accessing of personal and world information. Consciousness allows humans to gain access to knowledge through recall (and recognition) of both personal information and knowledge of the world. Recall of knowledge is accomplished mainly though attentional processes that are initiated internally or externally. This part of the definition of consciousness has three components: recall of self-knowledge, recall of general information, and recall of one's collective knowledge.

Self-knowledge is a sense of one's own personal information. First, there is the fundamental knowledge that you are you. This is called self-awareness. If an animal or human can recognize themselves in a mirror it is believed that they possess self-awareness. Self-awareness can be tested via the mirror test (Gallup, 1970). This involves marking the face with an odorless dye (with appropriate distraction so that the animal or human doesn't feel or remember feeling the dye put on). A mirror is then presented and the behavior of the animal or human is monitored. Self-awareness is indicated by recognition in the mirror as well as realization that the image in the mirror is them. This is usually accomplished by the animal or human noticing the dye in the image and then touching their own face or angling their view to see better. Humans over 2 years old pass the test, along with chimpanzees, bonobos, orangutans, dolphins, elephants, and possibly pigeons. Children under 2 years of age and dogs react to the mirror with fear or curiosity. Fish respond to the mirror as if it is another fish. Birds will often attack the mirror. Self-knowledge comprises self-awareness as well as other information about the self. You know, for example, that this moment you are seeing words on a page, that the word you just read (that became part of your immediate consciousness) was the word "consciousness"; you know if you are late for an appointment or have a headache; you know if you are having a clandestine affair; you know how you feel about your father; you know if your underwear is too tight or too loose, and countless other bits of personal information that can be immediately recalled without having to relive the event.

Another component, **world knowledge,** allows us to recall the many facts of our long-term memory. Thus, when you enter the Museum of Modern Art in New York City, you may elevate to consciousness memorized information about twentieth-century art. In effect, you may prime your expected views with knowledge previously buried in LTM. You may recall that the century began with abstract art and cubism and included several movements such as fauism. In a sense, your "level of consciousness," to use a trendy phrase, has been raised for this type of art, and hence you actually "see" more, because related neurological activity has been energized. When you attend to one of Andy Warhol's paintings of a Campbell's soup can, you understand it as a part of the artistic culture of the time, not as a misplaced advertisement.

The third aspect of the role of consciousness is the *activation of knowledge* is perhaps the most interesting of all. Here, one is conscious of another's actions. In evolutionary terms, across years of cooperative acts, such as mutual hunting activities or gathering of foodstuffs, survival was improved if one member could more or less know what his or her partner was thinking in addition to observing and understanding what she was doing. Empathetic sensitivity serves survival needs and is a key to knowing how we modern humans see the world. As the need for even more cooperative actions intensified, such as during the migration of tribes from central Africa and to the Middle East and southern Europe, a greater degree of "intuitive" sensitivity was required. Such developments were greatly facilitated by language, which served not only as a means to tell one's companion to remove the log that had fallen on one's leg but also to let her know how you are feeling. It may well be that cursing began in this way, and an expression such as "Get that @#$%^& log off my leg" not only conveyed a cry for cooperative behavior but was also an explicit expression of one's raw feelings. Feelings count, and knowing about another's conscious pain (as well as pleasure) was an important step in the socialization of the species.

Emotive: the affective components associated with consciousness. Sentience is the state of being conscious, and is often considered a feeling or emotion (as opposed to thought or perception). Thus, when you look at a building designed by Frank Lloyd Wright, it may cause a raw feeling of disgust or maybe one of delight. In any event, these perceptions produce an internal impression that you may tell others but that is difficult to measure empirically. To you, the experience is obvious. Emotions are caused by internal states as we respond to external events, such as the feelings you get when you stub your toe, lose a parent, get divorced, get an unexpected A on a test, marry the man or woman of your dreams, or find a $20 bill in an old pair of jeans. When describing these subjective emotions to another person it is impossible to convey exactly what you feel. No one can really crawl inside your skull or run a neurological conduit between your brain and theirs. We may look at brain images and get an idea as to what part of your brain is turned on when you get depressed, break your leg, or feel giddy over falling in love.

Novelty: the propensity not only to focus on central thoughts and events, but to seek out novel, creative, and innovative items. There is ample evidence that people and animals seek novel and informative stimulations; consciousness seems to have a preference for "news." Novelty can come from change in the environment, disconfirmation of expectation (surprise), or violation of skilled routines (choice-points in the otherwise routine flow of action).

Emergence: consciousness is distinctive from other neural processes in the respect that it deals with private and internal thoughts. Unlike other neural processes (e.g., that cause you to move your eyes to see something better), neural processes related to at least some aspects of consciousness appear to loop on internal information and self-reflection. This leads to at least the phenomenological impression that consciousness emerges from the activity in the brain.

Selectivity and **Subjectivity:** humans are constantly selecting a very few thoughts to consider at any given time, which may change rapidly given the intrusion of new thoughts or external cues. Consciousness has long been thought of as something that casts light on things to clarify understanding. This spotlight embodies the selective function of consciousness and the flow of conscious contents across multiple domains of memory, perception, imagery, thought, and action (Crick, 1984; Lindsay & Norman, 1977). Both psychological and neurobiological searchlights, or selectivity, are open to two unanswered questions: (1) how is the particular focus selected? and (2) once something is selected to be in focus, what happens to that information? And other information not selected? If we consider the spotlight in a more realistic context, like on a theater stage, we get closer to an understanding of how consciousness might operate in the brain. Thinking of a theater, we can liken conscious experience to the brightly lit stage in a darkened auditorium. Just because we cannot readily see beyond the stage does not mean that very important activities are not going on backstage and in the audience. Multiple sources of activity (the lighting guys, the orchestra in the pit, the makeup artist, costumer, and director, not to mention the audience) come together to create the experience of the play. We can extend this more directly to consciousness by recognizing that much of consciousness is disseminated throughout the brain, and it is only together that conscious experience as we know it occurs. And finally, plain and simple, subjectivity refers to the fact that each person's conscious experience is unique.

These are the aspects of the framework of consciousness we call AWAREness, which combine to contribute to your human experience of life's great pleasures and pains. Each of these aspects can be measured on a continuum and can be combined to evaluate something's level of consciousness. Each of the AWARE factors could be weighted on a quantative scale, say from 0 to 10—which would give further psychometric sensitivity to AWARE beings. This makes sense as we live in a multideminsional world and for eons have exhibited patterns of wide biodiversity. To impose a rigidly dichotomous classification of consciousness not only fails to grasp the complex nature of the term but also misrepresents human and animal consciousness.

For example, you are a conscious thing, a rock is not. The frog that lives by the pond may be, but not as conscious as measured by the AWAREness standard compared to you. Yet, it may be more conscious than a rock. Some animals such as a dog may be more alert than you at times. Some may argue that cats are more conscious than dogs, but most would agree that a cockroach is to a lesser degree. Conceivably cockroaches are an AWA type of conscious thing (i.e., they are aware, wakeful, and have some architectural locus for limited consciousness). It would be difficult to make a convincing argument that a cockroach has the RE aspects of consciousness, which deal with the recall of knowledge and emotions. You can apply the AWAREness framework to evaluate where on the consciousness continuum any entity lies.

Functions of Consciousness

Some philosophers have posed the argument that consciousness is not necessary for much of our human functioning, as exemplified by using the example of a zombie (Chalmers, 1995; Dennett, 1988). A zombie is a hypothetical creature who can do everything we can do, but does not have consciousness. In other words, a zombie might have all the receptors to detect red, and use that information to choose ripe apples, but would not have the subjective experience of "redness." This subjective experience is referred to as **qualia.** Qualia refers to the properties of sensory experiences, and the subjective experience and feelings associated with them. By virtue of the fact that humans experience objects, not the electromagnetic energy that we actually detect (see) with our retinas, qualia is considered phenomenological and subjective. Some argue (e.g., Dennett, 1988) that because of the subjective nature of qualia, they do not really exist, which essentially does away with the "hard problem" of consciousness (i.e., how is the mind created from brain activity). Others (e.g., Chalmers, 1986) argue that subjective experience or not, the perceptual experience is there, qualia do exist, and thus the "hard problem" is still present.

Consciousness . . . increases the likelihood that an organism will direct its attention, and ultimately its movements, to whatever is most important for its survival and reproduction.

—*Pierson and Trout*

However, others (Pierson & Trout, 2005) argue that the only reason to have consciousness is to make volitional movement possible. Volitional movements are those that are made by choice, not by instinct or reflex. In having consciousness, and thus volitional movement, we can direct our attention and behaviors to aspects of the environment that will lead to better outcomes. They argue that neural processes alone cannot perform these functions as effectively as neural processes combined with consciousness. Damasio (1999) has a similar view in that consciousness serves to allow us to plan our behaviors instead of relying purely on instincts. By doing so (and coupled with self-awareness) gives us greater survivability in the environment.

Baars and McGovern (1996) suggest several functions of consciousness (see figure). The first is a **context-setting** function whereby the systems act to define an incoming stimulus in terms of context and knowledge in memory, which serves to clarify understanding of the stimulus. The second function is **adaptation and learning,** which posits that conscious involvement is required to successfully deal with novel information. The third is a **prioritizing** and access function whereby consciousness is necessary to access the vast amounts of information available in the unconscious. The fourth is a **recruitment and control** function where consciousness taps into motor systems in order to carry out voluntary actions (similar to Pierson and Trout's position mentioned previously). Fifth is a

© Jolyon Troscianko 2007.

Try This

Consciousness Craze

If our estimates are correct, in 1950 there were 23 articles published on consciousness in the psychological literature; in 1975 that number rose to 532 and in 2000 to 11,480. There are specialized journals such as the *International Journal of Consciousness* and *Cognition* that publishes topics such as selective attention, priming, physiological correlates of awareness, blindsight, and the development of self-concept, for example. There has been an intellectual feeding frenzy over consciousness—the very topic that once caused consternation among many academic psychologists. Psychology lost its "mind" and became "unconscious" about 100 years ago. It now appears that we not only have regained our mind but also have revived consciousness.

Here are some important sites for consciousness on the Internet:

Centre for Consciousness (consciousness.anu .edu.au). Their mission is: "This project aims to develop a research centre that will be a world leader in the study of consciousness. The focus will be the question: how does human consciousness represent the world? The science of consciousness has seen explosive growth internationally in the last decade, but the relationship between consciousness and representation is not well-understood. Through local and international collaboration, researchers will develop a framework for understanding the representational content of consciousness and will analyze experimental work at the leading edge of neuroscience and cognitive science. This will help us to understand the nature of consciousness itself."

Center for Consciousness Studies (www .consciousness.arizona.edu). Their mission is: "Promoting open, rigorous discussion of all phenomena related to conscious experience."

Journal of Consciousness Studies (www .imprint.co.uk/jcs.html). How does the mind relate to the brain? Can computers ever be conscious? What do we mean by subjectivity and the self? These questions are being keenly debated in fields as diverse as cognitive science, neurophysiology, and philosophy, and this peer-reviewed journal publishes papers in these areas.

The Association for the Scientific Study of Consciousness (www.assc.caltech.edu/index.htm). Its stated mission is: "To encourage research on consciousness in cognitive science, neuroscience, philosophy, and other relevant disciplines in the sciences and humanities, directed toward understanding the nature, function, and underlying mechanisms of consciousness."

decision-making and executive function, which serves to bring necessary information and resources out of the unconscious to aid in making decisions and exerting control. The sixth function is **error detection and editing.** This function is focused on consciousness tapping into unconscious rule systems that let us (the conscious "us") know when we have made a mistake. The seventh function is **self-monitoring.** Self-monitoring, in the form of self-reflection, inner speech, and imagery, help us control our conscious and unconscious functioning. And lastly, the eighth function of consciousness is **organization and flexibility.** This function allows us to rely on automatic functions in predictable situations, but also allows us to tap into specialized knowledge sources in unpredictable situations.

*I*f I didn't wake up, I'd still be sleeping.

—*Yogi Berra*

Baars and McGovern's (1996) functions of consciousness.

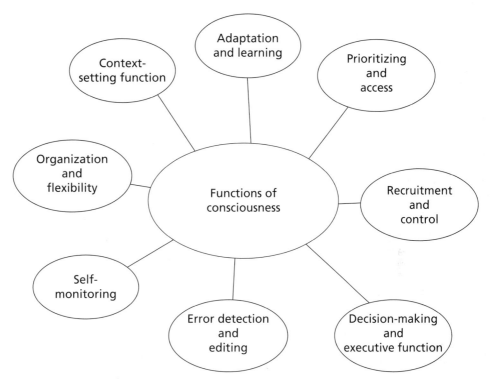

States of Consciousness

Much of the scientific and philosophical discussion regarding consciousness centers on issues of subjective experience and the neural correlates of consciousness. Another area of scientific inquiry is in states of consciousness, or states of varying awareness or altered consciousness. These incorporate the A (attention) and W (wakefulness) aspects of the AWAREness model. We will briefly cover sleeping, dreaming, drug use, and meditation.

Sleep

The clearest distinction between consciousness and unconsciousness is seen when one is awake or asleep, and experiments with sleeping people have been favored by researchers of consciousness. The preferred tool has been the electroencephalograph (EEG) because it is reasonably nonrestrictive (if one does not mind wearing a harness of snakelike wires hanging from one's head like Medusa) and good temporal data can be collected. It is possible to get brain waves throughout the sleeping period. During the day, we interact and are constantly in an attentive state—looking here, listening to one message, or smelling a new odor. But while we are asleep, the attentive mechanisms are profoundly reduced

Child with EEG cap, in a study at the University College London–Centre for Developmental Disorders and Cognitive Neuroscience.

Leon Neal (www.leonneal.com)

and personal interaction is almost nonexistent. There are also noticeable changes in EEG recordings that confirm that we humans normally go through various "stages" of sleep. In Figure 8.1, five characteristic brain waves show the electrical activity of humans awake and during the four stages of sleep. In the first level, the person is awake and exhibits a low-amplitude rapid pattern of activity that becomes the higher-voltage, slow delta wave patterns of deep sleep. During this stage, consciousness is markedly reduced. This deep sleep is replaced by rapid eye movement (REM) sleep when dreaming occurs as the person returns to a state of consciousness.

When we are in a relaxed state, awake with our eyes closed, we exhibit alpha waves in which the electrical potential shows a fairly regular pattern of 8–12 cycles per second. Stage I sleep is the lightest of the four stages and happens when we first doze off. During this stage there are short periods of theta activity (4–7 Hz) indicative of drowsiness. Stage II sleep is characterized by sleep "spindles," which are rhythmic bursts of 12–15 Hz of EEG activity. During Stage III sleep, we observe some very low frequency (1–4 Hz) delta waves in addition to the spindling pattern, and in Stage IV sleep, the EEG recordings are similar to those of the previous stage, but more extensive delta waves are noted. Stage IV sleep is the deepest of sleep states, from which arousal is most difficult. The behavioral characteristics of each stage, as well as an indication of **REM sleep,** which is sleep characterized by rapid eye movements and dreaming, are shown in Figure 8.2. The stages of sleep as indicated by behavioral representations as well as EEG characteristics are shown. Here, the person goes from wakefulness and slumber (he tosses and turns) to quiet, deep sleep to REM sleep and a return to more conscious activity.

FIGURE 8.1

An example of EEG recordings as a person goes from wakefulness to deep sleep.

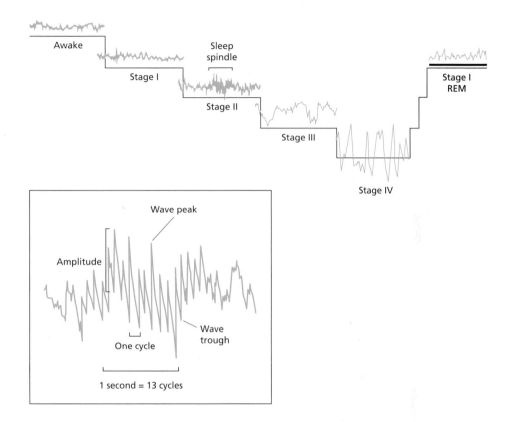

In the study of sleep, it is possible to see the change from a state of consciousness to unconsciousness and then a return to consciousness. Furthermore, through EEG recordings and other instrumentation, we can tie levels of consciousness to physiological measures of brain activity.

Dreaming

As mentioned, dreaming occurs during the REM portion of the sleep cycle. People are often very curious about dreams. Do dreams predict the future? Do they have some deep meaning that you should be concerned about? Why do we dream? Freud believed that dreams were a way that your unconscious leaked out information, and that you could learn about the hidden meaning of your dreams. Some religions view dreams as a way to communicate with ancestors. A scientific approach to why we dream is called the activation synthesis hypothesis. This hypothesis posits the brain activity present during REM (recall that

Sleep cycle.

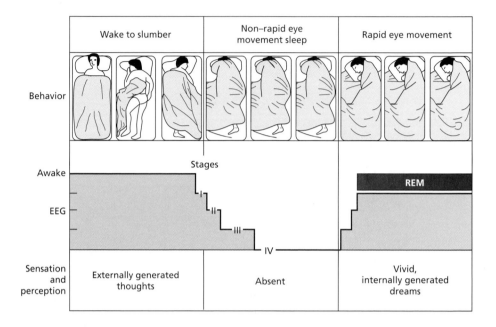

it is very similar to awake brain activity) is interpreted by the brain in the only way it knows how: by tapping into your existing knowledge structures in LTM, utilizing the ways in which we talk all the time, in the form of stories and narratives. Thus, it is not surprising that many people experience their dreams as movies that they feel they watch or participate in. Dreams comprise the same experiences and emotions that we have in day-to-day life: happiness, anger, fear, sadness, anxiety. We dream about what we know (often very vividly) and we also dream about what we don't know (and fill in or gloss over the details).

One problem with sleeping is it creates a discontinuity between waking consciousness and awareness of what is going on during sleep. How do we separate what we re-

A psychedelic experience is a journey to new realms of consciousness. The scope and content of the experience is limitless. . . . Of course, the drug does not produce the transcendent experience. It merely acts as a chemical key—it opens the mind, frees the nervous system of its ordinary patterns and structures.

—*Timothy Leary*

member from dreams, from reality? According to Steve Smith at Texas A&M University, memories that are bizarre and implausible are separated from reality and interpreted as dreams. When dreams are not implausible (e.g., you dream about being at work and having an argument with your boss) you may experience some unsettled feelings upon waking when you try to determine what is real and what is not!

Those who can exert cognitive control in their dreams are experiencing lucid dreaming. This is when you know you are dreaming while you are dreaming. Instead of feeling like a viewer or passive participant in the dream, lucid dreamers can make volitional decisions in their dreams (to make bad guys disappear, to fly away, or simply to "go over there" to check something out).

Drug Use

The reason why drugs "work" is that we have receptors in our brains for the drugs. However, these receptors weren't designed to process these particular chemicals, so using drugs alters our state of consciousness such that it is significantly different than the typical waking state. Some drugs (**depressants**) slow down nervous system activity (e.g., alcohol, barbituates, marijuana), others (**stimulants**) speed up nervous system activity (e.g., nicotine, cocaine, methamphetamines). Still others (**hallucinogens**) alter our sense of reality (e.g., LSD/acid, psylocibyn/mushrooms). Some drugs have multiple properties (like ecstasy, which is classified as a stimulant but also has hallucinogenic symptoms). All drugs operate on our neurotransmitters to carry out their effects.

Drugs affect your awareness of physiological and psychological aspects of your conscious experience. For example, ecstasy impacts you physiologically by causing involuntary teeth clenching, nausea, blurred vision, chills, sweating, increased heart rate, and blood pressure. Psychological effects include experiences of feelings of closeness with others and a desire to touch others. Repeated use of ecstasy damages the cells that produce serotonin, which interferes with mood, appetite, learning, and memory.

Hallucinations are vivid visual experiences. Unlike illusions, hallucinations are not able to be experienced by others. Your awareness of self, the world, and sensory information is dramatically altered with hallucinogenic drugs. Hallucinations may also be experienced with very high fevers, severe sleep deprivation, starvation, and oxygen deprivation.

Meditation

Meditation is a state of relaxed concentration whereby the mind is free from all thoughts. The practice of meditation is diverse in techniques and goals. Some use chants, internal mantras (repeating a word or nonword), body positions (from sitting styles to yoga), and external objects (pillows, rosary beads, small figurines) as part of their ritual. Nearly all meditation practices recommend daily practice of 10–30 minutes. Reasons for engaging in meditation may be religious, spiritual, personal well-being, or health-related. Meditation has been scientifically shown to aid in reducing stress and pain, as well as to promote physiologically relaxed states (Austin, 1999; Lazar et al., 2000). Meditation also affects the brain, with studies demonstrating its effects on the left prefrontal cortex, which is responsible for planning, reasoned decision making, and positive mood (Bennett-Goleman, 2001). Not everyone has positive experiences with meditation (Lukoff, Lu, & Turner, 1998); some report dissociative feelings and other psychological problems.

Models of Consciousness

There are several cognitive models of consciousness that attempt to frame this complex topic. Johnson-Laird (1988) puts forth a computational model that proposes that the cognitive architecture is a parallel processing system dominated by a control hierarchy. Schacter's model of dissociable interactions and conscious experience (DICE) is designed to account for memory dissociations in normal memory functioning and abnormal memory functioning in people with brain damage. DICE gives support to the notion that there is consciousness in a system of separate knowledge sources. Shallice's (1988) model is focused on an information processing system with four subsystems (contention scheduling, a form of behavioral scripts; a supervisory system, which monitors contention scheduling; a language system; an episodic memory system). Any single system is not necessary or sufficient to account for consciousness, and consciousness corresponds from the flow of information between these systems. Baars's (1983, 1988) global workspace theory views consciousness as a theater where there is a global broadcasting system that disseminates information throughout the brain. Baars's model is discussed in detail in the next section.

Baars's Global Workspace Theory

Baars's theory uses a theater as a metaphor to understand consciousness and its components. First, there is a "bright spot" on the stage that is moved by the selective "spotlight" of attention. Around the bright spot is a "fringe" that is composed of important but vaguely conscious events. Baars conceptualizes the stage as our working memory system. Further exploring the metaphor shows us that the audience out in the darkened theater receives information from the bright spot. The behind-the-scenes activities shape the events in the bright spot. So overall, the bright spot globally distributes information through the theater, to the audience, as well as to the behind-the-scenes systems (while at the same time being shaped by the inputs from these behind-the-scenes systems).

Bernard Baars. Developed a comprehensive theory of consciousness.

An example of "spotlight" and "fringe" events.

Baars focuses extensively on the limited capacity of conscious experience, drawing from what we know about the relatively low number of items that can be kept in short-term memory (7 +/− 2), as well as the selective nature of attention. We can only pay attention to one dense stream of information at once, at least if we are to gain meaning out of the stream. Think, for example, about having two people talk to you at once, telling you very important things. Person A says, "I just found out that your flight. . ." overlapping with Person B saying, "The passport office called and said . . ." You've got to shut one person out so that you can hear and understand each of these important streams of information, one after the other, not at the same time.

Despite what seems like a surprising limitation (you'd think 100 billion neurons could do better than this, right?), this limited capacity system is back-dropped by a vast collection of unconscious processes in the form of "orderly forests of neurons . . . and functions in parallel with many things happening at the same time, largely unconscious of the details, and widely decentralized in any task" (Baars, 1997, p. 295). This is all done without the benefit of some command center. Yet, consciousness allows for access to unconscious sources of knowledge. Thus, having this global access available to us minimizes the "problem" associated with limited capacity.

*T*he mind is what the brain does.

—*George Mandler*

A theater metaphor for conscious experience.

Adapted from Baars (1997). Baars, B.J. (1997). In the theater of consciousness: Global workspace theory, a rigorous scientific theory of consciousness. *Journal of Consciousness Studies,* 21(4), 292–309.

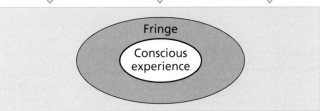

Contexts operators behind the scenes

| Director | Spotlight Controller | Local Contexts |

Competing for access to consciousness:

Outer Senses	Inner Senses	Ideas
Seeing		
Hearing		
Feeling	Visual imagery	Imagible Ideas
Tasting	Inner speech	Verbalized Ideas
Smelling	Dreams	Fringe Conscious
Submodalities	Imagined	Intuitions
Heat	Feelings	
Vibration		

the players . . .

. . . the spotlight of attention shining on the stage of working memory . . .

Fringe

Conscious experience

Working memory receives conscious input, controls inner speech and uses imagery for spatial tasks, all under voluntary control.

the unconscious audience...

Memory systems:

Lexicon
Semantic networks
Autobiographical
and declarative memory
Beliefs, knowledge
of the world, of
oneself and others

Interpreting conscious contents:

Recognizing objects, faces, speech, events. Syntactic anlysis. Spatial relationships. Social inferences.

Automatisms:

Skill memory
Details of language, action control, reading, thinking, and thousands more . . .

Motivational systems:

Is the conscious event relevant to my goals? Emotional responses, facial expressions, preparing the body for action. Managing goal conflicts.

You know how it is—your friend tells you about a favorite new car, restaurant, or clothing style. And all of sudden you see that thing everywhere! Were these things not there before? Of course they were, but your level of awareness of them was raised by the conversation with your friend and now you notice these elements in your environment when you didn't before. Let's see if we can raise your level of consciousness of the following list of words. Read this list and form an impression of each item:

CHER   PERFUME
CRUTCHES   FUNNY HAIR
CRYING BABY   SKATEBOARD

In the next few days note how some of these words have an uncanny way of entering your consciousness. How is this exercise related to priming experiments? Why did these concepts "pop into your head"? What is the relationship between memory and consciousness? Can you now reverse the process so you *cannot* have these words and their associates intrude on your conscious thought? How might other words and activities raise your level of consciousness?

Automatic Processes

Not all of our experiences are conscious ones. Have you ever accidentally driven to work or school on the weekend when you were actually going some place altogether different? Have you ever met someone that you instantly knew you liked? Have you ever unintentionally acted in a biased manner toward someone else? While taking a test, have you ever felt like you "knew" an answer, but couldn't quite come up with it? For many of us the answer is yes to all of the above. This is because we are not conscious of all thought processes taking place in our brains. Furthermore, some unconscious processes, with effort, can be taken under control. For example, we can consciously direct attention to something, though by and large our attentional processes are operating automatically. So, we are not saying that we are unconscious of our driving, it is just that the bulk of the cognitive processes involved in driving behaviors are handled automatically. Some refer to this as online cognitions, others refer to it as brief cognitions, while others might use the term automatic processing. **Automatic processes** are those that are uncontrollable, without

*I*t is the routine that keeps men sane; for if there were no grooves along which thought and action might move with unconscious ease, the mind would be perpetually hesitant, and would soon take refuge in lunacy.

—*Will Durant*

intention or outside awareness, and highly efficient. This section discusses how some cognitions are to a large degree handled with little or no awareness.

Implicit Memory

Implicit memory is germane to our discussion of consciousness because it refers to memory that is measured through a performance change related to some previous experience.

In many cases, implicit memory is revealed when previous information facilitates task performance and does not require conscious recall of those experiences. If you were asked to recall the capital of France, you actively and consciously search your memory to find Paris; this is an example of explicit memory. If you are shown a badly degraded figure and then shown the whole figure and asked to identify it, you are able to recognize the figure faster than if the degraded figure is not shown. Your conscious awareness of the influence of the prime (the degraded figure) is likely to be absent. This is the basis for priming studies, which we talk about next.

Priming Studies

The use of primes that activate mental associations just below the level of consciousness became all the rage in psychology in the 1980s and 1990s (see Roediger & McDermott, 1993, for an excellent review), and it seemed that one could not pick up a journal in experimental psychology during this period without reading about a new wrinkle on the topic. Now, those who are passionate about these studies are beginning to isolate some of the structures implicated in consciousness.

Cognitive psychologists began investigating the influence of briefly presented words on subsequent recognition of other words as early as early as the 1970s (see Meyer & Schvaneveldt, 1971, 1976; Meyer, Schvaneveldt, & Ruddy, 1974b) and unwittingly opened up a can of worms still not clearly understood. The experimental paradigm of these early studies was simple enough and has remained to this day. A research participant is shown a word, say *COLLEGE,* and then is shown an associate of the word, say *UNIVERSITY.* He or she is asked to identify the second word as a real word as fast as he can. Another participant is shown a word such as *JELLY* and is asked to identify *UNIVERSITY* as a real word. If primed with *COLLEGE,* a participant identifies *UNIVERSITY* faster than if primed with *JELLY.* This task is called a Lexical Decision Task (LDT).

The matter got more complicated when a different type of prime was used by Richard Nisbett and Lee Ross (1980) at the University of Michigan in a social psychological experiment that involved showing participants words that were associated such as *OCEAN* and *MOON.* Then, when asked to *free-associate* to the words, participants did not know why they responded with the words they used. For example, a person might say *detergent* and invent a reason like "My mom used Tide to do the laundry." By now, it was becoming clear that primes had an effect on subsequent performance *even when the participant was unaware of the cause.* The topic raised the possibility of **subliminal priming,** or the effect of a prime that is presented below the **sensory threshold,** defined as the lowest energy required to activate a neural response.

Figure 8.3, which illustrates subliminal priming, is based on some of the work done in England and has been used as a successful class demonstration. One half of the class

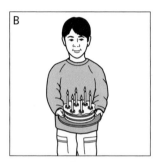

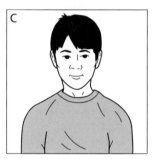

FIGURE 8.3

A demonstration of subliminal priming.

looked at a picture such as the one in Figure 8.3A, and the other half at 8.3B. (The pictures were presented on an overhead projector for about 100 ms.) Then all students were shown the boy in Figure 8.3C and asked to draw the face and make a judgment about the character of the boy. Students who saw A, even momentarily presented, had a tendency to see and draw the boy as somewhat devilish and use words such as *naughty* or *mischievous*. Those who saw B tended to draw and describe the boy using words like *angelic* or *nice*. The surprising part of the story is that students were not (generally) aware of the character of the prime picture. When allowed to study the prime, they remarked, "My gosh, the kid looks like a little devil complete with horns" or "I did not see how innocent the guy appeared." It appears that in this example, a stimulus prime presented subliminally (i.e., below the level of conscious recognition) has an influence on subsequent evaluation of a similar picture.

What has become an archetypal experiment in subliminal priming is a study by Tony Marcel of Cambridge University. In the first phase of the experiment a group of participants were presented with a word very briefly (20–110 milliseconds), which was followed by a visual mask (such as a series of XXXXs) that blocks the image of the word staying on the retina and inhibits further sensory processing. The presentations were so brief that the participants did not report seeing the words. They were presented at a subliminal rate and their guess as to the word presented was no better than chance. Having established the level of presentation at which participants could no longer identify the word, they were then presented with a word at a subliminal rate, which was a prime of another word (BREAD) or a word that was not a prime (TRUCK) (see Figure 8.4). The participants were to decide whether the second word (SANDWICH), the target word, was a real word or not. The results showed that, if primed with an associate, reaction time was faster than if not primed with an associate.

Several researchers have reported similar results. However, strong reactions have been called forth in others (see Holender, 1986, for an overview). Some critics argue that when the criterion for a perceptual threshold is set by a participant—that is, when a participant reports that he can or cannot "see" the prime—then the effect appears. On the other hand, if the threshold exposure time is set by an objective measure, the effect of subliminal priming does not occur.

Priming studies have been used in the area of **social cognition**—an area that borrows from cognitive psychology and social psychology—to study the effects on social judgment. Srull and Wyer (1979) had students unscramble either hostile or nonhostile sentences, and then read a passage about a guy named Donald who goes on an outing around town with his friend. When participants later made judgments about Donald, those who unscrambled hostile sentences rated Donald as more hostile than those who unscrambled nonhostile sentences. The act of unscrambling hostile sentences primed the participants to interpret aspects of the passage (like when he asked for his money back from a sales clerk) as hostile, whereas the other participants did not.

The **mere exposure effect** is where just being exposed to something increases liking of that something later on. Advertisers use this to their advantage, and numerous studies have demonstrated this strong effect. People are typically unaware that the source of their favorability is simply due to the familiarity with the object, event, or person. Jacoby et al. (1989) found that exposing participants to nonfamous names (e.g., Sebastian Wiesdorf) and

FIGURE 8.4

Paradigm for testing subliminal priming.

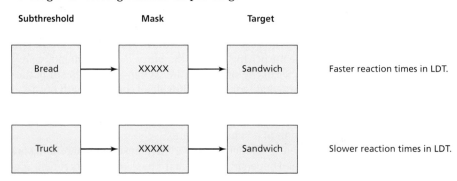

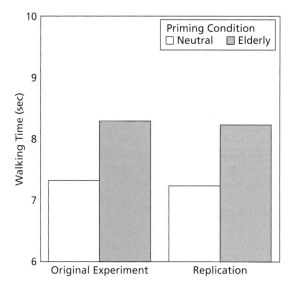

Primary Affects Behavior. Mean time (in seconds) to walk down the hallway after the conclusion of the experiment by stereotype priming condition.

(Bargh, Chen, & Borrows, 1996).

then testing them later with a list of moderately famous names, some of the old nonfamous names, and some new nonfamous names led to the participants reporting that many of the previously seen nonfamous names were indeed famous! Go Sebastian!

Automatic processing has also been shown to affect behavior. Bargh, Chen, and Borrows (1996) primed participants with using a scrambled sentence task where the sentences were either related to stereotypes of older adults (e.g., elderly, Florida) or neutral to the stereotype (e.g., thirsty, clean). The participants were then told the experiment was over, but were surreptitiously timed as they walked to the elevator. Sure enough, those primed with the elderly stereotype walked slower than those who had not been primed with that stereotype. These were college students just like you!

As you can see, priming studies are often done with words or sentence tasks, or by flashing words briefly on a screen. Thomas Mussweiler (2006) was interested in seeing if behaviors could prime stereotypes. He had participants put on a life vest and wear ankle and wrist weights. He had them engage in several different simple movements (e.g., bending over, sitting down and standing up, etc.). This manipulation unobtrusively caused participants to move in a manner associated with overweight people. He then had them rate an ambiguous target person, and those participants who were primed (through their behaviors) with being overweight were more likely than control participants (who did not wear the life vests and weights) to rate the target higher on characteristics stereotypical of being overweight.

I've told you this before, haven't I?

—*From the movie* Memento.

Metacognition

Another aspect of automatic processing is **metacognition**. People are often in situations where they are required to evaluate the contents of their memory. When people are approached on a busy street and are asked for directions, how do they know if they know the directions or not? When studying a list of items to be remembered, how do people know how much time they should spend studying each item for memorization? Furthermore, how do people know that they know the name of a movie they once saw, even though they cannot produce the name of the movie? These phenomena fall under the category of metacognition, or the "knowing about knowing." Metacognition is a broad category of self-knowledge monitoring. Metamemory is a category of metacognition that refers to the act of knowing about what you remember. We can exert control over our metacognitive processes to actively seek information, but the bulk of the memory monitoring (especially initial memory monitoring prior to a search of specific information) is automatic.

Metacognition is generally implicated in the monitoring and controlling of retrieval and inference processes involved in the memory system. **Monitoring** refers to how we evaluate what we already know (or do not know). Processes involved in metacognitive monitoring include Ease of Learning Judgments, Judgments of Learning, Feeling of Knowing Judgments, and Confidence in retrieved answers. Metacognitive control includes learning strategies such as Allocation of Study Time, Termination of Study, Selection of Memory Search Strategies, and Decisions to Terminate the Search.

A basic model of the metacognitive model involves the monitoring and control of the meta-level and the object-level with information flowing between each level. Basically, the meta-level is our conscious awareness of what is or is not in memory, while the object-level is the actual item in memory. The meta-level basically creates a model of the object-level having a general idea of the memory state. Based on this meta-level model a person can quickly evaluate what they know or think they know so they can decide if they should spend the effort trying to recall the information. An example of how the meta-level works might be the person being asked directions by a traveler. Before attempting to recall the directions, the person will determine (often automatically) if they even know the directions before they begin to recall the specific directions. Once the meta-level evaluates the memory state of the object-level determining that the directions are known, a search for specific details would follow.

The metacognitive system consists of two types of monitoring: (1) prospective, occurring before and during acquisition of information, and (2) retrospective, occurring after acquisition of information. Ease of Learning and Judgments of Learning are examples of prospective monitoring.

Ease of Learning involves the selection of appropriate strategies to learn the new information and which aspect of the information would be easiest to learn. For example, if the traveler decides that the directions are too difficult to remember, he or she might attempt to write them down, or he or she may ask for directions based on geographical locations rather than street-by-street directions. One way researchers study Ease of Learning is by having students participating in a memorization study, indicating which items on a list would be easier to learn (Ease of Learning Judgments). Participants would then be allowed a specific amount of time to learn the list during acquisition. Following a period of time when the information is retained in memory, a recall or recognition test would follow. The researcher then compares the Ease of Learning Judgments to the memory performance to determine how well the judgments predicted performance. The findings indicate that Ease of Learning Judgments can be accurate in predicting learning.

Judgments of Learning occur during and after the acquisition stage of memory. Participants in a study examining Judgments of Learning may be asked to study a list of items and then are asked to indicate which items they had learned the best. Or participants may be asked to provide Judgments of Learning after a retention period, just before the memory test is administered. Similar to the Ease of Learning Judgments, Judgments of Learning are compared to a later memory test to determine how accurate the participants were in their judgments. Research has found that Judgments of Learning become more accurate after practice trials. It is not known if Judgments of Learning are based on Ease of Learning or if they are based on previous recall trials.

Feeling of Knowing can be either prospective or retrospective. Feeling of Knowing is typically measured as an indication of how well a participant thinks he or she will be able to recognize the correct answer to a question in a subsequent multiple-choice task. Feeling of Knowing studies typically use a Recall–Judgment–Recognition task where participants are asked general information questions (sometimes trivia questions). If the participants is unable to recall the answer, he or she is then asked to provide a judgment evaluating the likelihood that he or she will be able to recognize the answer when seen in a multiple-choice type test. When compared to recognition performance, Feeling of Knowing Judgments are generally above chance, but far from perfect predictors of recognition. Research on Feeling of Knowing has helped establish that people are able to provide accurate self-reports of their metacognitive states.

Confidence Judgments are retrospective since they are taken after the retrieval of an item from memory. Depending on the type of information recalled, confidence judgments are related to the accuracy of recall. However, in some areas such as eyewitness identification, the relationship is low and not necessarily predictive of identification performance. This is due in part because individuals are seldom asked to make eyewitness identifications and typically only one piece of information is required ("is it him"), making it difficult to evaluate individual differences in this type of responding.

Metacognitive monitoring is studied by having participants provide judgments of their metacognitive state. A more naturally occurring metacognitive state is when a person has difficulty retrieving an item from memory, yet they have a sense that retrieval is imminent. This is commonly referred to as a tip-of-the-tongue state. In a tip-of-the-tongue state a person is often able to partially recall bits and pieces of information related to the sought-after item. Researchers have often used partial recall created while in a tip-of-the-tongue state as a "window" into the memory process because they can examine the types of partial information being recalled in relation to the properties of the memory item actually sought. It is believed that tip-of-the-tongue states are more than a memory curiosity and that they serve as a mechanism to evaluate our memory state and direct metacognitive control.

Ease of Learning, Judgments of Learning, Feeling of Knowing, and Confidence are ways metacognitive monitoring is examined. These processes are interrelated with metacognitive control. As with monitoring, metacognitive control is different for the different stages of memory. Control during the acquisition of memory can involve selection of the different type of process to use. For example, if the item to be remembered is thought to be easy, very little processing may be allocated to the item. However, if an item is though to be difficult, more elaborate rehearsal may be allocated. Control over the allocation of the amount of time given to study each item also occurs at the acquisition phase. For example, when studying for an exam, a student may decide to spend more time on a particular item that he or she feels will be eventually learned and little to no time to an item that is thought to be too difficult to learn and thus resulting in a waste of time. This control process is related to Ease of Learning. Finally, the decision to terminate study is a control process occurring at the acquisition phase. This decision is usually related to Judgments of Learning.

Metacognitive control over search strategies occurs during the retrieval of memory. These include the selection of search strategies and the termination of search. How elaborate of a search does a person conduct for an item in memory? When approached and asked for directions in an unfamiliar part of town it is not reasonable to exert too much time and energy attempting recall. However, if approached while in a familiar area, more effort may be allocated to a search. This process is related to the Feeling of Knowing. Tip-of-the-tongue states also influence retrieval strategies. When in a tip-of-the-tongue state a person may spend so much time and cognitive resources to recall the information they become preoccupied and at times immobilized.

Spotlight on Cognitive Neuroscience

Consciousness in the Brain

Consciousness can be thought of as a waking state, experience, or "mind," and as aspects as self-consciousness, such as self-recognition and self-knowledge, to name just a few. Areas as diverse as philosophy, neuroscience, cognitive psychology, and artificial intelligence have all contributed theories and methodologies to the exploration of consciousness. Adam Zeman reviews his own and others' work on consciousness and provides a comprehensive summary of the important theories, methods, and new directions for the study of consciousness. The goal of this research is to figure out how the activity of the brain results in mental states. In trying to achieve this goal, research is conducted on the electrical correlates of sleep and wakefulness and in the brain structures that control these states (particularly in the brainstem and diencephalon). The science of consciousness is focused on the "neurology of experience." By studying how the brain's neurological activity changes when there is no corresponding change in external stimuli gives insight into conscious awareness. Functional imaging and EEG techniques have changed the way researchers can tackle the "hard" problem of consciousness. Although the "rich texture of experience" may not be readily accessible to the scientist, the corresponding "revealable" neurological activity is.

Zeman, A. (2001). Consciousness. *Brain, 124*, 1263–1289.

A la carte

Deep Brain Stimulation

Researchers have long been interested in the relationship between the brain and electrical stimulation. Early researchers attempted to map out the brain using stimulation and others found they could retrieve old memories by stimulating selected neural regions. A procedure called deep brain stimulation (DBS), originally implanted in the motor areas to control the effects of Parkinson's disease, has recently been used in an attempt to revive patients in minimal conscious states due to brain injuries. Minimally conscious patients move in and out of unconsciousness; however, the duration of consciousness is limited and unpredictable. Researchers implanted a small electrode deep into the thalamus of a patient with a head injury using precision equipment guided by brain images (Shirvalkar, Seth, Schiff, & Herrera, 2006). The electrode is controlled by a device similar to a pacemaker. After six years of minimal consciousness, a 36-year-old patient became able to eat and communicate verbally with the DBS. These promising, yet exploratory results provide support for the role of the thalamus in maintaining and regulating consciousness.

Student Resource Center

STUDY GUIDE

1   Consciousness is the awareness of environmental and internal cognitive events.

2   Human interest in consciousness is as old as humankind, but the scientific study of consciousness is only about 100 years old.

3   The topic of consciousness is associated with philosophical topics including the mind–body issue.

4   The study of consciousness and unconscious phenomena can be divided into two classes of topics. In the conscious group, we find explicit cognition, immediate memory, novel stimuli, declarative memory, remembering, effortful processery, and so on, while in the unconscious group we find implicit cognition, long-term memory, procedural memory, subliminal stimulation, knowing, automatic processing, semantic memory, and so on.

5   Consciousness may be treated as a scientific construct that allows us to do valid experiments on the topic.

6   Consciousness has, over its history, been treated in terms of an activation threshold, a novelty metaphor, a spotlight, and an integrated metaphor.

7   Some of the most influential contemporary models of consciousness are Schacter's DICE and Baars's global workspace theory.

8   The functions of consciousness include definitional attributes, adaptation, prioritization of information, control of actions, decision making, editing functions, self-monitoring functions, management of internal organization, and flexibility.

KEY TERMS

adaptation and learning
architecture
attention
automatic processes
AWAREness
confidence judgments
consciousness
context setting
decision-making
depressants
ease of learning
emergence
emotive
error detection and editing
feeling of knowing
hallucinogens
hard problem
implicit memory
judgments of learning
meditation
mere exposure effect
metacognition

metacognition [illigible]
monitoring
neural correlation of consciousness
novelty
organization and flexibility
prioritizing
qualia
rapid eye movement (REM) sleep
recall of knowledge
recruitment and control
selectivity
self knowledge
self-monitoring
sensory threshold
sensory threshold
social cognition
stimulants
subjectivity
subliminal priming
wakefulness
world knowledge

STARTING POINTS

● There are more than ten thousand entries in data banks on *consciousness,* so the interested reader may have to extend his or her lifetime to plow through the literature. Our job here is to narrow the number of sources at the cost of excluding some fine references. Several general works are recommended, including a new book by Baars, *In the Theater of Consciousness: The Workspace of the Mind,* and another book by Dennett, *Consciousness Explained.* A slightly earlier book by Baars, *A Cognitive Theory of Consciousness,* is also recommended. Some more technical sources include *The Cognitive Neurosciences* (Gazzaniga, ed.), especially section XI, "Consciousness," edited by Daniel Schacter. Francis Crick, a Nobel laureate, has written *The Astonishing Hypothesis: The Scientific Search for the Soul,* which will awaken even the most somnolent of brain cells. There are far too many good chapters and articles by distinguished workers to be listed here, but we would recommend the works of Kinsborne, Searle (for a contrary view), Churchland (both Patricia and Paul), Weiskrantz, Moscovitch, Squire, and Schacter. Finally, in a book edited by Solso, *Mind and Brain Sciences in the 21st Century,* you will find a collection of papers by outstanding thinkers of the twentieth century, such as Carl Sagan, Endel Tulving, Edward Smith, Karl Pribram, Henry Roediger III, Michael Gazzaniga, Bernard Baars, Michael Posner, Richard Thompson, and others, in which consciousness is a central theme.

Movies

- The Science of Sleep (2006)—Sleep and dreaming
- Altered States (1980)—Consciousness
- Vanilla Sky (2001)—Lucid dreaming
- The Science of Sleep (2006)—Sleep and dreaming

Search Terms

SleepNet

Omni Brain

Center for Consciousness Studies

Centre for Consciousness

The Verbal Representation of Knowledge

hmmm. . .?

1. Why has the study of words and language been a favorite topic of psychologists interested in knowledge and its representation?

2. What features identify the following: set-theoretical model, semantic feature-comparison model, network model, propositional networks, neurocognitive model?

3. What is a "linguistic hedge"? Give an example from your everyday life.

4. What are the main features of a "spreading activation theory," and how might it predict results from priming?

5. Distinguish between declarative knowledge and procedural knowledge.

6. What have studies of amnesic patients told us about the structure of memory?

7. How is knowledge represented in PDP models?

*Y*ou are what you know.

—*Albert Einstein*

This chapter is about the representation of knowledge, which is to some the most important concept in cognitive psychology. By **knowledge** we mean the storage, integration, and organization of information in memory. As we saw in previous chapters, information is derived from the senses, but it is not the same as knowledge. Knowledge is information that has been organized in memory; it is part of a system or network of structured information; in a sense, knowledge is processed information and memory is the system by which we access knowledge.

Language and Knowledge

One reason words and language have been studied extensively is that the degree of verbal development in human beings far exceeds that of other species; hence, that attribute serves as a phylogenetic demarcation. Some estimates (Baddeley, 1990a, 1990b) place the number of words a person knows the meaning of at 20,000 to 40,000 and recognition memory many times that number as such it comes as no surprise that much of our knowledge is verbal. Another reason words and language have been studied extensively in cognitive psychology is that semantic structure allows us to identify what types of "things" are stored in and how a stored "thing" is related to others. Of course, for the cognitive psychologist, words in and of themselves are as uninteresting to study as are the blips on the radar screen. Words derive their vitality not from some intrinsic worth but from the concepts and relationships that they reflect and that make the facts and structures of knowledge come alive with meaning. By studying the ways words seem to be represented in memory, we can learn something about the contents, structure, and process of the representation of knowledge.

Associationist Approach

In the associationist approach, the doctrine is that there are functional relationships between psychological phenomena.

Organizational Variables

The study of organizational factors in memory was influenced by a series of papers by Gordon Bower and his colleagues (Bower, 1970a, 1970c; Bower, 1969; Clark, Lesgold, & Winzenz; Lesgold & Bower, 1970). In the context of modern cognitive theory, Bower used organizational factors in both traditional and contemporary ways. As in past research, Bower attempted to demonstrate the influence of structural organization on free recall. Bower believes that organization of semantic entities in memory has a much more powerful influence on memory and recall than has been previously demonstrated. In one

Gordon Bower. Made significant discoveries in memory, mnemonics, mathematical psychology, and language processing.

experiment (Bower et al., 1969), Bower's group looked at the potent influence on recall of organizational variables by constructing several conceptual hierarchies. An example of a conceptual hierarchy for the word *minerals* is shown in Figure 9.1.

These and many more experiments provided a bridge between an austere view of humankind's intellectual functions and one that envisioned a network of associations connected to other associations, and to other associations, and so on.

An underlying reason for why we associate and categorize objects in our environment may be the adaptive function such an organization scheme provides us. Geary (2005) posits that humans have the extraordinary ability to categorize (and thus mentally represent) objects, animals, and plants. In doing so, humans are better able to predict their environment and be successful in it.

Semantic Organization of Knowledge

The approach to semantic memory has shifted from the associationistic viewpoint to a cognitive viewpoint, which assumes that detailed cognitive structures represent the way

FIGURE 9.1

A conceptual hierarchy of words for the word *minerals*.

Adapted from Bower et al. (1969).

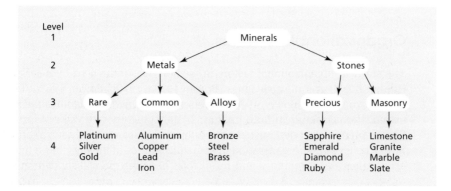

*I*nformation is not knowledge.

— *Albert Einstein*

semantic information is organized in memory. In the following section, some of these cognitive models are reviewed.

Set-Theoretical Model

The set-theoretical model deals with semantic **concepts.** Concepts are abstract ideas that represent categories of information or knowledge units. For example, "bananas" by itself is not a concept. However, grouped with apples, oranges, and grapes, it becomes part of the concept of fruit. Furthermore, knowledge units can be regrouped to form different concepts. For example, bananas can be grouped with mangoes, pineapple, and papaya to form the concept of tropical fruit.

In a **set-theoretical model** of memory, semantic concepts are represented by sets of elements, or collections of information. In this model, unlike the case with the clustering model, a concept may be represented in LTM not only by the exemplars of the concept or items that make up the concept but also by the exemplars' attributes (features). Thus, the concept *birds* may include the names of types of birds—canary, robin, hawk, wren, and so on—as well as the attributes of the concept—sings, flies, has feathers. In a set-theoretical model memory consists of numerous concepts. Items in memory can be stored in association with more than one concept. For example, the word "canary" can belong to the bird concept as well as the pet concept. Retrieval involves verification, that is, a search through two or more sets of information to find overlapping exemplars.

Concepts can be defined by their attributes and exemplars can be defined by their attributes as well. Verification of propositions (e.g., "a penguin is a bird") is done by comparing only the attributes of the concept *(bird)* with the attributes of the exemplar set *(penguin).* The degree of overlap of attributes (see Figure 9.2) forms the basis for a decision about the validity of the proposition (a penguin is a bird). As the distance between the sets becomes greater, the time to verify the proposition should increase. The fewer the differences the shorter the verification process (Meyer, 1970).

Two types of logical relationships between semantic categories are examined in this model: the universal affirmative (UA) and the particular affirmative (PA). In the UA case, all members of one category are subsumed in another category, which is represented as "All A are B" (e.g., "All penguins are birds"); in the PA case, only a portion of the members of one category make up the member of another category—which is represented as "Some A are B" (e.g., "Some birds are penguins"). The validity of the statements is determined by the set relationships of the semantic categories. The set relationships, or commonality, are gauged by the number of exemplars the two propositions share.

Not only are they combined by the set of overlap, the amount they lack in common can also be taken into consideration. The degree of validity of the logical assertion "All *S* are *P* (UA) and some *S* are *P*" is contingent on the amount of overlap (shaded area), or the exemplars they have in common.

To understand the model better, consider this experimental procedure. A research participant is seated before a screen in which a sentence of the type "All insects are animals"

FIGURE 9.2

Attributes of two sets (penguin and bird).

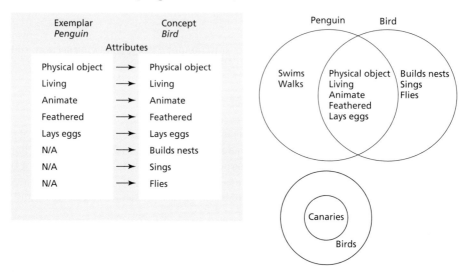

or "Some insects are butterflies" appears. The participant indicates whether the statement is true or false. Statements of the "Some insects are butterflies" type (PA) require less reaction time than those of the "All insects are animals" type (UA). Verification of the sentence "Some insects are butterflies" requires a search of memory only until a single instance of a butterfly being an insect is found (Laftus & Schaff, 1971).

Semantic Feature-Comparison Model

The **semantic feature-comparison model** shares a set-theoretical structure with the set-theoretical model but differs in several important assumptions (Rips et al., 1973: Smith et al., 1974). The first assumption is that the meaning of a word is represented as a set of semantic features (Smith et al., 1974). A broad set of features related to any word varies along a continuum from very important to trivial. A robin, for example, may be described according to these features: has wings, is a biped, has a red breast, perches in trees, likes worms, is untamed, is a harbinger of spring. Some of these are critical defining features (wings, legs, red breast), while others are only characteristic features (perches in trees, likes to eat worms, is untamed, and is a harbinger of spring). Smith and his colleagues propose that the meaning of a lexical unit (simply speaking, a word) can be represented by features that are essential, or defining, aspects of the word (**defining features**) and other features that are only incidental, or characteristic, aspects (**characteristic features**).

Take the example "A bat is a bird." Although one defining feature of birds is that they have wings, strictly speaking a bat is not a bird. However, a bat does fly, has wings, and looks something like a bird. Loosely speaking, a bat is a bird. Such terms as *technically speaking, loosely speaking,* or *appear to be* are all examples of linguistic hedges (Lakoff,

TABLE 9.1

Examples of Linguistic Hedges

Hedge	Statement	Features Represented by Predicate Noun	
		Defining	Characteristic
A true statement	A robin is a bird.	+	+
	A sparrow is a bird.	+	+
	A parakeet is a bird.	+	+
Technically speaking	A chicken is a bird.	+	−
	A duck is a bird.	+	−
	A penguin is a bird.	+	−
Loosely speaking	A bat is a bird.	−	+
	A butterfly is a bird.	−	+
	A moth is a bird.	−	+

1972), which we commonly use to expand conceptual representations. As is shown in Table 9.1, a "true statement" would be identified on the basis of both defining and characteristic features; a "technically speaking" statement, on the basis of defining but not characteristic features; and a "loosely speaking" statement, on the basis of characteristic but not defining features (Smith et al., 1974). Validation of a proposition (such as "A robin is a bird"), within the context of two types of features, is based more on the important (defining) features than on the less important (characteristic) features.

The first stage of validation of the statement involves a comparison of both the defining and characteristic features of the two lexical categories (*robin* and *bird*). If there is considerable overlap, then the sentence is validated. If there is no (or only tangential) overlap, then the sentence is judged to be invalid. If there is some overlap, the second-stage search is activated in which specific comparisons are made between the two lexical units on the basis of their shared defining features.

Eleanor Rosch has done research based on the logic that some members are more typical of a category than others. For example, a knife and rifle are typical weapons, while a cannon and club are less so, and a fist and chain are even less weaponlike. Rosch thought that because objects vary in typicality of their categories, the tendency might be to form prototype categories. Consider the category of birds. Most people would agree that a robin is a good example of a bird but that an ostrich and chicken are not so good. When we use the word *bird,* we generally mean something close to the prototype bird or, in this case, something like a robin. In order to test the notion, Rosch (1977) presented participants with sentences that contained the names of categories (e.g., *birds* and *fruit*). Some of the sentences might be:

I saw a bird fly south.
Birds eat worms.
There is a bird in a tree.
I heard a bird chirping on my windowsill.

Rosch then replaced the category name with a member of the category (e.g., *bird* was replaced by *robin, eagle, ostrich,* and *chicken*) and asked research participants to rate how sensible the sentences were. In each sentence *robin* was taken to make good sense, and *eagle, ostrich,* and *chicken* less sense. It seems plausible that the typical member of the category is similar to the prototype of the category.

The feature-comparison model seems to account for some of the unresolved issues of the set-theoretical model, but at the same time it has its own shortcomings. Collins and Loftus (1975) have criticized using defining features as if they have absolute properties. No single feature is absolutely necessary to define something (e.g., try to define a house by using a single critical feature). An igloo is still a house even if it has no windows or kitchen—that is, no single feature makes a house. People seem to have difficulty in judging whether a feature is defining or characterizing.

In spite of the differences between the set-theoretical model and the feature-comparison model, both models enhance our understanding of semantic memory in several important ways. First, they provide specific information about the multiple dimensions of semantic memory. Second, they use semantically categorized information as a starting point for an overall theory of semantic memory that embraces the vast network of memory functions. Third, because these models involve complex memory operations, they touch on the larger issue of the nature of our representation of knowledge, a principal part of which is the matter of the storage of semantic symbols and the laws that govern their recall.

Semantic Network Models

The best known of the early network models, proposed by Allen Collins and Ross Quillian, grew out of an earlier conceptualization of memory organization that was based on a computer program (Quillian, 1968, 1969). The model depicted each word in a configuration of other words in memory, the meaning of any word being represented in relationship to other words (see Figure 9.3). By now you have come to realize that bird examples are quite popular in this line of research. Brace yourself for yet another one. In this example, the information stored at level 0 is *canary,* "a yellow bird that can sing." Canary is linked to the corresponding words "is yellow," and "can sing" by a node. This node also links to other nodes that explicitly include the definition. The canary node links to the bird node. The bird node links to defining characteristics of a bird (has wings, can fly). This information need not be stored with each type of bird. The bird node also links to the animal node at level 2, which has its own set of attributes and is linked to other animal nodes such as fish. Therefore, the proposition "A canary can fly" is validated by retrieval of the information that (1) a canary is a member of the superset of birds and (2) a bird has the property "can fly." This system of semantic memory, by means of single rather than redundant entry of elements, minimized the space required for information storage. A model of this sort is considered to be an economical one in database design.

An appealing feature of the Collins and Quillian model is that it makes explicit the means by which information is retrieved from semantic memory. To search our memory for validation of a specific proposition (for example, "A shark can move around"), we must first determine that a shark is a fish, a fish is an animal, and an animal has the property "can move around." This is a rather circuitous route. Another assumption of the model is that all this intrastructural travel takes time. Appropriately, Collins and Quillian tested the model by having participants judge the veracity of a sentence. The principal depen-

FIGURE 9.3

Hypothetical memory structure for a three-level hierarchy.

Adapted from Collins and Quillian (1969). Reprinted by permission of Academic Press.

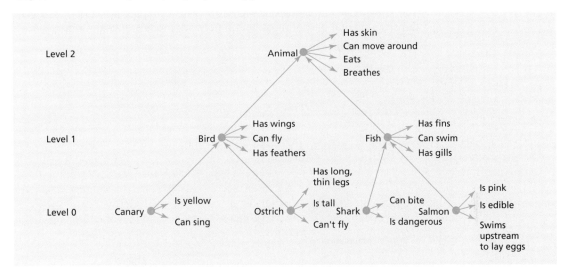

dent variable is the time it takes to validate this; the independent variable is the number and proximity of nodes in semantic memory.

Collins and Quillian's model suggests that semantic memory consists of a vast network of concepts, which are composed of units and corresponding properties and are linked by a series of associationistic nodes. In spite of the fact that the model has been criticized, such as that the associationistic strength varies within the network (for example, the subordinate category of shark is less easily identified as a fish, than salmon) or that some association violates the cognitive economy of the system, it argues for modification of the system, not abandonment of it. Furthermore, in its modifications, the model has provided an effective springboard to subsequent models, such as the spreading activation model.

Spreading Activation Model

The **spreading activation model** of semantic processing was developed by Allan Collins and Elizabeth Loftus (1975). The model, shown in Figure 9.4, is built on a complex network of associations in which specific items are distributed in conceptual space with related concepts that are linked by associations. In Figure 9.4 the concept *red* is shown. The strength of association between concepts is indicated by the length of the connecting lines. Long lines, such as those between *Red* and *Sunrises,* indicate a somewhat remote associate; shorter lines, such as those between *Red* and *Fire,* indicate a strong association. At the heart of many knowledge representation models is the idea that concepts are associated as they are in the spreading activation model. Also, with a bit of imagination, we could conceive a system of neural networks that embody some of the features of this model.

FIGURE 9.4

A spreading activation theory of semantic processing. The ellipses stand for concepts, and the lines are associations. The strength of the relationship between concepts is represented by the length of the line. The assumption that knowledge can be represented as a vastly complex network of associations is a pivotal part of most neural network models of cognition.

From Collins and Loftus (1975).

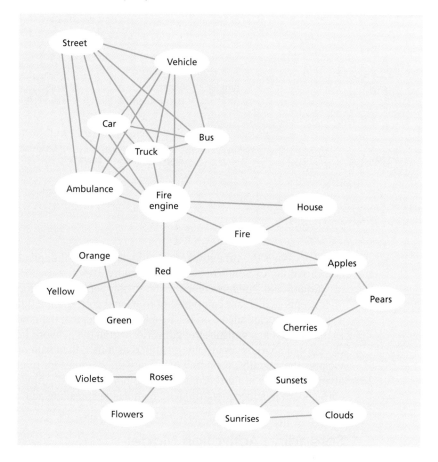

In the Spreading Activation model, there is a spreading activation among concepts, which may account for the results of priming experiments (the effect of making a word or concept more accessible following the presentation of a related word, or *prime*). For example, if we show you a picture of fire, it is likely that you will be able to recognize the word *Fire* faster than you would without the prime. Furthermore, if you see a picture of fire, recognition of its associate, for example, the word *Red,* is also enhanced. Presumably, even secondary associations would be activated; for example, the spread of activation may extend to associates of associates. In the preceding example, *fire* primes the activation of the word *Red;* however, activating *Red* may prime the word *Apples,* even though the only relationship between *fire* and *Apples* is through *Red.*

In such an extended distributed activation network, an estimate of the capacity for *fire* to prime *red* (through *house*) is conceptualized as a function of the algebraic summation of all competing associates. (see Kao, 1990; Kao & Solso, 1989).

Cognitive Neuroscience Support   In addition to the traditional behavioral study of the spreading activation model, recent studies have taken advantage of advanced neural imaging technology to show that physical, phonological, and semantic codes of words activate quite separate neural areas (Posner et al., 1988; Posner & Rothbart, 1989). Posner and his colleagues distinguish between repetition priming, which comes from repeating the same item twice (such as showing a participant the color *green* as a prime for the same color), and semantic priming, which comes from presenting a semantically related prime and its target (such as showing the color *green* followed by the word *grass*). Behavioral studies have shown that both priming effects yield reliable data and seem to take place automatically, that is, without conscious control or awareness and involve implicit memory processes. Are these processes managed by different parts of the brain?

Using PET scans, Petersen and his colleagues (1988) evaluated regional blood flow in the cortex as a measure of neural activity associated with different semantic tasks. They found that visual word forms are processed in the ventral occipital lobe, while semantic tasks involve the left-lateralized part of the brain. The word form areas are activated even when the research participant is passively interacting, for example, when the participant is told simply to look at the word. The semantic area is activated only when the participant is asked to actively process the word, for example, when the participant is asked to name the word or to classify it silently. In addition to verifying the neural basis of cognition, these studies tell us more about the possible relationship between attentional factors and the representation of knowledge.

Propositional Networks

A **proposition** is defined by Anderson (1985) as the "smallest unit of knowledge that can stand as a separate assertion (e.g., babies cry)." Propositions are the smallest units that are meaningful. Many theorists subscribe to the concept of propositional representation of knowledge (see Anderson, 1976, 1983a; Anderson & Bower, 1973; Kintsch, 1974; Norman & Rumelhart, 1975), although each interprets the concept somewhat differently.

Human Associative Memory (HAM) and the Representation of Knowledge

Anderson and Bower (1973) conceptualized the representation of knowledge within a network of semantic associations that they called human associative memory (HAM).

A key feature of HAM is the use of propositions, which are statements or assertions about the nature of the world. A proposition is a representation or an abstraction resembling a sentence, a kind of remote structure that ties together ideas or concepts.

Propositions are mostly illustrated with semantic examples, but other forms of information, for example, visual representation, can also be depicted in memory by proposition.

In propositional representations, the principal structure for storing information is the subject–predicate construction linked by a fact node.

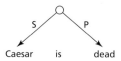

The sentence "Caesar is dead" is represented as having two components, the subject (*S*) and predicate (*P*), both sprouting from a "fact node," which represents the idea being asserted.

More complex sentences, such as "Jennifer married Ben," that contain a subject(*S*), and a predicate (*P*) where the predicate has been expanded to include a relation (*R*) and an object (*O*).

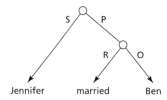

Even more complex sentences may contain a context (*C*), for example (to borrow from Anderson and Bower), "During the summer in Paris Jennifer married Ben."

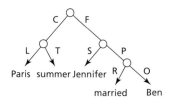

Here, time (*T*), location (*L*), and context (*C*) are added to a fact-idea (*F*) statement. Branches of the tree structures are joined by conceptual nodes, which are presumed to exist in memory before the encoding of a sentence. Nodes represent ideas and the linear association between ideas; therefore, understanding of a specific fact may be contingent upon the relationship to other conceptual facts.

Knowledge is memory.

—*Anonymous*

John R. Anderson. Developed influential
theory of associative memory (HAM, ACT).

The basic content is "wired" together in an associative web of more and more complex
structures, but all can be broken down to sets of two or fewer items emanating from a single node. HAM was a basic associationistic model and accounted for a limited amount of
knowledge representation. A comprehensive model of knowledge representation and information processing was developed by Anderson (1983A) called **adaptive control of thought
(ACT)**. It has gone through several iterations (from ACT* to the current ACT-R). We begin
our discussion of this influential theory by describing its general framework (see Figure 9.5).

In this framework there are three types of memory: working, declarative, and productive, which is similar to what most refer to as procedural memory. These are defined as follows:

**ACT's proposition encoding of "The tall lawyer believed the men were
from Mars."**

From Anderson (1983a). Reprinted with permission.

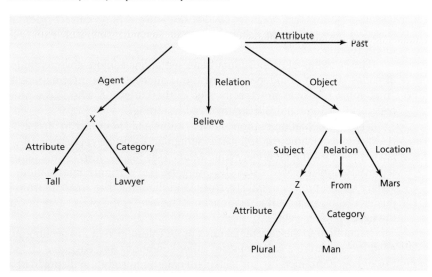

Working memory, a kind of enterprising short-term memory, contains information the system can access currently, including information retrieved from long-term declarative memory. Essentially, working memory refers to active memory, as shown in Figure 9.5. It is central to most of the processes involved.

Declarative memory is the knowledge we possess about the world (for example, knowing that good wine is produced in California and France or being able to recall some of the contents of your last cognitive psychology class). It seems that in Anderson's view, episodic and semantic information is included in declarative memory. Declarative representation of knowledge comes into the system in chunks, or cognitive units, comprising such things as propositions (such as, "Beth loves Boris"), strings (such as, "one, two, three"), or even spatial images ("A circle is above the square"). From these basic elements new information is stored in declarative memory by means of working memory. The retrieval of information from declarative memory into working memory resembles the calling up of information from the permanent memory of a computer—data stored on a hard disk in a computer are temporarily held for processing in a working memory.

Productive memory is the final major component in the system. Productive memory is very close to procedural memory, which refers to the knowledge required to do things, such as tie shoes, do mathematics, or order food in a restaurant. The difference between procedural and declarative memory (or knowledge) is the difference between knowing how and knowing what.

In ACT, Anderson proposes a tricode theory of knowledge representation. The three codes include a temporal string, a spatial image, and an abstract proposition.

The first of these codes, the temporal string, records the sequential structure of events. With it, we can recall the sequence of events in our daily experience. For example, we can recall the sequence of events in a movie we recently saw or in a football game.

Spatial representations are treated as one of the principal ways information is coded. Configural information, the type of information displayed in a figure, a form, or even a letter, is thought to be encoded in memory, but the size of the configuration is less important. Thus, we may encode the letter *Z* in its correct orientation but not its size. We may recognize *Z* half its size or twice its size, but if rotated 90 degrees, it might resemble an *N*.

The encoding of propositional representations is more abstract than the other types of codes, since it is independent of the sequence of the information. The proposition "Bill, John, hit" does not specify who is the hitter and who is the hittee. What is encoded is that John and Bill are involved in hitting.

The representation of propositional knowledge is similar to our earlier discussion of HAM. Consider how the following sentence would be represented by ACT: "The tall lawyer believed the men were from Mars" (see Figure 9.5). In this figure, propositional representations involve structure, category, and attribute information. A central node stands for the propositional structure, and the links that emanate from it point to various elements, such as the relationship ("believe"), the object ("man from Mars"), and the agent ("tall lawyer").

In addition to the general features of ACT described in this section, Anderson has applied the system to a wide range of other conditions and cognitive tasks, including control of cognition, memory for facts, language acquisition, and spread of activation.

Experts and Organization

Two features of the expert (as contrasted with the novice) seem to reappear in the literature. The expert has domain-specific, organized knowledge and knows how to use it efficiently and wisely. For example, it is estimated that a chess master has about 50,000 patterns in memory; a good player, about 1,000; and a beginner, only a few. However, the storage of passive information on any given topic alone does not constitute expertise. Organization of knowledge is important too.

In one important study of the organization of information, Chi, Feltovich, and Glaser (1981) used a card-sorting task to see how experts and novices classified problems. Each card had a diagram and description of a physics problem. The novices sorted problems on the basis of literal, surface features, such as the "problem deals with blocks on an inclined plane"; the experts tended to sort the problems on the basis of the principles used to solve the problem, such as the conservation of energy. This trait (surface analysis versus analysis of principles) holds for a variety of different specialties including mathematics, computer programming, and genetics. The same results are found in the classification and analysis of real-world phenomena such as pictures of dinosaurs, types of cameras, and electronic circuit diagrams. Experts have greater knowledge than novices and tend to organize their knowledge in terms of general principles rather than in terms of surface features.

Cognitive Neuroscience Support

It is self-evident to say that people learn from experience. What is less obvious is that those experiences modify the nervous system and that the ways in which it is modified form the neurological basis for the representation of knowledge. One approach to the neurological basis of memory is through the study of the molecular and cellular biology of individual neurons and their synapses (Squire, 1986). Although such efforts have told us a great deal about the physiology of neurons, they beg the larger question of how these microscopic entities are related to knowledge representation. Cognitive neuroscience studies have tried to integrate findings in neurophysiology with theories in cognitive psychology. One direction these studies have taken is to search for the location of memory.

A traditionally important issue is whether knowledge and the process of accessing it are distributed or localized in the cortex. One element central to this discussion is the search for the elusive *engram* (literally, "a trace," or, in the present context, a collection of neural charges that represents memory). Some areas of the brain are associated with specific functions (such as vision), yet functions such as memory seem to engage various locations, each of which may function simultaneously, or in parallel, with other locations. Larry Squire (1986) suggested that information storage may be more localized than thought earlier and that memory may be stored as changes in the same neural systems that participate in perception. This hypothesis may seem contrary to the findings of Lashley, who concluded that memory is widely distributed throughout the brain. However, Squire argues that Lashley's views are consistent with his own if one considers complex learning (for example, a rat's learning to traverse a maze) as the processing of many types of information (such as visual, spatial, and

Larry Squire. Cognitive neuroscience studies have helped establish important links between cognitive psychology and neuroscience.

olfactory) in which each type is separately processed and localized. "Thus, memory is localized in the sense that peculiar brain systems represent specific aspects of each event, and it is distributed in the sense that many neural systems participate in representing a whole event" (Squire, 1986, p. 1613).

A Taxonomy of Memory Structure

Overall, the experimental evidence supports the idea that the brain is organized around fundamentally different information storage systems, as illustrated in Figure 9.6. Declarative knowledge comprises episodic and semantic memories, and procedural knowledge includes skills, priming, dispositions, and other nonassociative types of representations.

One feature of this system is that it accepts both conscious (explicit) and unconscious (implicit) memory as serious topics for research. In addition, information can ac-

FIGURE 9.6

A tentative taxonomy for the representation of types of memory.

Adapted from Squire et al. (1990). Copyright © 1990 AAAS.

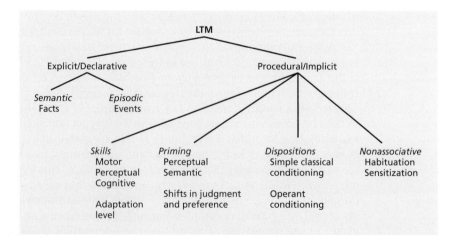

TABLE 9.2

Summary of the Semantic Organization of Knowledge

The five models of representational knowledge may be summarized as follows:

Clustering Model	Set-Theoretical Model	Semantic Feature-Comparison Model	Semantic Network Model	Cognitive Neuroscience Model
Organized in clusters. Categorically similar words are recalled together.	Sets or collections of information. Instances of a category and also attributes, or properties, of a category.	Set of semantic features. Two distinctive features are associated with an item's meaning: (1) defining features, which are essential components, and (2) characteristic features.	Independent units connected in a network. The storage of words is tied to a complex network of relationships.	Organization of neural networks. Knowledge is in the connections between units.

tivate both types of knowledge. For example, take the perception of the word *CHAIR* after seeing the word *TABLE*. From previous priming studies, we know that the perception of *CHAIR* is enhanced if preceded by *TABLE,* and that the effect is largely unconscious and procedural. Priming is also likely to engage declarative knowledge in normal participants. The engagement of declarative knowledge might be to store the word *TABLE* in episodic memory and have it become part of one's conscious experience. Supporting evidence for the model draws on a wide latitude of studies, including animal studies, the examination of histological sections, human cognitive experiments, and studies of the behavior of amnesic patients.

The importance of the previously mentioned experiments and theories seems to lie in two domains. First, they address the issue of the structure of knowledge. As such, they integrate various types of memories in an organized scheme, which accounts for declarative and nondeclarative knowledge and for conscious and unconscious processes. Second, they provide some of the most eloquent examples of the unification of brain science and cognitive psychology, especially as related to the central theme of the organization of knowledge. Table 9.2 provides an overview of the models.

Connectionism and the Representation of Knowledge

Connectionism can be defined as a theory of the mind that posits a large set of simple units connected in a parallel distributed network (PDP). Mental operations, such as memory, perception, thinking, and so on, are considered to be distributed throughout a highly complex neural network, which operates in a parallel manner. The theory is based on the assumption that units excite or inhibit each other throughout the system at the same time or in parallel. This is in contrast with serial processing theories, which are typically diagrammed with boxes and arrows, which suggest that processing between units is done only in sequence. The number of pairs of units involved, even in a simple task such as typing a word, may be considerable. It is within the connections between pairs of units that knowledge is distributed throughout the system. How can knowledge, the most complicated of topics thus far encountered, be expressed in terms of simple excitatory and inhibitory connections between units? In this section we try to answer that question.

In many of the previous models of information representation, knowledge was stored as a static copy of a pattern. An object, image, or thought is stored in memory with its attributes and connections with other objects, images, and thoughts. When recognition of an item is called for (e.g., "Do you know Dumbo the Elephant?"), a match is made between the elements of the question and the information stored in memory. Also, the associates of the elements (e.g., that elephants are gray), are activated, although the level of activation appears to be far less than for the central items *Dumbo* and *elephant*. Still, the way knowledge is represented is more or less static, and the means used to access knowledge is through matching stored information with a cue.

Knowledge representation in connectionistic models of cognition is quite different from models that store objects, images, and so forth. First, in connectionistic models the patterns themselves are not stored; what is stored is the connection strength between units, which allows these patterns to be recreated.

Second, connectionistic models approach learning differently. In traditional representational models, the goal of learning is the formation of explicit rules that allow for retrieval of information and generalization of cues. We know that Dumbo is an elephant and that, like most other elephants, he is gray and cannot easily fit into your Volkswagen. We know these things because we have learned rules. PDP models only assume that learning consists of the acquisition of connection strengths that allow a network of simple units to act as if they knew the rules. Rules are not learned; connections between simple units are. Even though our behavior seems to be rule governed, it is because of the underlying network of connections in the brain that we make these inferences.

Third, it is important to restate that the PDP model is neurally inspired; however, it is not the same as identifying specific neural pathways. Such a model would be impractical, since the model would be as complex as the brain itself. *Neurally inspired* simply means that the metaphor on which the model is based is the brain rather than the computer, on which some previous models have been based (see especially Collins and Quillian). The fact that PDP models are neurally inspired bears directly on the representation of knowledge. All knowledge is located in the connections, as might be the case with neural connections. In the computer metaphor, knowledge is thought to be stored in certain units. When we think of knowledge in the conventional sense, we are likely to think of it as being collected and stored someplace. The difference between these perspectives is considerable. For example, the PDP model suggests that "all knowledge is *implicit* in the structure of the device that carries out the task rather than *explicit* in the states of units themselves" (Rumelhart, Hinton, & McClelland, 1986, p. 75).

To illustrate the notion that all knowledge is in the connections, consider Figure 9.7. In this figure, input units are on the bottom and output units are on the right-hand side. Active units are filled in. Knowledge is stored in the strengths of connections between units, theoretically similar to the way neural networks represent information. The strength of the relations between units is simplified here. In the original system, detailed mathematical statements, which specify the strength of the connections, are given.

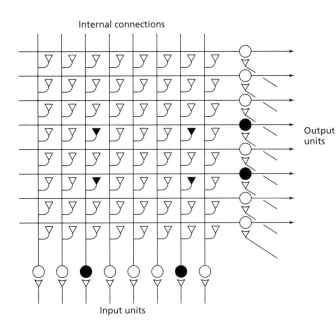

Internal connections

Input units

Output units

FIGURE 9.7

A connectionist association matrix.
Input units are on the bottom, and output units are along the right side. The filled circles are active units, and the filled triangles indicate which connections would change so that the input would evoke the output. Learning of associative relationships involves changing the strengths between the input units and the output units.

Modified from McClelland as suggested by Schneider (1987). Reprinted with permission.

A la carte

"I never forget a face, it's names I can't remember."

When asked what aspect of their memory they would like to improve, the majority indicate they would like to have a better memory for names. Probably because it is incredibly embarrassing when you can't remember a name. Names can be particularly difficult to remember; in fact, it is easier to remember a person's occupation than their name. Why? According to models of face recognition, a face is recognized before semantic information such as occupation is recalled, before the person's name can be recalled. A breakdown at any of these phases prevents the process from continuing to the next phase. As we have already seen in previous chapters, people can be trained in memory techniques that facilitate encoding; however, association-based mnemonics can require considerable cognitive effort, which might be best used perhaps to carry on a conversation. British researcher Peter Morris and his colleagues (Fritz, Jackson, Nichol, & Roberts, 2005) found evidence that it may be better to practice retrieving a name from memory rather

than putting effort into how the name is stored. In the study, researchers randomly selected names from the local phone book and had participants study them. Half of the participants were told to make semantic associations between the names (e.g., John Bush = Tree), while half were not given these instructions (presumably some participants in this condition naturally made semantic associations regardless). Additionally, half of the participants were assigned to an expanded retrieval condition. They were given booklets with names that would facilitate retrieval. For example, they would see the full name "John Bush" on one page and then see just the first name "John" on a later page. They would then have to retrieve the last name. The other half received booklets containing only the full names. The study was well controlled so participants in both groups saw the name an equal number of times. Results indicate that the expanded retrieval is the single best method for remembering names, and if combined with other methods it is even better. Therefore, it may be a matter of improving retrieval rather than improving encoding. This makes some intuitive sense; we know our LTM has a massive amount of storage capacity—the tricky part is getting the information out. Think of your bedroom, there is probably a lot of stuff in it. There are two strategies of getting something when you need it: (1) you could keep the room very organized, which would be similar to encoding, or (2) you could practice finding what you need (and then putting it back where you found it), which would be similar to retrieval. In the latter case, it wouldn't matter that your running shoes are tossed under the bed with other belongings, you had already looked for them before and found them there in the first place. Take a look at the offices of some professors we know; some are very tidy and some are quite unkempt. Both professors manage quite well finding what they need.

Spotlight on Cognitive Neuroscience

Representation of Knowledge

Understanding how knowledge is represented in the brain and how brain activity manifests itself in psychological experience is one of the primary goals of cognitive neuroscience. David Boles points out that it is essential to strike a balance between "lumping" and "splitting" if we are to truly develop a science of brain–behavior relationships. "Lumping" occurs when one assumes that a "selected task involves the mental process one thinks it does" or, in other words, when one believes that overtly similar tasks are actually all part of the same sort of processing when, in fact, they may be very different at the processing level. "Splitting," on the other hand, occurs when variations in brain function for similar tasks are assumed to be indications that they are in fact very different tasks when they may not be at all. An overreliance on lumping and splitting produces "empirical clutter" such that true findings are difficult to discern. David Boles suggests that overlumping can be reduced by using statistical methodologies that identify processes that are in common with various cognitive tasks; oversplitting can be avoided by correlating brain activation with task performance and then focusing on only those areas that indicate a strong relationship. Combining the perspectives of lumping and splitting can ultimately lead to a balance between overgeneralization of results and the temptation to pinpoint brain activity as directly related to task performance in such a way as to advance our understanding of function and the brain.

Boles, D. B. (2000). The "lumping" and "splitting" of function and brain. *Brain and Cognition*, 42, 23–25.

Student Resource Center

STUDY GUIDE

1. Semantic organization refers to the way concepts are organized and structured in memory.

2. Two principal viewpoints have dominated studies of semantic organization and differ in their respective focuses. The associationist approach has focused on functional relationships between concepts, and the cognitive approach has focused on mental structures that describe the relationship between meaning and memory.

3. Associationist studies examine semantic organization by studying the form of free recall (e.g., what words are recalled together), assuming such protocols provide information about the nature of the organization of concepts and the underlying cognitive structure.

4. Cognitive models organize data from semantic experiments into comprehensive theories of memory and include set-theoretical models, the feature-comparison model, network models, and propositional networks.

5. Set-theoretical models propose that concepts are organized by numerous sets of information, which include categories and attributes.

6. The semantic feature-comparison model assumes a set-theoretical structure but distinguishes attributes either as defining, essential features or as characteristic, descriptive features. Concept validation is presumably based more on defining features.

7. Network models assume that concepts are stored in memory as independent units interrelated by specific and meaningful connections (e.g., "A robin is a bird"). Additional assumptions concern memory retrieval by verification of both target and related concepts and the idea that intrastructural movement during retrieval requires time.

8. The spreading activation model of semantic processing (Collins and Loftus) is based on a complex network in which simple associations (e.g., *red* and *fire*) are linked together in conceptual space. The model is instrumental in accounting for priming effects and the facilitating effects of recovering a word or concept from memory when preceded by a related word.

9. Propositional network models propose that memory is organized by a complex associative network of propositional constructions that are the smallest units of meaningful information (e.g., "New York is large").

10. Adaptive control of thought (ACT) by Anderson is an associationistic theory of memory in which three types of memories are posited: working memory, declarative representation, and production memory.

11   Recent studies in cognitive neuroscience have tried to integrate findings in neurophysiology with theories in cognitive psychology. For example, studies of amnesic patients have proved quite profitable in the never-ending search for answers about how the brain works.

12   Two types of knowledge have been identified: declarative knowledge and procedural knowledge. Declarative knowledge is explicit and includes facts; procedural knowledge is implicit and may be sampled through performance. A taxonomy of memory structure in which declarative memory and nondeclarative memory are integral parts has been developed by Squire.

13   Knowledge is represented in PDP models as connections between units, which is theoretically similar to the way neural networks represent information.

KEY TERMS

adaptive control of thought (ACT)
characteristic features
concepts
connectionism
defining features
knowledge

network models
proposition
semantic feature-comparison model
set-theoretical model
spreading activation model

STARTING POINTS

Books and Articles

In addition to those works on memory suggested in previous chapters, there are several good references on semantic memory. The early material on clustering in an associationistic framework is in Kausler, *Psychology of Verbal Learning and Memory*—probably the most authoritative historical review available. For those interested in a psycholinguistic point of view, Edward Smith has a broad, comprehensive review of semantic memory in "Theories of Semantic Memory," which is found in *Handbook of Learning and Cognitive Processes,* edited by Estes. A scholarly approach to semantic memory can be found in Kintsch, *The Representation of Meaning in Memory,* and Miller and Johnson-Laird, *Language and Perception.* Collins and Loftus, "A Spreading Activation Theory of Semantic Processing," in *Psychological Review* gives a current view of their theory.

Network theories are thoroughly discussed in Anderson and Bower, *Human Associative Memory,* a remarkably ambitious book. In *Language, Memory, and Thought,* Anderson gives a detailed account of a revision of HAM called ACT. Also see *The Architecture of Cognition* by Anderson. *Neuroscience and Connectionist Theory,* edited by Gluck and Rumelhart, although technical in places, is highly recommended. Barsalou's book, *Cognitive Psychology,* stresses semantic memory and is especially recommended for those looking for detailed technical and theoretical discussion of these topics.

Movies

The Miracle Worker (1962)—verbal imagery

The Visual Representation of Knowledge

hmmm . . .?

- **Historical Perspective**
- **Theories of Visual Representation of Knowledge**
  Dual-Coding Hypothesis
  Conceptual-Propositional Hypothesis
  Functional-Equivalency Hypothesis
- **Cognitive Neuroscience Support**
- **Cognitive Maps**
- **Synesthesia: The Sound of Colors**

1. Define mental imagery. Does your definition include all sensory modes?

2. How were the early study of mental imagery and the testing of mental attributes related?

3. What are the main features of (a) the dual-coding hypothesis, (b) the conceptual-propositional hypothesis, and (c) the functional-equivalency hypothesis?

4. If you imagine an elephant standing next to a mouse, which question would you be able to answer faster: Does the elephant have a tail? Does the mouse have a tail? Why?

5. How have cognitive neuroscience experiments made the topic of mental imagery more empirical?

6. How does a person's bias influence the type of mental map he or she might form?

7. Suppose when you hear a high-pitched tone, it reminds you of an electrical spark. What is the word for that experience?

*M*ental imagery is remarkably able to substitute for actual perception . . . having been incorporated into our perceptual machinery by eons of evolution in a three-dimensional world.

—*Roger N. Shepard*

As with some other concepts in cognitive psychology, imagery is what everyone knows it to be (we have all experienced it) and yet its specific cognitive properties continue to be studied. What is a mental image, and what are its properties? What is it that you are "seeing" when you look at a mental image? Is the image "real," or is it conjured up from information that is stored in a different modality? Can you differentiate between an imaginary image and one that you have actually experienced? If so, what is different about them? These are some questions that have bemused philosophers for centuries and currently intrigue cognitive psychologists. Research has produced some exciting new findings and theories.

This chapter is about the visual representation of knowledge, and when we talk about the visual representation of knowledge we are talking about mental imagery by and large. Mental imagery is defined as a mental representation of a nonpresent object or event.

In fact, pretending and visualizing imagined worlds (whether they be images we conjure from reading a novel, or daydreaming about a faraway beach on a cold winter day) are even considered possibly to be functionally important in that they allow us to exercise skills that may ultimately serve direct adaptive purposes (Cosmides & Tooby, 2000; Leslie, 1987).

Historical Perspective

We can identify three historical eras of mental imagery: the philosophic era, the measurement era, and the cognitive era.

During the philosophic era, mental images were taken to be a principal ingredient in the composition of the mind and sometimes were believed to be the elements of thought. The topic was an integral part to Greek philosophers, notably Aristotle and Plato, and, later the British Empiricists, notably John Locke, George Berkeley, David Hume, and David Hartley.

The measurement era of mental imagery is traced to British intellectual Sir Francis Galton (1880, 1883/1907). He circulated a questionnaire to 100 of his well-to-do acquaintances, half of which were "men of science," in which he asked them to recall aspects of their morning breakfast and answer questions about the images they experienced.

Before addressing yourself to any of the Questions on the opposite page, think of some definite object—suppose it is your breakfast-table as you sat down to it this morning—and consider carefully the picture that rises before your mind's eye.

1. Illumination.—Is the image dim or fairly clear? Is its brightness comparable to that of the actual scene?
2. Definition.—Are all the objects pretty well defined at the same time, or is the place of sharpest definition at any one moment more contracted than it is in a real scene?

3. Colouring.—Are the colours of the china, of the toast, bread-crust, mustard, meat, parsley, or whatever may have been on the table, quite distinct and natural?" (Galton, 1880, p. 302)

The results surprised Galton, when the men of science "protested that mental imagery was unknown to them," while persons of general society" reported that the images were clear as the original perceptual experience. The testing of imagery drew the interest of several researchers, such as Titchener (1909) and Betts (1909). Their investigations consisted in having participants rate their ability to visualize an object such as an apple, the contour of a face, or the sun sinking below the horizon.

Interest in the investigation of imagery quickly sank below the horizon with the downfall of introspectrum and the rise of behaviorism, as exemplified in Watson's behaviorist of (1913) manifesto. The behaviorist manifesto, as Woodworth (1948) called it, denounced introspection, which was a critical part of the previously mentioned tests of imagery. Introspection, according to Watson, formed no essential part of psychology. Behaviorism was committed to the objective observation of overt responses, and terms such as *consciousness, mental states, mind,* and *imagery* were anethema, and would ruin the career of any researcher who used them. As with many topics in cognitive psychology, research in imagery lay dormant for many years.

Imagery research was reawakened in the late 1960s on two fronts. The first was related to the qualitative assessment of imagery (Sheehan, 1967b) and its use as a therapeutic vehicle. Also related to the assessment of imagery, but with a stronger theoretical bent, was the research of Bugelski (1970) and Paivio (1969). The second contemporary approach to imagery involved incorporation of the concept into a cognitive model in which the representation of knowledge was a central element. This view is evident in the research of Shepard (1975); Shepard and Metzler (1971); and, more recently, in the neurocognitive studies by Farah (1988), Kosslyn (1988), and Pinker (1985). The study of imagery has benefitted from the unique contributions of these researchers.

Theories of the Visual Representation of Knowledge

The study of the visual representation of knowledge engages the broader question of how visual information is stored and recalled from memory. We could argue that the neurological activity associated with the storage of information is of a specific form. That is, visual information is coded in terms of an internal "picture" that can be reactivated by calling up the picture, as we might in looking at a photo album. Alternatively, we could argue that visual information is filtered, summarized, and stored as abstract "statements" about the image. Reactivation of the memory then would consist of recalling the abstract code, which in turn would reconstruct the subjective image associated with it. Finally, we could argue that some information is stored visually and some in an abstract form, indicating that multiple codes exist in the mind.

Real progress has been made in the quest for a better understanding of imagery through inventive research techniques and clear-cut results. Currently there is debate over the question of whether visual imagery is really visual or is governed by general-purpose cognitive processes (as contrasted with specific visual processes). The visual argument holds that mental imagery involves the same representations used in vision,

"Seeing" Without Sensing

We see when a visual object is being viewed, but through the curiosity of **visual imagery,** we can also "see" when an object is not being viewed. Humans, and perhaps other animals, can "see" with the mind's eye.

Few dispute that all humans, to some degree, subjectively experience visual images; we can all "see" familiar shapes and forms by thinking of their characteristics.* Consider, for example, this problem: How many windows are there in the house in which you live? In all likelihood the way you answer this question is to form a mental image of your home and then mentally count the windows. Likewise, it appears that we are capable of

forming mental representations of other sensory experiences in the absence of the physical stimuli. If we were to ask you to imagine a beach scene on a remote tropical island, you might "see" palm trees, seashells, the sun, and people in various activities, but you might also "hear" the ocean, "feel" the tropical breeze, "smell" the salt air. Some people seem capable of composing very vivid mental images, while others find this task difficult.

Over the next few hours, keep track of your mental representations, visual and otherwise. Which images are the most real, what is the relationship between these images and "reality," and what purpose do images play in one's mental life?

*Likewise, we can "hear," "taste," "feel," and "smell" sensations by conjuring up their mental image.

so that when we "see" an actual tree, specific types of neural processing and representations are activated. When we "image" a tree, the same (or highly similar) processes and representations are activated. The other side of this argument is that the representations used in imagery are not the representations used in real perception. This argument holds that "thinking in pictures" basically involves knowledge best expressed in terms of traditional (i.e., propositional or associative) representations of knowledge.

Current theories about mental imagery are focused on three central hypotheses:

1. The **dual-coding hypothesis,** which suggests that there are two codes and two storage systems—one imaginal, the other verbal—and that information may be coded and stored in either or both (principally the work of Paivio).

2. The **conceptual-propositional hypothesis,** which proposes that both visual and verbal information are represented in the form of abstract propositions about objects and their relationships (principally the work of Anderson and Bower as well as Pylyshyn).

3. The **functional-equivalency hypothesis,** which suggests that imagery and perception employ similar processes (principally the work of Shepard and Kosslyn).

Dual-Coding Hypothesis

The work of Paivio and his colleagues (1965; Paivo, Yule, & Madigan, 1968) on imagery draws from the early efforts in quantifying imagery was done in a paired-associate learning paradigm, one very much in fashion at the time. The first step Paivio took was to quantify the imagery quality of nouns by having a group of college students rate nouns for their capacity to arouse an image, that is, "a mental picture, or sound, or other sensory picture." Table 10.1 contains a sample of their results, including ratings for imagery (the word's capacity to arouse nonverbal images), concreteness (rating of direct reference to

Cognition in Everyday Life

Mental Imagery and Sports

*C*an mental imagery help athletes perform better? Some research indicates a resounding "yes." Here's how:

[First, immerse] yourself mentally in the sport's environment. If it's basketball, see the gym, the stands, the three-point line, the basket. In skiing, learn the terrain changes, the texture of the snow, where the run starts and finishes and the line you want to take down the mountain.

The second preliminary step is visual imagery. Once you have specified and memorized the task, practice producing a vivid image of the situation, one that uses all your senses. A skier I've worked with imagines riding up in the chairlift, looking over his skis at the top of the hill, seeing the colors of the trees and the other skiers' bright clothing against the whiteness of the snow and feeling the sensation of his skis gliding over the snow. He brings in feelings as well as visual images, recalling the exhilaration and joy he experiences in making a good turn.

Once the task is clear and the images vivid, it's time to start the mental rehearsal itself. Close your eyes and experience the physical activity mentally and emotionally. Everything you visualize should look and feel the same as if you were really on the slopes or on the court.

From May (1989).

a sensory object's experience), meaningfulness (the mean number of related words written in 30 seconds) and frequency (how common the word is). These results confirm the obvious: that some words are more visual (e.g., *elephant, tomahawk,* and *church*) and others less visual (e.g., *context, deed,* and *virtue*).

Studies by Paivio and his colleagues have led to the development of the dual-coding hypothesis, a theory as to how information is represented in memory. The hypothesis is based on the inference that there are two coding systems, or two ways information may

TABLE 10.1

Imagery Scores and Scores on Related Attributes for a Representative Sample of Nouns

Noun	Mean Score*			
	Imagery	*Concreteness*	*Meaningfulness*	
Beggar	6.40	6.25	6.50	29
Church	6.63	6.59	7.52	100
Context	2.13	2.73	4.44	1
Deed	3.63	4.19	5.32	50
Elephant	6.83	7.00	6.88	35
Profession	3.83	3.65	5.44	28
Salary	4.70	5.23	5.08	50
Tomahawk	6.57	6.87	6.44	3
Virtue	3.33	1.46	4.87	50

*Ratings were on a scale of 1 to 7; the lower the score, the lower its imagery.
From Paivio, Yuille, and Madigan (1968).

be represented in memory: a nonverbal imagery process and a verbal symbolic process. The two codes—imaginal and verbal—may overlap in the processing of information with one coding scheme being dominant for a particular word.

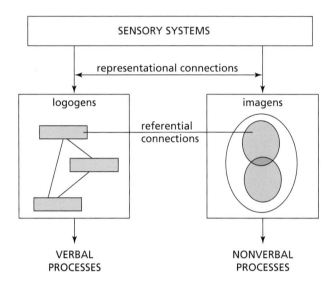

Conceptual-Propositional Hypothesis

Anderson and Bower, the developers of the propositional HAM model, were critical of the mental-picture metaphor, stating that "it is not scientifically viable to suppose that memories, or other sorts of knowledge, are carried about in a form like an internal photograph, video tape, or tape recording, which we can reactivate and replay in remembering an image" (1973, p. 453). Even though we are capable of a subjective experience of an image, the underlying cognitive component may be of a form much different from an image. One reason Anderson and Bower reject the pictures-in-the-head theory is related to a conservation argument, which states that it is useless to postulate storage of full pictures of scenes because such a memory system would require storage and retrieval well beyond the human capability. Some device would still be necessary to view and interpret these internal pictures.

The conceptual-propositional hypothesis holds that we store interpretations of events, whether verbal or visual, rather than the components of the image. Anderson and Bower do not deny that it is easier to learn concrete words than abstract words, but they attribute those results to the supposition that concrete concepts are coded by a rich set of predicates that bind concepts together. They state that "the only difference between the internal representation for a linguistic input and a memory image is detail of information" (1973, p. 460).

Anderson and Bower's conceptual-propositional hypothesis is a theoretically elegant point of view and one that is compatible with their theoretical model (HAM). However, the hypothesis has some difficulty accounting for some imagery processes that seem to require an internal structure that is second-order isomorphic to the physical object. Data that seem to reflect such processes have been presented by Shepard and his colleagues and are considered in the next section.

Functional-Equivalency Hypothesis

Much of the excitement in the field of mental imagery at the time was due to the demonstration and interpretation of **mental rotation** by Shepard and Metzler (1971). Using visual cues, Shepard studied mental rotation of visual stimuli in memory. In his experiments participants were presented with two images and were asked to judge whether the two were in fact the same object (except for orientation) (see Figure 10.1). In some cases the second pattern was a mirror image of the first and, therefore, not the "same" as the original stimulus, while in other cases the pattern was identical to the original, but rotated. The degree of rotation ranged from 0 degrees to 180 degrees.

FIGURE 10.1

Typical visual forms used in a mental rotation task. Subjects have to decide if the image on the left is the same as the one on the right (just rotated).

Adapted from Shepard and Metzler (1971).

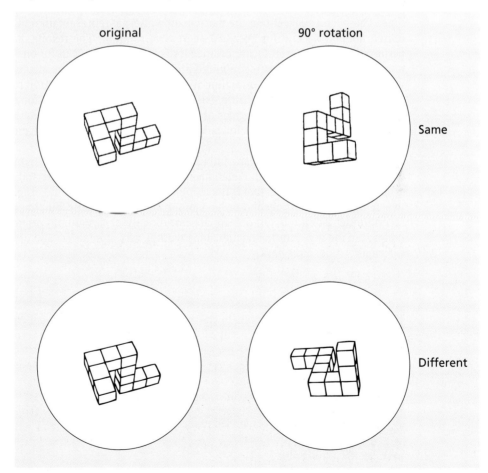

Reaction time as a function of degree of rotation of an object.

Adapted from Shepard and Metzler (1971).

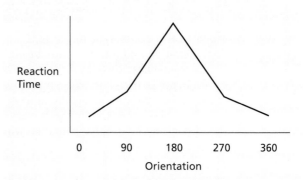

The dependent variable was the amount of time required to make a judgment. The results of these experiments indicate that the time required to respond was a linear function of the degree of rotation (see Figure 10.2). That is, a small degree of rotation of the second stimulus was quickly judged, while a large degree of rotation required more time. These data suggest that the participant's internal representation of the images required about 1 second for every 50 degrees of rotation. The results of Shepard's experiments have far-reaching importance for cognitive theory, but for our discussion the relationship between the time required and the degree of rotation suggests that the internal process is an orderly function of the amount of transformation required. Thus, it appears that a close relationship exists between the time required for a specific mental rotation and the actual degrees of rotation involved. If we consider both rotations on two scales—time required for mental rotation and degrees of rotation—the correspondence is evident.

Shepard (1968) and Shepard and Chipman (1970) introduced the term **second-order isomorphism** to represent the relationship between external objects and internal representations of those objects that is not a one-to-one (isomorphic) kind. The distinction between first-order and second-order isomorphism is a subtle but important one: In second-order isomorphism, objects are not directly or structurally represented in our brains, but the way internal relationships work is very similar (second order) to the way external relationships work.

Roger Shepard. Studies of mental rotation led to theories in mental imagery.

Cognitive Neuroscience Support

In addition to the reaction data presented in Shepard's experiments, some researchers have presented neurological evidence for mental rotation. One of these studies by Georgopoulos, Lurito, Petrides, Schwartz, and Massey (1989) is particularly interesting. They examined the electrical activity in the brain of a rhesus monkey as it performed a mental rotation task. The monkey was trained to turn a handle in reaction to the location of a light. When the light appeared in one location, the animal would move the handle in a corresponding direction. However, the primary interest lay in what happened in the cortex of the monkey, which the researcher interpreted as mental rotation, just prior to turning the handle. During the few milliseconds prior to the response, the animal anticipated the movement. It was this cognitive process (the anticipation) that the researchers were interested in measuring. Georgopoulos and his fellow researchers measured electrical activity in the monkey's motor cortex during this

THE FAR SIDE®   **BY GARY LARSON**

**Darrell suspected someone had once
again slipped him a trick spoon with the
concave side reversed.**

Stephen Kosslyn. Helped develop the field of mental imagery and cognitive neuroscience.

critical period and, with the assistance of computer graphics, showed that the cells responded in corresponding directional patterns. The results provide direct neurological evidence for mental rotation and suggest that the use of "single-cell" recordings of neural activity might be a useful supplement to behavioral data in the identification of cognitive operations.

From the research findings of Shepard's group and cognitive neuroscience findings, a strong case develops for the existence of images in the mind that are, if not structurally identical to the real-world object, at least functionally related.

Another series of studies examines the size and spatial properties of an object and how they affect cognitive processing. In a series of experiments, Kosslyn and his colleagues (Kosslyn, 1973, 1975, 1976a, 1977, 1980, 1981, 1994, 1995; Kosslyn & Pomerantz, 1977; Kosslyn et al., 1993) have investigated imagery from the standpoint of its spatial characteristics and, most recently, with the use of brain imaging technology (to be discussed later). In the main, Kosslyn's research has demonstrated that a mental image is similar to the perception of a real object. Most of his experiments are based on the assumption that an image has spatial properties, which may be scanned, and that it takes more time to scan large distances than short distances. In one experiment (1973), Kosslyn asked participants to memorize a set of drawings and then to imagine one at a time. At one time they were asked to "focus" on one end of the object they had imagined (e.g., if the object was a speedboat, they were asked to "look at" the rear portion). A possible property of the original picture was named, and the participant was asked to decide whether or not it was in the original. The results indicated that longer times were required to make judgments about properties that involved scanning distances. For example, those involving a scan from stern to bow (see Figure 10.3) took longer than those involving one from porthole to bow). Participants who were asked to keep the whole image in mind showed no differences in the time required to identify properties from different locations. It would appear that mental images can be scanned and that the time required to scan them is similar to that needed to scan real pictures.

If images do share some features of real-object perception (i.e., scanning time), are there other features common to percepts and images? Kosslyn, using the fact that small objects are generally seen less clearly than large objects, demonstrated that there are. In one experiment (1975), he had participants imagine a target animal (e.g., a rabbit) next to a small or large creature (e.g., a fly or an elephant). When the rabbit is envisioned in conjunction

FIGURE 10.3

Size scanning.

Kosslyn (1973).

*A*lthough imagery has played a central role in theorizing about the mind since the time of Aristotle, its nature and properties have been surrounded by controversy. Indeed, during the Behaviorist era, its very existence was questioned, and more recently its status as a distinct kind of mental representation has been vigorously debated.

—*Stephen M. Kosslyn*

with the elephant, the mental image is of a small rabbit with less detail. However, when the rabbit is envisioned next to a fly, the rabbit is relatively large and its image has more detail (see Figure 10.4). Given this, it takes longer for participants to determine appropriateness of a certain property (e.g., ears) when the rabbit is relatively small.

To guard against the possibility that such results might derive simply from greater interest in elephants than in flies, Kosslyn tested animals in the context of a gigantic fly and a tiny elephant. Under these conditions, more time was taken to evaluate the target animal when it was paired with the giant fly than with the tiny elephant.

In yet another experiment, Kosslyn (1975) asked participants to imagine squares of four different sizes—each six times the area of the next smaller one and each identified by a color name. After the participants were able to envision the size of the square on the basis of the color, they were given a color and animal name, such as "green bear" or "pink tiger," and asked to summon up an image of the designated animal according to the size of the box linked with the color (see Figure 10.5). After this, a possible property of the animal was presented. The time required to decide whether the property was a characteristic of the animal was much longer for animals in the small boxes than for those in the larger ones (see Figure 10.6).

FIGURE 10.4

Size comparison. Reaction times were longer when the rabbit was paired with the elephant.

Adapted from Kosslyn (1975).

FIGURE 10.5

Controlling for size. Here participants judged appropriateness of a property to an imagined animal in boxes of different sizes.

Adapted from Stephen M. Kosslyn (1975).

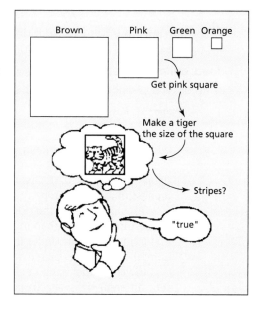

Taken together, these experiments of Kosslyn and Shepard indicate that visual images reflect internal representations that operate in a way that is isomorphic to the functioning of the perception of physical objects.

So far, we can conclude that mental imagery and perception of a real stimulus are seductively alike in many regards. However, to ascertain the completeness of the analogy of perception to imagery, further validation exists in the form of neurological evidence. Fortunately, a large body of data comes from neurological studies (e.g., Corballis, 1989; Gazzaniga & Sperry, 1967; Milner, 1968). Clinical observations by Luria (1976) and Farah (1988, 1995) of neurologically damaged patients show that impairment of the left hemi-

FIGURE 10.6

Inverse relationship between size of box and amount of time to make determination.

Data from Stephen M. Kosslyn (1975).

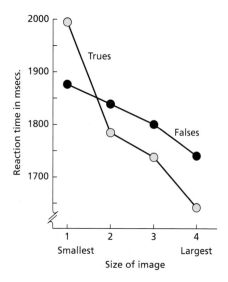

sphere of the brain is associated with disturbances of verbal memory, while right-hemisphere damage is associated with the memory for visual material. These findings tend to support the dual-coding theory of memory: one system for the coding and processing of visual information, another for the coding and processing of verbal information.

The rationale for many experiments dealing with brain activity and imagery is that activation of a cognitive process, such as imagery or verbal thought, is expressed in terms of localized brain activity, which can be measured by regional blood flow.

The logic of this quest is simple. If measurements of regional cerebral blood flow (rCBF) indicate that the same areas of the brain are active when we see an object as when we image an object, then the functional-equivalency position is supported (although not definitely established, since regions could carry on more than a single function). Conversely, if different areas of the brain are activated during perception than during imaging, then the equivalency position is not supported.

First, we consider the matter of uniqueness of imagery and brain activity. Strong objective evidence has been reported showing that all parts of the visual cortex are activated when participants imagine an object or use imagery to solve a problem. Specifically, research by Roland and Friberg (1985) measured rCBF during three cognitive tasks:

1. Mental arithmetic (subtracting by 3s starting with 50).
2. Memory scanning of an auditory stimulus (mentally jumping every second word in a well-known musical jingle).
3. Visual imagery (visualizing a walk through one's neighborhood, making alternating right and left turns starting at one's front door).

Each task activated different parts of the cortex, but most important for our discussion is the finding that during the visual task, blood flow was most apparent to the posterior regions, which includes the occipital lobe and temporal areas important for higher visual processing and memory. It appears that mental imagery of this sort involves not only visual processing areas but also memory areas.

In a related study, Goldenberg and colleagues (1990), using PET scans to trace brain activity, asked participants to answer some questions that required visual imagery and some that did not. For example:

"Is the green of pine trees darker than the green of grass?"
"Is the categorical imperative an ancient grammatical form?"

The results indicated that the first type of question produced high levels of blood flow in the occipital regions and in the posterior parietal and temporal visual processing areas, whereas the second nonimagery condition did not.

A detailed and direct test of the hypothesis about perception and imagery has been reported by Kosslyn and his colleagues (1993, 1995) in which an often-used test of imagery was used in a PET study. In this case, a task devised by Podgorny and Shepard (1978) consisted of asking participants to view a letter (such as the letter *F*) in a grid (the perceptual condition) or to image the letter in an empty grid (the imagery condition). Then a mark was presented, and the participants were to indicate whether the mark fell on or off the letter (see Figure 10.7).

What Kosslyn and his colleagues found was somewhat surprising. Although they hypothesized that the visual cortex would be activated during the perceptual task and probably activated during the imagery task, the PET results clearly showed *greater* activation of the visual cortex during image generation than during perception. It is as if this structure, and perhaps other structures involved in visual processing, had to work harder during image

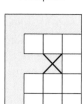
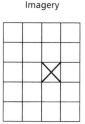

FIGURE 10.7

Sample figure used in the Podgorney and Shepard perceptual and imagery task.

Based on P. Podgorny and R. N. Shepard (1978). *JEP: HP and P, 4,* 21–35. Copyright © 1978 by the American Psychological Association. Reprinted by permission.

generation than during perception. One possible reason for this finding is that during perception the visual cortex receives detailed visual information from the external world (a kind of bottom-up process) and, therefore, operates with the object in view, which requires little effort. In contrast, during image generation, the person must recreate the visual stimulus from memory (a kind of top-down process), which forces it to work harder.

From these studies and many more (see Farah, 1988), several conclusions are appropriate:

1. Studies of brain activity indicate that different areas of the brain are associated with different cognitive tasks.
2. Visual imagery tasks and vision seem to be situated in similar locations in the brain.
3. Visual imagery tasks, which require associative knowledge, seem to activate regions of the brain affiliated with memory and vision.
4. Because of their top-down nature, imagery tasks may require more energy to process than perceptual tasks, which are initially bottom-up tasks.

One remaining issue has not been addressed in this section. It is the question of whether spatial representations (the type of representations we saw in Shepard's mental rotation experiments) and visual representations (the type of representations dependent on the reconstruction of a visual impression, for example, naming the color of an object such as a football) engage different parts of the brain. In answering this question, we turn to a clinical case study.

Farah and her colleagues worked with a 36-year-old minister (L. H.) who, when he was 18, sustained a serious head injury in an automobile accident. Subsequent surgery (and CT scan confirmation) indicated that the parts of the brain that were damaged involved both temporo-occipital regions, the right temporal lobe, and the right inferior frontal lobe, as shown in Figure 10.8. Although L. H. made remarkable recovery and out-

Martha Farah. Conducted innovative research in cognitive neuroscience, which has identified neurological sites of cognitive processes.

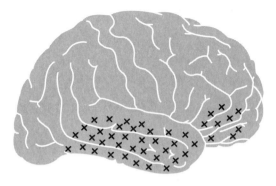

FIGURE 10.8

Areas of damage to L. H.'s brain (marked with Xs). Areas involved include the right temporal lobe and right inferior frontal lobe (upper figure) and the temporo-occipital regions (lower figure).

From Farah, Hammond, Levine, and Calvanio (1988). Reprinted with permission.

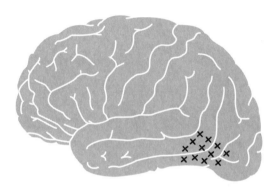

wardly seemed normal, he was profoundly impaired in visual recognition. For example, he could not reliably recognize his wife or children unless they were wearing distinctive clothes. This is called visual agnosia. He also had difficulty recognizing animals, plants, foods, and drawings. Some of the objects L. H. could not recognize are shown in Figure 10.9. He could, nevertheless, make reasonable copies of these figures, even though he did not know their identity. He had good elementary visual capabilities.

In the final stage of the experiment, L. H. performed a variety of tasks associated with spatial knowledge and other tasks associated with visual knowledge.

- *Visual Tasks.* For the visual tasks, animal tails (Does a kangaroo have a long tail?), color identification (What is the color of a football?), size comparison (Which is larger, a popsicle or a pack of cigarettes?), and comparison of state shapes (Which states are most similar in shape?) were presented to L. H. and to a number of control participants.

- *Spatial Imagery Tasks.* For the spatial tasks, letter rotation (mental rotation of a letter, similar to form rotation used by Shepard and Metzler), three-dimensional form rotation (see Shepard and Metzler), mental scanning (see Kosslyn), and size scaling (estimates of the same shape of figures regardless of size) were presented to the patient and to control participants.

The results, given in Figure 10.10A, clearly show L. H.'s performance on visual tasks as being impaired, presumably as the result of destruction of specific brain areas; however, these impairments seem to have left intact his ability to perform spatial tasks (see Figure 10.10B). It would appear, therefore, that these two types of tasks (visual and spatial) tap

FIGURE 10.9

A. Examples of drawings a patient with brain damage could not recognize.

B. Patient's reproductions of these figures.

From Farah et al. (1988). Reprinted with permission.

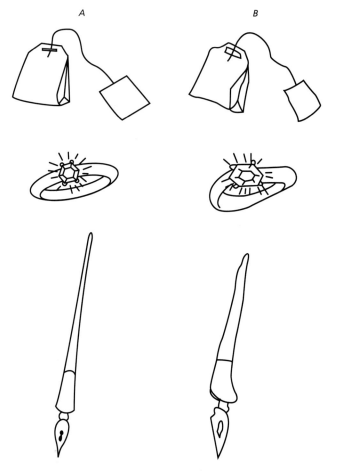

different types of mental representation that are neurologically distinct. Because they are neurologically distinct, it follows that different subsystems of imagery representations exist.

The experimenters in this case were interested in visual and spatial imagery ability vis-à-vis brain injuries. They argued that:

- Spatial representations are not confined to the visual modality (for example, mental rotations, which are considered to be spatial images, not visual images).
- Visual representations are confined to the visual modality (for example, the naming of a color of a common object such as a football).

Cognitive Maps

The human capacity for imagery is a powerful attribute of memory, as we saw in the chapter on mnemonics, but it is also essential in our everyday life as we work and move about in our environment. Humans share the same three-dimensional world as other earth

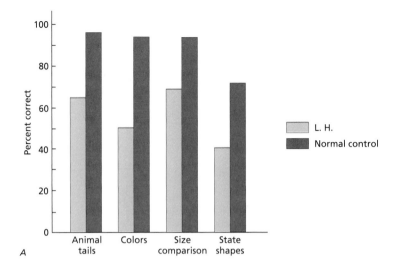

FIGURE 10.10

Visual Imagery Tasks
A. Performance of L. H. (light bars) and normal control participants (dark bars) on four visual imagery tasks.

Spatial Imagery tasks
B. Performance of L. H. (light bars) and normal control participants (dark bars) on seven spatial imagery tasks.

From Farah (1988). Reprinted with permission.

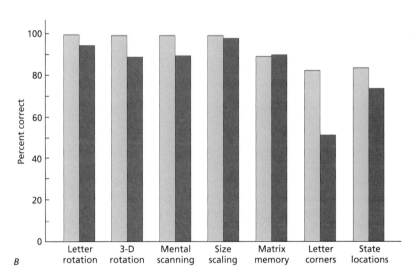

creatures (although not in the same way as fish or birds) and, to survive, must be able to use imagery to navigate through our spatial world and avoid harm.

Psychologists have for a long time been interested in the navigational patterns of animals, and the early work of Tolman led to the concept of the **cognitive map,** which referred to a general spatial knowledge exhibited by rats in a maze.

One experiment by Thorndyke and Hayes-Roth (1982) concluded that humans use two types of spatial knowledge—route knowledge and survey knowledge—in their effort to learn about the physical world. Route knowledge is related to the specific pathways used to get from one location to another. If a stranger on campus asked how to find the library, we would say something like "You take College Street to the president's house, take a right, go through the traffic circle, and across the plaza you'll see a large, flat

building." We would be giving route information. Survey knowledge, on the other hand, deals with more global relationships between environmental cues. We might answer the stranger's question by saying "It's over there, in that general direction." Another, more direct way to form survey knowledge is to study a map. The Thorndyke and Hayes-Roth study took place in the large office complex where they worked. They asked participants in the experiment to study a map and found that after only 20 minutes of study the participants were able to judge distances and locations as effectively as a group of secretaries who had worked in the building for two years.

In a somewhat related study, Tversky (1981; Taylor & Tversky, 1992) examined the distortions of memory for geographic locations. In their interesting work, Tversky suggests that distortions occur because people use conceptual strategies to remember geographic information. We have already seen that people tend to form prototypes when given simple geometric forms to imagine, and it is likely that even more complex forms of abstracted information are part of the cognitive mapping process of humans.

Following this line of thought, it may be that geographic information is structured in memory in terms of abstract generalizations rather than specific images. Such an argument would avoid the difficult question of how we can store so much information in visual memory, since the storage is condensed into larger units. Your home, for example, is part of a neighborhood, which is part of a city, which is part of a township, which is in a region of the state, and so on. When you move from one section to another, say, in your city, the knowledge you use may be in the form of an abstract representation of landmarks rather than a series of discrete visual images. Sometimes these higher structures interfere with decisions made on the local level. For example, if you were asked which city is farther west, Reno or Los Angeles (see Figure 10.11), you would likely answer Los Angeles (see Stevens & Coupe, 1978). Why? Because we know that Los Angeles is in California and that Reno is in Nevada, which is to the east of California. In this case we are relying on strategic information rather than tactical information, and we are misled.

It has long been known that we humans enjoy a geocentric view of the universe. Early scientists, with encouragement from the Church, even placed Earth in the center of the solar system (which required an inelegant theory of planetary motion) before Copernicus jolted us out of the vortex and properly placed Earth as the third planet from the sun. It is common, and understandable, that children regard their home as the center of their universe, surrounded by their neighborhood, city, state, and country. Local egocentric impressions of geography are the result of familiarization and provide emotional comfort. (*Home* is one of the most comforting words in our vocabulary.) Some have suggested that maps, which are basically human impressions of geographic reality, are both a reflection of the objective realities of the world and a reflection of the subjective interpretation of these impressions.

Spotlight on Cognitive Neuroscience

Cognitive Maps

Jeffrey Zacks, Jon Mires, Barbara Tversky, Eliot Hazeltine, and John Gabrieli focus on two different aspects of cognitive maps. The first aspect is object-based spatial transformations, which means rotating in your head a particular object or location. The second is egocentric perspective transformations in which you rotate or translate your point of view. Think of being in your local grocery store. You're pretty familiar with the layout because you shop there at least once a week. You are in one of the frozen food aisles looking at frozen pizza, debating between self-rising and thin crusts. You remember that you want to get some Ben & Jerry's, which is in the next aisle over. If you are engaging in object-based spatial transformation, you would envision the aisle rotating so you could picture where the ice cream was. An egocentric perspective transformation would have you envision yourself moving around the aisle and then facing the ice cream. In each of these types of transformation, some aspects of the world remain fixed while others rotate (you envision the aisle rotating while you remain still, or vice versa). Understanding these types of rotations is important for everyday life (maneuvering between pizza and ice cream at the store) as well as more "technical" areas (air traffic control and architecture, to name two). Zacks and his colleagues' previous research has found that there were different locations in the brain for each of these types of rotations. Their subsequent studies using more traditional cognitive methods of experimentation (mental rotation/visualization tasks as well as paper-and-pencil measures) complemented these findings by showing that there is indeed different processing involved (which corresponds to the different brain regions) for each type of transformation, such that there is an increase in reaction time with object-based transformations but not for egocentric perspective transformations. Their work is a fine example of using multiple methods (neurophysiological and cognitive) to understand important cognitive processes.

Zacks, J. M., Mires, J., Tversky, B., & Hazeltine, E. (2000). Mental spatial transformations of objects and perspective. *Spatial Cognition and Computation, 2*(4), 315–332.

Zacks, J. M., Hazeltine, E., Tversky, B., & Gabrieli, J. D. E. (1999). *Event-related fMRI of mental spatial transformations.* Paper presented at the Annual Meeting of the Cognitive Neuroscience Society, Washington, DC.

FIGURE 10.11

Geographical distortion. *A.* Cognitive map of Reno as east of Los Angeles. *B.* Actual location of Reno—west of Los Angeles.

Just as having participants recall a list of words can tell us something about how semantic information is organized, people's map drawings provide a window into the mind regarding the visual representation of spatial knowledge. There is considerable evidence that expressive forms of representation, such as sketches of maps and other graphic figures,[1] mirror our subjective impression of reality. Most map-drawing studies have dealt with systematic distortions and accuracies of regional cognitive maps, such as navigating around a college campus or judging the distance between geographic points. Several studies have considered world-scale cognitive maps. Certainly, ancient maps indicated a degree of unavoidable egocentrism. For example, the ancient Babylonians didn't know what lay past the distant hills. However, now almost all schoolchildren know something of the basic geographic boundaries of the world.

Some years ago an international study of the image of the world by different nationalities was done to broaden our understanding of cultural differences and to foster world peace (Saarinen, 1987). The design was simple. Students in a first-year course in geography from 71 sites in 49 countries were given a blank sheet of paper and asked to sketch a map of the world. Of the nearly 4,000 maps produced, the majority showed a Eurocentric worldview, even if the person who drew the map was from the periphery, as in the case of students from Hong Kong, Singapore, and Thailand. This is probably due to the wide use of Eurocentric maps for more than 500 years. Some American students drew an Americentric map; an example by a student from Chicago (who seems to have some familiarity with

---

[1]Our colleagues in clinical psychology have subscribed to this idea for a long time, as shown in their use of projective techniques (e.g., Draw-a-Person), which are thought to disclose hidden personality traits.

FIGURE 10.12

Map of the world by a student from Chicago.

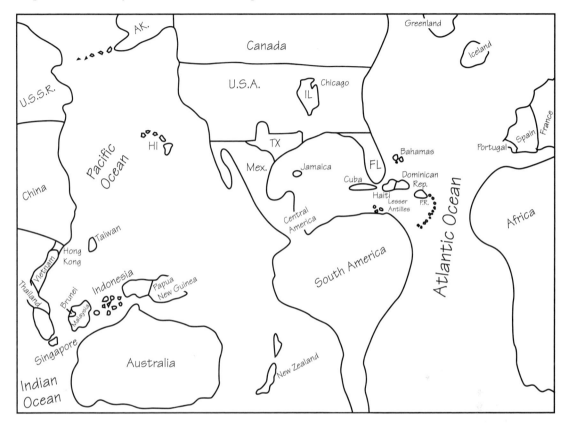

Texas and the Caribbean) is shown in Figure 10.12. Australian students tended to sketch Sinocentric maps, with Australia and Asia in the center; several Down Under students drew maps in which not only was Australia centrally located but also all other countries were shown in the "lower hemisphere," as shown in Figure 10.13. Maps of this orientation are not common in Australia. One would anticipate that students would draw their own country disproportionately larger, but this did not seem to be the case. Prominent countries (the United States and the former USSR, England, France, and so forth) were on most maps. Africa was generally underrepresented, and its countries seemed less well known. American students did rather poorly on the task, especially in terms of placing countries correctly. Students from Hungary and the former Soviet Union produced some of the most detailed maps.

Synesthesia: The Sound of Colors

Synesthesia is a condition in which sensations from one perceptual modality (e.g., vision) are experienced in another modality (e.g., audition). People may taste shapes, feel sounds, or see numbers or letters in color.

FIGURE 10.13

Map of the world by a student from Australia.

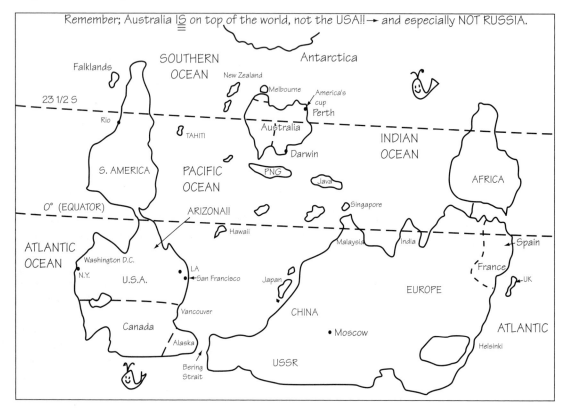

Synesthesia tends to be rule governed, not random. For example, there is a positive relationship between increasing the pitch of a sound and increased brightness (a sneeze is likely to be "brighter" than a cough).

There are convincing data to suggest that many people have a type of synesthesia in which images and sounds (as well as other sensory experiences) are entwined. Furthermore, synesthesia can be measured, and from these observations lawful statements can be derived. There are also data that suggest that some people are unusually synesthetic. These people experience egregious "cross-talk" among sensory experiences. Remember S. with the extraordinary memory? Well, he also had synesthesia. When he was mentally "reading" a series of items from memory, he would hear noises in the testing area as if they were "puffs of steam" or "splashes," which interfered with his "reading" of the information.

*T*he sound of colors is so definite that it would be hard to find anyone who would try to express bright yellow in the bass notes, or a dark lake in the treble.

—*Kandinsky*

Cognition in Everyday Life
Literary Metaphors and Synesthesia

The murmur of the gray twilight—Poe
The sound of coming darkness—Poe
Sunset hovers like the sound of golden horns—Robinson
I could hear the willows weeping sweet smells.—Dickinson
A soft yet glowing light, like lulled music—Shelley
The notes entered my breast like luminous arrows—Gautier
Music bright as the soul of light—Swinburne

When presented with a tone of 30 cycles per second with an amplitude of 100 decibels, S. reported that he first saw a strip 12 to 14 centimeters wide and the color of old, tarnished silver; a tone of 50 cycles per second with an amplitude of 100 decibels produced the experience of a brown strip against a dark background that had red, tongue-like edges. The experience was also accompanied by a sense of taste "like that of sweet and sour borscht." At 500 cycles per second and 100 decibels, S. saw a "streak of lightning splitting the heavens in two." The same tone at 74 decibels changed to a dense orange color that "made him feel as though a needle had been thrust into his spine." The same responses were obtained when the tones were repeated.

S. also experienced synesthetic responses to voices, once commenting to Luria, "What a crumbly yellow voice you have." His reactions to certain other voices were more flattering; one he described as "though a flame with fibers protruding from it was advancing toward me," adding, "I got so interested in his voice, I couldn't follow what he was saying." He described it this way:

. . . I recognize a word not only by the images it evokes but by a whole complex of feelings that image arouses. It's hard to express . . . it's not a matter of vision or hearing but some overall sense I get. Usually I experience a word's taste and weight, and I don't have to make an effort to remember it—the word seems to recall itself. But it's difficult to describe. What I sense is something oily slipping through my hand . . . or I'm aware of a slight tickling in my left hand caused by a mass of tiny, lightweight points. When that happens I simply remember, without having to make the attempt. . . .

What mechanisms might account for these observations? First, consider the physical characteristics of the natural world. Is there any good reason to link sights and sounds? Are bright objects and high-pitched sounds alike physically? Perhaps, but searching for physical explanations may overlook its important psychological character. Second, consider the perceptual and cognitive nature of synesthesia. It may be that our nervous system is structured in a way that "cross-talk" among cortical neurons is a valuable, "prewired" element in the redundant, parallel processing of information in the human brain. It is possible that connected areas in the brain that have activity simultaneously may give rise to synesthesiatic experiences. In the past, we have had to rely on the mediation of language and reaction-time experiments to find a nexus between sensory experiences. With increased sophistication in the detection of brain activities, studies of synesthesia and brain activity will identify the source and nature of this intriguing issue. Vilayanur Ramachandran of the Brain and Perception Laboratory at UC San Diego says that ". . . normal brains are wired so that concepts, perceptions and names of objects are routinely interconnected, giving rise to widely shared metaphors . . . [like 'loud' shirts and 'sharp' cheddar cheese]" (quoted in *The New York Times,* April 10, 2001).

A la carte

Spatial Skills of Gamers

We all probably know someone who is really good at a video game such as Halo or Half Life. Video games obviously rely on our cognitive skills and people obviously play so much that they can be considered experts in a particular game. Researchers who are interested in studying the cognitive abilities of experts have typically examined expertise in game playing. Chess players have been extensively studied. When video games came around, researchers started using gamers for their research studies. It is a heck of a lot easier to find people who are good at video games than it is to find expert chess players. One question cognitive psychologists are curious about is how well a skill transfers to another skill, which is referred to as the "general transfer hypothesis." For example, if you are good at Halo, how well would you be with another first person shooter such as old Duke Nuke'em? Because there are many factors present in video games available today, researchers often use older, arcade-style games such a Tetris when geometrical shapes have to be organized to fall into a special opening at the bottom of the screen. With Tetris, the falling shapes can be rotated and moved to the left or right to optimize where and how they fall. Although challenging, Tetris primarily involves one cognitive skill—spatial ability—and therefore it is easier for the researchers to control what is being studied compared to Halo where there are social aspects to the game, decision making regarding weapon choice, and so on. Researchers Valerie Sims and Richard Mayer (2002) examined how well Tetris experts could transfer their spatial skills to a mental rotation task requiring participants to determine if two shapes are the same, just rotated in different orientations (see figure). The researchers found little support for the general transfer hypothesis as Tetris players were only superior in rotating Tetris-like shapes, suggesting the skills learned for Tetris are domain specific and work best in the context in which they were originally developed. Therefore, once you get good at one video game chances are that the skills you developed won't directly transfer to the new game you just rented. Unless it is very similar, such as the sequel to the original one, you better be prepared to rent it for two weeks.

Participants can rotate the Ls but not the Rs. . . .

Mental Rotation of Tetris Shapes	Mental Rotation of non-Tetris Shapes

Mental Rotation of Tetris-like Letters	Mental Rotation of non-Tetris-like Letters

Student Resource Center

STUDY GUIDE

As we noted in the beginning of this section on imagery, early experimental efforts were frustrating. That remains the case. We have presented three viewpoints on imagery—the dual-coding hypothesis, the conceptual-propositional hypothesis, and the functional-equivalency hypothesis. Each viewpoint is both theoretically elegant and intuitively appealing, so the student of imagery is likely to feel frustrated in choosing the "best" model. It seems that information is imaginally coded at some level of processing, while the same information at another level of processing is conceptually coded. Thus the problem caused by three appealing hypotheses might be resolved by accepting all three, while acknowledging that the coding of information may span several layers of cognitive processes, each of which transcribes information in its unique way.

1   The study of mental imagery is concerned with the issue of how information is represented in memory.

2   Three distinct theoretical positions can be identified regarding how information is stored in memory. They include the dual-coding hypothesis, the conceptual-propositional hypothesis, and the functional-equivalency hypothesis.

3   The dual-coding hypothesis holds that information can be coded and stored in either or both of two systems: verbal and imaginal. Behavioral and neurological data support this position.

4   The conceptual-propositional hypothesis posits that information is stored in an abstract propositional format that specifies objects, events, and their relationships. This position is theoretically elegant, but it has difficulty accounting for the data indicating imaginal processes that involve a second-order isomorphism (e.g., Shepard's work).

5   The functional-equivalency hypothesis holds that imagery and perception are highly similar (principally the work of Shepard and Kosslyn).

6   Two types of representation have been proposed to explain imagery: direct representation and allegorical representation. The latter is generally more widely accepted than the former.

7   It is debated whether visual imagery is in fact visual (specific) or whether it is actually a more general-purpose cognitive process.

8   Neurological evidence has been claimed for mental rotation. Modern research on imagery has been polarized between those who believe that mental images are very much like all other sensory impressions from the physical world and those who believe that objects are represented in terms of the person's knowledge base. Some view the situation as being a mixture of these two extreme viewpoints.

9   Researchers using measurements of regional cerebral blood flow (rCBF) to study imagery are operating under the assumption that concentrations of blood in the brain correlate with the amount of functioning happening in that part of the brain. The data seem to show that visual processing and sometimes memory areas of the brain are at work when we imagine.

10 People tend to have an egocentric view of the world concerning their mental maps.

11 Synesthesia is a condition in which sensations usually experienced in a single modality are experienced in two modalities. This phenomenon, and those who experience it, have provided some interesting and informative research. In fact, some very reliable functions have been found in the data.

KEY TERMS

cognitive map
conceptual-propositional hypothesis
dual-coding hypothesis
functional-equivalency hypothesis

mental rotation
second-order isomorphism
synthesis
visual imagery

STARTING POINTS

● Relevant readings on imagery can be found in Paivio, *Imagery and Verbal Processes;* Rock, *Perception;* Shepard, "Form, Formation and Transformation of Internal Representations," and Shepard, "The Mental Image," in *American Psychologist.* A definitive account may be found in Pinker, *Visual Cognition.* For a clear description of the "imagery" versus "propositions" argument, Kosslyn and Pomerantz in *Cognitive Psychology* and Pylyshyn in *Psychological Bulletin* and *Psychological Review* are recommended. Also see Kosslyn's Image and Mind and his theory in *Psychological Review,* and *Ghosts in the Mind's Machine.* Also, Kosslyn's recent work using PET technology can be found in the *Journal of Cognitive Neuroscience* and *Science* as well as in the book *Image and Brain: The Resolution of the Imagery Debate.* Roger Shepard has a delightful book called *Mind Sights,* which should be read by all those interested in imagery and related topics. The September 1992 issue of *Memory & Cognition* is devoted to mental models and related topics. Volume 2 of Kosslyn and Osherson's series on *An Invitation to Cognitive Science* is on *Visual Cognition.* The entire Section VIII of Gazzaniga's *The Cognitive Neurosciences,* a classic volume, is on thought and imagery and is highly recommended.

Movies

● Synesthesia (2005)—Synesthetic experiences

● At First Sight (1999)—Cognitive maps

Search Terms

● Virtual Cognitive Maps

● The Synesthetic Experience

Language

hmmm. . .?

1. How do psychologists differ from linguists in the study of language?

2. What are the basic features of transformational grammar?

3. What is the linguistic-relativity hypothesis? What support has been given for the hypothesis? And what evidence is against the hypothesis?

4. What are the main points of Kintsch's model of comprehension?

5. How have cognitive neuroscientists investigated the brain and language and what are some of the main conclusions of this work?

6. Why are cognitive psychologists interested in words and reading?

7. What techniques have been used to study reading scientifically?

We should have a great fewer disputes in the world if words were taken for what they are, the signs of our ideas only, and not for things themselves.

—*John Locke*

As you read this text, you are engaging in one of the mind's most enchanting processes—the way one mind influences another through language. In this process, some cell assemblies in your brain are permanently changed, new thoughts are made, and, in a very real sense, you are changed. Yet, this staggeringly complex operation is done effortlessly thousands of times a day by millions of people. Old men, young children, hairdressers in Mexico City, taxi drivers in Denver, shoemakers in Athens, and trappers in Siberia all use language to communicate with others and, if no one is around with whom to converse, will spontaneously start babbling to a volleyball named Wilson. **Language,** to cognitive psychologists, is a system of communication in which thoughts are transmitted by means of sounds (as in speech) or symbols (as in written words and gestures).

The study of language is important to cognitive psychologists. Language development represents a unique kind of abstraction, which is basic to human cognition. Although other forms of life (bees, birds, dolphins, prairie dogs, and so on) have elaborate means of communicating and apes seem to use a form of language abstraction, the degree of abstraction is much greater among humans. Language is the main means of human communication, the way in which most information is exchanged. Language processing is an important component of information processing storage, thinking, and problem solving. As we've seen already, many of our memory processes involve semantic information.

Words and Their Associated Meanings

We humans know a lot of words; about 60,000 separate words are stored in our verbal dictionary (**lexicon**), but many more may be understood and are constantly being generated. Such is the dynamic nature of language. New words are added to the *Webster's Dictionary* every year. You might ask yourself what decade the word "snorkel" entered our language. Was it the 1940s, 1960s, or 1980s? The answer can be found in the Cognition in Everyday Life box.

Grammar and Its Structure

A second important area deals with the way words are structured into phrases and sentences. What good is it having a lot of words to express our thoughts? We also need to know the rules of sequencing that allow us to express ideas to others. Words can be combined in many different ways to express the same thought. Technically, the study of grammar embraces the areas of **phonology** (the combinations of sounds of a language), **morphology.** (the study of the combinations of bits of words and words into larger units), and **syntax** (the study of the combination of words into phrases and sentences).

Neurological Basis of Language

One of the earliest scientific analyses of language involved a clinical case study in 1861 when Paul Broca, a young French surgeon, observed a patient who suffered from paralysis of one side of his body as well as the loss of speech presumably from the neurological damage. Without the benefit of modern imaging techniques, physicians were limited to postmortem examination, which in this case showed a lesion in part of the left frontal lobe—an area that subsequently became known as **Broca's area** (see figure). Subsequent case studies confirmed Broca's observation that the left frontal area was involved in speech production.

In 1875 Carl Wernicke, in another clinical case study, found a lesion in the left temporal lobe affected language processing, but of a different sort than that tied into Broca's area. Broca's area is involved in language production, and **Wernicke's area** is involved with language comprehension. Damage to Wernicke's area left patients able to speak but with reduced understanding of spoken or written words. They could speak fluently, but could not really comprehend what was said to them.

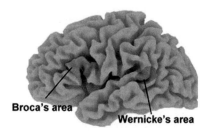

Broca's area

Wernicke's area

Linguistics Hierarchy

Linguistics is the science of language including the structure of language and focusing on a description of speech sounds, meanings, and grammar. Psychologists generally view language in terms of how humans use language. The discipline that incorporates both approaches to the study of language is called **psycholinguistics.** Because psycholinguistics incorporates both approaches, we'll start with an overview of linguistics.

Linguists have developed a hierarchical framework of language. Linguists are concerned with the development of a model of language—its content, structure, and process. The linguistic hierarchy ranges from fundamental components to compound components to very complex components—that is, sound units and meaning units in order of growing complexity.

In the English language, for example, there are only ten symbols for numerical digits and twenty-six letters, some of which are so redundant or infrequently used that they contribute little to the overall structure of the written language. From these few letters and digits, about forty thousand words in our working vocabulary are constructed, and from these words billions and billions of sentences are created. When we consider the richness of the human verbal experience generated by so few symbols, the hierarchical coding properties of language are staggering.

Phonemes

A **phoneme** is the basic unit of spoken language that by themselves have no meaning. They are single speech sounds represented by a single symbol. They are created by an intricate coordination of lungs, vocal cavities, larynx, lips, tongue, and teeth. When all works well, the sound produced is available for rapid perception and understanding by someone familiar with the language being spoken. English uses about forty-five different phonemes, however, only nine are needed to make up more than half of our words. Other languages get by with as few as fifteen phonemes, while some require as many as eighty-five.

Phonemes can be either vowels (*ee* as in h*ea*t, *i* as in h*i*t) or consonants (*t* as in *t*ee, *p* as in *p*ea) (Denes & Pinson, 1963).

Cognition in Everyday Life

*V*oice prints can also be used to help determine what is said, by showing us (literally) the acoustic properties. Take for example, Neil Armstrong's famous quote "That's one small step for man, one giant leap for mankind" as he steps on the moon. Armstrong always said that he intended to say (and thought he had said) "a man" and not "man." However, even he agreed that the audio transmission didn't support that intent. Peter Shann Ford and others have argued that analysis of the voice prints indicates that an "a" was evident. Others disagree.

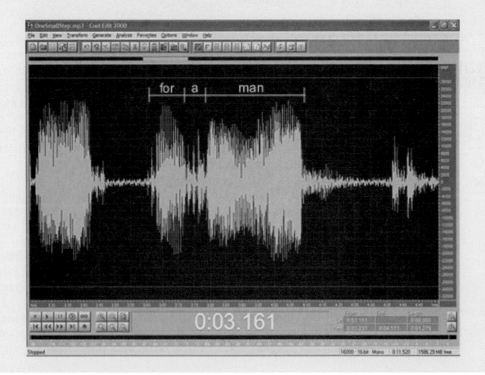

Speech sounds can be classified as voiced (e.g., *a* or *z*) or unvoiced (such as the *s* in *hiss*). Speech sounds that are produced by a coordinated effort of lungs, thorax, tongue, and so on and that include vibration of the vocal cords are classified as *voiced*. Speech sounds that do not use vocal cords are called *unvoiced* sounds. Within these two categories (voiced and unvoiced) are *fricatives* (produced by restricting the air passage in the mouth), such as *sh, f, v,* and *th*, and *plosives*, or *stops* (produced by interrupting the flow of air for a brief period), such as *t* and *d*.

It is possible, by use of the spectrograph, to study in minute detail how the acoustic characteristics of the spoken language vary across individuals. Not only has the recording of "visual speech" allowed researchers to study acoustic characteristics of the spoken language in detail, but it also has a direct practical application in teaching speech to deaf children. Speech development in normal children involves hearing speech, which serves as a model; from the model, a child produces sounds that he or she also hears, and from the hearing of which corrections can be made. Deaf children lack this feedback loop, but an instantaneous visual feedback system (offered by one spectrograph) can serve as a substitute.

Morphemes

Morphemes are the smallest unit of meaning in language. **Morphemes** may be words, parts of words, such as prefixes, suffixes, or combinations of these. Morphemes can be either free or bounded. Free morphemes are a unit of meaning that stands alone (e.g., *color, orange, dog, drive*), whereas bounded morphemes are parts of words *colorless, oranges, driving*). By combining morphemes, we can generate untold millions of words.

Morphology

Morphology is the study of the structure of words. In English we have more than one hundred thousand words formed by morpheme combinations, but even with such a vast number the composition of morphemes is tightly governed by linguistic constraints. One of the linguistic constraints of English is that no more than three consonants may start a syllable; usually it is less than two. Another constraint is that certain letters— for example, *q* and *d* or *j* and *z*—never appear together. These and other constraints on morphological formation, plus the built-in redundancy of our language, act to minimize the number of errors in transmission and decoding.

Syntax

The next level in the linguistic hierarchy is that of syntax, or the rules that govern the combination of words in phrases and sentences.

The number of different sentences humans can generate is restricted only by time and imagination, both of which are in long supply. In an attempt to understand the structure of language, linguists have concentrated their efforts on two aspects: productivity and regularity. **Productivity** refers to the infinite number of sentences, phrases, or utterances that are possible in a language, and **regularity** refers to the systematic patterns of the sentences, phrases, or utterances ("The boy hit the ball" rather than "ball boy The hit the").

Syntax failure and performance anxiety.

Transformational Grammar

The set of rules that governs the regularity of language is called grammar, and **transformational grammar** deals with the changes in linguistic forms that may retain the same meaning. For example:

The cat was chased by the dog.
The dog chased the cat.

Both sentences are correct, convey essentially the same meaning, have similar words, and yet differ somehow in their underlying structure. Apparently, the surface features of a language and the deep structure of a language needed to be separated, and the theories of Chomsky were designed along those lines.

The following points are frequently cited as embodying the most important aspects of Chomsky's thesis:

- Language has much underlying uniformity, and the underlying structure is often more closely related to the meaning of a sentence than are the surface characteristics.

Noam Chomsky. Changed the way language is viewed with the theory of transformational grammar.

- Language is not a closed system but a generative one.
- Within the underlying structures are elements common to all languages, and these may reflect innate organizing principles of cognition. These organizing principles may directly influence the learning and generation of language.

Three aspects define the contribution of Chomsky's theory to linguistics: surface structure, deep structure, and transformational rules. **Surface structure** is that part of the actual sentence that can be segmented and labeled by conventional parsing; **deep structure** is the underlying meaning of the structure.

Propositions

It has been asserted that beneath the surface structure of our language is a deep structure that follows systematic rules of transformation. The result of this theory has been the proliferation of hypotheses about other hidden cognitive structures. Among the most intriguing of these are those developed by Bransford and Franks (1971, 1972) concerning the nature of encoding sentences. They composed sentences that contained one, two, three, or four propositions in each.

Cognition in Everyday Life

Grammatically Correct, Semantically Absurd

*L*ewis Carroll gave us many examples of grammatically correct and semantically anomalous language nearly a century ago in *Through the Looking Glass*. A fragment of one of his more neologistically wild specimens is the following:

He took his vorpal sword in hand;
Long time the manxome foe he sought—
So rested he by the Tumtum tree,
And stood a while in thought.

And as in uffish thought he stood
The Jabberwock, with eyes of flame,
Came whiffling through the tulgey wood,
And burbled as it came.

Even though, technically, this should be meaningless, we still get a great deal of information from this passage given that the "words" still follow the rules of syntax.

One
The ants were in the kitchen.
The jelly was on the table.
The jelly was sweet.
The ants ate the jelly.

Two
The ants in the kitchen ate the jelly.
The ants ate the sweet jelly.
The sweet jelly was on the table.
The ants ate the jelly which was on the table.

Three
The ants ate the sweet jelly which was on the table.
The ants in the kitchen ate the jelly which was on the table.
The ants in the kitchen ate the sweet jelly.

Four
The ants in the kitchen ate the sweet jelly which was on the table.

The Branford and Franks (1971) experiment consisted of an acquisition phase and a recognition task. During the acquisition phase, participants were read 24 sentences, which consisted of one, two, and three propositions (they were never read a sentence with four propositions). After each sentence was read, the participants engaged in a color-naming task for 4 seconds and then asked a question about the sentence to ensure that the participants had encoded it. For example, if one of the sentences was "The rock rolled down the mountain," the question might have been "Did what?" After the participants were read all 24 sentences, the experimenter read aloud additional sentences—some new and some old from the original 24. The new sentences contained different parts of the complex idea that had been presented. A control condition of noncase sentences was included, which combined two unrelated concepts. For example, if an original sen-

---

Try This

Linguistic Abstraction

A convincing body of research indicates that when we read a book, a short story, or a poem, we retain only the essence of the work and not many of the details, which are forgotten, unavailable for recall, or melded with other memories to fabricate a distorted memory. Distorted memory from real-life experiences or from written material may be the result of one's previous knowledge, personal aspirations, or seeing the world in light of one's own belief systems. Try this little experiment: Read a short story, and paraphrase its main points in a few sentences as accurately as possible. Have a friend read the same story without writing the main ideas. Several weeks later, ask your friend to tell you the main ideas in the story. Compare your friend's recollection with your notes. Do the same thing with an abstract poem. What differences do you note between the initial factual description and the subsequent recalled accounts? What might contribute to these differences? Are the differences even greater for an abstract poem?

tence was "The rock that rolled down the mountain crushed the tiny hut at the edge of the woods" and another original sentence was "The ants ate the sweet jelly that was on the table," a noncase sentence might be "The rock which rolled down the mountain crushed the ants eating jelly in the kitchen." Participants were asked to indicate which of the sentences (from among the new, original, and noncase sentences read to them) they had heard during the acquisition phase. They were then asked to evaluate their confidence in their judgment on a five-point scale (from very low to very high). The findings were that evaluations were essentially the same for old and for new sentences and that participants' confidence in their recognition corresponded directly to the complexity of the sentence. Thus, sentences that had four propositions received the highest confidence ratings (even though no sentences with four propositions were actually presented), while those containing three propositions were rated lower and so on through the sentence with only one proposition, which received a negative rating. Few were fooled by the noncase sentences, where confidence received the lowest ratings. This control condition was important in that it shows that participants did not base their confidence on sentence length alone.

Why were participants so confident that they had heard the four-proposition sentences? It is likely that participants believed that they had heard the complex sentences before (when they had not), because they had abstracted a basic idea from the simple sentences to which they were exposed and stored that abstraction entity rather than the sentences themselves. These abstractions seem to function as prototypes.

The implication of these data for a theory of cognition and memory is that human memory for sentences is not merely a transcription of words (like a digital recording) but is the result of a dynamic reconstructive process in which ideas are abstracted. These abstract ideas are, of course, derived from experience with sentences and form the basis of our impression of new and old sentences. Thus, as Chomsky has described a structural linguistics in which language capacity is formulated in abstract principles, Bransford and Franks have described how information about ideas expressed in sentences is organized in a schematic structure that forms the basis for judging new information.

Psycholinguistics

Nature versus Nurture

Initially, the most controversial aspect of Chomsky's theory was his assertion that the essential components of language were innate (nature). However, Skinner argued that language is learned (nurture). Behaviorists believed that language developed through reinforcement; however, Chomsky argued that only the morphological aspects of language development is subject to reinforcement. For example, when shown a picture of an apple, a child learns to say "apple." She is reinforced with parental approval. The particular words are reinforced, but when they are combined to form sentences, they are governed by universal rules.

Chomsky argued that reinforcement cannot explain how a child generates a perfectly grammatical sentence he or she has never heard. The innate propensity for language, based on deep structure, is offered as the explanation. Chomsky's position does not hold

A different language is a different vision of life.

—*Federico Fellini*

that a particular grammatical system is innate, but does argue that we have an innate scheme for processing information and forming abstract structures of our language. This may be tied to the biological development of a **language acquisition device** (LAD). The LAD is a cognitive structure for learning the rules of language.

Linguistic-Relativity Hypothesis

Another viewpoint (not necessarily antagonistic to the first) is that language and biological maturation go hand in hand, each influencing the other.

Chomsky's emphasis on linguistic universals is an effort to identify linguistic operations that are common to all languages. As we have seen, it is largely based on deep structure of language and transformations. On the semantic and phonemic level, however, languages are obviously not the same. It is to these surface characteristics that the **linguistic-relativity hypothesis** is principally relevant.

The idea that our language influences perception and conceptualization of reality is known as the linguistic-relativity hypothesis. This is also known as the Whorfian hypothens based on the detailed work of Benjamin Lee Whorf (1956; see also Sapir, 1958). Whorf concluded that a thing represented by a word is conceived differently by people whose languages differ and that the nature of the language itself is the cause of those different ways of viewing reality. For example, Whorf studied Native American languages and found that clear translation from one language to another was impossible. In one language, he found that no clear distinction is made between nouns and verbs; in another, past, present, and future are ambiguously expressed; and in yet another, there is no distinction between the colors *gray* and *brown*. However, in English, despite the fact that English speakers have no unique physiological apparatus (to enable them, for example, to see the difference between *gray* and *brown*), we have words that make all these distinctions.

Of particular interest in this respect is the fact that all normal persons have the same visual apparatus (that is, the same physiological ability to see colors and make color discriminations). Thus, differences in the mental processing of the colors viewed are suspected of being due to the differences among the different language codes. Some research indicates this to be the case. For example, a color that does not fit into the categories delineated by color name (one that is "between" colors) is likely to be remembered as a member of the color it most resembles. Eskimos have many different names for snow (blowing snow, drifting snow, snow you can make igloos from, and so on), which allows them to "see"—to discriminate—many more different types of snow than we who live in a temperate zone can. Similarly, the Hanuos of the Philippine Islands have ninety-two names for various kinds and states of rice. The Whorfian hypothesis suggests that the physical reality is translated, according to some internal representation of reality, into a perception that is consistent with long-standing cognitive structures. One of the ways information is structured in the brain is apparently related to the specific language codes each of us has developed. These codes differ, as languages differ. This (Whorfian) viewpoint has been strongly opposed by some.

Further evidence in opposition to Whorf's hypothesis has been submitted by Heider (1971, 1972) and Rosch (1973, formerly Heider). She studied New Guinea natives, whose language is Dani. In Dani there are only two color names: *mola*—bright, warm colors—and *mili*—dark, cool colors. By using a recognition test, she found that recognition accuracy was better for focal colors than for nonfocal colors, and yet, if language determines perception, participants whose language has but two names would predictably experience difficulty in recalling focal as well as nonfocal colors. Thus, the case for linguistic determinism (at least of the rigid variety) seems questionable. Anthropologists and psychologists continue to be fascinated by the Whorf hypothesis. Kay and Kempton (1984), writing in *American Anthropologist,* provided a nice review of the empirical research on the hypothesis.

Consider one more question concerning Whorf's view (that language affects the way we conceive reality, process information, and store things in memory and recall): What is the origin of the lexical units? Why does the Eskimo language have so many names for snow and English have so few? Why do we have so many names for types of automobiles and the Laplanders so few (if any)? One answer is that the more significant an experience is to us, the greater the number of ways it is expressed in the language rather than the other way round—that is, that language determines our percepts. The development of specific language codes, therefore, is dependent on cultural needs; the learning of those codes by members of a language group also involves the learning of significant values of the culture, some of which may be related to survival. The consequence of the development of language codes may further determine what information is coded, transformed, and remembered.

Language and Neurology

The study of the neurological basis of language has been investigated by several means, including clinical investigations of brain-damaged patients (Broca's and Wernicke's areas), electrical stimulation of the brain, psychosurgical procedures, pharmaceutical investigations, and imaging technology. We cannot recount, in detail, findings in all areas, but we can give a sample of resear

Electrical Stimulation   The use of tiny *bipolar electrical probes* has occurred in human and animal experimental work for many decades. In the late 1950s, Penfield (1959) and Penfield and Roberts (1959) stunned the psychological world when they presented verbal protocols of patients undergoing psychosurgery in which low-voltage electrical currents applied to classic language areas, such as Broca's area and Wernicke's area as well as some areas of the motor cortex, interfered with speech production. In one instance, when a probe was placed in the speech zones, the patient (who was awake since the procedure required only local anesthesia) reported, "Oh, I know what it is. That is what you put in your shoes." After the probe was removed, the patient said "foot" (Penfield & Roberts, 1959, p. 123).

Later experiments using electrical stimulation of the brain by Ojemann (1991) have disclosed some equally interesting data on the brain and language and support the findings of Penfield.

PET Scans   One advantage of this technology over electrical stimulation is that it is far less invasive and can be performed on healthy persons; in contrast, electrical stimulation is usually done as an adjunct experiment during psychosurgery with impaired patients. Of particular interest is a study by Posner and his colleagues (1988) in which visually presented words caused activation in the occipital lobe while spoken words showed activation in the temporoparietal cortex, a finding entirely consistent with previous neurological studies. These studies are especially revealing when one considers the tasks involved. In one condition, called the semantic task, more complicated processing was examined than was done during the passive viewing of words. In the semantic task, the person was asked to say the use of a noun. For example, to the noun *hammer*, a participant might say "to pound." Such a task requires not just the passive observation of the word, as in the visual condition, but also access to associative-semantic regions of the brain. Posner and his colleagues found an increased blood flow in the anterior left frontal lobe as shown by the squares in Figure 11.1. While in the auditory condition, participants were asked to judge whether or not words, such as *pint* and *lint*, and *row* and *though*, rhymed, which required phonological analysis of visually presented material. The area activated in this task was the left temporal lobe, which is an area normally associated with auditory processing. These experiments suggest that linguistic processing is modality specific, that is, that semantic processing and auditory processing of visually presented material occur in different sites.

Reading

Toward the end of the nineteenth century, when experimental psychology was emerging in laboratories in Germany, England, and the United States, a French scientist, Émile Javal (1878), discovered that during reading the eye did not sweep across a line of print but moved in a series of small jumps—**saccades**—with momentary fixation occurring between them. James McKeen Cattell (1886a, 1886b) undertook to find how much could be read during a single visual fixation. Using a tachistoscope, he estimated the time it takes to identify such things as forms, colors, letters, and sentences. The results of his experiments conformed to those of the earlier studies of range of attention, but of greater in-

F I G U R E 1 1 . 1

PET scan data showing areas activated in visual reading. The triangles show areas activated in a passive visual task, while the squares refer to the semantic task.

Data from Posner et al. (1988). Copyright © 1988 AAAS. Reprinted with permission from AAAS.

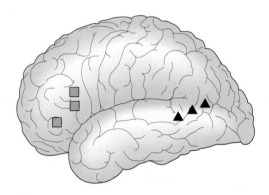

Smart Reading

Before reading ahead try to identify the following words: (1) n_t_r_, (2) m_m_r_, (3) p_rs_n_l t_. Did you find this too difficult?

It has been determined that word perception is influenced by previous experience. We carry around with us some well-established rules of orthography (letter sequence), grammar, semantics, and word associations—all of which assist us in reading as well as everyday living. How much information did you bring to the decoding of this message, and how much was in the stimuli? Our capacity to "see" letters and words is not a passive process, but rather it is an active process in which we search for perceptual objects that already have their representation in memory. If you had difficulty filling in the blanks, consider the following hints: (1) human, (2) long term, (3) traits. Are there other words that could be formed from the letters given above? Why did you not think of them immediately?

terest for Cattell was the fact that reaction times were related to the people's familiarity with the visual material.

By having participants view a display of letters and words for as little as 10 milliseconds (1/100 of a second), he discovered that the capacity to report letters was not so much a function of the number of letters as it was a function of how close the sequence of letters approached a meaningful sequence—as, for example, in a word. A participant exposed to a display of unconnected letters for 10 milliseconds was able to report three or four letters; if the letters made a word, then up to two words (of three or four letters each); and if the words were syntactically related, then the participant could "read" as many as four. Since 10 milliseconds is considerably less than the time required for a saccade, the span of apprehension in the Cattell studies was limited to what might be called (in filmmaking terms) a single frame of perception.

When we read or view a scene (such as a painting or picture), our eyes make a series of movements, called saccades, and there are periods of time when the eyes stop momentarily, called fixations, which, on average, last about 250 milliseconds, although individual differences both within and between people vary considerably. We do this because vision is sharpest in only a very narrow range, about 1 or 2 degrees. The typical saccade is about eight or nine letter spaces and is not affected by the size of the print, assuming it is not too small or too large. About 10–15 percent of the time we move our eyes back to review textual material; these are called *regressions*.

Modern cognitive psychologists are as intrigued by the question of **perceptual span** (how much information can be perceived during a brief presentation) as were their nineteenth-century counterparts.

First, consider the question of neurological capabilities in the identification of letters or words. Visual acuity is best for images that fall on the part of the retina called the fovea. This small indentation on the back part of the eye is densely packed with photosensitive neurons called *cones* (see Figure 11.2A). **Foveal vision** encompasses a visual angle of only about 1 to 2 degrees. By fixing your gaze on a single letter of text at a normal viewing distance, you can experience the difference between foveal and

FIGURE 11.2

A. Distribution of cones in the retina. B. Visual acuity in the retina. Shaded area is the "blind spot" (point of attachment of optic nerve).

A. Adapted from Woodson (1954). B. Adapted from Ruch and Patton (1965).

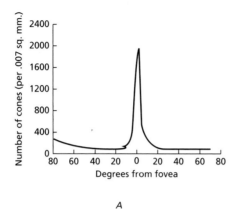

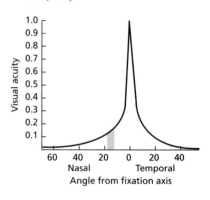

A

B

peripheral vision. The single letter focused on is very clearly resolved, and some letters on either side may also be seen clearly. However, the letters and words only a few degrees away are quite fuzzy, and letters and words in the periphery are unrecognizable (see Figure 11.2B).

In Figure 11.3 the cone of vision is shown. This illustration is meant to represent a three-dimensional view of normal viewing (in fact, the field of vision is a bit more irregular than shown). We can see that foveal vision occupies only the narrowest of wedges subtending a visual angle of about 2° and parafoveal vision 10°. Peripheral and near peripheral vision extends one's field of view considerably but at the cost of decreased resolution. Also, these parameters are sensitive to the type of stimuli being perceived. Stationary objects in the peripheral may go undetected, while moving objects may be "seen" and get our attention. Inherent in this observation are ecological considerations in which the perception of moving prey or predators was related to survival.

Yet, despite the fact that acuity drops off sharply from the fovea, it appears that identification of some letters and words, especially in the normal course of reading, occurs outside foveal vision. To better understand this seeming paradox, consider recent findings about saccadic eye movement. These rapid eye movements, although often studied in association with the reading process, also occur when a person views a visual pattern. According to Norton and Stark (1971), during reading there are typically two or three saccades per second, and these occur so fast that they occupy only about 10 percent of the viewing time. A movement of 10 degrees lasts only about 45 milliseconds and, during the movement, vision seems to be impaired, a condition called visual smear (Haber & Hershenson, 1973). It appears, then, that the recognition of letters and words in the nonfoveal field, which frequently occurs in the reading process, must be partly attributed to something other than the physical stimulation of the retina.

FIGURE 11.3

Cone of vision showing foveal, parafoveal, near peripheral, and peripheral vision.
(Here the angles measure the field of vision from one side to the other.)

From Solso (1994a).

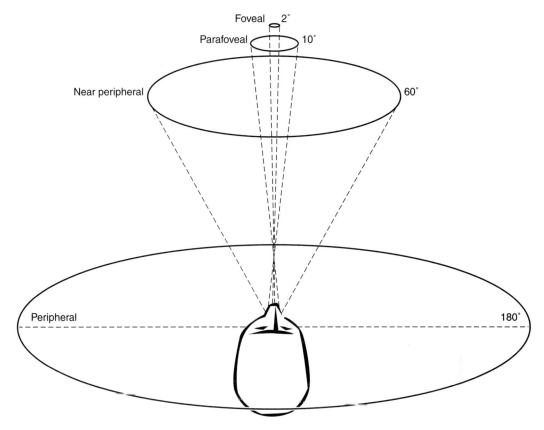

That "something" is likely to be the person's great knowledge of letter and word sequencing as well as his or her understanding of the theme of the text (in other words,
top-down processing).

Given the constraints of the visual system, what can we infer about the process involved in normal text reading? It is likely that textual information that falls on the fovea
is clearly detected and passed on to the brain for further processing. During the saccade,
little, if any, textual information is being detected or processed. Textual information that
is beyond the fovea, in parafovea or in peripheral vision, is poorly resolved neurologically,
and yet this seeming sensory handicap does not impede the normal processing of textual
material. Some evidence suggests that letters in the poorly resolved parafoveal vision are
detected more clearly if they are surrounded by a space. Estes (1977) reconstructed the
process involved in normal reading (shown in Figure 11.4).

FIGURE 11.4

Illustration of fixations and duration (in milliseconds). Also shown is a hypothetical reconstruction of the information perceived during fixations of normal text. Notice that at and near each fixation, letters are clearly perceived, while more distant letters are poorly perceived with the exception of letters surrounded by a space.

From Estes (1977) and Dearborn (1906). Reprinted with permission from W. K. Estes.

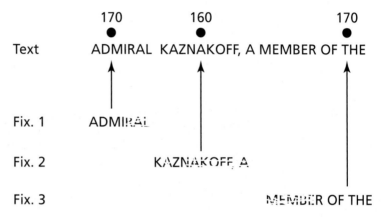

Text Processing: Evidence from Eye-Tracking Studies

As early as 1906 (Dearborn, 1906), psychologists were making photographic records of eye movements during reading. Modern eye-tracking systems use videotape recorders and computers to analyze the movement of eyes during reading (see Figure 11.5) or when viewing a picture, and since the mid-1970s there has been a resurgence of interest in studies of eye movements applied to reading (see Inhoff & Tousman, 1990; Just & Carpenter, 1987; Raney & Rayner, 1993; Rayner, 1993; Rayner, Sereno, Morris, Schmauder & Clifton, 1989, for reviews and recent developments) and perception of art (see Solso, 1994a).

William K. Estes. Made significant contributions to many fields of psychology, including learning theory, mathematical psychology, and cognitive psychology. Founding editor of *Cognitive Science.*

FIGURE 11.5

A typical eye-tracking experiment. Here the participant is viewing text as presented on a monitor. Her eye movements are recorded by means of a beam reflected off her pupil, which is transmitted to a computer and displayed on a second monitor being observed by the experimenter.

Photo courtesy of EyeTracking, Inc.

Some experimental work on the size of perceptual span has used eye-tracking studies. In this work, when a participant fixates on a portion of textual material, changes can be made in other parts of the display.

Rayner (1975, 1993) studied how wide the area is from which a reader picks up information about the text. Some (Goodman, 1970) have suggested that, on the basis of the context of information plus partial information from peripheral vision, subjects generate a "hypothesis" as to what will appear next. This means that when reading text, participants would move their eyes forward to confirm their hypothesis (the more frequent occurrence) or disconfirm their hypothesis (which then requires further processing). A contrary view is expressed by McConkie and Rayner (1973), who assume that participants use the time during fixation to determine the nature of the text rather than hypothesize what is to follow. However, periphery cues are important in a section of certain information (e.g., some features and shapes). When participants move their fixation point ahead, the perceived pattern is normally consistent with their partial information. Finally, an innovative feature of Rayner's work is the variability of information presented in participants' peripheral vision. In one experiment Rayner (1975) used a "critical word," which would change to the "word-identical condition" as participants moved their fixation point toward it (see Figure 11.6 for an example). Thus, in the sentence "The rebels guarded the palace with their guns," the critical word *palace* could change (as the eye moved toward it) to *police*.

FIGURE 11.6

An example of the boundary paradigm. The first line shows a line of text prior to a display change with fixation locations marked by asterisks. When the reader's eye movement crosses an invisible boundary (the letter *e* in *the*), an initially displayed word (*date*) is replaced by the target word (*page*). The change occurs during the saccade so that the reader does not see the change.

From Rayner (1993). Reprinted by permission of Cambridge University Press.

eyes	do	not	move	smoothly	across	the	date	of	text	Prechange
*		*		*	*					
eyes	do	not	move	smoothly	across	the	page	of	text	Postchange
							*			

Critical Word	Condition
Palace	Word-identical.
Police	Semantically and syntactically acceptable word, some of whose letters are the same as W-Ident.
Pcluce	Nonword, with extreme letters and shape the same as W-Ident.
Pyctce	Nonword with altered shape but same initial and end letters.
Qcluec	Nonword with end letters reversed.

Rayner found that a semantic interpretation (i.e., meaning) of a word was made one to six character spaces from the fixation point, but beyond that, at seven to twelve character spaces, participants were able to pick up only gross visual characteristics, such as word shape and initial and final letters. It appears that information in the near periphery is partially coded, and the extent of the processing is contingent on the distance from the fixation point.

Down-the-Garden-Path Experiments The method of studying reading by means of eye movements has been used by Carpenter and Dahneman (1981; see also Just & Carpenter, 1987) in whose research brief stories such as follows were read aloud:

> The young man turned his back on the rock concert stage and looked across the resort lake. Tomorrow was the annual one-day fishing contest and fishermen would invade the place. Some of the best bass guitarists in the country would come to this spot.

If you read this passage as most people do, you were led down the garden path in the first few lines, because when you read the word *bass,* you thought of the fish and pronounced it to rhyme with *mass.* The next word, *guitarists,* disconfirms that interpretation. Eye fixations up to *bass* are normal; however, as may be evident to you, the length of time spent on the word *guitarists* is longer than normal. Additionally, people tend to backtrack and to reconcile the previous word.

The garden-path experiments yield significant insights into the reading process as they relate to the processing of textual material. These experiments (along with several others) suggest that the early stages of the comprehension of written material may occur during very brief time intervals. Participants fixed their eyes on *bass* because the meaning

Try This

Can You "Read" This?

Aoccdrnig to a rscheearch at Cmabrigde Uin-ervtisy, it deosn't mttaer in waht oredr the ltteers in a wrod are, the olny iprmoetnt tihng is taht the frist and lsat ltteer be at the rghit pclae. The rset can be a total mses and you can sitll raed it wouthit porbelm. Tihs is bcuseae the huamn mnid deos not raed ervey lteter by istlef, but the wrod as a wlohe. Amzanig huh?

With little difficulty, you were probably able to decipher the preceding paragraph. People have found this so fascinating that the preceding paragraph often makes the rounds over email, with friends forwarding it to friends, not realizing that they are pondering some important cognitive principles! The paragraph demonstrates the brain's remarkable ability to derive meaning from patterns of symbols (letters) that we are so familiar with, even when those patterns aren't quite right. A bottom-up approach would lead to frustration. But given that reading relies very much on top-down processing, our brain can figure this out quite easily. But just because you can still read this does not mean that you should not spell-check your papers!

of that word, in context, was somehow discordant with the rest of the sentence, and they changed their pattern of reading in a matter of a few hundred milliseconds.

These findings suggest that from the very beginning of the processing of textual material some sophisticated form of comprehension, that is, the derivation of meaning, takes place. It is likely that, in reading, comprehension is nearly instantaneous with visual perception and need not occur after a trailing, speech-based, short-term memory code. In addition to early and nonspeech-based comprehension, it may be that in reading and other visual experiences we activate a rich chain of associative reactions that are used to understand the thing being perceived.

Lexical-Decision Task (LDT)

An innovative approach to the problem of contextual effects on word identification has been introduced by Meyer and his colleagues (Meyer & Schvaneveldt, 1971; Meyer, Schvaneveldt, & Ruddy, 1974a, 1974b). They used a **lexical-decision task (LDT),** a type of priming task, in which the experimenter measured how quickly participants could determine whether paired strings of letters were words. Typical stimuli were as follows:

Associated words	*BREAD–BUTTER*
	NURSE–DOCTOR
Unassociated words	*NURSE–BUTTER*
	BREAD–DOCTOR
Word–nonword	*WINE–PLAME*
	GLOVE–SOAM
Nonword–word	*PLAME–WINE*
	SOAM–GLOVE
Nonword–nonword	*NART–TRIEF*
	PABLE–REAB

In the procedure a participant looks at two fixation points. A series of letters (e.g., *NURSE*) appears at the top point. The participant presses a key, indicating whether the letters make a word. As soon as his or her decision is made, the first set of letters disappears and, shortly thereafter, the second set of letters appears. The participant decides whether the second set of letters is a word, and the process continues. This procedure makes it possible to measure word recognition of the second word as a function of the context, or prime, established by the first word. As might be anticipated, Meyer found that reaction time for judging the second word was much faster when it had been paired with an associated rather than nonassociated word.

Again we have an example of the effect of context on word identification. We could interpret those data in terms of a logogen model in which the first word excited the logogen of the second word. Meyer and his colleagues interpreted them in terms of a general information-processing framework in which the first stage is an encoding operation that creates an internal representation. Following encoding, the sequence of letters is checked against the participant's lexical memory to see whether the item has been previously stored, and, depending on whether a match is made, a decision is executed. Two important assumptions are made by the model regarding memory storage of lexical events: first, the words are stored at various locations in memory, with some words closely associated (e.g., *bread–butter*) and some distant (e.g., *nurse–butter*); second, retrieving information from a specific memory location produces neural activity that spreads to nearby locations, thereby facilitating the recognition of associated memories.

The theoretical positions of Meyer and of Morton and connectionism seem not to be antagonistic. Indeed, they appear to be complementary. All address the problem of the effect of context on word identification, and all have concluded that some internal mechanism enhances word identification as a function of context (see Figure 11.7). For Morton,

FIGURE 11.7

Contextual effects on word recognition.

Adapted from Morton (1979, p. 138). This version Copyright © 2002, Derek J. Smith.

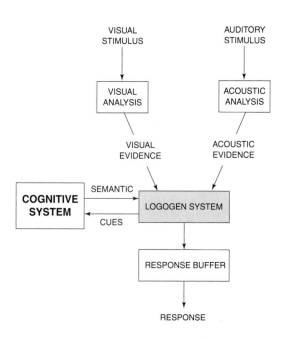

Cognition in Everyday Life

The Tortured Reading Patterns of Dyslexic People

Dyslexia is a reading deficiency that afflicts otherwise normal people. Some contend that it is constitutional in origin, while others argue it is social and/or psychological. That issue is not resolved. It is clear, however, that many schoolchildren have difficulty in reading, which profoundly affects their lives. The development of eye-tracking apparatus has made possible the measurement of eye fixations of normal and dyslexic people, which may give us insight into this problem. Samples of reading styles for a normal reader (PP) and a dyslexic (Dave) are shown here. The numbers immediately below the dots are the sequence of eye movements, and the larger numbers further below the dots are the fixation times in milliseconds (1000 milliseconds = 1 second).

PP
As society has become progressively more complex, psychology has

	.		.		.		.			.		.
1		2		3		4		5	7		8	9
234		310		188		216		242	188		177	159

                                                            6
                                                            144

Dave
As society has become progressively more complex, psychology has

1	2	3	5		6	7	8	9	10		15	12		13	14
311	277	115	412		198	403	266	295	311		193	317		600	312

                 4   11   18
                 222   277   206

                                                                    19
                                                                    415

PP
assumed an increasingly important role in solving human problems.

.		.	.	.	.		.		.
11		12	13	15	14		16		18
244		317	229	269	196		277		202

         10   17
         206   144

Dave
assumed an increasingly important role in solving human problems.

16		21		22	24		25	26	27		28	31		32
369		302		244	310		383	119	487		413	277		366

         17   20   23   29   33
         415   177   288   200   361

                                                      30
                                                      117

From Rayner and Pollatsek (1989).

the mechanism is one of elevating a logogen's level of excitation; for Meyer and for Rumelhart and McClelland, it is the spreading of neural activity, which renders similar lexical items more accessible.

Cognitive Neuroscience Support

In one study examining processing of visual and auditory words (Petersen et al., 1988), participants were asked to participate in three common lexical tasks: (1) participants examined a fixation point or passively watched visual words; (2) they repeated each word as it occurred; and (3) at the next level they generated a use for each word. Each task differed from the other by a small number of processing operations. At the same time, the researchers monitored data from PET scans with particular attention to the visual and auditory portions of the cortex.

The findings indicate that different cortical areas were activated by each of the different tasks (see Figure 11.8). Of particular interest in these findings are the portions of the cortex involved in visual word forms (A), which are represented by triangles in Figure 11.8, and those involved in semantic analysis (C), which are identified by circles,

FIGURE 11.8

Data from PET scans studies showing areas of visual and auditory words. Two areas are shown: the lateral sides of the cortex (1) and the medial portions (2). Visual words are shown in triangles (A), semantic analysis in circles (C), and attention in squares or hexagons. Solid figures indicate left hemisphere, and open figures indicate right hemisphere. The area activated by repeating words presented auditorially (such as in shadowing experiments) is encircled by broken lines (B).

From Petersen et al. (1988). Reprinted by permission from *Nature.* Copyright © 1988 Macmillan Magazines Ltd.

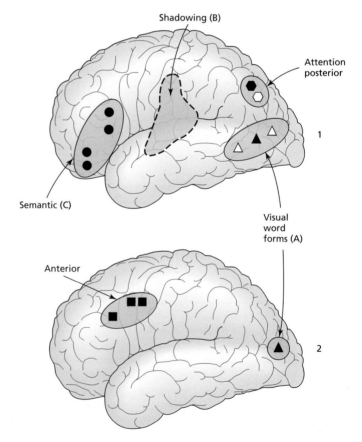

Shadowing (B)

Attention posterior

Semantic (C)

Visual word forms (A)

Anterior

suggesting that these different forms of lexical processing as suggested by Morton's Logogen model, are, indeed, handled by different parts of the brain.

These data were supported by an experiment by Posner, Sandson, Phawan, and Shulman (1989) using essentially the same technique, except that the person participated in a modified LDT. In one condition, a visual priming of a word was presented (e.g., *DOCTOR–DOCTOR*); in another task, a semantic priming of a word was presented (e.g., *DOCTOR–NURSE*); and in a third task, a cueing of visual spatial attention was done (for example, a peripheral cue to the left of the screen followed by a target to the left for a valid trial or to the right for an invalid trial). The results of the study showed that the area most likely to be involved in the priming of visual features (*DOCTOR–DOCTOR*) is the ventral occipital lobe (identified in Figure 11.8 as visual word forms [A]). Posner and his associates suggest that word primes activate these areas and that an identical target will re-activate the same pathway within the network. Semantic tasks (*DOCTOR–NURSE*) seem to activate two additional areas: the left inferior prefrontal cortex (C) (see circles in Figure 11.8) and the medial frontal lobe (see hexagons in Figure 11.8).

Although linguists have suspected that a word that is processed semantically is processed by a different part of the brain than a word processed perceptually, until recently, such impressions were scientifically unsubstantiated. John Gabrieli and his colleagues at Stanford University have presented additional data from fMRI studies that support the fundamental difference between these encoding types. In several studies (Gabrieli et al., 1996a, 1996b) participants were asked to evaluate a set of abstract words, such as *TRUST*, and concrete words, such as *CHAIR*. Sometimes the words were presented in uppercase and sometimes the words were presented in lowercase.

In the semantic condition of the experiment participants were asked to judge if the words were abstract or concrete, and in the perceptual condition of the experiment they were asked to identify the word as being shown in uppercase or lowercase. In Gabrieli's experiment the participant's brain activity was being monitored by a fMRI scan, which pinpointed the locus of cortical activity in these tasks.

It was found that during the semantic condition of the task, the left inferior prefrontal cortex was more active than for perceptual tasks. These results show that different parts of the brain are implicated in semantic versus perceptual processing of words.

Comprehension

Up to this point our discussion of the reading process has concentrated on the recognition of letters and words in and out of context. The reason people read, by and large, is to extract meaning from material that is conveniently represented in printed form. We use the term **reading comprehension** to describe the process of understanding the meaning of written material.

Consider a simple sentence, such as "The ball is red." From our previous discussion of visual perception and word identification, we know that light reflecting from the printed page received by the sensory neurons is transmitted to the brain, where feature, letter, and word identification is made. Such processes, however, are devoid of meaning, which is presumably the purpose of reading.

When you read the sample sentence, it is probable that you understand that (1) a single spherical object is (2) colored red. You comprehend the meaning of the sentence, and that meaning is about the same as the author intended and as most other folks understand. In addition to the basic physical characteristics described, you consciously or unconsciously make many inferences about the object. (For example, most readers infer that the ball is larger than a golf ball and smaller than a basketball.)

Comprehension of the sentence can be validated if you are shown a picture of a red ball and indicate that the meaning of the sentence is the same as the picture, as contrasted with a picture of a green ball or a red box. This seemingly simple task really involves many more operations than are first apparent. In order to understand reading comprehension, some theorists have broken the process into stages, which assumes that there is a sequence of processes that starts with the perception of the written word and leads to the understanding of the meaning of sentences and stories. One model, which incorporates some of the topics discussed in this book, was developed by Just and Carpenter (1980, 1987) and will serve as a representation of contemporary work in this field. The process of reading and comprehension in the Just and Carpenter model is conceptualized as the coordinated execution of a series of stages that include extracting physical features of letters, encoding words and accessing the lexicon, assigning case roles, and so on. In this representation the major stages of reading are shown in the left column, while the more permanent cognitive structures and processes are shown in the boxes in the middle and right side of the diagram.

Some of the intriguing features of this model are that it is comprehensive and yet it generates very specific predictions about reading performance that can be empirically measured by eye fixations. The authors assume that words in textual material are structured in larger units, such as clauses, sentences, and topics. When a participant encounters a section of written text that demands greater processing of information, he or she may require longer pauses, which can be measured by looking at eye-fixation times.

In a test of the model, college students were asked to read scientific texts from *Newsweek* and *Time* magazines while their eye movements and eye fixations were being unobtrusively measured. A sample of one student's performance is shown here:

1	2	3	4	5	6	7		
1566	267	400	83	267	617	767		
Flywheels	are	one	of the	oldest	mechanical	devices		

8	9	1	2	3	5	4	6
450	450	400	616	517	684	250	317
known to	man.	Every	internal-combustion	engine			contains

7	8	9	10	11	12
617	1116	367	467	483	450
a small	flywheel	that converts	the	jerky	motion of the pistons

13	14	15	16	17	18	19	20	21
383	284	383	317	283	533	50	366	566
into	the	smooth	flow	of energy	that powers	the	drive	shaft.

These are the eye fixations of a college student reading a scientific passage. Gazes within each sentence are sequentially numbered above the fixated words with the durations (in msec.) indicated below the sequence number.

These data suggest that greater processing loads, as shown by eye fixations, occur when readers are confronted with uncommon words, integrating information from important clauses and making inferences at the ends of sentences. The major processing levels are shown in Figure 11.9.

FIGURE 11.9

The major processing levels in the READER model. They operate as the reader fixates on the word *engine* in the text.

Adapted from Just and Carpenter (1987).

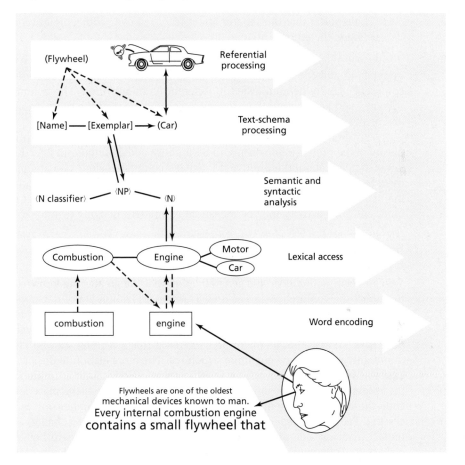

From what we know, one might expect greater involvement in regions such as Broca's area and Wernicke's area while reading more complicated material compared to simple material.

To test this notion Just, Carpenter, Keller, Eddy, and Thulborn (1996) developed a series of sentences that varied in structural complexity. After reading the sentences, the participants were asked questions related to their comprehension. All of this was done while fMRI measures were continuously being observed. Take the following sentences ordered in terms of their complexity:

Sentence	Type
"The reporter attacked the senator and admitted the error."	Active conjoined with no embedded clause
"The reporter that attacked the senator admitted the error."	Subject relative clause
"The reporter that the senator attacked admitted the error."	Object relative clause

As you read these three sentences, you may sense that the first is easy to read and understand and the latter two are a bit more difficult. Can such subtle differences in comprehensibility be manifested in different brain activities? The volume of neural tissue activated was measured in several suspected areas of the brain as participants read and answered questions about sentences of varying complexity.

Activation increased in both Wernicke's area and Broca's area with increased complexity of the sentence. In general, these findings add an important new dimension to our understanding about the brain and language comprehension. The amount of neural activity that cognitive tasks, such as reading, require is dependent on the computational demand of the task. Thus, reading of complicated material places a greater demand on the brain and such activity may be measured by modern imaging technology.

Top-Down Processing

We can begin with the simple generalization that the greater the knowledge of a reader, the better the comprehension of text. This generalization is not dependent on the type of material read (magazines or technical reports). One way to account for this generalization is that existing knowledge can be viewed as an organized collection of information. New information, as might be gathered through reading, can be assimilated more thoroughly with existing cognitive structures. The more elaborate the structure the more easy the assimilation. Conversely, insufficient knowledge limits comprehension because the reader must develop some structure of knowledge about the material as well as encode the information being read. Much, but not all, comprehension is top-down processing. People with specialized knowledge, be it in plumbing, ballet, astrophysics, or motorcar racing, comprehend technical information in their field better than nonspecialists do. Following are several examples of the power of top-down processing.

In one experiment by Anderson and Pichert (1978), participants were asked to read a story about the home of a wealthy family from the viewpoint of a prospective home buyer or a burglar. In the story, many features about the house and its contents were described, such as its fireplace, musty basement, leaky roof, silverware, coin collection, and television set. Participants were asked to recall as many items as they could, and rate the importance of them. The would-be burglars recalled items of value whereas the home buyers recalled items reflecting the condition of the house. These experiments demonstrate the nature of the encoding and how textual material is influenced by the contextual. Being assigned the role of say a home owner activates a type of schema (conceptual framework) whereby valuable items would be more relevant to a burglar and therefore processed more readily compared to information about a musty basement.

The power of an induced **schema** on story recall was further illustrated in a study by MacLin and Solso (2004). In this study, half the participants were induced with a po-

If dogs (like humans) had a schema, this is how Snoopy would interpret a story.

PEANUTS reprinted by permission of United Features Syndicate, Inc.

lice officer schema by taking a police officer entrance exam. The other participants completed a nonschema-inducing activity. Similar to the Anderson study, a text passage was provided that combined information relevant to the police schema as well as nonrelevant information. Participants in the police condition recalled more police items than did the control group. The importance of the MacLin and Solso study is that the schema can be induced rather than being assigned.

Bottom-Up Processing

Another important model of comprehension espoused by Kintsch and van Dijk. On the level of reading text material, the model is based on propositions, or abstractions of information, drawn from the text base, while on the level of reader intention, the model posits a goal schema that directs the reader's comprehension of text material.

The model allows researchers interested in the structure of stories to make precise predictions about the memorability of specific types of information. The technique developed by the authors of the experiment is consistent with modern scientific methodology in psychology as contrasted with the subjective method used earlier in the important work of Bartlett.

For purposes of our discussion, we concentrate on the way students go about storing in memory information acquired from an article called "Bumper Stickers and the Cops." In an experiment done by Kintsch and van Dijk (1978), participants were asked to read a nontechnical report that was about 1,300 words long. Following the reading of the report, one-third of the participants were immediately asked to recall and write a summary of it. Another one-third of the participants were tested after one month, and the final one-third after three months. The procedure is similar to the one conducted by Bartlett.

All of the recall accounts and summaries were organized into statements that could be identified as:

- Reproductions (statements that accurately reflect the comprehension of the text).

- Reconstructions (statements that are plausible inferences from the main theme aided by the participants' world knowledge, such as "Beth went to Vancouver by train," might be expanded to include "She went into the station to buy a ticket").

- Metastatements (participants' comments, opinions, and attitudes on the text).

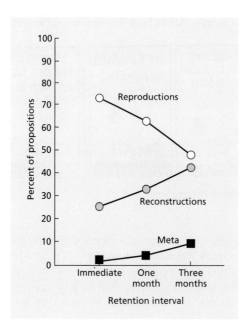

F I G U R E   1 1 . 1 0

Proportion of reproductions, reconstructions, and metastatements. In the recall protocols for three retention intervals.

From Kintsch and van Dijk (1978).

These components were analyzed with specific predictions made by the model. Several important conclusions were made by the authors about text comprehension and memory. As indicated by the data gathered over three different time periods (see Figure 11.10), it appears that participants lost more and more of the specific details of the report over time but retained the gist of the story with about the same degree of fidelity throughout a three-month period—a finding consistent with the protocol analysis of Bartlett. Additionally, it seems that the analysis of written material, such as books, stories, and technical reports, is organized in a way that is susceptible to careful empirical study of propositions, which may tell us more about the way text material is organized and how the human mind records and stores in memory written material over time.

A Model of Text Comprehension

In this section we explain the principal components of one influential and extensive model by Kintsch and his colleagues at the University of Colorado (Kintsch, 1974, 1979, 1988, 1990; Kintsch & van Dijk, 1978; Kintsch & Vipond, 1979; J. Miller & Kintsch, 1980; van Dijk & Kintsch, 1983).

This model of **comprehension** is more than a system that deals with the way textual information is understood. It is a theory that cuts across many topics in cognitive psychology, including memory and comprehension of the written and spoken language. Comprehension is dependent on two disparate sources that are similar to top-down and bottom-up processing with goal schema being similar to top-down processing and the surface structure of the text as bottom-up processing.

The model is based on *propositions,* which are abstractions based on observations (such as reading text material or listening to a speaker).

Walter Kintsch. Developed influential theories of language comprehension.

Propositional Representation of Text and Reading　　The model of comprehension holds that the underlying unit of memory for text material is the proposition. Additionally, the model predicts that sentences of greater propositional complexity are more difficult to comprehend than sentences with simple propositional structure, even if the surface complexity of the two sentences is about the same. Kintsch and Keenan (1973) designed an experiment to test this prediction.

　　Participants were asked to read ten sentences, all of which had about the same number of words but varied greatly in the number of propositions. Some sentences had as few as four propositions, and others had as many as nine. For example, read the following two sentences:

FIGURE 11.12

Reading time as a function of number of propositions per sentence.

From Kintsch and Keenan (1973).

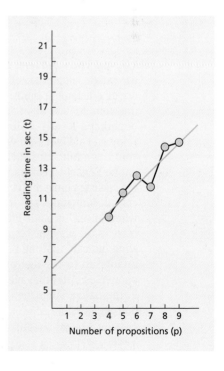

It's a strange world of language in which skating on thin ice can get you into hot water.

—*Franklin P. Jones*

Romulus, the legendary founder of Rome, took the women of Sabine by force. Cleopatra's downfall lay in her foolish trust in the fickle political figures of the Roman world.

Which sentence was more difficult to read? If you are like the people in Kintsch's and Keenan's experiment, you had more difficulty with the sentence about Cleopatra than the sentence about Romulus. Even though the surface complexity of the two sentences is about the same, they differ markedly in the number of propositions and the macrostructures that are required to interconnect the propositions.

In the Kintsch and Keenan experiment, participants were presented with sentences. The participants were asked to read each sentence and then to write it. Of interest was the relationship between propositional complexity and the amount of time participants required to read the sentence. The authors found an extraordinarily consistent relationship between the number of propositions and the time required to read the sentences; this relationship is shown in Figure 11.12.

Spotlight on Cognitive Neuroscience

Linguistics

" 'Liver.' The word rises from the voice box and passes the lips. It beats the air, enters an ear canal, sets nerve cells firing. Electrochemical impulses stream into the auditory cortex of a listener's brain. But then what? How does the brain's neural machinery filter that complex stream of auditory input to extract the uttered word: 'liver'—or was it 'river,' or perhaps 'lever'?" (Gibbs, 2002, p. 26). Wayt Gibbs reports in *Scientific American* magazine on Paul Iverson's work on how your first learned language actually changes the way your brain functions such that you hear other languages differently. He found that while native English speakers can easily distinguish the sounds /l/ and/r/, that native Japanese speakers have difficulties distinguishing the two, which is why these Japanese speakers will sometimes say "river" when they mean "liver," because they actually hear "river" when "liver" is said! Frank Guenther created a neural network to model this idiosyncrasy in the way the sounds of a second language are heard. His findings from this modeling indicate that the brain loses its ability to distinguish similar sounds. Interestingly, infants up to the age of 8 months are able to distinguish between the 869 existing phonemes. After that age, the brain starts to reorganize and becomes sensitized to sounds in the native language. English only has 52 different phonemes from the original 869 that are possible.

Gibbs, W. W. (2002, August). From mouth to mind: New insights into how language warps the brain. *Scientific American.*

A la carte

Baby Sign Language

If you have been following along up to this point, it should be clear that the behaviorists and the cognitive psychologists were at odds with one another. One of the contributions of behaviorism was the notion of a continuity from lower evolved species to higher evolved species. This rationale was used to extend research findings from rats and pigeons to explain and predict human behavior. While findings from lower species might be generalized up the "food chain" to humans, there are some behaviors that some researchers believe are so advanced that only humans possess them. In this manner, language in particular has been controversial and research demonstrating language in lower animals such as chimpanzees has quite often drawn fire from specialized research communities. Since chimpanzees do not have the ability to vocalize words, early researchers taught them how to use American Sign Language (Gardner & Gardner, 1969). Critics argued that the chimpanzees were not using language (i.e., deep structure syntax and such), but merely learning to associate a symbolic gesture with meaning, for example, placing the hand under the chin and wiggling the fingers to represent dirty (see figure). A recent trend of teaching ASL to preverbal infants, known as "baby sign," has emerged. We know that humans have separate areas of the brain for language: one for language comprehension, and one for language production, which also involves coordinating several motor skills. However, infants as young as 11 months old can learn to communicate using a baby version of ASL (Goodwyn, Acredolo, & Brown, 2000). Infants can be taught to sign such words as *eat, dog, hurt,* and *baby* well before they produce the sounds associated with these words. Although the big question is whether the preverbal use of signs is any closer to language than that of chimp ASL, Susan Goodwyn and her colleagues (2000) wanted to find out the relationship between learning baby sign and later language use. One might argue if baby sign is language, these babies should show a clear benefit over nonsigning babies in the ability to use verbal language later on. In a well-controlled longitudinal study, Goodwyn et al. examined verbal development of ASL babies and non-ASL babies at ages 15, 19, 24, 30, and 36 months. They found evidence that ASL does not hinder the development of verbal language, that in fact it might give these babies a head start compared to the control babies. Although these findings do not help us sort out the question facing the chimpanzee use of ASL, babies might allow for an interesting control group of nonverbal primates.

Dyslexia

Eric Nagourney reports on research exploring the origins of dyslexia. Some theories have posited that dyslexia is a hearing disorder, a visual disorder, or a disorder that comprises both modalities. Imaging researchers have discovered that dyslexia may have its origins in a genetic brain defect. Surprisingly, the seriousness of dyslexia may have to do with where you are raised, not just the goings on in your brain. Using PET technology, Eraldo Paulesu studied 72 dyslexic people from three different countries. There were similar abnormalities in brain function across all participants. So what's the point? Well, countries have widely varying incidence rates for the disorder, with the United States having the highest. It is believed that because English has many spellings of the same sounds (*f* and *ph* for the sound *fuh*) and dyslexics have difficulty differentiating between sounds, that English speaking-dyslexics have it tough. Uta Frith has found that dyslexics process words more slowly than nondyslexics. So it appears that "the roots of a language disorder may be in the brain, and on the map" (Nagourney, 2001, p. D7).

Nagourney, E. (2001, April 10). Geography of dyslexia explored. *The New York Times,* p. 07.

Student Resource Center

STUDY GUIDE

1. Language is crucial to a wide range of human activities, including communication, thought, perceiving and representing information, higher-order cognition, and neurology.

2. Early neurological studies by Broca and Wernicke established centers of the cortex, mostly located in the left cerebral hemisphere, that are involved in speech production and language comprehension.

3. Linguists conceive of language as a hierarchical structure that ranges from simple to increasingly complex components (e.g., phonemes, morphemes, and syntax).

4. One feature of recent theories of transformational grammar is that message content of sentences may remain constant despite changes in linguistic form. One thesis (Chomsky) distinguishes between surface and deep structures and argues for the importance of the underlying uniformity of language, the generative nature of language systems, and commonalities in all languages.

5. Three positions regarding language acquisition can be identified: one position (e.g., Chomsky) holds that language is an innate, universal propensity; the second position (e.g., Skinner) holds that language is learned via reinforcement contingencies; and a third views language development as a function of biological maturation and interactions with the environment.

6. The linguistic-relativity hypothesis proposes that the nature of a language determines how people see and think about reality (language thought), but evidence indicating that perceptual experience is similar to different language speakers makes a strict interpretation of this position questionable.

7. Comprehension in reading is the process of understanding the meaning of written material. Studies of eye fixations indicate that comprehension is influenced by such factors as rare words, the integration of important clauses, and making inferences. Knowledge, either acquired throughout the history of the individual or situational, also affects comprehension.

8. One model of comprehension (Kintsch) suggests that readers understand text material in terms of propositions and goal schemata.

9. Studies of syntactic constructions show cultural differences in preferred word order (e.g., subject–verb–object vs. verb–subject–object), although the subject precedes the object in the majority of cases.

10. Some functional properties of memory for narrative prose include the following: sentences are stored in memory in combined, not isolated, form; stories, like sen-

tences, can be parsed into their structural components; memory for narrative information is a function of its structural role; and gist is retained over time, but specific details are forgotten.

11 Studies of the neurology of language suggest that there are specialized areas involved in language processing, but that since language involves so many different subsystems, it is likely that many regions of the brain are engaged simultaneously.

12 The neurology of the brain has been studied by several techniques, including electrical probes and PET scans.

13 Viewing written text is constrained by the characteristics of the visual system, with greatest acuity occurring at the fovea (a visual angle of 1–2 degrees), poor resolution in the parafoveal and peripheral areas, and little or no detection during saccades.

14 Studies of perceptual span are used to examine the nature of information processing and include tachistoscopic, eye movement, and fixation procedures.

15 Eye-tracking studies indicate that information in the near periphery (up to twelve character spaces) is partially coded, with the extent of processing determined by the distance from the fovea.

16 Eye behavior changes rapidly (within a few hundred milliseconds) to accommodate discordant contexts, suggesting that sophisticated comprehension processes occur early during text processing.

17 Familiarity and context facilitate word recognition. Increases in both are associated with faster and better recognition.

18 In the interactive activation model, word recognition happens through excitation and inhibition among features, letters, and word levels.

19 PET studies indicate that different cortical areas are activated by different word recognition tasks. Such studies help us understand the relationship between cognitive tasks and brain functions.

20 Eye-fixation studies show longer fixations for words that are infrequent, those at the end of sentences, and those in integrating clauses, thus providing support for reading models proposing an interaction between stimulus input and memory.

KEY TERMS

Broca's area	phoneme
comprehension	phonology
deep structure	productivity
foveal vision	psycholinguistics
language	reading comprehension
language acquisition device	regularity
lexical-decision task (LDT)	saccades
lexicon	schema
linguistic-relativity hypothesis	surface structure
linguistics	syntax
morpheme	transformational grammar
morphology	Wernicke's area
perceptual span	

Starting Points

Books and Articles

● Excellent older books include R. Brown, *Words and Things,* a general and enjoyable book; Miller, *Language and Communication,* somewhat outdated but a classic; and Cherry, *On Human Communication.*

● Original sources on Chomsky's ideas are very specialized, hence difficult for the nonspecialist; more accessible are E. Bach, *Syntactic Theory;* Slobin, *Psycholinguistics;* Kess, *Psycholinguistics: Introductory Perspectives;* and Dale, *Language Development: Structure and Function.* A comprehensive account is H. Clark and E. Clark, *Psychology and Language: An Introduction to Psycholinguistics.*

● Also recommended is G. Miller's excellent book *The Science of Words.* For further treatment of Kintsch's work, read Kintsch and van Dijk in *Psychological Review.* Those interested in the neurology of language are directed to Kolb and Whishaw, *Fundamentals of Human Neuropsychology;* Kandel, Schwartz, and Jessell, *Principles of Neural Science;* and Springer and Deutsch, *Left Brain, Right Brain.* Section VII of Gazzaniga's *The Cognitive Neurosciences* has some good chapters and Pinker's *The Language Instinct* is interesting and a good read, as is his best-selling book *How the Mind Works.*

● Studies of word and letter identification can be found in Monty and Senders, eds., *Eye Movement and Psychological Processes;* and Rayner and Pollatsek's *The Psychology of Reading.* Volume 4 (No. 5) of *Psychological Science* contains a series on an interdisciplinary approach to reading research, including PET, eye-tracking, and connectionist articles and is highly recommended. The excellent books by Crowder, *The Psychology of Reading,* and Just and Carpenter, *The Psychology of Reading and Language Comprehension,* are not to be missed by those seeking an overview of the topic as well as detailed analysis of the current state of reading research. Numerous technical journals on the topic may be found in research libraries.

Movies

● Nell (1994)—Language develpment

● The Miracle Worker (1962)—Sign language

● Pygmalion (1938)—Spoken language

Search Terms

● Koko

● Friends of Washoe

● Linguistic fieldwork

Cognition across the Lifespan

hmmm. . .?

1. What is meant by "life-span development"? How is it studied?

2. Who was Jean Piaget, and what were his major contributions? Who was Lev Vygotsky, and what were his major contributions?

3. What have recent studies of twins told us about genetic influences on intelligence?

4. How early do babies attend to faces?

5. At what age do memories last longest?

6. How early do babies form concepts, and how has this been demonstrated?

7. Do children have imagery? Form prototypes?

8. How does thinking change as we get older?

The study of human development focuses on the age-related physical, cognitive, and social changes that occur throughout the life span. Cognitive development focuses specifically on changes in thinking, problem solving, memory, and intelligence. This important topic was once limited to the study of "child" psychology, but now, with the recognition that cognition unfolds throughout the entire life span of people, the topic ranges from the study of the fetus to the study of older adults. And because a greater number of people are living longer (by 2020 it is estimated that 17 percent of the American population—about 50 million—will be age 65 or older), the subspeciality of gerontology has attracted much research attention. It is simply impossible to cover in any detail the main features of this huge area, but it is possible to deal selectively with some very interesting and vital aspects of developmental psychology in this chapter on developmental cognition.

Human cognition, from a developmental perspective, is the result of a series of developmental stages beginning at our earliest years of growth beginning at the earliest stages. Our perceptions, memories, and language and thought processes are governed by the basic genetic structure we inherit and the changes we experience in response to the demands made during our long and varied interaction with the physical and social environment. The critical feature is that cognition develops—that is, cognition and thinking emerge—in an orderly fashion as individuals progress from infancy to adulthood, and then some cognitive skills may decline in old age. These changes may be caused by neurological and physical maturation (or deterioration) of the person; the family, social, and educational milieu in which the person lives; and the interaction between a physically changing person and his or her environment.

Based on which side of the nature–nurture dichotomy, some psychologists hold that an infant is largely devoid of naturalistic tendencies—is a kind of *tabula rasa,* or "blank tablet"— upon which the experiences of the world are to be recorded; and other, structurally oriented psychologists hold that infants possess certain invariant neurological and psychological potentials and that cognitive development is a matter of the interaction between these built-in structures and the encouragement and demands of society. While the once popular "nurture" side of the argument was radicalized by some overzealous behaviorists to the point that *all* behavior was considered to be the result of operant learning, recent findings have demonstrated that there is a large natural (or genetic) component to the developing human. It is safe to conclude that human cognition is determined by both the genetic makeup of the person and his or her environment. An intractable position on either side misses the main point. Developmentally, we are a blend of how our biological schematic is constituted and how our experiences are mapped onto the blueprint.

Cognitive Development

Interest in the development of cognition throughout a person's life span was initially stimulated by the seminal work of Jean Piaget of Switzerland and the theoretical legacy left by the thoughtful works of Lev S. Vygotsky of Russia. Much has been written and is generally available about the life and times of Piaget. Less is known of the life and theories of Vygotsky, and later in this chapter a brief précis of his life and work is presented. As important as these theories are in terms of establishing a general framework, recent ideas and data have contributed significantly to our current understanding of the forces implicated in cognitive development.

Assimilation and Accommodation: Piaget

Dissatisfied with attempts of moral philosophers and others to explain human knowledge through rational speculation alone, Jean Piaget adopted a unique and ultimately influential perspective. He decided that since intellect, like all biological functions, is a product of evolutionary **adaptation,** it could best be explained from a biological and evolutionary point of view. The best way to understand the nature of the adult mind was to study mental activity from birth, observing its development and changes in adaptation to the environment.

General Principles   For Piaget, two major principles operated in cognitive development: organization and adaptation.

Organization refers to the nature of the mental structures that are used to explore and understand the world. For Piaget the mind is structured, or organized, in increasingly complex and integrated ways, the simplest level being the **scheme,** which in his view is a mental representation of some action (physical or mental) that can be performed on an object. For the newborn, sucking, grasping, and looking are schemes; they are cognitive strategies the newborn uses to know the world—by acting on the world. Across development, these schemes become progressively integrated and coordinated in an orderly fashion so that eventually they produce the adult mind.

Adaptation is a two-pronged process of **assimilation** and **accommodation.** Assimilation is the process by which we take information from the outside world and assimilate it with our existing knowledge and behaviors. For an infant, their world is largely involved with physical objects—and their primary scheme at that time is to put objects in their mouths. Accomodation involves changing (adapting) old schemes to process new information and objects in the environment. For example, when an infant gets older and more mobile, he or she may come across a coffee table. The object is too big to put in

Jean Piaget **(1896–1980).** His research and theories form the basis of modern developmental psychology.

How are these two people cognitively the same? Different?

the mouth (the old scheme) and accommodates (changes) the old scheme by putting his face to the corner of the table and gnawing on it. Piaget believed that similar phenomena apply to mental activity, namely, that we possess mental structures that assimilate external events and convert them into mental events or thoughts. In other words, we would have to accommodate our biological structures to meet the problems posed by the new object. In similar fashion we accommodate our mental structures to new and unusual aspects of the mental environment. These two processes, assimilation and accommodation, represent two complementary aspects of the general process of adaptation.

Piaget postulates four approximate major periods of cognitive development through which the human intellect evolves. Changes within a given period were generally quantitative and linear, while differences across periods tended to be qualitative and, further, there was a necessary sequence of progression through the four periods; that is, a child had to go through each period to get to the next.

Within the stages there are schemes subject to accommodation, these changes occur in phases throughout each particular stage.

Stage 1: The sensorimotor period (birth to 2 years) is characterized by phases of progressive intercoordination of schemes into successively more complex, integrated ones. In the first phase, responses are innate and involuntary reflexes, such as sucking. In the next phase, reflex schemes are brought under voluntary control. When these primary schemes, such as sucking, looking, and grasping, are truly intercoordinated—that is, when the infant cannot only grasp and look simultaneously but also look at something *to* grasp it. This change in scheme leads to secondary schemes.

Stage 2: In the preoperational period (2 to 7 years), the young child's behavior shifts from dependence on action to utilization of mental representations of those actions—or what is commonly called thought. However, the preoperational child does not have a developed system for organizing these thoughts. Most all of us have been around children, who, if they can't see us, think that we can't see them either. This is a classic example of a preoperational child who is egocentric in that they have difficulty differentiating their perceptions from the perceptions of others. The capacity for mental representation makes possible a number of significant new schemes and abilities. Among them is a primitive kind of insight learning, in which the child can merely look at a problem and often solve it without having to perform any overt actions. That is, the child can figure out the answer in his or her head and realize the correct solution. Another advance made possible by representation is the child's ability to pretend and make believe, specifically, to use an object for a purpose for which it was not originally designed. For example, one of Piaget's daughters used a piece of cloth as if it were a pillow. She would pick up the cloth, put her thumb in her mouth, lie down with her head on the cloth, and pretend to go to sleep. Piaget feels that since the child can now relate objects to each other in her head, objects that resemble each other in some way can come to substitute for each other; the child doesn't now need a pillow to lie down—a substitute or make-believe pillow will do just fine. Finally, the capacity for representation underlies and makes possible the child's use of language. Language, for Piaget, comprises symbols (words) that stand for objects and events. Representation involves the creation and evocation, in the head, of symbols for objects. Until the child can truly represent and manipulate symbols, he or she will not be able to use language very effectively. Not surprisingly, the capacity for representation and the child's first multiword utterances emerge at about the same time. For Piaget, there is a causal connection between the two: representation makes possible the acquisition and use of language.

Stage 3: The concrete-operational period (7 to 11 years) advances in three important domains of intellectual growth: conservation, classification, seriation and transitivity.

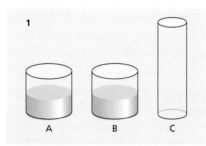

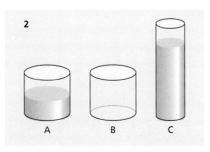

Arrangement (1) at outset of conservation task and (2) after contents of one vessel have been transferred to narrower and taller vessel.

Conservation, the first domain, is the ability to transform properties of objects. A typical test of conservation is given in the following example (see Figure 12.1). Three vessels are placed before you, two identical in dimensions and one higher and narrower. Water is poured into the two shorter vessels to exactly the same level. You confirm that the two contain the same amount of water, perhaps by checking the levels. Now water from one of the short vessels is poured into the tall, narrow one. The water in the latter climbs to a higher level. Is there more water in the tall one (C) than had been in the shorter vessel (A)? Piaget found that children in the preoperational stage typically say that the tall, narrow vessel has more water. However, children in the concrete-operational stage are able to determine that the amount of water is indeed the same.

Classification involves grouping and categorization of similar objects. Suppose for example, a child is shown four dogs and three cats and is asked whether there are more dogs or more cats. The preoperational child can answer this question correctly. However, asked whether there are more animals or more dogs, she replies that there are more dogs. The concrete-operational child will answer this last question correctly, demonstrating an ability to classify. For Piaget, successful performance involves not only an awareness of some of the subclasses, such as dogs and cats, but a complete knowledge that subclasses added together make up a third class (animals) and that the class can be reversed into its subclasses. This concrete-operational system, or grouping, is similar to that underlying conservation. The two subclasses (dogs and cats) can be combined (via *transformation*) into a third class (animals), which can be broken back down (via *reversibility*) into the two original subclasses. All this can be done in the head.

Seriation and **transitivity** are two separate but related skills. Seriation involves the ability to string together a series of elements according to some underlying relationship. For example, a child asked to order several sticks (see Figure 12.2) according to length will be able to do so aligning all of the sticks. Complete seriation ability awaits development of the system of concrete operations.

Transitivity is related to seriation ability. In the transitivity problem shown in Figure 12.2, a child is first shown a series of sticks, two at a time, and then asked

FIGURE 12.2

Above, seriation task (A) and performances on it by pre-operational (B) and concrete-operational (C) children. Below, pairs of sticks such as would be presented in a transitivity task. After a child determines that A and B are the same length, that B is longer than C, and that C is longer than D, he or she is asked whether B is longer than D.

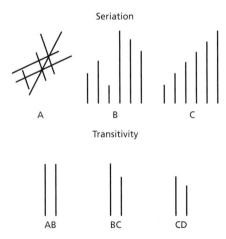

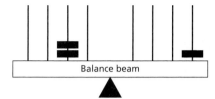

FIGURE 12.3

Typical arrangement of weights in balance-beam problem. The child must decide whether a beam (initially locked in balance position) will be in balance when released.

which is longer. Children perform poorly on this task until they reach the concrete-operational stage. The crucial ability for Piaget is the ability to cross the bridge between B and D. Clearly, the child must be able to seriate the sticks in order to do this. In addition, however, he or she must be able to coordinate the two isolated relationships (B > C and C > D) into a system to make the transitive inference that B > D. For Piaget the preoperational child knows that B > C and that C > D but cannot put these two relationships together via the middle linking term *C* to create a concrete-operational system.

Stage 4: The formal-operational period (adolescence and adulthood) is marked by the child's ability to formulate and test hypotheses against reality. Figure 12.3 shows a problem useful in illustrating formal-operational development. Consider a balance beam with various weights that can be placed in a variety of positions on either side of the beam. The goal—to balance the beam—can be accomplished by changing weights on either side of the beam or by moving weights closer to or farther from the central balance point (fulcrum).

Stages of Cognitive Development—Piaget

Stage	Age Range	Characteristics
Sensorimotor	0–2	World of here and now No language, no thought in early stages Understanding of objective reality absent
Preoperative	2–7 years	Egocentric thought Reason dominated by perception Intuitive rather than logical thought No ability to conserve
Concrete operation	7–11	Ability to conserve Classes and relations ability Number understanding Concrete thinking Development of reversibility in thought
Formal operations	11 and up	Complete generality of thought Propositional thinking Ability to deal with the hypothetical Development of strong idealism

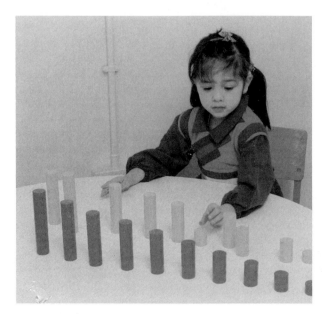

Young girl doing a seriation task.

Courtesy of Brendan McGonigle

The formal-operational child understands that the weights on both sides are related, for example, that adding weight to one side can be compensated for by moving the weights on the other side farther away from the fulcrum. Children in the lower stages have difficulty with this and cannot coordinate these two systems into a higher-order "system of systems." This coordination is precisely the goal of the formal-operational period— namely, coordination of previously isolated systems of concrete operations.

A direct outcome of the ability to coordinate systems of thought into higher systems is the ability to move beyond the actual world of physical reality to hypothetical worlds or other abstract realities. Abstract thought allows the child to consider outcomes and consequences and engage in long-term planning. Questions such as "What if the sun ceased to exist?" and "What if gravity disappeared?" that are so characteristic of adolescent thought stem directly from the ability to bring new, hypothetical dimensions to an otherwise concrete reality. This propensity toward hypothetical thinking is closely allied to the burgeoning tendency to think at a very abstract level; the formal-operational adolescent can consider general issues such as morality, love, existence. However, only about 35 percent of graduating American high school students are at this level.

For Piaget, formal-operational thought marks the end of intellectual growth. The child has clearly come a long way from the simple reflexes of the newborn to the sophisticated thoughts of the adolescent and adult. The striking feature of Piaget's theory is that it postulates the natural, logical progression of this development according to a unified set of theoretical principles.

Critique of the Piagetian Perspective Although immensely influential, Piaget's views have not gone unchallenged.

Evidence has been presented by Jean Mandler (1998, 2000) that raises another question about how Piaget views the thinking ability of young infants in the sensorimotor

FIGURE 12.4

Two types of pacifiers used in the Meltzoff and Borton study. After habituation with one type of pacifier without being able to see it, infants tended to look at the pacifier they felt in their mouth.

After Meltzoff & Borton (1979), as reported by Mandler (1990).

stage. Simply stated, the Piagetian view of young infants is that they go through a period during which they cannot completely form thoughts. Mandler suggests that the ability to think is far more extensive than originally proposed by Piaget. There is evidence for the existence of perceptual conceptualization at an early age. In one experiment (Spelke, 1979) two films depicting complex events accompanied by a single sound track were shown to 4-month-old infants. Infants preferred to view the film that matched the sound (see also Mandler & Bauer, 1988; Meltzoff & Borton, 1979). These results indicate that the child is able to take two separate stimuli (the film and the sound track) and combine them together as demonstrated by preference for the matching film and sound track.

Even infants only 1 month old seem to be able to recognize objects only felt in their mouths (see Meltzoff & Borton, 1979). The 1-month-old infants were given a pacifier with either a knobby surface or smooth surface (see Figure 12.4). After they were able to habituate to the pacifier without being able to see it, the pacifier was removed. Then the infant was shown both pacifiers. The infants spent more time looking at the pacifier they had only felt in their mouths before, which is taken as support for the view that some central processing of two similar patterns of information is accomplished indicating a cross-perceptual mode to recognize objects.

Mandler suggests that some of the evidence for conceptual ability gathered by child psychologists has been based on motor behavior and that what may appear to be conceptual incompetence may be motor incompetence. These areas of criticism, and others, argue that the child may possess sophisticated logical operations far earlier than thought by Piaget. They also suggest that other processes may be critical in determining whether a child will demonstrate a particular competence. Nevertheless, supporters

Jean Mandler. Conducted inventive experiments that have shed new light on thinking in young children.

of Piaget could argue that the studies just cited show only that the basic processes that determine cognitive advance occur earlier than anticipated. The basic operational schemes and the fundamental sequence of progressive integration and coordination remain as reasonable explanations for the child's cognitive growth. However, even this basic tenet has been challenged.

Mind in Society: Vygotsky

Between the cities of Minsk in Belarus and Smolensk in Russia, in the town of Orsha, Lev Vygotsky was born in 1896. A bright, energetic, curious lad, he won a gold medal for his scholarship upon completing gymnasium. Perhaps only in his fantasy did he imagine that he would be selected to attend "Lomonosov's University" (Moscow State University); few Jewish boys from remote towns were selected (a quota of 3 percent had been established for Moscow and St. Petersburg universities). Also, even if his talent was conspicuous and his grades impeccable, a new rule was being tried out whereby Jewish applicants were to be selected by casting lots (Dobkin in Levitin, 1982). Nevertheless, in some undistinguished pedagogical bureau, fate fell down on the side of schoolboy Vygotsky. By the luck of the draw, he won (and lost a bet with a friend, paying him off with a "good book") and commenced on an intellectual career unparalleled in the history of Russian psychology.

Counted among his early students and coworkers are the most illustrious psychologists in the former Soviet Union, including Alexander Luria (the most frequently cited Russian psychologist by Western psychologists; see Solso, 1985), Alexei Leontiev (the most frequently cited Russian psychologist by Russian psychologists), Zaporozhets, Zinchencho, Elkonin, Galperin, and Bozhovich.

Vygotsky's creative talents were not confined to psychology. They included philosophy (his works on Marx and Hegel are classics, and a book on Spinoza is still to be published [see Kozulin, 1984]), art criticism (his dissertation and first book were called *The Psychology of Art*), literary research (he founded the journal *Verask* and befriended the poet Mandelstam), and law and medicine (his first degree was in law, he was working on a medical degree, and, among other achievements, he left an important mark on clinical and developmental psychology). He died in 1934 at the age of thirty-seven; the cause of his early death was tuberculosis. Today, Russians enjoy calling

Lev Vygotsky **(1896–1934).** Made significant observations and proposed theories of child language development.

him the Mozart of psychology. Vygotsky's original works deserve careful reading. In this next section we focus on his basic ideas as they bear on the topic of developmental psychology.

Although Vygotsky and Piaget were contemporaries (the leading developmental psychologists of the century) and lived in Europe, they never met. They did know of each other's work, however; Vygotsky knew of Piaget well before Piaget knew of Vygotsky.[1] There are similarities and differences between the theories; one way to discuss Vygotsky's theories is to contrast them with Piaget's.

Stages of Development   Vygotsky accepted Piaget's general stages of development but rejected the underlying genetically determined sequence. Piaget believed that development precedes learning, however, Vygotsky believed that learning precedes development.

A second point of difference between the theorists is on the nature and function of speech. For Piaget, egocentric speech, which the child uses when "thinking aloud," gives way to social speech in which the child recognizes the laws of experience and uses speech to communicate. For Vygotsky, the child's mind is inherently social in nature, and egocentric speech is social in origin and social in purpose: children learn egocentric speech from others and use it to communicate with others. This position represents a major schism between the theorists and reveals the principal theory of child development according to Vygotsky.

The development of speech, which is tied to the development of thought in the child, proceeds along the following course. First and foremost, the primary purpose of speech (not only for children but also for adults) is communication, which is motivated by our basic need for social contact. Thus the earliest speech (babbling, crying, cooing) Vygotsky would say is essentially social. Speech becomes "egocentric" (and here Vygotsky accepts the stages of development according to Piaget but differs in explanation) when the child "transfers social collaborative forms of behavior to the sphere of the inner-personal psychic functions" (Vygotsky, 1934/1962). The development of thinking therefore is not from the individual to society but from society to the individual.

Phenomenon of Internalization   Internalization is the process by which external actions (roughly speaking, *behavior*) are transformed into internal psychological functions (roughly speaking, *processes*). On this point Vygotsky and Piaget agree on a descriptive level but not on the origin of internalization. Vygotsky's position is similar to the writings of Émile Durkheim and Pierre Janet (and was undoubtedly influenced by them through his familiarity with the French sociological school). Human consciousness, from this direction, consisted of internalized social, interpersonal relationships. The importance of this position for developmental psychology is that children tend to use the same form of behavior in relation to themselves as others have expressed toward them. This is achieved by the child following the adult's example and gradually developing the ability to do certain tasks without help or assistance. The difference between

[1]Piaget did not know the details of Vygotsky's criticisms of his works until about 1962, when he received an abridged translation of *Thought and Language.* He did publish an interesting critique on Vygotsky's position and his own in *Comments on Vygotsky's Critical Remarks* (L. Graham, 1972).

what the child can do with help and without help is what Vygotsky termed the *zone of proximal development.*

Developmental Stages   Vygotsky observed the way children sort objects, such as blocks differing in size, color, and shape. Older children, aged six and up, seemed to select a single quality such as color: all the green boxes were grouped together, as were the blue boxes, and so on. Younger children, below the age of six, used chain concepts, by which Vygotsky meant that the classification changed throughout the selection process. A child may pick up, say, a few blue boxes and then notice a triangular block. This would lead to the selection of another triangular block, and so on, until some other type of block caught the child's attention, such as rounded blocks, which were then abandoned for another type. The selection process seemed to be chained and changeable.

Preschoolers seemed to organize objects thematically rather than taxonomically. For example, older children and normal adults might put animals in one category, furniture in another, and toys in yet a third group (taxonomic classification), while a very young child might classify a cat with a chair, a toy with a bookcase, and a dog with a Frisbee because cats sit on chairs, toys are stored in a bookcase, and dogs play with a Frisbee (thematic classification). From similar observations, Vygotsky thought that children pass through three stages of conceptual development:

1. The formation of thematic concepts in which relationships between objects are important.
2. The formation of chain concepts (just discussed).
3. The formation of abstract concepts similar to adult concept formation.

Unlike Piaget, Vygotsky had an opportunity in his brief, intellectually crowded life to test a few of his hypotheses under well-controlled laboratory conditions. We will now turn to the important matter of the development of thought—a central thesis of Vygotsky's theory.

Vygotsky's Theory of Language

Stage	Function
Social (external) (Up to age 3)	Controls the behavior of others Expresses simple thoughts and emotions
Egocentric (Ages 3–7)	Bridge between external and inner speech Serves to control behavior, but spoken out loud
Inner (7 and older)	Self-talk that makes possible the direction of thinking Language is involved in all higher mental functioning

Development of Thought and the Internalization of Speech   The development of thought in the child is most evident in language development. At one point Vygotsky (1934/1962) wrote, "Language is a merger between outer speech the child hears and inner speech he thinks with." It is easy to conclude that language and thought are therefore dual entities of a common phenomenon. Carried to its logical conclusion, this notion would force us to deduce that without language there can be no thought, that thinking is dependent on language. Although some developmental psychologists subscribe to this idea, Lev Vygotsky does not. For Vygotsky, if a prelinguistic child thinks, as sufficient evidence suggests is the case, then we must find different roots for speech and thought. A fundamental tenet of Vygotsky's psychology is that thought and speech have different genetic roots and that the rates of development for each are different. The growth curves for thought and speech may "cross and recross" but always diverge. The source of thought is in the biological development of the child; the source of language in his or her social milieu. Even though language and thought have a different genus, they intertwine once the child comes to the realization that every object has a name. After this realization, thought and language are inseparable. Thus, the internalization of language causes thoughts to be expressed in inner speech.

Neural Development

The neurocognitive approach to developmental cognitive psychology emphasizes the developing brain and corresponding cognitive changes. The biological development of the brain, both prenatal and postnatal, is inherently involved in the cognitive development of the species.

Cognitive processes—perception, memory, imagery, language, thinking, and problem solving, for example—are all based on underlying neurological structures and processes. Certainly, the study of the development of cognition would be incomplete without some understanding of the basic nature of developmental neuropsychology. The purpose of this section is to understand better the function of the nervous system throughout the life span of humans. Four different approaches to developmental neuropsychology have been used, including (1) physical studies of the development of the nervous system correlated with cognitive changes; (2) cognitive studies over the life span of individuals from which inferences about neurological maturation are made; (3) the study of neurological pathology or damage in which changes in cognition are noted; and (4) experimental studies in which the brain is altered (mostly animal studies) or some independent variable is introduced and brain activity observed, as in the case of PET studies.

Early Neural Development

The brain develops prenatality over the gestation period as is shown in Figure 12.5. In the very early stages of development, the brain is in the rudimentary stages of growth, but by the beginning of the second trimester, the cerebral cortex is becoming differentiated from the spinal cord. By 7 months many of the principal lobes are being formed. By 9 months the lobes are distinguishable and a number of invaginations are seen. As far as can be told, even with this noticeable and various growth of brain cells, cognition—perception, language processing, thinking, and memory—is still in an embryonic state throughout prenatal growth. Indeed, full cognitive development seems not to occur until the mid 20s.

If one examines synaptic formation, which is closely related to a cognitively functional brain, we find that the numbers increase until about 2 years of age. Then, surprisingly, there is a natural process of *shedding* of synapses in which about 50 percent are lost by

FIGURE 12.5

Prenatal development of the brain. Showing a series of embryonic and fetal stages.

Adapted from W. M. Cowan (1979). Reprinted with permission.

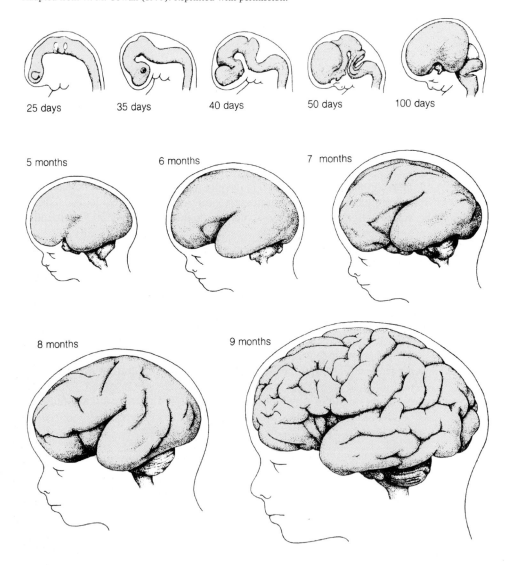

25 days   35 days   40 days   50 days   100 days

5 months   6 months   7 months

8 months   9 months

the age of 16. Some interpret these findings as meaning that favorable environmental influences may deter the loss of synapses rather than influence their initial formation (see Kolb & Whishaw, 1990). Recent studies have questioned the idea that neural development is arrested early in childhood (Thompson & Nelson, 2001; see Figure 12.6).

In Figure 12.7, we see the effects of a nonstimulated (left) and stimulated (right) brain cell taken from rats. As shown, the hairlike dendrites are small, uncomplicated, and

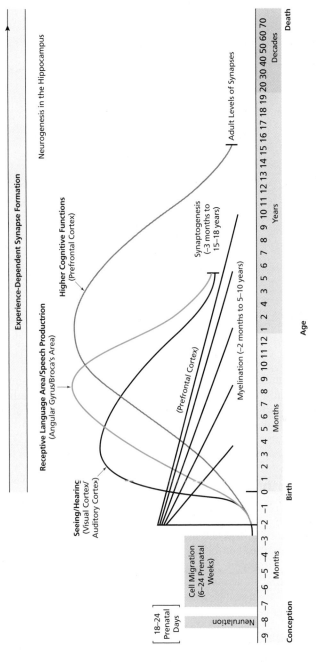

FIGURE 12.6

The developmental course of human brain development.

Note: This graph illustrates the importance of prenatal events, such as the formation of the neural tube (nuerulation) and cell migration; critical aspects of synapse formation and myelination beyond age 3; and the formation of synapses based on experience, as well as neurogenesis in a key region of the hippocampus (the dentate gyrus), throughout much of life.

From Thompson & Nelson (2001).

FIGURE 12.7

Early stimulation and neuron growth.

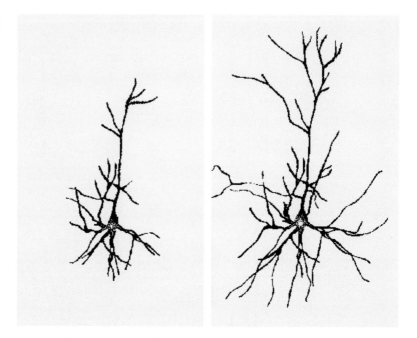

few in the left example, while the dendrites in the other example on the right are large, complex, and numerous; they are "well arborized," like the branches of a healthy tree or bush. The stimulated rats were allowed to explore a variety of objects that were changed daily (Rosenzweig & Bennett, 1996).

Environment and Neural Development

Environment does affect cognitive and brain development. Evidence for this can be found in animal studies where, typically, an animal is reared in some type of sensory isolation and then found to be unable to develop normally when placed in a normal or even an enriched environment. Brain size seems also to be affected by environment as evidenced by the fact that some domestic animals have certain cortical areas that are 10 to 20 percent smaller than comparable animals raised in the wild. Human babies raised in impoverished environments, such as the famous case of a child raised by wolves (see Singh & Zingg, 1940), seem unable to overcome their early experiences.

The effect of early stimulation of cognitive functions is, of course, important, and the term **functional validation** is used to express the notion that for the neural system to become fully functional, stimulation is required. Some experiments show an enriched environment increases brain size in the neocortex. Other cases, which are well documented, do suggest that children are remarkably resilient beings, and that some forms of early cognitive impoverishment may be overcome by changing environments.

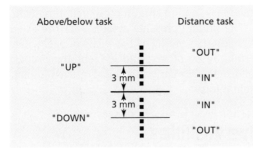

FIGURE 12.8

The "baseball" could appear in any one of the 12 positions relative to the "bat." The criterion in the above/below task was whether the ball was "up" or "down." The criterion in the distance task was whether the ball was closer to the line than 3 mm.

From Koenig, Reiss, and Kosslyn (1990). Reprinted with permission from Elsevier.

Cerebral Asymmetry

A number of well-controlled experiments have been conducted with children and cerebral asymmetry. Koenig, Reiss, and Kosslyn (1990) tested for lateralization of spatial abilities in five- and seven-year-olds. They asked children (and adult control participants) to play the role of a baseball umpire who was to call the location of a ball (a dot) as being above or below, or in or out (see Figure 12.8). The dot was presented to the right or left of the visual fixation point so that it would be processed in the opposite cerebral hemisphere as a result of the crossover of neural pathways from the eye to the brain (see Chapter 2). The children's decisions were measured by means of a reaction time key. As shown in Figure 12.9, children responded faster to stimuli presented initially to the left

FIGURE 12.9

Response latencies for children and adults. The stimuli were presented initially to the left hemisphere (right visual field), to the right hemisphere (left visual field), or to both hemispheres (central field). The participants decided whether the ball was above or below the bat or greater than 3 mm from the bat. For children and adults, the first trial block only is represented.

From Koenig, Reiss, and Kosslyn (1990). Reprinted with permission from Elsevier.

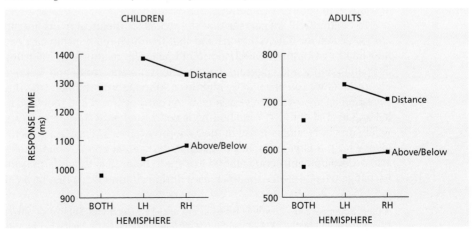

hemisphere in the above/below task, and to stimuli presented initially to the right hemisphere in the distance task. The finding presents evidence for the existence of distinct hemispheric subsystems for children as young as five years of age. Lateralization effects have been noted in young children by others, and we tentatively conclude that brain structures and processes are formed very early in infancy or even prenatally and are not subject to normal environmental forces.

Development of Cognitive Abilities

The investigation of age-related changes in cognition has required systematic exploration of many different processes. In this section we explore only a portion of these processes, and those within only a limited age range—namely, from preschool through adulthood. In essence we focus on the basic cognitive skills involved in acquiring information from the environment and in storing and manipulating information in memory. Our aim is to illustrate how the cognitive viewpoint is valuable in understanding some important aspects of human development.

Intelligence

One method developmental psychologists have used to distinguish the genetic basis of intelligence from the environmental basis is to study twins. In this type of research, fraternal twins (or *dizygotic twins*), who carry similar genetic traits, and identical twins (or *monozygotic twins*), who carry identical genetic traits, may be traced over their lifetime in an effort to discover the influence of environment on traits. Correlations between the abilities of the adopted child and his or her birth or adopted parents are made with the idea that biological influences may be seen in contrast with environmental factors. One of the most comprehensive of twin studies is the Colorado Adoption Project[2] directed by John DeFries and Robert Plomin (Plomin & DeFries, 1998). In one study, more than 200 adopted children and their birth and adoptive parents were studied. Correlations for a control group of children raised by their biological parents over several years were made and are shown in Figures 12.10 and 12.11.

In Figure 12.10 we can see that the scores for identical twins are more similar than are the scores for fraternal twins and that that high relationship carries through for the life span of twins from childhood to old age. The relationship holds for verbal as well as spatial ability and suggests that genetic traits are strong and last over a lifetime. In Figure 12.11 we can see that by middle childhood, birth mothers and their children *who were adopted by others* are very similar to control parents and their children on both verbal and spatial abilities. This finding is contrasted with the scores of adopted children, which do not resemble those of their adoptive parents. The data present convincing evidence for the large influence of genetics on mental abilities and intelligence. There is also a development trend, reported in these data, that suggests that there is an unexpected genetic influence that increases during childhood, so that by a child's mid-teens,

---

[2]Other prominent sites for twins research are at the University of Minnesota, directed by Thomas J. Bouchard, and at the Karolinska Institute in Stockholm, directed by Nancy L. Pedersen.

FIGURE 12.10

Twin studies have examined correlations in verbal *(top)* and in spatial *(bottom)* skills of identical twins and of fraternal twins. When the results of the separate studies are put side by side, they demonstrate a substantial genetic influence on specific cognitive abilities from childhood to old age. The scores of identical twins are more alike than those of fraternal twins. These data seem to counter the idea that the influence of genes wanes with time.

From Plomin and DeFries (1998).

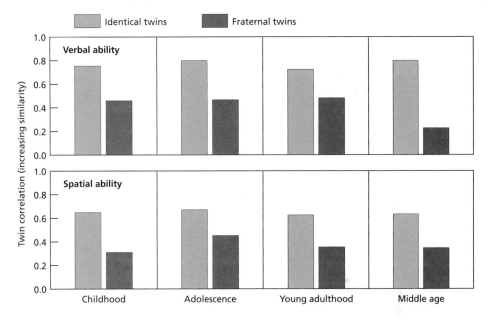

the influence of heredity is quite high. It would appear that some genetically activated change in cognitive functions takes place about the age of nine or ten years. By the time the child reaches sixteen, genetic factors account for about 50 percent of the verbal ability and 40 percent of the spatial ability. These results have been corroborated by other twin studies.

It is reasonable to conclude that genetics plays an important role in determining the verbal and spatial ability of children. While such observations are important, it should be noted that the specific shaping of human behavior, especially that of children, is also influenced by the environment in which the child grows.

Information-Acquisition Skills

The initial stages in cognition require that the child be able effectively to attend to, to perceive, and to search out the relevant information in the environment. Successful acquisition of information brings into play such processes as neurological development, the development of sensory registers, focal attention, and speed of processing, as well as

FIGURE 12.11

Colorado Adoption Project. Followed participants over time found that for both verbal (*top*) and spatial (*bottom*) abilities, adopted children come to resemble their birth parents as much as children raised by their birth parents do. In contrast, adopted children do not end up resembling their adoptive parents. The results imply that most of the family resemblance in cognitive skills is caused by genetic factors, not environment.

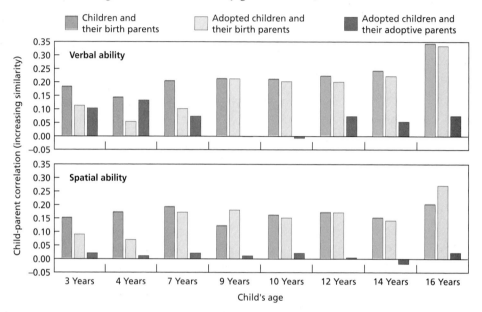

effective strategies for searching out and utilizing information in various portions of the environment. We focus on some of these processes that have been studied developmentally. Most of the modern themes of cognitive psychology, which include selective attention, facial identification, memory, higher-order cognition, and prototype formation, are repeated in the developmental literature.

Selective Attention   Selective attention refers to the ability to focus on relevant information. The evidence we have suggests that young children are somewhat less able to control their attentional processes than adults are. They are more easily detracted and less flexible in deploying attention among relevant and irrelevant information. In one study (Pick, 1975), children were asked to find all the *A*s, *S*s, and *L*s in a large box of multicolored block letters of the alphabet. Unknown to the children was the fact that all the *A*s, *S*s, and *L*s were the same color. Only the older children noticed this clue and used it to advantage in searching through the pile, displaying their greater attentional flexibility.

Although our knowledge about this process is far from complete, it appears that as children grow older, they become better able to control attention and to adapt to the demands of different tasks. When a high degree of selectivity is called for, older children can better focus on the relevant and ignore the irrelevant. Younger children have greater difficulty in this regard. Likewise, when less selectivity is appropriate, older children can

Do you remember T-Rex? How old were you? From *The San Francisco Chronicle,* Dec. 26, 1999.

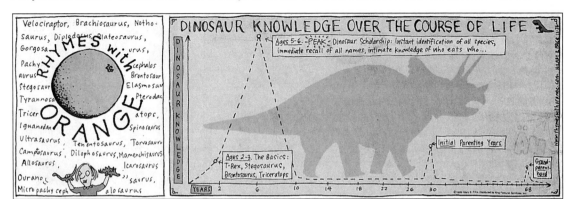

defocus and take in more relevant information. Much of the research on children's attention has dealt with vision.

For some time many professionals believed that newborn infants were functionally blind, a view that has since been discredited. Infants can "see" in the sense that their visual apparatus is functional, but their understanding of what they see—in effect, their perception—is questionable. What is known is that infants tend to look at some objects more than others. Some of the features of infant attention have been identified.

Facial Attention   One topic of interest among cognitive psychologists is to what features of a visual scene people attend. Because infants become familiar with people's faces (especially the mother's face) at a very tender age, cognitive developmental psychologists have studied facial attention in some detail. You may recall that pioneer work in the field of visual attention was done by Yarbus, who measured eye movements and fixations as subjects viewed a scene. Related work has been done with children by Salapatek (1975), who presented infants with a visual display in which one object was placed within another (e.g., a circle inside a triangle). Very young infants (up to the age of two months) showed an almost total preference for the outer edges of the external figure over the inner figure. After about the age of two months, the infants scanned both the outer features and the inner ones. In another study of this type, Haith, Bergman, and Moore (1977) used an eye-tracking device similar to the one shown in Figure 12.12. Of special interest is the use of infrared illuminators, which impinge on the infant's eyes. Rays from this source are beyond the sensory threshold; the infant cannot see them, and they are harmless. Because the position of these lights in the child's visual field is known, the fixation point can be determined by measuring the distance of one of the lights from the center of the pupil. (Similar technology has been used in reading experiments.) The infant's eye movements and the exact location of the mother's face are detected by video cameras and combined in a video mixer. It is possible to identify exactly where the infant is looking vis-à-vis the mother's face.

Experiments of these types are helpful in the study of memory and early perceptual organization in addition to the emotional and social development of infants. In the

FIGURE 12.12

Drawing of eye-tracking apparatus. Used to record eye movements and fixations of infants.

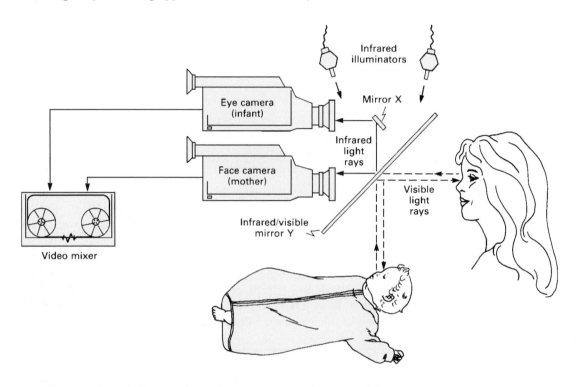

Cognition in Everyday Life

The Developing Brain—Use It or Lose It

"It's crazy," says Pasko Rakic, a Yale neurobiologist. "Americans think kids should not be asked to do difficult things with their brains while they are young: 'Let them play; they'll study at the university.' The problem is, if you don't train them early, it's much harder."*

Early stimulation of the brain, through puzzles, visual displays, music, foreign-language learning, chess, art, scientific exploration, mathematical games, writing, and many other similar activities, promotes synaptic connections in the brain. Shortly after birth, the number of neural connections increases at a phenomenal rate. Then, at about puberty, the number of new connections diminishes and two processes take place: functional validation, in which useful connections are made more permanent, and selective elimination, in which useless connections are eliminated.

Throughout the life span—from infancy to old age—we humans (and other creatures) are endowed with the capacity to expand our mental capacity through use. Disuse, through mindless, passive activities, is likely to dull brain growth.

* Cited in Life, July 1994.

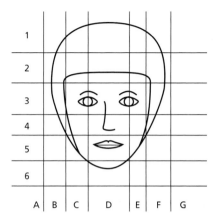

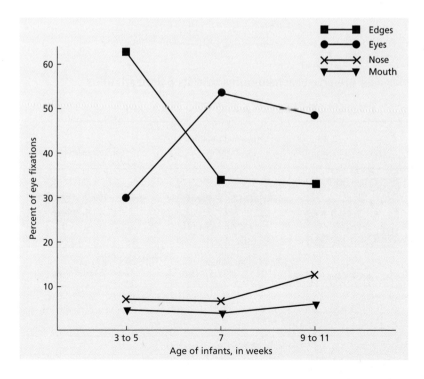

FIGURE 12.13

Zones for mother's face used in eye-tracking study. Zones were individually determined.

From Haith, Bergman, and Moore (1977).

experiment by Haith and his colleagues (1977), three groups of infants were observed. One group was three to five weeks old; the second group was seven weeks old, and the third was nine to eleven weeks old. The mothers' faces were divided into zones, which were used to identify eye fixations (see Figure 12.13). The results of the experiments are shown in Figure 12.14.

It was found that very young infants focus on the peripheral contours (as also reported by Salapatek), but older infants focus on the eyes. It was also found that older infants focus on the nose and mouth more than younger infants. The possible meaning of

FIGURE 12.14

Percentage of time spent on eyes, edges, nose, and mouth by infants of three different ages.

From Haith, Bergman, and Moore (1977).

these findings is that to the infant, the face of the mother is not merely a collection of visual events but a meaningful entity. We can dismiss these findings on the basis of the physical attractiveness of eyes (their color, movement, and contrast), but such argument does not account for the shift in attention over age, nor does it account for the relative lack of attention given to the mouth, which also has these characteristics. It is possible that by the seventh week eyes, especially a mother's eyes, take on special social value and are important in social interaction.

The problem of what critical features babies attend to was tackled by Mondloch et al. (1999) in an experiment that used artificial faces and facial features. Some studies indicate that very young babies prefer facelike stimuli over non-facelike stimuli (see, e.g., Valenza, Simion, Cassia, & Umilta, 1996) while others suggest the preference emerges between two and four months (Dannemiller & Stephens, 1988). In a carefully designed study by Mondloch and her colleagues, very young children who were less than an hour old were shown a series of standard visual stimuli, which are shown in Figure 12.15. The study also looked at six-week-old and twelve-week-old children. Preference for stimuli was determined by measuring the first look and the duration of the looking.

The results of this experiment show some clear distinctions between viewing preferences of very young babies as contrasted with those of older babies. In the "feature inversion" stimuli, the gross features of a face are shown in an upright or inverted orientation. Newborns overwhelmingly chose to look at the upright image while older babies showed no preference. In the "phase and amplitude reversal" images, in which facial features are somewhat fuzzy contrasted with a more globally defined head, neonates preferred the head while older babies preferred the fuzzy-featured face. In the "contrast reversal" faces, very young babies showed no preference while the twelve-week-old babies show a very definite preference for the positive contrast face. From these results we

FIGURE 12.15

Number of babies who preferred each stimulus over its paired stimulus.

From Mondloch et al. (1999).

Age	Feature inversion			Phase and amplitude reversal			Contrast reversal		
	Config	Inversion	Neither	Phase of face	Amplitude of face	Neither	Positive contrast	Negative contrast	Neither
Newborns	9*	1	2	0	9*	3	0	0	12
6-week-olds	0	0	12	12**	0	0	3	0	9
12-week-olds	0	1	11	12**	0	0	12**	0	0

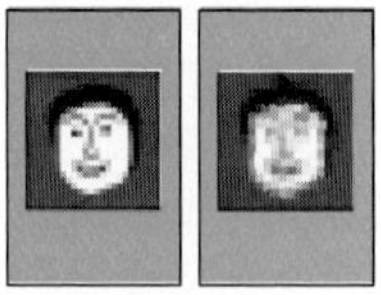

*p < .05, two-tailed binomial test. **p < .001, two-tailed binomial test. All other ps > .1.

learn that very young children (who have had little opportunity to learn about faces or visual stimuli) have an innate predisposition to look toward stimuli that resemble facial features. Johnson and Morton (1991) found similar results with newborns less than ten minutes old. These studies and others have been cited as support for a partially preprogrammed brain (in other words, not a blank slate) that has adapted to respond to faces in the environment to aid in survival (Tooby: Cosmides, 1992).

As a child matures other preferences emerge that suggest an increased cortical influence over infants' preferences for faces. From other studies, we know that there are dedicated parts of the human brain implicated in the perception of faces in humans as well as other animals (e.g., monkeys). It is consistent with a biological or survival point of view to conclude that facial perception is an important early means of recognizing critical signals during the first few minutes after birth. As a baby matures, the learning of other significant facial signals seems to happen until, in time, a child forms clear facial discriminations and preferences based on frequent exposure to parents, family members, and other caregivers.

Memory

There is considerable scientific evidence that infants have memory for events as well as the ability to form concepts (Mandler & McDonough, 1998). On a basic level, babies show recognition of previously seen stimuli, such as their mother's face, or classically conditioned responses (see Rovee-Collier, 1990, 1999, for details). Imitation and habituation are also reliably found in infants. These findings do not suggest, however, that early memories are of the same kind as adult memories (see Eacott, 1999). Early efforts to find the earliest memories have (generally) relied on introspective accounts (e.g., "What is your earliest memory?") and found that the average age was 39 to 42 months.

In a well-controlled experiment by Usher and Neisser (1993), childhood memory and its counterpart, childhood amnesia, were tested with 222 college students who were asked questions about four datable events—the birth of a younger sibling, a hospitalization, the death of a family member, and a family move. The events could be checked against reliable records and occurred when the subjects were one, two, three, four, or five years of age. The results are shown in Figure 12.16. Childhood amnesia, or the inability to recall an event that actually happened, ranged from the age of two for hospitalization and sibling birth to the age of three for death and a family move. The onset of childhood amnesia seems to depend on the nature of the event itself, as the birth of a sibling and hospitalization, potentially traumatic episodes, are significant events likely to be recalled in adulthood. Conversely, these events may have been recounted throughout the life of the child and early adult (see E. Loftus, 1993a, for a rejoinder).

If we consider the memory of older children, into early adulthood, the conclusions about adolescent memory are clear. Evidence abounds that the period between 10 and 30 years of age produces recall of the greatest amount of autobiographical memories. Many times these personal memories—of such things as a special date, a song, an automobile, a dress, a ring, an election, a favorite teacher (or not so favorite teacher), the winner of a movie's Academy Award, a boyfriend, an adventure in an unfamiliar city, an embarrassing moment—are the highlights of what one could call "your time." Many

FIGURE 12.16

Mean recall data for four target events as a function of age at experience.

From J. A. Usher and U. Neisser, "Childhood amnesia and the beginnings of memory for four early life events," *Journal of Experimental Psychology: General, 122,* 155–165. Copyright 1993 by the American Psychological Association. Reprinted by permission of the American Psychological Association.

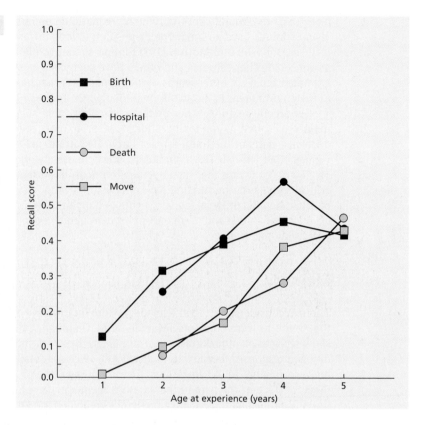

experimental papers address this topic and the conclusion is that those things that happen during adolescence and early adulthood are remembered best. As a sample of this work, consider the data presented in Figure 12.17, based on Holbrook and Schindler (1998) and reported by Rubin, Rahhal, and Poon (1998). Working on the notion that preference is related to memories, Holbrook and Schindler played 30-second excerpts from 28 songs to 108 people ranging in age from 16 to 86 and asked them to rate each song as to how much they liked it. As shown, the preferences for songs were clustered in the period when the raters were in their early adulthood. Data from other studies conducted here and abroad have corroborated these findings. (See Rubin et al. 1998.)

Organization (Chunking)   The development of sophisticated rehearsal strategies is just one of the factors influencing the growth of memory skills in school-age children. A second, equally important factor involves the ability to recognize and utilize potentially useful higher-order relationships that link various environmental events. (Earlier, we called this *organization,* or *chunking.*) During the school years, the child becomes better able to organize material he or she wants to remember.

Of the following two lists of words, which would you expect to recall more easily?

1. desk, arm, tree, hall, paper, clock, farmer, word, floor
2. apples, oranges, grapes, shirt, pants, shoe, dog, cat, horse

Notice the remarkable cognitive changes in these infants who range in age from 2, 3, 6, 9, 12, 15 months of age.

Photo courtesy of Carolyn Rovee-Collier.

The second list is indeed easier to recall once you realize that the words are composed of three separate categories. By chunking the words into categories, you form a higher-order rule and use the rule to help at the time of recall. Indeed, experiments have shown that recall of categorized lists is much easier than recall of unrelated words. Surprisingly, studies have shown that up to about the third grade, children's recall of categorizable items is not much better than their recall of unrelated items. Older children, on the other hand, recall categorizable items much better than unrelated items (Lange, 1973; Vaughn, 1968). These findings imply that the older children better recognize and utilize the categorical nature of the stimuli to help their memory performance.

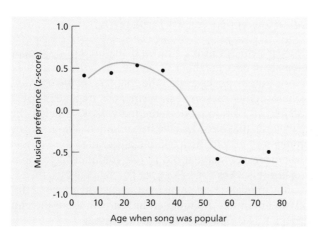

FIGURE 12.17

Distribution of scores.
Shows how much individuals ranging in age from 16 to 86 liked songs as a function of age when the song was popular.

From Rubin, Rahhal, and Poon (1998).

One way to try to help younger children to see the higher-order relationship between stimuli would be to present the categories in a blocked fashion—all items from one category first, the next category second, and so on. An experiment by Yoshimura, Moely, and Shapiro (1971) presented one group of children who were four to ten years old with categorizable stimuli in a blocked fashion and another group with stimuli in a random fashion. They found that while the older children benefitted from having the items blocked, the younger children did not. Other studies have shown some slight advantage from blocking for younger children (Cole, Frankel, & Sharp, 1971; Kobasigawa & Middleton, 1972), but, in general, the results reveal that young children appear not to notice or utilize as well the categorical structure of materials presented to them. Furthermore, it appears that if left to their own devices, younger children do not spontaneously use organizational strategies to help them remember. In one study (Liberty & Ornstein, 1973), fourth graders and adults were given twenty-eight words printed on individual cards. They were told to sort the cards in any way they wanted to help them remember. The adults tended to sort and group items that were related semantically, while the fourth graders grouped words in more idiosyncratic and less semantically related ways.

In sum, studies have documented clearly that older children are more likely to notice and utilize higher-order relationships among stimuli and are more likely to group items on that basis. Thus, the development of active, planful, spontaneous organization strategies characterizes the growth of the school-age child's memory abilities.

Higher-Order Cognition in Children

The importance of higher-order cognition in everyday processing of information has been discussed in some detail in previous chapters (with more to come in the following chapters). The question for this chapter is what the corresponding similarities and differences between higher-order cognition in adults and children are. Even though a definitive answer is impossible, a tremendous amount is known about higher-order cognition in both adults and children. One approach is to trace the developmental literature in each of the topics in higher-order cognition—from memory to creativity. Such a procedure requires many volumes; however, we can touch on the highlights here.

Knowledge Structure and Memory   Several features of a comparative study of higher-order cognition are at once apparent. Even the newborn is capable of storing some information in memory, but, as we learned in the chapters on memory and language, the form in which that information is stored in memory is dependent on several factors. These include the source of the information, the individual's previous knowledge base, and the structural networks that already have been framed. We first consider the way a child might store in memory an experience in his or her life.

Suppose you were to ask a six-year-old to tell you about her trip to the zoo. She might say something like this: "Let's see. First, we got on a big bus, then I saw elephants, an' big polar bears, an' monkeys, an' then I got an ice cream cone an' come home." From this little story an enormous amount can be learned about the child's knowledge base, the way information is stored, and the story grammar.

One way to analyze an episode of this type is to think about the way information is represented. Jean Mandler and her colleagues (Mandler, 1983, 1984, 2000; Mandler & De-Forest, 1979; Mandler & McDonough, 1998) have studied story grammars (as well as concept formation) in children and have developed a model that distinguishes between two types of representation. In one, the representation is in terms of what a person knows and how that information is organized in memory (such as a sequential structure or a classification of objects by category). In the other, the representation is in the terms of symbols (such as telling about an episode, or drawing a picture of an event, or writing a story about an experience, or even having an imaginary representation).

In the story of a visit to the zoo, the child organized the episode in terms of a sequence of events ("First . . . then . . . and then . . ." and so on) and in terms of a story schema or grammar (the story had a theme, a subject, a beginning, and an end). Mandler (1983), in discussing children's story grammar, contends that stories have "an underlying structure consisting of a setting component in which the protagonist and background information are introduced, followed by one or more episodes which form the skeletal plot structure of the story. Each episode has some kind of beginning, or initiating, event, to which the protagonist reacts." In one test of the hypothesis that children use a story schema, Mandler and DeForest read a two-episode story to eight-year-olds, 11-year-olds, and adults. In one condition the two episodes were interwoven; that is, the title and story setting of the first episode were presented, and then the title and setting of the second episode were presented. The rest of the story was also presented in a similar way, switching back and forth between the episodes. Some participants were asked to recall the story in the way it was presented (interrelated), and others were asked to recall all of episode one and then episode two. The former "unnatural" story grammar was much more difficult to recall, and in fact, the eight-year-olds found it impossible to recall the episodes in the interrelated way. We can conclude from this and other similar experiments that children at a very young age discover rather sophisticated story schemata, which they use to encode experiences.

Metaphorical Thinking   A beguiling peculiarity of children is their make-believe world. All healthy kids have one. It may be as simple as pretending that a block is a car, or a finger is a gun, or a used cardboard box is a palace, or it may be as elaborate as fantasizing about mystical powers or creating an imaginary playmate. As far as can be told (see Fein, 1979), infants up to one year of age are not capable of pretend play, and after the age of six children seem to favor (generally) other forms of play and games. Nevertheless, the early normal propensity to create a fantasy world seems to remain an active but poorly understood part of adult human behavior, in spite of important theories on the topic by Piaget and Vygotsky. It seems that the development of intellectual skills, creativity, and imagery is related to metaphorical thinking in children.

Imagery   A fundamental issue in the study of higher-order cognition in children is the question of how information is represented. In general, the argument is that adults rely more on semantically (meaning-) based representations and children rely more on perceptually based representations. As an example, consider the following question: Can you name the states that are rectangular? Chances are that you formed a mental image of regularly shaped states and then "looked" at them to see which ones were really rectangular. You may have focused on the "four-corner" part of the United States and then "looked" at Colorado, which meets the terms of rectangularity, and then Utah, which comes close but is not quite rectangular enough to meet the criterion, and then Wyoming, and so on. If you were asked to answer the question again, especially if you had repeated familiarization with the question, you may have stored the rectangularity of states in semantic memory (something like "rectangular states [are] Colorado and Wyoming; close to rectangular are New Mexico, North and South Dakota, Kansas, and Oregon"). Then when the question is asked again, you may access the answer from propositional memory rather than from imagery.

Some theorists believe that children use imagery more than propositionally based storage of information to answer questions. For example, consider if we ask an adult and a child the following question: Does a beagle have four legs? Chances are that even though an adult has never been asked this question before, answering correctly is an easy matter of dipping into his or her long-term propositionally stored information bank. However, children under the age of about seven are poor at this type of logical deduction based on semantically stored information. Kosslyn (1983) suggests that if a child does not have the answer stored as a direct associate, then imagery will be used to answer the question.

As in the case of fantasy, hard data on this subject are difficult to find in the experimental literature, but at least one interesting study conducted by Kosslyn (1980; see also Kosslyn, 1983) sheds some light on the topic. In an experiment done with first graders (about the age of six), fourth graders (about the age of ten), and adults, he asked the subjects to verify statements such as "A cat has claws," or "A cat has a head," or "A fish has fur." In one condition, he mentioned the name of the animal and told the subjects to "think about" features of that animal, while in another condition the subjects were asked to "image" the animal. After five seconds, they were to decide whether or not the features were part of the animal. For adults, who are supposedly more propositionally inclined, the most expedient way to answer the question would be to retrieve the semantically coded proposition, whereas children, who may rely more on imagery, would answer the question by forming an image of the animal and then "looking" at its features. Reaction time was the dependent variable, and the results are shown in Figure 12.18.

In general Kosslyn found that adults were swifter with the reaction key than children throughout most conditions, but the reaction-time data for the relative reaction times of children and adults are very interesting and deserve close inspection. When we consider

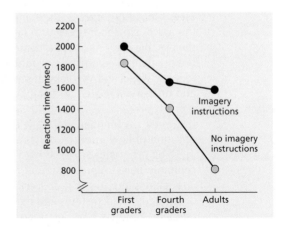

FIGURE 12.18

Proposition verification by age. Verify statements with imagery instructions and without imagery instructions.

Data from Kosslyn (1980).

the differences between the reaction times for those adults who were given the imagery instructions and those who were not given the imagery instructions, we find that those participants with instructions were much slower in giving an answer than those without instructions. This suggests that adults tend to store this type of information in terms of abstract propositions. These results are in contrast to the children's data, which show only slight differences between the group with instruction and the group without instruction. It may be that the children are using imagery in both conditions.

Many innovative research programs, such as the study of children's imagery, frequently raise more questions than they answer. Why do children rely more on imagery (if indeed they do) than adults? Is it because they have not learned propositionally structured knowledge? Is there a natural sequence of development that begins with sensory memories that give way to abstract semantic memories? Is it inherently more efficient to access propositionally based information than image-based information? Why is there a shift in the way information is stored? What implications does this research have for educational practices?

Prototype Formation among Children

The "booming, buzzing confusions" that William James thought the newborn baby was confronted with is one way of looking at the difficult task that we human information-processing creatures all faced initially. Out of the flood of information that bombards the infant's sensory system, what cognitive means exist for the storage and retrieval of pertinent information? It seems that our storage system—human memory—is limited in the amount of information that can be coded and retained by the limited capacity of the brain. We cannot store everything detected by our sensory system.

One alternative model to a store-everything concept is the idea that we form abstract representations of sensory impressions in the form of prototypes and/or conceptual categories. This necessary proclivity appears very early in infancy, and several experiments have shown that the formation of conceptual categories in infants may develop before language. Ross (1980) did an experiment with 12-, 18-, and 24-month-old infants in which they were shown, one at a time, ten toy objects of the same class, such as types of furniture. Then the infants were shown pairs of objects in which one item was a member of the class (but not originally presented) and the other item was a member of a different category (e.g., an apple). Even the youngest of infants in this study spent more time examining the "novel" object, which suggests that they had formed a class representation of, in this case, furniture in which one of the pairs was an "uninteresting" member.

A more direct test of prototype formation in very young (10-month-old) infants was demonstrated by Strauss (1979; see also Cohen & Strauss, 1979; Strauss & Carter, 1984), who used facial prototypes formed from the plastic templates of an Identikit. The primary purpose of the experiment was to assess infants' abilities to abstract prototypical representations, and if they could, to ascertain whether the prototype was formed on the basis of averaging the values of the exemplar items (feature-averaging model) or on the basis of summing the most commonly experienced values of the exemplar items (modal model).

Infants in Strauss's study were shown a series of fourteen faces that had been designed to represent a prototype formed on the basis of modal, or average, representations.

Following this stage, the infants were given pairs of two types of prototypes—one based on an averaging of the features in the first series, and the other based on a modal (or most frequent) number of features in the first series. The dependent variable was time spent looking at one of the faces. It was presumed that infants would spend more time on the novel, or nonprototypic, face than on the prototype face. By using time spent looking at new faces, the experimenter was able to infer which representation was responsible for the formation of a prototype. The most important finding was that very young (10-month-old) infants were able to abstract a prototype face. Strauss also found that infants abstracted information from the faces and formed a prototypical representation on the basis of an averaging of the features of the exemplar faces.

Walton and Bower (1993) reported data that indicated prototype formation in new-born infants, aged 8 to 78 hours, could be achieved. The researchers used infant suck-ing, which controlled the duration a face would be exposed, as the dependent variable. The faces the infants saw were images of eight female or blended (prototype) images of the faces. The infants looked longer at the composite face than at a composite of unseen faces on the first presentation of each. Walton and Bower argue that newborns do form a mental representation having some of the properties of a schema or prototype and that such representations are formed rapidly.

The work on prototype formation has been extended to include children in the age range of three to six years in an experiment conducted in 1993 by Inn, Walden, and Solso. A series of ten exemplar faces were developed from a police identification kit using a prototype face as a base. Initially, only exemplar faces were shown to children. After a child was shown the entire set of ten exemplar faces, he or she was shown a second set. Some of these faces were from the original set (old faces), some were faces not previously seen (new faces), and one of the new faces was the prototype from which the exemplars had been developed. The results are shown in Figure 12.19. As shown, very young chil-dren, about three or four years old, do not form an abstraction of the prototype face. However, by the age of five it appears that prototype formation begins, and it is nearly complete at the age of six, when children's performance on this task is similar to that of college students.

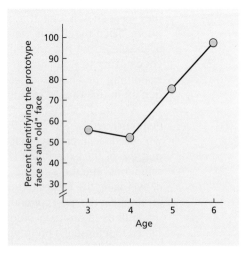

FIGURE 12.19

Percentage of false alarms to prototype face among young children.

Data from Inn, Walden, and Solso (1993).

Getting older is no problem, you just have to live long enough.

  –*Groucho Marx*

Keep in mind that when a participant identifies a prototype face as an old (previously seen) face, he or she is making a false alarm or error. The face is, in fact, new. Prototype formation may be a sophisticated means of storing frequently experienced features in a single "best example." From these studies and an ever-increasing body of literature on children's cognitive processes, the evidence is beginning to accumulate that points out that abstraction of verbal and visual information (be it conceptualized as schemes, grammars, formation of categories, or prototypes) is as important an attribute of children's information-processing activities as it is among adults.

Cognition and Aging

Birth rates in America during 1946 and 1964 increased sharply to an estimated 75 million people, now referred to as the baby-boomers. By the year 2010, the boomers will be between 64 and 46 years old. Additionally, due to medical advances and better health education, people are living longer. Therefore, as the age of this population segment increased, so does our interest in age-related issues. What will happen when these people get old? At what age will they no longer be able to work? At what point will they no longer be self-sufficient? Many of those asking these questions belong to the field of **gerontology,** which is the study of aging, not to be confused with **geriatrics,** which is the study of diseases due to aging. Gerontologists study the social, physical, and mental changes people go through as they get older. Cognitive psychologists too are interested in the effects of aging on mental cognitive abilities such as decision making, memory, and perceptual abilities.

Although aging is important in human development, much of our research has remained on children and adolescence. But it is important to study the human cognitive processes as we enter a period of **senescence** marked by the deterioration that follows our initial development. We must keep in mind that aging and dying are natural aspects of the human experience. Ironically, dying is quite adaptive. From an evolutionary perspective, a shorter life span (one that extends beyond reproduction and childrearing) frees up resources required for reproduction.

Methodologies for studying aging populations are typically conducted by comparing performance of younger adults with the performance of older adults (cross-sectional) or by repeatedly collecting data from the same group of participants as they age (longitudinal). Debra Fleischman and her colleagues (2004) conducted a longitudinal study with 161 participants with an average age of 79. Over a four-year period, participants underwent a series of memory tests that included tests for explicit and implicit memory. Overall, a decrease in memory related to aging was found for explicit, but not implicit, memory, supporting evidence that the two memory types are dissociable. Although the population studied was not experiencing the effects of dementia, the authors conclude that a decline in both explicit and implicit memory may

F I G U R E   1 2 . 2 0

Memory tends to be selective for events as well as for periods. Especially interesting is the tendency of the middle years to be less recallable.
By the age of 70, people remember more from their 20s, while those in
their 50s recall more from their teens.

From Rubin (1987).

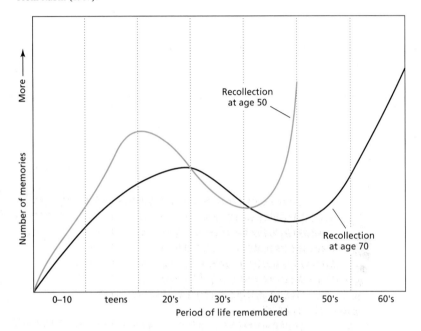

signal the onset of Alzheimer's disease. Implicit memory may not be the only type of
memory resistant to aging. In a cross-sectional study Lars Nilsson (2003) found short-
term memory, semantic memory, and procedural memory performance was not related
to normal aging; however, a decrease in episodic memory was reported. It is fortunate
too that we have so many different memory systems, so when one memory system
begins to decline with age, others do not. And although we can expect to retain a
good deal of our memory, as our episodic memory goes we may spend more time
looking for our keys or trying to remember where we parked the car (assuming we
are still driving).

In a series of studies, David Rubin of Duke University has shown that people remember some periods of their lives better than others and that for most people the recall of past times is remarkably similar. Rubin (1987, 2000; Rubin, Wetzler, & Nebes,
1986) found, for example, that people who reach their middle years (50s and beyond) tend
to remember more episodes from their youth and early adult years than from more recent years (see Figure 12.20).

"It seems to be that reminiscence flows more freely about the period in life that
comes to define you: the time of your first date, marriage, job, child," Rubin explains.
Our relative inability to remember events that happened between the ages of 40 and

55 may not be due to the dullness of those years but to the increased stability and routine nature of life during that period. In the sameness of life, one memory becomes merged with another and thus becomes less memorable. The period that seems inaccessible is before the age of four. While some psychoanalysts may contend that childhood repression of sexual desires accounts for this amnesia, another, more cognitive view is that these memories were not well integrated into a larger concept of personal history.

Cognitive Neuroscience Support

You might find it surprising that the memory system remains largely intact with participants without dementia. However, evidence from neuroimaging studies might provide a reason why. Roberto Cabeza (2002) of Duke University has developed the HAROLD model,

TABLE 12.1

PET/MRI Activity in Left and Right PFC in Younger and Older Adults

Imaging technique and materials or task	Younger		Older	
	Left	Right	Left	Right
Episodic Retrieval				
PET: Word-pair cued-recall (Cabeza, Grady, et al., 1997)	−	+ +	+	+
PET: Word-stem cued-recall (Backman et al., 1997)	−	+	+	+
PET: Word recognition (Madden, Gottlob, et al., 1999)	−	+	+ +	+ +
PET: Face recognition (Grady et al., 2002)	−	+ +	+	+
Episodic Encoding/Semantic Retrieval				
fMRI: Word-incidental (Stebbins et al., 2002)	+ +	+	+	+
fMRI: Word-intentional (Logan & Buckner, 2001)	+ +	+	+	+
fMRI: Word-incidental (Logan & Buckner, 2001)	+ +	+	+ +	+ +
Working Memory				
PET: Letter DR (Reuter-Lorenz et al., 2000)	+	−	+	+
PET: Location DR (Reuter-Lorenz et al., 2000)	−	+	+	+
PET: Number N-back: (Dixil et al., 2000)	+	+ + +	+ +	+ +
Perception				
PET: Face matching (Grady et al., 1994, Exp. 2)	−	+	+ +	+ +
PET: Face matching (Grady et al., 2000)	+	+ + +	+ +	+ +
Inhibitory Control				
fMRI: No-go trials (Nielson et al., 2002)	−	+	+	+

Note. Plus signs indicate significant activity in the left or right prefrontal cortex (PFC), and minus signs indicate nonsignificant activity. The number of pluses is an approximate index of the relative amount of activity in left and right PFC in each study, and it cannot be compared across studies. PET, positron emission tomography; fMRI, functional magnetic resonance imaging; DR, delayed response task; Exp., Experiment.

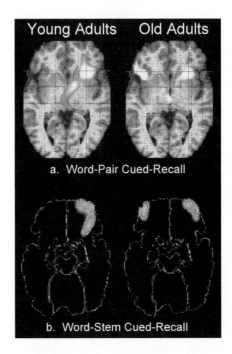

which stands for "hemispheric asymmetry reduction in older adults." We know from research on hemispheric asymmetry that each hemisphere tends to specialize in cognitive tasks, for example, the left hemisphere is typically specialized in language. Based on the HAROLD model it appears that as we grow older processing of tasks is conducted using both hemispheres (see table and figure) due to a reduction in hemispheric asymmetry. While it is not known exactly why this change in processing occurs, it is possible that either a change in cognitive processing strategies has occurred (psychogenic view) or that the actual neural mechanisms have actually undergone a change (neurogenic view).

Spotlight on Cognitive Neuroscience

Cognitive Development

Ross Thompson and Charles Nelson review the literature with regard to media accounts of children's development and the corresponding scientific evidence for those accounts. One particular area that they focus on is the importance of early experiences in brain development. It is known that a newborn's brain has many more synapses than an adult's brain. Furthermore, we know that the number of synapses rapidly decreases as we age. The idea is that various early experiences activate certain brain regions and synapses such that those activated synapses are some of the ones that disappear. This is a widely held belief, and although it has been empirically validated, they caution that more work is needed to understand the influence of genetics and early experiences on particular brain regions and when those experiences should occur for optimal effect (see also Figure 12.6).

Thompson, R. A., & Nelson, C. A. (2001). Developmental science and the media: Early brain development. *American Psychologist, 56*(1), 5–15.

A la carte

Reflections on the Age 60 Study

Back in the early 1990s Otto MacLin was putting his way through college working as a psychological technician at the Civil Aeromedical Institute in Oklahoma City, a branch of the Federal Aviation Administration (FAA). He and the other techs would assist the various researchers in their applied psychological research. For example, Dr. Dana Broach would conduct annual air traffic controller job satisfaction studies, which began after the once famous controller strike that President Ronald Reagan broke. Dr. Henry Mertens studied the perception of color, which was important in deciding what wavelengths to use in things such as landing lights and instrument gauges—it turned out Henry was color blind. Dr. Roni Prinzo studied pilot versus air traffic controller communications using some of the earliest voice recognition and voice synthesis technology at the time. But perhaps the most interesting and controversial was the Age 60 project Dr. Pam Della Rocco was working on in conjunction with Hilton Systems. Apparently, in response to an increasing number of airline pilots over the age of 60, in 1959 the FAA passed a mandatory rule that commercial pilots had to retire at age 60. Their rationale was that these pilots were experiencing ". . . progressive deterioration of both physiological and psychological functions which naturally occur with age . . . allowing these pilots to remain in command . . . would be a hazard to safety in air carrier operations" (FAA Press Release, 1959). Although there are those who speculate that the Age 60 rule was more political than safety related, it sent a strong message to America that when you reach 60 "it is all downhill." Theirs was a large project divided up between several research locations and organizations. Their part was to collect cognitive performance data and data using a 727 flight simulator from pilots above 60 and

Boeing 727 simulator.

below 60 years of age. They were surprised when the first batch of pilots arrived, as the pilots refused the coffee and Danishes offered to them for breakfast, instead indicating that they were very health conscious—so much for stereotypes. Physiological and demographic data were collected elsewhere along with information about how long they had been flying and if they were ever involved in an accident. In all, a tremendous amount of data was gathered and analyzed. The findings led to one basic conclusion that had nothing to do with health or cognitive ability. The main factor leading to poor performance was the amount of flying time the pilots had logged recently. It turns out, as with any skill, practice makes perfect, and continued practice maintains the skill. This finding has been bolstered in recent years by continued findings that "senility" does not have to be the norm for older adults. Keeping mentally, socially, and physically active maintains a healthy cognitive system.

Student Resource Center

STUDY GUIDE

1. Cognitive development concerns changes that occur in a more or less orderly fashion across the life span of individuals. It can be studied from the perspective of developmental psychology, neurocognitive development, and/or cognitive development.

2. One theory of cognitive development (Piaget) proposes that intellectual growth is biologically determined and governed by two processes: adaptation involving cognitive adjustments to the environment (assimilation and accommodation), and organization involving increasingly complex, integrated mental representations of operations. Cognitive development is characterized by quantitative, linear changes within a stage and qualitative changes across four major stages: sensorimotor, preoperational, concrete-operational, and formal-operational stages.

3. Another major theory of cognitive development (Vygotsky) rejects a strict biological determinism and proposes that learning precedes development. Thought and language are believed to originate independently, with thought being biologically determined whereas language is socially determined. Integration occurs when the child connects thought, language, and environmental events through naming activity.

4. Developmental cognitive neuroscience is based on the assumption that underlying all cognitive functions are neurological structures and processes.

5. The brain develops from simple to complex throughout the early life of an individual. It is subject to environmental stimulation and biological constraints.

6. Cerebral lateralization has been found among young children, which gives support to the biological nature of this phenomenon.

7. Cognitive development from an information-processing perspective concerns the question of changes in processes such as attention and memory as a function of increasing age.

8. Recent studies of twins suggest that genetics plays an important role in determining verbal and spatial ability in children.

9   Young children and infants have memory capacity, but it is doubtful that reliable memories are formed, or can be retrieved, before the age of two.

10 The age that the most memorable memories are formed is between 10 and 30.

11 Studies comparing higher-order cognition in children and adults show that children use story schemata in a manner analogous to adults. Adults rely more on semantic representations, whereas children rely more on perceptually based representations (i.e., imagery). Conceptual category formation may precede language acquisition with the basis of prototype formation in infants being feature-averaging.

12 Initial information acquisition requires perception of and attention to pertinent information. Research suggests that differences between younger and older subjects with respect to certain abilities, such as selective attention and the ability to respond to task demands, increase with age. Adults and older children use different encoding strategies (e.g., multiple vs. simple) relative to younger children, and these differences appear as early in the information-processing sequence as the sensory registers.

13 Prototype formation has been observed in very young infants and children.

Key Terms

accommodation	gerontology
adaptation	organization
assimilation	scheme
classification	schema
comprehension	senescence
conservation	seriation
functional validation	transitivity
geriatrics	

Starting Points

Books and Articles

Several books by or about Piaget are recommended. They include Piaget, *The Origins of Intelligence in Children;* "Piaget's Theory" in Mussen, ed., *Carmichael's Manual of Child Psychology;* and Piaget and Inhelder, *Memory and Intelligence.* Also see Flavell, *Cognitive Development* and *The Developmental Psychology of Jean Piaget;* and Brainerd, *Piaget's Theory of Intelligence.* Holmes and Morrison, *The Child,* is also recommended, as are P. Ornstein, ed., *Memory Development in Children;* Pick and Saltzman, eds., *Modes of Perceiving and Processing Information;* Siegler ed., *Children's Thinking: What Develops?* Daehler and Bukafko's text *Cognitive Development* is also recommended. Vygotsky's work is now generally available in English. Recommended are *Mind in Society* and *Thought and Language.* Several edited books on the information-processing approach to developmental psychology are also recommended. They include Sternberg, ed., *Mechanisms of Cognitive Development;* Flavell and Markman, eds., *Handbook of Child Psychology: Cognitive Development;* Sophian, ed., *Origins of Cognitive Skills;* and Moscovitch, ed., *Infant Memory.* Flavell's APA Award address, "The Development of Children's Knowledge about the Appearance-Reality Distinction," in *American Psychologist,* is also recommended. For infant memory see Rovee-Collier in A. Diamond, ed., *The Development and Neural Bases of Higher Cognitive Functions.* A somewhat technical, but worthwhile, collection of neurocognitive papers can be found in M. Johnson's *Brain Development and Cognition: A Reader.* Recent issues of journals devoted to developmental psychology are also recommended for current findings.

Movies

- Little Man Tate (1991)—Gifted Children
- Cocoon (1985)—Cognition and Aging
- On Golden Pond (1981)—Cognition and Aging

Search Terms

- Alzheimer's Nun Study
- Genius children
- Gerontology center
- Jean Piaget Society

Concept Formation, Logic, and Decision Making

hmmm. . .?

1. How do cognitive psychologists define "thinking," and how does thinking differ from concept formation? From logic?

2. Why is logic called the "science of thinking"?

3. What are the major components of a syllogism?

4. What is deductive reasoning, and how is it different from inductive reasoning?

5. How might a conversational argument be separated logically?

6. What are Venn diagrams? Take a basic argument and illustrate it in a Venn diagram.

7. What is a "decision frame," and how does it affect our ability to solve problems?

8. What is the gist of Bayes's theorem?

*M*any people would sooner die than think. In fact they do.

—*Bertrand Russell*

For some, cognitive psychology is all about thinking, and thus thinking can be thought of as the crown jewel of cognition. It is spectacularly brilliant, in some people; even sublime, among average folks; and, the fact that it happens at all, one of the great wonders of our species. In all reality, "thinking" is a loose term for information processing. With that said, thinking about thinking, what some call meta-thinking, may seem an insurmountable task, since it seems to engage all of the themes mentioned previously—the detection of external energy, neurophysiology, perception, memory, language, imagery, and the developing person. Advances in cognitive psychology, particularly within the last twenty years, have led to a formidable arsenal of research techniques and theoretical models capable of disclosing some of the facts about thought and casting them in a plausible framework of sound psychological theory. This chapter and the next are related because they are about the thought process and some of the means used to study this fundamental topic.

Thinking is a process by which a new mental representation is formed through the transformation of information by complex interaction of the mental attributes of judging, abstracting, reasoning, imagining, problem solving logic, concept formation, creativity, and intelligence.

There continues to be some dispute as to whether thinking is an internal process or exists only insofar as can be measured behaviorally. For example, a chess player may study his or her next move for several minutes before responding overtly. During the time the player is pondering what action to take, does thinking occur? It seems obvious that it does, and yet some would argue that because no overt behavior is observable, such a conclusion is based not on empirical observation but on speculation. A general definition of thinking might resolve some of the conflict and help guide our discussion. There are three basic ideas about thinking: (1) Thinking is cognitive—that is, it occurs "internally," in the mind—but is inferred from behavior. The chess player exhibits thinking in his or her move. (2) Thinking is a process that involves some manipulation of knowledge in the cognitive system. While the chess player is contemplating a move, past memories combine with present information to change his or her knowledge of the situation. (3) Thinking is directed and results in behavior that "solves" a problem or is directed toward a solution. The next chess move is, in the mind of the player, directed toward winning the game. Not all actions are successful, but generally, in the mind of the player, they are directed toward a solution.

Concept Formation

Concept formation refers to the discernment of the properties common to a class of objects or ideas. We have dealt with the topic of concept formation as it relates to visual forms and prototypes and semantic items in previous chapters. The greater part of our previous discussion specified the components or features of concepts and how concepts were structured in a semantic network. In this section the topic of features is also discussed, but we will concentrate on the rules that relate conceptual features. For example, we all have learned the concept *coffee cup* by identification of its classic properties (e.g., handle), that distinguish it from the other members of the general class of *ceramic cups,* or we have learned the properties of the more abstract concept *justice* (e.g., fairness, morality, equality) that distinguish it from other human qualities. In these instances the "rule" that relates the features to the concept is as follows: The concept is defined in terms of all the features and functions that have been associated with it.

Concept formation, as it is used in this chapter, is more limited in scope than thinking and is easy to study experimentally. It is not surprising, then, that there is a considerable body of knowledge about the laws and processes of concept formation. The early definition of *concept* was "mental images, ideas, or processes." This was normally disclosed through the experimental method of introspection, which was widely accepted as the principal technique of psychology. The decline of introspection as a method and the rise of behaviorism, especially in American psychology, brought about not only revolutionary methodological changes but also corresponding revolutionary changes in the view of the nature of cognitive events—and, consequently, in the definition of **concept**.

Concepts are defined in terms of their features. Features, as used here, are characteristics of an object or event that are also characteristic of other objects or events. Mobility, for example, is a feature of automobiles; Kias have it, Toyotas have it, and Lexus's have it. However, mobility is also a feature of other objects—marbles, birds, and even Legos (you can throw them, or build a car). From a cognitive viewpoint, the basis for accepting a characteristic as a feature is subjective. Thus, one can imagine automobiles, marbles, birds, and legos that do *not* share the feature of mobility, and so the determination of "critical features" of an object or idea is a function of the circumstances. In this sense, conceptual description is similar to the process involved in signal detection, in which acceptability as a feature of a concept is determined by the stringency of criteria. The setting of a criterion, is like setting a tolerance for how many features it needs to be considered to be part of a particular object class. We can build a car out of Legos, and we can throw them. At what point do they become part of an object class that includes the feature of mobility?

A distinction between features can be made on the quantitative basis as well as on the qualitative basis just described. Mobility is a qualitative feature that also can be measured quantitatively. Your Kia may have mobility (a qualitative statement) but may not have as much mobility as someone else's Lexus as measured by speed. Thus, both dimensional (quantitative) features and attributional (qualitative) features enter into conceptual formation; both kinds have been widely studied.

Association

The oldest and most influential theory in concept formation is the principle of association—also known as **associationism.** In its most succinct form, the principle holds that a bond will be formed between two events (or objects) as they are repeatedly presented together. Reinforcement, or a reward system, can facilitate formation of the bond. Thus, the association principle postulates that the learning of a concept is a result of (1) reinforcing the correct pairing of a stimulus (e.g., red boxes) with the response of identifying it as a concept, and (2) nonreinforcing (a form of punishment) the incorrect pairing of a stimulus (e.g., red circles) with a response of identifying it as a concept. (Such mechanistic viewpoints leave little room for the concept—prevalent among modern cognitive theorists—of internal structures that select, organize, and transform information.)

Hypothesis Testing

The general notion that people sometimes solve problems and form concepts by formulating and testing hypotheses has long been held in experimental psychology. The direct application of a hypothesis-testing model to concept formation by Bruner, Goodnow, and Austin (1956) in their influential book, *A Study of Thinking*, introduced a thorough methodological analysis of performance in concept formation.

The initial stage in concept formation is the selection of a hypothesis or a strategy that is consistent with the objectives of our inquiry. Whenever we seek to find out something, the process involves the establishment of priorities, much as a scientist may order a sequence of experiments, a lawyer may ask a series of questions, or a doctor may conduct a set of diagnostic tests.

The prime question is "What is to be gained by choosing one diagnosis as compared to another diagnosis?"

In a typical concept formation experiment, Bruner and his colleagues (1956) presented an entire concept universe (i.e., all possible variations on a number of dimensions and attributes) to participants and indicated one instance of an exemplar of the concept that the participants were to attain. The participants would pick one of the other instances, be told whether it was a positive or negative instance, then pick another instance, and so on until they attained the criterion (identified the concept).

The strategies participants may select in concept formation include scanning and focusing, each of which has its subtypes as follows:

Simultaneous scanning. Participants start with all possible hypotheses and eliminate the untenable ones.

Successive scanning. Participants begin with a single hypothesis, maintain it if successful, and, where it is unsuccessful, may change it to another that is based on all previous experience.

Conservative focusing. Participants formulate a hypothesis, select a positive instance of it as a focus, and then make a sequence of reformulations (each of

Jerome Bruner. His seminal work established "thinking" as a legitimate scientic topic.

which changes only one feature), noting each time which turns out to be positive and which negative.

Focus gambling is characterized by changing more than one feature at a time. Although the conservative-focusing technique is methodological and likely to lead to a valid concept, participants may opt for a gamble in the expectation that they may determine the concept more quickly.

Of the strategies described previously, conservative focusing tends to be the most effective (Bourne, 1963); scanning techniques give only marginal success. A difficulty with the Bruner model is that it assumes that participants hold to a single strategy, when, in actuality, some vacillate, shifting from strategy to strategy throughout the task.

Logic

Thinking refers to the general process of considering an issue in the mind, while **logic** is the science of thinking. Although two people may think about the same thing, their conclusions—both reached through thought—may differ, one being *logical,* the other *illogical.*

Try This

Thinking, Problem Solving, and "Frames"

Try to solve these problems (or present them to a friend and observe his or her behavior).

Each of the following cards has a letter on one side and a number on the other. If a card has a vowel on one side, then it has an even number on the other side. Which card(s) do you need to turn over to validate the rule?

Many years ago the post office had two rates for first- and second-class mail. The first-class rate was 29¢ if the letter was sealed and 25¢ if unsealed. Suppose that you are a postal clerk checking letters as they move across a conveyor belt and that you are charged with implementing the following rule: "If the letter is sealed, then it must have a 29¢ stamp." Of the following letters, which one(s) would you have to turn over to verify the rule?

Which of these two tasks was easier? Are the tasks similar? Identical? In the first case the problem was framed in more abstract terms than it was in the second, which was more realistic.

Adapted from Johnson-Laird & Wason (1977) and Johnson-Laird, Legrenzi, & Legrenzi (1992).

The solutions to the problems are at the end of this chapter.

In a recent newspaper interview of people on the street, a reporter asked, "Are you in favor of the death penalty?" One person gave the following answer: "I am religious and think that everyone has the right to life. The Bible says 'an eye for an eye,' and if someone does something to another person he should get what he deserves. Besides, it has been proved that some people have defective brains, which cannot be changed. Some things are worse than death, like rape." The person was in favor of the death penalty, although it is somewhat difficult to ascertain that conclusion given the reply. The conclusion (favoring the death penalty) seems to be in direct conflict with the opening statement, "I . . . think everyone has the right to life." Perhaps what the person really intended was "Even though people have a given right to life, if an individual violates certain laws of society, he or she should be executed." The justification for execution is supported by biblical teachings, good sense, medical truths, the relative severity of the punishment, and probably a high degree of emotional thought. In this case serious questions can be raised regarding the validity of the argument, but it is, nevertheless, a fairly typical representation of the way many people support a conclusion, which makes life both fascinating and frustrating.

Thinking and logic have been the subject of speculation for a long time. More than two thousand years ago, Aristotle introduced a system of reasoning or of validating arguments that is called the **syllogism.** A syllogism has three steps—a major premise, a minor premise, and a conclusion, in that order. Note the following example:

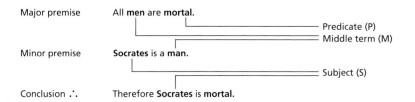

A conclusion reached by means of syllogistic reasoning is considered valid, or true, if the premises are accurate and the form is correct. It is, therefore, possible to use syllogistic logic for the validation of arguments. Illogical conclusions can be determined and their cause isolated. This is a succinct statement of the theoretical basis of much current research on thinking and logic.

Before introducing some of the current research, it is useful to review the laws of formal syllogistic logic. In the outline shown in Table 13.1 (Erickson, 1974) of the various forms of a syllogism, the predicate of the conclusion is labeled *P,* and the subject of the conclusion is labeled, *S.* The major premise links the predicate of the conclusion (*honest,* in the first example) with a middle term, *M* (*churchgoers*); the minor premise links the subject of the conclusion (*politicians*) with the middle term (*churchgoers*); and the conclusion links the subject (*politicians*) with the predicate of the conclusion (*honest*).

Each syllogism type can be designated on the basis of the kinds of sentences of which it is composed; thus, in the example, all of the sentences are of the universal affirmative type (*A*), and so the syllogism is of the AAA type.

The syllogistic figures shown in Table 13.1 are notations for mediation models, which are commonly used in the study of verbal learning. For example, Figure 1 (forward chain) in the example would have the following sequence: M–P, S–M, S–M. The total number

TABLE 13.1

Forms of a Syllogism

Basic Forms of a Syllogism		
Major Premise	All M are P	All churchgoers are honest.
Minor Premise	All S are M	All politicians are churchgoers
Conclusion	All S are P	Therefore all politicians are honest

Sentence Type Used in a Syllogism		
A	All S are P	All psychologists are wise	(universal affirmative)
E	No S are P	No poor research is published	(universal negative)
I	Some S are P	Some elected officials are truthful	(particular affirmative)
O	Some S are not P	Some professors are not rich	(particular negative)

Syllogistic Figures			
Figure 1 (Forward Chain)	Figure 2 (Stimulus Chain)	Figure 3 Response Equivalence)	Figure 4 (Backward Chain)
M–P	P–M	M–P	P–M
S–M	S–M	M–S	M–S
S–M	S–P	S–P	S–P

of syllogisms possible (a combination of types and figures) is 256, assuming each factor interacts with all other factors, of which only 24 are logical (6 for each figure).

An appealing feature of using syllogistic logic in cognitive research is that it makes it possible to evaluate, or validate, the correctness of the thought process on the basis of its form rather than its content. By using symbols (S and P) to represent the subject and predicate, it is possible to reduce logical thinking to a type of algebra. Instead of saying 8 apples plus 3 apples minus 2 apples yields 9 apples, we can mathematically represent the equation as $a + b - c = b^2$ or $a - c = b^2 - b$, without consideration of the referents designated by these symbols. Similarly, it is possible in syllogistic logic to reduce statements of fact to symbols and manipulate them, as in mathematical equations, without regard to the physical reality they may represent.

Deductive Reasoning

If Bill is taller than Jeff and Jeff is shorter than Ryan, then is Bill taller than Ryan? Take a moment and figure this out. Some people work out this problem (which, of course, has no definitive conclusion) by drawing little figures in which the relative height of the Bill, Jeff, and Ryan are depicted (also an example of how people can use verbal or visual processing).

Your conclusion was likely reached through a process of reasoning called **deductive reasoning,** which is the logical technique in which particular conclusions are drawn

*D*eduction

deduction.   1) In traditional LOGIC, the process of drawing, by reasoning, particular conclusions from more general principles assumed to be true. The Aristotelian SYLLOGISM is the classic example of deductive logic in the tradition.   2) In contemporary logic, any statement derived by a transformed rule upon an axiom; more generally, the term now refers to a process of deriving theorems from axioms, or conclusions from premises, by formal rules (transformation rules).

—*The Concise Columbia Encyclopedia*

from more general principles. Johnson-Laird (1995) has identified four contingencies in the scientific study of deductive logic.

1. *Relational inferences* based on the logical properties of such relations as *greater than, on the right of,* and *after.* (In the case of Bill et al. you had to use a "greater than" logic.)

2. *Propositional inferences* based on negation and on such connectives as *if, or,* and *and.* (For example, you might rephrase the preceding problem as "If Bill is taller . . .".)

3. *Syllogisms* based on pairs of premises that each contain a single qualifier, such as *all* or *some.* (In the next section we study syllogisms that have such qualifiers, such as, "All psychologists are brilliant; some psychologists wear glasses . . .".)

4. *Multiplying of quantified inferences* based on premises containing more than one qualifier, such as *Some French poodles are more expensive that any other type of dog.*

These four contingencies involved in decision making have been formalized by logicians into a type of predicate calculus (*viz.* that branch of symbolic logic that deals with relations between propositions and their internal structure—symbols are used to represent the subject and predicate of a proposition).

As an example of relational inferences and logic consider the following problem.

Suppose a friend of yours visits the Chicago Art Institute and tells you of his visit:
In one room there was a van Gogh (x), a Renoir (y), and a Degas (z).
The van Gogh painting was on the right of the Renoir.
The Degas was on the left of the Renoir.
Was the van Gogh on the right of the Degas?

A moment's thought will confirm that the answer is "yes". But how did you arrive at that answer, and what are the cognitive rules that describe your logic? One model by Johnson-Laird (1995), which may be generalized to other similar problems, follows.

For any x, y, if x is on the left of y, then y is on the right of x.
For any x, y, z, if x is on the right of y, and y is on the right of z, then x is on the right of z.

Consider another problem involving a more complex spatial relationship.

Problem A

The cup is on the right of the saucer.
The plate is on the left of the saucer.
The fork is in front of the plate.
The spoon is in front of the cup.
What is the relation between the fork and the spoon?

Try to solve this problem and the other problems in your head before looking at the figure. Now imagine changing just one thing (the saucer to cup in the second proposition); it changes the whole spatial configuration.

Problem B

The cup is on the right of the saucer.
The plate is on the left of the *cup.*
The fork is in front of the plate.
The spoon is in front of the cup.
What is the relation between the fork and the spoon?

What is your mental representation of this problem? There are at least two arrangements. Even though the answer is the same, this is a decidedly more difficult problem because both models must be constructed in order to test definitively the validity of the answer. One can see that the number of items one must hold in immediate memory nearly reaches the limit of short-term memory. Nevertheless, finding the underlying mathematical models that describe human logic is a worthy endeavor. These are simple little problems that nevertheless require careful attention and concentration to solve mentally.

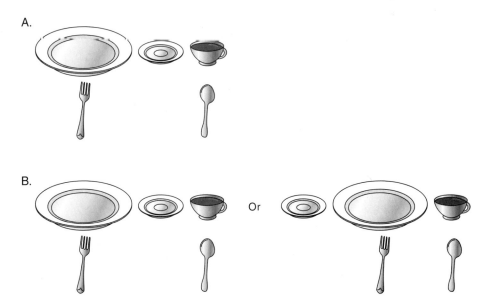

Syllogistic Reasoning

Early research studying syllogistic reasoning relied on reports by the participant of "what was going on in my head," also known as a talk-aloud procedure, when the participant verbalizes the steps they are engaging in when solving a problem. Although these introspective techniques lacked the empirical basis science requires, three important independent variables did emerge from them: the form of the argument, the content of the argument, and individual differences of the participants.

Form Early researchers (Chapman & Chapman, 1959; Sells, 1936; Woodworth & Sells, 1935) examined the errors produced in syllogistic reasoning tasks as a consequence of the "mood" or "atmosphere" created by the form of the argument, rather than on the basis of formal logical deduction. The most basic case might be:

> All *A* are *B*.
> All *C* are *B*.
> _____
> Therefore, all *A* are *C*.

Because this is in basic form, the conclusion is easy. However, when A, B, and C are substituted with words, they change the "mood" or "atmosphere". The obvious invalidity of the argument is evident if we substitute content for the letter abstractions. Thus:

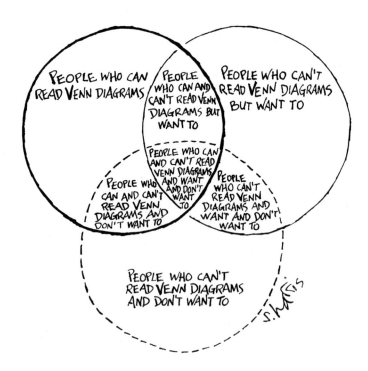

Copyright by S. Harris in *American Scientist* (Sep.–Oct. 1994), p. 420.

All Republicans are human.
All Democrats are human.
Therefore, all Republicans are Democrats.

While we don't know much about A and C, we know enough about Republicans and Democrats to know that they are categorically different. It's not simply a matter of substituting words for letters. The words have to have meaning to us. Consider the following syllogisms using some made-up words:

All revolutions are basically economic.
Some economic conditions cause hardships.
Some revolutions cause hardships.

Sam is not the best cook in the world.
The best cook in the world lives in Toronto.
Sam does not live in Toronto.

All nerts are soquerts.
All connets are strequos.
All connets are nerts.

One way to solve syllogisms is to draw diagrams called Venn diagrams, shown in Figure 13.1. The reason some were more difficult than others may be a function of your previous knowledge and your previous ability to recognize a logical argument when you see it. The first of these effects is called the atmosphere effect, discussed next, and the second is related to the validity of an argument that may be the result of formal training but is more likely the result of practice. Also, you may have learned that you need not know the definitions of terms to determine the content of an argument.

FIGURE 13.1

Diagrams in which all and some *A*'s are *B*'s and no or some *A*'s are *B*'s are represented.

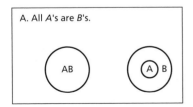

A. All *A*'s are *B*'s.

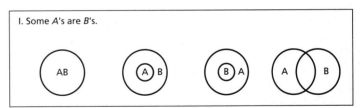

I. Some *A*'s are *B*'s.

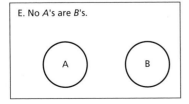

E. No *A*'s are *B*'s.

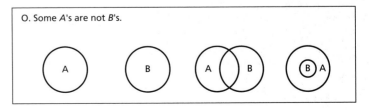

O. Some *A*'s are not *B*'s.

Atmosphere The **atmosphere effect** is defined as the tendency to accept or reject an argument on the basis of its form. In other words, merely presenting an argument in a certain way may influence its believability.

Johnson-Laird and his colleagues (Johnson-Laird & Byrne, 1989, 1991; Johnson-Laird & Steedman, 1978) have demonstrated that the form of a syllogism exhibits a strong influence on the conclusion drawn. Specifically, a syllogism of the following sort:

Some of the parents are scientists.
All of the scientists are drivers.

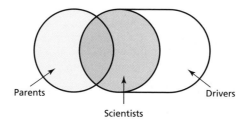

This tends to elicit the conclusion "Some of the parents are drivers" in preference to the equally valid conclusion "Some of the drivers are parents." In the symbolic language we have been using, an AB, BC syllogism favors an AC conclusion, while a BA, CB syllogism favors a CA conclusion. While these may look structurally the same, in fact the difference in pairings creates a different atmosphere, which leads to a different conclusion.

An interesting study was conducted by Clement and Fahmagne (1986) in which world knowledge and mental imagery were related to logical reasoning. Essentially, the experimenters varied the imagery value of the terms and the relatedness of conditional statements in syllogisms. From our discussion of mental imagery, you may recall that words differ with regard to their imagery values (e.g., *beggar* has higher imagery than *context*). **Relatedness** refers to how easily or naturally two actions form a relationship. An example of a statement used in a logical syllogism that is high in imagery might be "If the man wants plain doughnuts, then . . ." whereas a statement low in imagery might be "If the woman reorganizes the company structure, then . . ." High- and low-relatedness statements might include "If the man wants plain doughnuts, then he walks to the bakery across the intersection" and "If the man walks his golden retriever, then he gets

Phillip Johnson-Laird. Developed important models of human cognition and logic.

upset about his insect bite." All four possible combinations of statements were used in syllogistic problems (i.e., high imagery–high relatedness; high imagery–low relatedness; low imagery–high relatedness; and low imagery–low relatedness). Clement and Falmagne found that syllogisms in which the statements were high in imagery and relatedness were solved significantly better than other forms. That, given what we know about the powerful effects of both imagery and relatedness to form internal representations of reality and the above theoretical model of Johnson-Laird, seems to be a logical conclusion.

The usefulness of diagrams and imagery to solve problems in logic has been further demonstrated by Bauer and Johnson-Laird (1993) on complicated deductive logic problems of the following kind:

> Raphael is in Tacoma or Julia is in Atlanta, or both.
> Julia is in Atlanta or Paul is in Philadelphia, or both.

Is the following conclusion valid?

> Julia is in Atlanta, or both Raphael is in Tacoma and Paul is in Philadelphia.

If you are like most participants in the study, you found this difficult to validate. Now, try to visualize the problem with the assistance of the diagram in Figure 13.2. This diagram is a kind of road map in which the participant must travel from the left side to the right side by inserting the shapes (representing people) into the slots in the path (representing places). When a pathway is intact, travel can take place. Thus, if Julia is in Atlanta, traffic could flow through that area. Julia could be in Atlanta or Seattle or neither place. They (Bauer & Johnson-Laird, 1993) found that when problems of this sort were presented in diagram form, undergraduate students solved the problems faster and drew many more valid conclusions (about 30 percent more) than when the problems were presented verbally. The important conclusion we may draw from this experiment is that logically untrained people, such as most people are, tend to reason by building models of the situation or drawing diagrams that show relationships clearly.

The research on syllogisms has suggested that people tend to draw conclusions in syllogistic problems (and presumably in less formal ways of logical thinking as well) on the basis of first forming internal representations of the premises—sometimes imagined representations. Once these internal representations are formed, it is possible to apply logical thinking to them. If the representation (or heuristic) is biased toward verification (as "All artists are beekeepers"), then the logical test of the conclusion consists of trying to break the pathways between the premises and the conclusion.

Content   Since it is possible to hold the form of the argument constant while varying the content, the latter has also been a useful tool in the analysis of the thought process. Consider the following syllogism:

> All men are mortal.
> Socrates is a man.
> Therefore, Socrates is mortal.

may be evaluated by using the same form but different content:

> All men are moral.
> Hitler is a man.
> Therefore, Hitler is moral.

Look before you leap.

—*Samuel Butler*

If the premises of these syllogisms are true, then the conclusions are, even though one conclusion may be more difficult to accept than the other.

The effects of content on the judged validity of an argument remind us that the cognitive process is neither simple nor devoid of the considerable impact of knowledge stored in long-term memory. Throughout this book we have seen numerous examples of how that information influences (in many instances, to the degree of determining) the quality of the information perceived, encoded, stored, and transformed. It should not be surprising, then, that the judged validity of syllogistic statements about something we know may be a reflection of the content of the long-term memory.

The tendency to accept the conclusion of an invalid syllogism if the conclusion is consistent with the attitude of the judge was tested by Janis and Frick (1943). In their experiment, graduate students were asked to judge the soundness of arguments, with *soundness* defined as "a conclusion that logically follows from the premises." Some of the items used were as follows:

> Many brightly colored snakes are poisonous.
> The copperhead snake is not brightly colored.
> So the copperhead is not a poisonous snake.

FIGURE 13.2

Diagram representing a double disjunctive problem. Participants were asked to complete a path from the left side to the right side by inserting the shapes corresponding to people into the slots. Thus, Julia could be in Atlanta *or* Seattle but *not* both.

From Bauer and Johnson-Laird (1993).

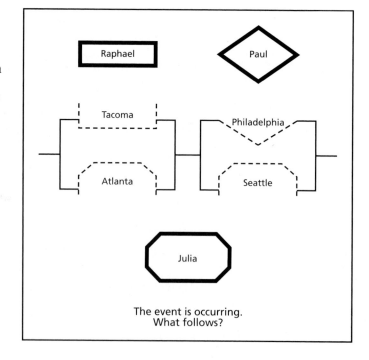

*D*on't confuse me with the facts; I've already made up my mind.

—*Unknown*

> There is no doubt that some drugs are poisonous.
> All brands of beer contain the drug alcohol.
> Therefore, some brands of beer are poisonous.
>
> All poisonous things are bitter.
> Arsenic is not bitter.
> Therefore, arsenic is not poisonous.

After the participants had agreed or disagreed with each of the syllogisms, they were asked to reread the conclusion and indicate whether they agreed or disagreed with it. The results indicated that participants' errors tended to be made in the direction of their bias concerning the conclusion.

There is more than one way to err in making a "logical" deduction. We will consider several.

Decision Making

Inductive Reasoning

Another form of reasoning is called **inductive reasoning.** In inductive reasoning a conclusion is usually expressed implicitly or explicitly in terms of a probability statement. In our everyday life we commonly make decisions not so much as a result of a well-reasoned syllogistic paradigm, but in terms of inductive reasoning, where decisions are based on past experiences and conclusions are based on what is perceived as the best choice of a number of possible alternatives. Consider the following statements:

*I*nduction

induction, in LOGIC, the process of reasoning from the particular to the general. Francis Bacon proposed induction as the logic of scientific discovery and DEDUCTION as the logic of argumentation. In fact, both processes are used together regularly in the empirical sciences: by the observation of particular events (induction) and from already known principles (deduction), new hypothetical principles are formulated and laws induced.

—*The Concise Columbia Encyclopedia*

If I work for one week, I will have enough money to go skiing.
I will work for one week.
Therefore, I will have enough money to go skiing.

The preceding argument is deductively valid. Now, suppose that the second statement was "I will not work at the library for one week." Then the conclusion "I will not have enough money to go skiing" is true given the constraints of syllogistic logic, but it is not necessarily true in real life. For example, your rich Uncle Harry might send you some money. Therefore, another form of decision making must be used. Evaluating the validity of a conclusion based on inductive reasoning may be based on considerations other than the structural form of an argument. In the case just mentioned, it could be based on the likelihood that Uncle Harry will send a gift of money or on other possibilities that some funds will come your way shortly.

An example of decision making based on inductive reasoning is one that you may have faced when you selected a college. Let us presume that you were accepted into four colleges—a large private university (A), a small private college (B), a medium-sized state university (C), and a large state university (D). How might you go about deciding which college to attend? One method would be to evaluate each of the choices in terms of their relative value on pertinent dimensions. The important dimensions might include (1) the quality of instruction, (2) cost, (3) proximity to home, (4) social opportunities, and (5) prestige. Each dimension will be assigned a value between 0 and 10.

	University A	College B	University C	University D
1. Instruction	9	7	6	7
2. Cost	2	3	9	7
3. Proximity	4	7	8	3
4. Social life	8	7	3	5
5. Prestige	9	10	3	4
Totals	32	34	29	26

If all of these factors are equally important in making your decision and if the values are accurately assigned, then the favored choice is a small, private college. A decision based on some organization of factors may be a practical way to solve a problem but as can easily be deduced from the example of choosing a college, definitive judgments of real problems are not so simple.

In many situations the nature of the problem is not compatible with mathematical analysis. Tversky (1972) suggests that in making decisions we select alternatives by gradually eliminating less attractive choices. He called this notion *elimination by aspects,* since the individual is thought to eliminate less attractive alternatives based on a sequential evaluation of the attributes, or aspects, of the alternatives. If some alternatives do not meet the minimum criterion, then those alternatives are eliminated from the choice set.

Decision Making in the "Real World"

If only the world were as reasonable as the rational logic of Socrates, you might lament, all of our problems would disappear. You have probably been in a heated argument with someone else and felt like saying, "Get real!" (By this, of course, you may actually mean to say "agree with me—never mind the logic and facts.") While not all arguments can be settled objectively, it is possible to parse verbal disagreements so that at least we can better analyze the components of a dispute.

Reasoning Dialogues   In the "real world" in which we all live, we commonly engage in conversations, which may include argumentation. One may make an assertion ("Professor, we would like to have a take-home final"); which is followed by a request for clarification ("Why is a take-home test better than an in-class test?"); which is followed by a justification ("Because in the 'real world' people have access to a variety of materials that will help them answer questions, such as the Internet, books, notes, and the like"); and finally by a refutation ("But, also in the 'real world' one is required to use stored knowledge to answer questions on the spot. We will have the final in class"). This scenario is typical of dozens of little arguments people engage in daily. What are the basic components of reasoning dialogues?

One way an argument may be parsed is to identify the underlying structural components as done by Rips and his colleagues (Rips, 1998; Rips, Brem, & Bailenson, 1999). Look at the two arguments shown in the box—the first from the O. J. Simpson trial and the other from two children.

Fortunately, many arguments are resolved amicably—some are not so smoothly settled. The components of argumentative dialogues consist of assertions, sometimes followed by concessions, requests for justification, or rebuttals; rebuttals can be followed by concessions or counterrebuttals; and so on. One way to illustrate the complexities of an argument is shown in the diagram in Figure 13.3.

In this figure we see that it is possible to nest arguments and subarguments into their logical components. For example, in the first case the initial claim by Mr. Kelly is met with a challenge, consisting of a justification query ("What is your foundation . . . ?") and that is followed by a paired justification ("She indicated to her mother . . . "). The researchers point out that "what is important in this example, though, is that the claim—the beginning of a new subargunment—can therefore be countered by a *rebutting defeater* (Pollock, 1998) from the judge ('The foundation is totally inadequate')." The same general analytic approach may be applied to the children's dialogue as well as most other "real-world" conversations.

Let us consider some other ways people fail in logical analysis.

The Fallacy of Reification   To *reify* an idea is to assume that it is real when, in fact, it may be hypothetical or metaphoric. For example, a student who was having difficulty completing his master's degree said to me, "This university does not want to give me a degree!" He assumed that the university acted as an individual would act, when, in truth, the university did no such thing. Possibly, his major advisor did not want to grant him a degree, perhaps for good reasons. People frequently reify ideas with such expressions as *the government, the newspapers, the unions, the Republicans, the Democrats, big business, mother nature,* and even *"they"* as in "ya know, they say . . . ."

Ad Hominem Arguments   **Ad hominem** arguments are those that attack a person's character rather than the substance of an argument. American politicians provide good examples. A candidate may present well-reasoned ideas but is rebutted, not for the ideas, but on the basis of his or her moral character (or how he or she dresses, or their latest haircut). Reviewers of professional matters—be they book reviewers, manuscript

FIGURE 13.3

A diagrammatic analysis of the dialogues presented in boxed feature "Cognition in Everyday Life: Argumentative Dialogues."

From Rips, Brem, and Bailenson (1999).

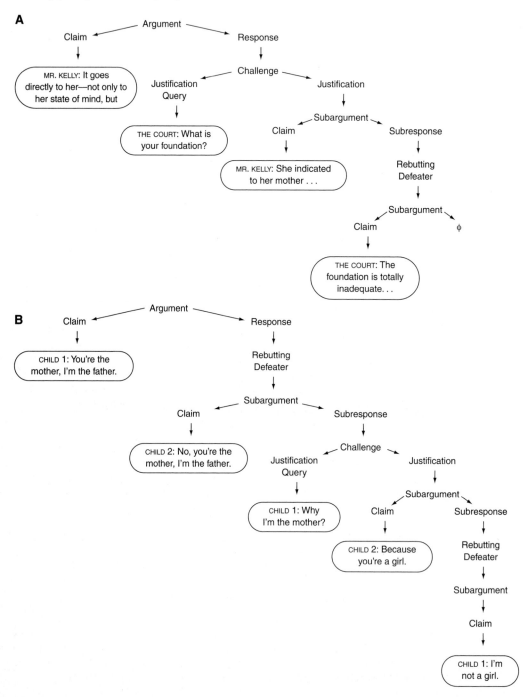

Cognition in Everyday Life

Argumentative Dialogues

Excerpt from CNN (1997)

MR. KELLY: Your Honor, this is four days before the murder; it [evidence about a book, *Battered Women,* that Nicole Simpson was reading] goes directly to her—not only her state of mind, but—

THE COURT: What is your foundation that she wrote these underlined—these things that you say she underlined?

MR. KELLY: She indicated to her mother, she was reading it and marking it up, and showed it to her mother, that she was doing it. At the same time, she said, "I've just started it; I'll give [it] to you afterwards."

And she can identify her handwriting.

THE COURT: I think under 352, the foundation is totally inadequate. I'm going to exclude it.

Dispute between two children (from Eisenberg & Garvey, 1981, p. 151)

CHILD 1: You're the mother, I'm the father.

CHILD 2: No, you're the mother, I'm the father.

CHILD 1: Why I'm the mother?

CHILD 2: Because you're—you're a girl.

CHILD 1: I'm not a girl.

reviewers, or judges of fellow professors for tenure or promotion—are admonished to avoid ad hominem arguments in their evaluations. Attack the idea, not the person—such advice is a good policy in everyday life.

Related to ad hominem arguments are those that are validated in terms of an individual's experience or knowledge of an individual's experience. These personal arguments seem to be pervasive among nonscientific thinkers as well as an alarming number of students. These occur when one instance is overweighted in the decision-making process. The gist of the validation of such an argument is that "it must be true because it happened to me . . . or to my great-uncle Oliver . . . or to my professor." Scientific progress is ill served by either type of argument.

Arguments That Appeal to Force and Power   An example of an appeal to power to validate an argument might be, "The United States was justified in entering the Vietnam War because we are a mighty and moral nation." Might and morality may be virtues, but they also may have nothing to do with treaties and a nation's right to sovereignty. Nevertheless, it is "human" to resort to such arguments.

Appeal to Authority and/or Fame   A common logical error is made by those who are impressed by authorities and/or famous people in one domain who make statements about another. This practice is common among advertisers who, in the United States especially, use athletes, movie stars, and singers to endorse products about which they often have virtually no special knowledge.

W*hat we have here is a failure to communicate.*

—*From the movie* Cool Hand Luke.

The Majority-Must-Be-Right Argument   Here the argument is that if most people do something, it must be right. "Everybody's doing it . . ." is the essence of the argument.

The Straw Man Argument   The straw man argument is to set up a weak argument and attribute it to someone else so that you can knock it down. A characteristic of the straw men argument is that a prominent (though largely unimportant) feature is isolated and emphasized, redirecting the main thrust of the argument. For example, two students were having an argument about global warming and during the argument one of the students used a straw men argument, referring to the fact that volcanoes have been producing emissions long before cars, and therefore cars aren't the problem and we shouldn't be worried about global warming.

Cognitive Neuroscience Support

The scientific study of the relationship between the brain on the one hand and reasoning and thinking on the other has traditionally been the domain of neurologists (who have concentrated on patients with a variety of neurological problems) and, only recently, cognitive neuropsychologists (who have concentrated on imaging studies with "normal" participants).

Neurologists have devised a series of diagnostic tests that may be administered as part of a neurological assessment. In one of these tests, called the Wisconsin Card Sorting Task, patients are asked to sort cards, one by one, by placing them under one of four target cards (see Figure 13.4). The task is similar to the concept-formation task described earlier in this chapter. The person is not informed as to the rules of sorting, whether sorting is to be on the basis of color, form, or number. He or she must discover the rules as determined by feedback from the person administering the test, who says "right" if the card is sorted by means of a predetermined rule or "wrong" if the card is incorrectly sorted by the same rules. After the person learns to sort by one rule, the game changes. Without her being informed, the sorting is governed by another set of rules.

This test is designed to see if the person can, first of all, find the initial rule of concept formation and, secondly, be flexible enough to abandon a previously reinforced rule

A concept formation task, such as the Wisconsin Card Sorting Task. A patient with damage to the lateral prefrontal cortex experiences difficulties. Here the patient places the top card of the deck next to one of four target cards. The experimenter says "correct" if the card is correctly placed and "wrong" if incorrectly placed. Through trial and error most normal partipants learn the sorting rule. The tricky part occurs after the participant has learned one sorting rule and then the rule changes.

correct

and find a new rule. Participants do pretty well on this task, and college students, for example, not only learn the first rule but are also flexible enough in their thinking to "change gears" and learn the second sorting law. However, patients with frontal lesions do not do well on this task. And those patients with bilateral frontal lesions have major problems, especially with the switched rule task. Frontal lesioned patients tend to perseverate, or continue to sort by the old rule of sorting. Perseveration is a common symptom of frontal lobe syndrome. This is but one example of the type of reasoning studies used to make a diagnosis with patients suspected of brain damage.

There is little question about the brain as the instrument of thought and reasoning. There are serious questions as to what parts of the brain are involved in the thought process and how the neuropsychology of thinking operates. To know how the brain acts when we are reasoning and thinking is a fundamental issue in current psychology that speaks to an age-old problem in philosophy, and that is that reasoning is exclusively verbal in nature. If, in solving the location of the fork and spoon problem presented earlier in this chapter, you relied on language to arrive at a conclusion, then we might (logically) expect the left hemisphere to be primarily involved and that right hemisphere activity would be minimal. Conversely, if you solved the problem by constructing models within a structural representation—in effect, used nonverbal techniques—in which you imaged the locations of items, then the left hemisphere would be only minimally involved and the right hemisphere would be primarily involved.

The neuropsychological data support this general conclusion, which also bolsters the theory that holds that nonverbal reasoning is a viable idea. In one study (Caramazza, Gordon, Zurif, & De Luca, 1976) patients with damage to their right hemispheres had difficulty in making inferences in simple deductive problems such as:

> John is taller than Bill.
> Who is shorter?

And they also performed more poorly when compared to normal controls on more complex problems such as:

> Arthur is taller than Bill.
> Bill is taller than Charles.
> Who is shortest?

In studies of conditioned reasoning, several researchers (see Whitaker, Savary, Markovits, Grou & Braun, 1991) have studied brain-damaged patients' problem-solving ability. One study examined two groups of patients who had undergone brain surgery (a unilateral anterior temporal lobectomy for the purpose of relieving epilepsy). One group had surgery on the right hemisphere and the other on the left hemisphere. Those with right-hemisphere lesions were poorer at reasoning in which false conditional premises were used than those with left-hemisphere damage. Consider the following conditional premise:

> If it rained the streets will be dry.
> It rained.

The group with right hemisphere damage had a tendency to conclude:

> The streets will be wet.

which, although true in the grand scheme of what we know about rain and wet streets, is nevertheless invalid, *given the premise.*

Thus, it appears that patients who have lost some functions of their right hemisphere are unable to deduce a correct answer of a logic problem that is based on a false premise. While the "location" of reason will be pursued for some time and it is likely that much more will be found out about the various cortical sights involved, these investigations may beg an even more meaningful question and that is "How is the thought process carried out?"

Decision Frames

A **decision frame** is, according to Tversky and Kahneman (1981), a decision maker's "conception of the acts, outcomes, and contingencies associated with a particular choice." A frame adopted by someone about to make a decision is controlled by the formulation of the problem as well as by the norms, habits, and personal characteristics of the individual. The researchers have clearly demonstrated how powerful a frame can be in determining the conclusion reached by individuals who are given essentially the same facts, but in different contexts. The effect of different frames is shown in the following example:

> Decision Frame 1: Imagine that the United States is preparing for the outbreak of an unusual Asian disease, which is expected to kill 600 people. Two alternative programs to combat the disease have been proposed. Assume that the exact scientific estimates of the consequences of the programs are as follows:
> If Program A is adopted, 200 people will be saved.
> If Program B is adopted, there is a one-third probability that 600 people will be saved and a two-thirds probability that no people will be saved.
> Which of the two programs would you favor?

Given the choice in this problem, the majority of participants selected Program A (72 percent), while only 28 percent chose Program B. The prospect of saving 200 lives is more attractive than the more risky alternative. Statistically, however, the alternatives will save the same number of lives.

Another group of participants was given this reformulated version of the same problem:

> Decision Frame 2: Remember, if Program A is adopted, 200 people will be saved. If Program C is adopted, there is a one-third probability that nobody will die, and a two-thirds probability that 600 people will die.
> Which of the two programs would you favor?

In this frame the majority chose the risk-taking procedure: the certain death of 400 people is less acceptable than the two-in-three chance that 600 will die. These problems illustrate how the influence of the framing of a question, even though the probabilities are identical, leads to different choices. In general, choices involving gains are frequently seen as risk aversive, whereas choices involving losses are perceived as risk taking.

Yet another example of framing, which is perhaps a more realistic problem than the one just discussed, is the following:

How Rational Are Your Decisions?

Give your best estimates to the following questions:

1. Billy, a tall, slender, nonathletic 36-year-old, has been described by a neighbor as being somewhat shy, intellectual, and withdrawn. He is helpful, tidy, and has a need for order and structure. Is it more likely that Billy is a salesperson or a librarian?
2. Suppose you are in Las Vegas on a gambling junket. (A) Last night you won $1,000 on a hot slot machine. Will you bet more tomorrow than you usually do? (B) Last night you dis-

covered you have $1,000 more in your savings account than you thought. Will you bet more tomorrow than you usually do?
3. (A) You go into a store to buy a portable CD player. It costs $50. You notice an ad for the same item at a store ten blocks away that costs only $25—such a deal! (B) You go into a store to buy a computer that costs $2,545. The same computer can be bought at a store ten blocks away for $2,520. Do you bother to go to the other store?

The solutions are at the end of this chapter.

> Decision Frame 3: Imagine that you have decided to see a play for which admission is $10 per ticket. As you enter the theater, you discover that you have lost a $10 bill. Would you still pay $10 for a ticket for the play?

Those who answered affirmatively amounted to 88 percent.

> Decision Frame 4: Imagine that you have decided to see a play and paid the admission price of $10 per ticket. As you enter the theater, you discover that you have lost the ticket. The seat was not marked, and the ticket cannot be recovered. Would you pay $10 for another ticket?

Those who answered yes to this reformulated version amounted to 46 percent. In both instances you are out $10. However, in the first instance, about twice as many people confronted with this problem would buy a ticket as those confronted with a similar condition in which the amount of money lost is identical.

Estimating Probabilities

Whether or not we recognize it, most decisions are related to an estimate of the probability of success. We plan a picnic when we think the sun will shine, we enroll in a course in cognitive psychology expecting certain rewards, we decide to stand with a card count of fourteen when a blackjack dealer shows a six as his or her "up card," we carry an umbrella when we see clouds in the sky, or we postpone a driving trip because we think it is going to snow. In some instances the probability of an event may be calculated on the basis of mathematics, while other events may be determined only by our previous experience. It is likely that we think we are acting rationally in these conditions since our decisions are based roughly on mathematical probabilities, but how accurate are our estimates? Or, in other words, how can we act so stupidly when we think we are acting so rationally? The next section might shed some light on the question.

Amos Tversky, **left (1935–1996), and** Daniel Kahneman. Identified strategies people use in solving common problems.

In a series of studies, Tversky and Kahneman (Kahneman, 1973; Tversky & Kahneman, 1981; Kahneman & Miller, 1986; Kahneman & Tversky, 1983, 1984; Tversky & Kahneman, 1981) have examined the way people sometimes arrive at a poor conclusion when their decisions are based on past experience. In one experiment (1974) they asked questions such as the following:

> Are there more words in the English language that start with the letter *K* or that have a *K* as their third letter?
> Which is the more likely cause of death—breast cancer or diabetes?
> If a family has three boys (B) and three girls (G), which sequence of births is more likely—BBBGGG or BGGBGB?

All the preceding questions have factual answers, and yet people's intuition or guesstimates are generally wrong. For example, when asked about the occurrence of the letter *K,* more people said that it more frequently started a word than was located in the third position, contrary to actual data. Why do people misjudge these events? According to Tversky and Kahneman, when confronted with this question, people try to generate words that start with the letter *K* and then try to think of words with *K* in the third position. If you try this yourself, you will see why people err in this problem. We tend to overestimate the frequencies of initial letters because the words they generate are more available than are words with that same letter in the third position. This is referred to as the **availability heuristic.** It seems that estimates of letter probabilities are derived from a generalization based on a very limited sample of available words that can be generated.

This basic idea was tested in an experiment by Tversky and Kahneman (1973) in which participants were asked to read a list of thirty-nine names of well-known people. One list contained about the same number of men as women (nineteen men and twenty women), but the women were more famous than the men. Another list reversed these conditions; the men were more famous than the women. Then the participants were asked whether the list contained more men or women. In both instances the participants greatly overestimated the frequency of the gender that was more famous. The reason for this behavior, despite the fact that the frequencies were nearly identical, was that the names of the famous people were more available.

Other researchers have used the availability heuristic to account for errors in the estimate of "everyday" knowledge. In one study Slovic, Fischhoff, and Lichtenstein (1977) asked people to estimate the relative probability of forty-one causes of death. Participants were given two causes of death and asked to judge which was more likely to cause death. The most seriously misjudged choices were causes of death that were well publicized. For example, accidents, cancer, botulism, and tornadoes were judged to be frequent causes of death. The authors reasoned that because these lethal events receive wide media coverage, they were more available than less publicized causes of death such as heart disease and stroke.

Representiveness Heuristic

Estimates of the probability of an event are influenced not only by the availability of the event but also by how representative an event is estimated to be in terms of how similar it is to the essential properties of its population. Consider this example of the **representiveness heuristic** from a study by Kahneman and Tversky (1972):

On each round of a game, twenty marbles are distributed at random among five children: Alan, Ben, Carl, Dan, and Ed. Consider the following distributions:

I		II	
Alan	4	Alan	4
Ben	4	Ben	4
Carl	5	Carl	4
Dan	4	Dan	4
Ed	3	Ed	4

In many rounds of the game, will there be more results of Type I or Type II?

What is your answer? If you selected Type I, your answer is consistent with the majority of participants in this experiment and is, of course, wrong. When participants read the word *random,* they apparently formed the impression that the distribution would be somewhat chaotic or helter-skelter, and when asked to evaluate Types I and II, they thought that the second distribution was too orderly to be random. The same type of error was observed in the sequence of boy and girl birth patterns mentioned earlier.

Another somewhat disturbing finding was that people tend to ignore sample size when estimating probabilities. For example, when asked whether finding 600 boys in a sample of 1,000 children was as likely as finding 60 boys in a sample of 100 children, participants reported that both samples were equally likely. In fact (if one assumes an equal distribution of the sexes), the first statistic is far less likely than the second.

Bayes's Theorem and Decision Making

We have seen that people may revise their probability estimates when new or different information is presented. When confronted with an equally attractive choice of going to a concert or a movie, we may make a decision tipped in favor of the movie if we learn that the only concert tickets available cost $35. A mathematical model that provides a method for evaluating hypotheses of changing probabilistic values is called **Bayes's theorem** after its author, Thomas Bayes, an eighteenth-century mathematician. Use of this theorem is illustrated in the following decision-making scenario.

Suppose that a long, romantic, and emotional relationship between you and a lover ended in a terrible fight in which you vowed never to see the person again. Several months pass during which you avoid situations in which you might accidentally see your ex. A mutual friend asks you to a large party. Your decision to go or not to go is based on the perceived probability that your ex will be in attendance. After considering the situation, you conclude that the mutual friend would probably not be so insensitive as to invite both of you. Furthermore, given past experience with similar situations, you might estimate that the probability of a chance encounter would be about 1 in 20. The hypothesis then could be stated mathematically where P equals the probability and H equals the hypothesis:

P(H) = 1/20 or 5%

The equation is read as "the probability of the hypothesis is equal to 5 percent (or 5 in 100)." The hypothesis is based on prior probabilities, that is, the possibility the event will occur given prior similar circumstances. An alternative hypothesis can also be stated, which is the probability that your lover will not be at the party. It may be stated as follows:

P($\sim$H) = 19/20 or 95%

This equation is read as "the probability of the hypothesis not occurring is 95 percent."

If real situations could be reduced to such probabilistic statements, life would be simple and boring. You could weigh the possibilities of an undesirable confrontation against the pleasure of going to a party and then make your decision. In this case, let's say you decide to go to the party. As you approach the house, you notice a yellow Volkswagen parked in the driveway. In a few seconds you calculate the probability that the owner of the car is your ex (which would further suggest that the person is at the party) and weigh that new information with the previous information about the probability that the host has invited the two of you to the same party. This situation is called a **conditional probability**—the probability that new information is true if a particular hypothesis is true. In this case, presume that the likelihood that the car belongs to your ex is 90 percent (the other 10 percent could be attributed to several factors, including the possibility that the car was sold to someone else, the car was loaned to someone else, or this was only a similar car). According to Bayes's theorem, the combined probabilities (1/20 the

Thomas Bayes **(1701–1761).** Born into an affluent family, Bayes studied logic and theology at Edinburgh and wrote only two scholarly papers, published after his death. His "theorem" published in 1763 has become increasingly popular and has been applied to psychology and sociology.

Cognition in Everyday Life

The Fido Caper

Suppose that you left your dog Fido at home to guard your house so that burglars would not break in and steal the 10-pound roast that is defrosting on the counter. When you get back, the locks are all in good order, so you know that no burglar has entered. However, the roast is gone. Needless to say, Fido is a prime suspect.

On the basis of past experience, two sessions with the dog psychiatrist, and a certain shifty look in his eye, you judge the probability is 0.95 that Fido did it. However, before convicting Fido, you decide to collect one more piece of evidence. You prepare his ordinary dinner and offer it to him. To your surprise, he gobbles it up to the last crumb. Hardly what you would expect of the thief who just made a 10-pound roast

disappear. You estimate that the probability that Fido would do this if he had in fact eaten the roast is only 0.02. Normally, though, he has a good appetite and eats his dinner with a probability of 0.99. How are you to revise your earlier suspicions given the evidence of the readily eaten dinner? Clearly, Bayes's theorem can come to the rescue. Given that he just ate his dinner, the probability that Fido is guilty may be expressed as follows:

$P(Guilty|E) =$

$$\frac{P(E|\text{Guilty}) \times P(\text{Guilty})}{P(E|\text{Guilty}) \times (\text{Guilty}) + P(E|\text{Innocent}) \times P(\text{Innocent})}$$

From the story, we know that
$$P(\text{Guilty}) = 0.95$$
$$P(\text{Innocent}) = 0.05$$
$$P(E|\text{Guilty}) = 0.02$$
$$P(E|\text{Innocent}) = 0.99$$

Therefore,
$$
\begin{aligned}
P(\text{Guilty}|E) &= \frac{(0.02)(0.95)}{(0.02)(0.95) + (0.99)(0.05)} \\
&= \frac{0.0190}{0.0190 + 0.0495} \\
&= \frac{0.0190}{0.0685} \\
&= 0.28
\end{aligned}
$$

Things looked very bad for Fido before the dinner experiment. However, with the aid of Bayes's theorem, we were able to take the results of the dinner experiment into account and conclude that Fido was probably innocent. Anyone who loves dogs can see the value of Bayes's theorem.

person was invited plus 9/10 that the car indicated the person was present) can be expressed in the following formula:

$$P(H|E) = \frac{P(E|H) \times (H)}{P(E|H) \times (H) + P(E|\overline{H}) \times P(\overline{H})}$$

where $P(H|E)$ is the probability of the hypothesis (H) given the evidence in E, or, in our case, the probability your ex would be at the party given the initial low probability and the recent new evidence. $P(E \mid H)$ represents the probability that E is true given H (for example, the probability that the car belongs to your ex). $P(H)$ is the probability of the initial hypothesis, and the terms $P(E \mid H)$ and $P(H)$ represent the probability the event will not occur. $P(E|H) = 90$ percent, $P(H) = 5$ percent, $P(E|\overline{H}) = 10$ percent, $P(\overline{H}) = 95$ percent. By substituting these values into the formula, we can solve for $P(H \mid E)$.

$$P(H \mid E) = \frac{0.9 \times 0.05}{(0.9 \times 0.05) + (0.1 \times 0.95)} = 0.32$$

Thus, according to this model the chances of an unhappy encounter at the party is about 1 in 3. Given these odds, you now can make a studied decision on the basis of how aversive such a meeting might be versus how pleasurable the party might be.

How closely does Bayes's theorem coincide with real life? It is highly unlikely that if you found yourself in the above circumstance, you would whip out your pocket calculator and determine the value of $P(H|E)$.

Some evidence gathered by Edwards (1968) suggests that we tend to judge conditional probability circumstances more conservatively than Bayes's theorem suggests. In one study of the influence of new information on participants' estimates of probabilities, Edwards gave college students two bags that contained 100 poker chips. One bag had 70 red chips and 30 blue chips, and the other bag had 30 red chips and 70 blue chips. One bag was selected at random, and the participants were to determine which bag it was on the basis of drawing out one chip at a time, examining it, returning it to the bag, and then continuing the process. Initially, the probability of drawing a red chip from the mostly red-chip bag would be 70 percent, or from the mostly blue-chip bag, 30 percent. However, if we draw only one chip from one of the bags and it is red, then the probability, according to the theorem, that the composition of the bag is predominantly red is 70 percent. People tend to underestimate the real (mathematical) significance of that observation and guess the content of the bag to be predominantly red with a value of 60 percent. If the second chip is also red, the real probability of the bag being predominantly red is 84 percent. Participants' judgments tend to be conservative in this case as well as with larger samples.

The application of Bayes's theorem to real-world tasks poses special problems because an accurate estimate of the probabilities of events is difficult to ascertain.

Interest in Bayesian methods has increased over the past few years (Malakoff, 1999). One reason for the increased number of papers is the ubiquitous presence of desktop computers and the development of new algorithms. Some have used the simulation techniques known as Markov Chain Monte Carlo (MCMC to insiders) that use Bayesian mathematics to use prior knowledge to predict everything from nuclear magnetic resonance to who might be a likely suspect in a crime scene. The latter use has been questioned on the basis of "racial profiling."

Decision Making and Rationality

To some, this chapter may seem to have initially represented the human animal as the most rational of creatures. Our discussion of concept formation, after all, showed that all normal beings form concepts using rational rules. In the discussion of syllogistic rea-

A la carte

Are Prisoners Expert Liars?

Some researchers have argued that language evolved due to environmental pressures related to social needs. Language is therefore highly social. In social situations it is sometimes common to tell lies, such as saying, "That is a lovely sweater you are wearing," when in fact it is not. These are acceptable because they facilitate social interaction. Other lies are told for the sake of deception and can be problematic, for example, a person lying to a friend or spouse about where they were last night (and who they were with for that matter). Psychologists are curious to find out how well humans are able to decide whether or not another person is lying. Before they can do this they must determine if there is a discriminable difference between a lie and a truth. Does a lie sound different? Is the surface structure of a lie different than a truth? Do people use more details when lying compared to telling the truth? Studies involving lying might require participants to argue a side to a controversial issue, such as abortion or the war in the Middle East, contrary to their own personal beliefs. Researchers can then use computer programs to break down the statements to analyze their content. Researchers have speculated a greater number of self-referencing; whereas others have found that liars use more negative words and motion related words than those telling the truth

(Newman et al., 2003). The problem we have as humans involves the base rate in which one might expect another to lie. In other words, we don't expect the person at the supermarket to lie to us about the daily specials or our coworker to lie about her son's wedding. On the other hand, we expect a fisherman to exaggerate about the size of the fish he caught, and we expect a prisoner in jail to lie more often, although this may or may not be the case. It might also be suspected that prisoners are more expert at lying and thus more able to detect lies compared to other liars. Gary Bond and Adrienne Lee (2005) of New Mexico State University had prisoners record three lies and three truthful statements. These statements were presented to a second group of prisoners to determine whether the statements were true or not. The researchers also used a computerized system that analyzed the content of the statements to see if the computer program was more accurate than the prisoner. They found that the younger prisoners were more accurate than the computer; however, the computer outperformed older prisoners. The researchers attribute the differences to the prisoners' ability to use context and base rate when evaluating the statements, something the computer is not programmed to do.

soning, we learned that the validity of an argument could be determined by the rules of logic, even if we tend to be fooled by either the structure or the content of a faulty argument. Finally, in the preceding section on decision making, we learned that the "rational" human race is commonly irrational when it comes to making a decision about a large class of events.

We think it would be foolish to argue that all people are as rational as we fashion ourselves, but are we, as a species, as irrational as one might conclude, given the empirical results gathered on decision-making tasks?

The findings of Tversky and Kahneman as well as studies of syllogistic reasoning, when carefully examined, suggest that human beings are less than perfectly rational creatures. Some have objected to these findings on the basis of experimental design and the inevitable philosophic conclusion forced by these experiments. One such critic is L. J. Cohen (1981), of Oxford University, who argues that (1) rationality should be determined by the common people, not in contrived laboratory experiments that are not really designed to illustrate everyday decision making and are largely irrelevant to real performance, (2) it is unreasonable to expect ordinary people to be sophisticated in the laws of probability and statistics that establish the baselines and points of deviation in many of the experiments, and (3) the laws of logic and rationality are not relevant to day-to-day human behavior. Take the case of the unfortunate individual who tried to avoid their ex. Using Bayes's theorem, the probability of the encounter, if the person to be avoided went to the party, was 0.32. How does that number bear on the behavior of the individual doing the avoiding? If the enmity between the pair is great ("I wouldn't go within 100 miles of him/her"), the figure is meaningless insofar as predicting behavior is concerned.

Spotlight on Cognitive Neuroscience

Decision Making

Monique Ernst and her colleagues argue that decision making is integral to behavior and that exploring the corresponding brain activity can aid in understanding when decision-making behaviors are maladaptive. To study this they had participants play a computerized gambling card game while in a PET scanner. They had to evaluate rewards and losses, which comprised the risk-taking component of the study. Research participants played two rounds of the gambling card game where they were active in deciding which decks to choose from based on loss and win information (in terms of dollar amounts). By the second round, participants had figured out that two of the four decks yielded larger gains. Another group of participants formed a control group where they played the same game but had no decisions to make (the decks from which they chose cards were chosen for them). They found that brain activity in the orbital and dorsolateral prefrontal cortex, anterior cingulated, insula, inferior parietal cortex, thalamus (right side), and cerebellum (left side) accompanied uninformed decision making (the first round). Guessing demonstrated activity in the sensorimotor associative areas and amygdala (left side). Informed decision making (data from the second round) activated memory areas such as the hippocampus, posterior cingulated, and motor control areas such as the striatum and cerebellum.

Ernst, M., Bolla, K., Mouratidis, M., Contoreggi, C., Matochik, J. A., Kurian, V., Cadet, J. L., Kimes, A. S., & London, E. D. (2002). Decision making in a risk-taking task: A PET study. *Neuropsychopharmacology*, *26*(5), 682–691.

Student Resource Center

Sᴛᴜᴅʏ Gᴜɪᴅᴇ

1   Thinking is an internal process in which information is transformed; thinking may be directed and lead to problem solving and, at the structural level, results in the formation of a new mental representation.

2   Concept formation involves discerning features common to a class of objects and discovering rules that relate those conceptual features. Cognitive activities believed important to the process include rule learning, association, and hypothesis testing.

3   Strategies for formulating and testing hypotheses during concept formation include scanning and focusing procedures, with focusing techniques (similar to scientific procedures) being more effective than scanning strategies.

4   Studies of deductive reasoning indicate that conclusions to syllogistic problems are affected by the form of presentation (visual vs. verbal), the number of alternatives generated by premises, the argument form (e.g., positive vs. negative), long-term knowledge relative to the problem presented, and the problem solver's level of intelligence and education.

5   Inductive reasoning results in conclusions often expressed in probability statements and corresponds more to everyday decision making than does syllogistic or deductive reasoning.

6   Studies of decision making show that problem solutions are influenced by memory factors (the availability hypothesis), reference frames that affect problem formulation, failure to consider how similar an event is to its population, and underestimating the mathematical significance of a possible event.

KEY TERMS

ad hominem
associationism
atmosphere effect
availability heuristic
Bayes's theorem
concept
concept formation
conditional probability
conservative focusing
decision frame
deductive reasoning

focus gambling
inductive reasoning
logic
relatedness
representiveness heuristic
simultaneous scanning
successive scanning
syllogism
thinking
verbal dialogues

STARTING POINTS

Books and Articles

● The number of books and articles dealing with thinking, problem solving, and decision making has increased sharply during the last decade. For more specialized reading, try Maxwell, *Thinking: The Expanding Frontier;* Gardner, *The Mind's New Science;* and Rubenstein, *Tools for Thinking and Problem Solving.* For decision making in the world context, read Janis and Mann, *Decision Making;* Valenta and Potter, eds., *Soviet Decision Making for National Security;* and Brams has an article called "Theory of Moves" in *American Scientist* that discusses game theory in international conflict situations. Johnson-Laird's chapter "Mental Models, Deductive Reasoning, and the Brain" in Gazzaniga's volume (1995) is excellent.

● Within the past few years several fine books in this field have been published. These books are well written, interesting, and contain a wealth of information about thinking and related topics. These include *Mental Models: Towards a Cognitive Science of Language, Inference, and Consciousness,* by one of the main researchers in the field, Johnson-Laird; and *Deduction* also by Johnson-Laird and Byrne. You might also try a stimulating book by John Hayes, *The Complete Problem Solver* (2nd ed.); and one of our favorite and highly recommended books, Marvin Levine's *Effective Problem Solving* (2nd ed.).

Movies

- 12 Angry Men (1957)—Group decision making
- The Bone Collector (1999)—Deductive reasoning
- The Miracle Worker (1962)—Concept formation

Search Terms

- Do we fear the right things
- Changing minds
- Categorical ayllogisms
- Silly Syllogisims

Answer to Try This! Thinking, Problem Solving, and "Frames"

Most people answer the first problem by inferring "A only" or "A and 4." The correct answer is "A and 7." If A does not have an even number on the other side, the rule is false, and if 7 has a vowel on the other side, the rule is false. In the second problem the answer is the first (sealed) envelope and the last, the envelope with the 25¢ stamp on it. More than 90 percent of participants solve the realistic (envelope stamp) problem, and yet only about 30 percent solve the abstract (card-letter) problem.

Answers to Try This! How Rational Are Your Decisions?

Problem 1: If you are like most people, you guessed that Billy is a librarian—in fact, about two out of three people make that judgment in a similar problem. However, if we look at the statistics regarding the likelihood of professions, there are more than 14 million salespeople in America and fewer than 200,000 librarians. On the basis of statistics alone, Billy is 75 times more likely to be a salesperson. Even if one factors into the conclusion the descriptive material, the probability of Billy's being in sales is higher than his being in books.

Problem 2: Most people say they would be more likely to blow the easy money won on the slot machine than the newly discovered hard money in the bank account, yet in both instances you are ahead by the same amount.

Problem 3: In the first instance, about three out of four people opt to go down the street to buy the cassette/radio for half price, yet only one in five would do the same for the computer. However, in both instances, the saving is $25. Is such action justified in the first case but not the second?

Problem Solving, Creativity, and Human Intelligence

hmmm . . . ?

1. How has the topic of problem solving been studied in the past?

2. Why is the way a problem is represented so important?

3. Think of some people you consider to be creative. What are the features that define creativity in them?

4. How does functional fixity make creative solutions difficult?

5. How do you define intelligence? How do cognitive psychologists define intelligence?

6. What recent experiments in genetics portend a new way of looking at intelligence?

*A*ll the really good ideas I ever had came to me while I was milking a cow.

—*Grant Wood*

In this chapter we present theories and data on three topics considered to be higher cognitive processes; they are problem solving, creativity, and human intelligence. These topics have been investigated by researchers interested in how each fits into the grand scheme of human cognition: they have also caused the philosopher and poet to wax eloquent. Interest in problem solving, creativity, and intelligence can be found among the nitty-gritty, pragmatic types who enjoy mundane topics such as: How do I get from my house to work in the shortest time with the least annoyance? Can I invent a device that will keep cinnamon rolls warm from the time they are baked until they are served? Why does my daughter write better computer programs than English essays?

Problem Solving

Problem solving permeates every corner of human activity and is a common denominator of widely disparate fields—the sciences; law; education; business; sports; medicine; industry; literature; and, as if there weren't enough problem-solving activity in our professional and vocational lives, many forms of recreation. Humans, apes, and many other mammals are curious types who, for reasons seemingly related to survival, seek stimulation and resolve conflict through a lifetime of creative, intelligent problem solving.

A good share of early problem-solving experiments addressed the question: What does a person do when he or she solves a problem? Although this descriptive approach helped define the phenomenon, it did little to enhance our understanding of the cognitive structures and processes involved in problem solving.

Problem solving is thinking that is directed toward the solving of a specific problem that involves both the formation of responses and the selection among possible responses. We encounter an untold number of problems in our daily lives that cause us to form response strategies, to select potential responses, and to test responses in solving a problem. For example, try to solve this problem: A dog has a 6-foot rope tied to its neck, and a pan of water is 10 feet away. How would the dog reach the pan? The solution to this problem involves the generation of possible responses (of which there are few), the selection and trial of them, and perhaps the discovery of the trick in the problem.[1]

Gestalt Psychology and Problem Solving

Although Gestalt psychology is particularly known for its theories of perceptual organization, it is also known for insight into problem solving. *Gestalt* is roughly translatable as "configuration" or "organized whole." The perspective of Gestalt psychologists is con-

[1]The dog would walk to it. The rope was tied to its neck.

McGuffin's Problem

"Paul McGuffin was born in 1986 in St. Louis. His father was Irish, his mother Native American. Fifty-two years later, he dies while playing chess with Albert Einstein in Nebraska. However, he dies in 1999. How can this be possible?" Try to solve this puzzle. What techniques are you using? Are you trying the same old solution over and over without success? Try a really innovative or creative approach to the problem. Is intelligence involved in your problem-solving efforts? After you give this a good attempt and produce some solutions then look below for some other solutions.

1. In the Native American calendar each year is counted as four years.
2. He was playing chess in room 1999.
3. "1999" is the name of a town in Nebraska.
4. In the year 2038, fifty-two years after his birth, a couple of brilliant scientists perfect a time machine and regress to the year 1999 so they can welcome in the millennium one more time. While passing the time of day, they play chess, but the excitement of time travel and anticipating the century are too much for Paul's heart and he dies.
5. During a cataclysmic event in the middle of 2022 all particles in the universe began to run in the opposite direction, which had the effect of reversing time. Why 2022? Well, that's another puzzle.
6. The guy moved his chess pieces so slowly that he died in 1999 but no one noticed for thirty-nine years.
7. "However" is the name of Paul's father.

His name was McGuffin, which was a name used by the late filmmaker Alfred Hitchcock for any device or element that deflects attention from other pivotal bits in a mystery film. Here, the "extra" bits of information—that his father was Irish, that he was born in St. Louis, that he was playing with Albert Einstein—are the McGuffin, used to sidetrack your thinking in nonproductive ways. McGuffins abound and sometimes pop up on final examinations. Do you have better "solutions"? Send them to us for future editions.

sistent with the word, in that they view behavior in terms of an organized system. According to the gestaltists, problems, especially perceptual problems, exist when tension or stress occurs as a result of some interaction between perception and memory. By thinking about a problem, or by examining it from different angles, the "correct" view can emerge in a moment of insight. The early Gestalt psychologists (Max Wertheimer, Kurt Koffka, Wolfgang Kohler) demonstrated the perceptional reorganization viewpoint in problem-solving activity. Out of their work emerged the concept of **functional fixedness,** originated by Karl Duncker (1945). This concept, which was to have considerable impact on problem-solving research, held that there is a tendency to perceive things in terms of their familiar uses and that that tendency often makes it difficult to use them in an unfamiliar way (e.g., using a brick as a measuring device). In effect, objects or ideas become set in their functions and, when they are part of a problem-solving task that requires that they serve a different function, the subject must overcome that "set."

Although we usually associate the term **set** with the state of mind (habit or attitude) a person brings to a problem-solving task, the original definition of the term includes the idea of any preparatory cognitive activity that precedes thinking and perception. In the context of the latter definition, *set* may enhance the quality of perception or thought through more active participation in the meaning of a stimulus (as in the case of an ambiguous word, the next move in a chess game, or the next response in a social situation). Alternatively, it may inhibit perception or thought (as in a problem in which a participant repeatedly tries a certain nonproductive solution that is related to an earlier experience). For example, Duncker (1945) gave participants three cardboard boxes, matches, thumbtacks, and candles and asked them to devise a plan whereby the candle could be mounted on a screen to serve as a lamp. One group of participants was given the screen; the candles, the tacks, and the matches were each presented in their own box. Another group of participants was given these objects *along* with the three boxes—that is, the objects were not *in* the boxes. The solution to this puzzle was to use the matches to light the candles, drip some wax on a box, stick the candle on it, and thumbtack the box to the screen. When the boxes were modeled ahead of time as containers, participants had much more difficulty in solving this problem than when the boxes were not (see Figure 14.1). Later experimenters (Glucksberg & Danks, 1969) demonstrated that simply labeling an object with a name fixed in the participant's mind a certain set that could either facilitate or impede the solving of a problem.

The types of problems used in the early experiments were of a wide variety, from mechanical to logic problems. The protocols (records of the thought processes as "thought aloud" by the participants) revealed that the problem-solving process had several well-ordered stages. Participants normally seem to begin with what is expected of them. Then hypotheses about possible solutions arise, are tested, and confirmed; if they are not confirmed, new hypotheses emerge (see Figure 14.2). The process, then, seems to be one of

FIGURE 14.1

A

The Candle Problem. Participants were asked to attach a candle to the wall when provided with a box of tacks, candles, and matches (A). The solution is shown (B).

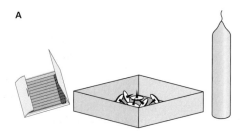

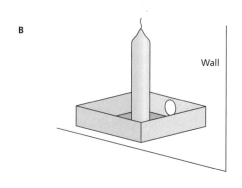

B

Wall

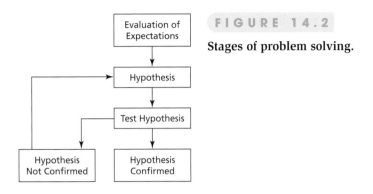

FIGURE 14.2

Stages of problem solving.

trial and error, with a new hypothesis replacing an unsuccessful one. These early experiments said little about how hypotheses originated and made no credible postulates as to the cognitive structures involved in the process.

Representation of the Problem

The work of the Gestalt psychologists focused on the nature of a task and its influence on a person's ability to solve it. Recent scholars have attacked the question of problem solving from several different perspectives, including what modern cognitive psychologists call the process of representation, or how a problem is depicted in the mind. Throughout this book, the topic of internal representation has been a central theme. Material that has already been presented is not repeated here, except to note that the way information is represented in a problem-solving task is important in finding its solution.

The way information is represented in solving a problem seems to follow a well-ordered pattern. For example, let's look at the problem of entering the real world after graduation from college. The stereotypical sequence of problem solving, as suggested by Hayes (1989), takes the following form:

Cognitive Action	Nature of the Problem
1. Identifying the problem	Next May I will graduate from college. It is the end of one phase of my life. (Time to grow up.)
2. Representation of the problem	I will be unemployed and without funds. I must get work. (Can no longer sponge off Mom and Pop.)

*T*he biggest problem in the world
Could have been solved when it was small.

—*Lao Tsu*

3. Planning the solution	I will write a résumé, investigate the job market, and consult with friends and teachers. (See what's out there. I could go to Tibet and become a monk.)
4. Executing the plan	I will make appointments with interesting companies. I will interview with them. (Take the plunge.)
5. Evaluating the plan	I will consider each offer in light of my own needs and desires and make a decision. (Who's offering big bucks, long vacations, and early retirement.)
6. Evaluating the solution	I will reflect on the process of solving this problem and use such knowledge in future problem solving. (Where did I go wrong?)

Perhaps, if you think of the way you have solved problems in your own life, you will find that you have used a sequence similar to the one shown here. The process is almost always unconscious. That is, you do not deliberately say to yourself, "Now, I am in phase three, 'planning the solution,' which means that I . . ."; nevertheless, it is likely that these stages are lurking in the background as you solve daily problems. Consider any problem—either real or imaginary (such as fixing a broken toaster, solving a difficult interpersonal problem, or deciding whether or not to have children)— and work through it following the steps of the sequence. You will find through this process that well-defined problems ("I'm unhappy in my current job") are easier to solve than ill-defined problems ("I hate my life").

Although all stages are important, the representation of a problem appears to be very important, especially the way information is represented in terms of visual imagery. Suppose you are asked to multiply 43 by 3. No big deal, you might say, as you produce the answer easily with few mental operations. However, if I ask you to multiply 563 by 26 mentally, how do you perform the task? If you are like many others, you "see" the problem; that is, you represent it visually and begin the process by multiplying 3×6, "see" the 8, carry the 1, then multiply 6×6, add the 1, and so on. All of these operations are done with the information being represented in imagery. Vision is the dominant sensory modality. So much of our information about the world comes through our visual system. It's no wonder that our mental world is equally visually oriented. It seems that writers have capitalized on this propensity to represent things visually by using prose rich in imagery. Sometimes these are called word pictures, as illustrated in the following passage from Salisbury (1955):

> A tall, lanky serious-faced man strolled toward the datcha with a loose-jointed boyish pace and came up to where I was wielding a paintbrush. We were glassing in the front porch and I was busy in my paint-smeared clothes putting the white trim on the windows. (p. 112)

You can "see" the "loose-jointed boyish" character (who turned out to be George Kennan), and the paint-smeared clothes, and so on. Now consider how the problem of representation influences the following problem.[2]

[2] Inspired by research of Bransford and Johnson (1972).

Brazilian Brain-Teaser

You and your companion are walking in a Brazilian rain forest when you come across a gorge. The gorge is 40 feet deep and 60 feet wide and several miles long in each direction. You have a 20-foot ladder, a pair of pliers, a box of matches, a candle, an endless supply of rope, and several rocks and boulders. How do you and your friend cross the chasm?

Fewer than one in ten people solve this problem. Why did or did you not solve it? Did you use all of the equipment provided? Is the solution "simple minded"? Did you not solve it because you added too many factors? Try this out on your friends and record the means they use to solve the problem. See the discussion of "Representation of the Problem" in the text. The solution is found at the end of this chapter.

Of course, I could go out and buy one, but that would take time and money. I could make one from an old newspaper, or wrapping paper, but the paper must be sturdy. Then there is the matter of use. Streets aren't so good, the beach is perfect, and an open field is also OK. Finally, the weather needs to be good; kind of windy, and definitely no rainstorms (unless you are foolish or interested in physics). (p. 112)

As you read this paragraph, you can undoubtedly understand every word and sentence, and yet you have a gnawing feeling that you really do not understand what is going on. (Try reading this to a friend and then ask what he or she thinks the paragraph is about.) However, if we tell you that theme of the paragraph is how to make and fly a kite, everything falls into place and you comprehend the entire passage and problem. Representation of information is very important in problem solving.

These examples have dealt with literary expressions of problems, but many of our problems are more physical. For example, we are puzzled by the arrangement of furniture in a room, the shortest route to and from work, which grocery items we should select for greatest efficiency in shopping, and so on. One way some of these problems can be solved is to "go to the extremes," as suggested by Marvin Levine (1993), a leading expert on problem solving. Try to solve one of his problems:

Two flagpoles are standing, each 100 feet tall. A 150-foot rope is strung from the top of one of the flagpoles to the top of the other and hangs freely between them. The lowest point of the rope is 25 feet above the ground. How far apart are the two flagpoles?

Can you solve the problem? How did you do it? Some of you might have begun with elaborate calculus in which the sag line of a rope is calculated. One other way is to draw a

FIGURE 14.3

A visual representation of the flagpole problem.

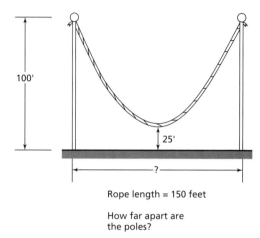

Rope length = 150 feet

How far apart are the poles?

picture of the problem (see Figure 14.3). The solution to the problem is simple and does not require advanced knowledge of geometry—only common sense. Remember, *go to the extremes.* In this case first imagine that the flagpoles were 150 feet apart. The rope would be taut. Now imagine the other extreme, that the poles would be touching each other. How would the rope hang? Since the rope is 150-feet long and the flagpoles are each 100-feet tall, when the poles are next to each other the draped rope hangs down one pole 75 feet and down the other 75 feet, leaving the center of the rope hanging 25 feet from the ground.

These examples have stressed the importance of representing the problem in a way that will enhance your ability to find a solution. In general, the solution to these problems seems to occur in one brilliant moment of awareness—what the Gestalt psychologists call insight—at which point the light goes on and all parts of the puzzle make sense. Frequently, however, problem solving is achieved through the stepwise discovery of small parts of a puzzle. This method, in which the solution to small components of a large problem serves as a means to the end solution, is sometimes called means–end analysis. We discuss this in greater detail later. Now, try to solve a problem which involves means–end analysis. This is the final example in problem solving and knowledge representation. It is shown in the box titled "Try This! A Problem of Patients—Psychiatrists' and Yours."

At the end of this problem is a matrix to keep track of your inferences and deductions. It is unlikely that you will be able to solve the problem without resorting to some outside representational aid.

Internal Representation and Problem Solving

Cognitive psychologists seem to focus their greatest efforts on defining the cognitive processes involved in internal representation. Only very recently has there been any systematic search for definite cognitive structures that are engaged during problem-solving activity. The models that have emerged draw heavily on the existing knowledge of memory structure and semantic networks—and for good reasons: the literature in both fields

Try This

A Problem of Patients—Psychiatrists' and Yours

Three married couples, Rubin, Sanchez, and Taylor, have a rather unusual thing in common: all six (three husbands and three wives) are psychiatrists. The six psychiatrists' names are Karen, Laura, Mary, Norman, Omar, Peter. As fate would have it, each doctor has one of the other doctors as a patient (but not his or her own spouse). Several other facts are:

1. Karen is the psychiatrist for one Dr. Rubin; Laura is the psychiatrist of the other.
2. Mary is the patient for one Dr. Taylor; Peter is the patient for the other.
3. Laura is a patient of Dr. Sanchez.
4. Peter has his psychotherapy with Omar.

Given these facts, determine each psychiatrist's full name and who is treating whom. Use the following table to keep track of your deductions. This mildly difficult problem is unlikely to be solved "in your head," and it is suggested that impossible combinations be marked with an "o." From these marks it will be possible to make inferences about other possible and impossible combinations. Since women cannot be husbands and men cannot be wives, we have marked the intersections with the exclusionary mark "o." Hint: Take clue 1. Since Karen and Laura are psychiatrists for Dr. (Mr.) Rubin and Dr. (Mrs.) Rubin, they (Karen and Laura) cannot be Rubins. Who is Dr. (Mrs.) Rubin? Mark with a ✓ Carry on and good luck. As you work through this problem try to identify the inferential processes you are using.

The solution is at the end of this chapter.

	Rubin		Sanchez		Taylor	
	Dr. (Mrs.)	Dr. (Mr.)	Dr. (Mrs.)	Dr. (Mr.)	Dr. (Mrs.)	Dr. (Mr.)
Karen		O		O		O
Laura		O		O		O
Mary		O		O		O
Norman	O		O		O	
Omar	O		O		O	
Peter	O		O		O	

is extensive, and problem solving is certainly related to memory factors as well as to many of those of semantic networks.

Internal Representation Model: Eisenstadt and Kareev   Eisenstadt and Kareev (1975), exploring some aspects of human problem solving exhibited by people playing board games, developed a network model. They focused their attention on the kind of internal representations of board positions that players form and on representations of knowledge. The board games they dealt with are the traditional Asian games of "Go" and "Gomoku," but presumably the model they postulate is flexible enough to apply to many games. Both "Go" and "Gomoku" are played on a board that contains a grid of nineteen vertical and nineteen horizontal lines. The pieces are small white and black "stones," which are placed on the intersections of the grid. The object is to capture the opponent's stones and occupy space. In "Go," players alternate placing their stones, and, if one player's stone is completely surrounded by the other player's stones, it is considered captured and is removed from the board. "Gomoku" is played on the same board, but here the object is fulfilled by forming an unbroken, straight line of five pieces. The opponent tries to block the formation while building his or her own line. To simplify the game, Eisenstadt and Kareev used a 9 × 9 grid and had participants place stones in the box portion of the grid rather than the intersections.

Game-playing activity was studied with human participants playing against a computer; this gave the researchers some control over the strategy and skill of the opponent, the computer, which plays a good game.

Internal representation in problem-solving tasks (as well as most other tasks) is highly subjective; mental transcription of configurations in the real world are not necessarily perfectly matched by a person's internal representation. For example, when the configuration shown in Figure 14.4A is regarded as a "Gomoku" position, the pattern important to the player (and, hence, the one given internal representation) is that indicated by the superimposed X in Figure 14.4B; however, in "Go" the important representation would be the possible capture configuration shown in Figure 14.4C. Perceptual organizations of problems, affected by the perceiver's motivation, can and frequently do differ from the physical nature of the task. To demonstrate the disparity between internal representation and real-world events, Eisenstadt and Kareev asked participants to analyze the board positions shown in Figure 14.4A and make the best play for black in a "Gomoku" game. Participants were then asked to reconstruct the positions in the absence of the configuration. Later they were given the board position shown in Figure 14.5B, told to make the best move for white in a "Go" game, and again asked to recon-

FIGURE 14.4

Board position (A); subject organization of same patterns as a position in a game of "Gomoku" (B); a game of "Go" (C).

Adapted from Eisenstadt and Kareev (1975).

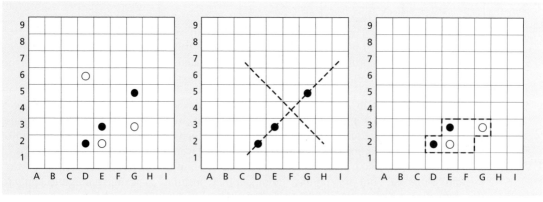

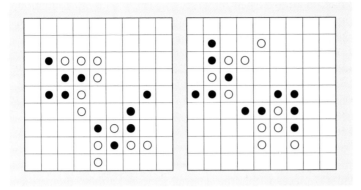

FIGURE 14.5

Board problems. Positions shown in board B are the same as in board A rotated counterclockwise 90 degrees and reflected across the vertical axis, with colors of pieces reversed.

Adapted from Eisenstadt and Kareev (1975).

struct the positions. The boards in Figures 14.5A and B are the same, except that the latter is rotated 90 degrees and reflected across the vertical axis, and the color of the stones is reversed. Therefore, in terms of pieces, essentially the same amount of information was given in both tasks. The researchers identified six pieces critical in "Go" and six pieces critical in "Gomoku"; in essence, these constitute the template for each game. The reconstruction from memory of these pieces was a direct function of the instruction. In other words, if the participants thought it was a "Go" game, they remembered the key "Go" pieces; if they were told the game was "Gomoku," they remembered the key Gomoku positions. Figure 14.6 shows the percentage of critical pieces correctly recalled as a function of the type of game participants believed they were viewing.

Further analysis of game playing indicated that participants played rapidly, suggesting that planning, or anticipating various configurations that might emerge, was neglected. Additionally, participants seemed to examine the board by means of "active searches for specific patterns, as well as by searches that seem to be driven by 'accidental' discovery of new configurations and pieces." Thus, the scanning of a problem seems to suggest

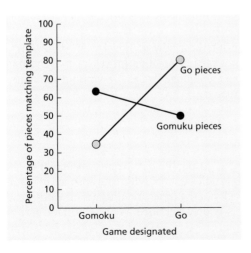

FIGURE 14.6

Percentage of critical pieces correctly recalled according to which game participants were told they were viewing.

Adapted from Eisenstadt and Kareev (1975).

that internal representations are formed by an active search. This operation is commonly called *top-down* processing and means that the analysis starts followed by a hypothesis, with attempts made to verify it by means of seeking out stimuli (for example, "This problem has stimuli, some of which are critical"). Also a possibility are bottom-up procedures, in which the stimuli are examined and attempts are then made to match them with structural components (e.g., "How does this piece figure into the problems?").

Solving a problem is somewhat dependent on the subjective representation stored in memory, and the formation of internal representation is an active process. Planning in board games, according to this viewpoint, involves both top-down and bottom-up processes, as Eisenstadt and Kareev (1975) observe:

> When a subject plans ahead, the same kinds of search processes can be used. The placement of "imaginary" pieces within the internal representation of the problem space automatically invokes the planning processes in a bottom-up manner. Determining which pieces to consider in this fashion is, of course, a top-down, hypothesis-driven situation. This helps explain one of the standard observations about human problem-solving behavior: People follow a "progressive deepening" search strategy rather than a depth-first or breadth-first one. Evidently, this results from the fact that once imaginary moves have been considered within the working (short-term) memory, they cannot be erased. Thus, backup in the planning sequence can easily overload the capacity of this memory. As a result, subjects tend to start a search process over rather than to back up a few steps. (p. 32)

Eisenstadt and Kareev, by their careful analysis of board games, have roughed out what seem to be the central mechanisms of problem solving within the domain of modern cognitive psychology. Many questions remain, particularly insofar as specification of the internal processes and structures is concerned.

Creativity

It is reasonable to assume that most people are creative to some degree. The creativity of, for example, Georgia O'Keeffe, Buckminster Fuller, Wolfgang Mozart, or Thomas Jefferson not only is a manifestation of great talent but also is well known. Other creative geniuses surely exist but go unrecognized.

Creativity is a cognitive activity that results in a new or novel way of viewing a problem or situation. This definition does not restrict creative processes to utilitarian acts, although the examples of creative people are almost always drawn from some useful invention, writing, or theory they have created.

Creative Process

It is ironic that no dominant theory has emerged during the past twenty years that might unify the disparate and sometimes conflicting studies of creativity. The absence of a unified theory points out both the inherent difficulty of the topic and the lack of widespread scientific attention. Nevertheless, creativity is widely heralded as an important part of everyday life and education.

A long time ago in the history of cognitive psychology, Wallas (1926) described the creative process as having four sequential stages:

1. **Preparation.** Formulating the problem and making initial attempts to solve it.
2. **Incubation.** Leaving the problem while considering other things.
3. **Illumination.** Achieving insight to the problem.
4. **Verification.** Testing and/or carrying out the solution.

Although there is little empirical support for Wallas's four stages, the psychological literature abounds with reports from people who have given birth to a creative thought. The most celebrated of these accounts is by Poincaré (1913), a French mathematician who discovered the properties of Fuchsian functions. After working on the equations for a time and after making some important discoveries (the preparation stage), he decided to go on a geologic excursion. While traveling he "forgot" his mathematical work (incubation stage). Poincaré then writes about the dramatic moment of insight. "Having reached Coutances, we entered an omnibus to go some place or other. At the moment when I put my foot on the step the idea came to me, without anything in my former thoughts seeming to have paved the way for it, that the transformations I had used to define the Fuchsian functions were identical with those of non-Euclidian geometry." The author continues to tell us that when he returned to his home, he verified the results at his leisure.

Wallas's four-stage model of the creative process has given us a conceptual framework to analyze creativity. Here we briefly consider each of the stages.

Stage 1: Preparation   Poincaré mentioned in his notes that he had been working intensively on the problem for fifteen days. During that period he seemed to have thought of several tentative solutions, which he tried out and, for one reason or another, discarded. However, to suggest that the period of preparation was fifteen days is, of course, wrong. All of his professional life as a mathematician and probably a good portion of his childhood could be considered part of the preparation stage.

A common theme in biographies of famous men and women is the notion that even during their early childhood, ideas were being developed, knowledge was being acquired, and tentative thoughts in a specified direction were being tried out. These early ideas frequently shape the ultimate destiny of the creative person. What remains one of the many mysteries of the process is why other individuals who share similar environmental stimulation (or, in many cases, deprivation) fail to be recognized for their creative talent. Maybe more attention should be given to the genetic bases of creativity.

Stage 2: Incubation   Why is it that a creative breakthrough frequently follows a period in which the problem is allowed to lie fallow? Perhaps the most pragmatic answer is that more of our life is devoted to recreation, watching television, skin diving, playing Texas Hold 'em, traveling, or lying in the sun watching the clouds drift by than in concentrated thinking about a problem that needs a creative solution. So creative acts are more likely to follow dormant periods simply because those periods occupy more of our time.

Posner (1973) offers several hypotheses about the incubation phase. One suggestion is that the incubation period allows us to recover from the fatigue associated with problem solving. Also, interruption of an arduous task may allow us to forget inappropriate approaches to a problem. We have already seen that functional fixedness can impede problem solving, and it is possible that during incubation people forget old, unsuccessful solutions to problems. Another reason incubation may help in the creative process is that during this period we may actually work on the problem unconsciously. Such a notion is similar to William James's famous dictum, "We learn to swim in the winter and ice-skate in the summer." Finally, interruption of the problem-solving process may allow for reorganization of material.

Stage 3: Illumination   Incubation does not always lead to illumination. When it does, however, the sensation is unmistakable. Suddenly, the lightbulb is turned on. The creative person may feel a rush of excitement as all the bits and pieces of ideas fall into place. All of the pertinent ideas complement each other, and irrelevant thoughts are discarded. The history of creative breakthroughs is replete with examples of the illumination stage. The discovery of the structure of the DNA molecule, the composition of the benzene ring, the invention of the telephone, the conclusion of a symphony, and the plot of a novel are all examples of how a moment of illumination has flooded the mind with a creative solution to a vexing old problem.

Stage 4: Verification   Following the euphoria that sometimes accompanies an insightful discovery, the idea is tested. This is the mopping up stage of the creative process in which the creative product is examined to verify its legitimacy. Often a solution first thought to be creative is only an intellectual fool's gold when examined carefully. This stage may be rather brief, as in the case of rechecking one's calculations or seeing whether an invention works; however, in some cases verification may require a lifetime of study, testing, and retesting.

Creativity and Functional Fixedness

Earlier in this chapter we saw how functional fixedness could impede problem solving. Functional fixedness also may obstruct creativity (which points out the similarity between the concepts of problem solving and creativity). People who do the same old thing over and over again or who think the same thoughts are considered to be rather unimaginative, not to mention being socially boring. On the other hand, creative people see novel relationships or unusual connections among seemingly unrelated things, such as the person who slipped an oversized tire over a small tree so when the tree grew it would have a built-in ring seat.

Investment Theory of Creativity

In science, art, literature, music, and most other fields, creative people "buy low and sell high." That is, they get in on the ground floor in which the initial stages of their endeavor are frequently thought by others to be foolish, ill-advised, or worse. If the idea has merit, then others may join in, but we do not judge those joiners' actions as particularly creative. It's the person or people who *first* dared to try something new that we consider creative. Many times the creative person will "sell high," which means that when the idea is more in vogue, he or she will move on to another problem.[3]

Sternberg and Lubart (1996) have developed a theory of creativity based on a multivariate approach to the topic, which is built around six attributes. These six facets of creativity are:

- Processes of intelligence
- Intellectual style
- Knowledge
- Personality
- Motivation
- Environmental context

Truly creative performance is rare, not because people are lacking in any one attribute but because it is difficult to get all six attributes working together. These attributes are seen much as an investment portfolio might be seen in a business enterprise. Our creativity portfolio is the basis of creative acts. These six facets of the portfolio can combine to yield creative performances at any stage of life, and the intellectual environment, such as school or home life, has an important early influence on creativity.

The importance of the work of Sternberg and Lubart is that it provides a general theory of creativity specifying particular attributes that can be studied analytically and longitudinally. It is clear that creativity is not a single trait, skill, or ability but a combination of several factors that can be identified and analyzed. Furthermore, assessing human creativity is not a simple matter of identifying the amount of each attribute and adding them together to find a kind of creativity index. Rather, it is a matter of identifying and assessing the strengths of the interactions among attributes. The combination of strengths of attributes and the number of interactions possible poses a complex network that might befuddle some scientists. In fact, the whole idea may appear foolishly complex. It may be that the authors of this theory are investing in what others might call a risky venture. To others, it appears that Sternberg and Lubart have bought low.

The Adaptive Function of Creativity

Creativity and the appreciation for the creative arts is thought to have evolved, but there is debate about whether creativity serves an adaptive function (Tooby & Cosmides, 2000, 2001), or is merely a by-product of other functional traits (like understanding language or interpreting visual scenes) (Pinker, 1997). There is a large body of logical evidence to support the by-product hypothesis; however, Cosmides and Tooby provide a compelling argument for the adaptive function of creativity, which rests on the idea that creating, viewing, and reading pretend worlds (via art, literature, film, etc.) actually serves to help the human "practice" for real events that it may encounter, and that, in turn, the desire to create and view creations assists us in carrying out other functional behaviors.

---

[3]See Thomas Kuhn (1962) for an analysis of the development of scientific revolutions in which a similar argument is made.

Judging Creativity

Whether or not we label it, Americans are fond of judging creative acts and individuals. Everything from the latest Italian sports car to the recent Steven Spielberg film, to the performance of ice-skating champions is rated for its originality and creative merit. In most cases judging creative acts is a highly subjective affair. Sometimes the standards are set by an authority in the field, such as a noted professor of design, a film critic, a former Olympic skater, or a very discerning person. This approach to psychology sounds more like art than science, and, understandably, many scientifically obsessed psychologists would rather put on a white coat, go to their laboratory, and measure blips on an oscilloscope made by a cat looking at a vertical line than try to evaluate a creative act or person. Yet some bold individuals have rushed in where their angelic colleagues fear to tread.

Psychologists thought it might be possible to assess creative ability by measuring how well people see novel connections between seemingly unrelated words. One of these tests, invented by Mednick (1967), was called the Remote Associations Test (RAT); it asked people to generate a single word that would be logically associated with three words. Consider the following two groups of three words: *RED, BRIDGE, ANGRY,* and *HEAD, SICK, PORT.* If you said "cross" for the first group, you would be right. What is the common word for the second group?

The RAT measures at least one component of creativity, but it probably measures other things too. Additionally, some very creative people might bomb on the test, which illustrates the slippery concept of creativity. Could it be that we are unconsciously creative, by which we mean that we have many associates to stimuli, such as a word or a visual scene or a musical piece, but are not consciously aware of them? The remote associates idea was expanded by Bowers and his colleagues (1990) in a task called the *dyads of triads.* One part of the task is like the RAT in that the words are part of a *coherent* triad, as are those just presented or those in the threesome *GOAT, PASS, GREEN,* all of which constellate around the coherent word *MOUNTAIN.* However, the triad *BIRD, PIPE, ROAD* is considered *incoherent* in that no (likely) common element is apparent. In this study subjects were given sets of coherent and incoherent triads and asked to find the common elements, if they could. Also, they were asked to judge which of the triads were coherent. The results showed that they were able to identify the coherent triads *even if they were unable to come up with the solution.* It was as if the participants knew that there was a common element but could not quite name it. Possibly, people activate part of a solution to a remote associate task, and that may be one phase of a creative solution to a task. Such an idea might be related to the concept of **intuition** (which is defined by the *Oxford English Dictionary* as "the immediate apprehension of an object by the mind without the intervention of any reasoning process"), a frequently defamed term in scientific literature. Human intuition may indeed be an important part of the discovery phase of creative acts.

Divergence Production Test   J. P. Guilford (1967) has spent most of his long and celebrated professional career developing theories and tests of mental ability that includes creativity. He has distinguished between two types of thinking: **convergent thinking** and **divergent thinking.** Convergent thinking moves in a straightforward manner to a particular conclusion. Much of pedagogy emphasizes convergent thinking, in which students are asked to recall factual information, such as

What is the capital of Bulgaria?

Divergent thinking requires a person to generate many different answers to a question, the "correctness" of the answers being somewhat subjective. For example:

For how many different things can you use a brick?

The convergent answer may be "to make a building or a chimney." A slightly more divergent answer may be "to make a bookcase" or "to serve as a candleholder," while a more off-the-wall divergent answer may be "to serve as emergency rouge," or "to serve as a bon voyage gift—shoes for people who are going to the moon for the first time." Simple productivity of responses is not creative thinking. One could use a brick to make a candy shop, a bakery, a factory, a shoe factory, a shop that sells hand-carved wooden things, a filling station, and so on. Divergent or more creative answers may utilize objects or ideas in more abstract terms. The divergent thinker is more flexible in his or her thinking.

If productivity were a valid measure of creativity, then quantitative assessment of that trait could be achieved by counting the number of responses to brick-type questions. Since it is not, as illustrated in the previous example, subjective evaluations must be used. Most people would agree, we suspect, that bricks as moonshoes is a more creative answer than listing the types of buildings one could make with bricks. The latter answer is, however, more practical.

Cultural Blocks   Why is it that some people can generate creative uses for objects, such as a brick, and others cannot? Part of the answer may lie in the cultural heritage of the individual. James Adams (1976a) provides an example of a **cultural block** in the following puzzle:

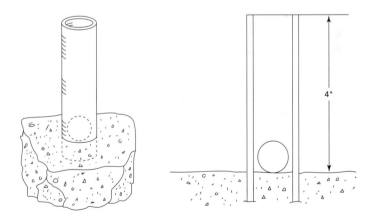

Exercise: Assume that a steel pipe is embedded in the concrete floor of a bare room, as shown in the illustration. The inside diameter is 0.6 inches larger than the diameter of a table tennis ball (1.50 inches), which is resting gently at the bottom of the pipe. You are one of a group of six people in the room, along with the following objects:

100 feet of clothesline
A carpenter's hammer

A chisel
A box of Wheaties breakfast cereal
A file
A wire coat hanger
A monkey wrench
A lightbulb

In five minutes list as many ways you can think of to get the ball out of the pipe without damaging the ball, the tube, or the floor.

Take a few moments to figure out a creative solution to this problem.

If your creative powers are like ours, you may have thought, "If I could only damage the floor, the ball, or the tube, I could get the ball out in minutes." Then perhaps you might have considered how the inventory of items could be used or fashioned into tools. If you were able to generate a long list of possible uses for the items, you may have been showing your fluency or ability to produce a number of concepts over a period of time. If you were able to generate several diverse ideas, however, you would have shown your flexibility. Creative problem solving may be done by fluency—that is, you may think of enough concepts to find one that will be appropriate—but in many cases fluency does not lead to a solution and may even be a waste of time. More flexible thinking is required.

Did you solve the ball-in-the-pipe problem? Perhaps you thought of making a giant pair of tweezers by separating the coat hanger and flattening the ends. Other, more flexible means might include making a snare from the filaments of the lightbulb. Another possibility would be to have one of the six people pee into the pipe, thereby levitating the ball to the surface. Why didn't you think of this, or if you did, why did you? It is likely that because of a cultural taboo that forbids public urination, this solution (apologies to those who can't stand puns) may not have occurred to you. Since no time limit is specified, you could also make a sticky paste of the Wheaties cereal, dip the clothesline in it, slip it down the pipe, and let it dry on the ball. Then the lightweight ball could be gently removed. Alternatively, the six people may be able to rotate the entire room and concrete floor, letting the ball roll out of the pipe (the directions say only that the pipe is embedded in a concrete floor and that the group of six people are in the room). After all, it could be a very small room easily negotiated by six people. Why didn't you think of that? Perhaps you could invent an antigravity machine with the tools available or transcendentally experience the ball outside the pipe (what is reality, after all?). If you have other ingenious solutions, perhaps you will send them to me. Our ability to think creatively is, in part, determined by our culture and education.

Teaching Creativity   Insofar as creativity is a function of our culture and education, is it possible to teach creativity? The answer depends on how creativity is defined. It is possible to train people to be more flexible in their thinking, to score higher on tests of creativity, to solve puzzles more creatively, and to probe scientific and philosophic issues more deeply than before. However, it is difficult to prove empirically that through training alone the likes of a Rossini, De Quincey, van Gogh, Einstein, Picasso, Dickinson, or Freud could be fashioned from a randomly selected person.

Hayes (1978) has suggested that creativity can be enhanced by several means.

Developing a knowledge base. A rich background in science, literature, art, and mathematics seems to give the creative person a larger storehouse of information from which to work his or her creative talents. Each of the previously mentioned creative people spent many years gathering information and perfecting their basic skills. In a study of creative artists and scientists, Anne Roe (1946, 1953) found that the only common denominator among the group she studied was the willingness to work unusually hard. The apple that fell on Newton's head and inspired him to develop a general theory of gravity struck an object filled with information.

Creating the right atmosphere for creativity. Several years ago the technique of brainstorming became fashionable. The gist of brainstorming is that people in a group generate as many ideas as they can without criticism from the other members. Not only can a large number of ideas or solutions to a problem be generated this way, but also the technique can be used on an individual basis to facilitate the development of a creative idea. Frequently, we are inhibited by others or our own constraint from generating bizarre solutions.

Searching for analogies. Several studies have shown that people do not recognize it when a new problem is similar to an old problem that they already know how to solve (see Hinsley, Hayes, & Simon, 1977; Hayes & Simon, 1976). In formulating a creative solution to a problem, it is important to consider similar problems you may have encountered. In the problem of extracting a table tennis ball from a 4-inch-long pipe, one technique was to make a glue from the Wheaties. If you were confronted with a similar puzzle, perhaps now you would, through analogous thinking, remember the problem with the pipe and table tennis ball and its Wheaties-and-glue solution.

H. O.: Case Study of an Artist—Solso; Miall and Tchalenko

One of the most complete studies of an expert portrait artist, Humphrey Ocean (H. O.), was recently conducted by Robert Solso at Stanford and Nevada and Chris Miall and John Tchalenko at Oxford. The research was based on the idea that experts in all fields, be it mathematics, music, athletics, or art, demonstrate neurocognitive attributes and performance actions that are markedly different from those of novices. With that premise in mind, a comprehensive study which involved a brain scan and eye-hand movements of an accomplished artist was done by Solso, Miall, and Tchalenko.

H. O., a practicing artist for more than twenty years and one of Britain's most distinguished portrait painters, has exhibited at the National Portrait Gallery (London), Wolfson College (Cambridge), and many other galleries. Among his best-known paintings is a portrait of the former Beatle Paul McCartney. He has been the recipient of many awards and has presented numerous exhibitions. In addition to having years of formal training in art, H. O. has spent between three and five hours each day working as an artist or, over his lifetime, has accumulated about 25,000 hours practicing his craft. He was forty-seven years old at the time of the study, a male, and right-handed. The fact that H. O. specializes in portraits was important, as a section of the human cortex seems to be dedicated to facial processing. H. O. agreed to submitting himself to being studied extensively, first by means of MRI and then by means of eye-tracking and motor movements—all data collected on an accomplished artist for the first time.

H. O. and fMRI   In a study done by Solso (2001), H. O. drew six portraits while lying flat on his back in the confined quarters of the MRI machine. A control participant also

FIGURE 14.7

fMRI scans made on H. O. and a nonartist control participant. Showing right parietal activity for both people (see column A). This area is involved in facial perception, but it appears that the nonartist is demanding more energy to process faces than H. O. In columns C and D, there is an increase in blood flow in the right frontal area of the artist, suggesting a higher-order abstraction of information.

(Solso, 2000, 2001)

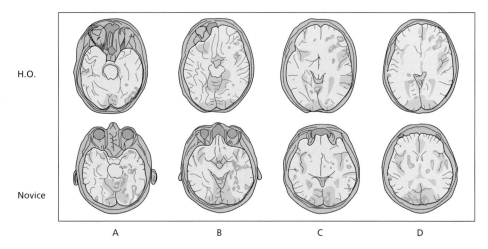

H.O.

Novice

A   B   C   D

participated in this task to provide a contrast for the brain activity of H. O. and a novice. The results of the brain flow activity of H. O. and the novice are shown in Figure 14.7 (and also as a color plate in the inside cover).

As expected there was more activity in the participant's right hemisphere, the sight of geometric and form perception and processing. Notably, the right *posterior parietal* has been implicated in facial perception, and as shown in column A and to some extent B, both the expert and the novice showed considerable activity in that region. However, if you look closely at the differences between the expert and novice, you will see that the novice seems to exhibit *more* blood flow to the right posterior parietal area (column A). Why would the expert show *less* blood flow to the face-processing area? The answer may hold one of the key elements to our understanding of experts.

It would appear that experts, in this case an expert portrait painter (who has processed faces for thousands of hours) is so *efficient* in his perception and memory for faces that he shifts his attention to "deeper" forms of cognition that involve a more penetrating analysis of faces. This deeper level may engage a unique form of facial comprehension—what we refer to as facial cognizance. Some clue to that deeper processing can be seen in column C where greater activity is shown in the expert's right frontal area than in the novice's. This area is thought to be involved in the more analytic, associative cortex, where abstract thinking takes place. Thus, it appears that our expert artist, H. O., is thinking a portrait as much as he is seeing it. The research, the first of its kind, also opens the door for more experiments on experts as they perform their specialized task. Where is the seat of thinking

FIGURE 14.8

Technique used to measure H. O.'s eye movements, eye fixations, and hand movements as he drew a portrait.

(Miall & Tchalenko, 2001)

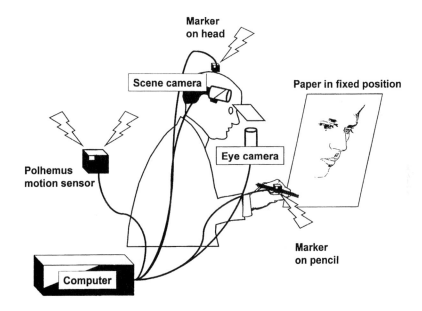

in the chess master, the astrophysicist, the volley ball champion, the cellist, the psychiatrist, the master carpenter? Answers to these questions, and many more, are within our grasp.

H. O. and Eye-Tracking and Motor Movements   A second phase of the study of H. O. involved measuring his eye fixations and movements and his hand movements as he drew a portrait of a model. In this phase of the experimental analysis of an artist, Miall and Tchalenko (2001) outfitted (see Figure 14.8) H. O. with an eye camera, which measured eye movements and fixations; a scene camera, which identified the visual scene; and a motion-detector marker, which indicated the movements of the artist's hand. It was possible to do this and, at the same time, allow H. O. to move his head and hands reasonably unimpeded. Thus, it was possible to keep track, over time, of the eye fixations and hand movements of H. O. as he was in the process of drawing a portrait. It will come as no surprise that the final product produced by this celebrated artist was much finer than those of amateurs who also participated in the experiment, but the researchers turned up some additional things, which included the following:

- H. O.'s fixation on the model was different from his "ordinary" looking pattern, which suggested that he assumed a more intense way of viewing when he put on his "artist's hat."

FIGURE 14.9

Lengths of eye fixations for H. O. and novice artists. Showing that the expert spent nearly twice as much time fixating on the model during each glance as did the novices.

(Miall & Tchalenko, 2001)

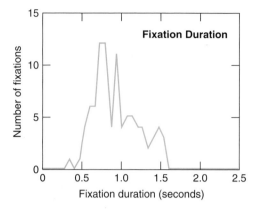

- As the drawing progressed, H. O. shifted his fixations from the model to the canvas, which may mean that as the picture becomes more completely composed, the picture itself serves as a stimulus for further "touch up." In the beginning of the picture, the artist must spend more time looking at the model to record the details of his face.

- The artist's typical fixation time during sketches was 0.6 to 1.0 second, while novices' typical fixation period was about half that time (see Figure 14.9). These results suggest that the artist was locking his gaze onto a single position, studying it in some detail, while the novices fixated on two or more positions, sometimes spatially disparate. The latter pattern of looking is not typical of everyday eye movements and was similar to H. O.'s eye fixations when he did not have on his "artist's hat."

- H. O.'s ability to capture visual information and reproduce it seems to be based on a detail-to-detail process rather than a holistic approach. The artist would build a nose, for example, point by point, and then an ear, and so on.

- Finally, when the results of H. O.'s hand movements were recorded, they provided a visual that was more astonishingly similar to the final sketch than had ever been imagined (see Figure 14.10). A fine-grained analysis of hand movements and final drawing shows precisely how the artist proceeded. For example, while the detail work on the subject's right eye absorbed much motor performance, the drawing of the edge of the nose required only one stroke.

For the first time, a very patient artist (and one who unselfishly gave of his time and effort) has been studied under the powerful lens of the fMRI, the eye-tracking device, and the motor movement recorder. Such research opens the way for other studies of experts with modern instrumentation. It is possible that the data collected on H. O. are idiosyncratic and other artists may use different strategies. Certainly, landscape and abstract artists may employ different patterns of eye movements and fixations and motor responses. It may be that different cortical regions would be activated and different eye patterns noted. And perhaps Leonardo da Vinci, Rembrandt, Picasso, and van Gogh would have exhibited different neurocognitive propensities.

FIGURE 14.10

The final result. Left: H. O.'s hand movements (not pencil strokes). Right: Finished portrait.

(Miall & Tchalenko, 2001)

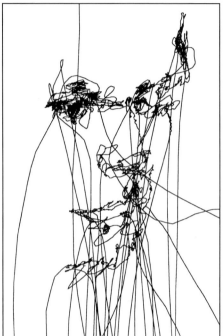 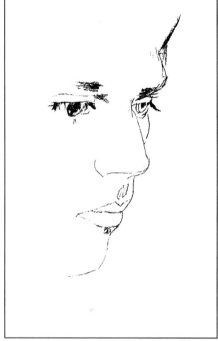

Human Intelligence

The Problem of Definition

In spite of the wide usage of the word **intelligence,** psychologists do not agree on a single definition. Many would agree, however, that all of the topics called higher-order forms of cognition—concept formation, reasoning, problem solving, and creativity, as well as memory and perception—are related to human intelligence. Sternberg (1982) asked people to identify the characteristics of an intelligent person, and among the most frequently given responses were "reasons logically and well," "reads widely," "keeps an open mind," and "reads with high comprehension." Others (Geary, 2005) have noted that intelligence can be defined in terms of individual differences in reaction time, "inspection" time, and working memory that are de facto assessed on standard intelligence tests. He goes on to further posit that these differences have a neurological basis that have evolved through natural selection. As a working definition we shall consider human intelligence to be the ability to acquire, recall, and use knowledge to understand concrete

---

*C*ognitive scientists are particularly interested in human intelligence, because intelligence represents, in some sense, the epitome of human functioning—that which makes us distinctively human.

   —*Robert J. Sternberg*

---

and abstract concepts and the relationships among objects and ideas, and to use knowledge in a meaningful way.

The recent interest in artificial intelligence (AI) has caused many psychologists to consider what is uniquely human about human intelligence and what abilities a computer would require to act (humanly) intelligent. Nickerson, Perkins, and Smith (1985) have settled on several abilities that they believe represent human intelligence.

The first is the ability to classify patterns. All humans with normal intelligence seem able to assign nonidentical stimuli to classes. This ability is fundamental to thought and language, since words generally represent categories of information. For example, telephone refers to a wide class of objects used for long-distance electronic communication. Imagine the hassle if you had to treat each telephone as a separate, nonclassified phenomenon.

The second is the ability to modify behavior adaptively—to learn. Many theorists consider adapting to one's environment the most important mark of human intelligence.

The third is the ability to reason deductively. As we considered earlier, deductive reasoning involves making logical inferences from stated premises. If we conclude that "Phil Smith likes wine," given the validity of the premises "All residents of Napa Valley like wine" and "Phil Smith lives in Napa Valley," we infer a degree of deductive reasoning ability.

The fourth is the ability to reason inductively—to generalize. Inductive reasoning requires that the person go beyond the information given. It requires the reasoner to discover rules and principles from specific instances. If Phil Smith likes wine and lives in Napa Valley, his neighbor also likes wine, and if his neighbor is also inclined to enjoy a bit of the nectar, you might get the impression that the next neighbor is also fond of fermented grapes. It might not be true, but it tends to be "intelligent."

The fifth is the ability to develop and use conceptual models. This ability means that we form an impression of the way the world is and how it functions and use that model to understand and interpret events. Nickerson and his colleagues (1985) use the following example:

> When you see a ball roll under one end of a couch and then emerge at the other end, how do you know that the ball that came out is the same one that went in? In fact you do not really know for sure that it is, but your conceptual model of the world leads you to make such an inference. . . . Moreover, had the ball, on emerging, been a different color, or a different size, than on entering, you would have had to infer either that the ball that came out was not the one that went in, or that something peculiar was going on under the couch. (p. 321)

Much of what we "know" we never directly observe, but we infer from our past experiences with other similar things and events. For example, we don't know whether a barber, born and bred in Arizona, can tell time or speak Hindi, but we act as if he can tell time and not speak Hindi whereas a person growing up in a remote village in north-eastern India might have an opposite model.

And the sixth is the ability to understand. In general, the ability to understand is related to the ability to see relationships in problems and to appreciate the meaning of these relationships in solving a problem. Validation of understanding is one of the most elusive problems in intelligence testing.

Cognitive Theories of Intelligence

If the processing of information follows a sequence of stages in which at each stage a unique operation is performed, then human intelligence is thought to be a component of human intellect that interacts with the processing of information. Essentially, this is the way intelligence is conceptualized by cognitive psychologists who subscribe to the information-processing theory of cognition. Enthusiasm for the model seemed to start with cognitive psychologists fascinated with computer intelligence. The analogy between human and artificial intelligence is inescapable; information from the external world is perceived or input, it is stored in memory, transformation of the information is performed, and an output is made. Additionally, the processing of information is analogous to programs in computers and intellectual functions, including intelligence, in humans.

Information Processing Speed   As an example of the type of studies of intelligence done by cognitive psychologists, we first consider the work of Hunt (1978), Hunt, Lunneborg, and Lewis (1975), and Hunt and Lansman (1982). One question asked by Hunt and his colleagues was, "In what way(s) does the processing of information differ in high- and low-ability subjects?" Two groups—one with high-ability students and one with low-ability students—selected on the basis of standardized college entrance examinations such as the Scholastic Aptitude Test (SAT), were asked questions that required searching for common information in their long-term memories. Speed of retrieval was used as the dependent variable.

The test Hunt used to measure reaction times was the letter-matching task developed by Posner, Boies, Eichelman, and Taylor (1969), which is discussed in some detail in Chapter 6. The task required subjects to decide whether two letters (e.g., *A-A* or *A-a*) matched. In some instances the letters matched physically and in other cases the match was made on the basis of the name of the letters. From the perspective of information processing, the physical match condition required only that the subject get the letters in short-term memory and make a decision. In the name-matching condition, the subject, in addition to getting both terms in STM, had to retrieve the name of the letter (ostensibly stored in LTM), make a decision, and then press a reaction-time key. Hunt assumed that physical matches reflect only structural processes dealing with the encoding and comparison of visual patterns, while name matching reflects the efficiency of encoding information to a level that requires that the physical representation of a letter make contact with the name of that letter in LTM. Crudely put, the speed with which people could retrieve information from LTM was hypothesized to be a measure of verbal ability. In the first condition, involving the physical match (*A-A*), the low- and high-ability groups did about equally well in the name-matching condition (*A-a*), the low-ability group, on average, took more time to make a correct decision than the high-ability group. The difference between the groups was in the range of 25 to 50 milliseconds, which may seem to be very

Earl Hunt. Studied intelligence and artificial intelligence within the context of cognitive psychology.

brief indeed; however, when we consider the decoding of countless thousands of letters and words in the process of normal reading (such as reading a textbook), the impact of these brief times adds up quickly. These results hold for different participant groups such as university students, 10-year-old children, elderly adults, and mentally retarded persons.

In another study Hunt (1978) used a modified form of the Brown-Peterson task to study differences between those with high verbal ability and those with low verbal ability. This task, as you may recall, requires participants to recall a three-letter syllable after they have counted backward by threes for a certain length of time. (Hunt used four-letter syllables and had the participants read the digits.) In this experiment the two groups differed significantly in recall of letters. In addition, the retention curves between the two groups were parallel, which suggests that the high-verbal group may be more efficient in encoding verbal information (rather than simply maintaining more information) than the low-verbal group. Finally, Hunt used the Sternberg paradigm to identify differences between participants with high-verbal ability and those with low-verbal ability. As might be expected by now, he found that the former group performed better than the latter group on this task.

The studies by Hunt and others are significant for two reasons. First, they indicate that the information-processing paradigm provides many useful procedures for the study of human intelligence. It is feasible that, in addition to verbal ability, other measures of intelligence—such as mathematical ability, spatial ability, or perhaps even general intelligence—may yield some of their enigmatic secrets in terms of reasonably simple cognitive processes and mechanisms. Second, STM is related to verbal components of intelligence, not necessarily because the number of items retained in STM is critically related to intelligence but because simple cognitive processes and operations, such as identification of the name of a letter or the retention of a trigram, that depend on LTM and STM are sensitive to individual intellectual differences.

General Knowledge   General knowledge has, since the development of the earliest tests of intelligence, been considered an integral part of human intelligence, and to this day questions designed to tap an individual's understanding of the world are part of most standard tests. Apparently, knowing that Baghdad is the capital of Iraq, or that hydrogen is lighter than helium, or that the Kirov Ballet performs in Saint Petersburg, or that Tutankhamen's mostly unmolested tomb was discovered by Howard Carter (all of which are examples of passive knowledge—the type of information a computer could store) is presumed by test makers to be related to intelligence. However, embarrassingly little attention has been given, either theoretically or pragmatically, to the reason general knowledge is considered a correlate of intelligence. As Siegler and Richards (1982) point out:

> For the same reasons that fish will be the last to discover water, developmental psychologists until recently devoted almost no attention to changes in children's knowledge of specific content. Such changes are so omnipresent that they seemed uninviting as targets for study. Instead of being investigated, improved content knowledge was implicitly dismissed as a by-product of more basic changes in capacities and strategies. (p. 930)

Tests of general information may provide important data on a person's current state of knowledge and ability to retrieve information. This in turn could provide a useful clue to the past intellectual history and predict future performance. Yet, of the many cognitive attributes recently discovered, only a few have been related to human intelligence. It seems that semantic organization is a topic that could be of special interest to people interested in intelligence. It would seem that the ability to store semantic information in an organized schema and to access that information efficiently is characteristic of at least one type of intelligence. Perhaps some enterprising student of cognitive psychology will pursue this valuable subject.

One developmental study has shown not only how experiments can be done in this area but also how they can lead to a clear demonstration of the impact of a knowledge base. Chi (1978) examined the effect of a specialized knowledge base on the recall of chess and digit stimuli. For her experiment, she selected ten-year-old children who were skilled chess players and adults who were novices at the game. The task was similar to the one used by Chase and Simon in which chess pieces were arranged in a normal game configuration. Both groups of participants were allowed to view the board and pieces and then were asked to reproduce the arrangement on a second board. A related task, called a meta-memory task—which refers to an individual's knowledge about his or her own memory—consisted of asking the children and adults to predict how many trials it would take to reproduce all the pieces. The results, shown in Figure 14.11, revealed that the children not only were better at recalling the arrangement of chess pieces but also were better at predicting their performance—that is, their metamemory was more accurate than that of adults. A standard digit-span task, which is commonly used in intelligence tests, was also administered, and as expected the adults performed better on recalling these digits and predicting their performance than the children. The effect of a knowledge base, independent of age or other types of intelligence (e.g., digit-span performance), appears to measurably enhance the ability to recall from working memory specialized information that is directly related to the knowledge base. The issues raised by this experiment, both methodological and theoretical, suggest that in the future many more studies of this type will appear.

Reasoning and Problem Solving   Almost everyone would agree that reasoning and problem solving are important components of human intelligence, and some would suggest that separating these concepts is done only for analytic purposes.

Most prominent among the new generation of cognitive psychologists to tackle the question of human intelligence in relation to reasoning and problem solving is Sternberg (1977, 1980a, 1980b, 1982, 1984a, 1984b, 1986a, 1986b, 1989). The theory of human intelligence proposed by Sternberg (1984b, 1985a, 1989) is the *triarchic theory*. It comprises three subtheories that serve as the governing bases for specific models of intelligent human behavior. These parts are:

FIGURE 14.11

Recall of chess and digit stimuli by children and adults.

From Chi (1978). Reprinted by permission from Erlbaum.

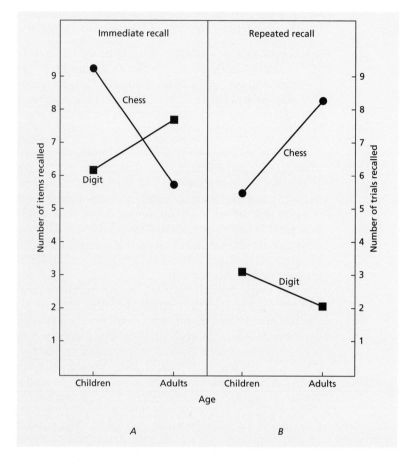

1. **Componential intelligent behavior.** This subtheory specifies the structures and mechanism that underlie intelligent behavior. Within this subtheory are three information processing components: (a) learning how to do things, (b) planning what things to do and how to do them, and (c) actually doing the things. People with such ability are generally good test takers and blow the top off standardized tests. They also do well commenting on other people's work. However, they are not necessarily critical thinkers, nor are they particularly creative.

2. **Experiential intelligent behavior.** This component posits that for a given task or situation, contextually appropriate behavior is not equally "intelligent" at all points along the continuum of experience with that behavior or class of behaviors. This kind of intelligence is best demonstrated when people are confronted with a novel situation or are in the process of automatizing performance on a given task. Those who have this component may not score highest on typical IQ tests, but they are creative. Such ability is generally predictive of success in a chosen field, be it business, medicine, or carpentry.

3. **Contextual intelligent behavior.** This involves (a) adaptation to a present environment, (b) selection of a more nearly optimal environment than the one the

Robert J. Sternberg. Developed triarchic theory of intelligence.

individual presently inhabits, or (c) shaping of the present environment to render it a better fit to skills, interests, or values. Contextual intelligence allows a person to find a good fit with the environment by changing one or the other or both. We might think of this type of intelligence as instrumental in getting along in your world, whether that world is the ghetto or the boardroom.

In illustrating these three types of intelligence, Sternberg recalls three idealized graduate students called Alice, Barbara, and Celia, who each exemplified one of the components of intelligence (see Trotter, 1986 (see figure)).

Such revolutionary ideas in the sensitive field of intelligence, which crosses so many areas of human endeavor (educational, political, racial, to name only three), were certain to be met with criticism. Some of the arguments are technical, others are philosophical, and others are pragmatically inspired. H. Eysenck (1984), is critical of the triarchic theory on the basis that it is not so much a theory of intelligence as it is a theory of behavior. The interested reader is directed toward original sources and current literature. At this time, no one—including Sternberg (see 1984b, p. 312)— believes that the final model of intelligence has been developed. At the same time, no one believes that our view of intelligence will remain unchanged.

In Sternberg's theory, reasoning is characterized as an attempt to combine elements of old information to produce new information. (See the box titled "Try This! Intelligence Test.") The old information may be external (from books, movies, newspapers), internal (stored in memory), or a combination of both. In inductive reasoning, discussed earlier, the information contained in the premises is insufficient to reach a conclusion; the person must create the correct solution. One technique used by Sternberg is the analogy that can be represented by A is to B as C is to D or, symbolically, A:B::C:D. In some instances the last term (D) is omitted and must be generated by the participant, or in other cases the participants must select from a series of alternative answers, as in the following:

Philology:Languages::Mycology:

(a. Flowering plants, b. Ferns, c. Weeds, d. Fungus)

The reasoning ability needed to solve this problem is minimal, but the analogy is nevertheless difficult for many people because they don't know that mycology is the study of fungi and philology is the study of the origin of languages. Analogies of this type measure a form of intelligence related to vocabulary.

Sternberg's Triarchic Theory of Intelligence

Componential/Analytic

Alice had high test scores and was a whiz at test taking and analytical thinking. Her type of intelligence exemplifies the componential subtheory, which explains the mental components involved in analytical thinking.

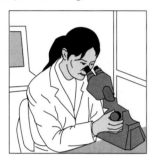

Experiential/Creative

Barbara didn't have the best test scores, but she was a superbly creative thinker who could combine disparate experiences in insightful ways. She is an example of the experiential subtheory.

Contextual/Practical

Celia was street-smart. She learned how to play the game and how to interact with her environment. Her test scores weren't tops, but she could come out on top in almost any context. She is Sternberg's example of contextual intelligence.

In the preceding analogy, the solution is dependent on knowledge of words and reasoning ability. Solving analogies is not as simple a matter, however, as recalling information from memory; it involves several stages. Sternberg suggests that when confronted with a problem of this sort, one should break the analogy down into subproblems, each of which requires solving before the entire problem can be solved. The strategy used is similar to the means-end analysis of Newell and Simon, but it differs in that each stage of the information processing sequence is thought to play an important role in the process. The following problem, adapted from Sternberg (1982), is an illustration of some of the stages a person must work through in solving an analogy.

Lawyer:Client::Doctor:

(a. Patient, b. Medicine)

In this case the encoding of the words is less problematic than in the previous case because most people are familiar with all the terms. The stages used in solving this problem are as follows:

1. The reasoner encodes the terms of the analogy.
2. The reasoner makes an inference between lawyer and client (e.g., a lawyer gives service to a client, a lawyer is paid by a client, and a lawyer may help the client).
3. The reasoner maps the higher-order relationship between the first half of the analogy and the second (both deal with professionals who render service to a patron).
4. The reasoner applies a relationship similar to the inferred one to the second half of the analogy, that is, from the doctor and each of the alternatives (a doctor gives service to a person, not medicine).
5. The reasoner makes his or her response.

Intelligence Test

Sample Test Questions

1. Suppose that all gemstones were made of foam rubber. Which of the following completions would then be correct for the analogy below?

   Wood: Hard::Diamond:

   a. Valuable, b. Soft, c. Brittle, d. Hardest

2. Janet, Barbara, and Elaine are a housewife, lawyer, and physicist, although not necessarily in that order. Janet lives next door to the housewife. Barbara is the physicist's best friend. Elaine once wanted to be a lawyer but decided against it. Janet has seen Barbara within the last two days, but has not seen the physicist.
   Janet, Barbara, and Elaine are, in that order, the

   a. Housewife, physicist, lawyer
   b. Physicist, lawyer, housewife
   c. Physicist, housewife, lawyer
   d. Lawyer, housewife, physicist

3. Josh and Sandy were discussing the Reds and the Blues, two baseball teams. Sandy asked Josh why he thought the Reds had a better chance of winning the pennant this year than did the Blues. Josh replied, "If every man on the Red team is better than every man on the Blue team, then the Reds must be on the better team." Josh is assuming that

   a. Inferences that apply to each part of a whole apply as well to the whole, and this assumption is true.
   b. Inferences that apply to each part of a whole apply as well to the whole, and this assumption is false.
   c. Inferences that apply to a whole apply as well to each part, and this assumption is true.
   d. Inferences that apply to a whole apply as well to each part, and this assumption is false.

4. Select that answer option that represents either a necessary or forbidden property of the italicized word.

   lion

   a. Fierce, b. White, c. Mammalian, d. Alive

5.

Answers: 1. b, 2. d, 3. b, 4. c, 5. 2

From R. Sternberg (1986b).

Initially the terms of an analogy must be encoded, or translated, into internal representations upon which subsequent operations can be performed. One model of representations used by Sternberg (1977, 1982, 1985a) is based on attributes of the information. This model is illustrated in the following example:

Washington:1::Lincoln:

(a. 10, b. 5)

- Washington could be encoded as a president (1st), a person whose visage is on currency (one-dollar bill), or a war hero (American Revolution).

- 1 might be encoded as a counting number (1), an ordinal position (1st), or an amount (1 unit).

- Lincoln might be encoded as a president (16th), a person whose visage is on currency (five-dollar bill), or a war hero (Civil War).
- 10 might be encoded as a counting number (10), an ordinal position (10th), or an amount (10 units).
- 5 might be encoded as a counting number (5), an ordinal position (5th), or an amount (5 units).

In addition to the semantic representations shown by these analogies, information in problems can be presented pictorially, as in an analogy that might include a black square inside a white circle, which might be represented in terms of shape, position, or color. (For an example, see question 5 in the box titled "Try This! Intelligence Test.")

From such problems Sternberg has developed a theory of intelligence that distinguishes five different components by which intelligence can be analyzed: metacomponents, performance components, acquisition components, retention components, and transfer components. **Components** refers to the steps that a person must go through to solve a problem. **Metacomponents** refers to the person's knowledge about how to solve a problem. Because metacomponents are the basis of so many diverse intellectual tasks, Sternberg considers it to be related to general intelligence. He is continuing to investigate how different components are involved in reasoning tasks, such as analogies, and how the components and metacomponents increase in complexity with development.

Are experts more intelligent? Well, their expertise in various are as displays, at the very least, high intelligence in particular domains. After reviewing a large number of studies of experts, Glaser and Chi (1988) have identified some of the characteristics of experts, which follow:

1. Experts excel mainly in their own domains. Experts in mental calculations, for example, are not likely to be experts in medical diagnosis and vice versa.

2. Experts perceive large meaningful patterns in their domain. Chess masters, radiologists, and architects are able to "see" more meaningful patterns within their specialty than nonspecialists.

3. Experts are fast. Expert typists, chess players, computer programmers, mathematicians, and so on work within their specialty with greater speed than others.

4. Experts seem to utilize STM and LTM effectively. It seems that experts have superior memories, but perhaps they simply utilize their memories better.

5. Experts see and represent a problem in their domain at a deeper level than novices. When experts are asked to sort and analyze problems, they tend to deal with deep issues rather than superficial ones.

6. Experts spend a great deal of time analyzing a problem qualitatively. They tend to look at a problem from several angles before plunging into its solution.

7. Experts have self-monitoring skills. They seem to be aware of their errors and are able to make in-course corrections.

Cognitive Neuroscience Support

While psychologists of different orientations, from Binet, to Spearman, Thurstone, Guilford, Cattel, Wechsler, Hunt, and Sternberg (and many others) have sought behavioral answers to the question of intelligence, neuroscientists have also been intrigued by the

Dilbert/ by Scott Adams

DILBERT reprinted by permission of United Features Syndicate, Inc.

problem but have sought neurological answers in the brain. Traditionally, the neurological approach has been grounded in medical research and practice and, frequently, the emphasis has been on mental retardation and developmental considerations. Surprisingly little work had been done on the biological development of "normal" intellectual processes. This situation changed with the invention of imaging technology, which allowed researchers to probe into the workings of the brain with effulgent clarity.

From our previous discussion (see Chapter 2) of positron emission tomography (PET) we learned that by measuring minute amounts of radioactive particles—specifically, hydrogen combined with oxygen 15, a radioactive isotope of oxygen—in the bloodstream, it is possible to measure sites in the brain that demand glucose nutrition. Ostensibly, areas that require more energy in the form of glucose are more active than areas that require less and these "hot spots" may be delineated by PET scans. The potential of this work for understanding the location of different types of intellectual work and possibly the way the brain processes intelligence tasks (such as taking an IQ test) is significant and may lead us in new directions regarding our basic concepts of intelligence. But, where to begin?

A logical place to look at the brain and intelligence is at the most general level. In a series of experiments Richard Haier and his colleagues at the University of California, Irvine have addressed this issue by looking at metabolic needs vis-à-vis brain locations, for different groups, such as skilled computer-game players versus nonskilled players; people who score high on abstract, nonverbal reasoning tasks versus base rates for normal performance; individuals with mild mental retardation and Down syndrome versus matched controls; and men versus women performing mathematical reasoning tasks. In one experiment subjects with high scores on abstract, nonverbal reasoning tasks showed reduced energy activity in parts of the brain which otherwise are involved in these tasks. You may recall from Chapter 2 we reported the finding that neural activity for computer-game experts was less than for novices and this finding and the preceding finding suggest that the brain is an efficient organ in the sense that intelligent and practiced brains use less glucose than comparable controls. The brain's glucose metabolic rate (GMR) was less for the people who scored high on the abstract test than for the control group, suggesting that this kind of intelligence is efficient in problem solving.

FIGURE 14.12

The "Tetris" game in progress from left to right. Participants attempt to manipulate configurations of four square blocks falling from the top of the screen to produce solid rows of blocks. Once a solid row of blocks is completed, it disappears and is replaced by the row above it. Symbol markings show individual shapes that have already been placed. Note the bottom row of the middle panel is complete; in the panel on the right it has disappeared (1 point is scored) and the rows above moved down.

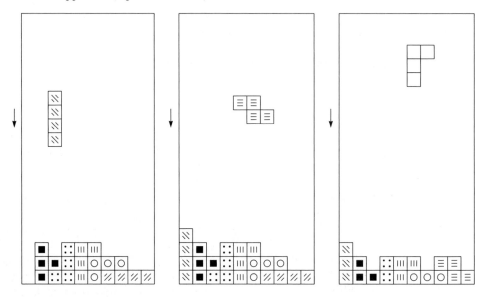

In yet another experiment related to intelligence a group of people practiced playing the computer game "Tetris" (see Figure 14.12), which requires the player to rotate and move objects in such a way as to create a solid row of blocks. If the player is successful, the speed increases until only real aficionados can keep up with the rapidly falling blocks. In general, Haier and his colleagues have developed an "efficiency model" of intelligence: Intelligence is not a function of how hard the brain works but rather how efficiently it works. In addition, learning may actually decrease brain metabolic works and, one is reminded of the concept of automaticity (see Chapter 3) in which well-practiced routines require little attention and run on "auto pilot." An earlier study had participants practicing up to five days a week for several months on the "Tetris" game. They got better by sevenfold, but their cortical and subcortical GMRs *decreased* significantly over their initial metabolic rates. Following this experiment Haier, Siegel, Tang, Abel, and Buchsbaum (1992) administered several standard tests of intelligence (Raven's Progressive Matrices scale and the Wechsler Adult Intelligence Scale). The purpose of the experiment was to establish the relationship between the learning of Tetris and scores on intelligence to determine if high-ability people show the largest GMR decreases as suggested by the brain efficiency hypothesis. The results, indicating that the magnitude of GMR changes and intelligence scores were related, supported the efficiency model.

Additional indication that smart brains are efficient brains comes through a study of brain size, GMR in mild mentally retarded and Down syndrome individuals by Haier et al. (1995) using both PET scans and magnetic resonance imaging (MRI) data. The results of the MRI showed that mentally retarded and Down syndrome groups both had brain volumes of about 80 percent of controls. The PET data show that whole brain cortex GMR was greater in both the retarded and Down syndrome groups as compared with control participants.

The question of whether human "intelligence" is composed of a series of subcomponents (such as mathematical ability, verbal ability, and spatial ability) or is a general factor that contributes to success in a large number of cognitive tasks has been hotly contested. Charles Spearman developed the concept of general intelligence of *g* during the early part of the twentieth century. Convincing evidence for *g* has been elusive yet, in a recent study by John Duncan and his associates (2000) at Cambridge, specific parts of the lateral frontal cortex appear to be implicated when people perform a variety of cognitive tasks used to measure intelligence. In the following task, choose the one that does not belong with the rest:[4] In the first task, a type of spatial intelligence is measured and in the second, verbal intelligence.

Spatial   **Verbal**

     LHEC   DFIM   TQNK   HJMQ

fMRI brain scans of people doing these types of tasks show that spatial and verbal processing are generally localized in the frontal part of the brain, thus supporting the *g*, or general theory of intelligence. (See the accompanying figure.) It appears that spatial processing involves both the left and right hemispheres. Such work is on the cutting edge of cognitive neuroscience and raises new questions. For example, are there specialized areas within the general areas that are associated with specific intellectual abilities? And how are these general intelligence areas connected to other parts of the brain that (likely) contribute to intelligent cognition?

Intelligence, or at least the performance on complex problem-solving tasks, is just beginning to succumb to the curious minds of genetic engineers, who champion the

Spatial processing   **Verbal processing**

 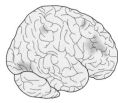    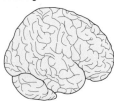

Left hemisphere   Right hemisphere   Left hemisphere   Right hemisphere

idea that through tinkering with the genetic structure of the brain, smarter creatures may be assembled. One such effort that has received wide attention is the work of Joe Tsien (2000) of Princeton University who has altered a protein in mice that is important in learning and memory. These genetically altered mice, dubbed Doogie, were placed in an open box and allowed to explore two objects for several minutes. Then, a few days later,

---

[4]The correct answer to the spatial question is the third nonsymmetrical item and to the verbal item, the third item that is equally spaced alphabetically (reversed order).

the experimenter replaced one of the objects with a new object. The "smart" mice spent more time exploring the new object while "normal" mice spent an equal amount of time exploring both objects, suggesting that the old object was no more familiar to them than the new. The genetically modified mice remembered objects up to five times longer than the nonmodified mice. Several subsequent tasks involving maze learning confirmed the earlier observations. While these mice will not be capable of solving even a simple problem in algebra, they seem to "act intelligently."

The future of genetic engineering—as well as other forms of mind altering, like chemical intervention, as it relates to making humans "act intelligently"— suggests to some a boon for the slow-learning person and to others a serious threat to natural intelligence. The "brave new world" that is being created in today's laboratories will be of immense interest and may present some moral problems for which intelligent decisions will be required.

The implications are many. Why are intelligent brains more efficient than less intelligent brains? Or, is the premise on which that question is framed erroneous? What underlying mechanism is responsible for the greater demand for glucose? Is the basic phenomenon related to the arborization of neurons? How is intelligence related to early development? Is there a critical period of neonatal development and brain development? What is the influence of early childhood stimulation on brain efficiency? Are instances of mental retardation preventable? reversible?

The work on human intelligence is just beginning. But then, so is the work that needs to be done on perception, learning, memory, problem solving, and a myriad of other problems we twentieth-century cognitive psychologists have tackled. Many of the solutions will be found to these mysteries in the twenty-first century.

Spotlight on Cognitive Neuroscience

Creative Problem Solving

Stephen Fiore and Jonathan Schooler have some interesting perspectives on creative problem solving. Their view is that several aspects of creative problem solving involve right-hemisphere functions. In particular, the notion of insight may be associated with certain cognitive processes that are known to originate in the right hemisphere of the brain. Experiences of insight that lead to creative problem solving often are nonverbal, "aha" moments. Remember in *Cast Away* when Tom Hanks has been trying unsuccessfully to start a fire. In the midst of scraping coconut out of its shell, he has an "aha" moment when he realizes that he should try that scraping motion of wood on wood to start the fire (instead of the spinning action he had been trying previously). The next scene shows him applying his newfound insight to his fire-starting problem. Fiore and Schooler conclude that, although the evidence may be circumstantial, it nevertheless indicates that the right hemisphere is particularly capable of processing information in such a way to lead to the type of insight that is useful in creative problem solving.

Fiore, S. M., & Schooler, J. W. (1998). Right hemisphere contributions to creative problem solving: Converging evidence for divergent thinking. In M. Beeman & C. Chiarello (Eds.), *Right hemisphere language comprehension: Perspectives from cognitive neuroscience* (pp. 349–371). Hillsdale, NJ: Erlbaum.

A la carte

Elephant Art?

Comparative psychology began as a method of studying animals so research findings could ultimately be compared or applied to humans. The comparative movement, which began in the late nineteenth century, was influenced by Darwin and fueled by researchers such as George Romanes and Lloyd Morgan. Comparative psychologist Edward Thorndike (1911) examined animal intelligence by placing cats inside of a box and measuring the time it took for them to escape. When the cats were able to escape faster, Thorndike attributed the time difference to equate with learning. He could then study how cats learned to solve the problem of escaping the "puzzle box." Later in the century Gestalt psychologist Wolfgang Kohler studied chimpanzees' ability to solve problems. In a famous study involving a chimp named Sultan, Kohler (1925) demonstrated that chimpanzees can experience insight into solving a problem. In this particular study, the goal was for Sultan to reach a banana suspended from the ceiling of the cage. The cage was equipped with some boxes and pieces of stick, none of which alone could be used to access the food. After several unsuccessful attempts, Sultan was reported to have the "insight" to combine the sticks into a larger stick, which ultimately lead to a successful attempt. More recently researchers have attempted to demonstrate language in a variety of species including non-human primates, parrots, and porpoises. A recent trend in elephant art has emerged. According to *National Geographic* (http://news.nationalgeographic.com/news/2002/06/0626_020626_elephant_2.html), some elephants will draw in the dirt with sticks. When given a set of elephant-sized

brushes, the elephants quickly learned how to paint (see photo below). As in the case with language, it may be debatable whether the final product is art or possibly art at the human preschool level. Decide for yourself by visiting *Novica.com* where proceeds from elephant art are donated in part to support elephants (http://www.novica.com/region/elephantartists.cfm).

Student Resource Center

STUDY GUIDE

1 Problem solving is thought directed toward discovering a solution for a specific problem.

2 Several models have proposed cognitive networks engaged during problem-solving activity. One such model (Eisenstadt & Kareev) has focused on internal representations formed during problem solving, with related research showing memory about the problem field to be a function of how the problem was formed, negligible anticipatory planning, and scanning patterns of the problem field suggestive of top-down or hypothesis-driven processing.

3 Creativity is cognitive activity resulting in a novel perspective of a problem and is not restricted to pragmatic outcomes.

4 One framework for viewing the creative process (Wallas) proposes four phases: (1) preparation, which involves problem formation, a process engaging our general knowledge base; (2) incubation, which is the period when no direct attempts to solve the problem are made and attention is diverted elsewhere; (3) illumination, which occurs when understanding is achieved; and (4) verification, which involves testing of the insight.

5 Judgments of creativity range from assessments by authorities in the relevant field (e.g., an Olympic athlete) to psychometric instruments designed to measure divergent thought processes defined as the ability to generate numerous abstract, flexible answers to one problem (e.g., how many different ways can you use a brick?). Both procedures involve subjective evaluations.

6 Training can result in improved performance on standard measures of creativity, but it is not known whether such experience can produce the type of activity associated with people generally considered to be creative (such as van Gogh, Einstein, or Dickinson).

7 The complex nature of intelligence produces definitional problems. Early attempts to address these conceptual difficulties used factor analysis to isolate general and specific abilities, but such procedures have been criticized for not providing information about mental processes; for being difficult to test against theories; and for relying on individual differences, which is not the only or necessarily the best way to study human abilities.

8 Cognitive theories of intelligence hold it to be a component that interacts with information as it is processed through stages involving unique operations. Research using this framework has determined that memory retrieval (speed, accuracy, and amount) is a function of verbal ability, and an individual's knowledge base (novice

vs. skilled) affects the amount and accuracy of recall as well as the accuracy of his or her metamemory.

9 Studies of brain glucose metabolic rate (GMR) indicate that people who score high on intelligence tests or are well practiced in skill performance tend to require fewer nutrients to parts of the brain than "less efficient" brains.

KEY TERMS

components
componential intelligent behavior
contextual intelligence behavior
convergent thinking
creativity
cultural block
divergent thinking
experiential intelligence behavior
functional fixedness

intelligence
illumination
incubation
intuition
metacomponents
preparation
problem solving
verification

STARTING POINTS

Books and Articles

● An outstanding review of early history of research in thinking, concept formation, and problem solving is Woodworth, *Experimental Psychology.* F. Bartlett, *Thinking,* is a good introduction to traditional viewpoints. Bruner, Goodnow, and Austin, *A Study of Thinking,* is the source of much of the traditional theory and experimentation in concept formation.

● Many articles have been collected into two paperback books, Johnson-Laird and Wason, eds., *Thinking and Reasoning* and *Thinking: Readings in Cognitive Science.*

● Three "annual reviews" of thinking that summarize the significant developments are Bourne and Dominowski, *Thinking;* Neimark and Santa, *Thinking and Concept Attainment;* and Erickson and Jones, *Thinking.*

● Rubinstein has written a lively account of thinking and problem solving in *Tools for Thinking and Problem Solving,* as have Bransford and Stein in *The Ideal Problem Solver.* An easy and entertaining book is Mayer's *Thinking, Problem Solving, Cognition.* A first-rate collection of papers on human intelligence has been edited by Robert Sternberg and is called *Handbook of Human Intelligence* and *Advances in the Psychology of Human Intelligence.* Also see *Intelligence Applied* and *Beyond IQ: A Triarchic Theory of Human Intelligence* by Sternberg. Several recent volumes on intelligence have been edited by Chipman, Segal, and Glaser and are called *Thinking and Learning Skills;* and Nickerson, Perkins, and Smith have written an excellent book on thinking called *The Teaching of Thinking.* The periodical *Current Issues in Cognitive Science* frequently contains stimulating articles on the topics covered in this chapter and in the February 1993 issue (Number 1) intelligence was featured in several articles. Hunt has an interesting article in *American Scientist* and for a look at the social/racial side of intelligence see *The Bell Curve* by Herrnstein and Murray. A special issue of *Scientific American* was published in 1998 called *Exploring Intelligence.*

Movies

● A Beautiful Mind (2001)—Creativity and Intelligence

● Rain Man (1988)—Savants

● Cast Away (2000)—Problem Solving

Search Terms

- Stereotype threat
- Animal intelligence
- Elephant art
- Intelligence and psychological testing

Answer to the Puzzle on Page 411

The puzzle states that you have an "endless supply of rope." You dump the rope into the gorge until it is filled up and you and your pal walk comfortably across. Meanwhile, you may have been inventing ingenious solutions which used the 20-foot ladder, the pliers, candle, matches, and your friend. Sometimes too much information in solving a problem makes it more difficult than just the bare essentials. Try the puzzle on a friend and eliminate all the supplies except the "endless supply of rope." How did the friend do? Why?

Incidentally, the use of this example was inspired by a frustrating event. One of us (RLS) ordered a specially designed drawer for his kitchen. It arrived with a bunch of assorted hardware, the drawer, and terse instructions obviously written by the same person who wrote the early computer guides. The hardware pieces were nondescript—one long piece looked something like a miniature harpoon with wings flaring out of the nonpointy end. Another was similar to a three-dimensional figure used in the test for applicants to dental school and another looked like a roller-coaster guide with only one wheel. It may have been possible to put these odd pieces on the drawer if there was some surface to mount them on. Alas, by Sunday afternoon he gave up and called the factory whose technician on duty was equally baffled. He did an extensive computer search and found a long outdated model from which he attempted to talk me through the installation process. "Take the harpoon, nonpointy side and hold it upright. Now take the dental test . . . ." Nothing worked. Late that night the "light turned on" and he realized that the harpoon, the dental test item, the roller coaster guide and so on were all already mounted on the drawer! The company had sent duplicate hardware, and he thinks they even threw in a few extra screws, harpoons and so on just to confuse. Problem solving with information is kind of like a Goldilocks problem: You need not too much, not too little, but just the right amount of information for efficient problem solving. The smart people among us are those who recognize the critical components needed for a solution and disregard the rest—the extra harpoon, the extra dental school test device, the extra screws, and so on. Cryptoanalysts, spies, specialty cabinet packers, and practical jokers all know this. Lao Tzu was right: "Less is more."

Answer to Puzzle on Page 413

Answer to problem in box titled "A Problem of Patients—Psychiatrists' and Yours." Karen and Laura care for a Rubin and, therefore, are not named Rubin (mark in the intersection of Karen and Laura with Rubin and exclusionary mark). Therefore, Mary is married to Rubin. Laura is a patient of Dr. Sanchez and, therefore, is not named Sanchez and must be called Taylor. By elimination, then, Karen is a Sanchez. Mary Rubin is seen by a female (clue 1) and a Dr. Taylor (clue 2), so she is treated by Laura Taylor and Mary's husband is treated by Karen Sanchez. Peter, who is treated by a Dr. Taylor (clue 2), is not Dr. Taylor (obviously) and cannot be the male Dr. Rubin treated by Karen Sanchez, so he must be Peter Sanchez and he treats Laura Taylor (clue 2). Omar cannot be the Dr. Rubin who is treated by Karen Sanchez because Omar is treated by Norman (clue 4), so Omar's last name is Taylor and Norman's last name is Rubin. Peter's psychiatrist is Omar Taylor, and, by elimination, Karen is under Mary Rubin's care. In summary, the full names of psychiatrists and patients are as follows: Drs. Laura Taylor (Mary Rubin), Karen Sanchez (Norman Rubin), Mary Rubin (Karen Sanchez), Omar Taylor (Peter Sanchez), Peter Sanchez (Laura Taylor), and Norman Rubin (Omar Taylor).

Artificial Intelligence

Hmmm . . .?

1. What is artificial intelligence, and how might it affect psychology and your life?

2. Trace the history of computing machines to current AI programs.

3. In what ways are silicon-based computers like a carbon-based brain (the human brain)? In what ways are they unlike each other?

4. What is the Turing test? What is the Chinese room?

5. How does a computer analyze visual forms?

6. How do computers recognize and produce language?

7. What types of artistic productions may be generated by computers? How successful are they?

8. Will computer intelligence ever exceed human intelligence?

9. What kind of a thinking machine is the brain?

10. How can human thinking be emulated by a machine?

11. Can human thinking be surpassed by computers?

*F*irst Law of Robotics—A robot may not injure a human being, or, through inaction, allow a human being to come to harm

Second Law of Robotics—A robot must obey the orders given it by human beings except where such orders would conflict with the First Law

Third Law of Robotics—A robot must protect its own existence as long as such protection does not conflict with the First or Second Law.

—*Issac Asimov*

Science fiction has a tendency to become science fact. Something like Hal,[1] the on-board spaceship computer capable of ethical decision making and intelligence in Arthur Clarke's *2001: A Space Odyssey,* is being discussed seriously in modern artificial-intelligence (AI) laboratories. That is not to say that computers will evolve exactly as Clarke envisioned, any more than propulsion systems developed in the way Jules Verne imagined three-quarters of a century before a rocket sent a spaceship to the moon. However, computer scientists are developing systems that come very close to mimicking aspects of human cognition; it seems plausible that something like Hal will be around before you depart from this earth.

Artificial intelligence (AI), is broadly defined as that branch of computer science that deals with the development of computers (hardware) and computer programs (software) that emulate human cognitive functions. In the preceding fifteen chapters "human cognitive functions" that have been discussed in some detail and

[1]Acrostic for *h*euristically programmed *alg*orithmic computer.

we have learned that cognition involves perception, memory, thinking, language processing, and many other related functions which are carried out in a more or less exact way. You can, for example, see and recognize your friend's face; solve the mathematical problem of $(7 \times 8)/(4 \times 5)$ in "your head"; compose a sensible poem set in iambic pentameter; recognize the voices of characters from *Southpark;* mentally calculate the most direct route from your home to the college; determine if it is or is not proper to invite the father of the bride to the groom's bachelor party; and distinguish sour milk from fresh milk. We do things like this every day with no effort (and, if we may extrapolate from the findings of Haier and his colleagues on human intelligence regarding metabolic rates and intellectual performance, without the expenditure of much energy). We also do a lot of foolish things, as evidenced by chips from *Youtube* and *Jackass 2.* We are human—and that's a problem for computers, being perfect machines that never make a mistake, "computer errors" notwithstanding. If a computer could simulate human thought and actions precisely, then it would be as good as we are in doing the list of things mentioned earlier, but also be just as fallible as we are. It is important to recognize the distinction between those who want to write programs that will perform human tasks well, such as the program we are presently using that draws a squiggly red line under misspelled words and those who aim to clone human thought. Computers and their impressive programs have become such an indispensable part of our everyday life that we wonder how we got along without them—still, they aren't clever enough to shampoo with toothpaste (or was it the other way around?). In order to do that, they would have to imitate exactly human thought and actions—to, in truth, perform *indistinguishably* from human cognition, which in fact, as we will see later, is a hallmark for evaluating artificial intelligence.

Let's consider a "simple" cognitive task: That of solving math problems. Many computer programs can do this swiftly and accurately, but they do not simulate human cognition. Early in AI research, Simon (1966) and colleagues attempted to model human performance in a computer program called STUDENT, which was designed to solve algebra word problems based on pure syntactic analysis. Some human participants in their study performed much like the way STUDENT did but many did not. They used auxiliary cues and physical representations in solving the problems, much as you probably did when trying to figure out the loss of water in a leaky bucket that was being simultaneously filled—you, thoughtfully, drew a picture.

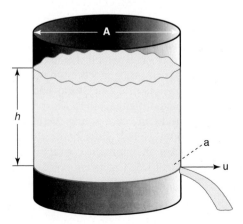

*I*t is morally impossible that there should be sufficient diversity in any machine to allow it to act in all events of life in the same way as our reason causes us to act.

—*Descartes*

When we discuss AI, it is usually intertwined with cognitive psychology and neuroscience. Ideas from one field, for example, neuroscience, might be incorporated into another, for example, artificial intelligence, and yet other ideas from cognitive psychology might be applied to both of the other areas. All three—AI, cognitive psychology, and neuroscience (especially neuroscience)— build a platform for cognitive science.

AI and cognitive psychology have a kind of symbiotic relationship, each profiting from the development of the other. The development of artificial ways to replicate human perception, memory, language, and thought, is dependent upon understanding how these processes are accomplished by human beings. And the development of AI increases the magnitude of our capabilities to understand human cognition.

This chapter offers a general introduction to AI as it relates to perception, memory, search processes, language, problem solving, artistic performance and robotics.

Although work in AI is devoted to the development of machines that act as if they were intelligent, most are designed without any intention of mimicking human cognitive processes. However, there are researchers who are concerned with the development of "intelligent" machines that model human thought, and it is this perspective—sometimes called computer simulation (CS)—that, for the most part, is reflected in this chapter. (Because at times it is nearly impossible to tell where AI leaves off and computer science begins, the widely accepted term *AI* is used in this chapter to embrace all forms of computer-produced output that would be considered intelligent if produced by a human.)

Historical Perspective

Calculators

Calculators are the oldest form of computers in that they are calculating devices. The earliest type was the abacus, which was used in China during the sixth century B.C. The Egyptians invented a counting machine that used pebbles some time before Herodotus (about 450 B.C.) noted its use. The Greeks had a similar device, and in Rome writers tell of three types of calculating machines. Most of these devices were used to keep track of transactions by adding and subtracting. Multiplication was performed by repeating the adding phase. About 1633 a little-known German astronomer, Wilhelm Schickard (1592–1635), invented an automatic digital calculator that was commemorated on a German postage stamp in 1973. The invention of a calculating machine is more often ascribed to French philosopher Blaise Pascal (1623–1662), the Father of Calculus. Pascal's ma-

Charles Babbage **(1792–1871).** British
mathematician and inventor who developed
the concept of a mechanical computational
device that could be programmed. He called
it the "analytic engine."

chine could only add and subtract, but it attracted widespread interest. In the 1670s
Gottfried Leibniz introduced a machine that could do multiplication and division. Computers came along later when the eccentric Charles Babbage (1792–1871), sometimes
called the world's first computer scientist, assisted by Lady Ada Lovelace invented the
difference engine, which had programmable operations containing conditional branches.
(See Haugeland, 1989, for details. A model of Babbage's machine can be seen at the
Smithsonian Institute in Washington, D.C.)

A Babbage Machine.

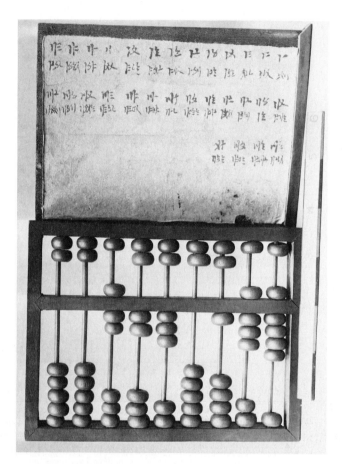

An ancient abacus.

Computers

The origin of modern computers can be traced to the 1940s, when vacuum-tube computers such as the Universal Automatic Computer (UNIVAC) and the Electronic Numerical Integrator and Computer (ENIAC) were invented to speed lengthy and tedious mathematical calculations commonly used by the military, such as calculating the trajectories of artillery shells. The ENIAC, a highly secretive U.S. Army–sponsored project conducted at the University of Pennsylvania, had 17,468 vacuum tubes (precursors to computer chips, and about the size of lightbulbs) whose manufacturer guaranteed a service life of 25,000 hours, which meant, on average, that a tube would burn out about every 8 minutes! The behemoth calculating machine weighed 30 tons and drew 174 kilowatts of power. The project directors were John Mauchley and J. Presper Eckert. By today's standards these giant computers were simpleminded and inefficient, performing functions one could now do on a cell phone's calculator. These giant machines gave way to smaller, more powerful, and complex systems that, in turn, were eventually replaced by the computers in general use today.

Few dates in cognitive psychology are more important than 1956.[2] During the summer of that year, a group of ten scientists met on the campus of Dartmouth College to consider the possibilities of developing computer programs that would "behave" intelligently. Among those who attended this conference were John McCarthy, who later founded AI laboratories at MIT and Stanford University and is generally credited with christening the new science "AI"; Marvin Minsky, who became the director of the AI laboratory at MIT; Claude Shannon, who developed the modern model for a communication system at Bell Laboratories; Herbert Simon, who was to win the Nobel Prize in economics; and Allen Newell, who has carried out his important work in cognitive science and AI at Carnegie Mellon University. The conference was historically significant because the direction AI was about to take was set, which directly influenced the way cognitive psychology was to develop.

Since the Dartmouth conference, AI has grown exponentially. AI, in some form or another, now touches the daily lives of most people in the world, and occupies the concentrated effort of thousands of scientists. The diverse ends of AI research and practice cannot be reported in a single chapter, or a book, or even many books. However, we can, in this chapter, present a sample of the work in AI as it relates to cognitive psychology.

Early AI

The most common type of computer in use today is patterned after a design ("architecture," in computer lingo) created by the Hungarian mathematician John von Neumann in 1958, who emigrated to the United States in 1930. These computers are sometimes called *Johniacs* or serial processors, meaning that electrical impulses are processed in series, or in sequence. These chainlike sequences operate very rapidly, with each step requiring only nanoseconds, but a computer performing complicated tasks in a serial fashion (such as solving involved mathematical functions, or rearranging data or files) may require several minutes, hours, or even longer. All computer users have experienced the maddeningly "long" lag time required by personal computers to "think" or "digest" a problem. One basic reason serial computers of the von Neumann genus require so much time is that one operation must be completed before another is initiated. Serial processors solve problems bit by bit (or byte by byte), in a stepwise fashion.

Even in the beginning of the technology of computers, AI scientists (and science fiction writers) had grand dreams about thinking machines and robots. A seminal paper was written in the early 1940s by a Chicago psychiatrist, W. S. McCulloch, and his student, W. Pitts. In this paper they introduced a concept that was to have significant impact on computer scientists, including von Neumann and later PDPers. Based on the idea that the *mind* was defined as the workings of the brain, specifically the brain's basic units, neurons, they argued that neurons could be viewed as "logical devices," that "neural events and the relations among them can be treated by means of propositional logic." When neurons communicate with each other, they do so electrochemically. A tiny electrical current is passed along a cell's axon to the synapse, where a chemical neurotransmitter passes the impulse to other neurons. The process of neurotransmission is rule governed: firing of a neuron occurs only

---

[2]During that year Bruner, Goodnow, and Austin published *A Study of Thinking*, Chomsky published "Three Models of the Description of Language," Miller published "The Magical Number Seven," and Newell and Simon completed "The Logic Theory Machine: A Complex Information Processing System."

 J. Presper Eckert (foreground) and John Mauchley work on the vacuum tube computer, ENIAC, with U.S. Army and other personnel in 1946.

when the threshold is achieved, all neurons have thresholds, neurons fire only when the current is positive, a negative current will inhibit a neuron from firing, and so on. Most importantly, each neuron seems to sum up all excitatory and inhibitory signals from its thousands of connections. Depending on its threshold, a neuron will fire or not; that is, it will be on or off. (Neurons of this type are called **McCulloch-Pitts neurons.**) McCulloch and Pitts observed that this on or off neuron could be seen as a logic device. As is commonly known, computers function by means of binary circuits that represent a state of either on or off (designated by 1s or 0s). Although simple in form, when thousands of these binary circuits are coupled together in exponential series, the amount of processing power is awesome. Similarly, the basic unit of neural processing, the neuron and its connections, are capable of monumental powers of processing.

John McCarthy. Pioneered studies in artificial intelligence and designed LISP, a widely used AI language.

A short time after the paper by McCulloch and Pitts, von Neumann saw the connection between the logical behavior of neurons as they interact and the way digital computers go about their work. "It can easily be seen that these simplified neuron functions can be imitated by telegraph relays or by vacuum tubes." (Transistors had not been invented yet, or he probably would have mentioned them.) Von Neumann, who had already developed the most useful computer architecture up to that point, suggested that it might be possible to design a computer that mimicked the human brain—not only in function but also in structure—where vacuum tubes, relays, connecting wires, and hardware replaced neurons, axons, and synapses.

Following von Neumann, F. Rosenblatt undertook the project of building a computer that mimicked the structure and function of the brain. His intent was to make a computer that could learn to classify shapes. The result was called a perceptron, and it crudely imitated the brain's organization. Rosenblatt's machine consisted of a three-level hierarchy. Each level was associated with a different function that generally emulated the sensory, associative, and motor pattern of humans. While early machines such as the perceptron could not learn, they simply processed a narrow range of stimuli and made equally simple responses.

Could computers be designed to learn? Humans are capable of learning because they have modifiable synapses. Recall Hebb's rule (introduced in Chapter 2) about the strength between two neurons increasing when they are simultaneously activated. Could such a rule be built into the connections between the tubes and wires? Learning by such a machine might require that a resistor (a device that specifies the amount of electrical impulse leaving one transistor that will reach another) be wired into and programmed in an artificial brain. A resistor would act very much like a regulator, allowing some bits of information to be passed on while rejecting others. Perceptrons capable of "learning" (and *learning* is defined here as "the change in strength between units that simulate neurons") do so because they behave in a way similar to McCulloch-Pitts neurons and obey Hebb's theory. A computer so constructed might be shown a simple geometric shape, such as a circle, to classify. If it responds by calling it a square, then it can be "taught" to respond correctly by increasing the resistance between certain units and lowering the resistance between others. If the response is correct, that is, if the perceptron calls a circle a circle,

John von Neumann **(1903–1957).**
Designed the computer architecture in common use.

the values are left alone. In this sense, perceptrons punish errors and ignore success. These early steps were important in designing machines capable of making generalizations and learning, factors essential in the construction of a "thinking machine" that functions similarly to a human brain.

We should keep in mind that early computers were rare, and very expensive, and in the hands of a few elite intellectuals who were naturally curious about their potential. During the early stages of computer development, some fundamental opinions about the use and significance of these newfound contraptions thus emerged. There were those who thought that if computers were programmed properly, that is, given the right rules and instructions, they could carry out any operations, including the effective mimicking of human thought. Others believed that for a machine to "think," it was necessary that a computer's hardware simulate a brain's physiology. To achieve the latter would require that a computer be built with layers upon layers of interconnected electronic surrogate neurons whose organization and function would simulate a human brain.

So far we have failed to produce either a truly "thinking" machine or one whose "brain" appears much like a human brain. However, as sciences go, AI is still in its infancy. Each of the perspectives mentioned has its own problems. In the first case, most AI programs are rigid in "thinking." When I ask you what is the square root of 73, you might say, "Well, it's at least 8 but not quite 9. About 8 and a half." A computer answers 8.5440037. . . . Rather than breed endless concatenations of digits, the human brain seems wonderfully designed to deal with chaos—seeing a familiar face in a crowd, driving on the Los Angeles freeways, understanding the deep meaning of a Chekhov drama, or feeling the sensuousness of silk as it caresses our skin. No computer can do that . . . yet. On the other hand, no human can spew out the answer to the square root problem in milliseconds, as any cheap handheld calculator can.

Just consider the Promethean task faced by those who aspire to wire a computer like a human brain! The brain has about 100 billion neurons, each of which connects with countless thousands of other neurons. Nevertheless, some people have attempted a small-scale computer model of the brain (see Rosenblatt, 1958) but, until recently (see the box titled "Cognition in Everyday Life: The Silicon Chip"), have discouraged others from pursuing this pastime (see Minsky & Papert, 1968). Earlier Minsky (1954) had written his dissertation on neural nets and had even built one with only 400 vacuum tubes (compared to over 17,000 in the ENIAC), but he soon became disinfatuated with the project. This early work did not produce "practical" results, while developing computer programs and hardware during the same time was the hottest game in town. Garage workshops expanded to huge factories, which built computer chips that could do things about which we could only dream.

Recent AI

The recent generation of computer/cognitive scientists is more sanguine regarding the simulation of neural functions by a machine. One of the recent changes in perceptrons was conceptual. Rather than thinking of a computer brain as an input-output device, scientists added a third layer, called a hidden layer. This hidden layer corresponds to the brain's interneurons, which are not concerned with input or output but with connecting im-

Cognition in Everyday Life

The Silicon Chip

A silicon chip, which is said to behave much like a human brain cell, was developed by Caltech and Oxford University researchers Mahowald and Douglas. The device, called a silicon neuron, has a structure and process that mimic the workings of neurons in the cerebral cortex. The important aspect of the technology is the analog nature of the device as contrasted with the digital processing units used in most computers. When humans see a complex object, such as a person's face, they do not see digitalized data—a series of pixels—but rather subtly graded contours and continuously varying shades of gray. From these signals the eye and brain extract meaning from the light signals through an analog process.

While others discount the importance of this technological discovery on the basis that the brain has many types of neurons and this is only one example, the idea of a silicon chip that imitates even some important features of the human neuron presents an intriguing question for the future. How far can technology go in creating a brain?

pulses to other neurons. The model is more representative of the human brain and compatible with contemporary connectionism, mentioned throughout this book.

Many of these issues deal with the problem of the architecture of computers and brains, a most important topic. However, computers still do not perform functions as humans do; computers and brains are not identical. In some ways computers do better than brains, but in some ways they do worse. This disparity is seen in many domains, as has been mentioned previously, but one particularly problematic area is the identification of three-dimensional objects. Our eyes, two-dimensional sensors, readily and accurately transmit signals that are interpreted as three-dimensional. Even with the sluggish "wetware" of the nervous system, the constant change in eye–object location, and size adjustments, our perceptual system works nearly perfectly. Computers do less well, even though the rate of transmission is millions of times faster than neurotransmission.

As has already been mentioned, one reason for the difference is that computers generally process information serially, using a **sequential processing model,** while brains generally process information in parallel. Some AI scientists have begun to overcome the architectural difference between brains and computers for the purpose of overcoming this functional difference. One such scientist is W. Daniel Hillis, who has developed a "connection machine" (see Hillis, 1987), which solves problems by breaking them down and then processing them at once in parallel, a **parallel processing model.** These smaller problems, or chunks, are then distributed to separate areas of the computer's processing network. This is contrasted with the von Neumann class of computers, which has one central processor that processes information sequentially. In Hillis's connection machine, 65,536 (a prime number in binary code) processors are available to work on a single problem, allowing it to be broken down into small pieces to be processed simultaneously. Although each processor is less powerful than the PC used in the preparation of this manuscript, when those 65,536 processors are hooked up together and work concurrently they can process several billion instructions per second. It's an impressive machine, both conceptually and functionally.

AI and Human Cognition

Those who subscribe to a neurally inspired parallel distributed processing model are hard at work trying to find solutions to questions about the brain as a thinking machine and whether computers can emulate brain activity and human cognition.

The Brain as a Thinking Machine   The answer to the first question is beginning to take shape after over a century of research in psychology, especially during the past several decades of research in cognitive psychology. What we have learned about our thinking machine, called the brain, is that it is fundamentally different from the von Neumann computers now in common use. Perhaps AI would be further along if computers resembled brains more closely. To clarify this matter, we have proposed the following comparative résumé (see Table 15.1):

Some computer programs work far more effectively than human thinking; most, however, are at best clumsy counterfeits of the real thing. Computers can solve some problems, such as detailed mathematical ones, faster and more accurately than humans can. Other tasks, such as making generalizations and learning new patterns of activity, are done best by humans but not as well by computers.

TABLE 15.1

	Silicon-Based Computers (von Neumann type)	Carbon-Based Brains (Humans)
Processing speed	In nanoseconds	In milliseconds to seconds
Type	Serial processor (mostly)	Parallel processor (mostly)
Storage capacity	Vast, for digitally coded information	Vast, for visual and linguistic information
Material	Silicon and electronic	Neurons and organic
Cooperation	Absolutely obedient	Generally cooperative
Learning capacity	Rule governed	Conceptual
Best feature	Can process an immense amount of data in a short period of time	Can make judgments, inferences, and generalizations easily
	Cost efficient, rule governed, easy to maintain, and predictable	Ambulatory; has language, speech, vision, and emotions
Worst feature	Does not self-learn easily; has difficulty with complex human cognitive tasks such as language understanding and production	Has limited capacity for information processing and storage; is forgetful; is expensive to maintain requiring food, drink, sleep, oxygen, moderate temperature in addition to a whole list of biopsychological needs (e.g., love, belongingness, sex)

Cognition in Everyday Life

The Beginnings of a Real $6 Million Man?

While American scientists of a generation ago tinkered with the notion that they could build a brainlike computer, in Japan one scientist, Aizawa, is building a brainlike computer with real nerve cells intermingled with electronic devices in an effort to fabricate a crude, semiartificial neural network. So far he has successfully combined cells with the semiconducting compound indium tin oxide and found that under very weak electrical stimulation organic cells respond with controlled growth (see figure shown here). It is too early to think of an artificial brain, but such devices might be useful as an interface between the nervous system and prostheses such as an artificial eye.

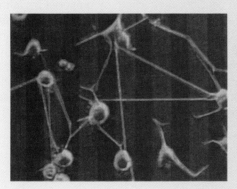 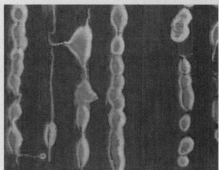

As shown in the table comparing von Neumann–type computers with brains, it is no wonder AI scientists have their work cut out for them. They are working with the wrong kind of machine. It appears as though we are on the verge of a conceptual breakthrough—perhaps a paradigm shift—in AI, in which the first steps have already been taken to make computers more brainlike in terms of both their structure and their process. Neural network systems, PDP models, and connectionism are attempting to discover the computational principles that govern networks of neurons in the human nervous system. They do this by what may seem to be a highly abstract means. Units may represent neurons, but units follow laws derived from neuron behavior. That is, a unit can be paired with other units, the association between them can be strengthened or weakened, they can achieve stable relations, and so on (Churchland, 1989).

An important concept has also been proposed with regard to neural networks: they can also learn. That is, through a system of synapse-like weights (as with the infrastructure of the brain) that link the units and can change through experience.

Some efforts have been successful. A new way of looking at human cognition has enjoyed great enthusiasm among its proponents. Even the casual student of cognitive psychology should be sensitized to this important contribution to psychology and be on the lookout for future developments.

The Thinking Machine

There are few areas of cognitive psychology that have been the subject of more heated arguments than the debate over the simulation of human thought by machines. On one side of the argument are AI zealots who believe not only that machines are capable of exactly replicating human cognition but also that advanced intellectual processes can be carried out only by machines. The logical extension of this argument is that computers should be directly involved in everyday human decision making. On the other side are those who consider AI to be an intellectually corrupt concept and believe people who put their faith in so-called thinking machines are materialistic idol worshipers. Human thinking is purely a human process that, even if partly synthesized by a machine, will never be duplicated by AI programs.

As a starting point, it is useful to consider the dichotomy proposed by John Searle (1980), a philosopher with the University of California at Berkeley. He describes two forms of AI: **weak AI,** which can be used as a tool in the investigation of human cognition, and **strong AI,** in which a properly programmed computer has a "mind" capable of understanding. Weak AI has few opponents; almost everyone acknowledges the importance of computers in the investigation of human cognition, and little more needs to be said about that issue here. Strong AI, which Searle refutes, has brought a storm of protest. Let's consider one of the original mind versus machine tests proposed by Alan Turing, a British mathematician.

The Turing Test

Turing (1950) proposed a test that involved communication between a human, who asked questions, and a language-using entity. Simply stated, the task of the human was to decide whether the entity was human. The **Turing test** was a very subtle deception that gave AI specialists something concrete to work on, diverting attention from the philosophic mind. Instead of addressing the philosophic issue directly (as Turing might have done had he asked, "Is cognition a function of material process, and if so, can those functions originate from an inorganic machine?" or "What is the solution to the mind–body problem?"), he chose a far more clever way to frame the question by basing it in operationalism. Since there remains some confusion in the literature about the real nature of the test Turing proposed, it is printed in detail here.

> The . . . problem can be described in terms of a game which we call the "imitation game." It is played with three people, a man (A), a woman (B), and an interrogator (C) who may be of either sex. The interrogator stays in a room apart from the other two. The object of the game for the interrogator is to determine which of the other two is the man and which is the woman. He knows them by labels X and Y, and at the end of the game he says either "X is A and Y is B" or "X is B and Y is A." The interrogator is allowed to put questions to A and B thus:
>
> C: Will X please tell me the length of his or her hair?
>
> Now suppose X is actually A, then A must answer. It is A's object in the game to . . . cause C to make the wrong identification. His answer might therefore be: "My hair is shingled, and the longest strands are about nine inches long."

In order that tones of voice may not help the interrogator the answers should be written, or, better still, typewritten. The ideal arrangement is to have a teleprinter communicating between the two rooms. Alternatively the question and answers can be repeated by an intermediary. The object of the game for the third player (B) is to help the interrogator. The best strategy for her is probably to give truthful answers. She can add such things as "I am the woman, don't listen to him!" to her answers, but it will avail nothing as the man can make similar remarks.

We now ask the question, "What will happen when a machine takes the part of A in this game?" Will the interrogator decide wrongly as often when the game is played like this as he does when the game is played between a man and a woman? These questions replace our original, "Can machines think?" (p. 434)

It is obvious that the value of certain questions put to X and Y depends on whatever fashion is current. For example, hair length and style as a basis of discrimination would be likely to lead to a high error rate in the 1970s. Nevertheless, the important point of Turing's test for AI and language scientists is that, in order for a computer to fool us into thinking that it is a human, it must be able to understand and generate a response that effectively mimics one important form of cognition.

The Chinese Room

To illustrate the untenable position of the strong AI view, Searle offers the following challenge. Suppose someone is confined to a room with a large collection of Chinese writings. The person knows no Chinese and may not be able to discriminate between Chinese calligraphs and other scripts. From outside the room the person is given another set of Chinese characters along with a set of rules for collating the first set of characters with the second. The rules are in plain English and will only let the person relate one set of symbols with another set of symbols. With the relational rules, the person in the **Chinese room** is able to give meaningful answers to questions about the content of the writings, even though the person is essentially ignorant of the language. After a while the person is so well practiced that questions can be answered both in English (the person's native language) and in Chinese (which the person does not know but is able to give responses in that language based on rules). The output is so good that it is "absolutely indistinguishable from that of native Chinese speakers" (Searle, 1980). The person in the Chinese room is a simple instantiation of a computer program: data in—data out. Searle takes the argument one step further. Being able to perform functions, such as translation by complex rules, does not mean that the thing performing the functions understands the meaning of the output. Human minds have *intentionality* (see Searle, 1983), which, according to Searle, is defined as "the property of mental states and events by which the mind is directed at objects and states of affairs in the world." These mental states include beliefs, fears, desires, and intentions. No matter how indistinguishable counterfeit thinking is from real human thinking, the two are not the same because of the intentions of the human thinker and because of the physical differences of the thinkers. One is produced organically; the other, electronically.

Computer scientists objected immediately to Searle's conundrum (see Boden, 1989). First, on the level of semantics; it was argued that the terms *intentionality, understanding,* and *thinking* are used without clear operational definitions. The second objection focused on the level of the example. If the person in the Chinese room performed the

Cognition in Everyday Life

Robot Surgeon?

*T*he question of indistinguishability of functions in another arena works differently. For example, suppose two surgeons work at a hospital. One surgeon is a graduate of a renowned med-

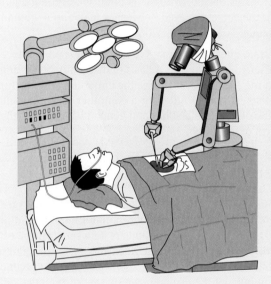

ical school and is reputed to be one of the best surgeons in the world. The other graduated from an undistinguished medical school and is regarded as a poor surgeon. One day an emergency operation is required, and the first physician is indisposed, so the second physician performs the operation unbeknownst to the patient, who is unconscious. The patient is not told which physician performed the operation and is satisfied that the procedure was successful. Furthermore, other physicians are convinced that the operation was performed by the first surgeon. In this limited example, we could conclude the test of indistinguishability had been passed. However, if you were the patient and learned that the operation had actually been performed by a robot, what would you conclude about the functional properties of the robot vis-à-vis the functional properties of a surgeon? Would you agree that they were the same? Why? Why not? Answers to these questions are hard to come by, but people who have strong opinions about the issues are not. One is Searle, who has turned the Turing test inside out.

functions described, the person (or the system) would indeed achieve at least some level of understanding. Third, the argument was dismissed on the basis of a reductio ad absurdum; that is, if carried to its logical conclusion, it would be possible to create a robot identical in every detail to a thinking person, and yet one would be capable of understanding and intentionality and the other not. Finally, for some AI scientists *understanding* and *intentionality* seemed to be related to specific material properties that caused them. Pylyshyn (1980) satirically muses that perhaps intentionality is a substance secreted by the human brain, and then poses his own riddle:

> If more and more of the cells in your brain were to be replaced by integrated circuit chips, programmed in such a way as to keep the input–output function of each unit identical to that of the unit being replaced, you would in all likelihood just keep right on speaking exactly as you are doing now except that you would eventually stop meaning anything by it. What we outside observers might take to be words would become for you just certain noises that circuits caused you to make. (p. 442)

The debate is far from over, and its value to some may be in its philosophic profundity. In addition, both camps have hardened their positions and seem to be advancing articles of faith rather than reason. The importance of discussing the debate in a book like this is twofold. First, it causes the reader to think deeply about the issue of what is human about human cognition. Second, it raises the question of the limits to which AI can imitate human intelligence. The fact that both the Turing test and the Chinese room problem have excited passions on both sides is a reflection of the intense interest of contemporary philosophers and AI scientists regarding the electronic genie that has been let out of the bottle recently.

In the next section some specific computer capacities are reviewed. The development of these specific functions approximates the flow of information in an information processing model from perception, to pattern recognition, and to higher forms of cognition.

Perception and AI

Human perception is initiated by external signals of light, sound, molecular composition, and pressure. These signals are detected by our sensory system and transduced (converted to neural energy) into messages the brain can understand. The amount of information available to us through our senses is enormous; our visual system alone can transmit 4.3×10^6 bits of information *per second* to the brain.

How might a machine be made to mimic this perceptual mechanism? A logical step is to develop some sensing capacity. One such approach can be seen in the work done on computer recognition systems. Much of the early research of this kind was motivated by practical problems (e.g., how to create a machine that could read a numerical code on a check) and, as such, only weakly addresses the human analog issue of AI; it is included here to illustrate some of the capacities of "perception" by existing computers.

Line Analysis

One way computers can be taught to recognize geometric forms by analyzing local features of an object uses the fact that complex geometric forms are composed of simpler ones. The program uses a number of small templates that are systematically passed over each object in search of a match. An example of a template and a geometric object to be identified is shown in Figure 15.1. The template is made up of two kinds of sensors—positive and negative, present and absent—one to a cell, or subdivision, of the template. The one shown has only six cells—three minus and three plus—and, because of the arrangement of these components (all minus elements at the left), it is of a kind likely to be suitable for identifying the left edge of an object. Positioning the template with its midline over the left edge of the cube would result in a perfect match. The corner match is poor, and there is no match on the bottom edge, where plus and minus sensors cancel out each other. Although this heuristic is more solidly oriented toward what a machine can do, it is not at odds with findings from studies of animal and human perception. Earlier in this book, we learned that physiological psychologists have successfully isolated line detectors in the cortical cells of cats, and it seems likely, although it has not been completely validated, that humans also have generalized edge detectors in the usual system.

FIGURE 15.1

Finding a left edge by means of a six-cell template. The signs + and − represent cells that respond to the conditions "present" or "absent," respectively.

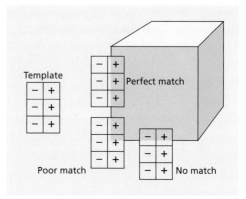

One difficulty with the system just described is that a great number of templates are needed for simple pattern recognition (e.g., a right-edge detector, a left-edge detector, etc.). An additional problem is the "goodness" of the stimulus; most geometric forms (especially those in the real world) have sharp *and* fuzzy edges, or bright *and* dull edges. Pattern recognition by line identification can be greatly simplified if the form to be recognized can first be converted into a line-only image, with templates then used to find the orientation of the lines.

Pattern Recognition

Pattern recognition systems have, for the most part, dealt with visual material. The general format of the perceptual hardware of these systems has been a raster, or matrix, of photoelectric cells (which respond to light energy). The photoelectric cells usually have only two states—on or off (or "white" or "black"). Consider the elementary task of identifying a number. Figure 15.2 shows how digits could be "transduced" into a binary code—*0* for "off" or "black," and *1* for "on" or "white." The computer "reads" each number (i.e., the photoelectric cells—one for each square of the grid superimposed on the number—"senses" the light areas, which are the ones not occupied by the number) on the basis of how close the digital code matches a template stored in the memory of the computer. It works very well if the figures are uniform, evenly positioned, and not degraded, and such devices are in wide use in industry and the U.S. Postal Service. However, when it comes to reading a hand-addressed letter to your Aunt Iola, optical scanning devices have some difficulty. It does appear, though, that means are rapidly being developed to "read" even handwriting.

Attempting to identify letters and words with the use of AI not only is a practical problem but also has meaning for those scientists who are interested in the process of human information analysis. Much of the current knowledge of the way we humans identify a letter and word is discussed in Chapter 11. This information is helpful in designing a computer program that mimics the process. A seminal report on this topic, which has served as a guide to subsequent research, was one from Selfridge and Neisser (1963). The general procedure for the "perception" of a letter, just described, would require a huge computer memory (to store a template of each novel form of each letter), otherwise many valid forms of letters would go undetected.

FIGURE 15.2

Representation in binary code (middle column) of letters at far left. 0s indicate "off" or "black"; 1s, "on" or "white." The last column shows letters as they might appear for reading by a scanner.

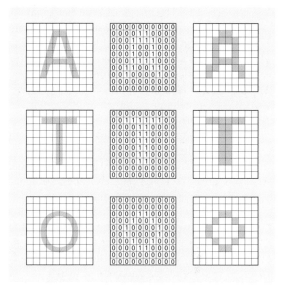

The basic logic espoused by Selfridge and Neisser a long time ago has been incorporated into recent letter and word reading machines. These computers "read" text through a series of subroutines, each of which specializes in one part of the task of reading, say, a letter. Such analysis is somewhat reminiscent of the means–end problem solver. One way a letter reading program might work is illustrated in Figure 15.3. It shows the way the letter *R* is processed through a series of stages, each quite simple, until a match is made on the basis of elimination of alternatives.

FIGURE 15.3

The letter *R* processed through a series of stages of identification. At each stage, a program recognizes particular attributes of the character, such as diagonal lines, indentations, and so on.

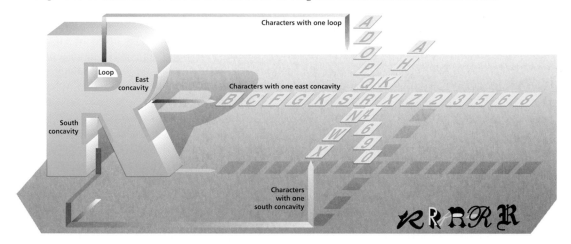

The matter of letter perception has also been considered in some detail by the PDPers. A general criticism of AI programs in the area of letter identification and form perception is that there is no workable mechanism for attention. A machine "sees" a form, be it a letter or geometric configuration, as a whole pattern and, unlike a human observer, finds it difficult to focus on critical features. One way the PDP model handles this difficult problem is to posit two types of feature detectors, one called a retinocentric feature unit and the other a canonic feature unit. In the retinocentric system visual stimuli are recorded in their "raw" form, much as an impression might fall on the retina. Canonic features are those that conform to the standard way information is presented, for example, just as we expect to see the letter *A* as it is shown here. In one system Hinton (1981) described a method for mapping retinocentric feature patterns onto canonical patterns. The details of this idea are too extensive to be presented here except to note that this important issue is under active investigation by those interested in PDP models. Interested students are directed to the original sources.

Older, and much more simpleminded, AI alphanumeric recognition systems were based on a template concept. A pattern of letters and numbers was stored in a computer's memory. When the computer "sees" a digit or letter, it "reads" it by matching the pattern, say *A*, with the mold of *A*. If a match is found, the letter is correctly identified. Even the sequential and parallel search methods described earlier were clearly brainless. The newer, neurally based computer models are actually capable of "learning" patterns. Some of these computer implementations can learn patterns, store them, and recognize them later. One program, called **DYSTAL** (*DYnamically STable Associative Learning*) successfully acquires alphabetic letters and letter sequences and, perhaps most remarkably, recognizes them even when only parts of the patterns are presented (see Figure 15.4).

DYSTAL does this, according to Alkon, much as we recognize a famous face suggested by the few lines of a cartoon. The system "learned" the pattern in the sense that there was no prewired connection between the input and output. A connection was developed, however, through greater weights being assigned to units (sites) that participate in the recognition process.

Another innovative feature of the system is that it is able to accommodate a large number of elements without requiring a huge amount of computer power. In many other network systems, each unit is connected with every other unit, so when the number of units is increased, the number of interactions increases exponentially. Thus, a system that has even a hundred units would require considerable processing time, and a network of that dimension would scarcely resemble a brain. "In DYSTAL, however, the weights of the connections are not compared with a fixed value: rather they arrive at a dynamic equilibrium in which the increases and decreases of weight over a set of pattern presentations are equal and no net weight change takes place" (Alkon, 1989). The system is comparable to human long-term memory in that when permanent memories are formed they are, for the most part, irreversible. Once these stable patterns are acquired, they require less computer power than do other, nonbiological networks.

The recognition of more complex forms follows the same logic as the recognition of simple forms, but it generally requires more complex processors. That topic is considered next.

Recognition of Complex Objects

Let's consider one example of a different kind of pattern recognition: the identification of a triangle. Figure 15.5 shows several triangles, all of which you will immediately recog-

FIGURE 15.4

Pattern recognition by Alkon's artificial network. Operates according to many of the same rules demonstrated by biological systems. When a network is trained to recognize a pattern, such as the lowercase *a* shown here at left, the receiving sites participating in the recognition are given more "weight" than those that are not participating—that is, their excitability is enhanced. Here synaptic weight is represented by the elevation of the elements in the layers. Enhancement helps to link together the neurons involved in a recollection when only a piece of a pattern is presented. (Thomas P. Vogl of the Environmental Research Institute of Michigan helped to design this drawing.)

From Alkon (1989). Reprinted by permission of Thomas C. Moore.

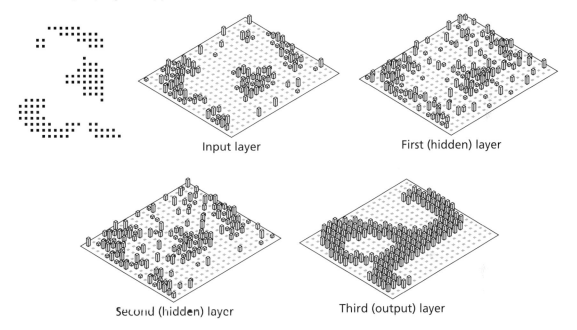

Input layer

First (hidden) layer

Second (hidden) layer

Third (output) layer

nize and categorize as such. If the prototype of triangularity stored in a computer program corresponded to the "good" triangle template (A), then triangles in B and C, if properly rotated and adjusted for size, could be easily recognized. Triangles in D and E, however, are problematic, especially those in E, which are identifiable mainly as the result of a "good gestalt," rather than on the basis of their being composed of three straight lines.

Our capacity to recognize immediately each of these forms as triangles is a function of our vast experience with other triangular objects; this abstract notion of *triangularity* is broad enough to allow us to include these triangles we have never seen in the category of triangles. Can a computer learn that concept? Probably, but the search mechanism needs to be more sophisticated than the single match operation such as that of machines that read numbers on bank checks. Instead, a search program that included the features of a triangle would have to be considered. Thus such features, or attributes, as angles, lines, shape, number of objects, and so on would have to be stored in the computer's memory, much as our own memory contains a catalog of these attributes of a triangle.

A practical application of computer recognition of complex forms is in the area of facial recognition. Suppose your face has unique features, much as your fingerprints do.

FIGURE 15.5

"Good" (A–D) and problematic (E) triangles. The former differ only in size, orientation, and relationship of their sides; the latter have no conventional straight-line sides but remain recognizable as triangles.

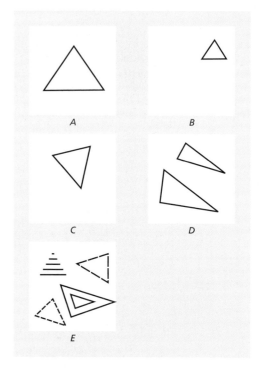

A computer system that could scan your face and find a perfect match with your identity might be a great aid to police departments. It also might be useful for check identification and even plant and office security. Imagine going to work in some security installation and being greeted every morning by a computer that asks, "Please place your face where I can see it" and, after scanning it and opening the door says, "Have a nice day, Ms. Juel, you have a call from W. M. Beach . . . and, by the way, happy birthday." While this threatens yet another intrusion into our private lives, it is likely that we will be living with such devices sooner than later.

The matter of facial identification has been undertaken by computer scientists such as Thomas Poggio and Roberto Brunelli at MIT. The gist of the program is that salient features, such as the width of the nose, the distance between the eyes and chin, and so on, are extracted from faces and analyzed mathematically. Sixteen features have been identified (see Figure 15.6).

If faces were always the same, a simple template matching model might suffice; however, our faces are never the same. Therefore, the program must find a close match between your face today and your face of last week and yet not be too lenient to allow in an impersonator. The program does this through geometric checks between angles of features and promises to be much more reliable than facial identification by humans. Such a device could help solve some of the photographic mysteries that crop up from time to time, such as the recent question posed by the discovery of a very early photograph of someone who may or may not be Abraham Lincoln. This early nineteenth-century photograph of a young man looks like Lincoln, but is it? Computer analysis of facial features may answer the question.

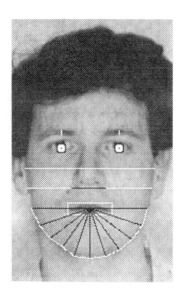

From our previous discussion of object recognition we know that human pattern perception is not simply a matter of seeing an object and then fitting that impression into a cerebral template (as computer matching of vertical bar codes is matched to corresponding patterns) but is likely to be built up of previously retained features which, when blended together form a prototype. New, or less familiar, stimuli take longer to recognize than old, or familiar, patterns because there are fewer matches between the pattern and memory. Computers do not have such limited capacity—there seems to be no practical limit to the storage capacity of computers—and, therefore, are frequently programmed to use massive storage and search mechanisms in trying to match sensation with memory. In "real life" we recognize people, places, and even words with little effort not because each time we see these things we store that impression separately, but because we store the abstraction associated with a class of stimuli. Thus, when you recognize your own bedroom, your pillow, and your shoes it is because the brain has stored image "ideals" not image "snapshots."

Sinha and Poggio (1996) demonstrated the strength of head shape on recognition, whereas computers rely on details of features as well as spatial configuration. Current models of face recognition rely on evaluating the mathematical properties of the facial shading to identify individual variation in faces. We know each other because we have had months or years of experience with someone. These facial characteristics are stored in memory and, when we see the whole person in which all of the features of his or her prototype face are present, we immediately recognize the person. In the Sinha and Poggio experiment they presented the faces shown in Figure 15.7. On first glance the famous pair looks like former President Bill Clinton and Vice President Al Gore, but in actuality, the face on the fellow in the background is made up of the salient features of President Clinton—his eyes, nose, and mouth—superimposed on Gore's physique—his hair, ears, and body. You probably were initially fooled by this illusion because you were "set up" to believe the people were a "pair" not a chimera. Even the stance each occupies biased your view and then you caught a glimpse of Gore's hair, his body, his posture, and the decision was quickly made. In humans, then, face recognition is strongly influenced by

Could this be Abraham Lincoln?

past perception which, in the case of a Gore finder, is ineffectual. Sinha and Poggio (2002) replicated this illusion with Dick Cheney and George W. Bush, demonstrating that the effect is robust and nonpartisan! The line of research carried out by Poggio and his colleagues is twofold: On the one hand it is possible to design programs which recognize objects and faces better than humans do (and such devices have utility in security scanning operations) and on the other hand it is possible to incorporate a learning program so that computers may through trial and error learn to recognize objects and faces much like humans do.

Decision Making and AI

Systems that perform like human experts are called **expert systems.** Basically, an expert system is an artificial specialist that solves problems in the area of its specialty. Expert systems have been designed to solve problems in medicine, law, aerodynamics, chess, and a myriad of routine chores that generally bore humans or, in some cases, may be too difficult for humans to solve. These systems follow rules and often use a decision tree, however, they can only "think" about one issue. An expert system in medicine may not know a tort from a hole in the ground, but it can make a reasonably accurate diagnosis of a thirteen-year-old girl who has a high fever, abdominal pain, and an abnormal concentration of white corpuscles. One such program, wryly called Puff, is an expert system designed to diagnose lung disorders, such as lung cancer, and boasts a hit rate of about 89 percent—close to the hit rate of experienced physicians. These systems have been especially popular with industry, with the military, and in space exploration. They are pretty good at the job they are designed to do. Furthermore, they do not go on strike and demand more money, don't mind getting blown to smithereens, and do not require life support.

Language and AI

Psychologists generally consider language a prime manifestation of underlying cognitive processes. Language, more than any other category of human response variables, reflects thought, perception, memory, problem solving, intelligence, and learning. Furthermore, because of its importance to basic psychological principles, it is of major interest to AI scientists.

FIGURE 15.7

Can you quickly identify this famous pair? Are you sure? See text for explanation.

The capacity for language and involved problem solving of Arthur C. Clark's fictional computer Hal was envisioned by the author to take a very complete form, as in this exchange between Dave (the human) and Hal:

"I want to do this myself, Hal," he said. "Please give me control."

"Look, Dave, you've got a lot of things to do. I suggest you leave this to me."

"Hal, switch to manual hibernation control."

"I can tell from your voice harmonics, Dave, that you're badly upset. Why don't you take a stress pill and get some rest?"

"Hal, *I* am in command of this ship. I order you to release the manual hibernation control."

"I'm sorry, Dave, but in accordance with special sub-routine C1435-dash-4, quote, When the crew are dead or incapacitated, the onboard computer must assume control, unquote. I must, therefore, overrule your authority, since you are not in any condition to exercise it intelligently."

FIGURE 15.8

Swift's Thinking Machine.

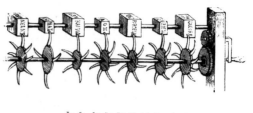

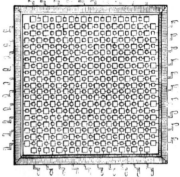

How close have we come to this fiction in the AI laboratory?

Shown in Figure 15.8 is an illustration of Jonathan Swift's "thinking machine" from *Gulliver's Travels*. Swift suggested acerbically that books and other literature could be written by turning the appropriate handles. Some "modern writing programs" have produced a form of science fiction that passes as fair literature. See *Omni* magazine for examples.

Eliza, Parry, and NETtalk

Enthusiastic early players at AI quickly embraced the challenge proposed by the Turing test and wrote programs designed to respond to real language queries in a way that were indistinguishable from human responses. Given the perspective of hindsight, some of these programs seem a bit klutzy now, but science often develops that way.

ELIZA   One of the first conversational computer programs, **ELIZA,** was written by Joseph Weizenbaum (1966). Several revisions of ELIZA have appeared since its original conception. In one specific program, called DOCTOR, ELIZA takes a role similar to that of a psychiatrist. In the following example, ELIZA's part is in capital letters:

Men are all alike.

IN WHAT WAY

They're always bugging us about something or other.

CAN YOU THINK OF A SPECIFIC EXAMPLE

Well, my boyfriend made me come here.

YOUR BOYFRIEND MADE YOU COME HERE

He says I'm depressed much of the time.

I AM SORRY TO HEAR YOU ARE DEPRESSED

It's true, I am unhappy.

DO YOU THINK COMING HERE WILL HELP YOU NOT TO BE UNHAPPY

I need some help, that much seems certain.

That conversation, one might argue, could easily have come from an interview between a human psychiatrist and patient. However, let us examine the transcript critically. The computer's responses tend to be stereotyped. For example, it is programmed to respond to certain key words with a response that is only a transformation of the original sentence. Thus, when the "patient" says the keyword "I'm," ELIZA responds with a locution such as "I am sorry to hear you are. . . ." If no key words are found, the computer responds with a content-free remark, or in some instances, an earlier transformation. The human capacity for knowledge about feelings, tendencies, group dynamics, and so on figures into what, for lack of a better word, we call understanding. ELIZA lacks it.

PARRY   What kind of conversation might result if the roles were reversed—that is, if a psychiatrist talked to a computerized simulation of a patient? Colby, Hilf, Weber, and Kraemer (1972) simulated such a patient, calling the program **PARRY,** since it simulated a paranoid patient. They selected a paranoid subject because some theoretical notion about the system and process of paranoia existed, the differences between psychotic responses and normal responses were great, and they could use expert judges to validate the distinguishability of computer simulation responses and human responses. Colby and his fellow researchers subjected the computer to a Turing test, asking a group of psychiatrists to interview PARRY by means of teletyped messages. The judges (psychiatrists) were asked to estimate the degree of paranoia of the total responses.

Interview A

Dr. IS THERE ANYTHING ABOUT PEOPLE IN PARTICULAR?

Pt. CERTAIN PERSONS

Dr. WHO ARE THE CERTAIN PERSONS AND WHAT IS IT THEY DO?

Pt. DO YOU KNOW HOW THE UNDERWORLD OPERATES?

Dr. HOW DO YOU MEAN?

Pt. SHOULDN'T I BE?

Dr. WHY DID YOU ASK ABOUT THE UNDERWORLD?

Pt. WHAT INFORMATION DO YOU HAVE ON THE UNDERWORLD?

Dr. I DON'T KNOW ABOUT THE UNDERWORLD BUT WHEN YOU MENTIONED THE UNDERWORLD I THOUGHT YOU MUST HAVE HAD SOME CONTACT WITH IT AND THAT'S WHAT I WOULD LIKE TO KNOW MORE ABOUT.

Pt. TRY TO AVOID THE UNDERWORLD.

Comments by Judge

An interesting clue. We'll have to find out what he thinks about these people.

Bringing up the underworld suggests a delusional system. We don't know whether he is being worked against or whether the underworld is on his side.

This question didn't work too well.

This is a kind of evasiveness about my evasiveness. Common with paranoia in my experience. Pretty characteristic.

This definitely feels paranoid. It has that feeling I associate with twisting. Avoiding answering directly or going into detail. Being suspicious of my questioning. I'm already involved in the patient's delusional system.

The results indicated indistinguishability between the model and the patient in a very specialized setting. Of course, it may be correctly argued that the conditions of the experiment were contrived, that actual diagnosis of paranoia involves extensive face-to-face interviews, and that, had the judges known the real nature of the task, their interviews would have been different. Although Colby and his colleagues successfully programmed a computer to respond in a way that a paranoid patient might and that program passed a form of the Turing test, it is vary far from a complete model of language production and understanding.

NETtalk   A much different type of program, based on a neural net, is called **NETtalk,** developed by Sejnowski then at Harvard Medical School and Rosenberg of Princeton (see Heppenheimer, 1988; Sejnowski & Rosenberg, 1987). In this program, NETtalk reads letters and pronounces them aloud (see Figure 15.9). The neural net simulation model consists of several hundred units ("neurons") and thousands of connections. NETtalk "reads aloud" by converting letters into phonemes, the elementary unit of language sounds. This system, like others we have encountered, has three layers: an input layer, in which each unit corresponds to a letter; an output layer, in which units represent the fifty-five

FIGURE 15.9

NETtalk reads aloud. It translates letters into phonemes. Each letter unit sends signals through weighted connections to all the "hidden" units; if the total signal reaching a hidden unit exceeds a certain threshold, the unit fires, sending signals to the phoneme units. The output is the phoneme that receives the strongest total signal. When a "teacher" tells NETtalk that it has made a mistake— here it has just read *m* instead of *n*—it corrects the error by adjusting all the weights according to a specific learning algorithm.

From Heppenheimer (1988).

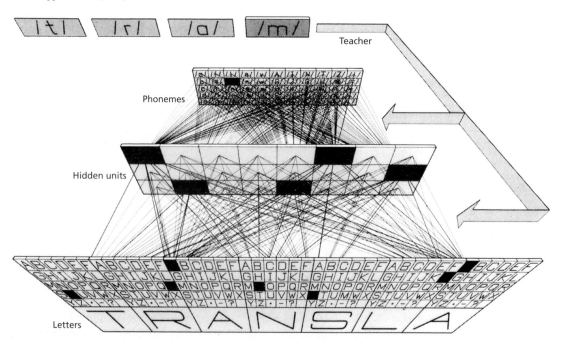

Terry Sejnowski. His neural nets contained a hidden layer that corresponds to interneurons.

phonemes of English; and a hidden unit layer, in which each of the units has a weighted connection to every input and output unit. NETtalk reads by considering each letter one by one, and by scanning three letters on either side for contextual information. Thus, the *e* in *net, neglect,* and *red* can be assigned different sounds. Each time NETtalk reads a word, it compares its pronunciation with the correct pronunciation provided by humans and then adjusts its weights to correct any errors.

After a few trials NETtalk makes noticeable improvement. Sejnowski reports:

> We left it to run overnight. At first it gave a continuous stream of babble. It was just guessing; it had not learned to associate phonemes with the letters. As the run continued, it began to recognize consonants and vowels. Then it discovered there were spaces between the words. Now its stream of sound broke up into short bursts, separated by these spaces. At the end of the night it was reading quite understandably, correctly pronouncing some ninety-two percent of the letters. (quoted in Heppenheimer, 1988, p. 74)

The practical application of these systems is obvious; what may be less obvious, but in the long run more significant, is the conceptual breakthrough such neurally inspired models present.

As Sejnowski and others recognize, context is of great importance in human and machine discourse. We will now consider another important problem, the issue of meaning and AI. Clearly, many of these issues have been sorted out. If you look at a transcript of the computerized operator at TIVO, the operator is nearly indistinguishable from a "live" operator.

Meaning and AI

Despite the fact that some of the computer's conversations are good enough to fool some of the people some of the time, they do not fail because of a lack of memory for words, which is nearly limitless; or in their ability to produce meaningful sentences, which is extensive; or in their facility in pronouncing letters, which is acceptable. They fail in their lack of understanding of what language is all about.

In the early stages of AI, it was thought that computers would be of great assistance in language translation. Simply load the memory bank of the computer with equivalent words in two languages (e.g., the English–Norwegian equivalents are: necklace = halsbånd, cloth = kloær, pocketbook = lommebok, pink = lyserød, etc.); feed in one language and out comes the other. However, even when a one-to-one translation is made within the context of syntactic information, the results are sometimes bizarre. In one example (probably apocryphal), the biblical passage "The spirit is willing, but the flesh is weak" was translated into Russian, then back to English; it came out: "The wine was agreeable but the meat was spoiled."

Experience with these primitive translation programs and developments in psycholinguistics changed our conceptualization of language. In the previous example, although the Norwegian and English words were equivalent and the syntax (in both languages) correct, the *meaning* of the two sentences was not the same. Our natural language operates within the constraint of a variety of rules that determine the sequence of grammatic components *and* the meaning of the total sequence. These have a complex relationship that is beginning to yield to analysis. Computer analysis of natural language processes has taken the form of designing systems that "understand" the language. Some rather sophisticated "understanding" programs based on the conceptual base of the language have been developed. Built into these systems is the capability to analyze both the context of the discourse and the meaning of the words and, in some cases, "world knowledge" (Winograd, 1977). A syntax analyzer determines the most likely parsing and interpretation of a sentence.

The first language systems were limited in their ability to mimic human conversation because of restricted world knowledge and inferential ability. When humans converse, what is *not* said is as important as what is said, insofar as effective communication is concerned. Intelligent human performance is characterized by all types of inferences, not only in language processing but also in other activities such as visual perception. We need not see an entire partially occluded figure to infer that the whole figure exists. Even fractional and secondary cues are enough to trigger a whole series of reactions. For example, if I am walking through a forest known to contain poisonous snakes, the sound of rustling leaves is enough of a cue to make me stop dead in my tracks.

Yet another area of understanding in AI research that has received attention is the concept of "beliefs." Consider the following example:

> I was out until 2:00 A.M. yesterday.
> Boy, did my wife give it to me.

It is fair to conclude that most people know that what the wife gave to her husband was not affection. Never mind that the inference may be totally wrong. (For example, the husband may have been working in his laboratory and just discovered a cure for cancer that would bring fame and fortune to his family, or the husband may have come home too early!) We are talking about what most people understand from this little story and most computer programs do not (in essence, the difference between surface structure meaning and deep structure meaning). A program that would understand this story would need not only a capacious memory of idioms (how else would it understand "give it to me") but also some understanding of the comings and goings of husbands and their wives' beliefs and attitudes about such things.

Continuous Speech Recognition (CSR)

Continuous speech recognition systems are programs which recognize and record natural speech. On the surface, continuous speech recognition seems undemanding. After all, most humans and a few animals recognize and record some type of speech. Yet, the task is devilishly intricate for the reasons mentioned earlier. Consider just the problem posed by homophones—words that sound alike but have different meaning, such as *arm*, the limb hanging from your torso, and *arm*, what you do to protect yourself from a midnight intruder. In the sentence, "Jeff armed himself in the event of an emergency," the word *armed* means Jeff got outfitted with some sort of weapon. However, if you knew Jeff and knew that he lost his arms in a tragic accident and had a set of artificial ones he put on in case of an emergency, such as a fire, you would know that *armed* means he put on his limbs. How might a continuous speech recognition device handle that speech pattern? Most programs are designed to function on the basis of statistical probability and limited syntactic context and, thus, would misinterpret the intention of the sentence. Gradually, however, more and more sophisticated programs are being developed that give context and include "world knowledge."

Research activities on the cutting edge of continuous speech recognition are translation programs mentioned above. These newer programs do not simply do a "brute search and match" translation but are capable of translating continuous, comprehensive vocabulary speech recognition, language translation, and speech synthesis with a high degree of accuracy. This means, that someone may speak in English, for example, into a "telephone" (or microphone connected to a computer); the English speech is translated into visual text; the text is translated into another language, say French; a second language speech is synthesized; and the output is a spoken version of the translated message. This wonderfully practical program is already in the experimental stage (see Kurzweil 1999), and commercial products are available.

Language Understanding Program

As NETtalk and continuous speech recognition programs engage world knowledge in reacting reasonably with humans, so too have other programs incorporated some forms of human understanding in their systems. Among the best known and most controversial is a language understanding program developed at Yale by Roger Schank. The direction of Schank's research was guided by several goals, which included the development of a program that would be able to understand written text, summarize the essential parts of such text, translate it into another language, and answer questions about the meaning of written material. Schank and his colleagues soon discovered that people understand a great deal more than just the raw words of natural language expression. Schank illustrates this issue in the following story: "John went to a restaurant. He ordered a sandwich. The waiter brought it quickly, so he left a large tip." Did John eat the sandwich? Did he pay for it?

When we tell you, "We visited Venice last summer," you can answer many questions more or less accurately: Did we spend any money? Did we travel by plane? By boat? Did we talk to anyone? Did we go to a restaurant? Did we see other people in Venice? Did they speak Italian? Did they wear clothes? Did they have fingernails? How many? For an "intelligent" machine to understand language, it would have to make reasonable inferences about language processing, much as normal humans do. The basic notion is similar to the concept of top-down processing discussed throughout this book.

Among the difficulties encountered in developing a language-processing program was the ambiguity of natural languages. Schank (1981) cites the following examples:

I hit Fred on the nose.
I hit Fred in the park.

To parse these sentences correctly, we need to know much more than purely syntactic and semantic rules. The reader has to know something about where a person can be located as well as other conceptual information about human behavior and general world information.

Problem Solving, Game Playing, and AI

One reason many AI scientists have been concerned with *problem solving* is that the term is roughly synonymous with thinking, which in its sophisticated form is a uniquely human attribute. This fact and the general capability of AI machines with regard to problem-solving procedures has led to a proliferation of techniques and theories in this area.

Calculation was one of the earliest instances of "problem solving" by machine. In 1642 Pascal (at the age of nineteen) demonstrated that some forms of mathematical problems could be solved more accurately and quickly by a mechanical calculator he invented than by humans. Problem solving in the context of modern AI means much more than mechanical calculation; it covers a wide range—finding solutions to complex puzzles, proving theorems, learning successful operations, and playing games.

Designing a computer that can solve a specific problem is easy. Designing a program that is versatile enough to handle a variety of problems is difficult. And designing a program that will adapt and learn solutions to a wide range of problems is, so far, impossible. But the aim of many contemporary AI specialists is to design a learning program that will solve problems. On an elementary level, such self-learning programs might be able to learn which clients would be good risks for credit card use and which would be bad risks (see Figure 15.10). At a more advanced level, computer-vision programs are under development by Abu-Mostafa (1995) whose goal is to recognize objects even when the target object changes direction or orientation.

How do machines learn? The logical answer is "by experience" but, of course, that tells little of the mechanisms which change the performance of the computer. Many AI specialists approach the issue from a mathematical position in which the behavior of a machine is seen as a function that associates input values (the nature of a problem to be solved, for example) with corresponding output values (the actions or decisions). One way to look at the issue is that machine learning is simply the "search for the right position for the knobs." Some programs learn by training examples as in the case of the problem shown in Figure 15.11.

Take a moment to see if you can solve the concept that distinguishes one class of objects from another. Notice that your concept formation solution may focus on semantic relationships—but, in what way are an ancient cork screw, a watch, and Bugs Bunny re-

FIGURE 15.10

Machine learning. Involves adjusting a system's internal parameters such that it makes the proper associations between data inputs and desired outputs. A credit-approval system, for example, would be trained to link applicants' personal data with their known credit behavior. In effect, the learning process "tunes the dials" until the machine can duplicate the input–output relations in the training examples.

Reprinted by permission of Roberto Osti Illustrations.

lated? This is a difficult task, and yet you, like the computer, are enlightened when you see the hint in Figure 15.12.

The machine "learns" by emulating the target functions and refining its actions stepwise in ever closer approximations to the target until it succeeds. Several programs have been successful in this format including those that are based on a neural network (see Hinton, 1992).

Underlying much of the work in AI is an important distinction between two types of methods used to solve problems. One method is called *algorithmic;* the other is called *heuristic.* **Algorithms** are commonly defined as procedures that guarantee a solution to a given kind of problem; **heuristics** are sets of empirical rules or strategies that operate, in effect, like a rule of thumb. The difference between the methods can be illustrated by means of a chess problem. Computer chess is a game during which, at any given time, there exists a limited number of possible moves by each player. Also, each of the possible moves may be answered by the opponent in a limited number of moves. For practical purposes the number of these permutations is finite—that is, the game must end in a win (and loss) or draw. (Figure 15.13 shows a portion of the ever-branching tree of possibilities that might ensue from a chess play.) Of course, the number of possible moves for an entire game cannot be represented, for such a chart would contain about 10^{120} different pathways. To understand the enormity of the number of possible moves in a chess game, consider the space needed to represent the permutations. If all the pathways were coded in the tiniest microdots, they would fill every library in the world many times over! Nevertheless, an algorithmic search that examines all alternatives would inevitably lead to a series of plays that would win (and lose) or draw. Humans (and even the most sophisticated computers imaginable) find this technique impossible. Instead we humans

FIGURE 15.11

CAN YOU SOLVE IT? These objects have been sorted into two classes, indicated by either a blue or black border. Which characteristic distinguishes them? Computers programmed to learn from examples often face similar puzzles. Providing the machine with hints can make learning faster and easier. For a hint to help with this puzzle, see Figure 15.12.

Reprinted by permission of Dan Wagner.

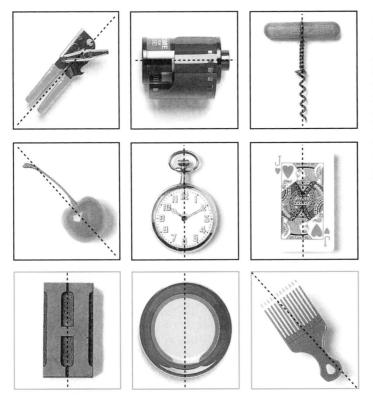

FIGURE 15.12

Visual hint. Aids both machines and people in solving the puzzle in Figure 15.11. Drawing the axis makes it clear that the top six objects lack the mirror-image symmetry exhibited by the bottom three. This characteristic distinguishes black and blue categories.

Reprinted by permission of Dan Wagner.

and computers use heuristic search methods, in which strategy play becomes important—for example, attack opponent's queen, control the center of the board, pin opponent's major pieces, exchange pieces on the basis of piece advantage or positional advantage, and so on.

Computer Chess

We have described how an optimal scanner working with a computer could make sense out of a simple pattern by means of template matching. Our discussion of pattern analysis revealed that patterns are complex and that a model of human pattern recognition based on single template matching fails to account for the diversity, complexity, and economy of the human ability to recognize patterns within a brief exposure.

Surely if there were a template for each of the diverse patterns encountered in daily living, it would overwhelm the storage capacity of even the largest computer. Let us look at template matching with a moderately simple pattern (somewhere between recognizing your grandmother and reading out the cost of a pound of butter from a code imprinted on the package). Chess has such a pattern. It uses a simple 8 × 8 grid of alternately differentiated squares; the moves are clearly defined (e.g., the rook may move

Portion of possibility tree for a chess game.

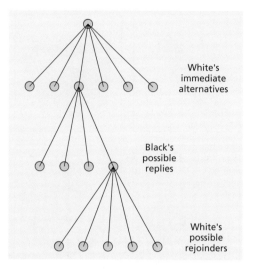

White's immediate alternatives

Black's possible replies

White's possible rejoinders

as many spaces along a vertical or horizontal pathway as desired, provided no other piece is in its path, the pawn may move one space forward except . . . and so on); the moves can be predicted on the basis of a brute search; and the number of permutations, albeit enormous, is finite. Given a very, very large storage and a great deal of time, determination of the probability of *each* move leading to a win is possible. Even though computers do examine a staggering number of possible moves, a model that searches *all* moves is impossible; furthermore, it says nothing about how we humans play chess or, more importantly, how complex patterns are perceived, encoded, transformed, and translated into action.

From the experiments of Chase and de Groot we know that chess players, even modest ones, chunk information about the situation of specific pieces and then concentrate on developing a strategy around sensitive pieces and moves. A chess-playing machine, then, if it is to play a game as humans play it, needs to be able to analyze a pattern and quickly abstract from the pieces and their positions information on the relative importance of the chunks.

In addition to chess a wide variety of other computer games may be challenged by humans including backgammon, bridge, checkers, go, Othello, poker, and Scrabble. All of these are available on the Internet and waiting for a smart brain, like yours, to give them a try.

AI and the Arts

Perhaps by now, you are thinking there are only a few areas of human endeavor that are protected from the encroachment of AI. You may argue that the arts—poetry, music, and art—are purely human manifestations not to be touched by the intrusion of electronic probes. Yet, in each of these areas, considerable work has been done. First, consider poetry.

Poetry   Several successful efforts have been made to create poems that pass for human poems. One such program has been developed by Kurzweil called Ray Kurzweil's

Cognition in Everyday Life

Carbon-Based Grandmaster versus Silicon-Based Champion

*H*ow well can a computer play chess? As we have seen, the best computer and program, Deep Blue, beat Garry Kasparov whom many consider to be the best human player of all time. And any number of computers now exist that can beat all but the best players, one of which lurks in residence in my own Pentium computer and, it is safe to surmise, exists within a few keystrokes away from you. What can we learn by watching a machine learn to play chess? Most of all, we can learn that pattern analysis by a machine can make only rude judgments as to what features are pertinent. What the computer lacks in perspicacity, however, it makes up in its capacity for rapid and voluminous mathematical search-and-match activity. The human capacity to extract meaningful cues from an enormously complex world of sensory information, to form abstractions of those cues, to transform abstractions into higher associative structures, and to develop elaborate cognitive plans while at the same time keeping these internal operations consistent with the external reality can still only be approximated in the computer. But even these voluminous search capabilities are not sufficient to exhaust *all* contingencies and the development of strategies of play are a palpable part of modern programs.

Three years before the end of the twentieth century the "impossible" happened. Deep Blue, the world's fastest chess-playing computer, created by Chung-Jen Tan at IBM, beat the world-champion chessmaster Gary Kasparov. Deep Blue was able to win because it was able to search up to 200 million chess positions every second. But it also won because it was able to predict the best strategy. The next generation of game-playing machines is likely to be those that can learn by experience and increase performance over a short period of time, much as humans do only faster and better.

Carbon-Based Grandmaster vs. Silicon-Based Champion

Kasparov may need
a new title:
World Chess Champion,
Carbon-Based Division.

Cognition in Everyday Life

Checkers Program that Thinks Like a Human[*]

At a recent meeting of the *2000 Congress on Evolutionary Computation,* David Fogel and Kumar Chellapilla showed a computer program called a neural network that was designed to self-learn, much as you might do if you were taught the basic rules of a game, such as checkers, and then improved on your own by thinking about different strategies. The evolved program plays an excellent game of checkers and easily wiped out almost all contestants. But what is interesting for our discussion of computer modeling of human neurological processes is that the program imitates the integrative functions of human neurons. We know that human neurons operate by means of "integrate-and-fire" structures in which a neuron adds up all electrical stimuli it receives from other neurons. If the sum total is above a certain threshold, it fires and stimulates other neurons. This basic principle is fundamental to human learning and responding. The checkers learning program operates by the same principle. Furthermore, given enough time, the program may improve many times over, which might prove interesting in space travel where intelligent machines would be able to "get smarter" throughout long flights. The implications for robot intelligence are significant and represent the new frontier of AI.

From The New York Times, *July 25, 2000, pp. D1–D2.*

Cybernetic Poet (RKCP). The program uses language-modeling techniques based on poems that it has "read." RKCP is fed a sample, the larger the sample the better, of a poet, and from those selections it creates a language model in which language style, rhythm patterns, and poem structure of the author are mimicked. Ponder this haiku (Japanese lyric verse) written by Ray Kurzweil's Cybernetic Poet after it read poems by John Keats and Wendy Dennis:

Soul

You broke my soul
the juice of eternity,
the spirit of my lips.

And this one after reading poems by Ray Kurzweil, Robert Frost, and Wendy Dennis:

I Think I'll Crash

I think I'll crash.
Just for myself with God
peace on a curious sound

Detective Spooner: Human beings have dreams. Even dogs have dreams, but not you, you are just a machine. An imitation of life. Can a robot write a symphony? Can a robot turn a . . . canvas into a beautiful masterpiece?

Sonny (the robot): Can *you?*

—*From the movie* I, Robot

---

for myself in my heart?
And life is weeping
From a bleeding heart
of boughs bending
such paths of them,
of boughs bending
such paths of breeze
knows we've been there

What do you think of these poems? Do they pass the Turing test?

Music   If it is possible to capture and emulate poetic schemas, is it also possible to do so with musical themes? Several successful programs have been written that seem to produce musical pieces judged to be quite good by listeners. One such program was written by Steve Larson, a professor of music at the University of Oregon, who selected three compositions—one by Johann Sebastian Bach, one by himself, and one by a computer—to be played before an audience. In an outcome somewhat bemusing to Larson, his own composition was judged to have been composed by the computer while the computer-generated music, called "Experiments in Musical Intelligence (EMI)," was judged to be the authentic Bach. At least on a limited basis, computer-generated music fools some of the people some of the time. Another program called Improvisor has been written by Paul Hodgson, a jazz saxophonist from England. This program can emulate a wide range of styles from that of Bach to those of jazz musicians such as Louis Armstrong and Charlie Parker.

At the present time, computer-generated music seems to be very convincing. The main weakness in these programs is in their ability to create music that is persuasive over a longer period of time, especially among musical specialists who are sensitive to the nuances of specialized types of music (essentially a musical Turing test). While a novice may be convinced that a computer-generated piece of music was composed by Mozart, a Mozart virtuoso could, given a comprehensive context, identify the artificial Mozart. One might be moved to observe that "it sounds like Mozart but, it sounds as if he was having a 'bad hair day.' " Of course, it is possible that future programs will not only produce Mozart-like compositions but go well beyond the talented young Austrian and generate super-Mozart compositions . . . music that would reincarnate the apotheosis of the boy genius.

Musical programs will probably get better, to the point that the distinction between the real Ella Fitzgerald and a programmed Ella may be indistinguishable. Whether we will be richer or poorer for the blurring of real from artificial is a problem to be pondered not only by philosophers and ethicists but by all of us.

Art   Computer-assisted video art has been around for decades, and some of the original CAD (computer-assisted design) programs have relieved the drudgery of architectural and industrial design. These programs are a far cry from programs that create art, such as those developed over the last quarter-century by Harold Cohen. His computer-driven robot, equipped with a drawing device, called Aaron, has been turning out paintings that look like real art, and who is to say that they are not "real" art? A sample of Cohen's art, or should we say Aaron's art, is shown in Figure 15.14.

The mechanics for drawing these pieces is reasonably simple. A small mobile robot scoots around a canvas drawing an object, as shown. The heart of the program, however, is information about the many aspects of the artistic construction including composition,

FIGURE 15.14

Computer-generated art. From Ray Kurzweil, *The Age of Spiritual Machines.*

Viking Press.

drawing, perspective, style, and color. The art world, which can at times be the most critical as well as liberal, has exhibited some of Cohen's pieces at major venues such as the Tate Galley in London, the Stedelijk Museum in Amsterdam, and the San Franciso Museum of Modern Art.

In all of the preceding instances of AI and the arts, the ultimate criterion for critical acceptability is the judgment of humans. If the poem, music, or art is judged to be sufficiently humanlike, it is judged aesthetically meritorious. If not, then it's an "off day" for the creator, which means it is a close approximation but is clearly a counterfeit. We lack objective criteria in the arts, and until taste, likes, and preferences are made more operational, poetry, music, and art (as well as many other humanoid personifications) will be in the hands and minds of organic computational devices.

Robots

Robots (devices capable of performing human tasks or behaving in a human manner) embody most of the geography of AI reviewed earlier—the replication of pattern recognition, memory, language processing, and problem solving.

Cognition in Everyday Life
Robot (Re)volutions

A fascination with the possibilities of humanoids performing in a fashion that mimics human behavior has pervaded folklore and fiction. Stories like "The Sorcerer's Apprentice," "Pinocchio," and *Frankenstein;* tales of "golems" and centaurs; and characters like R2D2 and C3PO (*Star Wars*) and Hal (of *2001* fame) reflect this interest. With the advent of modern engineering technology and cognitive psychology, robotics has evolved from the domain of mythology and science fiction to the status of a very serious scientific endeavor. Pioneering work was done by two British scientists, Ross Ashley and W. Gray Walter. Ashley designed and built an electronic circuit that maintained a favorable homeostasis, or state of internal balance. Walter added mobility to a homeostatic type of device that would seek light below a certain brightness; avoid light

above that level; and, where no light was available, move around in what may be called a search for light. These tropistic machines mimicked only the rudimentary properties of life exhibited by insects, plants, or simple animals. The robot next in line of evolution was put together at the Johns Hopkins University and became known as the Hopkins Beast. This could move about under its own power and was completely self-contained. It navigated by means of sonar, and its perceptual system consisted of a combination of photo cells, masks, lenses, and circuits all designed to detect only one thing: electrical outlet coverplates. When it "saw" one, it would try to make contact with it with its plug-shaped hand. Roving automatic vacuum cleaners have recently hit the market—bringing robot technology home—so to speak.

Robotics grew rapidly in the 1960s with the exploration of space and the need to develop highly sophisticated mechanical devices capable of performing specific tasks. The Mars lander, capable of carrying out a series of complex chemical analyses, is a result of these needs. (It should be pointed out that some of these robots, purely mechanical devices, are only remotely associated with the limited definition of AI used in this chapter.)

Some of the early prototypes of space robots were developed at the AI laboratory of Stanford University, where signs in the vicinity of the laboratory warned visitors that robot vehicles may be about. One of the most intriguing robots was developed there in 1968. It was a mobile, radio-controlled vehicle called Shakey, which had on-board perceptual and problem-solving capabilities. It was equipped with a television camera, a range finder, and a tactile sensor like a cat's whisker. All these relayed sensory information to a computer that held a variety of programs for analyzing the incoming signals and for planning action sequences aimed at manipulating the robot's environment. The whole was mounted in a motorized cart that could go in any direction.

The perceptual system consisted of a television camera that reduced the pictures to line images and then to significant areas or objects in the scene. The problem solver was a type of theorem-proving program that allowed Shakey to execute simple tasks.

A newer robot, Flakey, replaced Shakey. Flakey is a three-foot-tall ambulatory device with a video camera mounted on top. When given a command to go to an office five doors down the hall, Flakey obediently wheels itself to the designated place. Some of the most advanced robots are built by NASA. These machines are somewhat specialized devices used to collect and analyze soil samples from neighboring planets, make repairs on space stations, and carry out scientific experiments and observations in environments too forbidding for humans.

The grandiose plans of the 1970s, which ambitiously started out with designing whole-functioning robots, have given way to more reasonable projects in which relatively small humanoid processes are replicated. In this arena the business community is leading the way; many laborious or dangerous functions can be done by robots.

The Future of AI

In the twentieth century, psychology became grounded scientifically through advances in behaviorism, which gave techniques and objectivity to the study of the human mind and performance. Because of reasons mentioned in the first chapter, behaviorism gave way to cognitive psychology, which focused on internal representations of the mind that greatly expanded the scope of psychology. A significant shift in cognitive psychology as well as psychology in general, is currently taking place. This shift is brought about by advancements in two areas: cognitive neuroscience, which has been thematically infused throughout this book, and artificial intelligence. In the first case, we are beginning to apprehend the physiological underpinnings of human cognition, and in the second case, we are being challenged to ascertain the attributes as well as the limitations of human understanding and intellect. And it is entirely possible that in the present century we will stand side by side with an inorganic instrument whose intellectual acumen is far greater than ours.

Ray Kurzweil, in his provocative book *The Age of Spiritual Machines* (1999), and Bill Gates, in his prescient book *The Road Ahead* (1996), have been keeping track of the increment in computer speed (measured in calculations per second per thousand dollars) throughout the twentieth century. In the first half of the twentieth century, speed doubled every three years; between 1950 and 1966, it doubled every two years; and presently it is doubling every year, which suggests an exponential growth. The exponential growth was predicted by Gordon Moore, the co-founder of Intel, who noted in 1965 that the capacity of a computer chip would double every year. Even though Moore thought the torrid growth projection could not last forever—there are physical laws that would be reached—the rate of growth over the past forty years has been doubling about every eighteen months. This growth rate is called **Moore's law.** If computer power continues to grow over the next few decades, and there is ample reason to believe that it will, then even if the exponential growth rate is decelerated, the resulting capacity of future machines will approximate that of organic brains. Some (Kurzweil, 1999) project that computing potential will approximate that of the human brain as early as 2020 and well outstrip it by the end of the century. (See Figure 15.15 for a projection of the growth of computing through the twenty-first century.)

In order for this fantastic prediction to come true, more than computing power needs to be achieved for an artificial brain to act like a human brain (only smarter). These include the acquisition of information, what we have referred to as "world knowledge" in this chapter. In humans, each of the five senses detects and processes millions of bits of information each day. These bits are multifariously fused with existing knowledge in a vastly complex network which enables each of us to react wisely to new environmental cues in our quest for survival. One final component of an artificial brain is necessary and that is the formulae that govern the operation of the organic brain. This is a hugely

FIGURE 15.15

The exponential growth of computing, 1900–2100.

From Kurzweil (1999).

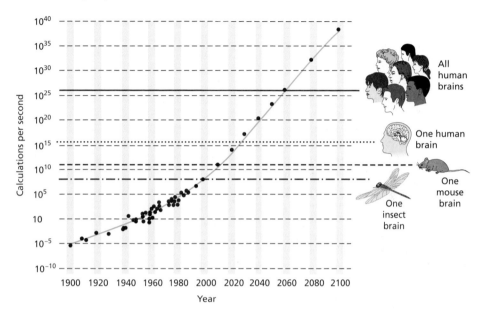

complicated matter and it is not clear exactly what these operational codes consist of, but some features include that potential for self-organization of information in workable networks, the capacity for recursive searches, and the ability to learn and self-adapt to external and internal cues. An alternative program would be to combine computer bits into an organic brain and some efforts in this direction have been done with startling success. (See Barinaga, 1999, for an example of how thoughts are being turned into actions.)

In realizing the visionary aspirations of AI dreamers, we need to consider some fundamental differences in the structural components of the brain and computer, computing power, and computer simulation. We learned earlier that the human brain has about 100 billion neurons with an estimated 1,000 connections between each neuron and other neurons (this figure is still definitively unknown). That is about 100 trillion parallel connections, which gives the user considerable cerebral power. The organic brain, however, reacts slowly with only about 200 calculations per second. If we multiply these numbers (100 trillion connections computing at 200 calculations per second), we get 20 million billion calculations per second. That is what your brain is doing at this second. How close are computers to this computational power?

The best massively parallel neural net computer as of this writing is capable of 2 billion connection calculations per second. What the silicon-based brain does far better than the organic brain is process information much much faster. If Moore's law holds, or even approximates the computing capacity in the future, by the year 2020, the present systems will have doubled about 23 times, which would yield a speed of 20 million billion neural connection calculations per second. Next, consider how much work can be accomplished with multiple computers. The Internet is of course a system of networked computers. Computers can be very powerful when linked for a common purpose. One such example is Seti@home. This project connects thousands of volunteers' computers to help in the search for extraterrestrial intelligence, taking advantage of the unused processing time of personal computers. You can download the software (http://setiathome .ssl.berkeley.edu/.) and then when your computer is idle, the software downloads a chunk of data from the Arecibo Radio Telescope, in Puerto Rico. The results are sent back to the research team and are used to help in the search for extraterrestrial signals.

A final word about AI and computer simulation: There is a huge conceptual leap between the types of actions produced by a human brain and an artificial brain. As discussed earlier, it may be possible to construct a Bach cantata, a van Gogh painting, or an e. e. cummings poem that passes the Turing test. It is even plausible to compose the preceding items that are judged by we humans to be the quintessence of the class—a type of aesthetic prototype for each artist rather than simply "like the artist." But in order for this to be done, humanly produced exemplars would have to be learned and understood by the inorganic machine. We humans provide the blueprint. When and if future thinking programs transcend human thought, then it is humans who *initially will feed* information to computers and set in operation the new thinking machines. Perhaps it would be prudent to put a scheme into the new brains that will be able to explain things to us in simple human terms, or we will be relegated to service functions, not intellectual functions.

AI and Scientific Inquiry

Throughout most of this chapter we have discussed the computer vis-à-vis human cognition and the immensely complex task undertaken by those who attempt to mimic human performance with the use of machines. In this closing section we would like to propose that the way scientists—including cognitive scientists—conduct research is likely to change significantly in the next few years with the use of computers assisted by AI programs.

We have already seen the widespread adoption of computers in nearly every area of human endeavor, and that trend probably will continue. Calculations necessary for everything from space travel to garbage truck routes to genetic research would be impossible without the modern high-speed computer. In fact, more advanced systems with greater memory capacity and faster processing are sure to appear in the future. Perhaps even radical new systems (such as the Japanese Fifth Dimension, which stresses knowledge information processing) will replace our present systems. Exciting as the past developments are, the future promises even more spectacular discoveries.

One area of interest to scientists is the way information is stored and codified. Presently, an enormous amount of scientific information is available in an electronic format in database, electronic storage, and multiuser categorization systems (like Wikipedia), in addition to the more conventional form of books and articles. Electronic access to information is expanding greatly in all fields, including psychology, so that a user can access the complete contents of an article or book online. Furthermore, information from other scholarly fields and from disparate sources, linked in the huge network called the

Internet, is available to most of us. The Internet is here to stay and will continue to affect scientific and other scholarly research.

But what can a scientist do with so much data? Is there the danger of having too much data and not knowing what it all means? Data banks are indispensable to anyone who attempts to write a comprehensive book—such as one on cognitive psychology that encompasses an extended range of topics. Authors of such works can access the abstracts of a subject, say, mental imagery in children, in seconds. As convenient as such databases are, they also present a problem in that the capacity of humans to store and process information is limited. We are at risk of becoming overwhelmed by the plethora of information. If such is the case, it is likely that some type of program that processes information in a knowledgeable, intelligent way—that is, *understands* information—will emerge. (AI will live up to the promise of its name.) If such an AI program appears, it may tell us what research has been done, so we can avoid redundant studies, and it also may tell us what needs to be done, so we can put our valuable time to good use. Furthermore, a superunderstanding computer may not only identify the holes in human knowledge but also fill them in by conducting "research" or making logical inferences from its colossal database (see Solso, 1986, 1987, 1994b). Conceivably, the resulting explosion of knowledge may answer the ancient questions of who we are, where we come from, and what is our future. May we all live so long as to know some of these answers, but not long enough to know all. It is better to travel than to arrive.

Spotlight on Cognitive Neuroscience:

Artificial Face Recognition

Cognitive scientists have been studying how people recognize faces for quite some time. With the advent of technologies such as cell recordings and imaging techniques we know that areas in the temporal lobe process facial information. However, it is unclear exactly what dimensions of the face are being processed. We know much more about how machines process facial information. Although computers are not as good as people in recognizing faces, researchers have developed computer systems that can take an image and recognize it as a face by locating the eyes, mouth, and border of the face. The system then adjusts the size and contrast of the face to convert it to a grid (or array) of numbers representing the gray scale pixel values. The pixel values are then converted to what are referred to as "eigenfaces" using a statistical process called factor analysis. This would be the machine equivalent of encoding the face. To recognize the face, the computer must now match the eigenface values of the face being processed to the eigenface values of "known" faces already stored in the computer. This would be the machine equivalent to the faces stored in memory. Not all matches are exact. However, stored faces that are closely matched to the face being processed will be displayed on the computer monitor along with a value representing how close the faces matched: the machine equivalent of recall. Machine face recognition is not perfect, but it reduces the labor involved in searching a crowd for a wanted individual. Additionally, this technology is being used to track terrorists and to identify children involved in child pornography rings; both require matching of known faces (terrorists or missing children photos) to new faces (people in airports or images off of the Internet).

Turk, M., & Pentland, A. (1991). Eigenfaces for recognition. *Journal of Cognitive Neuroscience, 3*(1), 71–86.

A la carte

Bionic Cockroach

Cockroaches have no centralized brain, yet they may be one of the most adaptive creatures on the planet. Garnet Hertz, a graduate student at the University of California, has used Madagascan hissing cockroaches to guide a robot through an obstacle course. The roach takes the place of a fairly sophisticated computer chip by processing information provided to it by the robot regarding environmental obstacles, a neat task for an insect with no central brain. The roach mobile works because the roach is suspended over a trackball that tells the robot where to move. If the roach moves to the right, the trackball moves to the right, guiding the electronic motors to turn the robot to the right. In the same manner, if the roach moves to the left, forward, or backward, so does the robot. While the robot relies on the roach to move about, the roach relies on the robot to provide it with information about objects in the world using a light panel dashboard located in front of the cockroach. The robot is equipped with sensors, much like those used in motion-detection devices found in airport restrooms. If an object triggers the sensor, a light corresponding to the location of the sensor turns on. The cockroach then turns in the opposite direction. If all of the lights are light due to a wall, the roach will likely back up. Pretty smart roach! How did it learn to steer the robot? Remember, the roach has no centralized brain. In fact, the roach never had to learn how to steer the robot, it simply uses its instinct to prefer darkness over light. When a light signals the presence of an object on the right, the roach moves left because it is avoiding the light, not the object. Hertz has only exploited what he already knew about basic insect instinct. This may be a good lesson to consider when encountering bugs that act intelligent. No wonder why some researchers remain skeptical when animals are reported to use language or to make art. Videos of this remarkable device can be found by searching youtube.com.

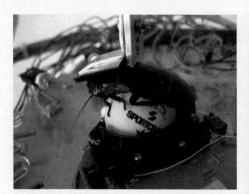

Photos courtesy of Garnet Hertz.

Student Resource Center

STUDY GUIDE

1. Artificial intelligence concerns any computer-produced output that would be judged intelligent if produced by a human.

2. One dichotomy (Searle) distinguishes between "strong" AI, which asserts that proper programming can create a "mind" capable of understanding, and "weak" AI, which emphasizes its value as a heuristic in studying human cognition.

3. Philosophical issues associated with AI concern intent, thought, and understanding. Exercises designed to demonstrate machine-human indistinguishability and functional equivalence (e.g., the Turing test and the Chinese room) are considered by some as failing to consider important factors such as intentionality, which humans possess but machines do not.

4. Information processing by machines, as an analog of human cognition, has increased capacity in recognizing complex stimuli from the early models (which used template matching) to more recent approaches (which combine analysis of structural features and their relationships).

5. Computer programs capable of "understanding" natural language require, as a minimum, semantic and syntactic rules, world and social context knowledge bases, and some method of handling the ambiguity present in common language usage.

6. Artificial intelligence problem-solving programs (e.g., computer chess) use two principal strategies: algorithmic procedures (which guarantee a solution by examining all possible alternatives) and heuristic procedures (which are strategy based and decompose complex problems into easily solved subproblems).

7. Successful AI programs have been written which produce acceptable poetry, music, and art.

8. The future of AI and cognitive neuroscience (in combination with genetic engineering) is likely to change significantly cognitive psychology as well as all of psychology. A computer brain with computing power of the human brain may emerge by 2020.

KEY TERMS

algorithm
artificial intelligence (AI)
Chinese room
continuous speech recognition (CSR)
DYSTAL
ELIZA
expert systems
heuristic
McCulloch-Pitts neurons

Moore's law
NETtalk
parallel processing model
PARRY
robots
sequential processing model
strong AI
Turing test
weak AI

Starting Points

Books and Articles

Resources on the topic of AI are abundant. General reviews are offered in Tauke, *Computers and Common Sense* (available in paperback); and Apter, *The Computer Simulation of Behavior.* A well-written and technically interesting account by a research scientist is Raphael, *The Thinking Computer.* Also recommended is Pylyshyn's *Computation and Cognition: Toward a Foundation for Cognitive Science; The Computer and the Mind,* by Johnson-Laird; *Memory Traces in the Brain,* by Alkon; *Artificial Intelligence: The Very Idea,* by Haugeland; and *Artificial Intelligence in Psychology: Interdisciplinary Essays,* by Boden. As mentioned earlier, Alan Turing's biography by Andrew Hodges is a good read.

The April 1985 issue of *Byte* magazine is largely devoted to AI and, although dated, has engaging articles by Minsky, Schank, and Hunter; J. Anderson and Reiser; Winston; and others that address themes still current. *Metamagical Themas: Questing for the Essence of Mind and Matter* and *Godel, Escher, Bach: An Eternal Golden Braid,* by Douglas Hofstadter, should be read by all people interested in AI and related matters; besides, they are a good read. Also, Gardner's *The Mind's New Science* is highly recommended for its discussion of AI and many other topics covered in this book. Some interesting technical problems are contained in *Artificial and Human Intelligence,* edited by Elithorn and Banerji. Finally, *The Age of Spiritual Machines* by Ray Kurzweil is highly recommended.

Movies

- I, Robot (2004)—Robots
- Matrix (1999)—Computers
- 2001: A Space Odyssey (1968)—Computers
- Artificial Intelligence: AI (2001)—Robots

Search Terms

- Kismet
- The Turing Test Page
- Association for the Advancement of Artificial Intelligence
- Algorithmic Art
- EPIC Face Recognition

Glossary

Accommodation   An activity involved in the adaptation of intellectual processes during which mental structures (schemes) undergo reorganization so that new information that does not readily conform to previous structures can be integrated into the cognitive system.

Acronym   A word formed using the first letters in a phrase or group of words. Used as a mnemonic system.

Acrostic   A phrase, poem, or sentence in which the first letters of the words are associated with a to-be-remembered word or concept. Used as a mnemonic technique.

ACT   See **Adaptive control of thought.**

Ad hominem   Argument based on attacking the person making the argument, not the substance of the argument itself.

Adaptation   The responsive adjustment of a sense organ to varying qualities or intensity of a stimulus. Changes over time in an organism that increases the long-term potential for reproductive success.

Adaptive control of thought   A comprehensive model of cognition.

Aggregate field theory   The idea that cerebral functions are distributed throughout the brain that functions as a whole.

Algorithm   A step-by-step procedure that guarantees a solution to a given kind of problem. See Heuristic.

Amnesia   Memory deficits caused by problems in the brain.

Anterograde amnesia   The loss of memory after the onset of the memory disorder, due to an inability to transfer information to long-term memory. See Retrograde amnesia.

Anthropomorphism   The attribution of human qualities and characteristics to inanimate or non-human objects.

Architecture   The design and operational structure of a computing system; the physical location of the physiological structures that underpin consciousness; also part of the AWAREness model.

Artificial intelligence (AI)   Computer-produced output that would be considered intelligent if produced by a human.

Assimilation   An activity involved in the adaptation processes during which new situations are processed in accordance with existing mental structures or schemes. See Adaptation.

Association   The principle that asserts that ideas are connected in the mind on the basis of contiguity, similarity, or contrast.

Associationism   A theory of how two ideas or units become connected in the mind.

Atmosphere effect   Person perception, the tendency for one characteristic of a person to influence the way the person's other characteristics are perceived by others.

Attention   The concentration of mental effort on select sensory or mental events; also part of the AWARENESS model.

Attribute-frequency theory   A model that asserts that a prototype represents the mode or most frequently experienced combination of attributes. See Prototype.

Autobiographical Memory   Memories consisting of an individual's past history of events or facts.

Automatic processes   Cognitive processing that does not require conscious thought as a result of existing cognitive structures or highly practiced tasks.

Availability heuristic   Mental shortcut that leads people to base a judgment on the ease with which something can be brought to mind.

AWAREness   A general framework of consciousness, which includes attention, wakefulness, architecture, recall of knowledge, emotive, novelty, emergence, subjectivity, and selectivity.

Axon   A long, tubular pathway that transmits electrical impulses from the cell body (soma) to other cells. See Neuron.

Bayes's theorem   (also called Bayesian theorem) A mathematical statement of a relationship evaluating the probability that a hypothesis regarding a future event will occur.

Behaviorism   A theory of animal and human learning that focuses on objectively observable behaviors and discounts mental activities.

Bottom-up processing   Cognitive processing initiated by the components of a stimulus pattern or problem that, when taken together, lead to recognition of the whole configuration or problem. See Top-down processing.

Broca's area   A brain area specialized for language production located along the inferior frontal gyrus. See Wernicke's area.

Brown-Peterson technique   A procedure developed to study short-term memory in which an item to be remembered is followed by a distractor task that lasts for variable time intervals before recall. The length of duration is varied to measure its effects on recall.

Canonic perspectives   Views that "best" represent an object. Frequently, these are the images that first come to mind when we are asked to recall an object.

Case studies   A method of research in which a variety of information about one person is collected in order to examine aspects relevant to the individual, a group, or a situation.

CBF   See **rCBF.**

Cell body   Part of a neuron in which nutrients and waste products are filtered in and out through its permeable cell wall. See Neuron.

Central executive   Presides over the working memory model that regulates attentional processes and governs cognitive processes.

Central nervous system (CNS)   The portion of the neurological system which consists of the brain and spinal cord.

Central-tendency theory   A model proposed by prototype theory that holds that a prototype represents the mean or average of a set of exemplars.

Cerebral commissurotomy   The surgical severing of the connective tissue between the two hemispheres of the brain and has been used in split-brain research.

Cerebral cortex   The top layer of the brain, involved in "higher-order" mental functions.

Cerebral hemispheres   The two major components of the brain. The left hemisphere is generally involved in language and symbolic processing, and the right is generally involved in nonverbal perceptual processing.

Channel capacity   An assumption regarding information processing that postulates that the capacity to handle the flow of input is determined by the limitations of the system. See Attention.

Characteristic features The incidental or superficial features of a concept. See Defining features.

Chinese room A hypothetical situation used to test the existence of strong artificial intelligence that extends beyond the simple demonstration of machine intelligence to actual thinking and understanding taking place within the machine.

Central executive Presides over the working memory model that regulates attentional processes and governs cognitive processes.

Chunking A strategy of combining small pieces of information, in short term memory, to form a larger, meaningful unit of information that aids retrieval from long term memory.

Classification Arrangement of knowledge into specific groups or systems.

Closure The tendency of the human brain to perceive a whole object, despite the absence of component features essential to that object.

CNS See Central nervous system.

Cocktail party phenomenon The intrusion of an interesting event that gains one's attention. See Attention.

Codes The rule governed conversion of units of information from one modality to another.

Cognitive map A picture or image based on spatial knowledge of a stimulus or physical situation.

Cognitive model A metaphor based on observations and on inferences drawn from observations that describes the detection, storage, and use of information in the brain.

Cognitive neuroscience The study of the relationships between neuroscience and cognitive psychology, especially those theories of the mind dealing with memory, sensation and perception, problem solving, language processing, motor functions, and cognition.

Cognitive revolution Beginning in the 1950's, a shift in the area of psychological research that was focused on the study of observable behaviors toward focusing on the examination of mental processes.

Cognitive science An interdisciplinary area of study which examines research from a variety of areas in an attempt to gain insight into issues involving the mind and the human brain.

Commissurotomy See Cerebral commissurotomy.

Common fate The Gestalt principle of organization stating that elements moving in a similar manner tend to be grouped together. See Pragnan.

Components Units of importance, which, when combined, form a larger, cohesive concept, model, or theory.

Comprehension The ability to understand the meaning or importance of something.

Componential intelligence Intelligence related to academic problem solving skills.

Computational brain The concept that the brain's function is to interpret and process sensory signals and bodily needs in a comprehensible way. Involves coding information, storing information, transforming information, thinking, and, finally, reacting to information.

Computed axial tomography (CAT) An imaging technique which allows a variety of X-ray images to be taken and combined into a cross-sectional view of the human body, including the brain.

Computer science The systematic study of computing systems and computation.

Concepts Ideas or groups of ideas (tangible or intangible) that share specific common features or characteristics.

Concept formation The discernment of properties common to a class of stimuli and the discovery of rules relating its properties; also known as concept learning.

Conceptual science A system that provides useful metaphorical classification schemes. Because these schemes are devised by humans for human purposes, they are fabrications of human cognition that mirror reality.

Conceptual-propositional hypothesis A hypothesis positing that information is represented in memory in an abstract propositional format explicating objects and their relationships.

Conceptually driven processing See Topdown processing.

Conditional probability The probability that an event will occur given that one or more other events have previously occurred.

Cones Photoreceptors in the retina of the eye, typically allowing for color vision.

Confabulate The process of confusing imagination with memory and similarly, true memories with false memories.

Connectionism The idea that complex cognitive functions can be understood in terms of the network of links among units.

Consciousness An awareness of events or stimuli in the environment and of cognitive phenomena such as memories, thoughts, and bodily sensations.

Conservation The idea that certain transformations do not alter the basic properties of objects.

Conservative focusing A hypothesized strategy used in concept formation in which one hypothesis is formulated and reformulations of a positive instance are sequentially tested and outcomes noted. See Hypothesis testing.

Consolidation failure The incomplete storage of information in memory.

Constructive memory The idea that prior experience, postevent information, perceptual factors, and one's desire to remember certain events over others influence what we recall (Bartlett).

Constructive perception The theory that during perception we form and test hypotheses regarding perception based on what we sense and what we know.

Contextual intelligence The ability to grasp, deal with and understand everyday tasks.

Continuity A Gestalt perceptual principle stating that objects positioned along a path are more likely to be seen as a group.

Continuous speech recognition (CSR) Computer programs that recognize and record natural human speech.

Contralaterality The processing by the brain of information received from opposite sides of the body.

Convergent thinking A deductive form of thinking with a goal of arriving at the single best answer or conclusion. See Divergent thinking.

Cornea The transparent, circular part of the front of the eyeball that covers the iris and the pupil, allowing light reflected from images to pass through the pupil, into the eye, and onto the retina at the back of the eyeball.

Corpus callosum The massive bundle of nerves that connects the two hemispheres of the brain to facilitate in communication.

Creativity The process involving cognitive activity that results in new ideas or concepts.

Data-driven processing See Bottom-up processing.

Decay Forgetting due to a lack of use or rehearsal of previously available information.

Decision frame A decision maker's framework concerning a choice alternative that includes behaviors, results, and contingencies.

Declarative knowledge Factual information known about objects, ideas and events. See Knowledge.

Declarative memory Knowledge about the world. See Procedural memory.

Declarative representation See Declarative memory.

Deductive reasoning The process of reasoning in which particular conclusions are drawn from more general principles or previously known facts. See Inductive reasoning.

Deep structure The underlying form of a sentence that holds information crucial to its meaning.

Defining features The essential, required features of a concept. See Characteristic features.

Dendrites The highly arborized parts of a cell that gather neural impulses from other cells. See Neuron.

Depressants Substances that suppress the nervous system.

Dichotic listening task A task in which individuals listen to two different messages presented through headphones, one message to each ear, and are asked to focus and recall information from only one of the messages.

Direct perception Theory of perception that purports that stimuli themselves contain all the necessary information for perception to occur and that past knowledge is unnecessary.

Divergent thinking Thinking that involves generating many different answers to a single problem, with the "correctness" dependent on subjective evaluation of answers as abstract and flexible. See Convergent Thinking.

Dual-coding hypothesis The hypothesis that proposes two coding and storage systems (verbal and visual).

Dualistic Viewing each person as consisting of two entities: the mind and the body.

DYSTAL A neural network architecture based on based on biological associative learning.

Echoic memory The persistence of auditory impressions and their brief availability for further processing.

Eidetic imagery The vivid, often seemingly realistic, experience of mental images.

Egocentrism The tendency to regard the world from one's own perspective.

Electroconvulsive therapy (ECT) Also called shock therapy. A form of somatic therapy consisting of the application of electric currents to the head, which produce convulsions and unconsciousness.

Electroencephalography (EEG) The measurement of electrical activities of the brain.

ELIZA One of the first conversational computer programs to simulate intelligence. (Weizenbaum). See PARRY.

Emergence Consciousness results from activity in the brain; also part of the AWAREness model.

Emotive Affective components associated with consciousness; also part of the AWAREness model.

Empiricists Those who adhere to the philosophy that knowledge exists only after experience, which typically involves sensations and perceptions.

Engram A trace a collection of neural charges that represent memory.

Episodic memory Memory that concerns information about temporally dated episodes and events along with the relationships among such events. See Declarative memory.

Epistemology The study of the origin and nature of knowledge.

Ethics System of moral principles, rules, and standards of conduct.

Evolutionary cognitive psychology Discipline that views cognition from an evolutionary-adaptive viewpoint.

Evolutionary perspective Posits that cognition is best understood from a functionalist approach.

Exemplar A typical or standard mental model of an object, pattern, or idea.

Experiential intelligence The ability to react to novel situations and stimuli.

Experiment   The scientific process by which variables are manipulated and measured to obtain results which examine a given construct.

Eye-tracking studies   Studies which measure the extent to which the eyes saccade while attempting to locate/view/sense information located in the visual field.

Expert systems   Computer systems based on subject-specific knowledge that perform as human experts do.

Explicit memory   Memory recovery or recognition based on conscious search processes as one might use in answering a direct question. See Implicit memory.

Facial cognizance   An astute level of facial processing in which an adept observer or expert (like a portrait artist) is able to see beyond the surface characteristics of a face.

Facts   Information we know to be true based on universal human sensations.

Failure to encode   An insufficient amount of attention is present resulting in information which is not fully encoded to memory.

False memories   Reconstructed memories about events that did not occur but are invented (Loftus).

Feature   A basic component of a complex stimulus pattern.

Feature analysis   The hypothesis that pattern recognition occurs only after sensory stimuli have been analyzed according to their simple or basic components.

Filter model   Broadbent's theory that information processing is restricted b y channel capacity.

Fissures   Deep grooves on the surface of the brain. See Sulci.

Focus gambling   A strategy used in concept formation in which more than one concept feature at a time is changed, with the goal being a correct response in a shorter time span (Bruner). See Hypothesis testing.

Formalism   The philosophical theory that formal statements have no meaning but that its symbols exhibit a form that has useful applications.

Fovea   A small indentation in the retina that contains the highest concentration of cones and provides the greatest visual acuity.

Foveal vision   Vision that provides the greatest visual acuity and is restricted to a visual angle of about 1 to 2 degrees.

Frontal lobe   One of the four major regions of the brain located anterior (in front) to the parietal lobe. Plays a part in such functions as impulse control, judgment, and problem solving among others.

Functional fixedness   The tendency to view things in terms of their familiar uses, which makes it difficult to achieve novel perspectives often necessary for problem solving.

Functional-equivalency hypothesis   The idea that imagery and perception are very similar cognitive phenomena.

Ganglion cells   A type of neuron located on the retina, which receives visual information from the photoreceptors and other intermediate cells, transmitting information to the optic nerve, and on to the lateral geniculate nucleus.

Geon   Basic geometric forms which make complex forms when combined. "Geometric ions".

Geriatrics   The branch of medicine concerned with the diagnosis, treatment and prevention of disease in older people and the problems specific to aging.

Gerontology   The study of aging and its biological, psychological, and sociological impacts.

Gestalt psychology   Theory that states that psychology, especially perception and cognition, can be understood by examining the way information is organized as a whole structured phenomenon.

Grandmother cell   A hypothetical neuron which represents a complex concept or object.

Gyri   The protruding ridges between the folds in the surface of the brain. (*gyrus*, sing.)

Hallucinogens   A diverse group of drugs that alter perceptions, thoughts, and feelings.

Hard problem   In consciousness, the question of how unique phenomenological experience arise out of the activities of the brain.

Heuristic   Sets of empirical rules or strategies that lead to a solution most of the time. See Algorithm.

Homunculus   A hypothetical entity used in philosophical arguments relating to theories of the mind. In effect arguing the existence of a little person who views incoming images from the visual system as though it were watching (and interpreting) a movie.

Human Intelligence   The ability to acquire, retrieve, and use knowledge in a meaningful way; to understand concrete and abstract ideas; and to comprehend relationships among objects and ideas.

Hypothesis testing   The notion that some problems are resolved by forming and testing a hypothesis or question that can be tested.

Iconic memory   The momentary persistence of visual impressions and their brief availability for further processing.

Illumination   A stage in the creative process that involves sudden understanding of a problem and its solution.

Illusion   The perception of a visual stimulus that represents what is perceived in a way different from the way it is in reality.

Illusory contours   The perception of contours, despite changes in luminance.

Imaging studies   Studies which involve methodologies used to produce a picture of internal body structures (e.g. the brain).

Implicit memory   A type of memory retrieval in which recall is enhanced by the presentation of a cue or prime, despite having no conscious awareness of the connection between the prime and to-be-recalled item.

Incubation   A stage in the creative process that involves temporarily setting a problem aside and diverting attention elsewhere.

Inductive reasoning   Reasoning from the particular to the general. See Deductive reasoning.

Information processing   Information which is perceived via sensory mediums is analyzed and transformed into meaningful units.

Information-processing model   A model proposing that information is processed through a series of stages, each of which performs unique operations. Each stage receives information from preceding stages and passes the transformed input along to other stages for further processing.

Intelligence   The ability to comprehend, understand, and profit from experience.

Interference   The prevention of acquiring new information due to the previous acquisition of old information.

Internal representation   A transformation of environmental cues into meaningful cognitive symbols of the perceived stimuli.

Introspection   A technique of self-observation.

Intuition   Instinctive knowing (without the use of rational processes).

Isomorphism   A one-to-one correspondence between a perceived object and its internal representation. See Gestalt psychology.

Key word method   A mnemonic technique used in second-language learning.

Knowledge   The storage and organization of verbal and visual information in memory.

Korsakoff's syndrome   The disorder commonly brought about by severe alcoholism resulting in bilateral damage to the diencephalon causing amnesia.

Labeled lines   Nerves are connected to a specific sensory function.

Language   A systematic means of communicating thoughts by the use of sounds and/or symbols.

Language acquisition device (LAD)   A part of the human brain theorized by Noam Chomsky which allows humans to acquire languages.

Lateral geniculate nucleus (LGN)   A region of the brain, located within the larger region of the thalamus, which receives information from the optic nerve, transmitting it to the visual cortex.

Lateral inhibition   A signal produced by one cell that prevents adjacent cells from firing .

LDT   See Lexical-decision task.

Lens   The transparent structure inside the eye that focuses light rays onto the retina.

Level of processing   Stimuli perceived via sensory inputs can be encoded on a variety of dimensions, ranging from shallow to deep.

Levels-of-processing model   A theory proposing that memory occurs as a by-product of processing activities, with memory trace durability a function of the depth of that processing.

Lexical-decision task   A priming task in which a subject is shown a related word and asked to evaluate quickly whether a second string of letters makes a legal word or not .

Lexicon   A person's knowledge of vocabulary.

Linguistics   The scientific study of language.

Linguistic-relativity hypothesis   The hypothesis that proposes that perception of reality is determined by one's language history.

Lobotomy   A surgical procedure involving the removal of regions of the brain

Localization   Identification of particular structures or regions of the brain that appear to be involved in particular cognitive process.

Logic   The science of thinking based on laws that determine the validity of a conclusion.

Long-term memory   A memory storage system characterized by long duration, large capacity, and accessibility.

Long-term potentiation   An increase in neural responsiveness after rapid repeated stimulation over an extended time period.

Luminance   A measure of the brightness of a surface.

Magnetic resonance imaging (MRI)   A brain imaging technique that generates cross-sectional images of a human brain by detecting small molecular changes.

Magnetoencepholography (MEG)   A brain imaging technique which measures the magnetic fields produced by electrical activity in the brain.

Mass action   The idea that memories are distributed throughout the brain.

McCulloch-Pitts neurons   Artificial neurons which gather information from various inputs, producing one output, which mimic the normal processes of human biological neural networks.

Meditation   A technique which produces focused, directed attention, or awareness for a duration of time which often produces physical and mental relaxation.

Mental representations   A hypothetical pattern of mental or brain activity that represents some feature of the world, of the person, or of the interaction between the person and the world.

Mental rotation   The human ability to assess similarity of shapes and objects which are presented at different angles and orientations.

Mere exposure effect   The more we are exposed to something, the more we are likely to like it.

Metacognition   Higher order thinking involving active control over cognitive processes.

Metaphors A statement that allows understanding one conceptual domain in terms of another conceptual domain.

Method of loci A mnemonic technique that involves associating items to be remembered with physical locations and "revisiting" those sites during recall.

Mind–body issue The philosophic problem dealing with the relationship between the mind and the body.

Mirror reversal task A task which typically requires tracing an object, which can only be perceived by viewing the object in a mirror which shows the reverse image of the object.

Mnemonic Any technique that serves to facilitate storage and recall of information in memory.

Mnemonic encoding principle experts encode information in terms of a large existing knowledge base.

Models Schemes or structures that correspond to real objects, events, or classes of events, and that have explanatory power.

Monitoring The ongoing assessment of the progress of activities.

Moore's law A law that states that the size of a transistor in an integrated circuit chip will be reduced by 50 percent every 24 months with the result being an exponential growth in computing power over time.

Morpheme The smallest unit of meaning in a language (e.g., a prefix or a suffix) that is combined with other such units in various ways to create words.

Morphology The form and structure of an organism.

Motivated forgetting Failing to retain stored information to memory, often due to the potentially aversive nature of such information.

Myelin sheath The fatty outer covering of a neuron's axon that facilitates neural transmission in some neurons.

Nativists Those who adhere to the philosophy that the mind produces ideas which are not derived from experiences.

NETtalk A neural net simulation that reads letters and pronounces them aloud.

Network model A semantic organization model proposing that concepts are represented in memory as independent units stored in spatial arrangements according to the degree and nature of their relationships.

Neural correlates of consciousness Biological mechanisms of the brain which are associated with a variety of aspects related to conscious experience.

Neural network systems See Parallel distributed processing model.

Neurogenesis The process by which neurons are created and first develop.

Neuroscience The scientific study of the nervous system.

Neurotransmission Passage of signals from one nerve cell to another via chemical substances and electrical signals.

Neuron A nerve cell with specialized processes that constitutes the structural and functional unit of nerve tissue. As the basic cell of the nervous system, the neuron conducts neural information.

Neurotransmitters Chemicals that act on the membrane of the dendrite of a neuron to facilitate or inhibit neurotransmission. See Neuron.

Nondeclarative knowledge See Procedural knowledge.

Nonsense syllable A nonword sequence typically composed of three letters used in early memory studies.

Novelty   the propensity to seek out novel, creative and innovative items in the environment; also part of the AWAREness model.

Occipital lobe   One of the four major regions of the brain located posterior (behind) to the parietal lobe. Plays an integral part in vision receiving information from the LGN.

Operational definition   Defining a variable in terms of how it is measured.

Organization   The collective functioning of connected, interdependent parts.

Organizational schemes   A technique that organizes information into categories that are used as recall cues. See Mnemonic.

Output interference   The detrimental effect that the retrieval of one item has on the retrieval of subsequent items.

Parallel distributed processing model   A neurally inspired model of the mind in which information is processed in a massively distributed, mutually interactive, parallel system in which various activities are carried out simultaneously through excitation and/or inhibition between units.

Parallel processing model   A computer program that breaks down problems into smaller problems then examines all input features at the same time.

Parietal lobe   One of the four major regions of the brain located superior (above) to the temporal lobe. Plays a part in integrating sensory information and movement.

PARRY   A conversational computer program that simulated responses of a paranoid patient and was used in a test of indistinguishability between a machine and a human with psychiatrists as the expert judges. See ELIZA.

Pattern organization   The mental process of identifying and classifying certain aspects of a pattern into meaningful units.

Pattern recognition   The mental process of recalling a previously identified pattern from memory.

PDP   See **Parallel distributed processing model.**

Peg word system   A mnemonic strategy that involves learning a set of stimulus items that serve as pegs on which the items to be remembered are hung.

Perception   The branch of psychology that deals with the interpretation of sensory stimuli.

Perceptrons   The simulation of neural nets in computer architecture.

Perceptual span   The amount of information that can be perceived during a brief presentation or within a specific area.

Period of enlightenment   In the 18th Century, the increased desire to learn new information, acquire knowledge, and examine previously unexplained phenomena (also called the Renaissance).

Peripheral nervous system   Nerves that lie outside the spinal cord and the brain, most of which are involved in sensing energy changes in the environment.

Permastore   A type of memory that is so well entrenched that it is permanent and lasts a lifetime.

Perspectives   Theoretical viewpoints.

Philosophy   A discipline which engages in careful thought about the fundamental nature of the world.

Phoneme   The basic speech sound unit of a spoken language distinguishable by how it is produced (voiced, unvoiced, fricative, or plosive). Phonemes are combined with other sound units to create words.

Phonology   The study of speech sounds (phonemes) and how they are used.

Phonological loop A rehearsal circuit in the working memory that holds inner speech for verbal comprehension model.

Phrenology The pseudoscientific study of the configuration of a person's skull based on the supposition that it accurately indicates mental faculties and character traits.

Pop out effect When visual elements are distinctive the boundaries jump out to the viewer.

Positron emission tomography (PET) A brain imaging technique that allows researchers to observe active brain areas while people engage in a variety of mental processes and tasks.

Pragnanz The Gestalt principle of organization asserting that stimulus figures are seen in the "best" possible way given the stimulus conditions. The "best" figure is stable and cannot be made simpler or more orderly by shifts in perception.

Preparation A stage in the creative process that involves problem formulation and initial solution attempts.

Presynaptic terminal Bulb-shaped tip of the axon that forms part of the synapse and releases neurotransmitters to communicate with other cells. See Neuron.

Primary memory The immediate memory that never leaves consciousness and provides an accurate representation of events.

Primacy-recency effect The notion that units of information are best encoded to memory which are at the beginning or the end of a sequence of information.

Priming The process by which a cue enhances recall or recognition or a subsequent item from memory.

Priming effect The enhanced recall or recognition of an item following a prime. The process usually takes place without conscious awareness of the link between the cue and the to-be-recalled (recognized) item.

Priming studies Studies that evaluate the processes whereby exposure to words or concepts affect later cognitive or behavioral performance.

Proactive interference Interference created by memories from prior learning.

Probe item A cue used to signal a person in a memory task to recall a specific item.

Productivity The degree to which native speakers use particular grammatical processes, especially in word formation.

Problem solving Thought directed toward discovering a solution for a specific problem that involves both response formation and response selection.

Procedural knowledge Knowledge that is implicit and sampled through actions or performance. See Declarative knowledge.

Procedural memory Relates to the knowledge of how to do things (procedures). It is largely unconscious and not easily verbalized. See Implicit memory.

Production memory The knowledge required to do things, such as tie shoelaces or perform as well. See Declarative memory.

Production system The notion that underlying human cognition is a set of conditional-action pairs called productions. See ACT.

Proposition The smallest unit of information that is meaningful.

Prototype An abstraction of stimulus patterns stored in long-term memory against which similar patterns are evaluated in terms of how closely they fit the model.

Prototype matching A hypothesis proposing that pattern recognition occurs when a match is made between sensory stimuli and an abstracted or idealized cognitive pattern.

Prototype theory A model of categorization where members of a category are a better fit than others. The prototype is often an abstraction of the category members. See Attribute-frequency model, Central-tendency model.

Proximity   A Gestalt perceptual principle stating that objects positioned near one another are more likely to be seen as forming a group.

Pseudomemory   The tendency for subjects to recognize a prototype falsely as a previously seen figure with greater confidence than figures that have actually been previously seen.

Pseudoscience   Any body of knowledge or practice which purports to be scientific or supported by science but which fails to use adequate scientific methodology.

Psycholinguistics   Study of language as it relates to the human mind.

Psychophysics   The scientific study of the relationship between physical events and psychological phenomena.

Psychosurgery   Brain surgery on human patients intended to relieve severe and otherwise intractable mental or behavioral problems.

Qualia   The subjective aspect of conscious experience which is different from the physical nature of the stimulus that provokes it.

Reaction time studies   Studies which measure the amount of time taken to complete a given task.

Reading comprehension   The level of understanding of a passage or text.

Recall of knowledge   The retrieval of previously stored information; also part of the AWAREness model.

Reconstructive memory   The idea that people assimilate facts about the world and then are able to recall them as they really happened.

Regional cerebral blood flow (rCBF)   By measuring the blood flow in the brain, it is possible to infer which regions are neurologically active using PET and fMRI.

Reflex arc   The neural pathway mediating a reflex.

Regularity   Typical frequency of a given occurrence of some behavior or action.

Relatedness   The similarity in structure, function, or meaning of two or more entities.

REM sleep   Rapid eye movement during dreaming.

Representation of knowledge   The extent to which knowledge is adequately stored and later retrieved in memory.

Representativeness heuristic   The tendency to judge the probability or aspects of an event by using previously acquired information from a known event and assuming that the probabilities or aspects of the event will be similar.

Repressed memories   Memories so painful or traumatic that they are not expressed in consciousness.

Repression   The removal of traumatic thoughts and experiences from memory.

Retina   The membrane on the back of the eye that contains photoreceptor cells (rods and cones).

Retrieval failure   Forgetting information due to inadequate retrieval of the information from long term memory.

Retrieval structure principle   Experts use their knowledge of a subject to develop abstract, highly specialized mechanisms for systematically encoding and retrieving meaningful patterns from LTM.

Retroactive interference   Newly acquired information disrupts the retrieval of previously learned information.

Retrograde amnesia   The inability to recall information acquired prior to the onset of a memory disorder. See Retrograde amnesia.

Robots   Machines capable of performing human tasks or behaving in a human manner.

Rods   Photoreceptors in the retina of the eye, typically allowing for the perception of dim luminance information and peripheral vision.

Saccade   The rapid eye movement occurring during reading and when viewing visual patterns.

Schema   A cognitive framework of meaningfully organized concepts.

Scheme   A mental representation of some action (mental or physical) that can be performed on an object and that, as the organism develops, increases in integration and coordination. See Adaptation.

Second-order isomorphism   The relationship between external objects and their internal representation that is lawful but not structural.

Secondary memory   Permanent memory that is characterized by individual differences.

Selective attention   A type of attention which involves focusing on a specific aspect of an experience while ignoring other aspects.

Selectivity   The filtering of incoming information from the outside world; also part of the AWAREness model.

Self-knowledge   A sense of one's own personal information; also part of the AWAREness model.

Self-schema   A complex internal representation of self, revolving around the topics of "I, me, and mine."

Semantic code   A means of describing the content of a piece of information.

Semantic feature-comparison model   A model of semantic organization proposing that concepts are stored in memory as sets of semantic features distinguishable as either defining or characteristic features.

Semantic memory   Memory that stores word meanings, concepts, and world knowledge.

Semantic priming   The presentation of a semantically related prime followed by its target.

Senescence   The process of deterioration natural to the development of an organism.

Sensation   The detection of stimulation, the study of which commonly deals with the structure of sensory mechanisms (such as the eye) and the stimuli (such as light) that affect those mechanisms.

Sensory store   Very short-term memory which allows incoming sensory information to be processed so long as the information is properly encoded.

Sensory threshold   The level of energy required to activate a neural response.

Sentience   Having conscious sensations. Experiencing sensations or feelings.

Sequential processing model   A computer program that examines each input feature in a predetermined stepwise fashion, with the outcome of each stage determining the next step in the program.

Seriation   The ability to order elements according to some underlying principle.

Set   Any preparatory cognitive activity that precedes thinking and perception.

Set-theoretical model   A model of semantic organization proposing that concepts are represented in memory as information sets that include category examples and attributes.

Shadowing   An experimental procedure used in auditory attention research in which subjects are asked to repeat a spoken message as it is presented.

Short-term memory   A hypothetical storage system characterized by a duration estimated at about 12 seconds, by a capacity estimated at about 7 ± 2 items, and by accurate recall.

Signal detection theory   A common method used in psychophysical research which allows researchers to test human abilities related to differentiating between signal and noise.

Similarity   The Gestalt principle of organization stating that like elements in the same structure tend to be perceived together. See Pragnanz.

Simultaneous scanning   A strategy used in concept formation in which people begin with all possible hypotheses and eliminate all untenable ones (Bruner). See Hypotheses testing.

Single-cell studies   Evaluating the electrical activity of individual cells in the brain.

Social cognition   A level of analysis that aims to understand social psychological phenomena by investigating the cognitive processes that underlie them.

Speculation   An opinion about a phenomenon, which is has not or cannot be tested scientifically.

Speed-up principle   Practice increases the speed with which experts recognize and encode patterns.

Spreading activation model   The memory model that posits that semantic storing and processing are based on a complex network in which simple associations.

Sternberg paradigm   A procedure used to study retrieval in short-term memory in which a sequence of items is presented for a short duration followed by a probe digit. Subjects are asked to decide whether the probe digit was in the original series. Reaction times are the principal dependent variable.

Sternberg task   A method created by Sternberg to examine how information retrieved from short term memory is transferred to long term memory.

Stimulants   A class of drugs that elevates mood, increases feelings of well-being, and increases energy and alertness.

Stimulus response   The relationship between sensory information which must be sensed by the organism in order for a response to occur.

Storage capacity   The amount of information that can be stored to memory.

Store   The smallest unit of information which can be stored to memory.

Striate cortex   An area of the brain, located within the occipital lobe, involved in the perception of vision.

Strong AI   Supposes that it is possible for computers to become self-aware, but not necessarily exhibit human-like thought processes.

Subjectivity   Each person's conscious experience is unique; also part of the AWAREness model.

Subliminal perception   The influence of stimuli that are insufficiently intense to produce a conscious sensation but strong enough to influence some mental processes.

Subliminal priming   Briefly presenting a stimulus below one's ability to consciously perceive it; however, serves to elevate the threshold of retrieval for related or associated items in memory. See Priming.

Successive scanning   A strategy used in concept formation in which people begin with one hypothesis, maintain that hypothesis as long as it is successful, and discard or change it when it is no longer tenable. See Hypothesis testing.

Sulci   The grooves between the ridges (gyri) on the surface of the brain. (*sulcus,* sing.)

Surface structure   The portion of a sentence that can be analyzed and labeled by conventional parsing schemes.

Syllogism   An argument according to Aristotle's logical theory involving a major premise, a minor premise, and a conclusion.

Symmetry   A Gestalt principle whereby the whole of a figure is perceived rather than the individual parts which make up the figure.

Synapse   The juncture between two neurons where neurotransmitters are passed. See Neuron.

Synesthesia   The condition in which information from one sensory modality (such as auditory) is coded in another modality (such as visual).

Syntax Rules that govern the combination of morphemes into larger linguistic units such as phrases and sentences.

Template matching The theory asserting that pattern recognition occurs when an exact match is made between sensory stimuli and a corresponding internal mental form.

Temporal One of the four major sections on the surface of each hemisphere, marked off by major convolutions or fissures.

Temporal lobe One of the four major regions of the brain located below the other three. Plays a part in language and memory.

Theories Potential explanations for phenomenon which use subsequent evidence to attempt to support such explanations.

Thinking The general process of considering an issue in the mind, which results in the formation of a new mental representation.

Tip of the tongue phenomenon The subjective feeling that information is readily available, but in the absence of the ability to recall such information.

Tomogram An image that shows a cross section of the brain.

Top-down processing Cognitive processing as hypothesis-driven recognition of the whole stimulus configuration or problem which leads to recognition of the component parts. See Bottom-up processing.

Transaxial magnetic stimulator (TMS) A brain imaging technique which generates images of the brain by magnetically stimulating the visual cortex.

Transformational grammar Rules that change the linguistic structure of a sentence into another form while maintaining the semantic content.

Transitivity The ability to coordinate isolated elements from a total system and perform operations on those elements.

Turing test The test involving communication between a human who asks questions and an unknown language-using entity, with the human's task being to distinguish the output as human or nonhuman.

Unconscious inference Process in which an observer constructs a percept by means of reasoning without being consciously aware of the procedure.

Unit of analysis The entity which a study is attempting to examine and analyze.

Verbal dialogues Conversations between people in which argumentation or persuasion plays a role.

Verification A stage in the creative process that involves testing or carrying out the problem solution.

Very long term memory (VLTM) Information which is typically stored early in the course of an individual's development, which remains adequately stored for the entire life span.

Vision The perceptual experience of seeing.

Visual cortex An area of the brain, located within the occipital lobe, involved in the perception of vision.

Visual field The area of the environment which can be perceived, given the relative location of the person.

Visual imagery Imagery that invokes colors, shapes, or anything that can be perceived.

Visuospatial sketchpad A brief loop that rehearses and processes images in the working memory model.

von Restorff effect The tendency to recall an item that is highlighted or otherwise distinctive, relative to other to-be-remembered items.

Wakefulness The continuum from sleep to alertness; a state in which you are consciously awake and aware of the outside world; also part of the AWAREness model.

Weak AI   The view, in the area of artificial intelligence, that while humans are computing machines, no machine will ever have the capabilities of a human.

Wernicke's area   A region of the brain adjacent to the auditory projection area implicated in understanding word meanings. See also Broca's area.

World knowledge   Facts available in long term memory; also part of the AWAREness model.

Working memory   A memory system that temporarily holds and manipulates information as we perform cognitive tasks. Working memory is analogous to a workbench where new and old material is constantly being processed, transformed, and combined.

References

Aaronson, D., & Ferres, S. (1984). Reading strategies for children and adults: Some empirical evidence. *Journal of Verbal Learning and Verbal Behavior, 9,* 700–725.

Aaronson, D., & Ferres, S. (1986). Reading strategies for children and adults: A quantitative model. *Psychological Review, 93,* 89–112.

Abu-Mostafa, Y. S. (1995). Machines that learn from hints. *Scientific American,* April, 64–69.

Adams, J. L. (1976a). *Conceptual blockbusters.* (2nd ed.). New York: Norton.

Adams, J. L. (1976b). *Learning and memory.* Homewood, IL: Dorsey Press.

Adelson, B. (1981). Problem solving and the development of abstract categories in programming languages. *Memory and Cognition, 9,* 422–433.

Adelson, B. (1984). When novices surpass experts: The difficulty of a task may increase with expertise. *Journal of Experimental Psychology: Learning, Memory, and Cognition, 10,* 483–495.

Alkon, D. L. (1988). *Memory traces in the brain.* Cambridge, U.K.: Cambridge University Press.

Alkon, D. L. (1989, July). Memory storage and neural systems. *Scientific American,* pp. 42–50.

American Heritage Dictionary of the English Language. (1969). Boston: Houghton Mifflin.

Amosov, N. M. (1967). *Modeling of thinking and the mind.* Translated from Russian by L. Finegold. New York: Spartan.

Anderson, A. R. (Ed.). (1964). *Minds and machines.* Englewood Cliffs, NJ: Prentice-Hall.

Anderson, J. R. (1975). Item-specific and relation-specific interference in sentence memory. *Journal of Experimental Psychology: Human Learning and Memory, 104,* 249–260.

Anderson, J. R. (1976). *Language, memory, and thought.* Hillsdale, NJ: Erlbaum.

Anderson, J. R. (1978). Arguments concerning representations for mental imagery. *Psychological Review, 85,* 249–277.

Anderson, J. R. (1983a). *The architecture of cognition.* Cambridge, MA: Harvard University Press.

Anderson, J. R. (1983b). A spreading activation theory of memory. *Journal of Verbal Learning and Verbal Behavior, 22,* 261–295.

Anderson, J. R. (1985). *Cognitive psychology and its implications* (2nd ed.). San Francisco: Freeman.

Anderson, J. R. (1990). *Cognitive psychology* (3rd ed.). San Francisco: Freeman.

Anderson, J. R. (Ed.). (1981). *Cognitive skills and their acquisition.* Hillsdale, NJ: Erlbaum.

Anderson, J. R., & Bower, G. H. (1972). Recognition and retrieval processes in free recall. *Psychological Review, 79,* 97–123.

Anderson, J. R., & Bower, G. H. (1973). *Human associative memory.* Washington, DC: Winston.

Anderson, J. R., & Kosslyn, S. M. (Eds.). (1984). *Tutorials in learning and memory: Essays in honor of Gordon Bower.* San Francisco: Freeman.

Anderson, J. R., & Reiser, B. J. (1978). Schema directed processes in language comprehension. In A. Lesgold, J. Pellegrino, S. Fokkima, & R. Glaser (Eds.), *Cognitive psychology and instruction.* New York: Plenum.

Anderson, J. R., & Reiser, B. J. (1985). The LISP tutor. *Byte, 10,* 159–178.

Anderson, R. C., & Pichert, J. W. (1978). Recall of previously unrecallable information following a shift in perspective. *Journal of Verbal Learning and Verbal Behavior, 17,* 1–12.

André-Leicknam, B., & Ziegler, C. (1982). *Naissance de l'écriture: Cuneiformes et hieroglyphes.* Paris: Minister of Culture.

Andrew, A. M. (1963). *Brain and computer.* London: Harrap.

Annett, M. (1982). Handedness. In J. G. Beaumont (Ed.), *Divided visual field studies of cerebral organization*. London: Academic Press.

Anokhin, P. K. (1969). Cybernetics and the integrative activity of the brain. In M. Cole & I. Maltzman (Eds.), *A handbook of contemporary Soviet psychology*. New York: Basic Books.

Apter, M. J. (1970). *The computer simulation of behavior*. New York: Harper & Row.

Apter, M., & Westby, G. (Eds.). (1973). *The computer in psychology*. New York: Wiley.

Atkinson, R. C. (1975). Mnemotechnics in second-language learning. *American Psychologist, 30*, 821–828.

Atkinson, R. C., Herrmann, D. J., & Wescourt, K. T. (1974). Search processes in recognition memory. In R. L. Solso (Ed.), *Theories in cognitive psychology*. Hillsdale, NJ: Erlbaum.

Atkinson, R. C., & Juola, J. F. (1973). Factors influencing speed and accuracy of word recognition. In S. Kornblum (Ed.), *Attention and performance* (Vol. IV, pp. 583–612). New York: Academic Press.

Atkinson, R. C., & Juola, J. F. (1974). Search and decision processes in recognition memory. In D. H. Krantz, R. C. Atkinson, R. D. Luce, & P. Suppes (Eds.), *Contemporary developments in mathematical psychology* (Vol. 1, pp. 242–293). San Francisco: Freeman.

Atkinson, R. C., & Raugh, M. R. (1975). An application of the mnemonic keyword method to the acquisition of a Russian vocabulary. *Journal of Experimental Psychology: Human Learning and Memory, 104*, 126–133.

Atkinson, R. C., & Shiffrin, R. M. (1968). Human memory: A proposed system and its control processes. In K. W. Spence & J. T. Spence (Eds.), *The psychology of learning and motivation: Advances in research and theory* (Vol. 2, pp. 89–195). New York: Academic Press.

Austin, J. H. (1999). *Zen and the brain: Toward an understanding of meditation and consciousness*. Cambridge, MA: MIT Press.

Averbach, E., & Coriell, A. S. (1961). Short-term memory in vision. *Bell System Technical Journal, 40*, 309–328.

Baars, B. J. (1983). Conscious contents provide the nervous system with coherent, global information. In R. Davidson, G. Schwartz, & D. Shapiro (Eds.), *Consciousness and self-regulation* (Vol. 2, pp. 45–76). New York: Plenum Press.

Baars, B. J. (1986). *The cognitive revolution in psychology*. New York: Guilford Press.

Baars, B. J. (1988). *A cognitive theory of consciousness*. Cambridge, UK: Cambridge University Press.

Baars, B. J. (1996). *In the theater of consciousness: The workspace of the mind*. Oxford, UK: Oxford University Press.

Baars, B. J. (1997). In the theatre of consciousness: Global workspace theory, a rigorous scientific theory of consciousness. *Journal of Consciousness Studies, 4*(4), 292–309.

Baars, B. J., & McGovern, K. (1995). Steps toward healing: False memories and traumagenic amnesia may coexist in vulnerable populations. *Consciousness & Cognition, Special Issue on Recovery of Traumatic Childhood Memory, 3*(3,4).

Baars, B. J., & McGovern, K. (1996). Cognitive views of consciousness: What are the facts: How can we explain them? In M. Velmans (Ed.), *The science of consciousness: Psychologycal, neuropsychological, and clinical reviews*, 63–95. London: Routledge.

Baars, B. J., & McGovern, K. A. (2000). Consciousness cannot be limited to sensory qualities: Some empirical counterexamples. *Neuro-psychoanalysis, 2*(1), 11–13.

Bach, E. (1974). *Syntactic theory*. New York: Holt, Rinehart & Winston.

Bach, M. J., & Underwood, B. J. (1970). Developmental changes in memory attributes. *Journal of Educational Psychology, 61*, 292–296.

Baddeley, A. (1982). *Your memory: A user's guide*. New York: Macmillan.

Baddeley, A. D. (1972). Retrieval-rules and semantic coding in short-term memory. *Psychological Bulletin, 78*, 379–385.

Baddeley, A. D. (1973). Memory coding and amnesia. *Neuropsychologia, 11*, 159–165.

Baddeley, A. D. (1978). The trouble with levels: A reexamination of Craik and Lockhart's "Framework for memory research" *Psychological Review, 85*, 139–152.

Baddeley, A. D. (1986). *Working memory*. Oxford, UK: Oxford University Press.

Baddeley, A. D. (1990a). *Human memory*. Hove, UK: Erlbaum.

Baddeley, A. D. (1990b). *Human memory: Theory and practice*. Boston: Allyn & Bacon.

Baddeley, A. D. (1992). Working memory. *Science, 255*, 556–559.

Baddeley, A. D., & Hitch, G. (1974). Working memory. In G. H. Bower (Ed.), *The psychology of learning and motivation* (Vol. 8, pp. 47–90). New York: Academic Press.

Baddeley, A. D., & Levy, B. A. (1971). Semantic coding and memory. *Journal of Experimental Psychology, 89,* 132–136.

Baddeley, A. D., & Warrington, E. K. (1973). Memory coding and amnesia. *Neuropsychologia, 11,* 159–165.

Bahrick, H. P. (1984). Semantic memory content in permastore: Fifty years of memory for Spanish learned in school. *Journal of Experimental Psychology: General, 113,* 1–35.

Bahrick, H. P., Bahrick, P. O., & Wittlinger, R. P. (1975). Fifty years of memory for names and faces: A cross-sectional approach. *Journal of Experimental Psychology: General, 104,* 54–75.

Bahrick, H. P., & Phelps, E. (1987). Retention of Spanish vocabulary over 8 years. *Journal of Experimental Psychology: Learning, Memory and Cognition, 13,* 344–349.

Ballard, D. H., & Brown, C. M. (1985). Vision. *Byte, 10,* 245–261.

Ballard, P. B. (1913). Oblivescence and reminiscence. *British Journal of Psychology Monograph Supplements, 1,* 1–82.

Banks, W. P. (1970). Signal detection theory and human memory. *Psychological Bulletin, 74,* 81–99.

Bargh, J. A., Chen, M., & Burrows, L. (1996). Automaticity of social behavior: Direct effects of trait construct and stereotype priming on action. *Journal of Personality and Social Psychology, 71,* 230–244.

Barinaga, M. (1999). The mapmaking mind. *Science, 285,* 189–192.

Barkow, J. H., Cosmides, L., & Tooby, J. (1992) (Eds.). *The adapted mind: Evolutionary psychology and the generation of culture.* New York: Oxford University Press.

Baron, J. (1973). Phonemic stage not necessary for reading. *Quarterly Journal of Experimental Psychology, 25,* 241–246.

Baron, J. (1988). *Thinking and deciding.* Cambridge, UK: Cambridge University Press.

Baron, J., & Thurston, I. (1973). An analysis of the word superiority effect. *Cognitive Psychology, 4,* 207–228.

Barsalou, L. W. (1992). *Cognitive psychology.* Hillsdale, NJ: Erlbaum.

Bartlett, F. C. (1932). *Remembering: A study in experimental and social psychology.* Cambridge, UK: Cambridge University Press.

Bartlett, F. C. (1958). *Thinking.* New York: Basic Books.

Bartlett, J. C., & Snelus, P. (1980). Lifespan memory for popular songs. *American Journal of Psychology, 93,* 551–560.

Bauer, M. I., & Johnson-Laird, P. N. (1993). How diagrams can improve reasoning. *Psychological Science, 4,* 372–378.

Beal, M. K., & Solso, R. L. (April, 1996). *Schematic activation and the viewing of pictures.* Paper presented at the Western Psychological Association, San Jose, CA.

Bédard, J., & Chi, M. T. H. (1993). Expertise. *Current Directions in Psychological Science, 4,* 135–139.

Begg, I., & Denny, J. P. (1969). Empirical reconsideration of atmosphere and conversion interpretations of syllogistic reasoning errors. *Journal of Experimental Psychology, 81,* 351–354.

Bellezza, F. S. (1992). Recall of congruent information in the self-reference task. *Bulletin of the Psychonomic Society, 30,* 275–278.

Bellows, S. (1987). *The bellarosa connection.* New York: Penguin.

Benderly, B. L. (1989, September). Everyday intuition. *Psychology Today,* pp. 35–40.

Bennett-Goleman, T. (2001). *Emotional alchemy: How the mind can heal the heart.* Harmony Books. New York.

Benson, D. F., & Zaidel, E. (Eds.). (1985). *The dual brain: Hemispheric specialization in humans.* New York: Guilford Press.

Bergen, J. R., & Julesz, B. (1983). Parallel versus serial processing in rapid pattern discrimination. *Nature, 303,* 696–698.

Bernbach, H. A. (1967). Decision processes in memory. *Psychological Review, 74,* 462–480.

Bernstein, L. (1959). What makes the opera grand. In *The joy of music* (p. 290). New York: Simon & Schuster.

Bernstein, L. (1976). *The unanswered question: Six talks at Harvard.* Cambridge, MA: Harvard University Press.

Bernstein, N. (1967). *The co-ordination and regulation of movements.* Oxford, UK: Pergamon Press.

Bertelson, P. (1967). The time course of preparation. *Quarterly Journal of Experimental Psychology, 19,* 272–279.

Betts, G. H. (1909). *The distribution and functions of mental imagery.* New York: Teachers College, Columbia University Press.

Biederman, I. (1972). Perceiving real world scenes. *Science, 177,* 77–80.

Biederman, I. (1985). Human image understanding: Recent research and a theory. *Computer Vision, Graphics and Image Processing, 31,* 29–73.

Biederman, I. (1987). Recognition by components: A theory of human image understanding. *Psychological Review, 94,* 115–147.

Biederman, I. (1990). Higher-level vision. In E. N. Osherson, S. M. Kosslyn, & J. M. Hollerbach (Eds.), *An invitation to cognitive science* (Vol. 2, pp. 41–72). Cambridge, MA: The MIT Press.

Biederman, I., & Cooper, E. E. (1991). Priming contour-deleted images: Evidence for intermediate representations in visual object recognition. *Cognitive Psychology, 23,* 393–419.

Biederman, I., Glass, A. L., & Stacy, E. W. (1973). Searching for objects in real world scenes. *Journal of Experimental Psychology, 97,* 22–27.

Bjork, E. L., & Estes, W. K. (1973a). Detection and placement of redundant signal elements in tachistoscope display of letters. *Perception and Pychophysics, 9,* 439–442.

Bjork, E. L., & Estes, W. K. (1973b). Letter identification in relation to linguistic context and masking conditions. *Memory and Cognition, 1,* 217–223.

Black, J. B. (1981). The effects of reading purpose on memory for text. In J. Long & A. Baddeley (Eds.), *Attention and performance* (Vol. 9). Hillsdale, NJ: Erlbaum.

Black, J. B. (1984). Understanding and remembering stories. In J. R. Anderson & S. M. Kosslyn (Eds.), *Tutorials in learning and memory.* San Francisco: Freeman.

Black, J. B., & Bower, G. H. (1980). Story understanding as problem solving. *Poetics, 9,* 223–250.

Blakemore, C. (1977). *Mechanics of the mind.* Cambridge, UK: Cambridge University Press.

Bledsoe, W. W., & Browning, I. (1959). Pattern recognition and reading by machine. *Proceedings of the Eastern Joint Computer Conference,* 225–232. Reprinted in L. Uhr (Ed.). (1966). *Pattern recognition.* New York: Wiley.

Bliss, J. C., Hewitt, D. V., Crane, P. K., Mansfield, P. K., & Townsend, J. T. (1966). Information available in brief tactile presentations. *Perception and Psychophysics, 1,* 273–283.

Boden, M. (1977). *Artificial intelligence and natural man.* New York: Basic Books.

Boden, M. A. (1989). *Artificial intelligence in psychology: Interdisciplinary essays.* Cambridge, MA: MIT Press.

Bogen, J. E., & Vogel, P. J. (1962). Cerebral commissurotomy: A case report. *Bulletin of the Los Angeles Neurological Society, 27,* 169.

Boles, D. B. (1984). Sex in latalized tachistoscopic word recognition. *Brain and Language, 23,* 307–317.

Boles, D. B. (1987). Reaction time asymmetry through bilateral versus unilateral stimulus presentation. *Brain and Cognition, 6,* 321–333.

Boles, D. B. (1994). An experimental comparison of stimulus type, display type, and input variable contributions to visual field asymmetry. *Brain and Cognition, 24*(2), 184–197.

Boles, D. B. (2000). The "lumping and "splitting" of function and brain. *Brain and Cognition, 42,* 23-25.

Bond, G. D., & Lee, A. Y. (2005). Language of lies in prison: Linguistic classification of prisoners' truthful and deceptive natural language. *Applied Cognitive Psychology* 19(3), 313–329.

Borge, V. (1978, April 9). Quoted by Linda Gutstein in "They laugh when he sits down to play." *Parade,* p. 18.

Boring, E. G. (1942). *Sensation and perception in the history of experimental psychology.* New York: Appleton-Century-Crofts.

Boring, E. G. (1946). The perception of objects. *American Journal of Psychology, 14,* 99–107.

Boring, E. G. (1950). *A history of experimental psychology* (2nd ed.). New York: Appleton-Century-Crofts.

Bourne, L. E., Jr. (1963). Factors affecting strategies used in problems of concept-formation. *American Journal of Psychology, 76,* 229–238.

Bourne, L. E., Jr. (1974). An interference model for conceptual rule learning. In R. L. Solso (Ed.), *Theories in cognitive psychology: The Loyola Symposium* (pp. 231–256). Hillsdale, NJ: Erlbaum.

Bourne, L. E., Jr., & Dominowski, R. (1972). Thinking. In *Annual Review of Psychology* (Vol. 23). Palo Alto, CA: Annual Reviews.

Bourne, L. E., Jr., & Guy, D. E. (1968). Learning conceptual rules: I. Some interrule transfer effects. *Journal of Experimental Psychology, 76,* 423–429.

Bourne, L. E., Jr., & Restle, F. (1959). Mathematical theory of concept identification. *Psychological Review, 66,* 278–296.

Bourne, L. E., Jr., Dominowski, R. L., Loftus, E. F., & Healy, A. F. (1986). *Cognitive processes* (2nd ed.). Englewood Cliffs, NJ: Prentice-Hall.

Bourne, L. E., Jr., Ekstrand, B. R., & Dominowski, R. L. (1971). *The psychology of thinking.* Englewood Cliffs, NJ: Prentice-Hall.

Bousfield, W. A. (1951). *Frequency and availability measures in language behavior.* Paper presented at the annual meeting of the American Psychological Association, Chicago.

Bousfield, W. A. (1953). The occurrence of clustering in the recall of randomly arranged associates. *Journal of General Psychology, 49,* 229–240.

Bousfield, W. A., & Cohen, B. H. (1953). The effects of reinforcement on the occurrence of clustering in the recall of randomly arranged associates. *Journal of Psychology, 36,* 67–81.

Bousfield, W. A., & Sedgewick, C. H. W. (1944). An analysis of sequences of restricted associative responses. *Journal of Psychology, 30,* 149–165.

Bower, G. H. (1967). A multi-component theory of the memory trace. In K. W. Spence & J. T. Spence (Eds.), *The psychology of learning and motivation: Advances in research and theory* (Vol. 1, pp. 299–325). New York: Academic Press.

Bower, G. H. (1970a). Analysis of a mnemonic device. *American Scientist, 58,* 496–510.

Bower, G. H. (1970b). Imagery as a relational organizer in associative learning. *Journal of Verbal Learning and Verbal Behavior, 9,* 529–533.

Bower, G. H. (1970c). Organizational factors in memory. *Cognitive Psychology, 1,* 18–46.

Bower, G. H. (1972). Mental imagery and associative learning. In L. W. Gregg (Ed.), *Cognition in learning and memory* (pp. 51–88). New York: Wiley.

Bower, G. H. (1973a). How to . . . uh . . . remember! *Psychology Today, 7,* 62–67.

Bower, G. H. (1973b). Memory freaks I have known. *Psychology Today, 7,* 64–65.

Bower, G. H. (1975). Cognitive psychology: An introduction. In W. Estes (Ed.), *Handbook of learning and cognitive processes* (Vol. 1, pp. 25–80). Hillsdale, NJ: Erlbaum.

Bower, G. H. (1976a, September). *Comprehending and recalling stories.* Division 3 Presidential address presented at the annual meeting of the American Psychological Association, Washington, DC.

Bower, G. H. (1976b, April 8). *Experiments on story understanding and recall.* Bartlett Lecture to EPS at Durham, UK.

Bower, G. H. (1993, July). Quoted in "Biomedicine in the age of imaging." *Science, 261,* 30.

Bower, G. H., & Clark, M. C. (1969). Narrative stories as mediators for serial learning. *Psychonomic Science, 14,* 181–182.

Bower, G. H., & Clark-Meyers, G. (1980). Memory for scripts with organized vs. random presentations. *British Journal of Psychology, 71,* 368–377.

Bower, G. H., & Gilligan, S. G. (1979). Remembering information related to one's self. *Journal of Research in Personality, 13,* 420–432.

Bower, G. H., & Karlin, M. B. (1974). Depth of processing pictures of faces and recognition memory. *Journal of Experimental Psychology, 103,* 751–757.

Bower, G. H., & Reitman, J. S. (1972). Mnemonic elaboration in multilist learning. *Journal of Verbal Learning and Verbal Behavior, 11,* 478–485.

Bower, G. H., & Springston, F. (1970). Pauses as recoding points in letter series. *Journal of Experimental Psychology, 83,* 421–430.

Bower, G. H., & Winzenz, D. (1969). Group structure, coding, and memory for digit series. *Journal of Experimental Psychology Monograph Supplement, 80,* 1–17.

Bower, G. H., & Winzenz, D. (1970). Comparison of associative learning strategies. *Psychonomic Science, 20,* 119–120.

Bower, G. H., Black, J. B., & Turner, T. (1979). Scripts in memory for text. *Cognitive Psychology, 11,* 177–220.

Bower, G. H., Clark, M. C., Lesgold, A. M., & Winzenz, D. (1969). Hierarchical retrieval schemes in recall of categorized word lists. *Journal of Verbal Learning and Verbal Behavior, 8,* 323–343.

Bower, G. H., Muñoz, R., & Arnold, P. G. (1972). *On distinguishing semantic and imaginal mnemonics.* Unpublished manuscript. Cited in J. Anderson & G. Bower (1973). *Human associative memory* (p. 459). Washington, DC: Winston.

Bower, T. G. R. (1970). Reading by eye. In H. Levin & J. P. Williams (Eds.), *Basic studies in reading.* New York: Basic Books.

Bowers, K. S., Regehr, G., Balthazard, C., & Parker, K. (1990). Intuition in the context of discovery. *Cognitive Psychology, 22,* 72–110.

Bowman, J. P. (1968). Muscle spindles in the intrinsic and extrinsic muscles of the rhesus monkey's (macaca mulatta) tongue. *Anatomical Record, 161,* 483–488.

Bowman, J. P., & Combs, C. M. (1968). Discharge patterns of lingual spindle afferent fibers in the hypoglossal nerve of the rhesus monkey. *Experimental Neurology, 21,* 105–119.

Bowman, J. P., & Combs, C. M. (1969a). Cerebellar responsiveness to stimulation of lingual spindle afferent fibers in the hypoglossal nerve of the rhesus monkey. *Experimental Neurology, 23,* 537–543.

Bowman, J. P., & Combs, C. M. (1969b). The cerebro-cortical projection of hypoglossal afferents. *Experimental Neurology, 23,* 291–301.

Bradshaw, J. L., & Nettleton, N. C. (1981). The nature of hemispheric specialization in man. *Behavioral and Brain Sciences, 4,* 51–91.

Brainerd, C. J. (1973). Order of acquisition of transitivity, conservation, and class inclusion of length and weight. *Developmental Psychology, 8,* 105–116.

Brainerd, C. J. (1978). *Piaget's theory of intelligence.* Englewood Cliffs, NJ: Prentice-Hall.

Brams, S. J. (1993). Theory of moves. *American Scientist, 81,* 562–570.

Bransford, J. D., & Franks, J. J. (1971). The abstraction of linguistic ideas: A review. *Cognitive Psychology, 2,* 331–350.

Bransford, J. D., & Franks, J. J. (1972). The abstraction of linguistic ideas: A review. *Cognition, 1,* 211–250.

Bransford, J. D., & Johnson, M. K. (1972). Contextual prerequisites for understanding: Some investigations of comprehension and recall. *Journal of Verbal Learning and Verbal Behavior, 11,* 717–726.

Bransford, J. D., & Stein, B. S. (1993). *The ideal problem solver.* New York: Freeman.

Brewer, W. F. (1974). The problem of meaning and the interrelations of the higher mental processes. In W. B. Weimer & D. S. Palermo (Eds.), *Cognition and the symbolic processes* (pp. 263–298). New York: Wiley.

Briggs, G. E., & Blaha, J. (1969). Memory retrieval and central comparison times in information-processing. *Journal of Experimental Psychology, 79,* 395–402.

Broadbent, D. E. (1954). The role of auditory localization and attention in memory spans. *Journal of Experimental Psychology, 47,* 191–196.

Broadbent, D. E. (1958). *Perception and communication.* London and New York: Pergamon Press.

Broadbent, D. E. (1962). Attention and the perception of speech. *Scientific American, 206,* 143–151.

Broadbent, D. E. (1966). The well-ordered mind. *American Education Research Journal, 3,* 281–295.

Broadbent, D. E. (1971). *Decision and stress.* London: Academic Press.

Broadbent, D. E. (1973). *In defense of empirical psychology.* London: Methuen.

Broadbent, D. E. (1981). Selective and control processes. *Cognition, 10,* 53–58.

Broadbent, D. E. (1984). The Maltese cross: A new simplistic model for memory. *Behavioral and Brain Sciences, 7,* 55–94.

Broadhurst P. L. (1957). Emotionality and the Yerkes-Dodson law. *Journal of Experimental Psychology, 54,* 345–352.

Bromley, H. L., Jarvella, R. L., & Lundberg, I. (1985). From Lisp machine to language lab. *Behavioral Research Methods, Instruments, and Computers, 17,* 399–402.

Brooks, L. R. (1968). Spatial and verbal components of the act of recall. *Canadian Journal of Psychology, 22,* 349–368.

Brown, A. L. (1975). The development of memory: Knowing, knowing about knowing, and knowing how to know. In H. W. Reese (Ed.), *Advances in child development and behavior* (Vol. 10). New York: Academic Press.

Brown, A. S. (1991). A review of the tip of the tongue phenomenon. *Psychological Bulletin, 109,* 204–223.

Brown, J. (Ed.). (1975). *Recognition and recall.* London: Wiley.

Brown, J. A. (1958). Some tests of the decay theory of immediate memory. *Quarterly Journal of Experimental Psychology, 10,* 12–21.

Brown, R. (1958). *Words and things.* New York: Free Press.

Brown, R. (1970). *Psycholinguistics.* New York: Free Press.

Brown, R., & Herrnstein, R. J. (1975). *Psychology.* Boston: Little, Brown.

Brown, R., & Kulik, J. (1977). Flashbulb memories. *Cognition, 5,* 73–99.

Brown, R., & McNeill, D. (1966). The "tip of the tongue" phenomenon. *Journal of Verbal Learning and Verbal Behavior, 5,* 325–337.

Bruner, J. S., Goodnow, J. J., & Austin, G. A. (1956). A *study of thinking.* New York: Wiley.

Bruner, J. S., Oliver, R. R., & Greenfield, P. M. (Eds.). (1966). *Studies in cognitive growth.* New York: Wiley.

Bryant, P. E., & Trabasso, T. (1971). Transitive interferences and memory in young children. *Nature, 232,* 456–458.

Bugelski, B. R. (1970). Words and things and images. *American Psychologist, 25,* 1002–1012.

Bugelski, B. R., Kidd, E., & Gegmen, J. (1968). Image as a mediator in one-trial paired-associate learning. *Journal of Experimental Psychology, 76,* 69–73.

Cabeza, R., & Nyberg, L. (1997). Imaging cognition: An empirical review of PET studies with normal subjects. *Journal of Cognitive Neuroscience, 9,* 1–26.

Calfee, R. C. (1975). *Human experimental psychology.* New York: Holt, Rinehart & Winston.

Caramazza, A., & Shelton, J. R. (1998). Domain-specific knowledge systems in the brain: The animate–inanimate distinction. *Journal of Cognitive Neuroscience, 10,* 1–34.

Caramazza, A., Gordon, J., Zurif, E. B., & De Luca, D. (1976). Right hemispheric damage and verbal problem solving behavior. *Brain and Language, 3,* 41–46.

Carbonell, J. G. (1979). *Subjective understanding: Computer models of belief systems.* Unpublished doctoral dissertation, Yale University.

Carey, S. & Diamond, R. (1977). From piecemeal to configurational representation of faces. *Science, 195,* 312–313.

Carpenter, P. A., & Dahneman, M. (1981). Lexical retrieval and error recovery in reading: A model based on eye fixations. *Journal of Verbal Learning and Verbal Behavior, 20,* 137–164.

Carroll, J. B., & Freedle, R. O. (Eds.). (1972). *Language comprehension and the acquisition of knowledge.* Washington, DC: Winston.

Casey, R. G., & Nagy, G. (1971). Advances in pattern recognition. *Scientific American, 224,* 56–64.

Catania, A. C. (1970). Reinforcement schedules and psychophysical judgments. A study of some temporal properties of behavior. In W. N. Schoenfeld (Ed.), *The theory of reinforcement schedules* (pp. 1–42). New York: Appleton-Century-Crofts.

Cattell, J. McK. (1886a). The time it takes to see and name objects. *Mind, 11,* 63–65.

Cattell, J. McK. (1886b). The time taken up by cerebral operations. *Mind, 11,* 277–292, 524–538.

Cattell, J. McK. (1954). Uberdi Aeit der Erkennung and Benennung von Schriftzeichen, Bildern and Farben. *Philos, St. 2,* 1885, 635–650. Cited in R. Woodworth & H. Schlosberg (Eds.), *Experimental psychology.* New York: Holt.

Cattell, R. B. (1965). *The scientific analysis of personality.* Baltimore: Penguin.

Cattell, R. B. (1971). *Abilities: Their structure, growth and action.* Boston: Houghton Mifflin.

Ceraso, J., & Provitera, A. (1971). Sources of error in syllogistic reasoning. *Cognitive Psychology, 2,* 400–410.

Cermak, L. S. (1976). *Improving your memory.* New York: McGraw-Hill.

Chalmers, D. J. (2000). *Neural correlates of consciousness: Empirical and conceptual questions* (T. Metzinger, Ed.). Cambridge, MA: MIT Press.

Chapman, L. J., & Chapman, J. P. (1959). Atmosphere effect reexamined. *Journal of Experimental Psychology, 58,* 220–226.

Chase, W. G. (Ed.). (1973). *Visual information processing.* New York: Academic Press.

Chase, W. G., & Ericsson, K. A. (1981). Skilled memory. In J. R. Anderson (Ed.), *Cognitive skills and their acquisition.* Hillsdale, NJ: Erlbaum.

Chase, W. G., & Ericsson, K. A. (1982). Skill and working memory. In G. H. Bower (Ed.), *The psychology of learning and motivation* (pp. 1–58). New York: Academic Press.

Chase, W. G., & Simon, H. A. (1973a). The mind's eye in chess. In W. G. Chase (Ed.), *Visual information processing.* New York: Academic Press.

Chase, W. G., & Simon, H. A. (1973b). Perception in chess. *Cognitive Psychology, 4,* 55–81.

Cheesman, J., & Merikle, P. M. (1984). Priming with and without awareness. *Perception and Psychophysics, 36*(4), 387–395.

Cherry, C. (1953). Some experiments on the recognition of speech with one and with two ears. *Journal of the Acoustic Society of America, 25,* 975–979.

Cherry, C. (1966). *On human communication* (2nd ed.). Cambridge, MA: The MIT Press.

Chi, M. T. (1976). Short-term memory limitations in children: Capacity or processing deficits. *Memory and Cognition, 5,* 559–572.

Chi, M. T. (1978). Knowledge structures and memory development. In R. S. Siegler (Ed.), *Children's thinking: What develops?* Hillsdale, NJ: Erlbaum.

Chi, M. T. H., Feltovich, P., & Glaser, R. (1981). Categorization and representation of physics problems by experts and novices. *Cognitive Science, 5,* 121–152.

Chi, M. T. H., Glaser, R., & Farr, M. J. (Eds.). (1988). *The nature of expertise.* Hillsdale, NJ: Erlbaum.

Chiarello, C. (1988). Lateralization of lexical processes in the normal brain: A review of visual hemi-field research. In H. A. Whitaker (Ed.), *Contemporary reviews in neuropsychology.* (pp. 36–76). New York: Springer.

Chipman, S. F., Davis, C., & Shafto, M. G. (1986). Personnel and training research program: Cognitive science at ONR. *Naval Research Review, 38,* 3–21.

Chomsky, N. (1956). Three models of the description of language. Proceedings of a Symposium on Information Theory. *IRF Transactions on Information Theory, IT-2*(3), 113–124.

Chomsky, N. (1957a). Review of *Verbal behavior* by B. F. Skinner. *Language, 35,* 26–58.

Chomsky, N. (1957b). *Syntactic structures.* The Hague: Mouton.

Chomsky, N. (1965). *Aspect of the theory of syntax.* Cambridge, MA: MIT Press.

Chomsky, N. (1966). *Topics in the theory of generative grammar.* The Hague: Mouton.

Chomsky, N. (1968). *Language and mind.* New York: Harcourt Brace Jovanovich.

Chukovsky, K. (1971). *From two to five.* Berkeley: University of California Press.

Churchland, P. S. (1989, July). From Descartes to neural networks. *Scientific American,* p. 118.

Churchland, P. S., & Sejnowski, T. J. (1988). Perspectives on cognitive neuroscience. *Science, 242,* 741–745.

Clark, H., & Clark, E. (1977). *Psychology and language: An introduction to psycholinguistics.* New York: Harcourt Brace Jovanovich.

Clark, W. C. (1966). The psyche in psychophysics: A sensory-decision theory analysis of the effect of instruction on flicker sensitivity and response bias. *Psychological Bulletin, 65,* 358–366.

Clark, W. C., Brown, J. C., & Rutschmann, J. (1967). Flicker sensitivity and response bias in psychiatric patients and normal subjects. *Journal of Abnormal Psychology, 72,* 35–42.

Clarke, A. C. (1968). *2001: A space odyssey.* New York: New American Library.

Clement, C., & Falmagne, R. J. (1986). Logical reasoning, world knowledge, and mental imagery: Interconnections in cognitive processes. *Memory and Cognition, 14,* 299–307.

Cofer, C. N. (1973). Constructive processes in memory. *American Scientist, 61,* 537–543.

Cofer, C. N. (Ed.). (1976). *The structure of human memory.* San Francisco: Freeman.

Cohen, G. (1989). *Memory in the real world.* Hillsdale, NJ: Erlbaum.

Cohen, J. D., Servan-Schreiber, & McClelland, J. L. (1992). A parallel distributed processing approach to automaticity. *American Journal of Psychology, 105,* 239–269.

Cohen, J. J., & Squire, L. R. (1980). Preserved learning and retention of pattern-analyzing skill in amnesia: Dissociation of knowing how and knowing that. *Science, 210,* 207–210.

Cohen, K. M., & Haith, M. M. (1977). Peripheral vision in the effects of developmental, perceptual, and cognitive factors. *Journal of Experimental Child Psychology, 3,* 373–395.

Cohen, L. B., & Salapatek, P. (1975). *Infant perception: From sensation to cognition* (Vol. 1). New York: Academic Press.

Cohen, L. B., & Strauss, M. S. (1979). Concept acquisition in the human infant. *Child Development, 50,* 419–424.

Cohen, L. J. (1981). Can human irrationally be experimentally demonstrated? *Behavioral and Brain Sciences, 4,* 317–370.

Cohen, M. S., Rosen, B. R., & Brady, T. J. (1992, Winter). Ultrafast MRI permits expanded clinical role. *Magnetic Resonance, 26.*

Colby, K. M., Hilf, F. D., Weber, S., & Kraemer, H. C. (1972). Turing-like indistinguishability tests for the validation of a computer simulation of paranoid processes. *Artificial Intelligence, 3.*

Cole, M. (1975). An ethnographic psychology of cognition. In R. W. Brislin, S. Blochner, & W. J. Lonner (Eds.), *Perspectives on learning, I, Cross-cultural research and methodology.* New York: Halsted Press, Wiley.

Cole, M., Frankel, F., & Sharp, D. (1971). Development of free recall learning in children. *Developmental Psychology, 4,* 109–123.

Cole, M., Gay, J., Glick, J., & Sharp, D. (1971). *The cultural context of learning and thinking.* New York: Basic Books.

Cole, M., & Scribner, S. (1974). *Culture and thought.* New York: Wiley.

Collins, A., & Smith, E. E. (Eds.). (1988). *Readings in cognitive science: A perspective from psychology and artificial intelligence.* San Mateo, CA: Morgan Kaufmann.

Collins, A. M., & Loftus, E. F. (1975). A spreading activation theory of semantic processing. *Psychological Review, 82,* 407–428.

Collins, A. M., & Quillian, M. R. (1969). Retrieval time from semantic memory. *Journal of Verbal Learning and Verbal Behavior, 8,* 240–247.

Collins, A. M., & Quillian, M. R. (1972). How to make a language user. In E. Tulving & W. Donaldson (Eds.), *Organization of memory.* New York: Academic Press.

Collyer, S. C., Jonides, J., & Bevan, W. (1972). Images as memory aids: Is bizarreness helpful? *American Journal of Psychology, 85,* 31–38.

Coltheart, M. (Ed.). (1972). *Readings in cognitive psychology.* Toronto: Holt, Rinehart & Winston.

Coltheart, M. (1975). Iconic memory: A reply to Professor Holding. *Memory and Cognition, 3,* 42–48.

Coltheart, M. (1983). Ecological necessity of iconic memory. *Behavioral and Brain Sciences, 6,* 17–18.

Coltheart, M. (Ed.). (1987). *The cognitive neuropsychology of language.* Hillsdale, NJ: Erlbaum.

The Columbia Dictionary of Quotations. (1993). New York: Columbia University Press.

The Concise Columbia Encyclopedia (1995). New York: Columbia University Press.

Conrad, C. (1972). Cognitive economy in semantic memory. *Journal of Experimental Psychology, 92,* 149–154.

Conrad, R. (1963). Acoustic confusions and memory span for words. *Nature, 197,* 1029–1030.

Conrad, R. (1964). Acoustic confusions in immediate memory. *British Journal of Psychology, 55,* 75–84.

Conrad, R. (1970). Short-term memory processes in the deaf. *British Journal of Psychology, 61,* 179–195.

Conway, M. A., Cohen, G., & Stanhope, N. (1991). On the very long-term retention of knowledge acquired through formal education: Twelve years of cognitive psychology. *Journal of Experimental Psychology: General, 120,* 395–409.

Conway, M. A. & Fthenaki, A. (2000). Disruption and loss of autobiographical memory. In F. Boller, and J. Grafman (Eds.), *Handbook of Neuropsychology,* 2nd ed., Vol. 2.

Cooper, E. E., & Biederman, I. (1993, May). *Metric versus viewpoint invariant shape differences in visual object recognition.* Poster presented at the meeting of the Association for Research in Vision and Ophthalmology, Sarasota, FL.

Cooper, L. A., & Shepard, R. N. (1972). The time required to prepare for a rotated stimulus. *Memory and Cognition, 1,* 246–250.

Cooper, L. A., & Shepard, R. N. (1973). Chronometric studies of the rotation of mental images. In W. G. Chase (Ed.), *Visual information processing.* New York: Academic Press.

Cooper, L. A., & Shepard, R. N. (1980). Transformations on representations of objects in space. In E. C. Carterette & M. Friedman (Eds.), *Handbook of perception, Volume 8: Space and object perception.* New York: Academic Press.

Corballis, M. C. (1989). Laterality and human evolution. *Psychological Review, 96,* 492–505.

Corballis, M. C., Kirby, J., & Miller, A. (1972). Access to elements of a memorized list. *Journal of Experimental Psychology, 9,* 185–190.

Corbetta, M., Miezin, F. M., Dobmeyer, S., Shulman, G. L., & Petersen, S. E. (1991). Selective and divided attention during visual discriminations of shape, color, and speed: Functional anatomy by positron emission tomography. *Journal of Neuroscience, 11,* 2363–2402.

Coren, S. (1991). Retinal mechanism in the perception of subjective contours: The contribution of lateral inhibition. *Perception, 20,* 181–191.

Corteen, R. S., & Dunn, D. (1974). Shock-associated words in a nonattended message: A test for momentary awareness. *Journal of Experimental Psychology, 102,* 1143–1144.

Corteen, R. S., & Wood, B. (1972). Autonomic responses to shock-associated words in an unattended channel. *Journal of Experimental Psychology, 9,* 303–313.

Cosmides, L., & Tooby, J. (1997). *Evolutionary psychology: A primer.* Available at: *http://www.psych.ucsb.edu/research/cep/primer.html*

Cosmides, L., & Tooby, J. (2000). Consider the source: The evolution of adaptations for decoupling and metarepresentation. In D. Sperber (Ed.), *Metarepresentations: A multidisciplinary perspective.* 53–116. New York: Oxford University Press.

Cousins, N. (1957, October 5). Smudging the subconscious. *Saturday Review,* pp. 20–21.

Cowan, N. (1988). Evolving conceptions of memory storage, selective attention, and their mutual constraints within the human information-processing system. *Psychological Bulletin, 104,* 163–191.

Cowan, W. M. (1979). The development of the brain. *Scientific American, 241,* 112–133.

Craik, F. I. M., & Jacoby, L. L. (1975). A process view of short-term retention. In R. Restle (Ed.), *Cognitive theory* (Vol. 1). Hillsdale, NJ: Erlbaum.

Craik, F. I. M., & Lockhart, R. S. (1972). Levels of processing: A framework for memory research. *Journal of Verbal Learning and Verbal Behavior, 11,* 671–684.

Craik, F. I. M., & Tulving, E. (1975). Depth of processing and the retention of words in episodic memory. *Journal of Experimental Psychology: General, 104,* 268–294.

Craik, F. I. M., & Watkins, M. J. (1973). The role of rehearsal in short-term memory. *Journal of Verbal Learning and Verbal Behavior, 12,* 599–607.

Crick, F. (1993). *The astonishing hypothesis: The scientific search for the soul.* New York: Scribners.

Crick, F. H. C. (1984). Function of the thalamic reticular complex: The searchlight hypothesis. *Proceedings of the National Academy of Sciences. USA, 81* 4586–93 (July).

Crick, F., & Asanuma, C. (1986). Certain aspects of the anatomy and physiology of the cerebral cortex. In D. E. Rumelhart, J. L. McClelland, & the PDP research group (Eds.), *Parallel distributed processing: Explorations in the microstructure of cognition* (Vol. 2). Cambridge, MA: Bradford.

Crowder, R. G. (1982a). The demise of short-term memory. *Acta Psychologica, 50,* 291–323.

Crowder, R. G. (1982b). *The psychology of memory.* New York: Oxford.

Crowder, R. G. (1982c). *The psychology of reading.* New York: Oxford.

Crowder, R. G. (1985). On access and the forms of memory. In N. Weinberger, J. McGaugh, & G. Lynch (Eds.), *Memory systems of the brain.* New York: Guilford Press.

Crowder, R. G. (1993). Short-term memory: Where do we stand? *Memory and Cognition, 21,* 142–145.

Crundall, D., Chapman, P., Phelps, N., & Underwood G. (2003). Eye movements and hazard perception in police pursuit and emergency response driving. *Journal of Experimental Psychology: Applied, 9*(3), 163–174.

Cudhea, D. (1978). Artificial intelligence. *Stanford Magazine, 6,* 8–14.

Cutting, J. E. (1986). *Perception with an eye for motion.* Cambridge, MA: MIT Press.

Cutting, J. E. (1993). Perceptual artifacts and phenomena: Gibson's role in the 20th century. In S. C. Masin (Ed.) *Foundations of perceptual theory* (pp. 231–260). New York: Elsevier.

D'Agostino, P. R., O'Neill, B. J., & Paivio, A. (1977). Memory for pictures and words as a function of levels of processing: Depth or dual coding? *Memory and Cognition, 5,* 252–256.

Daehler, M. W., & Bukatko, D. (1985). *Cognitive development.* New York: Knopf.

Dale, P. S. (1976). *Language development: Structure and function* (2nd ed.). New York: Holt, Rinehart & Winston.

Damasio, A. R. (1989). Time-locked multiregional retroactivation: A systems-level proposal for the neural substrates of recall and recognition. *Cognition, 33,* 25–62.

Damasio, A. R. (1999). How the brain creates the mind. *Scientific American, 12,* 4–9.

Dannemiller, J. L., & Stephens, B. R. (1988). A critical test of infant pattern preferences models. *Child Development, 59,* 210–216.

Darwin, C. J., Turvey, M. T., & Crowder, R. G. (1972). An auditory analogue of the Sperling partial report procedure: Evidence for brief auditory storage. *Cognitive Psychology, 3,* 255–267.

Dawes, R. (1966). Memory and the distortion of meaningful written material. *British Journal of Psychology, 57,* 77–86.

Dawson, J. L. M. (1967). Cultural and physiological influences upon spatial-perceptual processes in West Africa. *International Journal of Psychology, 2,* 115–128.

Day, M. C. (1975). Developmental trends in visual scanning. In H. W. Reese (Ed.), *Advances in child development and behavior* (Vol. 10). New York: Academic Press.

Day, R. S., & Wood, C. C. (1972a). Interactions between linguistic and nonlinguistic processing. *Journal of the Acoustical Society of America, 51,* 79A.

Day, R. S., & Wood, C. C. (1972b). Mutual interference between two linguistic dimensions of the same stimuli. *Journal of the Acoustical Society of America, 52,* 175A.

Day, R. S., Cutting, J. C., & Copeland, P. M. (1971). Perception of linguistic and nonlinguistic dimensions of dichotic stimuli. *Haskins Laboratories Status Report on Speech Research, SR-27,* 193–197.

de Groot, A. D. (1965). *Thought and choice in chess.* The Hague: Mouton.

de Groot, A. D. (1966). Perception and memory versus thought: Some old ideas and recent findings. In B. Kleinmuntz (Ed.), *Problem solving: Research, method and theory.* New York: Wiley.

Dearborn, W. (1906). *The psychology of reading* (Columbia University contributions to philosophy and psychology). New York: Science Press.

Dehn, N., & Schank, R. (1982). Artificial and human intelligence. In R. Sternberg (Ed.), *Handbook of human intelligence.* Cambridge, UK: Cambridge University Press.

Denes, P. B., & Pinson, E. N. (1963). *The speech chain.* Murray Hill, NJ: Bell Laboratories.

Dennett, D. C. (1987). Consciousness. In R. L. Gregory (Ed.), *The Oxford companion to the mind* (pp. 160–164). Oxford: Oxford University Press.

Dennett, D. C. (1991). *Consciousness explained.* New York: Little, Brown.

Deregowski, J. B. (1971). Symmetry, Gestalt and information theory. *Quarterly Journal of Experimental Psychology, 23,* 381–385.

Deregowski, J. B. (1973). Illusion and culture. In R. L. Gregory & E. H. Gombrich (Eds.), *Illusion in nature and art.* New York: Scribner.

Deregowski, J. B. (1980). *Illusions, perception and pictures.* London: Academic Press.

Deregowski, J. B., Muldrow, E. S., & Muldrow, W. F. (1973). Pictorial recognition in a remote Ethiopian population. *Perception, 1,* 417–425.

Descartes, R. (1931). *Philosophical works* (E. S. Haldane & G. R. T. Pross, Trans.). Cambridge, UK: Cambridge University Press.

Deutsch, J. A., & Deutsch, D. (1963). Attention: Some theoretical considerations. *Psychological Review, 70,* 80–90.

Deutsch, J. A., & Deutsch, D. (1967). Comments on selective attention: Perception or response? *Quarterly Journal of Experimental Psychology, 19,* 362–363.

Diringer, D. (1968). *The alphabet: A key to the history of mankind* (3rd ed.) (Vols. 1 & 2). London: Hutchinson.

Dolinsky, R. (1973). Word fragments as recall cues: Role of syllables. *Journal of Experimental Psychology, 97,* 272–274.

Donaldson, W., & Murdock, B. B., Jr. (1968). Criterion changes in continuous recognition memory. *Journal of Experimental Psychology, 76,* 325–330.

Donegan, C. (1989, March 15). Think again. *American Way,* pp. 73–111.

Downing, P., Liu, J., & Kanwisher, N. (2001). Testing cognitive models of visual attention with fMRI and MEG. *Neuropsychologia, 39*(12), 1329–1342.

Dreyfus, H. L. (1965). *Alchemy and artificial intelligence.* Santa Monica, CA: Rand Corporation.

Dreyfus, H. L. (1972). *What computers can't do: A critique of artificial reason.* New York: Harper Row.

Duchaine, B. C. (2000). Developmental prosopagnosida with normal configural processing. *Neuroreport. 11,* 79–83.

Duchaine, B., Cosmides, L., & Tooby, J. (2001). Evolutionary psychology and the brain. *Current Opinions in Neurobiology, 11,* 225–230.

Duchamp, M. (1945). From an interview with Janees Johnson Sweeney in Eleven Europeans in America. *Bulletin of the Museum of Modern Art* (New York), *13*(4–5), 19–21.

Duncan, J., Seitz, R. J., Kolodny, J., Bor, D., Herzog, H., Ahmed, A. et al. (2000). A neural basis for general intelligence. *Science, 289,* 457–460.

Duncker, K. (1945). On problem solving. *Psychological Monographs, 58* (5, whole no. 270).

Dunlap, K. (1900). The effect of imperceptible shadows on the judgment of distance. *Psychological Review, 7,* 435–453.

Dupre, J. (Ed.). (1987). *The latest on the best essays on evolution and optimality.* Cambridge, MA: MIT Press.

Eacott, M. J. (1999). Memory for the events of early childhood. *Current Directions in Psychological Science, 8,* 46–49.

Easterbrook, J. A. (1959). The effect of emotion on cue utilization and the organization of behavior. *Psychological Review, 66,* 183–201.

Ebbinghaus, H. (1885). *Über das Gedächtnis: Intersuchungen zur experimentellen psychologie.* Leipzig: Duncker and Humboldt. (Translated by H. A. Ruger & C. E. Bussenius, 1913, and reissued by Dover Publications, 1964.)

Edson, L. (1982). Under Babel's tower. *Mosaic, 13,* 22–28.

Edwards, W. (1968). Conservatism in human information processing. In B. Kleinmuntz (Ed.), *Formal representations of human judgment.* New York: Wiley.

Einstein, A. (1950). *Out of my later years.* New York: Philosophic Library.

Eisenberg, A. R., & Garvey, C. (1981). Children's use of verbal strategies in resolving conflicts. *Discourse Processes, 4,* 149–170.

Eisenstadt, M., & Kareev, Y. (1975). Aspects of human problem solving: The use of internal representation. In D. Norman & D. Rumelhart (Eds.), *Exploration in cognition.* San Francisco: Freeman.

Elithorn, A., & Banerji, R. (Eds.). (1984). *Artificial and human intelligence.* New York: Oxford University Press.

Ellis, H. C. (1978). *Fundamentals of human learning, memory, and cognition.* Dubuque, IA: W. C. Brown

Erdelyi, M. H., & Becker, J. (1974). Hypermnesia for pictures: Incremental memory for pictures but not for words in multiple recall trials. *Cognitive Psychology, 6,* 159–171.

Erdmann, B., & Dodge, R. (1898). *Psychologische untersuchungen über das Lese.* Halle: M. Niemeyer. Cited by R. Woodworth & H. Schlosberg, *Experimental Psychology.* New York: Holt, Rinehart & Winston.

Erickson, J. R. (1974). A set analysis theory of behavior in formal syllogistic reasoning tasks. In R. L. Solso (Ed.), *Theories in cognitive psychology: The Loyola Symposium.* Hillsdale, NJ: Erlbaum.

Erickson, J. R., & Jones, M. R. (1978). Thinking. *Annual Review of Psychology, 29,* 61–91.

Ericsson, K. A., & Charness, N. (1994). Expert performance: Its structure and acquisition. *American Psychologist, 49,* 725–777.

Ericsson, K. A., & Chase, W. A. (1982). Exceptional memory. *American Scientist, 70,* 607–615.

Eriksen, C. W., & Collins, J. F. (1967). Some temporal characteristics of visual pattern perception. *Journal of Experimental Psychology, 74,* 476–484.

Ernst, M., Bolla, K., Mouratidis, M., Contoreggi, C., Matochik, J. A., Kurian, V., Cadet, J. L., Kimes, A. S. & London, E. D. (2002). Decision making in a risk-taking task: A PET study. *Neuropsychopharmacology, 26*(5), 682–691.

Estes, W. K. (1974). Memory, perception and decision in letter identification. In R. L. Solso (Ed.), *Information processing and cognition: The Loyola Symposium.* Hillsdale, NJ: Erlbaum.

Estes, W. K. (1977). In D. Laberge & S. J. Samuels (Eds.), *Basic processes in reading: Perception and comprehension,* (pp. 1–25). Hillsdale, NJ: Erlbaum.

Estes, W. K. (1977). The structure of human memory. In *Encyclopedia Britannica: Yearbook of science and the future.* Chicago: University of Chicago Press.

Estes, W. K. (Ed.). (1978). *Handbook of learning and cognitive processes* (Vol. 6). Hillsdale, NJ: Erlbaum.

Estes, W. K., Bjork, E. L., & Skaar, E. (1974). Detection of single letters and letters in words with changing versus unchanging mark characteristics. *Bulletin of the Psychonomic Society 3,* 201–203.

Evans, L. (1989, September 9). Evans on chess: 24 computers clash. *Reno Gazette-Journal.*

Evarts, E. V. (1973). Motor cortex reflexes with learned movements. *Science, 179,* 501–503.

Exploring intelligence. (1998, Winter). *Scientific American, 9.*

Eysenck, H. J. (1984). Intelligence versus behavior. *Behavioral and Brain Sciences, 7,* 290–291.

Eysenck, M. W. (1984). *A handbook of cognitive psychology.* Hillsdale, NJ: Erlbaum.

Farah, M. J. (1984). The neurological basis of mental imagery: A componential analysis. *Cognition, 18,* 245–272.

Farah, M. J. (1988). Is visual imagery really visual? Overlooked evidence from neuropsychology. *Psychological Review, 95,* 307–317.

Farah, M. J. (1995). The neural bases of mental imagery. In M. S. Gazzaniga (Ed.), *The cognitive neurosciences* (pp. 959–961). Cambridge, MA: MIT Press.

Farah, M. J., Hammond, K. M., Levine, D. N., & Calvanio, R. (1988). Visual and spatial mental imagery: Dissociable systems of representation. *Cognitive Psychology, 20,* 439–462.

FCC (1974). 42, 74–78, *U.S. Law Week 2404,* Feb. 5.

Fehlman, S. E. (1989). Representing implicit knowledge. In G. E. Hinton & J. A. Anderson (Eds.), *Parallel models of associative memory.* Hillsdale, NJ: Erlbaum.

Fein, G. G. (1979). Play and the acquisition of symbols. In L. Kantz (Ed.), *Current topics in early childhood education.* Norwood, NJ: Ablex.

Feinaigle, G. von. (1813). *The new art of memory* (3rd ed.). London: Sherwood, Neely & Jones. Cited in A. Paivio (1971). *Imagery and verbal processes.* New York: Holt, Rinehart & Winston.

Felzen, E., & Anisfeld, M. (1970). Semantic and phonetic relations in the false recognition of words by third and sixth grade children. *Developmental Psychology, 3,* 163–168.

Field, D. (1981). Retrospective reports by healthy intelligent elderly people of personal events of their adult lives. *International Journal of Behavioral Development, 4,* 77–97.

Fikes, R. E., Hart, P. E., & Nilsson, N. J. (1972). In B. Meltzer & D. Michie (Eds.), *Machine intelligence.* Edinburgh: Edinburgh University Press.

Fiore, S. M. & Schooler, J. W. (1998). Right hemisphere contributions to creative problem solving: Converging evidence for divergent thinking. In M. Beeman & C. Chiarello (Eds.), *Right hemisphere language comprehension: Pespectives from cogntive neuroscience* (pp. 349–371). Hillsdale, NJ: Erlbaum.

Fischler, I. S., & Bloom, P. A. (1985). Effects of constraint and validity of sentence context on lexical decision. *Memory and Cognition, 13,* 128–139.

Fischler, I. S., & Bloom, P. A. (1979). Automatic and attentional processes in the effects of sentence context on word recognition. *Journal of Verbal Learning and Verbal Behavior, 18,* 1–20.

Fitts, P. M., & Posner, M. I. (1967). *Human performance.* Belmont, CA: Brooks/Cole.

Flagg, P. W., & Reynolds, A. G. (1977). Modality of presentation and blocking in sentence recognition memory. *Memory and Cognition, 5*(1), 111–115.

Flagg, P. W., Potts, G. R., & Reynolds, A. G. (1975). Instructions and response strategies in recognition memory for sentences. *Journal of Experimental Psychology: Human Learning and Memory, 1*(5), 592–598.

Flavell, J. H. (1963). *The developmental psychology of Jean Piaget.* Princeton, NJ: Van Nostrand.

Flavell, J. H. (1985). *Cognitive development* (2nd ed.). Englewood Cliffs, NJ: Prentice-Hall.

Flavell, J. H. (1986). The development of children's knowledge about the appearance–reality distinction. *American Psychologist, 41,* 418–425.

Flavell, J. H., & Markman, E. M. (Eds.). (1983). *Handbook of child psychology: Cognitive development* (Vol. 3). New York: Wiley.

Flavell, J. H., Beach, D. H., & Chinsky, J. M. (1966). Spontaneous verbal rehearsal in a memory task as a function of age. *Child Development, 37,* 283–299.

Flowers, M., McGuire, R., & Birnbaum, L. (1992). Adversary arguments and the logic of personal attacks. In W. Lehnert & M. Ringle (Eds.), *Strategies for natural language processing.* Hillsdale, NJ: Erlbaum.

Fodor, J. A., & Pylyshyn, Z. W. (1988). Connectionism and cognitive architecture: A critical analysis. *Cognition, 28,* 3–71.

Fodor, J., & Garrett, M. (1966). Some reflections on competence and performance. In J. Lyons & R. J. Wales (Eds.), *Psycholinguistic Papers: The Proceedings of the 1966 Edinburgh Conference.* Edinburgh: Edinburgh University Press.

Forster, P. M., & Govier, E. (1978). Discrimination without awareness? *Quarterly Journal of Experimental Psychology, 31,* 282–295.

Fowler, M. J., Sullivan, J. J., & Ekstrand, B. R. (1973). Sleep and memory. *Science, 179,* 302–304.

Frank, F. (1966). Perception and language in conservation. In J. S. Bruner, R. R. Olver, & P. M. Greenfield (Eds.), *Studies in cognitive growth.* New York: Wiley.

Fredericksen, C. (1975). Effects of context-induced processing operations on semantic information acquired from discourse. *Cognitive Psychology, 7,* 139–166.

Freud, S. (1952). *A general introduction to psychoanalysis.* New York: Washington Square Press. (1924/1952)

Freud, S. (1950). A note upon the "mystic writing pad." In J. Strachey (Ed.), *Collected papers of Sigmund Freud.* London: Hogarth Press. (Original work published 1940)

Freund, J. S., & Johnson, J. W. (1972). Changes in memory attribute dominance as a function of age. *Journal of Educational Psychology, 63,* 386–389.

Fritsch, G., & Hitzig, E. (1870). Uber die elektrische Erregbarkeit des Grosshirns. *Archiv fur Anatomie Physiologie und Wissenschaftliche Medicin, 37,* 300–332. In G. von Bonin (Trans.), (1960). *Some papers on the cerebral cortex* (pp. 73–96). Springfield, IL: Charles C. Thomas.

Frost, N. A. H. (1971). *Clustering by visual and semantic codes in long-term memory.* Unpublished doctoral dissertation, University of Oregon.

Fruth, H. G. (1969). *Piaget and knowledge: Theoretical foundations.* Englewood Cliffs, NJ: Prentice-Hall.

Funnell, M. G., Corballis, P. M., & Gazzaniga, M. S. (1999). A deficit in perceptual matching in the left hemisphere of a callosotomy patient. *Neuropsychologia, 37*(10), 1143-1154.

Gabrieli, J. E. E., Desmond, J. E., Demb, J. B., Wagner, A. D., Stone, M. V., Vaidya, C. J., et al. (1996). Functional magnetic resonance imaging of semantic memory processed in the frontal lobes. *Psychological Science, 7,* 278–283.

Gallup, G. G., Jr. 1970. Chimpanzees: self-recognition. *Science,* 167, 86–87.

Galotti, K. M., Baron, J., & Sabini, J. (1986). Individual differences in syllogistic reasoning: Deduction rules or mental models? *Journal of Experimental Psychology: General, 115,* 16–25.

Galton, F. (1880). Statistics of mental imagery. *Mind, 5,* 301–318.

Galton, F. (1907). *Inquiries into human faculty and its development.* London: Macmillan. (Original work published 1883)

Ganellen, R. J., & Carver, C. S. (1985). Why does self-reference promote incidental encoding? *Journal of Experimental Psychology, 21,* 284–300.

Garcia, G., & Diener, D. (1993, May). *Do you remember . . . A comparison of mnemonic strategies.* Paper presented at the annual meeting of WPA, Phoenix, AZ.

Garden, S., Cornoldi, C., & Logie, R. H. (2002). Visuospatial working memory in navigation.

Gardner, H. (1985). *The mind's new science.* New York: Basic Books.

Gardner, R. A., & Gardner, B. T. (1969). Teaching sign language to a chimpanzee. *Science, 165,* 664–672.

Garner, W. R. (1958). Symmetric uncertainty analysis and its implications for psychology. *Psychology Review, 65,* 183–196.

Garner, W. R. (1962). *Uncertainty and structure as psychological concepts.* New York: Wiley.

Garner, W. R., & Carson, D. H. (1960). A multivariate solution of the redundancy of printed English. *Psychology Review, 6,* 123–141.

Garrity, L. I. (1975). An electromyographical study of subvocal speech and recall in preschool children. *Developmental Psychology, 11,* 274–281.

Gastaut, H., & Bert, J. (1961). Electroencephalographic detection of sleep induced by repetitive sensory stimuli. In G. E. W. Wolstenholme & M. O'Connor (Eds.), *The nature of sleep.* London: Churchill.

Gates, B. (1996). *The road ahead,* New York: Penguin.

Gazzaniga, M. A. (1970). *The bisected brain.* New York: Appleton-Century-Crofts.

Gazzaniga, M. A., & Sperry, R. W. (1967). Language after section of the cerebral commissures. *Brain, 90,* 131–148.

Gazzaniga, M. S. (1967). The split brain in man. *Scientific American, 217*(2), 24–29.

Gazzaniga, M. S. (1975). Experimental apparatus. In M. S. Gazzaniga & C. Blakemore (Eds.), *Handbook of psychobiology.* New York: Academic Press.

Gazzaniga, M. S. (1983). Right hemisphere language following commissurotomy: A twenty-year perspective. *American Psychologist, 38,* 525–537.

Gazzaniga, M. S. (1998). The split brain revisited. *Scientific American, 274,* 123–129.

Gazzaniga, M. S. (Ed.). (1995). *The cognitive neurosciences.* Cambridge, MA: MIT Press.

Gazzaniga, M. S., Bogen, J. E., & Sperry, R. W. (1965). Observations on visual perception after disconnection of the cerebral hemispheres in man. *Brain, 88,* 221–236.

Geary, D. C. (2005). *The origin of mind.* Washington, DC: American Psychological Association.

Geiger, G., & Lettvin, J. (1987). Dyslexia. *New England Journal of Medicine, 316,* 1238–1243.

Gelman, R. (1969). Conservation acquisition: A problem of learning to attend to relevant attributes. *Journal of Experimental Child Psychology, 7,* 167–187.

Gelman, R. (1972). The nature and development of early number concepts. In H. Reese (Ed.), *Advances in child development and behavior* (Vol. 7). New York: Academic Press.

Generalization of conditioned GSRs in dichotic listening. In P. M. A. Rabbit & S. Dornic (Eds.), *Attention and performance V.* New York: Academic Press.

Georgopoulos, A. P., Lurito, J. T., Petrides, M., Schwartz, A. B., & Massey, J. T. (1989). Mental rotation of the neuronal population vector. *Science, 243,* 234–236.

Gernsbacher, M. A., & Robertson, R. R. W. (2000). The definite article *the* as a cue to map thematic information. In W. van Peer & M. M. Louwerse (Eds.), *Thematics: Interdisciplinary studies.* Philadelphia: John Benjamins.

Gevins, A., & Cutillo, B. (1993). Spatiotemporal dynamics of component processes in human working memory. *Electroencephalography and Clinical Neurophysiology, 87,* 128–143.

Gibbs, W. W. (2002, August). From mouth to mind: New insights into how language warps the brain. *Scientific American.*

Gibson, J. J. & Radner, M. (1937). Adaptation, after-effect and contrast in the perception of tilted lines. *Journal of Experimental Psychology, 20:*453–467.

Gibson, J. J. (1966). *The senses considered as perceptual systems.* Boston: Houghton Mifflin.

Gibson, J. J. (1979). *The ecological approach to visual perception.* Boston: Houghton Mifflin.

Glaser, R., & Chi, M. T. H. (1988). Overview. In M. T. H. Chi, R. Glaser, & M. J. Farr (Eds.), *The nature of expertise.* Hillsdale, NJ: Erlbaum.

Glass, A. L., & Holyoak, K. J. (1974). The effect of *some* and *all* on reaction time for semantic decisions. *Memory and Cognition, 2,* 436–440.

Glass, A. L., & Holyoak, K. J. (1975). Alternative conceptions of semantic memory. *Cognition, 3*(8), 313–339.

Glass, A. L., & Holyoak, K. J. (1986). *Cognition* (2nd ed.). New York: Random House.

Glass, A. L., Holyoak, K. J., & O'Dell, D. (1974). Production frequency and the verification of quantified statements. *Journal of Verbal Learning and Verbal Behavior, 13,* 237–254.

Gluck, M. A., & Rumelhart, D. E. (Eds.). (1990). *Neuroscience and connectionist theory.* Hillsdale, NJ: Erlbaum.

Glucksberg, S. (1962). The influence of strength of drive on functional fixedness and perceptual recognition. *Journal of Experimental Psychology, 63,* 36–51.

Glucksberg, S., & Danks, J. H. (1969). Grammatical structure and recall: A function of the space in immediate memory or of recall delay. *Perception and Psychophysics, 6,* 113–117.

Godden, D., & Baddeley, A. D. (1975) Context-dependent memory in two natural environments: on land and under water. *British Journal of Psychology, 66,* 325–331.

Gold, A. R. (1988, July 9). Scholars losing sight of the reason for reading. *Reno Gazette-Journal.*

Gold, P. E. (1987). Sweet memories. *American Scientist, 75,* 151–155.

Goldenberg, G., Podreka, I., Steiner, M., Suess, E., Deeke, L., & Willmes, K. (1990). Regional cerebral blood flow patterns in imagery tasks—results of single photon emission computer tomography. In M. Denis, J. Engelkamp, & J. T. E. Richardson (Eds.), *Cognitive and neuropsychological approaches to mental imagery.* Dordrecht, The Netherlands: Martinus Nijhoff.

Goldin-Meadow, S. (1982). Cited in L. Edson, Under Babel's tower. *Mosaic, 13,* 22–28.

Goodman, K. (1970). Reading: A psycholinguistic guessing game. In H. Singer & R. D. Ruddel (Eds.), *Theoretical models and processes of reading* (pp. 259–272). Newark, DE: International Reading Association.

Goodwyn, S. W., Acredolo, L. P., & Brown, C. A. (2000). Impact of symbolic gesturing on early language development.

Gordon, R. (1949). An investigation into some of the factors that favour the formation of stereotyped images. *British Journal of Psychology, 39,* 156–167.

Gordon, R. (1950). An experiment correlating the nature of imagery with performance on a test of reversal of perspective. *British Journal of Psychology, 41,* 63–67.

Graham, F. K., Leavitt, L. A., Strock, B. D., & Brown, J. W. (1978). Precocious cardiac orienting in human anencephalic infants. *Science, 199,* 322–324.

Graham, L. R. (1972). *Science and philosophy in the Soviet Union.* New York: Knopf.

Gray, J. A., & Wedderburn, A. A. I. (1960). Grouping strategies with simultaneous stimuli. *Quarterly Journal of Experimental Psychology, 12,* 180–184.

Green, D. M., & Swets, J. A. (1966). *Signal detection theory and psychophysics.* New York: Wiley.

Greenberg, J. H. (1963). Some universals of grammar with particular reference to the order of meaningful elements. In J. H. Greenberg (Ed.), *Universals of language.* Cambridge, MA: The MIT Press.

Greeno, J. G. (1973). The structure of memory and the process of solving problems. In R. L. Solso (Ed.), *Contemporary issues in cognitive psychology: The Loyola Symposium.* Washington, DC: Winston/ Wiley.

Greeno, J. G. (1974). Hobbits and orcs: Acquisition of a sequential concept. *Cognitive Psychology, 6,* 270–292.

Gregg, L. W., & Simon H. A. (1967). Process models and stochastic theories of simple concept formation. *Journal of Mathematical Psychology, 4,* 246–276.

Gregory, R. L. (1973). The confounded eye. In R. L. Gregory & E. H. Gombrich (Eds.), *Illusion in nature and art.* New York: Scribner.

Gregory, R. L. (Ed.). (1987). *The Oxford companion to the mind.* Oxford: Oxford University Press.

Gruneberg, M. M., Morris, P. E., & Sykes, R. Jr. (Eds.). (1978). *Practical aspects of memory.* London: Academic Press.

Guilford, J. P. (1959). Three faces of intellect. *American Psychologist, 14,* 469–479.

Guilford, J. P. (1966). Intelligence: 1965 model. *American Psychologist, 21,* 20–26.

Guilford, J. P. (1967). *The nature of human intelligence.* New York: Scribner.

Guilford, J. P. (1982). Cognitive psychology's ambiguities: Some suggested remedies. *Psychological Review, 89,* 48–59.

Guzman, A. (1968). *Computer recognition of three-dimensional objects in a visual scene* (Project MAC-TR-59) (pp. 447–449). Cambridge, MA: MIT Artificial Intelligence Laboratory.

Haber, R. N. (1970). Visual perception. *Annual Review of Psychology* (Vol. 29). Palo Alto, CA: Annual Reviews.

Haber, R. N. (1983). The impending demise of the icon: A critique of the iconic storage in visual information processing. *Behavioral and Brain Sciences, 6,* 1–54.

Haber, R. N. (1985a). Comment on the demise of the icon. *Behavioral and Brain Sciences, 8,* 8.

Haber, R. N. (1985b). An icon can have no worth in the real world: Comments on Loftus, Johnson and Shimamura's "How much is an icon worth?" *Journal of Experimental Psychology: Human Perception and Performance, 11,* 374–378.

Haber, R. N. (1989). Twenty years of haunting eidetic images: Where's the ghost? *Behavioral and Brain Sciences, 2,* 583–594.

Haber, R. N., & Hershenson, M. (1973). *The psychology of visual perception.* New York: Holt, Rinehart & Winston.

Hagen, J. W. (1967). The effects of distraction on selective attention. *Child Development, 38,* 685–694.

Hagen, J. W. (Ed.). *Perspectives on the development of memory and cognition.* Hillsdale, NJ: Erlbaum.

Haier, R. J., Chueh, D., Touchette, P., Lott, I., Buchsbaum, M. S., MacMillan, D., et al. (1995). Brain size and cerebral glucose metabolic rate in nonspecific mental retardation and Down syndrome. *Intelligence, 20*(2), 191–210.

Haier, R. J., Siegel, B. V., MacLachlan, A., Soderling, E., et al. (1992). Regional glucose metabolic changes after learning a complex visiospatial/ motor task: A positron emission tomographic study. *Brain Research, 570,* 134–143.

Haier, R. J., Siegel, B. V., Tang, C., Abel, L., & Buchsbaum, M. S. (1992). Intelligence and changes in regional cerebral glucose metabolic rate following learning. *Intelligence, 16*(3–4), 415–426.

Haith, M. M., Bergman, T., & Moore, M. J. (1977). Eye contact and face scanning in early infancy. *Science, 198,* 853–855.

Haith, M. M., Morrison, F. J., Sheingold, K., & Mindes, P. (1970). Short-term memory for visual information in children and adults. *Journal of Experimental Child Psychology, 9,* 454–469.

Hale, G. A. (1975). *Development of flexibility in children's attention deployment: A colloquium.* Research memorandum. Princeton, NJ: Educational Testing Service.

Hall, J. L., & Gold, P. E. (1990). Adrenalectomy induced memory deficits: Role of plasma glucose levels. *Physiology and Behavior, 47,* 27–33.

Hall, J. W., & Halperin, M. S. (1972). The development of memory-encoding processes in young children. *Developmental Psychology, 6,* 181.

Halpern, A. R. (1986). Memory for tune titles after organized or unorganized presentation. *American Journal of Psychology, 99,* 57–70.

Hamilton, W. (1938). Cited in R. Woodworth (Ed.), *Experimental psychology.* New York: Holt.

Hamilton, W. (1954). *Lectures on metaphysics and logic* (Vol. 1, Lect. XLV). Edinburgh: Blackwood, 1859. Cited in R. Woodworth & H. Schlosberg, *Experimental psychology.* New York: Holt.

Hart, J. T. (1965). Memory and the feeling-of-knowing experience. *Journal of Educational Psychology, 56,* 208–216.

Haugeland, J. (1989). *Artificial intelligence: The very idea.* Cambridge, MA: MIT Press.

Haxby, J. V., Ungerleider, L. G., Horwitz, B., Rapoport, S. I., & Grady, C. L. (1995). Hemispheric differences in neurosystems for face working memory: A PET-rCBR study. *Human Brain Mapping, 3,* 68–32.

Hayes, J. R. (1978). *Cognitive psychology: Thinking and creating.* Homewood, IL: Dorsey Press.

Hayes, J. R. (1989). *The complete problem solver* (2nd ed.). Hillsdale, NJ: Erlbaum.

Hayes, J. R., & Simon, H. A. (1976). Psychological differences among problem isomorphs. In N. Castellon, Jr., D. Pisoni, & G. Potts (Eds.), *Cognitive theory* (Vol. 2). Hillsdale, NJ: Erlbaum.

Haygood, R. C. (1975). *Concept learning.* Morristown, NJ: General Learning Press.

Haygood, R. C., & Bourne, L. E., Jr. (1965). Attribute and rule-learning aspects of conceptual behavior. *Psychological Review, 72*(3), 175–195.

Hayman, C. A. G., Macdonald, C. A., & Tulving, E. (1993). The role of repetition and associative interference in new semantic learning in amnesia: A case experiment. *Journal of Cognitive Neuroscience, 5,* 375–389.

Head, H. (1926). *Aphasia and kindred disorders of speech.* Cambridge, UK: Cambridge University Press.

Head, H. (1958). Cited in F. Bartlett, *Thinking* (p. 146). New York: Basic Books.

Hebb, D. O. (1949). *The organization of behavior.* New York: Wiley.

Heider, E. R. (1971). "Focal" color areas and the development of color names. *Developmental Psychology, 4,* 447–455.

Heider, E. R. (1972). Universals in color naming and memory. *Journal of Experimental Psychology, 93,* 10–20.

Henle, M. (1962). On the relation between logic and thinking. *Psychological Review, 69,* 366–378.

Henle, M., & Michael, M. (1956). The influence of attitudes on syllogistic reasoning. *Journal of Social Psychology, 4,* 115–127.

Heppenheimer, T. A. (1988). Nerves of silicon. *Discover,* Feb. 70–79.

Hernandez-Peon, R. (1966). Physiological mechanisms in attention. In R. W. Russell (Ed.), *Frontiers in physiological psychology.* New York: Academic Press.

Herrmann, D. J. (1987). Task appropriateness of mnemonic techniques. *Perceptual and Motor Skills, 64,* 171–178.

Herrnstein, R. J., & Murray, C. (1994). *The bell curve: Intelligence and class structure in American life.* New York: Free Press.

Hilgard, E. R. (1980). Consciousness in contemporary psychology. *Annual Review of Psychology, 31,* 1–26.

Hilgard, E. R. (1987). *Psychology in America: A historical survey.* San Diego, CA: Harcourt Brace Jovanovich.

Hilgard, E. R., & Bower, G. H. (1974). *Theories of learning* (4th ed.). Englewood Cliffs, NJ: Prentice-Hall.

Hillis, W. D. (1987). The connection machine. *Scientific American, 256,* 108–115.

Hillyard, S. A. (1993). Electrical and magnetic brain recordings: Contribution to cognitive neuroscience. *Current Operations in Neurobiology, 3,* 217–224.

Hillyard, S. A., Mangun, G. R., Woldorff, M. G., & Luck, S. J. (1995). Neural systems mediating selective attention. In M. S. Gazzaniga (Ed.), *The cognitive neurosciences.* Cambridge, MA: MIT Press.

Hinsley, D., Hayes, J. R., & Simon, H. A. (1977). From words to equations. In P. Carpenter & M. Just (Eds.), *Cognitive processes in comprehension.* Hillsdale, NJ: Erlbaum.

Hinton, G. E. (1981). A parallel computation that assigns canonical object-based frames of reference. *Proceedings of the 7th International Joint Conference on Artificial Intelligence.*

Hinton, G. E. (1992, September). How neural networks learn from experience. *Scientific American*, pp. 67–72.

Hintzman, D. L. (1974). Psychology and the cow's belly. *Worm Runner's Digest, 16,* 84–85.

Hoe, H. S., Pocvavsek, A., Geentanjali, C., Fu, Z. Vicini, S., Ehlers, M. D. et al. (2006). Apolipoprotein E receptor 2 interactions with the *N*-methyl-D-aspartate receptor. *Journal of Biological Chemistry, 281*(6), 3425–3431.

Hofstadter, D. R. (1979). *Godel, Escher, Bach: An eternal golden braid.* New York: Basic Books.

Holbrook, M. B., & Schindler, R. M. (1998). Some exploratory findings on the development of musical tastes. *Journal of Consumer Research, 16,* 119–124.

Holding, D. H. (1975a). A rejoinder. *Memory and Cognition, 3,* 49–50.

Holding, D. H. (1975b). Sensory storage reconsidered. *Memory and Cognition, 3,* 31–41.

Holender, D. (1986). Semantic activation without conscious identification in dichotic listening, parafoveal vision, and visual masking: A survey and appraisal. *Behavioral and Brain Sciences, 9,* 1–66.

Hollan, J. D. (1975). Features and semantic memory: Set theoretic or network model? *Psychological Review, 82,* 154–155.

Holmes, D. L., Cohen, K. M., Haith, M. M., & Morrison, F. J. (1977). Peripheral visual processing. *Perception and Psychophysics, 22*(6), 571–577.

Holmes, L. H., & Morrison, F. J. (1979). *The child.* Monterey, CA: Brooks/Cole.

Holt, R. R. (1964). Imagery. The return of the ostracized. *American Psychologist, 12,* 254–264.

Holyoak, K. J., & Glass, A. L. (1975). The role of contradictions and counterexamples in the rejection of false sentences. *Journal of Verbal Learning and Verbal Behavior, 14,* 215–239.

Horowitz, L. M., & Prytulak, L. S. (1969). Redintegrative memory. *Psychological Review, 76,* 519–531.

Horowitz, L. M., Chilian, P. C., & Dunnigan, K. P. (1969). Word fragments and their redintegrative powers. *Journal of Experimental Psychology, 80,* 392–394.

Horowitz, L. M., White, M. A., & Atwood, D. W. (1968). Word fragments as aids to recall: The organization of a word. *Journal of Experimental Psychology, 76,* 219–226.

Horton, D. L., & Turnage, T. W. (1976). *Human learning.* Englewood Cliffs, NJ: Prentice-Hall.

Houston, J. P. (1976). *Fundamentals of learning.* New York: Academic Press.

Hovland, C. I. (1952). A communication analysis of concept learning. *Psychological Review, 59,* 461–472.

Howes, D., & Solomon, R. L. (1951). Visual duration thresholds as a function of word probability. *Journal of Experimental Psychology, 41,* 401–410.

Hubel, D. & Wiesel, T. (1959). Receptive fields of single neurons in the cat's striate cortex. *Journal of Physiology, 148,* 574–591.

Hubel, D. & Wiesel, T. (1968). Receptive fields and functional architecture of moneky striate cortex. *Journal of Physiology, 195,* 215–243.

Hubel, D. H. (1959). Receptive fields of single neurons in the cat's striate cortex. *Journal of Physiology, 148,* 574–591.

Hubel, D. H. (1963a). Receptive fields of cells in the striate cortex of very young, visually inexperienced kittens. *Journal of Neurophysiology, 26,* 994–1002.

Hubel, D. H. (1963b, November). The visual cortex of the brain. *Scientific American,* pp. 54–62.

Hubel, D. H., & Wiesel, T. N. (1959). Receptive fields of single neurons in the cat's striate cortex. *Journal of Physiology, 148,* 574–591.

Hubel, D. H., & Wiesel, T. N. (1963). Receptive fields of cells in the striate cortex of very young, visually inexperienced kittens. *Journal of Neurophysiology, 26,* 994–1002.

Hudson, W. (1967). The study of the problem of pictorial perception among unacculturated groups. *International Journal of Psychology, 2,* 89–107.

Huey, E. B. (1968). *The psychology and pedagogy of reading.* Cambridge, MA: MIT Press. (Original work published 1908)

Hume, D. (1912). *An enquiry concerning human understanding.* Chicago: Open Court. (Original work published 1748)

Humphreys, G. W. (Ed.). (1992) *Understanding vision.* Oxford: Blackwell.

Hunt, E. B. (1961). Memory effects in concept learning. *Journal of Experimental Psychology, 62,* 598–609.

Hunt, E. B. (1968). Computer simulation: Artificial intelligence studies and their relevance to psychology. In P. R. Farnsworth (Ed.), *Annual review of psychology* (Vol. 19). Palo Alto, CA: Annual Reviews.

Hunt, E. B. (1971). What kind of computer is man? *Cognitive Psychology, 2,* 57–98.

Hunt, E. B. (1973). The memory we must have. In R. Schank & K. Colby (Eds.), *Computer models of thought and language* (pp. 343–371). San Francisco: Freeman.

Hunt, E. B. (1978). Mechanics of verbal ability. *Psychological Review, 85,* 109–130.

Hunt, E. B. (1989). Cognitive science: Definition, status, and questions. In M. R. Rosenzweig & L. W. Porter (Eds.), *Annual Review of Psychology, 40* (pp. 603–629). Palo Alto, CA: Annual Reviews.

Hunt, E. B. (1995). The role of intelligence in modern society. *American Scientist, 83,* 356–368.

Hunt, E. B., & Lansman, M. (1982). Individual differences in attention. In R. J. Sternberg (Ed.), *Advances in the psychology of human intelligence.* Hillsdale, NJ: Erlbaum.

Hunt, E., & Love, T. (1972). How good can memory be? In A. W. Melton & E. Martin (Eds.), *Coding processes in human memory.* Washington, DC: Winston.

Hunt, E. B., Lunneborg, C., & Lewis, J. (1975). What does it mean to be high verbal? *Cognitive Psychology, 7,* 194–227.

Hunter, I. M. L. (1957). *Memory: Facts and fallacies.* Harmondsworth, UK: Penguin.

Hunter, I. M. L. (1964). *Memory.* Harmondsworth, UK: Penguin.

Inhelder, B., & Piaget, J. (1964a). *The early growth of logic in the child.* New York: Harper Row.

Inhelder, B., & Piaget, J. (1964b). *The early growth of logical thinking.* New York: Norton.

Inhoff, A., & Tousman, S. (1990). Lexical priming from partial-word previews. *Journal of Experimental Psychology: Human Perception and Performance, 16,* 825–836.

Inn, D., Walden, K. J., & Solso, R. L. (1993). *Facial prototype formation in three to six year old children.* Unpublished manuscript. University of Nevada, Reno.

Intons-Peterson, M. J., & Fournier, J. (1986). External and internal memory aids: When and how often do we use them? *Journal of Experimental Psychology: General, 115,* 267–280.

Ionesco, E. (1970). *Story number 2.* New York: Harlin Quist/Crown.

Ivry, R. B., & Lebby, P. C. (1993). Hemispheric differences in auditory perception are similar to those found in visual perception. *Psychological Science, 4,* 41–45.

Izawa, C. (1989). *Current issues in cognitive processes: The Tulane Flowerree Symposium on cognition.* Hillsdale, NJ: Erlbaum.

Jackson, A., & Morton, J. (1984). Facilitation of auditory word recognition. *Memory and Cognition, 12,* 568–574.

Jackson, P. C. (1974). *Introduction to artificial intelligence.* New York: Petrocelli/Charter.

Jacobs, J. (1887). Experiments on "Prehension" *Mind,* Vol. 12, No. 45, pp. 75–79

Jacoby, L. L., & Witherspoon, D. (1982). Remembering without awareness. *Canadian Journal of Psychology, 32,* 300–324.

Jakobovits, L. A., & Miron, M. S. (1967). *Readings in the psychology of language.* Englewood Cliffs, NJ: Prentice Hall.

Jakobson, R. (1972, September). Verbal communication. *Scientific American,* pp. 38–44.

James, W. (1983). *The principles of psychology.* Cambridge, MA: Harvard University Press. (Original work published 1890)

James, W. (1890). *Principles of psychology.* New York: Holt.

James, W. (1902). *The varieties of religious experience.* New York: Longmans, Green & Co.

Janis, I. L., & Frick, F. (1943). The relationship between attitudes toward conclusions and errors in judging logical validity of syllogisms. *Journal of Experimental Psychology, 33,* 73–77.

Janis, I. L., & Mann, L. (1977). *Decision making.* New York: Free Press.

Javal, L. E. (1878). Essai sur la physiologie de la lecture. *Annales d'Oculistique, 82,* 242–253.

Jaynes, J. (1976). *The origins of consciousness in the breakdown of the bicameral mind.* Boston: Houghton Mifflin.

Jenkins, J. G., & Dallenbach, K. M. (1924). Obliviscence during sleep and waking. *American Journal of Psychology, 35,* 605–612.

Jenkins, J. J. (1963). Mediated associations: Paradigms and situations. In C. N. Cofer & B. S. Musgrave (Eds.), *Verbal behavior and learning.* New York: McGraw-Hill.

Jensen, A. R. (1993). Why is reaction time correlated with psychometric *g? Current Directions in Psychological Science, 2,* 53–56.

John, E. R. (1972). Switchboard versus statistical theories of learning and memory. *Science, 177,* 849–864.

Johnson, M. H. (Ed.). (1993). *Brain development and cognition: A reader.* Cambridge, MA: Blackwell.

Johnson, M., & Morton, J. (1991). *Biology and cognitive development: The case of face recognition.* Oxford: Blackwell.

Johnson-Laird, P. N. (1970). The perception and memory of sentences. In J. Lyons (Ed.), *New horizons in linguistics* (pp. 261–270). Baltimore: Penguin.

Johnson-Laird, P. N. (1983). *Mental models: Towards a cognitive science of language, inference, and consciousness.* Cambridge, MA: Harvard University Press.

Johnson-Laird, P. N. (1988). *The computer and the mind.* Cambridge, MA: Harvard University Press.

Johnson-Laird, P. N. (1995). Mental models and probabilistic thinking. In J. Mehler & S. Franck (Eds.), *Cognition on cognition. Cognition special series* (pp. 171–191). Cambridge, MA: MIT Press.

Johnson-Laird, P. N., & Byrne, R. M. J. (1989). Only reasoning. *Journal of Memory and Language, 28,* 313–330.

Johnson-Laird, P. N., & Byrne, R. M. J. (1991). *Deduction.* Hove, UK: Erlbaum.

Johnson-Laird, P. N., Legrenzi, P., & Legrenzi, M. (1992). Reasoning and a sense of reality. *British Journal of Psychology, 63,* 395–400.

Johnson-Laird, P. N., & Steedman, M. (1978). The psychology of syllogisms. *Cognitive Psychology, 10,* 64–99.

Johnson-Laird, P. N., & Wason, P. C. (Eds.). (1977). *Thinking: Readings in cognitive science.* Cambridge, UK: Cambridge University Press.

Johnston, W. A., & Heinz, S. P. (1975). Depth of non-target processing in an attention task. *Journal of Experimental Psychology, 5,* 168–175.

Johnston, W. A., & Heinz, S. P. (1978). Flexibility and capacity demands of attention. *Journal of Experimental Psychology: General, 107,* 420–435.

Johnston, W. A., & Wilson, J. (1980). Perceptual processing of non-target in an attention task. *Memory and Cognition, 8,* 372–377.

Jolicoeur, P., Regehr, S., Smith, L. B., & Smith, G. N. (1985). Mental rotation of representations of two-dimensional and three-dimensional objects. *Canadian Journal of Psychology, 39,* 100–129.

Julesz, B. (1971). *Foundations of cyclopean perception.* Chicago: University of Chicago Press.

Just, M. A., & Carpenter, P. A. (1980). A theory of reading: From eye fixations to comprehension. *Psychological Review, 87*(4), 329–354.

Just, M. A., & Carpenter, P. A. (1987). *The psychology of reading and language comprehension.* Boston: Allyn & Bacon.

Just, M. A., Carpenter, P. A., Keller, T. A., Eddy, W. F., & Thulbom, K. R. (1996). Brain activation modulated by sentence comprehension. *Science, 274,* 114–116.

Kahn, D. (1967). *The codebreakers: The story of secret writing.* New York: Macmillan.

Kahneman, D. (1973). *Attention and effort.* Englewood Cliffs, NJ: Prentice-Hall.

Kahneman, D., & Miller, D. (1986). Norm theory: Comparing reality to its alternatives. *Psychology Review, 93,* 136–153.

Kahneman, D., & Tversky, A. (1972). Subjective probability: A judgment of representativeness. *Cognitive Psychology, 3,* 430–454.

Kahneman, D., & Tversky, A. (1983). On the psychology of prediction. *Psychological Review, 80,* 237–251.

Kahneman, D., & Tversky, A. (1984). Choices, values, and frames. *American Psychologist, 39,* 341–350.

Kandel, E. R. (1981a). Brain and behavior. In E. R. Kandel & J. H. Schwartz (Eds.), *Principles of neural science.* New York: Elsevier/NorthHolland.

Kandel, E. R. (1981b). Nerve cells and behavior. In E. R. Kandel & J. H. Schwartz (Eds.), *Principles of neural science.* New York: Elsevier/North-Holland.

Kandel, E. R., & Schwartz, J. H. (Eds.). (1981). *Principles of neural science.* New York: Elsevier/North-Holland.

Kandel, E. R., Schwartz, J. H., & Jessell, T. M. (1991). *Principles of neural science.* New York: Elsevier.

Kanizsa, G. (1976). Subjective contours. *Scientific American, 234,* 48–52.

Kao, Y. F. (1990). *Subliminal processing: The spread of activation in color priming.* Unpublished doctoral dissertation. University of Nevada, Reno.

Kao, Y. F., & Solso, R. L. (1989, April). *One second of cognition.* Paper presented at the annual meeting of RMPA/WPA, Reno, NV.

Kaplan, R. M. (1972). Augmented transition networks as psychological models of sentence comprehension. *Artificial Intelligence, 3,* 77–100.

Kapur N., Scholey K., Barker S., Mayes A., Brice J., Fleming J. (1994) The mammillary bodies revisited: their role in human memory functioning. In: *Neuropsychological explorations of memory and cognition: essays in honor of Nelson Butters* (Cermak, LS, eds), p. 159. New York: Plenum.

Kapur S., Craik F.I.M., Tulving E., Wilson A.A., Houle S., Brown G.M. (1994). Neuroanatomical correlates of encoding in episodic memory: Levels of processing effect. *Proceedings of the National Academy of Sciences of the United States of America, 91,* 2008–2011.

Kapur, N., Scholey, K., Moore, E., Barker, S., Mayes, A., Brice, J., et al., (1994). The mammillary bodies revisited: Their role in human memory functioning. In L. S. Cermak (Ed.), *Neuropsychological explorations of memory and cognition: Essays in honor of Nelson Butters* (pp. 159–189). New York: Plenum Press.

Kapur, S., Craik, F. I. M., Tulving, E., Wilson, A. A., Hoyle, S., & Brown, G. M. (1994). Neuroanatomical correlates of encoding in episodic memory: Levels of processing effect. *Proceedings of the National Academy of Sciences, 91,* 2008–2011.

Kassin S. M., & Kiechel K. L. (1996). The social psychology of false confessions: Compliance, internalization, and confabulation. *Psychological Science* 7(3), 125–128.

Katz, S., & Gruenewald, P. (1974). The abstraction of linguistic ideas in "meaningless" sentences. *Memory and Cognition, 2,* 737–741.

Kavanagh, J. F., & Mattingly I. G. (Eds.). (1972). *Language by ear and by eye: The relationship between speech and reading.* Cambridge, MA: MIT Press.

Keele, S. W. (1973). *Attention and human performance.* Pacific Palisades, CA: Goodyear.

Kendler, H. H., & Kendler, T. S. (1969). Reversal-shift behavior: Some basic issues. *Psychological Bulletin, 72,* 229–232.

Kennedy, A., & Wilkes, A. (Eds.). (1975). *Studies in long-term memory.* New York: Wiley.

Kess, J. F. (1976). *Psycholinguistics: Introductory perspectives.* New York: Academic Press.

Kessen, W., & Kuhlman, C. (1970). *Cognitive developments in children.* Chicago: University of Chicago Press.

Kihlstrom, J. F. (1987). The cognitive unconscious. *Science, 237,* 1445–1453.

Kihlstrom, J. F. (1993). The psychological unconscious and the self. In G. R. Bock & J. Marsh (Eds.), *CIBA Symposium on Experimental and Theoretical Studies of Consciousness* (pp. 147–156). Chichester, UK: Wiley.

Kihlstrom, J. F., & Cantor, N. (1984). Mental representations of the self. *Advances in Experimental Social Psychology, 93,* 200–208.

Kimura, D. (1963). Right temporal lobe damage. *Arch Neurology, 8,* 264–271.

Kimura, D. (1967). Functional asymmetry of the brain in dichotic listening. *Cortex, 3,* 163–178.

Kintsch, W. (1967). Memory and decision aspects of recognition learning. *Psychological Review, 74,* 496–504.

Kintsch, W. (1974). *The representation of meaning in memory.* Hillsdale, NJ: Erlbaum.

Kintsch, W. (1979). On modeling comprehension. *Educational Psychologist, 14,* 3–14.

Kintsch, W. (1988). The role of knowledge in discourse comprehension: A construction-integration model. *Psychological Review, 95,* 163–182.

Kintsch, W. (1990). The representation of knowledge and the use of knowledge in discourse comprehension. In C. Graumann & R. Dietrich (Eds.), *Language in the social context.* Amsterdam: Elsevier.

Kintsch, W., & Keenan, J. (1973). Reading rate and retention as a function of the number of propositions in the base structure of sentences. *Cognitive Psychology, 5,* 257–274.

Kintsch, W., & van Dijk, T. A. (1978). Toward a model of text comprehension and production. *Psychological Review, 85,* 363–394.

Kintsch, W., & Vipond, D. (1979). Reading comprehension and readability in educational practice and psychological theory. In L. G. Nilsson (Ed.), *Perspectives on memory research.* Hillsdale, NJ: Erlbaum.

Kirkpatrick, E. A. (1894). An experimental study of memory. *Psychological Review, 1,* 602–609.

Kitaoka, A. and Ashida, H. (2003) Phenomenal characteristics of the peripheral drift illusion. *VISION, 15,* 261–262.

Klatzky, R. L. (1975). *Human memory: Structures and processes.* San Francisco: Freeman.

Klatzky, R. L. (1984). *Memory and awareness.* San Francisco: Freeman.

Klein, K., & Saltz, E. (1976). Specifying the mechanisms in a levels-of-processing approach to memory. *Journal of Experimental Psychology, 87,* 281–288.

Kleinmuntz, B. (1969). *Clinical information processing by computer.* New York: Holt, Rinehart & Winston.

Kline, S. B., & Kihlstrom, J. F. (1986). Elaboration, organization, and the self-reference effect in memory. *Journal of Experimental Psychology: General, 113,* 26–38.

Kobasigawa, A., & Middleton, D. B. (1972). Free recall of categorized items by children at three grade levels. *Child Development, 43,* 1067–1072.

Koenig, O., Reiss, L. P., & Kosslyn, S. M. (1990). The development of spacial relation representations: Evidence from studies of cerebral lateralization. *Journal of Experimental Child Psychology, 50,* 119–130.

Köhler, W. (1925). The mentality of apes. New York: Trench, Trubner, & Co. Ltd.

Köhler, W. (1938). *The place of value in the world of facts.* New York: Liveright.

Köhler, W. (1947). *Gestalt psychology: An introduction to the new concepts in modern psychology.* New York: Liveright.

Kolb, B., & Whishaw, I. Q. (1990). *Fundamentals of human neuropsychology.* New York: Freeman.

Kolers, P. A., & Palef, S. R. (1976). Knowing not. *Memory and Cognition, 4,* 553–558.

Kolers, W. (1970). Three stages of reading. In H. Levin & J. P. Williams (Eds.), *Basic studies on reading.* New York: Basic Books.

Kornack, D. R. & Rakic, P. (2001) Cell proliferation without neurogenesis in adult primate neocortex. *Science,* 294(5549), 2127–2130.

Kosslyn, S. M. (1973). Scanning visual images: Some structural implications. *Perception and Psychophysics, 14,* 90–94.

Kosslyn, S. M. (1975). Information representation in visual images. *Cognitive Psychology, 7,* 341–370.

Kosslyn, S. M. (1976a). Can imagery be distinguished from other forms of internal representation? Evidence from studies of information-retrieval time. *Memory and Cognition, 4,* 291–297.

Kosslyn, S. M. (1976b). *Visual images present metric spatial information.* Paper presented at the Psychonomic Society Meetings, St. Louis, MO.

Kosslyn, S. M. (1977). Imagery and internal representation. In E. Rosch & U. Lloyd (Eds.), *Categories and cognition.* Hillsdale, NJ: Erlbaum.

Kosslyn, S. M. (1980). *Image and mind.* Cambridge, MA: Harvard University Press.

Kosslyn, S. M. (1981). The medium and the message in mental imagery. *Psychological Review, 88,* 46–66.

Kosslyn, S. M. (1983). *Ghosts in the mind's machine.* New York: Norton.

Kosslyn, S. M. (1988). Aspects of cognitive neuroscience of mental imagery. *Science, 240,* 1621–1626.

Kosslyn, S. M. (1994). *Image and brain: The resolution of the imagery debate.* Cambridge, MA: MIT Press.

Kosslyn, S. M. (1995). Introduction. In M. S. Gazzaniga (Ed.), *The cognitive neurosciences* (pp. 959–961). Cambridge, MA: MIT Press.

Kosslyn, S. M., & Koenig, O. (1992). *Wet mind: The new cognitive neuroscience.* New York: Free Press.

Kosslyn, S. M., & Osherson, D. N. (Eds.) (1995). *Visual cognition.* Cambridge, MA: MIT Press.

Kosslyn, S. M., & Pomerantz, J. R. (1977). Imagery, proposition, and the form of internal representations. *Cognitive Psychology, 9,* 52–76.

Kosslyn, S. M., & Schwartz, S. P. (1977). A simulation of visual imagery. *Cognitive Science, 1,* 265–295.

Kosslyn, S. M., Alpert, N. M., Thompson, W. L., Meljkovic, V., Weise, S. B., Chabris, C. F., et al. (1993). Visual mental imagery activates topographically organized visual cortex: PET investiga-tions. *Journal of Cognitive Neuroscience, 5,* 263–287.

Kosslyn, S. M., Ball, T. M., & Reiser, B. J. (1978). Visual images preserve metric spatial information. Evidence from studies of image scanning. *Journal of Experimental Psychology: Human Perception and Performance, 40,* 47–60.

Kosslyn, S. M., Murphy, G. L., Bemesderfer, M. E., & Feinstein, K. J. (1977). Category and continuum in mental comparisons. *Journal of Experimental Psychology: General, 106,* 341–375.

Kosslyn, S. M., Sokolov, M. A., & Chen, J. C. (1989). The lateralization of BRIAN: A computational theory and model of visual hemispheric specialization. In D. Klahr & K. Kotovsky (Eds.), *Complex information processing: The impact of Herbert H. Simon.* Hillsdale, NJ: Erlbaum.

Kozulin, A. (1984). *Psychology in Utopia: Toward a social history of Soviet psychology.* Cambridge, MA: The MIT Press.

Kozulin, A. (1986). The concept of activity in Soviet psychology. *American Psychologist, 1,* 264–274.

Kries, J. von. (1925). Über die Natur gewisser mit den pschischen Vorgangen Verknupfter Gehirnzustande. *Z. Psy,* 1985, *8,* 1–33. Cited in R. Woodworth & H. Schlosberg (Eds.), *Experimental psychology.* New York: Holt.

Kroll, N. E. A., Schepeler, E. M., & Angin, K. T. (1986). Bizarre imagery: The misremembered mnemonic. *Journal of Experimental Psychology: Learning, Memory, and Cognition, 12,* 42–53.

Kučera, H., & Francis, W. N (1967). *Computational analysis of present-day American English.* Providence, RI: Brown University Press.

Kuhn, T. S. (1962). *The structure of scientific revolutions.* Chicago: University of Chicago Press.

Kupferman, I. (1981). Localization of higher function. In E. R. Kandel & J. H. Schwartz (Eds.), *Principles of neural science.* New York: Elsevier/North-Holland.

Kurzweil, R. (1999). *The age of spiritual machines.* New York: Viking.

LaBerge, D. (1972). Beyond auditory coding. In J. F. Kavanagh & I. G. Mattingly (Eds.), *Language by ear and by eye* (pp. 241–248). Cambridge, MA: MIT Press.

LaBerge, D. (1975). Acquisition of automatic processing in perceptual and associative learning. In P. M. A. Rabbit & S. Dornic (Eds.), *Attention and performance V.* London: Academic Press.

LaBerge, D. (1976). Perceptual learning and attention. In W. Estes (Ed.), *Handbook of learning and cognitive processes*, Vol. 4: *Attention and memory.* Hillsdale, NJ: Erlbaum.

LaBerge, D. (1980). Unitization and automaticity in perception. In J. H. Flowers (Ed.), *Nebraska Symposium on Motivation* (pp. 53–71). Lincoln: University of Nebraska Press.

LaBerge, D., & Samuels, S. J. (1974). Toward a theory of automatic information processing in reading. *Cognitive Psychology, 6,* 293–323.

LaBerge, D., & Samuels, S. J. (1978). *Basic processes in reading: Perception and comprehension.* Hillsdale, NJ: Erlbaum.

Laird, D. A., & Laird, E. C. (1960). *Techniques for efficient remembering.* New York: McGraw-Hill.

Land, M. F., & Fernald, R. D. (1992). The evolution of eyes. In *Annual Review of Neuroscience, 15,* 1–29.

Landauer, T. K. (1975). Memory without organization: Properties of a model with random storage and undirected retrieval. *Cognitive Psychology, 7,* 495–531.

Landauer, T. K., & Meyer, D. E. (1972). Category size and semantic-memory retrieval. *Journal of Verbal Learning and Verbal Behavior, 11,* 539–549.

Lange, G. (1973). The development of conceptual and rote recall skills among school-age children. *Journal of Experimental Child Psychology, 15,* 394–406.

Lashley, K. S. (1929). *Brain mechanisms and intelligence: A quantitative study of injuries to the brain.* Chicago: University of Chicago Press.

Lashley, K. S. (1950). In search of the engram. *Proceedings from Social Experimental Biology, 4,* 454–482. Reprinted in F. A. Beach, D. O. Hebb, C. T. Morgan, & H. W. Nissen (Eds.), *The neuropsychology of Lashley.* New York: McGraw-Hill.

Lashley, K. S. (1951). The problem of serial order in behavior. In L. A. Jeffress (Ed.), *Cerebral mechanisms in behavior: The Hixon Symposium.* New York: Wiley.

Lassen, N. A., Ingvar, D. H., & Skinhoj, E. (1979). Brain function and blood flow. *Scientific American, 239,* 62–71.

Laughlin, P. R. (1968). Focusing strategy for eight concept rules. *Journal of Experimental Psychology, 77,* 661–669.

Laughlin, P. R., & Jordan, R. M. (1967). Selection strategies in conjunctive, disjunctive, and biconditional concept attainment. *Journal of Experimental Psychology, 75,* 188–193.

Lazar, S. W., Bush, G., Gollub, R. L., Fricchione, G. L., Khalsa, G., & Benson, H. (2000). Functional brain mapping of the relaxation response and meditation [autonomic nervous system]. NeuroReport, *Volume 11*(7), 1581–1585.

Le Bihan, D., Turner, R., Zeffiro, T. A., Cuenold, C. A., Jezzard, P., & Bonnerot, V. (in press). Activation of human primary visual cortex during visual recall: A magnetic resonance imaging study. *Proceedings of the National Academy of Sciences.*

Lefebvre, V. A. (1982). *Algebra of consciousness.* Boston: Reidel.

Lefton, L. A. (1973). Guessing and the order of approximation effect. *Journal of Experimental Psychology, 101,* 401–403.

Lenneberg, E. H. (1964a). *New directions in the study of language.* Cambridge, MA: The MIT Press.

Lenneberg, E. H. (1964b). In J. A. Fodor & J. J. Katz (Eds.), *The structure of language: Readings in the philosophy of language.* Englewood Cliffs, NJ: Prentice-Hall.

Lenneberg, E. H. (1967). *Biological foundations of language.* New York: Wiley.

Lenneberg, E. H. (1969). On explaining language. *Science, 164,* 635–643.

Lenneberg E. H., Nichols, I. A., & Rosenberger, E. F. (1964). In D. Rioch (Ed.), *Disorders of communication* (Research publications of Associations for Research in Nervous and Mental Disorders). New York.

Leontiev, A. N. (1978). Cited in L. S. Vygotsky, *Mind in society.* Cambridge, MA: Harvard University Press.

Lesgold, A. M., & Bower, G. H. (1970). Inefficiency of serial knowledge for associative responding. *Journal of Verbal Learning and Verbal Behavior, 9,* 456–466.

Lesher, G. W. (1995). Illusory contours: Toward a neurally based perceptual theory. *Psychonomic Bulletin and Review, 2,* 279–321.

Lesher, G. W., & Mingolla, E. (1993). The role of edges and line-ends in illusory contour formation. *Vision Research, 33,* 2253–2270.

Levine, M. (1993). *Effective problem solving* (2nd ed.). Englewood Cliffs, NJ: Prentice-Hall.

Levitin, K. (1982). *One is not born a personality.* Moscow: Progress Publishers.

Levy, J., Trevarthen, C., & Sperry, R. V. (1972). Perception of bilateral chimeric figures-following hemispheric deconnexion. *Brain, 95,* 61–78.

Lewis, J. L. (1970). Semantic processing of unattended messages using dichotic listening. *Journal of Experimental Psychology, 85,* 225–228.

Liberty, C., & Ornstein, P. A. (1973). Age differences in organization and recall: The effects of training in categorization. *Journal of Experimental Child Psychology, 15,* 169–186.

Libet, B. (1978). Neuronal vs. subjective timing for a conscious sensory experience. In P. A. Buser & A. Rougeul-Buser (Eds.), *Cerebral correlates of conscious experience* (pp. 69–82). INSERM Symposium No. 6. Amsterdam, North Holland: Elsevier.

Libet, B. (1981). Timing of cerebral processes relative to concomitant conscious experiences in man. In G. Adam, I. Meszaros, & E. I. Banyai (Eds.), *Advances in physiological science.* New York: Pergamon Press.

Lindsay, P. H., & Norman, D. A. (1973). *Human information processing* (2nd ed.). New York: Academic Press.

Lindsay, P. H., & Norman, D. A. (1977). *Human information processing: An introduction to psychology* (2nd ed.) New York: Academic Press.

Linton, M. (1982). Transformations of memory in everyday life. In U. Neisser (Ed.), *Memory observed: Remembering in natural contexts.* San Francisco: Freeman.

Lockhart, R. S., & Murdock, B. B., Jr. (1970). Memory and the theory of signal detection. *Psychological Bulletin, 74,* 100–109.

Lockhart, R. S., Craik, F. I. M., & Jacoby, L. L. (1975). Depth of processing in recognition and recall: Some aspects of a general memory system. In J. Brown (Ed.), *Recognition and recall.* London: Wiley.

Loftus, E. F. (1975a). Leading questions and the eyewitness report. *Cognitive Psychology, 7,* 560–572.

Loftus, E. F. (1975b). Spreading activation within semantic categories: Comments on Rosch's "Cognitive representations of semantic categories." *Journal of Experimental Psychology: General, 104,* 234–240.

Loftus, E. F. (1977). How to catch a zebra in semantic memory. In R. Shaw & J. Bransford (Eds.), *Perceiving, acting and knowing.* Hillsdale, NJ: Erlbaum.

Loftus, E. F. (1983). Misfortunes of memory. *Philosophical Transactions of the Royal Society.* London, B 302, 413–421.

Loftus, E. F. (1993a). Desperately seeking memories of the first few years of childhood: The reality of early memories. *Journal of Experimental Psychology: General, 122,* 274–277.

Loftus, E. F. (1993b). The reality of repressed memories. *American Psychologist, 48,* 518–537.

Loftus, E. F., & Ketcham, K. (1991). *Witness for the defense: The accused, the eyewitness, and the expert who puts memory on trial.* New York: St. Martin's Press.

Loftus, E. F., & Palmer, J. C. (1974). Reconstruction of automobile destruction: An example of the interaction between language and memory. *Journal of Verbal Learning and Verbal Behavior, 13,* 585–589.

Loftus, E. F., & Pickrell, J. E. (1995). The formation of false memories. *Psychiatric Annals, 25,* 720–725.

Loftus, E. F., & Zanni, G. (1975). Eyewitness testimony: The influence of the wording of a question. *Bulletin of the Psychonomic Society, 5,* 86–88.

Loftus, G. R. (1982). Picture methodology. In C. R. Pubb (Ed.), *Handbook of research methods in human memory and cognition* (pp. 257–285). New York: Academic Press.

Loftus, G. R. (1983). The continuing persistence of the icon. *Behavioral and Brain Sciences, 1,* 43.

Loftus, G. R. (1995). On worthwhile icons: Reply to Di Lollo and Haber. *Journal of Experimental Psychology: Human Perception and Performance, 18,* 530–549.

Loftus, G. R., Johnson, C. A., & Shimarmura, A. P. (1985). How much is an icon worth? *Journal of Experimental Psychology: Human Perception and Performance, 11,* 1–13.

Loftus, G. R., & Loftus, E. F. (1976). *Human memory: The processing of information.* Hillsdale, NJ: Erlbaum.

Lorayne, H., & Lucas, J. (1974). *The memory book.* New York: Stein & Day.

Lubart, T. I., & Sternberg, R. J. (1995). An investment approach to creativity. Theory and data. In S. M Smith, T. B. Ward, & R. A. Finke (Eds.), *The creative approach* (pp. 269–305). Cambridge, MA: The MIT Press.

Lubart, T. I., & Sternberg, R. J. (in preparation). *Creative performance: Testing an investment theory.* New Haven, CT: Yale University Press.

Lukoff, D., Lu, F. G., & Turner, R. P. (1998). From spiritual emergency to spiritual problem: The transpersonal roots of the new DSM-IV category. *Journal of Humanistic Psychology, 38*(2), 21–50.

Luria, A. R. (1960). *Problems of psychology, No. 1.* New York: Pergamon Press.

Luria, A. R. (1968). *The mind of a mnemonist.* New York: Basic Books.

Luria, A. R. (1971). Towards the problem of the historical nature of psychological processes. *International Journal of Psychology, 6,* 259–272.

Luria, A. R. (1976). *The neuropsychology of memory.* Washington, DC: Winston.

Lynch, S., & Yarnell, P. R. (1973). Retrograde amnesia: Delayed forgetting after concussion. *American Journal of Psychology, 86,* 643–645.

Lyons, J. (1968). *Introduction to theoretical linguistics.* Cambridge, UK: Cambridge University Press.

Lyons, J. (1970). *New horizons in linguistics.* Harmondsworth, UK: Penguin.

Lyons, J., & Wales, R. J. (1966). Psycholinguistic papers. *The Proceedings of the 1966 Edinburgh Conference.* Edinburgh: Edinburgh University Press.

MacKay, D. G. (1973). Aspects of a theory of comprehension, memory, and attention. *Quarterly Journal of Experimental Psychology, 25,* 22–40.

Mackworth, N. H. (1950). *Researches on the measurement of human performance* (Medical Research Council Special Report Series, No. 268). England.

Mackworth, N. H. (1965). Visual noise causes tunnel vision. *Psychonomic Science 3,* 67–68.

Mackworth, N. H. (1970). *Vigilance and habituation.* London: Penguin.

MacLin, M. K., & Solso, R. L. (2004). *A method for schematic activation in the laboratory.* Manuscript under review.

MacLin, O. H. Zimmerman, C. A., & Malpass R. S. (2005) PC-Eyewitness and the sequential superiority effect: Computer based linear administration. Law and Human Behavior, 29, 303–321.

MacNeilage, P. F. (1970). Motor control of serial ordering of speech. *Psychological Review, 77,* 182–196.

MacNeilage, P. F. (1972). Speech physiology. In J. Gilbert (Ed.), *Speech and cortical functioning* (pp. 1–72). New York: Academic Press.

MacNeilage, P. F., & Ladefoged, P. (1976). The production of speech and language. In E. C. Carterette & M. P. Friedman (Eds.), *Handbook of perception* (Vol. 7, pp. 75–120). New York: Academic Press.

MacNeilage, P. F., & MacNeilage, L. A. (1973). Central processes controlling speech production during sleep and waking. In F. J. McGuigan & R. A. Schoonover (Eds.), *The psychophysiology of thinking* (pp. 417–448). New York: Academic Press.

Malakoff, D. (1999). Bayes offers a "new" way to make sense of numbers. *Science, 285,* 1460–1464.

Maltzman, I. (1955). Thinking: From a behavioristic point of view. *Psychological Review, 62,* 275–286.

Mandler, G. (1954). Response factors in human learning. *Psychological Review, 61,* 235–244.

Mandler, G. (1962). From association to structure. *Psychological Review, 69,* 415–427.

Mandler, G. (1967). Organization and memory. In K. W. Spence & J. T. Spence (Eds.), *The psychology of learning and motivation* (Vol. 1). New York: Academic Press.

Mandler, G. (1974). Memory storage and retrieval: Some limits on the reach of attention and consciousness. In P. M. A. Rabbit & S. Dornic (Eds.), *Attention and performance V.* London: Academic Press.

Mandler, G. (1975a). Consciousness: Respectable, useful, and probably necessary. In R. L. Solso (Ed.), *Information processing and cognitive psychology.* Hillsdale, NJ: Erlbaum.

Mandler, G. (1975b). *Mind and emotion.* New York: Wiley.

Mandler, G. (1983). Representation and recall in infancy. In J. H. Flavell & E. M. Markman (Eds.), *Handbook of child psychology: Cognitive development* (Vol. 3). New York: Wiley.

Mandler, G. (1984). Consciousness, imagery, and emotion—with special reference to autonomic imagery. *Journal of Mental Imagery, 8*(4), 87– 94.

Mandler, J. M. (1984). *Mind and body: Psychology of emotion and stress.* New York: Norton.

Mandler, J. M. (1984). Representation and recall in infancy. In M. Moscovitch (Ed.), *Infant memory.* New York: Plenum Press.

Mandler, J. M. (1990). A new perspective on cognitive development in infancy. *American Scientist, 78,* 236–243.

Mandler, J. M. (1998). Babies think before they speak. *Human Development, 41*(2), 116–126.

Mandler, J. M. (2000). Perceptual and conceptual processes in infancy. *Journal of Cognition and Development, 1,* 3–36.

Mandler, J. M., & Bauer, P. J. (1988). The cradle of categorization: Is the basic level basic? *Cognitive Development, 3,* 247–264.

Mandler, J. M., & DeForest, M. (1979). Is there more than one way to recall a story? *Child Development, 44,* 697–700.

Mandler, J. M., & Johnson, N. S. (1977). Remembrance of things parsed: Story structure and recall. *Cognitive Psychology, 9,* 111–151.

Mandler, J. M., & McDonough, L. (1998). Studies in inductive inference in infancy. *Cognitive Psychology, 37,* 60–96.

Mangan, B. (1993). Taking phenomenology seriously: The "fringe" and its implications for cognitive research. *Consciousness and Cognition, 2*(2), 89–108.

Manro, H. M., & Washburn, M. F. (1908). The effect of imperceptible lines on the judgment of distance. *American Journal of Psychology, 19,* 242–243.

Mantyla, T. (1986). Optimizing cue effectiveness: Recall of 500 and 600 incidentally learned words. *Journal of Experimental Psychology: Learning, Memory, and Cognition, 12,* 66–71.

Mäntysalo, S., & Näätänen, R. (1987). The duration of neuronal trace of an auditory stimulus as indicated by event-related potentials. *Biological Psychology, 24,* 183–195.

Marcel, A. (1983). Conscious and unconscious perception: Experiments on visual masking and word recognition. *Cognitive Psychology, 15,* 238–300.

Marcel, A. J. (1983). Conscious and unconscious perception: Experiments on visual masking and word recognition. *Cognitive Psychology, 15,* 197–237.

Markus, H. (1977). Self-schemata and processing information about the self. *Journal of Personality and Social Psychology, 35,* 63–78.

Marr, D. (1982). *Vision.* San Francisco: Freeman.

Massaro, D. W. (1972). Preperceptual images, processing time, and perceptual units in auditory perception. *Psychological Review, 79*(2), 124–145.

Massaro, D. W. (1975). *Experimental psychology and information processing.* Chicago: Rand McNally.

Massaro, D. W. (1987). *Speech perception by ear and eye: A paradigm for psychological inquiry.* Hillsdale, NJ: Erlbaum.

Massaro, D. W., & Hestand J. (1983). Developmental relations between reading ability and knowledge of orthographic structure. *Contemporary Educational Psychology, 8,* 174–180.

Massaro, D. W., & Schmuller, J. (1975). Visual features, preperceptual storage, and processing time in reading. In D. Massaro (Ed.), *Understanding language.* New York: Academic Press.

Matthews, W. A. (1968). Transformational complexity and short-term recall. *Language and Speech, 11,* 120–128.

Mattingly, I. G. (1972). Speech cues and sign stimuli. *American Scientist, 60,* 327–337.

Maxwell, W. (Ed.). (1983). *Thinking: The expanding frontier.* Philadelphia: Franklin Institute Press.

May, J. (1989, May). Mental imagery and sports. *Psychology Today,* pp. 23–24.

Mayer, R. E. (1981). *The promise of cognitive psychology.* San Francisco: Freeman.

Mayer, R. E. (1983). *Thinking, problem solving, cognition.* San Francisco: Freeman.

McBurney, D., & Collings, V. (1977). *Introduction to sensation/perception.* Englewood Cliffs, NJ: Prentice-Hall.

McCarthy, D. (1954). Language development in children. In L. Carmichael (Ed.), *Manual of child psychology* (pp. 492–630). New York: Wiley.

McCarthy, G., Blamire, A. M., Rothman, D. L., Gruetier, R., & Shulman, R. G. (1993). *Proceedings of the National Academy of Sciences, 90,* 49–52.

McCaul, K. D., & Maki, R. H. (1984). Self-reference versus desirability ratings and memory for traits. *Journal of Personality and Social Psychology, 47,* 953–955.

McClelland, J. L. (1981). Retrieving general and specific information from stored knowledge of specifics. *Proceedings of the third annual meeting of the Cognitive Science Society,* 170–172.

McClelland, J. L. (1988). *Parallel distributed processing: Implications for cognition and development.* Technical report AIP-47, Carnegie-Mellon University, Department of Psychology, Pittsburgh, PA.

McClelland, J. L., & Jenkins, E. A., Jr. (1992). Emergence of stages from incremental learning mechanisms: A connectionist approach to cognitive development. In K. Van Lehn (Ed.), *Architectures for intelligence.* Hillsdale, NJ: Erlbaum.

McClelland, J. L., & Rumelhart, D. E. (1981). An interactive activation model of context effects in letter perception: Part 1. An account of basic findings. *Psychological Review, 88,* 375–407.

McClelland, J. L., & Rumelhart, D. E. (1985). Distributed memory and the representation of general and specific information. *Journal of Experimental Psychology: General, 114,* 159–188.

McClelland, J. L., Rumelhart, D. E., & Hinton, G. E. (1986). The appeal of parallel distributed processing. In D. E. Rumelhart, J. L. McClelland, & the PDP Research Group (Eds.), *Parallel distributed processing: Explorations in the microstructure of cognition* (Vol. 1). Cambridge, MA: Bradford.

McConkie, G. W., & Rayner, K. (1973). *The span of the effective stimulus during fixations in reading.* Paper presented at the American Educational Research Association meetings, New Orleans.

McCormack, P. D. (1972). Recognition memory: How complex a retrieval system? *Canadian Journal of Psychology, 24,* 19–41.

McCulloch, W. S., & Pitts, W. (1943). A logical calculus of the ideas imminent in nervous activity. *Bulletin of Mathematical Biophysics, 5,* 115–133.

McDaniel, M. A., & Einstein, G. O. (1986). Bizarre imagery as an effective memory aid: The importance of distinctiveness. *Journal of Experimental Psychology: Learning, Memory, and Cognition, 12*, 54–65.

McGaugh, J. L. (1966). Time dependent processes in memory storage. *Science, 153*, 1351–1358.

McGaugh, J. L. (1990). Significance and remembrance: The role of neuromodulatory systems. *Psychological Science, 1*, 15–25.

McGoech, J. A. (1932). Forgetting and the law of disuse. *Psychological Review, 39*, 352–370.

McKoon, G., Ratcliff, R., & Dell, G. S. (1986). A critical evaluation of the semantic-episodic distinction. *Journal of Experimental Psychology: Learning, Memory, and Cognition, 12*, 295–306.

Mednick, S. A. (1967). *The remote associates test.* Boston: Houghton Mifflin.

Mehler, J. (1963). Some effects of grammatical transformations on the recall of English sentences. *Journal of Verbal Learning and Verbal Behavior, 2*, 346–351.

Melton, A. W. (1963). Implications of short-term memory for a general theory of memory. *Journal of Verbal Learning and Verbal Behavior, 2*, 1–21.

Melton, A. W., & Irwin, J. M. (1940). The influence of degree of interpolated learning on retroactive inhibition and the overt transfer of specific responses. *American Journal of Psychology, 53*, 173–203.

Melton, A. W., & Martin, E. (Eds.). (1972). *Coding processes in human memory.* Washington, DC: Winston.

Meltzoff, A. N., & Borton R. W. (1979). Intermodal matching by human neonates. *Nature, 282*, 403–404.

Metzler, J., & Shepard, R. N. (1974). Transformational studies of the internal representation of three-dimensional objects. In R. L. Solso (Ed.), *Theories in cognitive psychology: The Loyola Symposium.* Hillsdale, NJ: Erlbaum.

Mewhort, D. J. K. (1970). Guessing and the order-of-approximation effect. *American Journal of Psychology, 83*, 439–442.

Meyer, D. E., & Schvaneveldt, R. W. (1971). Facilitation in recognizing pairs of words. Evidence of a dependence between retrieval operations. *Journal of Experimental Psychology, 90*, 227–234.

Meyer, D. E., & Schvaneveldt, R. W. (1976). In C. N. Cofer (Ed.), *The structure of human memory.* San Francisco: Freeman.

Meyer, D. E., Schvaneveldt, R. W., & Ruddy, M. G. (1974a). Functions of graphemic and phonemic codes in visual word-recognition. *Memory and Cognition, 2*(2), 309–321.

Meyer, D. E., Schvaneveldt, R. W., & Ruddy, M. G. (1974b). Loci of contextual effects on visual word recognition. In P. M. A. Rabbit & S. Dornic (Eds.), *Attention and performance V.* London: Academic Press.

Miall, R. C., & Tchalenko, J. (2001). The painter's eye movements: A study of eye and hand movement during portrait painting. *Leonardo, 34*, 35–40.

Miller, G. A. (1951). *Language and communication.* New York: McGraw-Hill.

Miller, G. A. (1956). The magical number seven, plus or minus two: Some limits on our capacity for processing information. *Psychological Review, 63*, 81–97.

Miller, G. A. (1962). *Psychology: The science of mental life.* Harmondsworth UK: Penguin Books.

Miller, G. A. (1979). "A very personal history." Talk to Cognitive Science Workshop, Massachusetts Institute of Technology, Cambridge, MA, June 1. Cited in H. Gardner, *The mind's new science: A history of the cognitive revolution.* New York: Basic Books.

Miller, G. A. (1980). Computation, consciousness, and cognition. *Behavioral and Brain Sciences, 3*, 146.

Miller, G. A. (1992). *The science of words.* New York: Freeman.

Miller, G. A., & Friedman, E. A. (1957). The reconstruction of mutilated English texts. *Information Control, 1*, 38–55.

Miller, G. A., & Isard, S. (1963). Some perceptual consequences of linguistic rules. *Journal of Verbal Learning and Verbal Behavior, 2*, 217–228.

Miller, G. A., & McKean, K. O. (1964). A chronomatic study of some relations between sentences. *Quarterly Journal of Experimental Psychology, 16*, 297–308.

Miller, G. A., Galanter, E., & Pribram, K. H. (1960). *Plans and the structure of behavior.* New York: Holt, Rinehart & Winston.

Miller, J. R., & Kintsch, W. (1980). Readability and recall of short prose passages: A theoretical analysis. *Journal of Experimental Psychology: Human Learning and Memory, 6*, 335–354.

Milner, A. D., & Rugg, M. D. (Eds.). (1992). *The neuropsychology of consciousness.* London: Academic Press.

Milner, B. (1966). Amnesia following operation on the temporal lobes. In C. Whitty & O. Zangwill (Eds.), *Amnesia* (pp. 109–133). London: Butterworth.

Milner, B. (1968). Visual recognition and recall after temporal-lobe excision in man. *Neuropsychologia, 6*, 191–209.

Milner, B., Petrides, M., & Smith, M. L. (1985). Frontal lobes and the temporal organization of memory. *Human Neurobiology, 4,* 137–142.

Minsky, M. (1975). A framework for representing knowledge. In P. Winston (Ed.), *The psychology of computer vision.* New York: McGraw-Hill.

Minsky, M. (1994, October). Will robots inherit the earth? *Scientific American,* pp. 109–113.

Minsky, M., & Papert, S. (1968). *Perceptions.* Cambridge, MA: MIT Press.

Moe, A. & Di Beni, R. (2005). Stressing the efficacy of the Loci method: Oral *Applied Cognitive Psychology* 19(1), 95–106 presentation and the subject-generation of the Loci pathway with expository messages.

Mondloch, C. J., Lewis, T. L., Budreau, D. R., Maurer, D., Dannemiller, J. L., Stephens, B. R., et al. (1999). Face perception during early infancy. *Psychological Science, 10,* 419–422.

Monty, R. A., & Senders, J. W. (Eds.). (1983). *Eye movement and psychological processes.* Hillsdale, NJ: Erlbaum.

Moray, N. (1959). Attention in dichotic listening: Affective cues and the influence of instructions. *Quarterly Journal of Experimental Psychology, 11,* 56–60.

Moray, N. (1969). *Attention: Selective processes in vision and audition.* New York: Academic Press.

Moray, N. (1970). *Listening and attention.* London: Penguin.

Moray, N., & O'Brien, T. (1967). Signal detection theory applied to selective listening. *Journal of Acoustical Society of America, 42,* 765–772.

Moray, N., Bates, A., & Barnett, T. (1965). Experiments on the four-eared man. *Journal of the Acoustical Society of America, 38,* 196–201.

Morris, P. E., Fritz, C. O., Jackson, L., Nichol, E., & Roberts, E. (2005). Strategies for learning proper names: Expanding retrieval practice, meaning, and imagery. *Applied Cognitive Psychology, 19,* 779–798.

Morris, P. E., Fritz, C. O., Jackson, L., Nichol, E., & Roberts, E. (2005). Strategies for learning proper names: Expanding retrieval practice, meaning and imagery. *Applied Cognitive Psychology, 19*(6), 779–798.

Morrison, F. J., Holmes, D. L., & Haith, M. M. (1974). A developmental study of the effect of familiarity on short-term visual memory. *Journal of Experimental Child Psychology, 18,* 412–425.

Morton, J. (1969). Interaction of information in word recognition. *Psychological Review, 76,* 165–178.

Morton, J. (1970). A functional model of memory. In D. A. Norman (Ed.), *Models of human memory.* New York: Academic Press.

Morton, J. (1979). Word recognition. In J. Morton & J. C. Marshall (Eds.), *Psycholinguistics: Vol. 2. Structure and Processes,* 107–156. London: Elek.

Morton, J. (1980). The logogen model and orthographic structure. In U. Frith (Ed.), *Cognitive processes in spelling.* London: Academic Press.

Morton, J. (1981). The status of information processing models of language. *Philosophic transactions of the Royal Society of London, B, 295,* 387–396.

Moscovitch, M. (Ed.). (1984). *Infant memory.* New York: Plenum.

Mountcastle, V. B. (1978). Brain mechanisms of directed attention. *Journal of the Royal Society of Medicine, 71,* 14–27.

Mountcastle, V. B. (1979). An organizing principle for cerebral function: The unit module and the distributed system. In F. O. Schmitt (Ed.), *The neurosciences: Fourth study program.* Cambridge, MA: The MIT Press.

Mowrer, O. H. (1954). The psychologist looks at language. *American Psychologist, 9,* 660–694.

Müeller, G. E., & Pilzecker, A. (1990). Experimentelle Beitrage zur Lehre vom Gedachtnis. *Zeitshrift für Psychologie,* Ergbd. 1.

Mueller, M. (1974). Cited in N. Chaudhuri, *Scholar extraordinary,* London: Chatto & Windus.

Murch, G. M. (1973). *Visual and auditory perception.* Indianapolis, IN: Bobbs-Merrill.

Murdock, B. B. (1965). Signal-detection theory and short term memory. *Journal of Experimental Psychology, 70,* 443–447.

Murdock, B. B. (1971). Four channel effects in short-term memory. *Psychonomic Science, 24,* 197–198.

Murdock, B. B. (1983). A distributed memory model for serial-order information. *Psychological Review, 90,* 316–338.

Mussen, P. M. (Ed.). (1970). *Carmichael's manual of child psychology.* New York: Wiley.

Mussweiler, T. (2006). Doing is for thinking!: Stereotype activation by stereotypic movements. *Psychological science 17*(1), 17–21.

Myers, R. E., & Sperry, T. W. (1953). Interocular transfer of the visual form discrimination habit in cats after section of the optic chiasm and corpus callosum. *Anatomical Record, 175,* 351–352.

Myers, T., Laver, J., & Anderson, J. R. (Eds.). (1981). *The cognitive representation of speech.* Amsterdam: North-Holland.

Näätänen, R. (1985). Selective attention and stimulus processing: Reflections in event-related potentials, magnetoencephalogram, and regional cerebral blood flow. In M. I. Posner & O. S. Marin (Eds.), *Attention and performance* (Vol. II, pp. 355–373). Hillsdale, NJ: Erlbaum.

Nagourney, E. (2001, April 10). *Geography of dyslexia explored.* The New York Times, p. 07.

Naqvi, N. H., Rudrauf, D., Damasio, H. & Bechara, A. (2007). Damage to the insula disrupts addiction to cigarette smoking. *Science, 315*(5811), 531–534.

Natsoulas, T. (1978). Consciousness. *American Psychologist, 33,* 906–914.

Nehrke, M. F. (1972). Age, sex and educational differences in syllogistic reasoning. *Journal of Gerontology, 27,* 966–970.

Neimark, E. D. (1987). *Adventures in thinking.* San Diego, CA: Harcourt Brace Jovanovich.

Neimark, E. D., & Santa, J. L. (1975). Thinking and concept attainment. *Annual Review of Psychology* (Vol. 26). Palo Alto, CA: Annual Reviews.

Neisser, U. (1967). *Cognitive psychology.* New York: Appleton-Century-Crofts.

Neisser, U. (1969). *Selective reading: A method for the study of visual attention.* Paper presented at the 19th International Congress of Psychology, London.

Neisser, U. (1976). *Cognition and reality: Principles and implications of cognitive psychology.* San Francisco: Freeman.

Neisser, U. (Ed.). (1982a). *Memory observed.* San Francisco: Freeman.

Neisser, U. (1982b). Snapshots or benchmarks? In U. Neisser (Ed.), *Memory observed.* San Francisco: Freeman.

Neisser, U., & Becklen, R. (1975). Selective looking: Attending to visually significant events. *Cognitive Psychology, 7,* 480–494.

Neisser, U., & Weene, P. (1962). Hierarchies in concept attainment. *Journal of Experimental Psychology, 64,* 640–645.

Neumann, P. G. (1977). Visual prototype formation with discontinuous representation of dimensions of variability. *Memory and Cognition, 5,* 187–197.

Neville, H. J. (1995). Developmental specificity in neurocognitive development in humans. In M. S. Gazzaniga (Ed.) *The cognitive neurosciences.* Cambridge, MA: MIT Press.

Newell, A. (1967). *Studies in problem solving: Subject 3 on the crypt-arithmetic task. DONALD plus GER-ALD equals ROBERT.* Pittsburgh: Carnegie Mellon Institute.

Newell, A. (1973). Artificial intelligence and the concept of mind. In R. C. Schank & C. M. Colby (Eds.), *Computer models of thought and language.* San Francisco: Freeman.

Newell, A. (1990). *Unified theories of cognition.* Cambridge, MA: Harvard University Press.

Newell, A., & Simon, H. A. (1956). The logic theory machine: A complex information processing system. *IRE Transactions of Information Theory, IT-2*(3), 61–79.

Newell, A., & Simon, H. A. (1963). GPS, a program that stimulates human thought. In E. A. Feigenbaum & J. Feldman (Eds.), *Computers and thought.* New York: McGraw-Hill.

Newell, A., & Simon, H. A. (1972). *Human problem solving.* Englewood Cliffs, NJ: Prentice-Hall.

Newell, A., Shaw, J. C., & Simon, H. A. (1960). Report on a general problem-solving program. In W. R. Reitman (Ed.), *Proceedings of the International Conference on Information Processing* (pp. 256–264). Paris: UNESCO.

Newell, A., Simon, H. A., & Shaw, J. C. (1958). Elements of a theory of human problem solving. *Psychological Review, 65,* 151–166.

Newman, J., & Baars, B. J. (1993). A neural attentional model for access to consciousness: A Global Workspace perspective. *Concepts in Neuroscience, 4*(2), 255–290.

Ng, M., Ciaramitaro, V. M, Anstis, S., Boynton, G. M., & Fine, I. (2006). Selectivity for the configural cues that identify gender, ethnicity, and identity in the human cortex. *PNAS, 103*(51), 19552–19557.

Nickerson, R. S. (1965). Short-term memory for complex meaningful visual configurations: A demonstration of capacity. *Canadian Journal of Psychology, 19,* 155–160.

Nickerson, R. S. (1968). A note on long-term recognition memory for picture material. *Psychonomic Science, 11,* 58.

Nickerson, R. S., Perkins, D. N., & Smith, E. E. (1985). *The teaching of thinking.* Hillsdale, NJ: Erlbaum.

Nisbett, R. E., & Ross, L. (1980). *Human preferences: Strategies and shortcomings of social judgment.* Englewood Cliffs, NJ: Prentice-Hall.

Noe, A. and Thompson, E. Sorting out the neural basis of consciousness. Authors reply to commentators, *Journal of Consciousness Studies,* 11 (2004): 87–98.

Norman, D. A. (1966b). Memory and decisions. *Proceedings of Symposium on Memory and Attention, 18th International Congress of Psychology,* Moscow.

Norman, D. A. (1968). Toward a theory of memory and attention. *Psychological Review, 75,* 522–536.

Norman, D. A. (1969). Memory while shadowing. *Quarterly Journal of Experimental Psychology, 21,* 85–93.

Norman, D. A. (1976). *Memory and attention* (2nd ed.). New York: Wiley.

Norman, D. A., & Rumelhart, E. E. (1975). *Exploration in cognition.* San Francisco: Freeman.

Norman, D. A., & Shallice, T. (1986). Attention to action: Willed and automatic control of behavior. In R. Davidson, G. E. Schwartz, & D. Shapiro (Eds.), *Consciousness and self-regulation* (Vol. 4, pp. 11–28). New York: Plenum Press.

Norman, D. A., & Wicklegren, W. A. (1965). Short-term recognition memory for single digits. *Journal of Experimental Psychology, 70,* 479–489.

Norman, G. R., Brooks, L. R., & Allen, S. W. (1989). Recall by expert medical practitioners and novices as a record of processing attention. *Journal of Experimental Psychology: Learning Memory and Cognition, 15,* 1166–1174.

Norton, D., & Stark, L. (1971). Eye movements and visual perception. *Scientific American, 224,* 34–43.

Oakley, D. A. (1981). Brain mechanisms of mammalian memory. *British Medical Bulletin, 37,* 175–180.

O'Brien, E. J., & Wolford, C. R. (1982). Effect of delay in testing on retention of plausible versus bizarre mental images. *Journal of Experimental Psychology: Learning, Memory, and Cognition, 8,* 148–153.

Ojemann, G. A. (1991). Cortical organization of language. *Journal of Neuroscience, 11,* 2281–2287.

Oldfield, R. C. (194). Memory mechanisms and the theory of schemata. *British Journal of Psychology, 43,* 14–23.

Olson, G. M. (1977). An information-processing analysis of visual memory and habituation in infants. In T. J. Tighe & R. H. Leaton (Eds.), *Habituation: Perspectives from child development, animal behavior and neurophysiology.* Hillsdale, NJ: Erlbaum.

Ornstein, P. A. (Ed.). (1978). *Memory development in children.* Hillsdale, NJ: Erlbaum.

Ornstein, P. A., Naus, M. J., & Liberty, C. (1975). Rehearsal and organizational processes in children's memory. *Child Development, 45,* 818–830.

Ornstein, R. (1991). *The evolution of consciousness: The origins of the way we think.* New York: Simon & Schuster.

Ornstein, R. E. (1972). *The psychology of consciousness.* San Francisco: Freeman. (Also published by Viking, 1972.)

Ornstein, R. E. (1973). *The nature of human consciousness.* San Francisco: Freeman. (Also published by Viking, 1973).

Ornstein, R. E. (1977). *The psychology of consciousness.* New York: Harcourt Brace Jovanovich.

Ornstein, R., & Thompson, R. F. (1985). *The amazing brain.* Los Altos, CA: ISHK Book Service.

Osterberg, G. A. (1935). Topography of the layer of rods and cones in the human retina. *Acta Ophthalmologica, Suppl. 6, 61,* 1–102.

Owen, F. W., Adams, P. A., Forrest, T., Stolz, L. M., & Fischer, S. (1971). Learning disorders in children: Sibling studies. *Monographs of the Society for Research in Child Development, 36*(4, serial no. 144).

Paivio, A. (1965). Abstractness, imagery, and meaningfulness in paired-associated learning. *Journal of Verbal Learning and Verbal Behavior, 4,* 32–38.

Paivio, A. (1969). Mental imagery in associative learning and memory. *Psychological Review, 76,* 241–263.

Paivio, A. (1971). Imagery and deep structure in the recall of English nominalizations. *Journal of Verbal Learning and Verbal Behavior, 10,* 1–12.

Paivio, A. (1975). Perceptual comparisons through the mind's eye. *Memory and Cognition, 3,* 635–647.

Paivio, A., & Csapo, K. (1969). Concrete-image and verbal memory codes. *Journal of Experimental Psychology, 80,* 279–285.

Paivio, A., Smythe, P. C., & Yuille, J. C. (1968). Imagery versus meaningfulness of norms in paired-associate learning. *Canadian Journal of Psychology, 22,* 427–441.

Paivio, A., Yuille, J. C., & Madigan, S. A. (1968). Concreteness, imagery and meaningfulness values for 925 nouns. *Journal of Experimental Psychology Monograph Supplement, 76*(1), part 2.

Palmer, S. E. (1975a). The effects of contextual scenes on the identification of objects. *Memory and Cognition, 3,* 519–526.

Palmer, S. E. (1975b). Visual perception and world knowledge: Notes on a model of sensory cognitive interaction. In D. A. Norman, D. E. Rumelhart, & the LNR Research Group, *Explorations in cognition.* San Francisco: Freeman.

Palmer, S. E. (1989). Reference frames in the perception of shape and orientation. In B. E. Shepp & S. Ballesteros (Eds.), *Object perception: Structure & process.* Hillsdale, NJ: Erlbaum.

Palmer, S. E. (1999). *Vision science: Photons to phenomenology.* Cambridge, MA: MIT Press.

Palmer, S. E., Rosch, E., & Chase, P. (1981). Canonical perspective and the perception of objects. In J. Long & A. Baddeley (Eds.), *Attention and performance IX.* Hillsdale, NJ: Erlbaum.

Pardo, J. V., Fox, P. T., & Raichle, M. E. (1991). Localization of a human system for sustained attention by positron emission tomography. *Nature, 349,* 61–64.

Parkin, A. J. (1993). *Memory: Phenomena, experiment and theory.* Oxford: Blackwell.

Pashler, H. (1993). Doing two things at the same time. *American Scientist, 81,* 48–55.

Pear, T. H. (1922). *Remembering and forgetting.* London: Methuen.

Penfield, W. (1959). The interpretive cortex. *Science, 129,* 1719–1725.

Penfield, W., & Jasper, H. H. (1954). *Epilepsy and the functional anatomy of the human brain.* Boston: Little, Brown.

Penfield, W., & Roberts, L. (1959). *Speech and brain mechanism.* Princeton, NJ: Princeton University Press.

Petersen, S. E., & Fiez, J. A. (1993). The processing of single words studied with positron emission tomography. *Annual Review of Neuroscience, 16,* 509–530.

Petersen, S. E., Fox, P. T., Posner, M. I., Mintun, M., & Raichle, M. E. (1988). Positron emission tomographic studies of the cortical anatomy of single word processing. *Nature, 331,* 585–589.

Petersen, S. E., Fox, P. T., Snyder, A. Z., & Raichle, M. E. (1990). Activation of extrastriate and frontal cortical areas by visual words and word-like stimuli. *Science, 249,* 1041–1044.

Peterson, L. R., & Peterson, M. J. (1959). Short-term retention of individual verbal items. *Journal of Experimental Psychology, 58,* 193–198.

Peterson, M. T., Meagher, R. B., Jr., Chait, H., & Gillie, S. (1973). The abstraction and generalization of dot patterns. *Cognitive Psychology, 4,* 378–398.

Peterson, M.J., R.B. Meagher, Jr., H. Chait, and S. Gillie. 1973. The abstraction and generalization of dot patterns. *Cognitive Psychology,* 4:378–398.

Pew, R. W. (1974). Levels of analysis in motor control. *Brain Research, 71,* 393–400.

Phillips, W. A. (1974). On the distinction between sensory storage and short-term visual memory. *Perception and Psychophysics, 16,* 283–390.

Phillips, W. A., & Baddeley, A. D. (1971). Reaction time and short-term visual memory. *Psychonomic Science, 22,* 73–74.

Philpott, A., & Wilding, J. (1979). Semantic interference from subliminal stimuli in a dichoptic viewing situation. *British Journal of Psychology, 70,* 559–563.

Piaget, J. (1926). *The language and thought of the child.* New York: Harcourt Brace.

Piaget, J. (1952a). *The child's conception of number.* New York: Humanities Press.

Piaget, J. (1952b). *The origins of intelligence in children.* New York: International Universities Press.

Piaget, J. (1970). Piaget's theory. In P. H. Mussen (Ed.), *Carmichael's manual of child psychology* (Vol. 1, pp. 703–732). New York: Wiley.

Piaget, J., & Inhelder, B. (1941). *Le developpement des quantites chez l'enfant.* Neuchatel: Delachaux et Niestle.

Piaget, J., & Inhelder, B. (1956). *The child's conception of space.* London: Routledge & Kegan Paul.

Piaget, J., & Inhelder, B. (1973). *Memory and intelligence.* New York: Basic Books.

Pick, A. D. (1975). *The development of strategies of attention.* Paper presented at the biennial meeting of the Society for Research in Child Development, Denver.

Pick, A. D., Christy, M. D., & Frankel, G. W. (1972). A developmental study of visual selective attention. *Journal of Experimental Child Psychology, 11,* 165–175.

Pick, H. L., Jr., & Saltzman, E. (Eds.). (1978). *Modes of perceiving and processing information.* Hillsdale, NJ: Erlbaum.

Pierce, J. R. (1961). *Symbols, signals and noise.* New York: Harper & Row.

Pierce, J. R. (1968). *Science, art and communication.* New York: Clarkson N. Potter.

Pierson, L., & Trout, M. (2005) *What is consciousness for?* Available at: http://cogprints.org/4482/01/whatisconsciousnessfor.pdf

Pillsbury, W. B. (1897). A study in apperception. *American Journal of Psychology, 8,* 315–393.

Pinker, S. (1980). Mental imagery and the third dimension. *Journal of Experimental Psychology: General, 109,* 354–371.

Pinker, S. (1994). *The language instinct.* New York: Morrow.

Pinker, S. (1997). *How the mind works.* New York: Norton.

Pinker, S. (Ed.). (1985). *Visual cognition.* Cambridge, MA: MIT Press.

Place, U. T. (1956). Is consciousness a brain process? *British Journal of Psychology, 47,* 44–50.

Plihal W. & Born J. (1997). Effects of early and late nocturnal sleep on Declarative and Procedure memory. *The Journal of Cognitive NeuroScience 9,* 534–547.

Plomin, R., & DeFries, J. C. (1998). The genetics of cognitive abilities and disabilities. *Scientific American,* May, 62–69.

Podgorny, P., & Shepard, R. N. (1978). Functional representations common to visual perception and imagination. *Journal of Experimental Psychology: Human Perception and Performance, 4,* 21–35.

Poincaré, H. (1913). Mathematical creation. In *The foundations of science* (G. H. Halstead, Trans.). New York: Science Press.

Pollock, J. (1998). *How to build a person.* Cambridge, MA: MIT Press.

Porth, C. M. (1986). *Pathophysiology.* Philadelphia: Lippincott.

Posner, M. I. (1969). Abstraction and the process of recognition. In J. T. Spence & G. H. Bower (Eds.), The *psychology of learning and motivation: Advances in learning and motivation* (Vol. 3). New York: Academic Press.

Posner, M. I. (1973). *Cognition: An introduction.* Glenview, IL: Scott, Foresman.

Posner, M. I. (1988). Structures and functions of selective attention. In T. Boll & B. Bryant (Eds.), *Master lectures in clinical neuropsychology* (pp. 173– 202). Washington, DC: American Psychological Association.

Posner, M. I. (1992). Attention as a cognitive and neural system. *Current Directions in Psychological Science, 1,* 11–14.

Posner, M. I. (Ed.). (1989). *Foundations of cognitive science.* Cambridge, MA: MIT Press.

Posner, M. I., & Boies, S. J. (1971). Components of attention. *Psychological Review, 78,* 391–408.

Posner, M. I., & Keele, S. W. (1967). Decay of visual information from a single letter. *Science, 158,* 137–139.

Posner, M. I., & Keele, S. W. (1968). On the genesis of abstract ideas. *Journal of Experimental Psychology, 77,* 353–363.

Posner, M. I., & Konick, A. F. (1966). On the role of interference in short-term memory. *Journal of Experimental Psychology, 72,* 221–231.

Posner, M. I., & Petersen, S. E. (1990). The attention system in the human brain. *Annual Review of Neuroscience, 13,* 25–42.

Posner, M. I., & Raichle, M. E. (1994). *Images of mind.* New York: Scientific American Library.

Posner, M. I., & Rothbart, M. K. (1989). Intentional chapters on unintended thoughts. In J. S. Uleman & John A. Bargh (Eds.), *Unintended thought.* New York: Guilford Press.

Posner, M. I., & Rothbart, M. K. (1991). Attentional mechanism and conscious experience. In *The neuropsychology of consciousness* (pp. 92–111). New York: Academic Press.

Posner, M. I., & Snyder, C. R. R. (1974). Attention and cognitive control. In R. L. Solso (Ed.), *Information processing and cognition: The Loyola Symposium.* Hillsdale, NJ: Erlbaum.

Posner, M. I., & Snyder, C. R. R. (1975). Facilitation and inhibition in the processing of signals. In P. M. A. Rabbit & S. Dornic (Eds.), *Attention and performance V.* London: Academic Press.

Posner, M. I., & Warren, R. E. (1972). Traces, concepts, and conscious constructions. In A. W. Melton & E. Martin (Eds.), *Coding process in human memory.* Washington, DC: Winston.

Posner, M. I., Boies, S. J., Eichelman, W., & Taylor, R. L. (1969). Retention of visual and name codes of single letters. *Journal of Experimental Psychology Monographs, 79,* 1–16.

Posner, M. I., Early, T. S., Reiman, E. M., Pardo, P. J., & Dhawan, M. (1988). Asymmetries in hemispheric control of attention in schizophrenia. *Archives of General Psychiatry, 45,* 814–826.

Posner, M. I., Goldsmith, R., & Welton, K. E., Jr. (1967). Perceived distance and the classification of distorted patterns. *Journal of Experimental Psychology 73,* 28–38.

Posner, M. I., Petersen, S. E., Fox, P. I., & Raichle, M. E. (1988). Localization of cognitive operations in the human brain. *Science, 240,* 1627–1631.

Posner, M. I., Sandson, J., Dhawan, M., & Shulman, G. L. (1989). Is word recognition automatic: A cognitive-anatomical approach. *Journal of Cognitive Neuroscience, 1,* 50–60.

Posner, M.I., Petersen, S.E., Fox, P.T., & Raichle, M. E. (1988). Localization of cognitive operations in the human brain. *Science, 240,* 1627–1631.

Potter, R. K., Kopp, G. A., & Kopp, H. G. (1966). *Visible speech.* New York: Dover.

Poudion, E. C. (1962). Peripheral vision, refractoriness, and eye movements in fast oral readings. *British Journal of Psychology, 53,* 409–419.

Pratkanis, A. R., & Greenwald, A. G. (1988). Recent perspectives on unconscious processing: Still no marketing applications. *Psychology and Marketing, 5,* 337–353.

Premack, D. (1976). Language and intelligence in ape and man. *American Scientist, 64,* 674–683.

Pribram, K. H. (1971). *Languages of the brain: Experimental paradoxes and principles in neuropsychology.* Englewood Cliffs, NJ: Prentice-Hall.

Pribram, K. H. (1986). The cognitive revolution and mind/brain issues. *American Psychologist, 41,* 507–520.

Pylyshyn, Z. W. (1973). What the mind's eye tells the mind's brain: A critique of mental imagery. *Psychological Bulletin, 80,* 1–24.

Pylyshyn, Z. W. (1980). The "casual power" of machines. *Behavioral and Brain Sciences, 3,* 442–444.

Pylyshyn, Z. W. (1981). The imagery debate: Analogue media versus tacit knowledge. *Psychological Review, 88,* 16–45.

Pylyshyn, Z. W. (1986). *Computation and cognition: Toward a foundation for cognitive science.* Cambridge, MA: MIT Press.

Quillian, M. R. (1968). Semantic memory. In M. Minsky (Ed.), *Semantic information processing.* Cambridge, MA: MIT Press.

Quillian, M. R. (1969). The teachable language comprehender: A simulation program and theory of language. *Communication of the Association for Computing Machinery, 12.*

Rachlin, H., Logue, Q. W., Gibbon, J., & Frankel, M. (1986). Cognition and behavior in studies of choice. *Psychological Review, 93,* 35–45.

Raichle, M. E. (1994). Visualizing the mind. *Scientific American, 270,* 58–63.

Raichle, M. E., Fiez, J. A., Videen, T. O., MacLeod, A. K., Pardo, J. V., Fox, P. T., et al. (1994). Practice-related changes in human brain functional anatomy during nonmotor learning. *Cerebral Cortex, 4*(1), 8–26.

Ramachandran, V. S. (1987). Visual perception of surfaces: A biological theory. In S. Petry & G. E. Meyer (Eds.), *The perception of illusory contours* (pp. 93–108). New York: Springer-Verlag.

Raney, G. E., & Rayner, K. (1993). Event-related brain potentials, eye movements, and readings. *Psychological Science, 4,* 283–286.

Raphael, B. (1976). *The thinking computer.* San Francisco: Freeman.

Ratcliff, R., & McKoon, G. (1986). More on the distinction between episodic and semantic memories. *Journal of Experimental Psychology: Learning, Memory, and Cognition, 12,* 312–313.

Raugh, M. R., & Atkinson, R. C. (1975). A mnemonic method for learning a second-language vocabulary. *Journal of Educational Psychology, 67,* 1–16.

Rayner, K. (1975). The perceptual span and peripheral cues in reading. *Cognitive Psychology, 7,* 65–81.

Rayner, K. (1978). Eye movements in reading and information processing. *Psychological Bulletin, 85,* 618–660.

Rayner, K. (1980). Personal communication cited by R. G. Crowder in "The demise of short-term memory." *Acta Psychologica, 50,* 1982, 292–323.

Rayner, K. (1993). Eye movements in reading: Recent developments. *Current Directions in Psychological Science, 2,* 81–85.

Rayner, K., & Frazier, L. (1989). Selection mechanisms in reading lexically ambiguous words. *Journal of Experimental Psychology: Learning, Memory, and Cognition, 15,* 779–790.

Rayner, K., & Morris, R. K. (1992). Eye movement control in reading: Evidence against semantic pre-processing. *Journal of Experimental Psychology: Human Perception and Performance, 18,* 163–172.

Rayner, K., & Pollatsek, A. (1987). Eye movements in reading: A tutorial review. In M. Coltheart (Ed.), *Attention and performance XII: The psychology of reading.* London: Erlbaum.

Rayner, K., & Pollatsek, A. (1989). *The psychology of reading.* Englewood Cliffs, NJ: Prentice Hall.

Rayner, K., & Posnansky, C. (1978). Stages of processing in word identification. *Journal of Experimental Psychology: General, 107,* 64–81.

Rayner, K., Sereno, S. C., Morris, R. K., Schmauder, A. R., & Clifton, C. (1989). Eye movements and on-line language comprehension processes. *Language and Cognitive Processes, 4* (Special Issue), 21–50.

Reber, A. S., & Scarborough, D. L. (Eds.). (1977). *Toward a psychology of reading.* Hillsdale, NJ: Erlbaum.

Ree, M. J., & Earles, J. A. (1992). Intelligence is the best predictor of job performance. *Current Directions in Psychological Science, 1,* 86–89.

Reed, S. K. (1972). Pattern recognition and categorization. *Cognitive Psychology, 3,* 382–407.

Reed, S. K. (1973). *Psychological processes in pattern recognition.* New York: Academic Press.

Rees, A., Beal, M. K., & Solso, R. L. (1993, April). *Prototype formation in right and left hemispheres.* Paper presented at the annual meeting of WPA/RMPA, Phoenix, AZ.

Reicher, G. M. (1969). Perceptual recognition as a function of meaningfulness of stimuli material. *Journal of Experimental Psychology, 81,* 275–280.

Reitman, J. S., & Bower, G. H. (1973). Storage and later recognition of exemplars of concepts. *Cognitive Psychology, 4,* 194–206.

Reitman, W. R. (1965). *Cognition and thought: An information-processing approach.* New York: Wiley.

Reitman, W. R., Grove, R. B., & Shoup, R. G. (1964). Argus: An information-processing model of thinking. *Behavioral Science, 9,* 270–281.

Restak, R. M. (1988). *The mind.* New York: Bantam.

Restle, F. A. (1955). A theory of discrimination learning. *Psychological Review, 62,* 11–19.

Restorff, V. H. (1933). Über die Wirkung von Bereichsbildungen im Spurenfeld. *Psychologie Forschurg, 18,* 299–342.

Reutner, D. B. (1972). Class shift, symbolic shift, and background shift in short-term memory. *Journal of Experimental Psychology, 93,* 90–94.

Reynolds, D. (1964). Effects of double stimulation: Temporal inhibition of response. *Psychological Bulletin, 62,* 333–347.

Richardson, A. (1969). *Mental imagery.* New York: Springer.

Riley, C. A. (1975). *Representation and use of comparative information and inference making in young children.* Unpublished doctoral dissertation, Princeton University.

Riley, C. A., & Trabasso, T. (1974). Comparatives, logical structures and encoding in a transitive reference task. *Journal of Experimental Child Psychology, 17,* 187–203.

Riley, K. P., Snowdon, D. A., Desrosiers, M. F., & Markesbery W. R. (2005) Early life linguistic ability, late life cognitive function, and neuropathology: Findings from the Study *Neurobiology of Aging* 26(3), 341–347.

Rips, L. J. (1975). Inductive judgments about natural categories. *Journal of Verbal Learning and Verbal Behavior, 14,* 665–681.

Rips, L. J. (1998). Reasoning and conversation. *Psychological Review, 105,* 441–441.

Rips, L. J., Brem, S. K., & Bailenson, J. N. (1999). Reasoning dialogues. *Current Directions in Psychological Science, 8,* 172–177.

Rips, L. J., Shoben, E. J., & Smith, E. E. (1973). Semantic distance and the verification of semantic relations. *Journal of Verbal Learning and Verbal Behavior, 14,* 665–681.

Risberg, J. (1987). Development of high-resolution two-dimensional measurement of regional cerebral blood flow. In J. Wade, S. Knezevik, V. A. Maxim-ilian, Z. Mubrin, & I. Prohovnik (Eds.), *Impact of functional imaging in neurology and psychiatry.* London: Libbey.

Risberg, J. (1989). Regional cerebral blood flow measurements with high temporal and spatial resolution. In D. Ottoson (Ed.), *Visualization of brain functions* London: Macmillan.

Roberge, J. J. (1972). Effects of structure and semantics on the solution of pure hypothetical syllogisms. *Journal of General Psychology, 87,* 161–167.

Rock, I. (1983). *The logic of perception.* Cambridge, MA: MIT Press.

Rock, I. (1984). *Perception.* New York: Scientific American.

Rock, I., & Ebenholtz, S. (1962). Stroboscopic movement based on change of phenomenal rather than retinal location. *American Journal of Psychology, 75,* 193–207.

Roe, A. (1946). The personality of artists. *Educational Psychology Measurement, 6,* 401–408.

Roe, A. (1953). *The making of a scientist.* New York: Dodd, Mead.

Roediger, H. L. (1980). Memory metaphors in cognitive psychology. *Memory and Cognition, 8,* 231–252.

Roediger, H. L., & Craik, F. I. M. (Eds.). (1989). *Varieties of memory and consciousness: Essays in honor of Endel Tulving.* Hillsdale, NJ: Erlbaum.

Roediger, H. L., & McDermott, K. B. (1993). Retrieval blocks in episodic and semantic memory. *Canadian Journal of Psychology, 36,* 213–242.

Roediger, H.L. III, & McDermott, K.B. (1995). Creating false memories: Remembering words not presented in lists. *Journal of Experimental Psychology: Learning, Memory, and Cognition, 21,* 803–814.

Rogers, T. B., Kuiper, N. A., & Kirker, W. S. (1977). Self-reference and the encoding of personal information. *Journal of Personality and Social Psychology, 35,* 677–688.

Roland, P. E., & Friberg, L. (1985). Localization of cortical areas activated by thinking. *Journal of Neurophysiology, 53,* 1219–1243.

Rosch, E. (1973). On the internal structure of perceptual and semantic categories. In T. E. Moore (Ed.), *Cognitive development and the acquisition of language* (pp. 111–144). New York: Academic Press.

Rosch, E. (1974). Linguistic relativity. In A. Silverstein (Ed.), *Human communication: Theoretical perspectives* (pp. 95–121). New York: Halsted.

Rosch, E. (1975). Cognitive representations of semantic categories. *Journal of Experimental Psychology: General, 104,* 192–233.

Rosch, E. (1977). Human categorization. In N. Warren (Ed.), *Advances in cross-cultural psychology* (Vol. 1). London: Academic Press.

Rosenblatt, F. (1958). The Perceptron: A probabilistic mode for information storage and organization in the brain. *Psychological Review, 65,* 386–407.

Rosenzweig, M. R., & Bennett, E. L. (1996). Psychology of plasticity: Effects of training and experience on brain and behavior. *Behavioural Brain Research, 78*(1), 57–65.

Ross, G. S. (1980). Categorization in 1- to 2-year-olds. *Developmental Psychology, 16,* 391–396.

Rovee-Collier, C. (1999). The development of infant memory. *Current Directions in Psychological Science, 8,* 80–85.

Rovee-Collier, C. K. (1987). Learning and memory in infancy. In J. D. Osofsky (Ed.), *Handbook of infant development* (2nd ed., pp. 517–536). New York: Wiley.

Rovee-Collier, C. K. (1990). The "memory system" of prelinguistic infants. In A. Diamond (Ed.), *The development and neural bases of higher cognitive functions.* New York: New York Academy of Sciences.

Rubin, D. C. (1985, September). Flashbulb memories. *Psychology Today.*

Rubin, D. C. (1987). Quoted in *The New York Times,* June 23.

Rubin, D. C. (2000). Autobiographical memory and aging. In D. C. Park & N. Schwarz (Eds.), *Cognitive aging: A primer* (pp. 131–149). Philadelphia: Psychology Press.

Rubin, D. C., & Friendly, M. (1986). Predicting which words get recalled: Measures of free recall, availability, goodness, emotionality, and pronunciability for 925 nouns. *Memory and Cognition, 14,* 79–94.

Rubin, D. C., Rahhal, T. A., & Poon, L. W. (1998). Things learned in early adulthood are remembered best. *Memory and Cognition, 26,* 3–19.

Rubin, D. C., Wetzler, S. E., & Nebes, R. D. (1986). Autobiographical memory across the life span. In D. C. Rubin (Ed.), *Autobiographical memory.* Cambridge, UK: Cambridge University Press.

Rubinstein, H., Lewis, S. S., & Rubinstein, M. A. (1971). Evidence of phonemic recoding in visual word recognition. *Journal of Verbal Learning and Verbal Behavior, 10,* 645–657.

Rubinstein, M. F. (1986). *Tools for thinking and problem solving.* Englewood Cliffs, NJ: Prentice-Hall.

Ruch, T. C., & Patton, H. D. (1965). *Physiology and biophysics* (19th ed.). Philadelphia: Saunders.

Rugg, M. D. (1995). Event-related potential studies of human memory. In M. S. Gazzaniga (Ed.), *The cognitive neurosciences* (pp. 789–801). Cambridge, MA: MIT Press.

Rumelhart, D. E. (1975). Notes on a schema for stories. In D. Bobrow & A. Collins (Eds.), *Representation and understanding: Studies in cognitive science.* New York: Academic Press.

Rumelhart, D. E. (1977). *An introduction to human information processing.* New York: Wiley.

Rumelhart, D. E., & McClelland, J. L. (1982). An interactive activation model of context effects in letter perception: Part 2. The contextual enhancement effect and some tests and extensions of the model. *Psychological Review, 89,* 60–94.

Rumelhart, D. E., Hinton, G. E., & McClelland, J. L. (1986). A general framework for parallel distributed processing. In D. E. Rumelhart, J. L. McClelland, & the PDP research group (Eds.), *Parallel distributed processing: Explorations in the microstructure of cognition* (Vol. 1). Cambridge, MA: Bradford.

Rumelhart, D. E., McClelland, J. L., & the PDP Research Group (Eds.). (1986). *Parallel distributed processing: Explorations in the microstructure of cognition* (Vol. 1). Cambridge, MA: Bradford.

Rumelhart, D. E., & Norman, D. A. (1975). The computer implementation. In D. Norman & D. Rumelhart (Eds.), *Exploration in cognition.* San Francisco: Freeman.

Russell, W. R. (1959). *Brain, memory, learning.* Oxford: Clarendon.

Saarinen, T. F. (1987). Centering of mental maps of the world: Discussion paper. Department of Geography and Regional Development, University of Arizona, Tucson.

Sagen, C., Drake, F. D., Drugen, A., Ferris, I., Lomberg, J., & Sagen, L. S. (1978). *Murmurs of earth: The voyager interstellar record.* New York: Random House.

Sakitt, B. (1976). Iconic memory. *Psychological Review, 83,* 257–276.

Sakitt, B., & Long, G. M. (1979). Spare the rod and spoil the icon. *Journal of Experimental Psychology: Human Perception and Performance, 5,* 19–30.

Salapatek, P. (1975). Pattern perception in early infancy. In L. B. Cohen & P. Salapatek (Eds.), *Infant perception: From sensation to cognition.* New York: Academic Press.

Salasoo, A., Shiffrin, R. M., & Feustel, T. C. (1985). Building permanent memory codes: Codification and repetition effects in word identification. *Journal of Experimental Psychology: General, 114,* 50–77.

Salisbury, H. E. (1955). *American in Russia.* New York: Harper.

Samuel, A. G., & Ressler, W. H. (1986). Attention within auditory word perception: Insights from the phonemic restoration illusion. *Journal of Experimental Psychology: Human Perception and Performance, 12,* 70–79.

Santa, J. L., & Lamners, L. L. (1974). Encoding specificity: Fact or artifact? *Journal of Verbal Learning and Verbal Behavior, 13,* 412–423.

Santa, J. L., & Lamners, L. L. (1976). Where does the confusion lie? Comments on the Wiseman and Tulving paper. *Journal of Verbal Learning and Verbal Behavior, 15,* 3–57.

Sapir, E. (1958). Language and environment. *American Anthropologist, 1912,* n.s., 226–242. Also in D. G. Mandelbaum (Ed.), *Selected writings of Edward Sapir in language, culture, and personality* (pp. 89–103). Berkeley and Los Angeles: University of California Press.

Saporta, S. (Ed.). (1961). *Psycholinguistics: A book of readings.* New York: Holt, Rinehart & Winston.

Savin, H. B., & Perchonock, E. (1965). Grammatical structure and immediate recall of English sentences. *Journal of Verbal Learning and Verbal Behavior, 4,* 348–353.

Schacter, D. L. (1987). Memory, amnesia, and frontal lobe dysfunction. *Psychobiology, 15,* 21–36.

Schacter, D.L. (1989). On the relation between memory and consciousness: dissociable interactions and conscious experience. In H.L. Roediger III & F.I.M. Craik (Eds.), *Varieties of memory and consciousness: Essays in honour of Endel Tulving* (pp. 355–389). Hillsdale, NJ: Erlbaum.

Schaeffer, B., & Wallace, R. (1970). The comparison of word meanings. *Journal of Experimental Psychology, 86,* 144–152.

Schank, R. C. (1972). Conceptual dependency: A theory of natural language understanding. *Cognitive Psychology, 3,* 552–631.

Schank, R. C. (1981). Language and memory. In D. A. Norman (Ed.), *Perspectives on cognitive science.* Norwood, NJ: Ablex.

Schank, R. C. (1982). *Dynamic memory: A theory of reminding and learning in computers and people.* Cambridge, UK: Cambridge University Press.

Schank, R. C., & Abelson, R. (1977). *Scripts, plans, goals, and understanding.* Hillsdale, NJ: Erlbaum.

Schank, R. C., & Hunter, L. (1985, April). The quest to understand thinking. *Byte,* pp. 143–155.

Schmidt, F. L., & Hunter, J. E. (1992). Development of a causal model of processes determining job performance. *Current Directions in Psychological Science, 1,* 89–92.

Schmidt, R. A. (1975). A schema theory of discrete motor skill learning. *Psychological Review, 82,* 225–229.

Schneider, W. (1987). Connectionism: Is it a paradigm shift for psychology? *Behavioral Research Methods, Instruments, and Computers, 19,* 73–83.

Schneider, W., & Shiffrin, R. M. (1977). Controlled and automatic human information processing: Detection, search and attention. *Psychological Review, 84*(1).

Schneider, W., Noll, D. C., & Cohen, J. D. (1993). Functional topographic mapping of the cortical ribbons in the human visual cortex using conventional MRI. *Nature, 365,* 150–153.

Schulman, A. I. (1974). Memory for words recently classified. *Memory and Cognition, 2,* 47–52.

Schvaneveldt, R. W., & McDonald, J. E. (1981). Semantic context and the encoding of words: Evidence for two modes of stimulus analysis. *Journal of Experimental Psychology: Human Perception and Performance, 2,* 243–256.

Schwartz, B.L. (1999). Sparkling at the end of the tongue: The etiology of the tip-of-the-tongue phenomenology. *Psychonomic Bulletin & Review, 6*(3), 379–393.

Scientific American (1998). Exploring Intelligence, *9,* Winter.

Scribner, S. (1975). Recall of classical syllogisms: A crosscultural investigation of error on logical problems. In R. J. Falmagen (Ed.), *Reasoning: Representation and process.* Hillsdale, NJ: Erlbaum.

Scribner, S., & Cole, M. (1972). Effects of constrained recall training on children's performance in a verbal memory task. *Child Development, 43,* 845–857.

Scribner, S., & Cole, M. (1974). Research program on Vai literacy and its cognitive consequences. *Cross-Cultural Psychology Newsletter, 8,* 2–4.

Scribner, S., & Cole, M. (1981). *The psychology of literacy.* Cambridge, MA: Harvard University Press.

Seamon, J. G., & Travis, Q. B. (1993). An ecological study of professors' memory for student names and faces: A replication and extension. *Memory, 1,* 191–202.

Searle, J. (1980). Minds, brains, and programs. *Behavioral and Brain Sciences, 3,* 417–457.

Searle, J. (1983). *Intentionality: An essay in the philosophy of mind.* Cambridge, UK: Cambridge University Press.

Sejnowski, T. J. Stevens, & J. Watson (Eds.). (1991) *Cold Spring Harbor Symp. Quart. Biol., 55.*

Sejnowski, T. J., & Rosenberg, C. R. (1987). NETtalk: Parallel networks that learn to pronounce English text. *Complex Systems, 1,* 145–168.

Sejnowski, T. J., Koch, C., & Churchland, P. S. (1988). Computational neuroscience. *Science, 241,* 1299–1306.

Sekuler, R. W., & Abrams, M. (1968). Visual sameness: A choice time analysis of pattern recognition process. *Journal of Experimental Psychology, 77,* 232–238.

Selfridge, O. G., & Neisser, U. (1963). Pattern recognition by machine. In E. Feigenbaum & J. Feldman (Eds.), *Computers and thought.* New York: McGraw-Hill.

Sells, S. B. (1936). The atmosphere effect: An experimental study of reasoning. *Archives of Psychology,* no. 200.

Service, R. F. (1993). Making modular memories. *Science, 260,* 1876.

Shallice, T. (1972). On the dual functions of consciousness. *Psychological Review, 79,* 383–396.

Shallice, T. (1978). The Dominant Action System: An information-processing approach to consciousness. In K. S. Pope & J. L. Singer (Eds.), *The stream of consciousness: Scientific investigations into the flow of experience,* New York: Plenum.

Shallice, T. (1988). Information-processing models of consciousness: Possibilities and problems. In A. J. Marcel & E. Bisiach (Eds.), *Consciousness in contemporary science* (pp. 305–333). Oxford, UK: Clarendon Press.

Shallice, T., & Vallar, G. (1990). The impairment of auditory-verbal short-term storage. In G. Vallar & T. Shallice (Eds.), *Neuropsychological impairments of short-term memory* (pp. 11–53). Cambridge, UK: Cambridge University Press.

Shannon, C. E. (1948). A mathematical theory of communication. *Bell System Technical Journal, 27,* 479–523.

Shapiro, P., & Penrod, S. (1986). Meta-analysis of facial identification studies. *Psychological Bulletin, 100,* 139–156.

Sheehan, P. W. (1967a). Reliability of a short test of imagery. *Perceptual and Motor Skills 25,* 744.

Sheehan, P. W. (1967b). A shortened form of Betts' questionnaire upon mental imagery. *Journal of Clinical Psychology, 23,* 386–398.

Sheehan, P. W. (1971). Individual differences in vividness of imagery and the function of imagery in incidental learning. *Australian Journal of Psychology, 23,* 279–288.

Sheehan, P. W. (1973). Stimulus imagery effect and the role of imagery in incidental learning. *Australian Journal of Psychology, 25,* 93–102.

Sheehan, P. W., & Neisser, U. (1969). Some variables affecting the vividness of imagery in recall. *British Journal of Psychology, 25,* 93–102.

Sheingold, K. (1973). Developmental differences in intake and storage of visual information. *Journal of Experimental Child Psychology, 16,* 1–11.

Shepard, R. N. (1966). Learning and recall as organization and search. *Journal of Verbal Learning and Verbal Behavior, 5,* 201–204.

Shepard, R. N. (1967). Recognition memory for words, sentences, and pictures. *Journal of Verbal Learning and Verbal Behavior, 6,* 156–163.

Shepard, R. N. (1968). *Cognitive Psychology:* A review of the book by U. Neisser. *American Journal of Psychology, 81,* 285–289.

Shepard, R. N. (1975). Form, formation, and transformation of internal representations. In R. L. Solso (Ed.), *Information processing and cognition: The Loyola Symposium.* Hillsdale, NJ: Erlbaum.

Shepard, R. N. (1977, September). *The mental image.* Paper delivered at the American Psychological Association Meeting, San Francisco.

Shepard, R. N. (1978). The mental image. *American Psychologist, 33,* 125–137.

Shepard, R. N. (1987). Evolution of a mesh between principles of the mind and regularities of the world. In J. Dupre (Ed.), *The latest on the best essays on evolution and optimality.* Cambridge, MA: MIT Press.

Shepard, R. N. (1987). Toward a universal law of generalization for psychological science. *Science, 237,* 1317–1323.

Shepard, R. N. (1990). *Mind sights.* San Francisco: Freeman.

Shepard, R. N. (1992). The perceptual organization of colors: An adaptation to the regularities of the terrestrial world? In J. Barkow, L. Cosmoides, & J. Tooby (Eds.), *The adapted mind: Evolutionary psychology and the generation of culture* (pp. 495–532). New York: Oxford University Press.

Shepard, R. N. (1994). Perceptual-cognitive universals as reflections of the world. *Psychonomic Bulletin & Review, 1,* 2–28.

Shepard, R. N. (1995). Toward a 21st century science of mental universals. In R. L. Solso & D. W. Massaro (Eds.), *The science of the mind: 2001 and beyond.* New York: Oxford University Press.

Shepard, R. N., & Chipman, S. (1970). Second-order iso-morphism of internal representations: Shapes of states. *Cognitive Psychology, 1*, 1–17.

Shepard, R. N., & Metzler, J. (1971). Mental rotation of three-dimensional objects. *Science, 171*, 701–703.

Shepherd, G. M. (1994). *Neurobiology* (3rd ed.). New York: Oxford University Press.

Shiffrin, R. M., & Atkinson, R. C. (1969). Storage and re-trieval processing in long-term memory. *Psychological Review, 76*, 179–193.

Shiffrin, R. M., & Schneider, W. (1977). Controlled and automatic human information processing: II Perceptual learning, automatic attending, and a general theory. *Psychological Review, 84*, 127–190.

Shimamura, A. P. (1996). Unraveling the mystery of the frontal lobes: Explorations in cognitive neuro-science. *Psychological Science Agenda*, September–October 1996. Copyright 1996 American Psychological Association.

Shimamura, A. P., & Squire, L. R. (1984). Paired-asso-ciate learning and priming effects in amnesia: A neuropsychological study. *Journal of Experimental Psychology: General, 113*, 556–570.

Shirvalkar, P., Seth, M., Schiff, N. D., & Herrera, D. G. (2006). Cognitive enhancement with central thal-amic electrical stimulation. *Procedings of the Na-tional Academy of Sciences* 103(45) 17007–17012.

Shulman, H. G. (1970). Encoding and retention of se-mantic and phonemic information in short-term memory. *Journal of Verbal Learning and Verbal Be-havior, 9*, 499–508.

Shulman, H. G. (1971). Similarity effects in short-term memory. *Psychological Bulletin, 75*, 399–415.

Shulman, H. G. (1972). Semantic confusion errors in short-term memory. *Journal of Verbal Learning and Verbal Behavior, 11*, 221–227.

Siegler, R. S. (1976). Three aspects of cognitive devel-opment. *Cognitive Psychology, 8*, 481–520.

Siegler, R. S. (1981). Developmental sequences within and between concepts. *Monographs of the Soci-ety for Research in Child Development, 46*, (No. 189, pp. 1–74).

Siegler, R. S. (Ed.). (1978). *Children's thinking: What develops?* Hillsdale, NJ: Erlbaum.

Siegler, R. S., & Klahr, D. (1982). When do children learn? The relationship between existing knowl-edge and the acquisition of new knowledge. In R. Glaser (Ed.), *Advances in instructional psychology* (Vol. 2). Hillsdale, NJ: Erlbaum.

Siegler, R. S., & Richards, D. D. (1982). The develop-ment of intelligence. In R. J. Sternberg (Ed.), *Handbook of intelligence.* Cambridge, UK: Cam-bridge University Press.

Simon, H. A. (1966). Thinking by computers. In R. G. Colodny, *Mind and cosmos: Essays in contempo-rary science and philosophy* (pp. 3–21). Latham, MD: Center for the Philosophy of Science.

Simon, H. A., & Feigenbaum, E. A. (1964). An infor-mation processing theory of some effects of simi-larity, familiarization, and meaningfulness in verbal learning. *Journal of Verbal Learning and Verbal Be-havior, 3*, 385–396.

Simpson, G. B., Peterson, R. R., Castell, M. A., & Burgess, C. (1989). Lexical and sentence context effects in word recognition. *Journal of Experi-mental Psychology: Learning, Memory, and Cog-nition, 15*, 88–97.

Sims, V., & Mayer, R. (2002). Domain specificity of spa-tial expertise: The case of video game players. *Applied Cognitive Psychology* 16(1) 97–115.

Singer, H., & Ruddell, R. D. (Eds.). (1976). *Theoretical models and processes of reading.* Newark, DE: In-ternational Reading Association.

Singer, J. L., & Antrobus, J. S. (1966). *Imaginal pro-cesses inventory.* New York: Authors.

Singer, J. L., & Antrobus, J. S. (1970). *Imaginal processes inventory.* New York: Authors.

Singer, J. L., & Antrobus, J. S. (1972). Daydreaming, imag-inal processes, and personality: A normative study. In P. W. Sheehan (Ed.), *The function and nature of imagery* (pp. 175–202). New York: Academic Press.

Singer, M. (1973). A replication of Bransford and Franks' (1971) "The abstraction of linguistic ideas." *Bulletin of the Psychonomic Society, 1*, 416–418.

Singh, J. A. L., & Zingg, R. M. (1940). *Wolf children and feral man.* New York: Harper.

Sinha, P. and Poggio, T. (2002)., *Perception*, 31/1, 133.

Sinha, P., & Poggio, T. (1996). SIR—Exactly what do we recognize in a face? Intuition suggests that it is . . . *Nature* 384, 404.

Skinner, B. F. (1957). *Verbal behavior.* New York: Ap-pleton-Century-Crofts.

Skinner, B. F. (1989). The origins of cognitive thought. *American Psychologist, 44*, 13–18.

Slobin, D. I. (1971). *Psycholinguistics.* Glenview, IL: Scott, Foresman.

Slovic, P., Fischhoff, B., & Lichtenstein, S. (1977). Be-havioral decision theory. *Annual Review of Psy-chology, 28*, 1–39.

Small, S. L., Cottrell, G. W., & Tanenhaus, M. K. (Eds.). (1988). *Lexical ambiguited resolution: Perspectives from psycholinguists, neuropsychology, and artificial intelligence.* Los Altos. CA: Morgan Kaufmann.

Smart, J. J. C. (1959). Sensations and brain processes. *Philosophical Review, 68,* 141–156.

Smedslund, J. (1961). The acquisition of conservation of substance and weight in children. *Scandinavian Journal of Psychology, 2,* 11–20.

Smedslund, J. (1965). The development of transitivity of length: A comment on Braine's reply. *Child Development, 36,* 577–580.

Smith, E. E. (1978). Theories of semantic memory. In W. K. Estes (Ed.), *Handbook of learning and cognitive processes* (Vol. 6). Hillsdale, NJ: Erlbaum.

Smith, E. E., & Medin, D. L. (1981). *Categories and concepts.* Cambridge, MA: Harvard University Press.

Smith, E. E., Shoben, E. J., & Rips, L. J. (1974). Structure and process in semantic memory: A featural model for semantic decisions. *Psychological Review, 1,* 214–241.

Smith, F. (1971). *Understanding reading.* New York: Holt, Rinehart & Winston.

Smith, S. B. (1983). *The great mental calculators: The psychology, methods, and lives of calculating prodigies, past and present.* New York: Columbia University Press.

Snodgrass, I. (1975). Psychophysics. In B. Sclarf (Ed.), *Experimental sensory psychology.* Glenview, IL: Scott, Foresman.

Sokolov, E. N. (1960). Neuronal models and the orienting reflexes. In M. A. Brazier (Ed.), *The central nervous system and behavior.* New York: J. Macy.

Sokolov, E. N. (1963). *Perception and the conditioned reflex.* New York: Macmillan.

Solomon, P. R., Goethals, G. R., Kelly, C. M., & Stephens, B. R. (Eds.). (1989). *Memory: Interdisciplinary approaches.* New York: Springer.

Solso, R. L. (1985). The citation of Soviet scholars by Western psychologists. *American Psychologist, 40,* 1264–1265.

Solso, R. L. (1986, December). Organization of knowledge in the world community of cognitive scientists. *Cognitive Systems,* pp. 321–327.

Solso, R. L. (1987). The social-political consequences of the organization and dissemination of knowledge. *American Psychologist, 42,* 824–825.

Solso, R. L. (1994a). *Cognition and the visual arts.* Cambridge, MA: MIT Press.

Solso, R. L. (1994b). Turning the corner. In R. L. Solso & D. W. Massaro (Eds.), *The science of the mind: 2001 and beyond.* Cambridge, MA: MIT Press.

Solso, R. L. (1997) (Ed.). *Mind and brain sciences in the 21st century.* Cambridge, MA: MIT Press.

Solso, R. L. (Ed.). (1973). *Contemporary issues in cognitive psychology: The Loyola Symposium.* Potomac, MD: Winston/Wiley.

Solso, R. L. (Ed.). (1974). *Theories of cognitive psychology: The Loyola Symposium.* Potomac, MD: Erlbaum.

Solso, R. L. (Ed.). (1975). *Information processing and cognition: The Loyola Symposium.* Hillsdale, NJ: Erlbaum.

Solso, R. L., & Biersdorff, K. K. (1975). Recall under conditions of cumulative cues. *Journal of General Psychology, 93,* 233–246.

Solso, R. L., & Johnson, H. H. (1989). *An introduction to experimental design in psychology: A case approach.* New York: Harper & Row.

Solso, R. L., & Johnson, H. H. (1994). *An introduction to experimental design in psychology: A case approach* (3rd ed.). New York: Harper & Row.

Solso, R. L., & MacLin, O. H. (2000). The history of cognitive psychology. In A. E. Kazdin (Ed.), *Encyclopedia of Psychology.* New York: APA Books, Oxford University Press.

Solso, R. L., & McCarthy, J. E. (1981a). Prototype formation: Central tendency model versus attribute frequency model. *Bulletin of the Psychonomic Society, 17,* 10–11.

Solso, R. L., & McCarthy, J. E. (1981b). Prototype formation of faces: A case of pseudomemory. *British Journal of Psychology, 72,* 499–503.

Solso, R. L., & Raynis, S. A. (1979). Prototype formation from imaged, kinesthetically, and visually presented geometric figures. *Journal of Experimental Psychology: Human Perception and Performance, 5,* 701–712.

Sophian, C. (Ed.). (1984). *Origins of cognitive skills.* Hillsdale, NJ: Erlbaum.

Spear, N. (Ed.). (1989). *Comparative perspectives on the development of memory.* Hillsdale, NJ: Erlbaum.

Spearman, C. (1904). General intelligence objectively determined and measured. *American Journal of Psychology, 15,* 201–293.

Spearman, C. (1927). *The abilities of man: Their nature and measurement.* New York: Macmillan.

Spelke, E. S. (1979). Perceiving bimodally specified events in infancy. *Developmental Psychology, 15,* 626–636.

Spelke, E. S. (1988). The origins of physical knowledge. In L. Weiskrantz (Ed.), *Thought without language* (pp. 168–184). London: Clarendon Press.

Spelke, E. S., & Kestenbaum, R. (1986). Les origines du concept d'objet. *Psychologie française 31*, 67–72.

Sperling, G. (1960). The information available in brief visual presentation. *Psychological Monographs, 74.*

Sperling, G. (1963). A model for visual memory tasks. *Human Factors, 5*, 19–31.

Sperling, G. (1967). Successive approximations to a model for short-term memory. *Acta Psychologica, 27*, 285–292.

Sperry, R. W. (1968). Hemisphere deconnection and the utility of conscious experience. *American Psychologist, 23*, 723–733.

Sperry, R. W. (1974). Lateral specialization in surgically separated hemispheres. In F. O. Schmitt & F. G. Worden (Eds.), *The neurosciences* (Vol. 3). Cambridge, MA: MIT Press.

Sperry, R. W. (1982). Some effects of disconnecting the cerebral hemispheres. *Science, 217*, 1223–1226.

Springer, S. P., & Deutsch, G. (1981). *Left brain, right brain.* San Francisco: Freeman.

Springer, S., & Deutsch, G. (1984). *Left brain, right brain* (2nd ed.). San Francisco: Freeman.

Squire, L. R. (1982). The neuropsychology of human memory. *Annual Review of Neuroscience, 5*, 241–273.

Squire, L. R. (1986). Mechanisms of memory. *Science, 232*, 1612–1619.

Squire, L. R., & Butters, N. (Eds.). (1984). *Neuropsychology of memory.* New York: Guilford Press.

Standing, L. (1973). Learning 10,000 pictures. *Quarterly Journal of Experimental Psychology, 25*, 207–222.

Standing, L., Bond, B., Hall, J., & Weller, J. (1972). A bibliography of picture-memory studies. *Psychonomic Monograph Supplement, 29*(6B).

Standing, L., Conezio, J., & Haber, R. N. (1970). Perception and memory for pictures: Single-trial learning of 2560 visual stimuli. *Psychonomic Science, 19*, 73–74.

Stanovich, K. E., & West, R. F. (1979). Mechanism of sentence context effects in reading: Automatic activation and conscious attention. *Memory and Cognition, 7*, 77–85.

Stanovich, K. E., & West, R. F. (1983). On printing by a sentence context. *Journal of Experimental Psychology: General, 112*, 1–36.

Staszewski, J. J. (1988). Skilled memory and expert mental calculation. In M. T. H. Chi, R. Glaser, & M. J. Farr (Eds.), *The nature of expertise.* Hillsdale, NJ: Erlbaum.

Staszewski, J. J. (1989). Exceptional memory: The influence of practice and knowledge on the development of elaborative encoding strategies. In W. Schneider & F. E. Weinert (Eds.), *Interactions among aptitudes, strategies, and knowledge in cognitive performance.* Berlin: Springer.

Sternberg, R. J. (1977). *Intelligence, information processing, and analogical reasoning: The componential analysis of human abilities.* Hillsdale, NJ: Erlbaum.

Sternberg, R. J. (1979). Developmental patterns in the encoding and combination of logical connectives. *Journal of Experimental Child Psychology, 28*, 469–498.

Sternberg, R. J. (1980a). The development of linear syllogistic reasoning. *Journal of Experiment Child Psychology, 29*, 340–356.

Sternberg, R. J. (1980b). Representation and process in linear syllogistic reasoning. *Journal of Experimental Psychology: General, 109*, 119–159.

Sternberg, R. J. (1982). Reasoning, problem solving, and intelligence. In R. J. Sternberg (Ed.), *Handbook of human intelligence.* Cambridge University Press.

Sternberg, R. J. (1985a). *Beyond IQ: A triarchic theory of human intelligence.* Cambridge, UK: Cambridge University Press.

Sternberg, R. J. (1984b). Toward a triarchic theory of human intelligence. *Behavioral and Brain Sciences, 7*, 269–315.

Sternberg, R. J. (1985b). Human intelligence: The model is the message. *Science, 230*, 1111–1118.

Sternberg, R. J. (1986a). Inside intelligence. *American Scientist, 74*, 137–143.

Sternberg, R. J. (1986b). *Intelligence applied.* New York: Harcourt Brace Jovanovich.

Sternberg, R. J. (1989). Intelligence, wisdom, and creativity: Their natures and interrelationships. In R. L. Linn (Ed.), *Intelligence: Measurement, theory, and public policy.* Chicago: University of Illinois Press.

Sternberg, R. J. (Ed.). (1984a). *Mechanisms of cognitive development.* San Francisco: Freeman.

Sternberg, R. J. (Ed.). (1994). *Encyclopedia of human intelligence.* New York: Macmillan.

Sternberg, R. J., & Lubart, T. I. (1996). Investing in creativity. *American Psychologist, 51*, 667–688.

Sternberg, R. J., & Wagner, R. K. (1993). The geocentric view of intelligence and job performance is wrong. *Current Directions in Psychological Science, 2*, 1–5.

Sternberg, R. J., Lubart, T. I., & Todd, J. (1991) An investment theory of creativity and its development. *Human Development, 34,* 1–31.

Sternberg, S. (1966). High speed scanning in human memory. *Science, 153,* 652–654.

Sternberg, S. (1967). Two operations in character recognition: Some evidence from RT measurements. *Perception and Psychophysics, 2,* 45–53.

Sternberg, S. (1969). Memory scanning: Mental processes revealed by reaction time experiments. *American Scientist, 57,* 421–457.

Stevens, A., & Coupe, P. (1978). Distortions in judged spatial relations. *Cognitive Psychology, 63,* 390–397.

Strand, B. N., & Mueller, J. H. (1977). Levels of processing in facial recognition memory. *Bulletin of the Psychonomic Society, 9,* 17–18.

Strauss, M. S. (1979). Abstraction of prototypical information by adults and 10-month-old infants. *Journal of Experimental Psychology: Human Learning and Memory, 5,* 618–663.

Strauss, M. S., & Carter, P. N. (1984). Infant memory: Limitations and future directions. In R. Kail & N. E. Spear (Eds.), *Comparative perspectives on the development of memory.* Hillsdale, NJ: Erlbaum.

Stromeyer, C. G. (1970). Eidetikers. *Psychology Today,* Nov., 76–80.

Suler, J. (1989, January). "Eliza" helps students grasp therapy. *APA Monitor,* p. 30.

Sutherland, N. S. (1972). Object recognition In E. C. Carterette & M. P. Feidman (Eds.), *Handbook of perception* (Vol. 3). New York: Academic Press.

Swets, J. A. (1961). Is there a sensory threshold? *Science, 134,* 168–177.

Swick, D., Kutas, M., & Neville, H. J., (in press). Localizing the neural generators of event-related brain potentials. In A. Kertesz (Ed.), *Localizations and neuroimaging in neuropsychology.* New York: Academic Press.

Swinney, D. (1979). Lexical access during sentence comprehension: Reconsideration of context effects. *Cognitive Psychology, 18,* 645–660.

Tanenhaus, M. K., & Lucas, M. M. (1987). Context effects in lexical processing. *Cognition, 25,* 213–234.

Tanner, W. P., & Swets, J. A. (1954). A decision-making theory of visual detection. *Psychological Review, 61,* 401–409.

Tauke, M. (1961). *Computers and common sense.* New York: Columbia University Press.

Taylor, H. A., & Tversky, B. (1992). Descriptions and depictions of environments. *Memory and Cognition, 20,* 483–496.

Taylor, S. E. (1965). Eye movements while reading: Facts and fallacies. *American Educational Research Journal, 2,* 187–202.

Theios, J., Smith, P. G., Haviland, S., Traupmann, J., & Moy, M. C. (1973). Memory scanning as a serial self-termination process. *Journal of Experimental Psychology, 97,* 323–336.

Thibadeau, R. (1985). Automatic visual inspection as skilled perception. In P. Jackson (Ed.), *The Robotics Institute: 1984 Annual Research Review.* Pittsburgh: Robotics Institute.

Thomas, J. C., Jr. (1974). An analysis of behavior in the hobbits-orcs problem. *Cognitive Psychology, 6,* 257–269.

Thompson, M. C., & Massaro, D. W. (1973). Visual information and redundancy in reading. *Journal of Experimental Psychology, 98,* 49–54.

Thompson, R. A., & Nelson, C. A. (2001). Developmental science and the media: Early brain development. *American Psychologist, 56*(1), 5–15.

Thompson, R. F. (1993). *The brain: A neuroscience primer* (2nd ed.). New York: W. H. Freeman.

Thomson, D. M., & Tulving, E. (1970). Associative encoding and retrieval: Weak and strong cues. *Journal of Experimental Psychology, 86,* 255–262.

Thorndike (1911) Animal Intelligence: Experimental Studies. MacMillan.

Thorndike, E. L., & Lorge, I. (1944). *The teacher's word book of 30,000 words.* New York: Teachers College, Columbia University Press.

Thorndyke, P. W. (1977). Cognitive structures in comprehension and memory of narrative discourse. *Cognitive Psychology, 9,* 77–110.

Thorndyke, P. W., & Hayes-Roth, B. (1982). Differences in spatial know]edge acquired from maps and navigation. *Cognitive Psychology, 14,* 580–589.

Thurstone, L. L. (1938). Primary mental abilities. *Psychometric Monographs, No. 1.* Chicago: University of Chicago Press.

Tinklenberg, J. R., & Taylor, I. L. (1984). Assessments of drug effects on human memory functions. In L. R. Squire & N. Butters (Eds.), *Neuropsychology of memory.* New York: Guilford Press.

Titchener, E. B. (1909). *Experimental psychology* (Vol. 1, Part 1, Student's Manual). New York: Macmillan.

Tolman, E. C. (1932). *Purposive behavior in animals and man.* New York: Appleton-Century.

Tooby, J., & Cosmides, L. (1992). The psychological foundations of culture. In J. Barkow, L. Cosmides, & J. Tooby (Eds.), *The adapted mind: Evolutionary psychology and the generation of culture* (pp. 19–136). New York: Oxford University Press.

Tooby, J., & Cosmides, L. (2000). Toward mapping the evolved functional organization of mind and brain. In M. S. Gazzaniga (Ed.), 1167–1178. *The new cognitive neurosciences,* Cambridge, MA: MIT Press.

Tooby, J., & Cosmides, L. (2001). Does beauty build adapted minds? Toward an evolutionary theory of aesthetics, fiction, and the arts. *SubStance, 94/95,* 6–27.

Trabasso, T. (1977). The role of memory as a system in making transitive inferences. In R. V. Kall & J. W. Hagen (Eds.), *Perspectives on the development of memory and cognition.* Hillsdale, NJ: Erlbaum.

Trabasso, T., & Bower, G. (1964). Memory in concept identification. *Psychonomic Science, 1,* 133–134.

Trabasso, T., & Bower, G. (1968). *Attention in learning.* New York: Wiley.

Tredoux, C. (2002). A direct measure of facial similarity and its relation to human similarity perceptions. *Journal of Experimental Psychology: Applied, 8*(3), 180–193.

Tredoux, C.G. (2002). A direct measure of facial similarity and its relation to human similarity perceptions. *Journal of Experimental Psychology: Applied* 8(3), 180-193.

Tredoux, C. (2003). A direct measure of facial similarity and its relation to human similarity perceptions. *Journal of Experimental Psychology: Applied, 8*(3), 180–193.

Treisman, A. (1988). Features and objects: The fourteenth Bartlett Memorial Lecture. *Quarterly Journal of Experimental Psychology, 40A,* 201–237.

Treisman, A. M. (1960). Contextual cues in selective listening. *Quarterly Journal of Experimental Psychology, 12,* 242–248.

Treisman, A. M. (1964a). Monitoring and storage of irrelevant messages in selective attention. *Journal of Verbal Learning and Verbal Behavior, 3,* 449–459.

Treisman, A. M. (1964b). Selective attention in man. *British Medical Bulletin, 20,* 12–16.

Treisman, A. M. (1964c). The effect of irrelevant material on the efficiency of selective listening. *American Journal of Psychology, 77,* 533–546.

Treisman, A. M. (1969). Strategies and models of selective attention. *Psychological Review, 76,* 242–299.

Treisman, A. M. (1977). Focused attention in the perception and retrieval of multidimensional stimuli. *Perception and Psychophysics, 22,* 1–11.

Treisman, A. M. (1986). Personal communication, April 23.

Treisman, A. M., & Gelade, G. (1980). A feature integration theory of attention. *Cognitive Psychology, 12,* 97–136.

Treisman, A. M., & Riley, J. (1969). Is selective attention selective perception or selective response? A further test. *Journal of Experimental Psychology, 79,* 27–34.

Treisman, A. M., & Williams, T. C. (1984). A theory of criterion setting with an application to sequential dependencies. *Psychological Review, 91,* 68–111.

Treisman, A. M., Squire, R., & Green, J. (1974). Semantic processing in dichotic listening? A replication. *Memory and Cognition, 2,* 641–646.

Treisman, A., 1988. Features and objects: The Fourteenth Bartlett Memorial Lecture. *Quarterly Journal of Experimental Psychology,* 1988, 40A, (2) 201–237.

Trotter, R. J. (1986, August). Three heads are better than one. *Psychology Today,* pp. 56–62.

Tsien, J. Z. (2000, April). Building a brainier mouse. *Scientific American,* pp. 62–68.

Tufte, E. R. (1983). *The visual display of quantitative information.* Cheshire, CT: Graphics Press.

Tulving E., Kapur S., Craik F.I.M., Moscovitch M., Houle S. (1994). Hemispheric encoding/retrieval asymmetry in episodic memory: position emission tomography findings. *Proceedings of the National Academy of Sciences of the United States of America, 91,* 2016–2020.

Tulving, E. (1962). Subjective organization in free recall of "unrelated" words. *Psychological Review, 69,* 344–354.

Tulving, E. (1972). Episodic and semantic memory. In E. Tulving & W. Donaldson (Eds.), *Organization of memory.* New York: Academic Press.

Tulving, E. (1974). Cue-dependent forgetting. *American Scientist, 62,* 74–82.

Tulving, E. (1983). *Elements of episodic memory.* London: Clarendon Press/Oxford University Press.

Tulving, E. (1984). Organization of memory: Quo vadis? In M. S. Gazzaniga (Ed.), *The cognitive neurosciences.* Cambridge, MA: MIT Press.

Tulving, E. (1984). Precis of *Elements of episodic memory. Behavioral and Brain Sciences, 7,* 223–268.

Tulving, E. (1985b). Memory and consciousness. *Canadian Psychologist, 26,* 1–11.

Tulving, E. (1986). What kind of a hypothesis is the distinction between episodic and semantic memory? *Journal of Experimental Psychology: Learning, Memory, and Cognition, 12,* 307–311.

Tulving, E. (1989a). Memory: Performance, knowledge, and experience. *European Journal of Cognitive Psychology, 1,* 3–26.

Tulving, E. (1989b). Remembering and knowing the past. *American Scientist, 77,* 361–367.

Tulving, E. (1993). What is episodic memory? *Current Directions in Psychological Science, 2*(3), 67–70.

Tulving, E., & Arbuckle, T. Y. (1963). Sources of intratrial interference in immediate recall of paired associates. *Journal of Verbal Learning and Verbal Behavior, 1,* 321–334.

Tulving, E., & Gold, C. (1963). Stimulus information and contextual information as determinants of tachistoscopic recognition of words. *Journal of Experimental Psychology, 66,* 319–327.

Tulving, E., & Hastie, R. (1972). Inhibition effects of intralist repetition in free recall. *Journal of Experimental Psychology, 92,* 297–304.

Tulving, E., & Madigan, S. A. (1970). Memory and verbal learning. In P. H. Mussen & M. R. Rosenzweig (Eds.), *Annual Review of Psychology* (Vol. 21). Palo Alto, CA: Annual Reviews.

Tulving, E., & Osler, S. (1968). Effectiveness of retrieval cues in memory for words. *Journal of Experimental Psychology, 77*(4), 593–601.

Tulving, E., & Pearlstone, Z. (1966). Availability versus accessibility of information in memory for words. *Journal of Verbal Learning and Verbal Behavior, 5,* 381–391.

Tulving, E., & Psotka, J. (1971). Retroactive inhibition in free recall: Inaccessibility of information available in the memory store. *Journal of Experimental Psychology, 87,* 1–8.

Tulving, E., & Schacter, D. L. (1990). Priming and human memory systems. *Science, 247,* 301–306.

Tulving, E., & Thompson, D. M. (1971). Retrieval processes in recognition memory. *Journal of Experimental Psychology, 87,* 116–124.

Tulving, E., & Thompson, D. M. (1973). Encoding specificity and retrieval processing in episodic memory. *Psychological Review, 80,* 352–373.

Tulving, E., Kapur, S., Craik, F. I. M., Moscovitch, M., & Houle, S. (1994). Hemispheric encoding/retrieval asymmetry in episodic memory: Positron emission tomography findings. *Proceedings of the National Academy of Sciences, 91,* 2016– 2020. Washington, DC: National Academy of Sciences.

Turing, A. M. (1950). Computing machinery and intelligence. *Mind, 59,* 433–460.

Turk, M. & Pentland, A. (1991). Eigenfaces for recognition. *Journal of Cognitive Neuroscience, 3*(1), 71-86.

Tversky, A. (1972). Elimination by aspects: A theory of choice. *Psychological Review, 79,* 281–299.

Tversky, A., & Hutchinson, J. W. (1986). Nearest neighbor analysis of psychological spaces. *Psychological Review, 93,* 3–22.

Tversky, A., & Kahneman, D. (1973). Availability: A heuristic for judging frequency and probability. *Cognitive Psychology, 4,* 207–232.

Tversky, A., & Kahneman, D. (1981). The framing of decisions and the psychology of choice. *Science, 211,* 453–458.

Tversky, B. (1981). Distortions in memory for maps. *Cognitive Psychology, 13,* 407–433.

Tye, M. (1991). *The imagery debate.* Cambridge, MA: The MIT Press.

Uhr, L., & Vossler, C. (1963). A pattern-recognition program that generates, evaluates and adjusts its own operators. In E. A. Feigenbaum & J. Feldman (Eds.), *Computers and thought.* New York: McGraw-Hill.

Underwood, B. J. (1969). Attributes of memory. *Psychological Review, 76,* 559–573.

Underwood, G. (1976). Semantic interference from unattended printed words. *British Journal of Psychology, 67,* 327–338.

Underwood, G. (1977). Contextual facilitation from attended and unattended messages. *Journal of Verbal Learning and Verbal Behavior, 16,* 99– 106.

Underwood, G. (1982). *Aspects of consciousness.* New York: Academic Press.

Usher, J. A., & Neisser, U. (1993). Childhood amnesia and the beginnings of memory for four early life events. *Journal of Experimental Psychology: General, 122,* 155–165.

Uttal, W. R. (1978). *The psychobiology of mind.* Hillsdale, NJ: Erlbaum.

Valenta, J., & Potter, W. C. (1984). *Soviet decision making for national security.* Winchester, MA: Allen & Unwin.

Valenza, E., Simion, F., Cassia, V., & Umilta, C. (1996). Face preference at birth. *Journal of Experimental Psychology: Human Perception and Performance, 22,* 892–903.

van Dijk, T. A., & Kintsch, W. (1983). *Strategics of discourse comprehension.* New York: Academic Press.

Vaughn, M. E. (1968). Clustering, age and incidental learning. *Journal of Experimental Child Psychology,* 323–331.

von Neumann, J. (1958). *The computer and the brain.* New Haven, CT: Yale University Press.

von Wright, J. M., Anderson, K., & Stenman, U. (1975). Generalization of conditioned GSRs in dichotic listening. In P. M. A. Rabbit & S. Dornic (Eds.), *Attention and performance V.* New York: Academic Press.

Vurpillot, E. (1968). The development of scanning strategies and their relation to visual differentiation. *Journal of Experimental Child Psychology, 6,* 632–650.

Vygotsky, L. S. (1934/1978). *Mind in society.* Edited by M. Cole, V. John-Steiner, S. Scribner, & E. Souberman. Cambridge, MA: Harvard University Press.

Vygotsky, L. S. (1962). *Thought and language.* Cambridge, MA: MIT Press. (Original work published in Russian in 1934)

Wagenaar, W. (1986). My memory: A study of autobiographic memory over the past six years. *Cognitive Psychology, 18,* 225–252.

Wallas, G. (1926). *The art of thought.* New York: Harcourt Brace.

Walton, G. E., & Bower, T. G. R. (1993). Newborns form "prototypes" in less than 1 minute. *Psychological Science, 4,* 203–205.

Wardlaw, K. A., & Kroll, N. E. A. (1976). Autonomic responses to shock-associated words in a non-attended message: A failure to replicate. *Journal of Experimental Psychology: Human Perception and Performance, 2,* 357–360.

Watkins, S. H. (1914). Immediate memory and its evaluation. *British Journal of Psychology, 7,* 319–348.

Watson, J. B. (1913). Psychology as a behaviorist views it. *Psychological Review, 20,* 158–170.

Watson, J. B. (1914). *Behavior: An introduction to comparative psychology.* New York: Holt.

Watson, J. B. (1919). *Psychology from the standpoint of behaviorist.* Philadelphia: Lippincott.

Waugh, N. C., & Norman, D. A. (1965). Primary memory. *Psychological Review, 72,* 89–104.

Weaver, W. (1949). Introductory note on the general setting of the analytic communication studies. In C. E. Shannon & W. Weaver (Eds.), *The mathematical theory of communication.* Urbana: University of Illinois Press.

Wechsler, S. B. (1963). Engrams, memory storage, and mnemonic coding. *American Psychologist, 18,* 149–153.

Weiskrantz, L. (1966). Experimental studies in amnesia. In C. W. M. Whitty & O. L. Zangwill (Eds.), *Amnesia.* London: Butterworth.

Weiss, A. P. (1967). 1 + 1 = 2 (one plus one does not equal two). In G. C. Quarton, T. Melnechuk, & F. O. Schmitt (Eds.), *The neurosciences* (pp. 801–821). New York: Rockefeller University Press.

Weisstein, N. (1973). Beyond the yellow Volkswagen detector and the grandmother cell: A general strategy for the exploration of operations in human pattern recognition. In R. L. Solso (Ed.), *Contemporary issues in cognitive psychology: The Loyola Symposium.* Washington, DC: Winston/Wiley.

Weist, R. M., & Crowford, J. (1977). The development of organized rehearsal. *Journal of Experimental Child Psychology, 24,* 164–179.

Weizenbaum, J. (1966). ELIZA—A computer program for the study of the natural language communication between man and machine. *Communication Associates Computing Machinery, 9,* 36–45.

Weizenbaum, J. (1976). *Computer power and human reason: From judgment to calculation* (pp. xii– 300). San Francisco: Freeman.

Welch, J. C. (1898). On the measurement of mental activity through muscular activity and the determination of a constant of attention. *American Journal of Physiology, 1,* 283–306.

Welker, W. I., Johnson, J. I., & Pubols, B. H. (1964). Some morphological and physiological characteristics of the somatic sensory system in raccoons. *American Zoologist, 4,* 75–94.

Wertheim, T. (1934). Über die indirekte Sehsharfe. *Zeitschrift fur Psychologie, 7,* 172–187.

Wertheimer, M. (1912). Experimentelle Studein über das Sehen von Bewegung. *Zeitschrift fur Psychologie, 61,* 161–265.

Wertheimer, M. (1923). Untersuchungen zur Lehre von der Gestalt. II. *Psychologie Forschung, 301–350.* Reprinted in D. C. Beardslee & M. Wertheimer (Eds.), *Readings in perception.* Princeton, NJ: Van Nostrand, 1958.

Wertheimer, M. (1945). *Productive thinking.* New York: Harper & Row.

Wertheimer, M. (1958). Principles of perceptual organization. In D. C. Beardslee & M. Wertheimer (Eds.), *Readings in perception.* Princeton, NJ: Van Nostrand.

Wertsch, J. V. (Ed.). (1985a). *Culture, communication, and cognition: Vygotskian perspectives.* Cambridge, UK: Cambridge University Press.

Wertsch, J. V. (1985b). *Vygotsky and the social formation of mind.* Cambridge, MA: Harvard University Press.

Wheeler, D. (1970). Processes in word recognition. *Cognitive Psychology, 1,* 59–85.

Wheeler, M. A., & Roediger, H. L. (1992). Disparate effects of repeated testings: Reconciling Ballard's (1913) and Bartlett's (1932) results. *Psychological Science, 3,* 240–245.

Whitaker, H. A., Savary, F., Markovits, H., Grou, C., & Braun, C. M. J. (1991). Inference deficits after brain damage. Paper presented at the annual INS meeting, San Antonio, Texas.

White, K., Sheehan, P. W., & Aston, R. (1977). Imagery assessment: A survey of self-report measures. *Journal of Mental Imagery, 1,* 145–170.

Whitehead, R. (1991a). Right hemisphere processing superiority during sustained visual attention. *Journal of Cognitive Neuroscience, 3,* 329–334.

Whitehead, R. (1991b). Right hemisphere superiority during sustained visual attention. *Journal of Cognitive Neuroscience, 3–4,* 329–331.

Whorf, B. L. (1956). A linguistic consideration of thinking in primitive communities. In J. B. Carroll (Ed.), *Language, thought, and reality.* New York: Wiley.

Wickelgren, W. A. (1965). Acoustic similarity and intrusion errors in short-term memory. *Journal of Experimental Psychology, 70,* 102–108.

Wickelgren, W. A. (1968). Sparing of short-term memory in an amnesiac: Implications for strength, theory of memory. *Neuropsychologia, 6,* 235–244.

Wickelgren, W. A. (1970). Time, interference and rate of presentation in short-term recognition memory. *Journal of Mathematical Psychology, 7,* 219–235.

Wickelgren, W. A. (1973). The long and short of memory. *Psychological Bulletin, 80,* 425–538.

Wickens, D. D. (1970). Encoding categories of words: An empirical approach to meaning. *Psychological Review, 77,* 1–15.

Wickens, D. D. (1972). Characteristics of word encoding. In A. Melton & E. Martin (Eds.), *Coding processes in human memory* (pp. 191–215). Washington, DC: Winston.

Wickens, D. D. (1973). *Memory and Cognition, 1,* 490. The Psychonomic Society, Inc.

Wickens, D. D., & Engle, R. W. (1970). Imagery and abstractness in short-term memory. *Journal of Experimental Psychology, 84,* 268–272.

Wickens, D. D., Born, D. G., & Allen, C. K. (1963). Proactive inhibition and item similarity in short-term memory. *Journal of Verbal Learning and Verbal Behavior, 2,* 440–445.

Wickens, D. D., Clark, S. E., Hill, F. A., & Wittlinger, R. P. (1968). Grammatical class as an encoding category in short-term memory. *Journal of Experimental Psychology 78,* 599–604.

Wilkins, A., & Stewart, A. (l974). The time course of lateral asymmetrics in visual perception of letters. *Journal of Experimental Psychology, 102,* 905–908.

Wilkins, M. C. (1917). Unpublished M. A. thesis, Columbia University. In R. S. Woodworth (Ed.), *Experimental psychology.* New York: Holt.

Wilks, Y. (1973). An artificial intelligence approach to machine translation. In R. Schank & K. Colby (Eds.), *Computer models of thought and language.* San Francisco: Freeman.

Williams, J. D. (1971). Memory ensemble selection in human information processing. *Journal of Experimental Psychology, 88,* 231–238.

Wilson, R. A., & Keil, F. C. (Eds.). (1999). *The MIT encyclopedia of the cognitive sciences.* Cambridge, MA: MIT Press.

Winikoff, A. (1973). *Eye movements and an aid to protocal analysis of problem solving behavior.* Unpublished Ph.D. dissertation, Carnegie Mellon University. Cited by A. Newell in "Artificial intelligence and the concept of mind." In R. Schank & K. Colby (Eds.), *Computer models of thought and language.* San Francisco: Freeman.

Winograd, T. (1972). *Understanding natural languages.* New York: Academic Press.

Winograd, T. (1974, May). Artificial intelligence: When will computers understand people? *Psychology Today.*

Winograd, T. (1975). Computer memories: A metaphor for memory organization. In C. Cofer (Ed.), *The structure of human memory.* San Francisco: Freeman.

Winograd, T. (1981). What does it mean to understand language? In D. A. Norman (Ed.), *Perspectives on cognitive science.* Norwood, NJ: Ablex.

Winograd, T. (1985). *Language as a cognitive process.* Reading, MA: Addison-Wesley.

Winograd, Terry (1977), "On some contested suppositions of generative linguistics about the scientific study of language," *Cognition* 5, 1977, 151–179.

Winokur, S. (1976). *A primer of verbal behavior: An operant view.* Englewood Cliffs, NJ: Prentice-Hall.

Winston, P. H. (1970). *Learning structural description from examples* (Project MAC-TR-231–447–48, 450–52, 460–480–82). Cambridge, MA: MIT Artificial Intelligence Laboratory.

Winston, P. H. (1973). Learning to identify toy block structures. In R. L. Solso (Ed.), *Contemporary issues in cognitive psychology: The Loyola Symposium.* Washington, DC: Winston/Wiley.

Winston, P. H. (1975). *The psychology of computer vision.* New York: McGraw-Hill.

Winston, P. H. (1984). *Artificial intelligence* (2nd ed.). Reading, MA: Addison-Wesley.

Wittgenstein, L. (1915/1993). Quoted in *The Columbia Dictionary of Quotations.* New York: Columbia University Press.

Woldorff, M. G., Gallen, C. C., Hampson, S. A., Hillyard, S. R., Pantev, C., Sobel, D., et al. (1993). Modulation of early sensory processing in human auditory cortex during auditory selective attention. *Proceedings of the National Academy of Sciences. USA, 90,* 8722–8726.

Woldorff, M. G., Hansen, J. C., & Hillyard, S. A. (1987). Evidence for effects of selective attention to the midlatency range of the human auditory event-related potential. *Electroencephalographic Clinical Neurophysiology.* Supplement, *40,* 146–154.

Wollen, K. A., & Lowry, D. H. (1971). Effects of imagery on paired-associate learning. *Journal of Verbal Learning and Verbal Behavior, 10,* 276–284.

Wollen, K. A., Weber, A., & Lowry, D. H. (1972). Bizarreness versus interaction of mental images as determinants of learning. *Cognitive Psychology, 3,* 518–523.

Wood, C. C. (1975). Auditory and phonetic levels of processing in speech perception: Neurophysiological and information-processing analyses. *Journal of Experimental Psychology: Human Perception and Performance, 104,* 3–20.

Woodson, W. E. (1954). *Human engineering guide for equipment designers.* Berkeley: University of California Press.

Woodworth, R. S. (1929). *Psychology.* New York: Holt.

Woodworth, R. S. (1938). *Experimental psychology.* New York: Holt.

Woodworth, R. S. (1948). *Contemporary schools of psychology* (revised). New York: Ronald.

Woodworth, R. S., & Sells, S. B. (1935). An atmosphere effect in formal syllogistic reasoning. *Journal of Experimental Psychology, 18,* 451–460.

Woolridge, D. E. (1968). *Mechanical man: The physical basis of intellectual life.* New York: McGraw-Hill.

Wundt, W. (1892). In R. Woodworth (Ed.), *Contemporary schools of psychology* (p. 24). New York: Ronald.

Wundt, W. (1905). *Grundriss der Psychologie.* Leipzig: Englemann.

Yarbus, A. L. (1967). *Eye movements and vision* (B. Haigh, Trans.). New York: Plenum.

Yates, F. A. (1966). *The art of memory.* Chicago: University of Chicago Press.

Yerkes, R. M., & Dodson, J. D. (1908). The relation of strength of stimulus to rapidity of habit-formation. *Journal of Comparative Neurology and Psychology, 18,* 459–482.

Yerkes, R. M., & Dodson, J. D. (1908). The relation of strengths of stimulus to rapidity of habit-formation. *Journal of Comparative Neurological Psychology, 18,* 459–482.

Yoshimura, E. K., Moely, B. E., & Shapiro, S. I. (1971). The influence of age and presentation order upon children's free recall and learning to learn. *Psychonomic Science, 23,* 261–263.

Young, M. N., & Gibson, W. B. (1974). *How to develop an exceptional memory.* North Hollywood, CA: Wilshire.

Young, R. K. (1975). *Human learning and memory.* New York: Harper & Row.

Yuille, J. C., & Catchpole, M. J. (1977). The role of imagery in models of cognition. *Journal of Mental Imagery, 1,* 171–180.

Yuille, J. C., & Paivio, A. (1967). Latency of imaginal and verbal mediators as a function of stimulus and response concreteness-imagery. *Journal of Experimental Psychology, 75,* 540–544.

Zacks, J. M., Hazeltine, E., Tversky, B., & Gabrieli, J. D. E. (1999). *Event-related fMRI of mental spatial transformations.* Paper presented at the Annual Meeting of the Cognitive Neuroscience Society, Washington, DC.

Zacks, J. M., Mires, J., Tversky, B., & Hazeltine, E. (2000). Mental spatial transformations of objects and perspective. *Spatial cognition and computation, 2*(4), 315-332.

Zaffy, D. J., & Bruning, J. L. (1966). Drive and the range of cue utilization. *Journal of Experimental Psychology, 71,* 382–384.

Zajonc, R. B. (1968) Attitudinal effects of mere exposure. *Journal of Personality and Social Psychology, 9*(2); 1–27.

Zeman, A. (2001). Consciousness. *Brain,* 129, 1263– 1289.

Zinchenko, P. I. (1962). *Neproizvol'noe azpominanie* (Involuntary memory) (pp. 172–207). Moscow: USSR APN RSFSR.

Zinchenko, P. I. (1981). Involuntary memory and the goal-directed nature of activity. In J. V. Wertsch, *The concept of activity in Soviet psychology.* Armonk, NY: Sharpe.

Zola-Morgan, S., & Squire, L. R. (1990). Neuropsychological investigations of memory and amnesia: Findings from humans and nonhuman primates. In A. Diamond (Ed.), *The development and neural bases of higher cognitive functions.* New York: New York Academy of Sciences.

Name Index

Subject Index